The Windows CE Technology Tutorial

The Windows CE Technology Tutorial

Windows Powered Solutions for the Developer

Chris Muench

 **Addison-Wesley**

Boston • San Francisco • New York • Toronto • Montreal
London • Munich • Paris • Madrid
Capetown • Sydney • Tokyo • Singapore • Mexico City

Many of the designations used by manufacturers and sellers to distinguish their products are claimed as trademarks. Where those designations appear in this book and Addison Wesley Longman, Inc. was aware of a trademark claim, the designations have been printed in initial capital letters or all capitals.

The author and publisher have taken care in the preparation of this book, but make no expressed or implied warranty of any kind and assume no responsibility for errors or omissions. No liability is assumed for incidental or consequential damages in connection with or arising out of the use of the information or programs contained herein.

The publisher offers discounts on this book when ordered in quantity for special sales. For more information, please contact:

Pearson Education Corporate Sales Division
One Lake Street
Upper Saddle River, NJ 07458
(800) 382-3419
corpsales@pearsontechgroup.com

Visit AWL on the Web: *www.awl.com/cseng/*

Library of Congress Cataloging-in-Publication Data

Muench, Chris.
    The Windows CE technology tutorial: windows powered solutions for the developer / Chris Muench.
        p.   cm.
    ISBN 0-201-61642-4
    1. Microsoft Windows (Computer file). 2. Operating systems (Computers)   I. Title.
    QA76.76.O63 M8445   2000
    005.4'469—dc21   00–022369

ISBN 0-201-61642-4
Text printed on recycled and acid-free paper
1 2 3 4 5 6 7 8 9 10—MA—0403020100
First printing, April 2000

For Bettina and Alisa,
who mean more to me than anything else

Contents

Preface   *xvii*

Acknowledgments   *xxiii*

Foreword   *xxv*

Part 1   **Ready . . . Set . . . Go!**   *1*

Chapter 1   **Why Windows CE?**   *3*

1.1   What Is Windows CE?   *4*
     1.1.1   No Legacy 16-Bit APIs   4
     1.1.2   Modular to Fit into Small Devices   4
1.2   Windows CE versus Embedded Windows NT   *7*

Chapter 2   **Preparing Your PC for Windows CE**   *11*

2.1   Choosing the Right PC   *11*
     2.1.1   Get at Least a Pentium II or K6-2 with 300MHz   12
     2.1.2   Use Windows 2000 Professional or Windows 2000 Server   12
     2.1.3   Get a Lot of RAM   12
     2.1.4   Use the New Dual- or Multi-Monitor Support   12
     2.1.5   Get a Big Hard Disk   13
     2.1.6   Use a Network Interface Card (NIC)   14
     2.1.7   Use DVD-ROM Instead of CD-ROM   15

2.2   Choosing the Right Windows CE Device   *15*

2.3   Summary   *19*

Chapter 3   **Installing Your PC**   *21*

3.1   Installing the Operating System   *23*

3.2   Installing the Development Tools   *24*
   3.2.1   Office 2000   26
   3.2.2   Visual Studio 98   26
   3.2.3   The eMbedded Visual Tools 3.0   26
   3.2.4   The Windows CE Platform SDKs   26
   3.2.5   ActiveSync 3.1   27

3.3   Setting Up Your Windows CE Device to Connect
   to the Workstation   *28*
   *3.3.1   Create a Direct Dial-Up Connection Using
       115K Baud   28*
   *3.3.2   Setting the Default Connection for
       the PC-Link   29*
   3.3.3   Test Your Connection to the PC   30
   *3.3.4   Optional Steps: Using a LAN Card to
       Connect to Your PC   31*

Chapter 4   **The Windows CE Development Tools**   *35*

4.1   Windows CE Tools   *35*
   4.1.1   Remote File Viewer   35
   4.1.2   Remote Heap Walker   36
   4.1.3   Remote Process Viewer   40
   4.1.4   Remote Registry Editor   41
   4.1.5   Remote Spy++   41
   4.1.6   Remote Zoomin   42
   4.1.7   The Control Manager   43

4.2   eMbedded Visual C++ versus eMbedded
   Visual Basic   *44*

4.3   The eMbedded Visual Basic Environment   *46*
   *4.3.1   Creating, Downloading, and Debugging a
       Small eVB Application   47*

4.4   The eMbedded Visual C++ Environment   *49*
   *4.4.1   Creating, Downloading, and Debugging
       a Small C++ Application   50*
   4.4.2   Using the Windows CE Platform Manager   54

4.5 Choosing the Right Framework for Your Task   *57*

4.6 Basic Windows CE Development Tips   *61*
    4.6.1 Compile-Time Version Checking   61
    4.6.2 Compile-Time Platform Detecting   62
    4.6.3 Runtime Version Checking   63
    4.6.4 Accessing Debug Messages in ActiveX Controls   69
    4.6.5 Debugging ActiveX Controls   70

Chapter 5   **The Thread-Example Pocket-CD-Manager**   *71*

5.1 The Pocket-CD-Manager Feature List   *71*

5.2 Creating the Framework of Your Application   *73*

5.3 Differences between the Desktop and Windows
    CE Versions   *76*
    5.3.1 stdafx.h   77
    5.3.2 PCDM.CPP   77
    5.3.3 Mainfrm.cpp   78
    5.3.4 PCDMDoc.cpp   78
    5.3.5 PCDMView.cpp   78
    5.3.6 Resources   78
    5.3.7 Differences in Project Settings   78

5.4 The User Interface of the Pocket-CD-Manager   *81*
    5.4.1 "File"   81
    5.4.2 "Help"   81

5.5 Creating a Prototype of PCDM   *82*
    5.5.1 Creating the Desktop Version of the Prototype   83
    5.5.2 Porting the Desktop Prototype to Windows CE   89
    5.5.3 Preparing the DeluxeCD Database   89
    *5.5.4 Converting the Desktop eVB Project to
        an eVB Project   91*
    5.5.5 Migrating Forms and Code   92
    *5.5.6 Migrating ADO Desktop to ADO for
        Windows CE   102*

5.6 Summary   *107*

Chapter 6   **COM for Windows CE**   *111*

6.1 A Short Introduction to COM   *111*
    6.1.1 How Does COM Work?   112
    6.1.2 Versioning   113
    6.1.3 Early Binding No Longer Necessary   113

6.1.4   *Communicating EXE to EXE   114*
6.1.5   *Making Remote Communication Seamless   114*

6.2   COM Activation Methods   *114*
6.2.1   *In-Place Activation   115*
6.2.2   *ActiveX Controls   115*
6.2.3   *Inproc: In-Process Activation   116*
6.2.4   *EXE to EXE   116*
6.2.5   *MTS or DLLHOST.EXE   116*
6.2.6   *DCOM   117*
6.2.7   *COM+ Services   117*

6.3   Creating a Small COM Server   *117*
6.3.1   *Creating a COM Server for Windows CE   118*
6.3.2   *Generating the Desktop-Equivalent COM Server   122*
6.3.3   *Calling the COM Server in C++   123*
6.3.4   *Using #import   123*
6.3.5   *Calling the COM Server in Visual Basic   126*

6.4   Creating an ActiveX Control   *127*
6.4.1   *Creating an ActiveX Control for Windows CE   127*
6.4.2   *Generating the Desktop Equivalent   133*
6.4.3   *Using the Control in eMbedded Visual C++   133*
6.4.4   *Using the Control in eMbedded Visual Basic   137*

6.5   Creating the Wrapper Controls for the PCDM   *140*

6.6   DCOM: Distributed COM   *141*

6.7   deviceCOM: The Industrial Version of DCOM   *141*
6.7.1   *Installation of deviceCOM   142*
6.7.2   *Starting DCServer as a COM Surrogate   144*
6.7.3   *A Small deviceCOM Example   146*
6.7.4   *Other Features of deviceCOM   152*

6.8   Summary   *153*

Part II   Windows CE in Detail   *155*

Chapter 7   The Windows CE User Interface   *157*

7.1   The Command Bar   *158*
7.1.1   *Adding a Command Bar to an Application   159*
7.1.2   *PCDMUI: Including the Command Bar   167*
7.1.3   *Testing the Control in eMbedded Visual Basic   182*
7.1.4   *Calling the Control from the PCDM Application   185*

7.1.5   Summary   189

7.2   The Command-Band   *190*

7.2.1   Adding the Command-Band to an Application   190

7.2.2   Updating the PCDMCommander Class   195

*7.2.3   Testing the New PCDMCommander Class
in eMbedded Visual Basic   202*

*7.2.4   Using the PCDMCommander Class
in the PCDM Application   204*

7.2.5   Summary   206

7.3   Special Palm-size PC Considerations   *206*

*7.3.1   Small Example Showing the Application
Menu Bar   207*

7.3.2   Updating Your PCDMCommander Class   210

*7.3.3   Testing the New Class in eMbedded
Visual Basic for Palm-size PC 2.0   216*

7.3.4   Verifying Your PCDM Application   218

7.4   The List View Control   *219*

*7.4.1   Including the List View Control in an
Application   220*

*7.4.2   Adding the List View Control to
PCDMUI.DLL   222*

*7.4.3   Testing the New CPCDMList Class in
Visual Basic   231*

*7.4.4   Using the New CPCDMList Class in the
PCDM Application   233*

7.4.5   Summary   242

7.5   Other Supported Common Controls   *243*

7.6   Common Controls That Are Not Supported   *245*

7.7   Printing in Windows CE   *246*

7.8   The Hardware Buttons on Palm-size PCs   *250*

7.8.1   The Action and Escape Keys   250

7.8.2   The Application Launch Keys   250

7.9   The Soft Input Panel   *252*

7.9.1   A Simple Application Showing the SIP   252

7.9.2   ShowSIP( ) for PCDMDLL.DLL   255

7.9.3   Testing the New PCDMUI in Visual Basic   257

7.10   Ink Control   *258*

7.10.1   Creating a Small Ink Control Application   259

7.10.2   Other Ink Control Functions   262

Chapter 8   **Storage**   *263*

8.1   The Windows CE Registry   *264*
      *8.1.1   Adding CPCDMAccessReg to the
              PCDMDLL.DLL   265*
      *8.1.2   Testing the New CPCDMAccessReg in eMbedded
              Visual Basic   269*

8.2   The File System   *269*
      8.2.1   No Drive Letters   270
      8.2.2   The Name "Storage Card" Can Be Localized   270
      8.2.3   "My Documents" on a Palm-size PC   272

8.3   The Object Store   *272*
      *8.3.1   A Simple API Application Accessing the Object
              Store   274*
      *8.3.2   A Simple MFC Application Accessing the Object
              Store   277*
      *8.3.3   Adding Object Store Access to the
              PCDMDLL.DLL   280*
      *8.3.4   Testing the New Class in eMbedded
              Visual Basic   293*
      *8.3.5   Adding the PCDMAccessDB Class to the PCDM
              Application   296*

8.4   ADO for Windows CE   *304*
      8.4.1   A Simple Application Using ADO   309
      8.4.2   Adding ADO to the PCDMAccessDB Class   319
      *8.4.3   Retesting ADO Changes in eMbedded Visual
              Basic   334*

8.5   Pocket-Access Files   *334*
      *8.5.1   Copying an Access 2000 Database to the
              Emulation   334*
      *8.5.2   Synchronizing Pocket-Access with Access 2000
              Databases   339*
      8.5.3   Updating the PCDM to Use the New Database   344

Chapter 9   **Remote and Connectivity**   *347*

9.1   Using RAS as TCP/IP Provider   *349*
      *9.1.1   Install the Communication Cable between
              Two PCs   349*
      *9.1.2   Setting the Baud Rate of the Communication Cable
              to 115K   351*

9.1.3   Set Up Windows 2000 Incoming Connections   352

9.1.4   Windows 2000 Server in a Domain Environment   357

9.2   Remote API   *361*

9.2.1   A Small RAPI Example   362

9.2.2   Converting ObjectStoreIt to a Desktop Application   365

9.2.3   Updating Your PCDM Application with RAPI   366

9.2.4   Testing the Class in Visual Basic for the Desktop   368

9.3   ActiveSync: Keep in Sync with Your Data   *369*

9.3.1   The Concept of ActiveSync   370

9.3.2   Creating an ActiveSync Service Provider for the PCDM   371

9.3.3   Some Debugging Tips   404

9.3.4   Summary   405

9.4   Distributed COM   *405*

9.5   Winsock   *408*

9.5.1   A Tiny Winsock Example   409

9.5.2   The PCDM Application   418

9.6   IrDA or Infrared: The Wireless Wire   *418*

9.6.1   Adding IrDA Support to Your Winsock Example   419

9.6.2   Adding IrDA Support to the PCDMDLL   424

9.6.3   Test the New PCDMDLL in eMbedded Visual Basic   432

9.6.4   Implementing "Send to . . ."/"Receive . . ." in the PCDM Application   433

9.7   HTTP: Integration of the Internet   *440*

9.7.1   Wininet: The Client Internet API   441

9.7.2   A Small Wininet Example   441

9.7.3   The Web Server Issue   445

Chapter 10   Graphics and Sounds   *447*

10.1   Loading Bitmaps   *448*

10.1.1   Using LoadBitmap( )   449

10.1.2   Using SHLoadDiBitmap( )   449

10.1.3   Using Custom Code   450

10.1.4   Adding a Picture Class to the PCDMUI.DLL   457

10.2   Displaying Bitmaps Using GDI   *459*

10.2.1   Updating OnDraw of the PCDMPicture Class   460

10.2.2   *Testing the PCDMPicture Class in eMbedded
Visual Basic   462*

10.2.3   *Updating the PCDM Application   462*

10.3   Playing Sounds Using the Windows CE API   *463*

10.3.1   *Adding a Sound to the PCDM Application   464*

10.4   DirectX on Windows CE   *464*

Chapter 11   **Miscellaneous Topics**   *465*

11.1   Enhancements for Pocket PC Devices   *465*

11.1.1   *Window Size Must Be Calculated
Differently   466*

11.1.2   *Only Full-Screen Dialog Boxes   467*

11.1.3   *A Tiny Example   468*

11.1.4   *Summary   473*

11.2   Creating Help Files for Your Application   *473*

11.2.1   *Creating a Help File for the PCDM
Application   474*

11.2.2   *Calling the Help File from within the PCDM
Application   478*

11.3   Creating a Control Panel Application   *479*

11.4   Adding an Icon to the Taskbar   *482*

11.4.1   *Adding a Taskbar Icon to Your PCDM
Application   482*

11.5   Installation for Windows CE   *484*

11.5.1   *Installation Targeting Windows CE   485*

11.5.2   *The Installer Information File (.INF)   485*

11.5.3   *Creating the Installer File for Your PCDM
Application   485*

11.5.4   *Creating a CEF Installation for PCDM   498*

11.5.5   *Writing a Custom SetupDLL   500*

11.5.6   *CF-Card Instant-Installer for the Pocket PC   503*

11.5.7   *Creating an Installation for the Desktop   510*

11.6   Rules to Make Your App Logo-Compliant   *527*

11.6.1   *Logo Requirements of All Target Platforms   528*

11.6.2   *Special H/PC Logo Requirements   530*

11.6.3   *Special Palm-size PC Requirements   530*

Chapter 12   **Conclusions and Visions** *533*

12.1   A Word about Your PCDM Application *533*

12.2   What's Next? *534*
      12.2.1   *How Small Will It Become?* *536*
      12.2.2   *The Dark Side of the New World* *536*
      12.2.3   *What Can You Do to Take Part?* *537*

12.3   Where Is the Technology Now? *537*

Part III   **Appendices** *539*

Appendix A   **Frequently Asked Questions** *541*

Appendix B   **The PCDMUtils Class** *545*

Appendix C   **Glossary and Abbreviations** *557*

Appendix D   **Tips and Tricks for Unicode versus ANSI** *565*

Index *569*

Preface

Welcome to the World of Windows CE

Windows CE is probably the most underestimated technology Microsoft has ever produced. At present, Windows CE is most commonly used in palm-size and handheld PCs, but in fact it is capable of much more. The embedded environment Windows CE is targeting holds a nearly unlimited reservoir of opportunities for software developers and original equipment manufacturers.

Windows CE was written from scratch but is modeled after its bigger brother Windows. This book will help you to understand the differences between these two brothers and will guide you step by step through all the major technologies of Windows CE.

Back in 1996, when Windows CE was still in diapers, I was already working on several hardware and software products, using this program as the base technology. At that time I was working as a technology ambassador for Siemens at Microsoft, which entailed dual responsibilities: to evangelize Windows CE at Siemens and to deliver feedback from Siemens to Microsoft. During my time at Microsoft I made friends in all departments of the Windows CE team. The Microsoft DRG (Developer Relations Group) made sure that I always had the latest Windows CE devices running the newest beta build of their next-generation software. The Windows CE Marketing and the Tools Team provided me with the latest versions of SDKs (Software Development Kits) and compilers. Many of those technologies were still in beta when I wrote this book. By the end of 1998 I had collected so much information and knowledge about Windows CE that I thought it would make a useful book for others.

How Is This Book Different from Others?

The title tells you that this book is a technology tutorial. But what is a technology tutorial? A tutorial explains something by walking the reader step by step through an example. This book is a technology tutorial because it uses the tutorial method to walk you through all the essential technologies of Windows CE. Traditional technology books generally discuss a technology in a more theoretical way—for example, by explaining the Application Programmable Interface (API) calls and their parameters. However, during my years of experience as a developer, I found that even the worst example is better than the best theoretical explanation.

During the course of this book you will find innumerable tiny examples and step-by-step explanations showing you how to recreate each example from scratch. At first the explanations will be very detailed, but as you proceed through the book, you'll find that they come to focus more on the essentials.

In addition, this book emphasizes the importance of Windows 2000. This new operating system will quickly become essential for developers, industrial users, and end-customers in the business sector.

The book also stresses the importance of the Common Object Model (COM) approach for Windows CE. COM is the best way of preparing any application for the digital and "distributed-technology" age we will face in the near future—and which I will discuss more fully in Chapter 12.

The "Thread Example": A Real-Life Application

Another big feature of this book is the "thread example." The thread example is a Pocket-CD-Manager (PCDM) application. It allows you to synchronize a database of your CDs with the "Microsoft Deluxe CD Player" on your desktop and manage it with your Windows CE device. The PCDM will, with very few exceptions, explore all the technologies of Windows CE. This example, which gets its name because it weaves through the book like a red thread, is a real-life application that you will create from scratch. At the end of the book the application will be ready for deployment, including a redistributable setup.

How to Read This Book

This book is meant for developers who want to bring their desktop programming experience to Windows CE but have not yet worked on Windows CE. In other words, it is aimed at Win32 professionals who are Windows CE beginners.

To guide you through the technologies of Windows CE, the book contains 12 chapters, each focusing on one area of Windows CE. The order of the chapters is determined by the real-life thread example. As in any tutorial, you will create this real-life example from start to finish. The sample application is a Pocket-CD-Manager that will synchronize a CD library database on your Windows CE device with the library of the Deluxe CD Player on your Windows 2000 desktop. To be more specific, you will learn how to

- Set up your development machine (Chapters 1–3)
- Create the first steps of the application by choosing the framework, creating the application base structures, and designing a prototype in eMbedded Visual Basic (Chapters 4–5)
- Create the framework for two components used in the sample application introducing COM on Windows CE (Chapter 6)
- Include the UI elements like CommandBar, CommandBand, and ListView, among others (Chapter 7)
- Add storage capacity to the application using Registry, ObjectStore, and Active Data Objects (ADO) (Chapter 8)
- Add support for remote technologies like Remote Application Programmable Interface (RAPI), infrared communication, and ActiveSync (Chapter 9)
- Create a fancy About Box, using graphic APIs on Windows CE (Chapter 10)
- Wrap up the application by adding advanced feature support for palm-size PCs, creating a setup to install the application on Windows CE and to distribute it, and using the Windows Installer Technology (MSI) (Chapter 11)

If you follow all the steps, you will end up with a fully functional Pocket-CD-Manager application.

One goal of this book is to keep the sample code as simple as possible. Therefore you will not check each and every error condition, and some code will look a bit "crude." For example, instead of using dynamically allocated and growing lists, the book will rely upon fixed-dimension arrays.

Besides the thread example, each chapter also contains a tiny code snippet that shows the technology at work. This will allow you to jump to any chapter if you are just interested in a specific technology.

To summarize, the technology section of each chapter will have several sub-sections, including all or parts of the following:

- An introduction to the technology
- A small code snippet giving you a quick glance at the technology
- A sub-section wrapping the technology into a COM component
- A small Visual Basic code snippet using the COM component of the previous sub-section
- A sub-section adding the COM component to the main PCDM application
- A summary highlighting the main caveats, gotchas, and remarkable facts of the technology

The book contains countless examples and sample code. To save space, I provide only the technology-specific code and not all the plumbing code that the eMbedded Visual C++ (eVC) wizards create. If you have to change any code, the new code will be printed in **boldface**. Most of the code is embedded in step-by-step procedures that explain exactly what you have to do to add the code to the example. Since many of those procedures will have repeated content (for example, adding a method to a COM component), they will become progressively simpler and less detailed as the book progresses.

```
// Code lines themselves are printed in fixed letter spaces.
```

The Companion CD

All source code printed in the book can also be found on the companion CD in the directory Sources. Chapter and section numbers structure this directory. An extra sub-directory contains the sources of the thread example. Inside this directory you will find sub-directories named PCDMUI, for the user interface component; PCDMDLL, containing the core technology component; and PCDMCE, the main thread-example application.

Other directories include tools, helpers, and some redistributables you can use to evaluate certain third-party technologies like DeviceCOM, InstallShield for CE, the Microsoft Installer SDK, and the latest ActiveSync. The source code on the CD was created using the latest Microsoft eMbedded Visual Tools. I removed all temporary eVC files but kept the executables and DLLs so that you can run the application without having to recompile them. If you open the source code, you will find the book-specific code between two remark lines:

```
// <BOOK_ADDON Chapter=x.x.x> ***************************************
// </BOOK_ADDON Chapter=x.x.x> **************************************
```

The thread-example code adds the step number after the chapter number to the remark tag. If you are familiar with Extended Markup Language (XML), you will recognize that we are using XML syntax to mark the code of the book. Using a Visual Basic macro, you could highlight the areas where the book has added code.

The Beginning at the End

The final chapter will give you some general ideas about where to go from here and what the digital future may bring. In case you do not know what to do with Windows CE, just read it, and you should come away with at least one idea that leads to a great digital-age product.

Acknowledgments

- Scott Henson (Microsoft), Sam Henderson (Microsoft), and especially Phil Aiken (Microsoft) for helping me through the jungle of Microsoft and feeding me with the latest Windows CE gadgets and devices.
- Dan Benson (Siemens TTB) for his great initial copyedit and review.
- Dave Tobias (AMD), Chris DeHerrera, and Jason Dunn, for doing an excellent job reviewing this book and keeping me on track.
- Chris Stirrat (Microsoft) and Matt Woodmark (Microsoft) for their help with the ADOCE chapter.
- Charles Wu (Microsoft) for help with the ActiveSync chapter.
- Mike Shappell (Microsoft) and Rodney Rushing (Microsoft) for their help with Microsoft eMbedded Visual Tools issues.
- Mike Thomson (Microsoft) for help regarding the Windows CE system.
- Rebecca Bence and Gary Clarke (Addison-Wesley) for being so patient in guiding me through my first experience as an author.
- Lori Sargent for encouraging me to write the book.
- Rainer Besold (Siemens) and the Siemens A&D PT1 team for their support.
- My wife Bettina and my daughter Alisa for being so understanding and supportive with me during this time- and evening-consuming marathon.

Chris Muench

Foreword

Over the past four years, while developing Windows CE, I have had the pleasure of meeting and working with people throughout the "Embedded Industry." For the most part, these individuals have been in companies not directly associated with the traditional desktop computing industry. They include people like William Baxter (BSQUARE), Mark Morneault (AMD-Advanced Micro Devices), Tom Wong (Mainbrace), Tony Fadell (formerly with Philips), Blake Krikorian (ID8Group), Eric Carpenter (ARM-Advanced RISC Machines), Chris Muench (Siemens), and many, many others.

Collectively, these people are industry drivers who share common entrepreneurial, evolutionary, and even revolutionary ideas about the future of computing—outside the desktop. They represent a wide variety of technology and business initiatives that might seem to have little in common—such as DSP modules, licensable CPU cores, custom hardware boards, companion chipsets, development tools, software integration services, packaging and design innovations, and software applications, drivers, and components. They innovate, collaborate, and compete vigorously. Although they act independently, they share—and seek to realize—a common vision of a highly connected world of embedded devices improving all aspects of our lives.

Windows CE has contributed to this dynamic by bringing these people together and accelerating the pace of innovation in the embedded industry. But Windows CE is not the lone catalyst of change; many of CE's competitors are realizing the potential of this new realm. The result is a fast-growing, highly complex "technology solution space" with orders of magnitude and more opportunity than the PC desktop could provide. Although many in the traditional desktop and server software industries are just beginning to recognize this emerging market opportunity, it is moving forward at an accelerated rate.

To understand the potential of this market, one has only to think of the many contributing factors that characterize the embedded computing industry. In desktop PC and server computing, there is only one or two of each CPU type, hardware design, and operating system configuration; when considering market share, one could argue that x86, Windows, and the PC-99 hardware specification together constitute the single most significant platform. The majority of the industry is thus geared toward innovation against standard platforms. Moreover, the resulting technology solutions are limited to a few specific form factors—primarily desktop computers and servers.

In contrast, the embedded industry offers more of each of these variables—more CPU types (both the number of core architectures as well as the number of custom chipsets per architecture), application-specific integrated circuits (ASICs), application-specific semiconductor parts (ASSPs), and application-specific custom parts (ASCPs); more hardware boards [many custom varieties, but human-machine interface (HMI)- and peripheral component interconnect (PCI)-based derivatives, too]; and more operating systems configurations (Windows CE, for example, is designed to be custom-configured to meet the needs of any specific solution). Perhaps most important, no limits are placed on the form factor of a solution. Just think of the possibilities:

At work: Pick a sector of industry, such as manufacturing, and imagine an integrated manufacturing and information system with automated failure reporting, adjustments for demand changes, wireless diagnostic communication with inspection personnel, productivity measure reporting, automatic ordering of parts when supplies run low, and a state-of-the-art user interface (UI) for man–machine interfaces. Couple this with development tools such as Visual Basic (VB) and you add the ability to reconfigure and adapt to industry demands almost instantaneously.

At home: How about a digital music system available throughout the home? Or programmable, compatible audio and video appliances that interface with anyone's digital cable, satellite, set-top box, or residential gateway connections? Other possibilities include the addition of 1394, wireless, and other home networks, which include central media servers, home-to-auto RF garage sockets, and automated security, lighting, watering, heating, and utility conservation measures.

On the go: How many times have you wished you could download your address book from Outlook to your cell phone? How about five days of standby; color displays; Internet connectivity; interfacing with home, work, and public phone systems; synchronizing information with other phones locally; and so on? The options are many, and the technology to accomplish these and many other features is here today.

There are countless opportunities to add value throughout this industry, each with its own unique set of hardware, software, and form-factor requirements.

Seeing the possibilities is one challenge, but implementing them is quite another. Today the embedded industry is truly a rich and complex technology environment. It demands great flexibility and, in particular, the ability to customize in all aspects of design. Windows CE was designed with this very challenge in mind. It is a fully customizable and modular operating system that can be configured to work in less than 500KB of memory by eliminating many unneeded operating system features. Or it can be configured as a high-end implementation with a complete Windows graphical user interface (GUI), a Win32 programming model, and a multi-threaded, multi-task, message-based operating system similar to its desktop brethren. Or it can be literally anything in between. It is fully compatible with popular networking protocols and standards such as TCP/IP for interoperability with existing systems and networks. And in all cases, no matter the custom configuration needed, Windows CE supports a plethora of CPU architectures, enabling a wide selection of hardware to suit the needs of the specific design.

All of this adds up to one thing for the developer: building technology solutions for the emerging embedded market is an exciting new frontier that has yet to be tamed, or "matured," as those in the industry would say. As with all new frontiers, there is much to be discovered and much to learn. And the learning curve is particularly challenging. Fortunately, the new references and other learning materials that are starting to appear can significantly lower this learning curve.

Chris Muench has created one very good source with *The Windows CE Technology Tutorial*. The approach Chris takes in this book is uniquely pragmatic, designed to help developers hit the ground running, as opposed to devoting countless hours to reading before getting started. His abundant use of examples and his emphasis on the "way things work" rather than "what they are" makes the book immediately useful, both as an advanced reference and as a place for someone just getting started.

Of course, there are other sources of help. There are training sessions and seminars, there are other books, and for those learn-it-the-hard-way people, one can simply get the Platform Builder and start building today against an ordinary PC. Personally, however, I recommend the fastest and easiest path up the learning curve—because if there is one thing that's consistent in this industry, it's that it moves at lightning speed, making time-to-market the single most important criteria for success. If you want to get up to speed quickly, you will find *The Windows CE Technology Tutorial* a great asset.

Randy Kath
Director, Windows CE Embedded Platforms
Microsoft Corporation

Part I

Ready . . .
Set . . . Go!

1
Chapter

Why Windows CE?

Developing applications and systems for Windows CE has a lot in common with the art of creating and taking care of bonsai trees. In each case:

- The goal is to produce small but nicely designed versions of their big brothers.
- The end products require as much, if not more, care than their brothers.
- They will not survive unless you optimize their resources.

Are you ready to step into the world of bonsai development?

The first part of the book will give you the basic tools you will need to write successful Windows CE applications. You will find step-by-step discussions of how to:

- Set up your PC to work optimally with Windows CE Tools
- Install the Development Tools and Windows CE Tools
- Set up the Emulation Environment for the target platform
- Choose the right platform for your task
- Install this device and test its connection to your development PC
- Use the Windows CE Remote Tools
- Choose the right technology framework for your task

You will also learn more about the thread example that you will be following through the rest of the book.

Before we start setting up our workstation and getting ready to develop for Windows CE, I would like to introduce you to this program and summarize the challenges that you will face over the next several chapters. You may have heard about Windows CE if you have been following Microsoft's publicity efforts for this new operating system. The press, on the other hand, has shown little interest in the topic. There have been some magazines for handheld (H/PC), palm-size PC (Ps/PC), and Pocket PC owners, but there has been little coverage of Windows CE topics for developers. Microsoft has devoted great resources to the development of Windows CE, and I am pretty sure that ultimately computer publishers will follow suit by introducing new Windows CE periodicals. Indeed these periodicals may have been launched by the time this book is published.

1.1　What Is Windows CE?

Windows CE is a new operating system. It is not a port from Windows NT or Windows 9x, though you may sometimes hear this from the press and maybe even from some "Microsofties." The Windows CE APIs are modeled after those of Windows NT, but internally Windows CE is a new code base.

This is a very important statement you should always keep in mind when working with Windows CE. Once you've become familiar with its APIs and its design criteria, you will be convinced that it's a new operating system. Below are the two most important criteria.

1.1.1　No Legacy 16-Bit APIs

Windows CE looks nearly like a cleaned-up version of Windows NT. Have you taken a look at the Windows NT APIs lately? Do you know how many old 16-bit calls still exist under Windows NT in order not to break any old applications? If Microsoft had modeled Windows CE after Windows NT, Windows CE would not only be much bigger but also slower and clumsier.

For developers this means that if there is a new 32-bit call originally replacing the old 16-bit call, Windows CE has only implemented the 32-bit call and does not even stub-out the old call as NT does. A good example is "CreateWindow()": under Windows CE only the new "CreateWindowEx()" call exists.

1.1.2　Modular to Fit into Small Devices

Windows CE was designed to run in the smallest devices that care very much about their memory footprint of ROM and RAM. Adjustments for different and smaller displays can also be added to this criterion. If Microsoft had to decide between functionality and size, it decided to optimize for size. You will find new core DLLs that do not exist under Windows NT. They contain some functions of many Window NT core dynamic link libraries (DLLs) like "kernel32.dll", "user32.dll", and "gdi32.dll". Most of the core functions are in the "COREDLL.DLL", the very heart of Windows CE.

The functions in the "COREDLL.DLL" are the least common denominator of Windows CE. In other words, all CE devices must include this DLL. If you create an application that only uses functions of the "COREDLL.DLL", your application will run on every device that claims it is running Windows CE. Of course, the device needs to have some way of installing your application and enough RAM to host it, but if these frame conditions are met, your application will run. If you try to look for this DLL in the Windows directory, you may not see it because many vendors decided to protect the DLL.

Here is a tip on how you can get the properties of this DLL to see how big it is and when it was created:

Create a copy of any file on your Windows CE device and rename it "COREDLL.DLL" and then try to copy it to the \Windows directory. Windows CE will prompt you to confirm replacement of the existing (hidden) DLL file. Included in this confirmation box is the size of "COREDLL.DLL" and the date it was created/stored on the device.

WARNING: Do not actually confirm the replacement process. This might render your device unusable until you cold-reset it. Normally your Windows CE device should refuse the copy process because the "COREDLL.DLL" is in use.

For Windows CE 2.11, H/PC Professional devices, the "COREDLL.DLL" is about 393K. In the remaining chapters of the book you will learn which DLL(s) are required to be on the Windows CE device to support particular technologies.

Why is Windows CE so interesting for developers in all areas of application and system development? The reasons can be found in several key features of Windows CE.

Windows CE is the smallest version of Windows that you can get. This makes it the perfect system for smaller PC-like devices, such as those used in vertical applications that need to have the Windows look and feel but cannot afford the memory footprint of the desktop version. Windows CE is likewise a good choice for devices that do not have any user interface (so-called headless devices) but that require the Win32 API to allow fast and easy development of custom applications.

Windows CE is the fastest version of Windows. Once cold-booted, Windows CE starts and stops instantly, providing the "instant on" that is needed in many vertical applications, such as medical devices, automation controllers, or personal organizers. With Version 3.0, Windows CE even allows for real-time applications.

Windows CE is the most reliable version of Windows. This is a highly debated topic, and not everybody will agree. But here are some points that argue in favor of this thesis:

- Windows CE was designed and developed from the ground up. It includes only the latest APIs and, unlike Windows NT, does not carry old legacy code.

- When Microsoft developed Windows CE, it eliminated all 16-bit related calls, which were one of the major reasons for Windows NT's instability.

- The Windows CE team also eliminated redundant code. If there was one way to develop a feature, Microsoft eliminated all other ways to do it. Sometimes this strategy results in more work for the developer, but it keeps the code size small and eliminates errors on the developer side.

- In Windows CE, an application will always be optimized for the smallest possible size. Smaller code is not only faster, but is also more controllable and thus more reliable.

Windows CE covers a much larger market than a desktop operating system. The potential market for Windows CE is much broader than that for desktop PCs. Figure 1.1 compares the cost per operating system for a pyramid of operating system

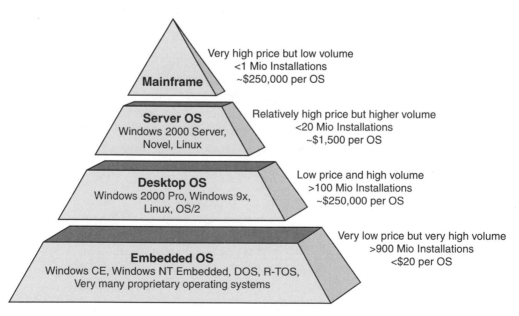

Figure 1.1   The operating system segmentation pyramid

units. You can see that the end result is pretty close to the same money volume, but the segmentation and the variety increase the further you go down the pyramid. Windows CE is at the very bottom. If you are beginning to imagine what you might do with Windows CE, just wait until you read Chapter 12, which should give you even more ideas.

Windows CE offers the greatest flexibility that an operating system can provide. Windows CE is foremost an operating system for the embedded space. In this market, it is imperative to have the ability to design hardware and software that conform exactly to the needs of your target application. Windows CE offers this flexibility through its high level of componentization. Unlike PC-based operating systems, it does not require standard hardware. Instead it offers support for a wide variety of CPUs—and will continue to support more CPUs in the future—and it offers standard driver support for a large variety of new technologies, including Universal Serial Bus (USB), Digital Versatile Disk (DVD), infrared, Ethernet, and Global Positioning System (GPS) devices.

1.2   Windows CE versus Embedded Windows NT

Another frequently asked question concerns the differences between Windows CE and the new embedded version of Windows NT. Table 1.1 lists several differences between the two operating systems. Microsoft uses Figure 1.2 to illustrate the functions or uses for which each OS is best suited.

Given that embedded Windows NT can be run without a keyboard and display adapter, there are overlapping areas and applications where either operating system (OS) could be used. Most of the time, however, the requirements of size or for server services will determine your choice of OS.

If you are still uncertain whether Windows CE is the right operating system for your application, ask yourself the following questions:

- Can I do without strict security in my application and my network connections?
- Is memory size an issue?
- Does my application have to be instantly available?
- Is power consumption of any concern?
- Does my application require execution in real-time?

If the majority of your answers are "Yes," Windows CE is the perfect choice for your task.

Table 1.1   Differences between Windows CE and Embedded Windows NT

Feature	Windows CE	Embedded NT
Minimum Memory Usage	512K for OS, 4K for RAM,	6MB for OS 24MB for RAM
Support for Spindle-Less Operation (No Hard Drive)	Yes	Yes
Support for Headless Operation (No UI)	Yes	Yes
Instant On (No Boot)	Yes	No
Networking Support	Limited	Full
Plug and Play	No	No
COM Support	Limited until Version 3.0, see Chapter 6.	Full
Transaction Server Support	No	Yes
Message Queuing Support	Client in Version 3	Client and server
Support for SQL Databases	Limited	Full
Maximum Number of Processes	32	Unlimited
Server Service Support	HTTP in Version 3.0	HTTP, FTP, File Server, Print Server, and SQL Server
Support for Hard Drives	Generally, no, but drivers for Adaptec PC-Card SCSI and PC-CARD ATA Flash Disks are available.	Full
PC (Intel) Hardware Required	No	Yes
Support for Other CPUs Than i386	Yes	No
Multimedia Support	Limited; DirectX will come over time starting with 2.12.	Full
Touch Screen Support	Built in	Third party
Unicode Support	Full	Full
Developer Support	Limited Win32 APIs	Full Win32 API
Optimized for Low Power Consumption	Yes	No

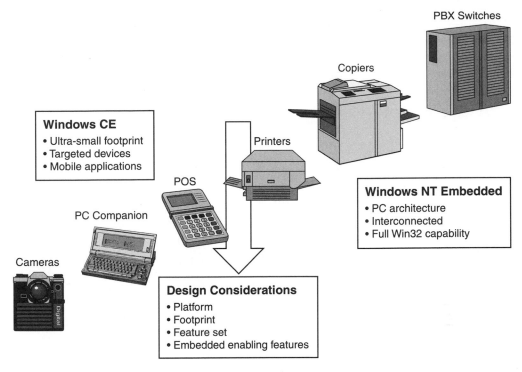

Figure 1.2   How to position the two operating systems

2 Chapter

Preparing Your PC for Windows CE

Before we step into the world of Windows CE, we need to set up our environment to work most efficiently. Getting the right development workstation is one part of assuring maximum productivity. This chapter will describe the setup of your development workstation in great detail because I believe that a stable installed workstation is the most important foundation for solid development.

2.1 Choosing the Right PC

You might think that since Windows CE works so well with smaller devices, you can use one of your old 486 machines for development work. This is not the case. Development of Windows CE applications requires a professional workstation, the same type that you would choose for regular Windows development.

Microsoft recommends a Pentium 90 MHz, NT4, Windows 95 or Windows 98, 32MB RAM, and about 610MB for the complete Windows CE Toolkit installation. I have worked with the Windows CE Tools since their first beta build and have found that for the greatest efficiency you should at least double these minimal requirements. Therefore, here are my recommendations.

2.1.1   Get at Least a Pentium II or K6-2 with 300MHz

You will not get any smaller ones these days anyway, and faster is better. Every minute you have to wait for the computer to complete a task you lose in productivity.

2.1.2   Use Windows 2000 Professional or Windows 2000 Server

The new Windows 2000 Operating System (formerly known as Windows NT5) has many advantages in terms of productivity and usability. It also has numerous enhancements that help developers become more productive, including, for example, dual- or multi-monitor support (see below). Although, in general, Windows 2000 Professional is perfect for your development workstation, Windows 2000 Server has some unique advantages that make it my primary platform.

- The integrated terminal server—a very nice feature for presenting your work on a different machine without copying the whole development environment over to that machine. Even the Windows CE Emulators that come with the Windows CE Tools work in the terminal server environment.
- A more flexible Web server—where Windows 2000 Professional includes only the Personal Web Server (PWS), Windows 2000 Server comes with the full-fledged Internet Information Server 5.0 (IIS5).

I strongly advise against the use of Windows 95 or Windows 98. The Windows CE tools include very nice emulation support for some Windows CE classes of devices. These emulations do not work under Windows 9x. Another reason to avoid Windows 9x is the well-known fact that the compiler sometimes hangs unexpectedly during development.

2.1.3   Get a Lot of RAM

You should have at least 128MB RAM. Every time the system has to swap memory to the hard drive, your system slows, and you lose productivity. RAM has become very cheap on the market, and the cost for one hour of your time has probably gone up. So everything you can do to increase your productivity is worth the money.

2.1.4   Use the New Dual- or Multi-Monitor Support

Multi-monitor support is one of the features of Windows 2000 that can really increase the productivity of Windows CE developers. In the current version of the Windows CE

Tools, the emulator will always be at the screen coordinates (0, 0). In a single-monitor environment you have no choice but to move your development environment either to the right of the emulation, in the case of the palm-size PC (Ps/PC) emulation, or below the emulator, in the case of the handheld (H/PC) emulation. In either case, you loose valuable screen estate. With a dual-monitor solution you can win back this estate by using the second monitor for your development and the primary monitor for the emulator.

Here is the hardware that I recommend for a dual-monitor setup.

- Two graphic cards, preferably a 3DFX Banshee AGP with 16MB VRAM as primary video card and a Matrox G200 PCI as secondary.
- Two monitors, at least one of which should be a 21-inch monitor.

There is a trick to perfectly configuring the Windows 2000 dual-monitor environment: The primary graphic card will always have the coordinates (0, 0). In most cases, this means that if you are using an Advanced Graphics Port (AGP) and a PCI graphic card, the system will boot from the AGP card, and as soon as Windows 2000 is fully loaded, the screen coordinates of the AGP card will be (0, 0). AGP cards are normally faster than PCI cards and should be used for the development screen rather than the emulator screen. Windows 2000 lets you configure the primary monitor via Display Properties. Choose the Matrox card as your primary card by selecting the option "Use this device as the primary monitor," as shown in Figure 2.1, to get the screen coordinates (0, 0) on the Matrox card. Remember that the emulator will always use (0, 0) as its top left corner.

Select a low resolution for this monitor—say, 800×600—and connect your smaller monitor to this card. Select a higher resolution for your development screen, and connect it to your 21-inch monitor. With this configuration you can have the full 21-inch screen estate for development without covering the emulator. Figure 2.2 shows a schematic of how your setup might look.

If you want the emulation monitor to the left or right of your development monitor, you simply need to drag the monitor to the corresponding position in Display Properties (see Figure 2.1).

2.1.5 Get a Big Hard Disk

Your hard disk should have plenty of space. Partition it generously because you might want to install samples from different sources without playing CD-ROM disk jockey. The hard disk should also be very fast because the compilers will do a lot of their work on this drive. I recommend at least a 10GB drive connected either to an Enhanced Integrated Drive Electronics (EIDE) with Ultra 33DMA or to a SCSI3 U2W controller. Here you can take advantage of another feature of Windows 2000.

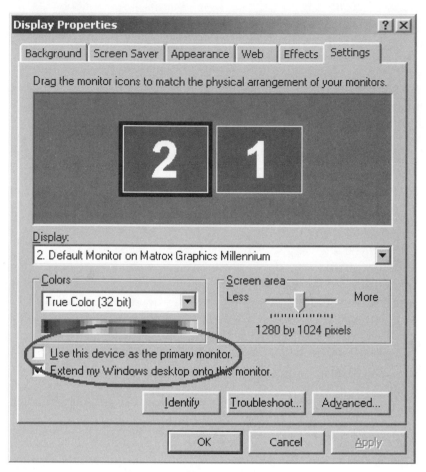

Figure 2.1   The display properties of Windows 2000

With Windows 2000 you can format the whole 10GB hard drive with one partition. Windows NT 4, on the other hand, does not support boot partitions greater than 2GB.

2.1.6   Use a Network Interface Card (NIC)

Microsoft does not require this option for developing Windows CE applications, but it will save you a lot of setup pain if you have an Ethernet adapter in your PC. During the setup of Windows 98, Windows NT, or Windows 2000, the setup will try to install a network on your PC. Without an NIC, you will not be able to install the TCP/IP protocol that you need for Remote Access Service (RAS). As you will learn in Chapter 10, RAS is necessary to use the Winsock functionality of Windows CE.

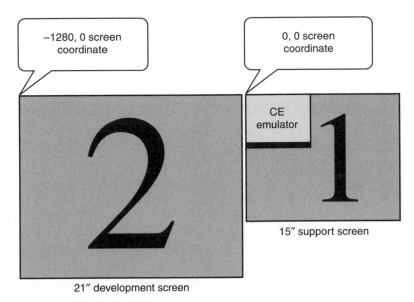

Figure 2.2   The dual monitor scenario

Another reason for an NIC is that debugging, application downloading, and all other ActiveSync features are much faster over an Ethernet connection than over a serial cable. NICs are very cheap, so cost should not be an issue.

2.1.7   Use DVD-ROM Instead of CD-ROM

This is not really a requirement so much as a good recommendation. Microsoft has already started shipping the Microsoft Development Network (MSDN) Library CDs on DVD, and many more tools and vendors will follow. You do not need a DVD encoder card, just the plain drive. The price difference between a CD-ROM and a DVD-ROM is under $50 and should not be the reason for choosing the old drive.

2.2   Choosing the Right Windows CE Device

There are many Windows CE devices to choose from. Which one you buy really should depend on what you are planning to do with it or the applications you want to develop. Table 2.1 compares these devices from a developer's perspective in order to help you choose the one that best meets your needs. It does not, however, show the general enhancements that Microsoft added from one device to the next device. It does not include the AutoPC, which is not discussed in this book.

Table 2.1   Choosing the Right Windows CE Device

Pros	Cons	Devices	Uses
Palm-size PC (Ps/PC) Version 1.0			
Full Windows CE 2.01, yet still small and lightweight, even fitting into a shirt pocket, making the computer "wearable."	Only a four-color gray scale. Slower than newer devices. No ADO, MFC, Active Template Library (ATL), or eVB.	Casio E10/E11, Philips NINO, Everex Freestyle.	Great for outdoor use or where carrying space is scarce or in applications without a keyboard or large screen requirements.
Relatively long battery life.			
Display offers good outdoor visibility.	No Ethernet support in the box.		
Palm-size PC (Ps/PC) Version 1.1			
Windows CE 2.11. Adds color to the 1.0 devices. Supports ADO, MFC, ATL, and eVB. Runs Windows CE 2.11 on par with H/PC Pros. Adds Ethernet support.	Shorter battery life than V1.0 devices. Outdoor visibility of color devices is not as good as the gray-scale 1.0 devices.	HP Journada 420, Casio E15 (BW), Casio E100/105 (Color), Compaq Aero, Philips Nino 500, Everex Freestyle, Compaq Aero 2100.	Same as V1.0. Vertical applications requiring a color display, such as color presentation applications.
Handheld PC (H/PC) Version 1.0			
Windows CE 1.0. First available devices. Very cheap now. Very good readable	No Ethernet support. Only a four-color gray-scale display. Poor Windows CE	Casio A10/A11, NEC MobilePro 750, Philips Velo 1.	Outdoor applications for roaming sales managers.

Pros	Cons	Devices	Uses
display, even outdoors.	services (H/PC Explorer). Cannot run the new development tools in Microsoft eMbedded Visual Tools 3.0.		Games in the "Gameboy" style.

Handheld PC (H/PC) Version 2.0

Pros	Cons	Devices	Uses
Windows CE 2.0. Ethernet, color display, a bigger screen than palm-size PCs, and eVB support.	Shorter battery life than palm-size PCs. No ADO. Outdoor visibility of color devices is very poor.	Sharp Mobilon, NEC MobilePro 400/450, Casio A20, HP 620LX and 660LX, Philips Velo 500.	Same as 1.0 devices. Vertical applications requiring color like those for realtors or doctors.

Handheld PC (H/PC) Professional Version 3.0

Pros	Cons	Devices	Uses
Windows CE 2.11. ADO support. Bigger display and keyboards. USB support, Pocket Access, IMAP support.	Bigger devices are not as wearable as the older, smaller ones were.	HP Journada 820, Sharp Mobilon Pro, Vadem Clio, NEC MobilePro 800, IBM Workpad, Compaq Aero 8000.	Replacement for notebook in conferences or on short trips and as a presentation device and e-mail client in the office.

CEPC—A standard Desktop PC running Windows CE

Pros	Cons	Devices	Uses
The most flexible Windows CE device. "All-you-can-eat" component selection of any version of Windows CE.	Development platform only. No handheld or palm-size PC-specific add-ons like ADO, IE4, or Pocket-Office available.	The CEPC parts list will not fit here. For a complete listing, see: http://msdn.microsoft.com/library/techart/guide.htm#guide_topic3.	Development. Embedded system platform.

If you are planning to create a smart application that runs on all devices (except on Windows CE Version 1.0 devices), your best choice would be an H/PC Professional with a screen size of at least 640 × 480 pixels.

You can test and run applications written for the Ps/PC, H/PC Version 2.0, and, of course, the H/PC Professional on the H/PC Professional platform. Palm-size PCs have screen resolutions of approximately 240 × 320 pixels and will not display correctly on H/PC Version 2.0 devices because their maximal horizontal screen resolution is 240. Since all H/PC Pros are in color, you can even test the applications you want to run on the Ps/PC 1.1 devices. There are some special Ps/PC functions you have to test on a Ps/PC in case you use them in your application. The H/PC Professional is therefore an excellent development platform for Windows CE. Its bigger keyboard, larger screen, and USB support for a mouse are additional benefits.

 Remember: If you are targeting any device other than the H/PC Pro, you must use this device to make your final system tests. If you are targeting all devices, as does the thread example of this book, you will need to get all those devices to test on.

2.3 Summary

Let's summarize what you need for an optimal development workstation for Windows CE.

Table 2.2 Hardware Components for a Windows CE Development Workstation

Component	Minimum (as stated by Microsoft)	Recommended
High-Speed Desktop PC	90MHz Pentium	450MHz Pentium II
Lots of RAM	64MB	128MB
Big Hard Drive	1GB	10GB
Two Graphic Cards	One card, just SVGA	One 3DFX Banshee (AGP) One Matrox Millennium G200 (PCI)
DVD/CD-ROM	CD-ROM 4x	DVD-ROM 2x
Network Card	Not required	3COM Etherlink III 10/100 (PCI)
A Windows CE Device	You choose	Ps/PC: Casio E105
		H/PC Pro: NEC MobilePro 800
Windows CE Ethernet Card	Not required	Socket LP Compact Flash (compatible with all Windows CE devices)

3
Chapter

Installing Your PC

Everybody who has installed Microsoft Tools before knows that the order in which you install your system can be crucial to a smooth development ride. It is no different with Windows CE Tools. To Microsoft's credit, it has dramatically improved the installation for the new eMbedded Visual Tools. You have almost nothing to do other than install the tools. Table 3.1 lists the software components you need to purchase in order to have an

Table 3.1 Software Components for a Windows CE Development Workstation

Software	Part of
Windows 2000	Operating system
Visual Studio 98	Visual Studio
eMbedded Visual Tools 3.0	eMbedded Visual Tools CD1
MSDN	MSDN

For the book you will also need the following:

Office 2000	Office 2000
InstallShield for Windows Installer	InstallShield tools
InstallShield for CE	InstallShield tools

optimal working installation. The components listed in Table 3.2 are free or come with software that you already have purchased.

Selecting an operating system is your first and most important decision. As the eMbedded Visual Tools 3.0 release notes explain, eMbedded Visual Tools support all Microsoft operating systems, but they have limitations when used with some of them. Table 3.3 compares the available Microsoft operating systems and explains why I recommend Windows 2000 Professional as the prime choice for Windows CE development. Note that there are no non-Microsoft operating systems on the list because Windows CE Tools do not run on any other platform.

Table 3.2   Setup Components for a Windows CE Development Workstation

Software	Part of
Palm-size PC SDK 1.0	CE SDK
Palm-size PC SDK 1.1	CE SDK
Palm-size PC SDK 2.0	CE SDK
H/PC 2.0 SDK	CE SDK
H/PC Pro (3.0) SDK	CE SDK
ActiveSync 3.1	Free to download from the Web

Table 3.3   Decision Table for Operating Systems

Operating System	Pros	Cons	Remarks
Windows 95	Cheap, easy to install.	No emulation for CE devices, slower than NT, does not scale well (machines with more than 64MB RAM do not gain anything), poor security.	Worst choice for an OS. It offers no advantages over any other OS.

Operating System	Pros	Cons	Remarks
Windows 98	Cheap, easy to install, dual monitor support, IrDA support.	Same as Windows 95.	Better than Windows 95 but still no emulation support. If you are going to write an IrDA application (see Section 9.6), you can only use Windows 98 or Windows 2000.
Windows NT4	Very solid, emulation support, scales very well.	Difficult to install and get everything running smoothly (for example, SP3 has to be installed twice, and the boot partition has to be 2GB). No dual monitor support.	Good choice if you just want to develop for Windows CE and your hardware does not have any new options you would like to use (USB, IrDA, AGP Graphic Card).
Windows 2000	All of NT4, plus emulation support (even on terminal server), support for new hardware like USB and IrDA, dual monitor support, and very easy to set up.	None.	Has all the advantages of the other operating systems and none of their disadvantages. This makes it your prime choice.

3.1   Installing the Operating System

Having decided to use Windows 2000 as the operating system for your Windows CE development workstation, you will next need to install the system. This section will explain how to do so.

   If you want a clean installation, which is what I recommend, you should let Windows 2000 format your hard drive. The best and fastest way to set up your hard drive is to let Windows 2000 format one partition for the whole drive as Windows NT File System (NTFS). This arrangement will give you the best security and reliability that you can get with Windows 2000. The system also supports FAT32, but since Windows 2000 cannot put its native security on such a drive, I do not recommend using FAT32. In case you want to dual-boot the machine with Windows 9x, you might consider using removable hard drives instead.

 Do not install Windows 2000 and Windows 9x on the same partition as dual boot. The "Program Files" folder will be used by both operating systems and will lead to conflicts.

Windows 2000 is very easy to install. Just use the default settings, and the very good Plug-and-Play of Windows 2000 will take care of all your hardware.

If you are using the Windows CE Services 3.0, you do not even have to install the RAS (Remote Access Services) subsystem except when

- You want to access your desktop PC with your CE device using a modem.
- You want to access or use any service that uses the TCP/IP protocol such as browsing the Intranet/Internet, using DCOM/deviceCOM, or using applications that are using pure Winsock (Windows Sockets).

In these cases, you must install the RAS subsystem because Transmission Control Protocol/Internet Protocol (TCP/IP) is necessary. (See Chapter 9, "Remote and Connectivity.")

3.2 Installing the Development Tools

The next steps are fairly straightforward. The only important thing is the order in which you install the applications. For a perfect installation, I recommend following the order shown in Table 3.4.

Table 3.4 Installation Order of the Tools

Software	Remark
1) Install Windows 2000.	I recommend a clean install to get a well-defined state.
2) Install Office 2000 (typical).	You will need this package for procedures described later in the book.

Software	Remark
3) Install Visual Studio 98.	You will also need eVC and eVB later in the book. However, for pure Windows CE development, Visual Studio is no longer necessary.
VS will ask for server extensions if you selected "Custom" in the setup.	You do not have to install any server extensions. You do not need them for the book, but you can install them if you want to experiment with them.
4) Install MSDN.	Visual Studio 98 will ask for MSDN automatically.
5) Install the latest VS98 Service Pack.	I recommend working with the latest service pack. Even if it costs you some time in switching over, it will be worth your while. It becomes increasingly difficult to keep up with the latest technologies if the developer does not keep up with the latest generation of tools.
6) Install the eMbedded Visual Tools 3.0.	Install all features of the eMbedded Visual Tools.
7) Install InstallShield for Windows Installer.	Section 11.5 will explain how to create a setup for Windows CE Software. If you have the full version of InstallShield 2000, you do not need to install the version that comes with VS98.
8) Install the H/PC SDK, Ps/PC SDK, and H/PC Pro SDK.	I recommend installing the SDKs in the order of their release date, to ensure that a patch for an older SDK, shipped in a newer release, can be applied.
9) Install ActiveSync 3.1.	Install the latest version of ActiveSync.

 If you have the Terminal Server option in the "Application Mode" installed on your Windows 2000 Server workstation, you must either use the "Add/Remove Programs" applet in the control panel to install all the tools, or set the PC to "Install" mode. You can adjust this setting by starting a DOS console and typing in the command "Change User/Install". When you are done with the installation, you have to switch back to the regular execute mode with "Change User/Execute". The "Add/Remove Programs" applet does that for you. If you are using Windows 2000 Professional or if you have installed Terminal Services in "Administration Mode," you do not need to follow this procedure.

Below are some tips for the installation of the tools mentioned above.

3.2.1 Office 2000

When you are done with the installation, configure Outlook 2000 to obtain a valid Outlook profile. Taking this step will enable you to install ActiveSync correctly later on. If you want, you can install PhotoDraw 2000 and Publisher 2000. These tools are not needed for this book, but if you want to use them, they will not disrupt the installation process.

3.2.2 Visual Studio 98

I recommend installing VS98 with the custom settings and selecting the complete Visual C. Doing so will save you the trouble of later having to install parts of eVC that you may need.

During the installation of VS98 the setup will ask you to install MSDN. If you have subscribed to MSDN, install the quarterly updated MSDN CDs when VS98 requests the MSDN CDs. Do not forget to install the latest service pack of Visual Studio.

3.2.3 The eMbedded Visual Tools 3.0

Select the "complete" options during the setup and your installation will work fine, but do not install any SDK from the setup. The installation of the SDKs will be started automatically, so just cancel them. I also recommend using the default directory because the book will occasionally point to files on your hard drive.

3.2.4 The Windows CE Platform SDKs

Let setup install the tools to their default directory. You can use "typical" to install the SDKs. The best order for installing the SDKs is by Windows CE version number, beginning with the oldest, as shown in Table 3.5.

Once you have installed the SDKs, test their emulation environments by starting "Start Menu/Program/Windows CE Platform SDK (H/PC)/Desktop Handheld PC

Table 3.5 **Windows CE Versions of the Platform**

Platform	Windows CE Version
H/PC Version 2.0	2.0
Palm-size PC Version 1.0	2.01
H/PC Pro (H/PC Version 3.0)	2.11
Palm-size PC Version 1.1	2.11
Palm-size PC Version 2.0	3.0

Emulation" and "Start Menu/Program/Windows CE Platform SDK (Palm size/ PC)/Desktop Palm-size PC Emulation". Both should come up without trouble.

3.2.5   ActiveSync 3.1

The installation of ActiveSync 3.1 is really almost painless. Just install it, and you will be able to immediately connect to your Windows CE device. You should see a small icon in the tray, as illustrated in Figure 3.1. This icon will display the status of your connection to the device.

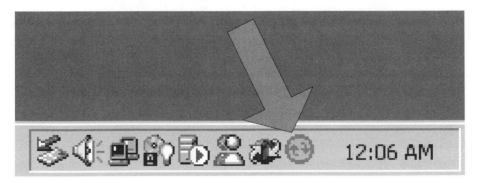

Figure 3.1   Tray icon showing the status of your device connection

3.3 Setting Up Your Windows CE Device to Connect to the Workstation

This step prepares your Windows CE device to connect to your workstation. Microsoft has made this step fairly simple, but because you changed the default communication speed to 115K baud, you have to take one additional step to hook up your device. The steps below are the same on all devices.

3.3.1 Create a Direct Dial-Up Connection Using 115K Baud

1. Go to "Start/Programs/Communication" and select "Remote Networking" on your Windows CE device.
2. In the upcoming Windows double tab, the "Make New Connection" icon and the "Make New Connection" wizard will pop up. (See Figure 3.2.)
3. Name the connection "115K," and select the "Next" button.

On the next page, the "Serial Cable on COM1:" should already be selected in the drop-down box.

4. Tab on the "Configure . . ." button and you will be able to set the parameter for the cable in an upcoming dialog box. (See Figure 3.3.)

The only thing you have to change at this point is the Baud Rate.

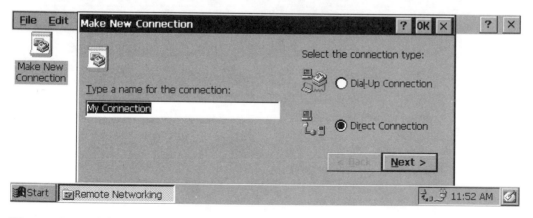

Figure 3.2 The "Make New Connection" wizard

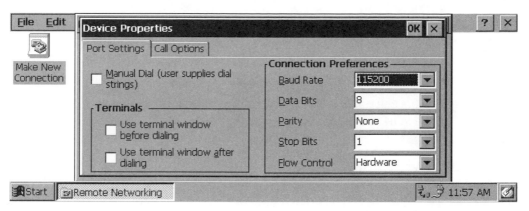

Figure 3.3 Configuring the serial cable

5. Set it to 115200, and close the dialog box using the "OK" button in the upper right corner of the dialog box.

6. Back in the wizard, tab on the "Finish" button, and you will see a new icon in the Remote Networking Window labeled "115K".

3.3.2 Setting the Default Connection for the PC-Link

Now you have to tell the Windows CE device to use your new connection as default setting for the PC-Link.

1. Start the Windows CE control panel by selecting it in the Start Menu under "Settings". You will find an icon for "Communication" there.

2. Double-tab this icon, and you will see the dialog box of the "Communication Properties". In the first tab you can give a name to the device.

 This device name is very important in networking with Windows CE. Without a valid name, you will not be able to connect to a remote server using the networking redirector (for example, \\MYServer).

3. Name your device "MYCE", enter "CEDevice1" as the device description, and then select the "PC Connection" tab.

This tab declares what connection should be used as the default when connecting to a PC. The current default setting depends on the Windows CE version.

4. You want to change this setting, so click on the "Change . . ." button.

In the dialog box, you can only change one setting: the way of connecting to your desktop PC. As soon as you tab on the drop-down box, you will see the "115K" entry that you created in the first step.

5. Select this entry and close the dialog box. Close the "Connection Properties" with the "OK" button in the upper left corner.

3.3.3 Test Your Connection to the PC

The last step is to test your connection to the PC.

1. Connect the communication cable that came with your Windows CE device to the PC in the COM1 port and hook it up to your Windows CE device.

As soon as you plug in the cable on both sides, the Windows CE device will try to connect to the PC. If it is successful and if you set all parameters correctly, you may get a password dialog box on the Windows CE screen asking you for a user name, password, and domain name. However, this dialog box will appear only if you are using a network connection via an Ethernet card or a modem using RAS. If you are using a standard serial cable and ActiveSync, you will not be prompted to enter credentials.

2. Enter "CEPC" as the user name and a small "a" as the password.

As you can see in Table 3.6, if your PC is running Windows 2000 Professional or Windows NT 4.0 Workstation, you do not have to enter a domain name. If you installed a server operating system and you have upgraded your server to a domain controller (DC), you need to enter the domain name. If you are running a regular server, you must enter the machine name of your server as the domain name.

Table 3.6   Domain Name Entries by Operating System

Operating System	Domain Name Entry
You installed Windows 2000 Professional, Windows NT 4.0 Workstation, or Windows 9x.	Leave it empty.
You installed regular Windows 2000 Server or Windows NT 4.0 Server.	Enter the machine name of the PC.
You upgraded your Windows 2000 Server or Windows NT 4.0 Server to a domain controller (DC).	Enter the domain name of the server.

There is one special case in which you must enter a domain name even for a Windows 2000 Professional or Windows NT 4.0 workstation installation. If you joined your workstation to a domain controller and the CEPC account is on the domain, you must enter the name of that domain controller. In general, I would not recommend this arrangement. For example, if the connection to the domain controller were broken—because the network or the DC was down, or because you were working from home with cached DC credentials—your Windows CE device would not be able to connect to your workstation.

Once you are logged in, ActiveSync wants to synchronize your Outlook data with your Windows CE Device.

3.   If ActiveSync asks you if you want to set up a partnership, select "Yes".

4.   In "Number of Partnerships," the wizard's next page, you can choose whether to synchronize your device with just one or a maximum of two workstations. You can choose what you need here; it does not really matter for the various examples in this book.

5.   Select "Next" to choose the synchronization settings.

In the next page of the wizard, you can select what you want to synchronize between your PC and your Windows CE device. I will come back to these options in discussing ActiveSync and Active Data Objects (ADO) in Chapter 9. For now you can select whatever you want. I recommend using the defaults. (See Figure 3.4.) Once the partnership is established successfully, you are set up and ready to go.

3.3.4   Optional Steps: Using a LAN Card to Connect to Your PC

ActiveSync, the Windows CE Development Tools, and the Remote tools also work using a LAN connection between the Windows CE device and your development workstation. This is a new feature of Windows CE 2.0 and does not work with older Windows CE 1.0 devices.

To use this feature you need a NE2000-compatible Ethernet PC-Card for the Windows CE device. If you own a Windows CE device running Windows CE 2.11 or higher, you can also use the Proxim Wireless LAN Card "RangeLAN2". The setup is fairly simple:

1.   Plug in your Ethernet card into the PC-card slot, and a dialog box will pop up, asking you for the TCP/IP configuration data.

2.   If you have a Dynamic Host Control Protocol (DHCP) server running in your network, you just need to select "OK," and the card will work immediately.

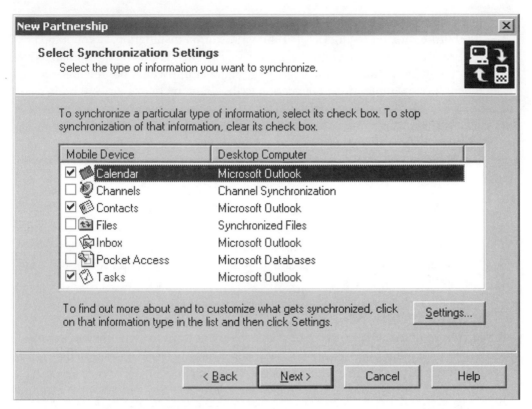

Figure 3.4 The ActiveSync options

If you do not have a DHCP server, you will need to enter an IP address manually. This address has to be in the same sub-net as your PC workstation so that the two devices can communicate. Windows 2000 will automatically provide a generated IP address to your workstation during setup if you selected the typical installation option. To verify your IP address, open a DOS box and enter "IPCONFIG". You will get a small list of data similar to the one shown in Table 3.7.

Table 3.7   IPCONFIG Results

Adapter domain name	(empty)
DNS servers	192.100.3.10
IP address	192.100.3.11
Sub-net mask	255.255.0.0
Default gateway	192.100.3.1

The important data you should see are the IP address (192.100.3.11 in this example) and the sub-net mask (255.255.0.0).

3.   To connect to a machine with the data above, you should set the IP address on the Windows CE device to 192.100.3.12 and the same sub-net mask as the PC (255.255.0.0).

If your PC and Windows CE device are connected to a network with multiple machines, you will have to get an IP address from your IT administrator to make sure it will not conflict with an existing PC. Once you enter the IP address, the LAN card will be ready to use. But instead of using the PC-Link to start the communication with your PC, you must use the "ActiveSync" feature of the Windows CE device.

4.   You can start ActiveSync by selecting "Start Menu/Programs/Communication/ ActiveSync".

A dialog box will ask you what method you want to use to connect to your PC.

5.   Choose "Network Connection" and press the "Connect . . ." button.

Very quickly you will see whether you set up your Windows CE device correctly. Watch the connection message on your PC screen. On the Windows CE device, you will get a dialog box, as shown in Figure 3.5. This dialog box will stay open until you

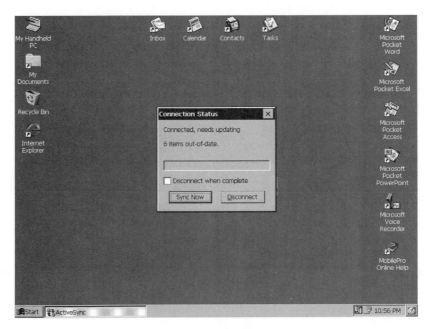

Figure 3.5   The ActiveSync connection dialog box

disconnect from your PC. You can minimize the dialog box by tapping on the "ActiveSync" button in your Start Bar.

 Important note: The Ethernet connection will fail if there is no WINS server in your network and you do not have the network protocol NetBEUI installed on your desktop PC. ActiveSync uses the WINS server or NetBEUI name resolution services to locate the desktop machine.

4
Chapter

The Windows CE Development Tools

You are now ready to take your first steps using the Windows CE tools. Along with the eMbedded Visual Tools, Microsoft includes a series of tools that helps you understand, debug, and get a deeper look inside the Windows CE operating system used by your device. This part of the book will briefly introduce these tools and give you some tips on how to use them most efficiently.

4.1   Windows CE Tools

You can find the remote tools in the eMbedded Visual C++ environment in the "Tools" menu. eMbedded Visual Basic includes the same tools but stores them in a sub-menu named "Remote Tools" in the "Tools" menu. Each of the remote tools requires a little server on your Windows CE device. If you are connected with ActiveSync over Ethernet or serial cable, the tools will check whether this server is available on the device. If the server is missing, the tools will automatically send down the correct version of the server from the PC to the Windows CE device.

4.1.1   Remote File Viewer

The Remote File Viewer lets you explore inside your Windows CE device or emulation environment. (See Figure 4.1.) It looks like the standard Windows File Explorer,

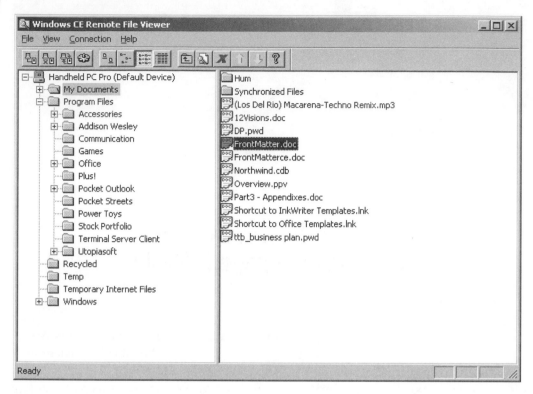

Figure 4.1 The Remote File Viewer

but the Remote File Viewer offers a far more limited range of features than those available with Windows File Explorer. With the yellow arrows, you can import and export files between the Windows CE device and the desktop. The file viewer also allows you to delete and rename files on the Windows CE device.

4.1.2 Remote Heap Walker

The Remote Heap Walker (see Figure 4.2) can be a very useful tool for detecting memory leaks. Unfortunately, it is a very basic tool and lacks many desirable features, such as a configurable automatic refreshing of the heap list and process list; additional details on any process—for example, total usage of the heap; or memory or sorting of the heap list by any of its columns.

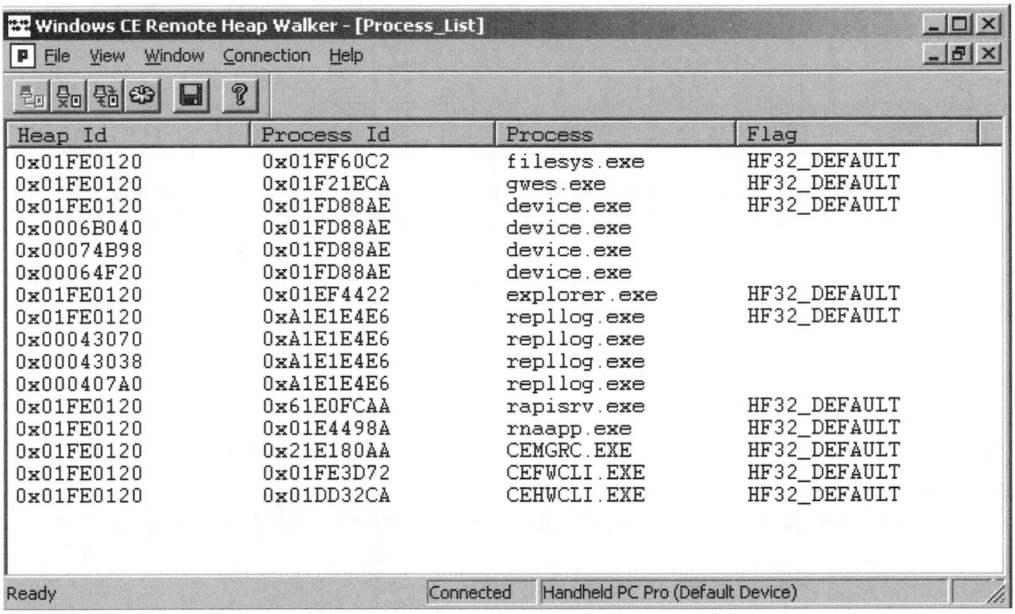

Figure 4.2   The Remote Heap Walker

How to Detect Memory Leaks

Because the Heap Walker is a pretty basic tool, you will have to make some convoluted steps to detect memory leaks. Here is a method that worked for me:

1.   Double-click the process you want to monitor, and the heap list will appear.

The task should be in an idle state, or at least you should know what it is doing. An active task could change the heap permanently and is therefore hard to diagnose.

2.   Use the "Save" button in the toolbar to save the contents of the heap list to the disk.

Refresh the screen after about 30 seconds and save the new screen to the disk, but this time use a different file name.

3.   Repeat the last step for about 10 minutes.

At the end of this process you should have 20 files on your disk. Now you can either use a tool like WinDiff to compare two files or Access to compare all of them. I prefer to use Access.

1. Open Access and create a new blank database.
2. Select "File/Get External Data/Import" and the first heap list file in the upcoming dialog box.

After you select the file, the "Import Text Wizard" will pop up.

3. On the first page, do not change anything. Just press "Next" because the Heap Walker will save the data in a file with fixed-width alignment.

On the second page, you have to create break lines to help Access find the fields in the file.

4. Set the break lines right before the field starts, as shown in Figure 4.3, and press "Next".

On the following page you can just press "Next" because this is the first import of a heap list file, and you have to create a new table.

The next page allows you to name the fields, which you should do if you intend to use this Access database again.

5. For leak detection, it is not necessary to do anything on this page, so just press "Next".
6. On the following page you will be asked to add a primary key. It is very important to select "No Primary Key".

Any key you add here would render the table useless for memory-leak detection because it would refuse to import more files into the table.

7. The last page of the wizard asks for a name for the new table. Call it "HeapListFiles".

You will find the new table in the "Tables" section of the Access object. Now you need to import the other heap list files into the same table.

8. Select "File/Get External Data/Import" again and then select the next file of your heap list files.
9. Skip the first page and select the same break lines in the second page as mentioned above.
10. On the third page, select the existing table "HeapListFiles", and press "Next".

The final page will only ask for confirmation.

11. When you press "Finish", the data will be imported into your "HeapListFiles" table.

12. Repeat the last four steps for each of your heap list files.

Once all the files are imported, you can check the lists for memory leaks.

13. Open the table "HeapListFiles", and sort it by the "Field1" (Address) column.

If you imported all 20 files you should see every address 20 times in the "Field1" column.

If you have no memory leaks, the values in "Field2" for a given address should be the same. If the values change, either you have a memory leak, or else you did not undertake the process when the system was in an idle state. Once you have located the address of the leak, you can use the eMbedded Visual C++ (eVC) debugger to find the part in your code that is causing it.

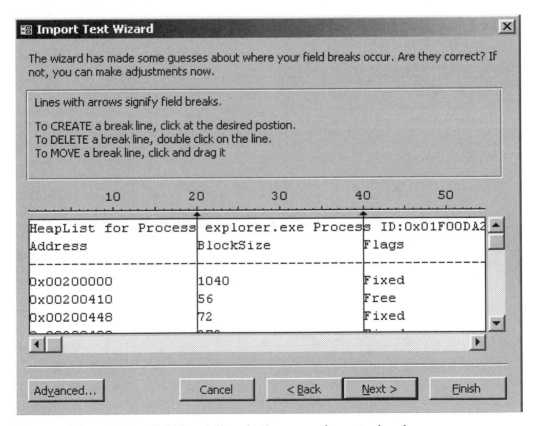

Figure 4.3 Setting field break lines in the access import wizard

4.1.3 Remote Process Viewer

The Remote Process Viewer is a very useful tool. It shows you all running threads of a given process and all modules (DLLs) that the process has in use (see Figure 4.4). It also allows you to kill a selected process.

 Be careful when killing any specific process. If you kill a process that is necessary to communicate with the desktop, you might, in effect, cut the cable to your device.

The Remote Process Viewer is easy to use, but it does not offer a lot of interaction. To view the threads and modules of a given process, simply select the process in the top list. Remember that you can only kill processes, not threads. To kill a process, select the process in the top list and click on the big red "X" in the toolbar.

Process	PID	Base Pr...	# Threads	Base Addr	Access Key	Window
NK.EXE	21FF7FE2	3	4	02000000	00000001	
filesys.exe	01FF60C2	3	1	04000000	00000002	
gwes.exe	01F21ECA	3	13	06000000	00000004	
device.exe	01FD88AE	3	32	08000000	00000008	
explorer...	01EF4422	3	4	0A000000	00000010	Control...
repllog.exe	A1E1E4E6	3	7	0C000000	00000020	ReplLog
rapisrv.exe	61E0FCAA	3	3	0E000000	00000040	Pegasus...
rnaapp.exe	01E4498A	3	2	10000000	00000080	Connect...
CEMGRC.EXE	21E180AA	3	3	12000000	00000100	
CEFWCLI.EXE	01FE3D72	3	1	14000000	00000200	
CEPWCLI.EXE	C1D886D6	3	2	16000000	00000400	

Thread ID	Current PID	Thread Priority	Access Key
01FE3EEA	21E180AA	3	00000101
E1E1EE76	21E180AA	0	00000101
C1E18CAA	01FD88AE	3	00000109

Module	Module ID	Proc C...	Global...	Base Addr	Base Size	hModule	Full Path
TLCESR...	81DDC400	1	3	00F10000	24576	81DDC400	\Windo...
WINSOC...	81F6ACF8	1	8	01CF0000	30720	81F6ACF8	\Windo...
coredl...	81FF7580	4	93	01F90000	403456	81FF7580	\Windo...

Figure 4.4 The Remote Process Viewer

4.1.4   Remote Registry Editor

The Remote Registry Editor is one of my personal favorites. This tool allows you to add, change, and delete registry keys in your Windows CE device, emulation, or development workstation registry. (See Figure 4.5.) It even allows you to cut, copy, and paste keys and entries between the registries. The registry keys' export feature, which you might know from the desktop "RegEdit" version, is also quite helpful. You will use this tool several times in the coming chapters to set registry keys for needed functions.

   To modify a registry key, use the tree view to navigate to the location you want to modify. Then click the node with the right mouse button and select the action you want to perform on the key. If the key has values, you can also click with the right mouse button on them and perform some actions.

4.1.5   Remote Spy++

If you are familiar with the Spy++ program in the Desktop Windows Platform SDK you will easily be able to use this tool. It will not work in an emulation environment.

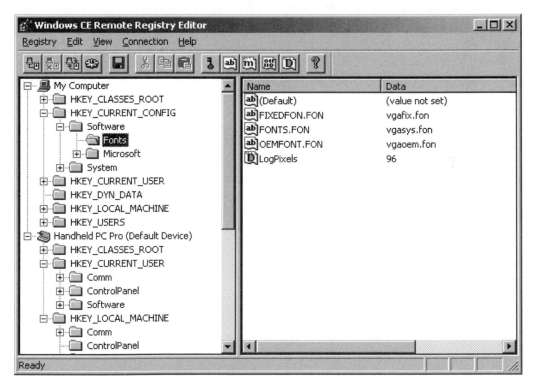

Figure 4.5   The Remote Registry Editor

The tool supports nearly every activity that it performs in the desktop version, such as viewing messages and properties of a given window. It even includes a windows finder similar to that found in the desktop version. (See Figure 4.6.)

4.1.6 Remote Zoomin

The Remote Zoomin allows you to view the screen on your Windows CE device on the desktop and is a great tool to create user documentation. It just grabs the screen content and transports it to your development workstation. (See Figure 4.7.) You can save the content to disk as screen shots. Zoomin also allows you to print out the screen content.

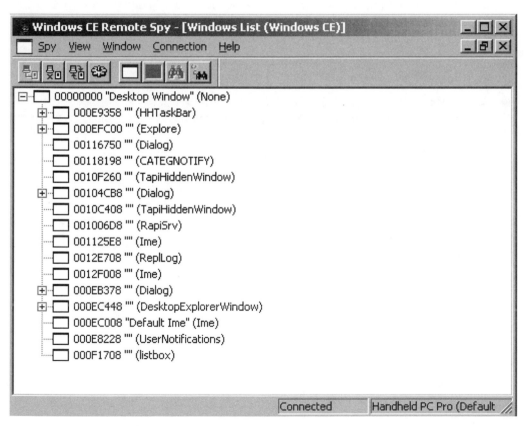

Figure 4.6   The Remote Spy++ in action

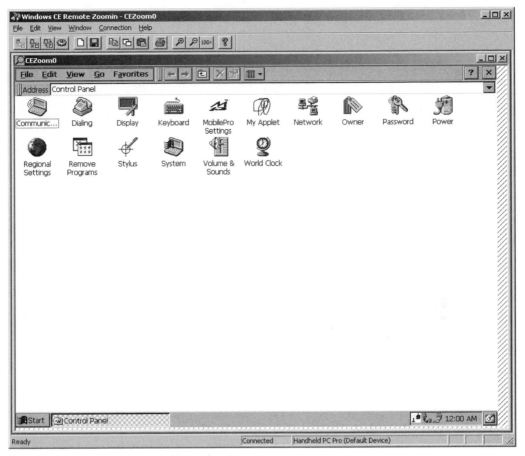

Figure 4.7   The Remote Zoomin

4.1.7   The Control Manager

The Control Manager would be a useful tool for Visual C++ developers, too, but is currently only accessible through the "Remote Tools" menu in eMbedded Visual Basic (eVB). It allows you to view, install, and remove ActiveX controls on your Windows CE device. (See Figure 4.8.) With the yellow arrows you can import and export files to and from the Windows CE device and the desktop. The Remote File Viewer also allows you to delete and rename files on the Windows CE device. You will use this tool later in the book several times to install some of the controls that you will be writing.

This tool is very easy to work with. Just select the platform you are working with and open its node in the tree view. Once you have selected the correct device, you will see all the controls available for and installed on the device in the right pane of the

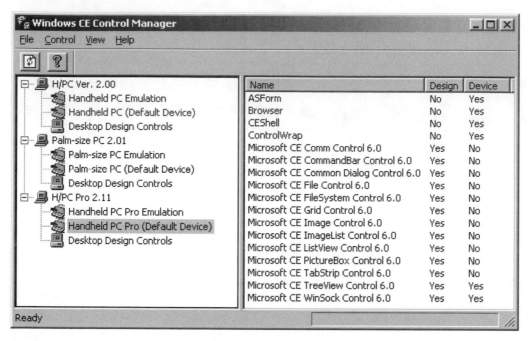

Figure 4.8 The Control Manager

control manager. You can then click with the right mouse button on a control and perform an action on it. Unless you are using a desktop, you cannot create new controls with eMbedded Visual Basic. You have to create them using eMbedded Visual C++. In addition, you have to have a desktop version of the corresponding Windows CE version registered on your desktop in order to see the ActiveX controls for Windows CE or to be able to add them to the Control Manager. The book will cover this and all other known issues in detail in Chapter 6, "COM for Windows CE."

Unfortunately, the Control Manager does not offer an "Update" function. If you have changed an ActiveX control, you have to uninstall it from the target and then reinstall it—an unpleasant task for an ActiveX control developer.

4.2   eMbedded Visual C++ versus eMbedded Visual Basic

Now for a nearly religious topic: What is the best development environment for Windows CE? In the section discussing different devices, I advised you to choose the device that best fits the task at hand. The same is true for choosing your development environment. Both Basic and C++ have unique features that will help you determine which to select for your development task. Table 4.1 provides a decision table regarding the two languages and their corresponding tools.

You should select a language by asking yourself several questions and answering each of them with either "C++" or "Basic". Once you have completed this process, simply choose a language based on whether the "Cs" or the "Bs" predominate. If your

Table 4.1   Decision Table for C++ versus Basic

Feature	eMbedded Visual C++	eMbedded Visual Basic
Requires runtime	Only if you are using ATL or MFC	Always
Result runs on emulation	Yes	Yes
Result runs on H/PCs	Yes	Yes
Result runs on palm-size PC	Yes	Not on old V1.0 devices
Result is processor independent	No	Yes
Debugging support for desktop emulation	Yes	Yes
Debugging support for Windows CE devices	Yes	Yes (only H/PCs)
Development of COM components (COM server or ActiveX controls)	Yes	No
Hosting ActiveX controls	Yes (but hard to develop)	Yes (easy to develop)
Development of drivers	Yes	No
Development of ActiveSync filter	Yes	No
Rapid development, testing, and deployment	No	Yes
Degree of freedom	High (no boundaries)	Low (limited eVB syntax and possibilities)
Support for embedded devices	Yes (all versions)	Since Windows CE 2.11
Support for remote services	Yes	Yes (using Winsock control)

questions have resulted in an even split, flip a coin. Here are some questions to consider.

Which language do I know better?

Is my task more user interface (Basic) or body code (C++)?

Does my application have to run on older palm-size PC devices?

Yes = C++; No = Basic

What is my company standard?

Do I have to write a lot of ActiveX controls or COM servers?

Yes = C++; No = Basic

Do I have enough space on my device to download the big VB runtime?

Yes = Basic; No = C++

Do I have to write low-level drivers, services, or applications with no user interface (UI)?

Yes = C++; No = Basic

There is a new Basic runtime that does not require any forms, but if you need scalable and high-speed services, I do not recommend using it.

You can also decide to use a mix of both languages by creating the general UI in Basic and developing the core functionality as ActiveX controls in eVC. The book's thread example will use this type of development style, at least for testing the COM components.

4.3 The eMbedded Visual Basic Environment

So far you have set up your PC, installed software, and prepared to take your first steps as a Windows CE developer. But before you actually begin development, you need to make sure that your development tools are working, especially the debugger.

To test whether eVB is working correctly, you will build a tiny application, download it to the device, and try to hit a breakpoint in the code. This test will familiarize you with the development environment.

4.3.1   Creating, Downloading, and Debugging a Small eVB Application

First, you need to create a new application from scratch.

1.   Start the eMbedded Visual Basic environment from the "Microsoft eMbedded Visual Tools" menu in the "Start menu".

As soon as eMbedded Visual Basic is fully loaded, you will see the "New Project" dialog box, shown in Figure 4.9.

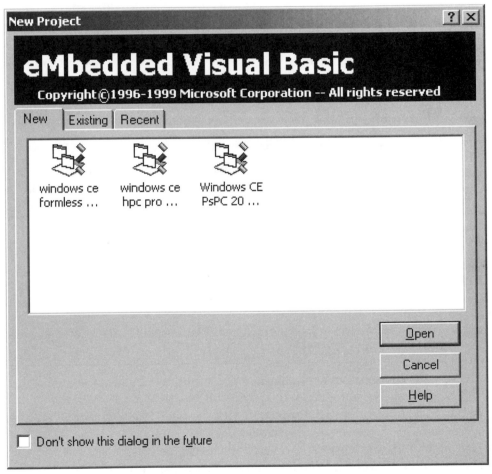

Figure 4.9   The eMbedded Visual Basic "New Project" dialog box

2. You are going to create a "Windows CE HPC Professional Project". Select this project type in the dialog box and click the "Open" button.

3. Select the project properties in the "Project" menu and change the "Run on Target" setting to "Handheld PC Pro (Default Device)".

eMbedded Visual Basic has created a new project with "Form1" as its default startup form. To ensure that your Windows CE device is ready to run your new application, you have to check the runtime availability.

4. In the "Tools/Remote Tools" menu, select the menu item "Download Runtime Files".

eMbedded Visual Basic will now connect to your Windows CE device and check whether you lack any components that you will need to run an eVB application. If a component is missing, eVB will download, install, and register it. You have to select this menu item only once to prepare your device for eVB. If you change your device, buy a new one, or have to cold-reset your device, you must reselect this menu item again.

5. Create a button on the form and name and label it "Test" by changing the properties "(Name)" and "Caption" to "Test".

6. Create a text box under the "Test" button, but do not change any properties.

7. Double-click the button and the code window for the button will come up.

8. Type the following lines in the "Test_Click" subroutine:

```
Private Sub Test_Click()
    Dim I
    I=14
  MsgBox "It Works!"
    Text1.Text = I
End Sub
```

9. Set a breakpoint in the line with the MsgBox.

So far, the eVB environment works much as you would expect it to. All the features you learned to love in VB for the desktop are available for Windows CE development. Probably the next thing you would do on the desktop would be to press the "Run" button, and that is just what you do in Windows CE!

If your workstation, your Windows CE device, the remote connection, and your eVB installation are working correctly, you should see the eVB form with the "Test" button in the upper left corner of your H/PC Professional screen. If you tab on the "Test" button, you will find that the debugger works just as expected.

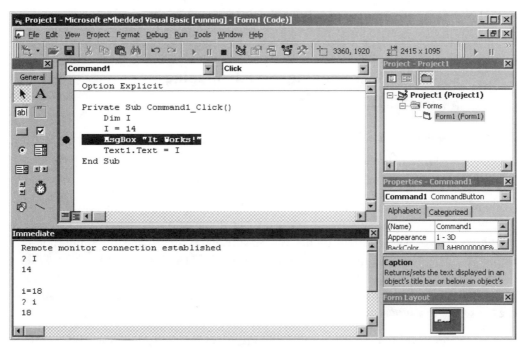

Figure 4.10   The eMbedded Visual Basic debugger

In the immediate window you can print values and enter commands. In Figure 4.10, note that I first printed out the variable "i" and then changed it to "18" and printed it out again.

As soon as you press the "Run" button in the debugger, you will see the message box "It Works!" on your Windows CE device. And as you close the message box the text box will contain the value 18 because you changed it in the debugger's window.

Congratulations! If everything worked as above, your eMbedded Visual Basic installation is set up properly. Now you are ready to start your first serious eVB application. Before you do, I need to discuss eMbedded Visual C++.

4.4   The eMbedded Visual C++ Environment

eMbedded Visual C++ (eVC) is the other development environment you want to make sure is set up correctly. For this reason you are going use eVC to build the very same application that you just created using eMbedded Visual Basic. This procedure will also introduce the new features of Windows CE's eVC Toolkit.

4.4.1 Creating, Downloading, and Debugging a Small C++ Application

1. Start the eVC environment at "Start/Programs/Microsoft Microsoft eMbedded Visual Tools/eMbedded Visual C++ 3.0".
2. Once eVC is loaded, select the "New . . ." item in the "File" menu.

You are probably familiar with the upcoming dialog box, with the exception that the eVC dialog shows only "WCE . . ." project types. Each of the project templates for Windows CE has a counterpart on the Win32 side and basically has the same functionality. For your application, you will use the WCE MFC AppWizard (EXE). Later in the chapter you will get help in deciding which framework to use for your development job. For this little test application, the MFC framework provides the fastest means to get to a quick result.

3. Enter "MyFirst" in the field for the Project Name and select the "WCE MFC AppWizard (EXE)".

As you can see in Figure 4.11, the eVC Toolkit adds a number of processor types to the platform list. This, by the way, is an interesting faux pas on Microsoft's part because it usually calls "H/PCs," "palm-size PCs," and "H/PC Pros" platforms rather than processors. It would have been much better had the company listed the target platforms in that list instead of the processors. The irritations increase if you try to find a way to compile for the processor "WCE (x86)" because none of the platform choices in the selection bar supports the Intel x86 processor.

4. After you click the "OK" button, the WCE MFC AppWizard will start. Compared to the AppWizard for Win32, this wizard offers fewer options, but the core questions remain the same.
5. On the first page of the wizard, select "Dialog Based", and press the "Next" button. Actually, you could also press the "Finish" button, since you are not going to change any value in the upcoming pages.

You might want to browse quickly through the pages to see what options you can choose from, especially the last page in which the wizard asks if you want to use the MFC DLL as a shared DLL or prefer to bind it statically to the application. Since binding the MFC statically will increase your application's size and thus its memory footprint, I always recommend choosing "Shared DLL".

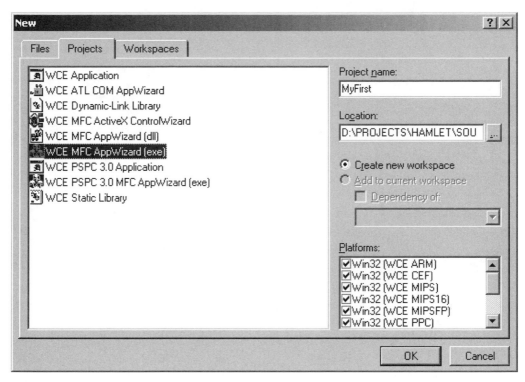

Figure 4.11   The eMbedded Visual C++ new project dialog box

Speed and Memory Space

Windows CE devices have two major problems that you should keep in mind: speed and memory space. Linking the MFC statically in your application wastes a lot of space on the device. Most current devices have the MFC in ROM. Windows CE has a very nice feature in that it does not load a DLL into program memory, but instead executes the functions inside the DLL "in place," in its storage location—hence in ROM. This feature is commonly referred to as "XIP" (eXecute In Place). Regarding speed, the bigger an application is, the longer it takes to load and run. You always want to keep your application as small as possible in order to get the highest speed possible.

Once the wizard has finished its job of creating the frame for your application, you will get an eVC environment that looks similar to the one in Figure 4.12. Figure 4.12 shows the "MyFirst" dialog box that was created by the AppWizard. Open this dialog box and insert a button and an edit box.

    6.   Name the button "Test" by changing its "Caption" property.

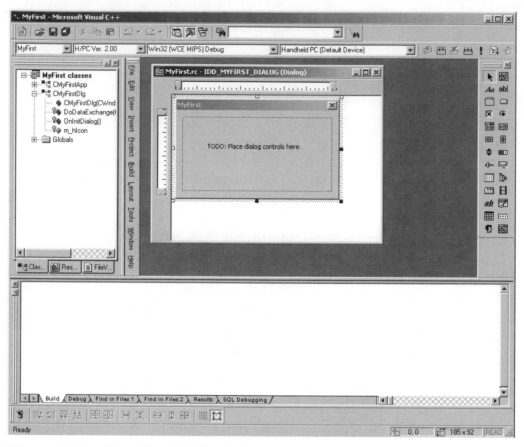

Figure 4.12 The eMbedded Visual C++ development environment

 Having read this far, you have probably noticed that I am always eager to optimize my screen estate. One nice feature of eMbedded Visual C++ 3.0 is that it allows you to drag the menu bar to a different location and even dock it vertically. The location I selected for the menu bar saves space on top of my screen and gives me about two more lines of C++ code.

7. Select the "Test" button with the right mouse button and then select "Events . . .".

8. In the upcoming "Message and Event Handler" dialog box, press the "Add Handler and Edit" button.

9.   In the upcoming dialog box, just press "OK".

The next window you will see is the source window of "MyFirstDlg.cpp" and the function "void CMyFirstDlg::OnButton1()".

10.   Enter the following code between the braces:

```
void CMyFirstDlg::OnButton1()
{
        int m_i=14;
        MessageBox(L"It Works");
        //CDialog::DoDataExchange(pDX);
        CWnd *Edit=GetDlgItem(IDC_EDIT1);
        CString stEdit;
        stEdit.Format(L"%d",m_i);
        Edit->SetWindowText(stEdit);
}
```

So far you have done nothing different from what you would have done for a Win32 project. Even such Visual C++ 6.0 features as ToolTips, Auto-complete, and Type-Complete appear in eMbedded Visual C++. The next steps, though, are different and are Windows CE-specific.

11.   Before you can compile the project you have to select the correct platform (CPU) and device (platform). (I wish Microsoft would get its wording right.)

You can use the toolbars in the eVC environment to set those values. The toolbar contains four combo boxes that you normally use by working from the left to the right. First, select your project. Since you only have one in your small application, the project "MyFirst" is pre-selected. The second combo box contains all the platforms you have installed. It should contain "H/PC Version 2.0", "Palm-size PC 2.01", "Palm-size PC 2.11", "Palm-size PC 3.00", and "H/PC Pro 2.11".

12.   Select the "H/PC Pro 2.11" option.

The next combo box contains the processor type.

 Other than eMbedded Visual Basic, which is processor-neutral in Visual C++, you must specifically set the processor type you are going to target.

13.   Choose the debug version of the processor that you have in your device.

If you are not sure which processor is in your device, you can look at the "System Properties" in your device's control panel. The processor type can be found in the "Device" tab of "System Properties".

You will also find that the processor type "CEF"—Common Executable Format (CEF)—is not actually a processor, but rather an executable format used on newer devices. Instead of compiling for the real processor in your Windows CE device, you can compile to the CEF P-Code. As soon as the CEF file gets downloaded to the Windows CE device, an Install-Time-Compiler will compile the CEF file into the native binary required on the target CE device. The big benefit of CEF is that one CEF file can run on all the CPUs of one platform. This reduces the size of your setup file dramatically.

The last combo box tells the eVC environment which device to target. With eMbedded Visual C++, it is possible to use an Ethernet LAN connection for downloading and debugging even without using ActiveSync as transport.

4.4.2 Using the Windows CE Platform Manager

Here is how to set up a direct TCP/IP link to your Windows CE device. In the "Tools" menu, find a new entry called "Configure Platform Manager" next to the Windows CE remote tools. If you select this item, you will find a dialog box that allows you to add and configure new devices (see Figure 4.13).

1. Select the "H/PC Pro 2.11" node and press "Add Device".
2. Name the device "MyCE" and press the "Properties" button.

The upcoming "Device Properties" dialog box will select the transport "Windows CE Services" by default. If you want to use Windows CE Services, you can do so and exit from this dialog box. But Windows CE Services has two major disadvantages:

- Your device has to be continuously connected while you are developing, either via the PC-Link (serial connection) or ActiveSync. But on occasion this link can be disconnected because errors on the line disrupt ActiveSync.
- You can only connect to one device at a time.

You want to use the pure "TCP/IP" transport for this example.

3. Select the "TCP/IP" transport and click on the "Advanced" button.

In the "Advanced" dialog box you will find the CE Services again selected as the default.

4. Change the server component to "Manual Server" and close the box with "OK" to get back to "Device Properties".

If you press the "Test" button in "Device Properties", eVC will tell you which components it requires to use this transport and the command needed to start the server. If your H/PC Professional does not include these components, you can find them on your hard drive in the directory "\Windows CE Tools\WCE211\MS HPC Pro\ PlatMan\target\<your Processor>".

   Once you download the components for your device, you can test the connection using the parameters you get from the "Test" dialog box. I strongly recommend that you make a hard copy of that dialog box to preserve the long and time-consuming connection string.

 You can create a hard copy of a dialog box by pressing the key combination "ALT-PrintScrn" on your desktop machine. Then start the Paint application and select "Paste" from the edit menu. Save the picture to a safe location.

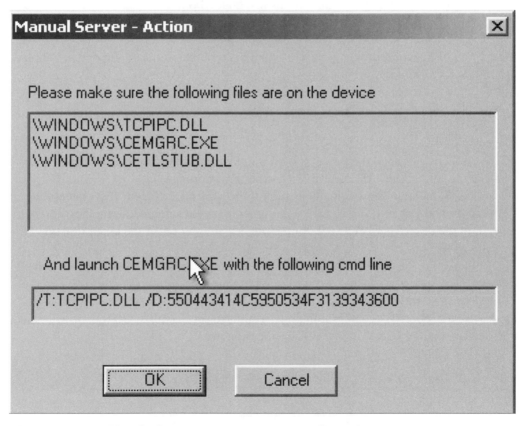

Figure 4.13   The platform manager transport configuration

The main advantage of pure TCP/IP transport is that you can use it to do all remote functions, including those provided by the remote Windows CE tools described earlier in the chapter. Even eVB can use this transport.

 You can find a small setup program in the directory "Tools\TCPTransport Setup" on the CD-ROM that creates a registry entry into your Windows CE device for the "Run" command in the "Start" menu. After you have installed the tool, you can go to the "Start" menu and select the "Run" option. You will find the complicated parameter in the "Open Combo Box". Just change the /D: address, and it will be easy to launch the server again at any time.

Now back to the little sample application and the target device combo box. You will find your new device "MyCE" in this last dialog box.

5. Select it, and you are ready to compile for the first time.

At the end of the compilation, you will find a dialog box similar to the one in the platform manager's configuration connection test. If you look closely, you will see that the /D: option differs only in the first number behind the colon.

6. Select "Run" on the device again and change the number to the corresponding value.

eCE will then download the successfully compiled "MyFirst.exe". Next, set a breakpoint in the line of the "MessageBox", and start the application.

eCE will try to locate the local version of the MFCCE211d.dll. Just cancel this dialog box, and you will see your first application on the screen. Tab on the "Test" button on the device, and eCE will hit the breakpoint you set in the OnButton1() function.

You can now test all the debugger functions you learned to love for Win32 development, such as the ToolTips on "m_I" showing the value, changing the value in the "Auto Watch" window, or dragging and dropping a variable in the "Watch" window, as shown in Figure 4.14. Congratulations! You have successfully written, downloaded, and debugged your first Windows CE application in eVC.

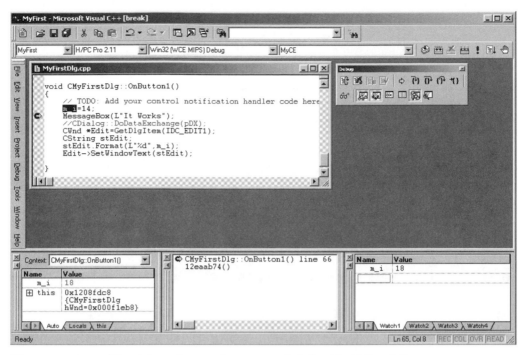

Figure 4.14   The debugging environment of eMbedded Visual C++

4.5   Choosing the Right Framework for Your Task

The next question you need to ask yourself is:

Which framework should I choose for my development task?

In writing applications for the desktop, you probably became accustomed to choosing from among a wide range of frameworks. With Version 2.11, Windows CE finally reached the point of parity with the desktop. Now all frameworks for the desktop are also available for Windows CE. If, however, you are targeting older devices such as H/PCs and palm-size PCs of the first generation, you will find that they are not, in all cases, available.

Table 4.2 shows which frameworks are available for various Windows CE devices. If you are wondering why ADO, COM, DCOM, and HTML are in this table, the reason is simple: these technologies are central to Microsoft's strategy for the future and will play a key role in your choice of framework. COM and DCOM, for example, can only be developed in C using ATL, MFC, or pure C. ADO is a very important technology to access data of all kinds. I am convinced that today every data access application should use ADO. And HTML is the most universal of all frameworks. Unfortunately, it is also the most limited framework in regard to Windows CE, although I hope that Microsoft will enhance CE's HTML framework in the future by introducing such features as scriptlets, DHTML, and client- and server-side scripting, which you already know and love from the desktop.

You might also be surprised that ADO is not part of Windows CE 2.11 for embedded development. The reason for this is that the internal structure of Microsoft separates the Windows CE core team from the platform teams like handheld, palm-size, AutoPC, and WebTV. Each of those teams can create extra features that the core OS team may eventually adopt. Not every platform supports every processor type, but the core OS—and therefore the embedded version of Windows CE—has to. ADO was

Table 4.2   Available Frameworks by Device

Device	Pure C	ATL	MFC	eVB	ADO	COM	DCOM	Java	HTML
H/PC V1.0 (Pegasus)	Yes	No	No	No	No	No	No	No	Yes
H/PC V2.0 (Mercury)	Yes	Yes	Yes	Yes	No	Yes (Inproc)	No	Yes	Yes
H/PC V3.0 (Jupiter)	Yes	Yes	Yes	Yes	Yes	Yes (Inproc)	No	Yes	Yes
Palm-size PC V1.0 (Gryphon)	Yes	No	No	No	No	No	No	No	Yes (Mobile Channels)
Palm-size PC V1.1 (Wyvern)	Yes	Yes	Yes	Yes	Yes	Yes	No	Yes	Yes
Palm-size PC V2.0 (Rapier)	Yes	Yes	Yes	Yes	Yes	Yes	No	Yes	Yes
Embedded (CE 2.11) (Birch SP1)	Yes	Yes	Yes	No	No	Yes	No	Yes	Yes
Embedded (CE 2.12) (Birch SP2)	Yes	Yes	Yes	Yes	Yes	Yes	Yes	Yes	Yes

developed and tested by the handheld team, and H/PCs are available only for ARM, SH3, and MIPS. To put ADO into the core OS, the core team has to test it on all other CPUs—including x86, PPC, and SH4. The H/PCs run on Windows CE 2.11, which has to be finished before the H/PC can ship. The new component, whether it be ADO or any other feature, goes to the core team so they can incorporate it into the next version. Sometimes a technology developed by a platform team does not get into the core OS because Microsoft decides that it is a feature unique to the platform it was developed for. An example of this is the form technology that was developed for the AutoPC. The future of the AutoPC's speech engine is still being debated at Microsoft. I am strongly hoping that it will be approved for inclusion in the core.

Once you know which devices you are going to target, you can start the decision process for your framework. Table 4.3 provides a decision table to help you in making the fundamental choice among frameworks.

Table 4.3   Framework Decision Table

Framework	Pros	Cons
Pure C	Result application can be very small because no runtime is required. Highest level of freedom for the developer. Supports all devices. You can write one binary that runs on all Windows CE devices. Since you have to do everything yourself, you can optimize your code to run at high speed.	You write a lot of code yourself that ATL and MFC could do for you. You have to take care of all Unicode issues. You will not have any problems if you only target Windows CE, but if your application needs to run on Win9x as well, you will be in trouble.
	Pure C is the best framework for drivers and high-speed applications like action games and industrial software or applications that have to run on all devices.	
ATL	Optimized for small components. Helpful wizards guide you through the development cycle. Very easy to use.	Not useful for bigger applications. UI design is painful. Requires at least one runtime: "ATLCE.DLL".

(continued)

Table 4.3 (continued)

Framework	Pros	Cons
	ATL is great for writing ActiveX controls and COM servers.	
MFC	Easy to use for fast development. UI design is very easy. Great for bigger applications and ActiveX hosts. Great partner inside ATL objects. MFCCE.DLL is shipping in most of the devices running Windows CE 2.11. Easy to learn for C++ developers and easy to migrate from desktop.	Big runtime DLL required: "MFCCE.DLL". Very complicated to use MFC for components. If used in ATL components, it requires two runtimes. Each new version of MFCCE.DLL has a new version number in the DLL name, such as "MFCCE211.DLL." Thus you could have multiple MFCs on your device, eating up valuable space.
	MFC is great for rapid development of mid-size to large applications. It provides the best parity to the desktop and hides a lot of the Unicode issues with Windows CE.	
eVB	Very easy to learn. Result code is processor neutral and very small. Can host ActiveX controls very easily. New formless runtime allows for headless applications.	Very big runtime. Cannot host ActiveX controls written with an ATL/MFC combination. No support for older devices. No support for writing ActiveX controls or DLLs.
	eVB is great for prototyping, utilities, ActiveX containers, and smaller applications.	

You should also ask yourself the following questions before deciding on a framework:

Do I only have to write COM components (COM servers or ActiveX controls)?

(Yes = Choose ATL)

Do I have to write a prototype for a quick review?

(Yes = Choose eMbedded Visual Basic)

Do I have to write a fairly large application with a lot of UI, communication, and data access?

(Yes = Choose MFC)

Do I have to write a real-time application, driver, or high-speed action game?

(Yes = Choose Pure C/C++)

Does my application have to run on all available devices with Windows CE 2.0?

(Yes = Choose Pure C/C++)

The last question could even be answered for Windows CE 1.0. All Windows CE applications written for Version 1.0 will run under any newer device. The drawback is that you cannot use any of the new features like ADO, the new CommandBand, color, printing support, or COM. You also have to install the old Visual Studio 97 and the Visual C++ Tools for Visual C++ Version 1.0. This book will not cover this option because it differs too much from the new Microsoft eMbedded Visual Tools and would probably fill another complete book.

The remainder of the book will use various frameworks, depending on which is best suited for a given task. It will also give tips and examples using different frameworks in order to compare results.

 One more thing: It is very difficult to switch from one framework to another because frameworks are fundamentally different. You should make a firm decision before you start coding. But as an experienced Win32 developer you certainly know that already.

4.6 Basic Windows CE Development Tips

Throughout the book you will find many code samples that include macros and defines that make it easier to work with Windows CE code. The most commonly used macros and defines are described below.

4.6.1 Compile-Time Version Checking

To specify at compile time what code has to be compiled for what version of Windows CE, use the define:

```
#if UNDER_CE=<CEVersion>
```

or

```
#if _WIN32_WCE=<CEVersion>
```

This preprocessor definition is very helpful when you are writing code that needs to run on both Windows CE devices and the desktop. You can even give a version number of CE to differentiate code segments targeted for specific versions of Windows CE.

In this book, the version number is rarely used because the goal here is to have one binary that will run on all Windows CE versions. The desktop variation of the binary is different, so you use this define to separate its code from the Windows CE code. Likewise, you will not find much code in the else branch of this "#if" because this book and its examples focus on Windows CE development.

4.6.2 Compile-Time Platform Detecting

Another problem is the compile-time detection of the target platform. Since Microsoft does not offer any help in this matter, I came up with a rather simple solution. Create a new include file called "Platform.h" in all "include" directories under "\Windows CE Tools\WCE<VersionNumber>\<Platform>\include" and add only one define to it:

```
#define <Platform> <PlatformVersion>
```

For example, in the "Wyvern" platform "include" directory (. . .\WCE211\ms palm size pc\. . .), use:

```
#define PALM_PC 2
```

In the "Rapier" platform "include" directory (. . .\WCE300\ms palm size pc\. . .), use:

```
#define PALM_PC 3
```

To exlude all code that does not run on a Pocket PC, you can add the following directives to your code:

```
#if PALM_PC>2
#endif
```

The $(CePlatform) Compiler Preprocessor Definition

If you do not need an exact definition of the platform and you can live with the platform category, you can also use the $(CePlatform) definition of the compiler. Table 4.4 shows the definitions to which this macro will be translated during the compile time.

With this in mind you can either include or exclude code for a certain platform by surrounding it with "#if . . . #endif" statements. In other words, the following code will be compiled only if the compiler is set to compile against a Pocket PC or palm-size PC platform:

```
#ifdef PSPC
// your pocket PC-specific code goes here
#endif
```

4.6.3 Runtime Version Checking

Doing runtime version checking is a bit tricky because you are dealing with different versions of Windows CE, platforms, and processors. The easiest part to get is the version number of Windows CE. It can be obtained with the standard Windows API function "GetVersionEx" that fills in the structure "_OSVERSIONINFO":

```
typedef struct _OSVERSIONINFO{
    DWORD dwOSVersionInfoSize;
    DWORD dwMajorVersion;      // contains CE Major Version i.e. 2
    DWORD dwMinorVersion;      // contains CE Minor Version i.e. 01
    DWORD dwBuildNumber;       // contains CE Build Number i.e.
                               // 8292 for H/PC Professional
```

Table 4.4   **Translations of the $(CePlatform) Definition at Compile Time**

On Platform	Result
Pocket PC	WIN32_PLATFORM_PSPC
Palm-size PC	WIN32_PLATFORM_PSPC
Handheld PC (Versions 1.0 and 2.0)	Not supported by the macro
Handheld PC 3.0 (Professional editions)	WIN32_PLATFORM_HPCPRO
Any embedded or OEM device not certified for one of the categories above	WIN32_PLATFORM_UNKOWN

```
    DWORD dwPlatformId;        // contains VER_PLATFORM_WIN32_CE
    TCHAR szCSDVersion[ 128 ];// contains Service Pack info
} OSVERSIONINFO;
```

In addition, you have to check the platform, which can be done with the function "SystemParameterInfo(SPI_GETPLATFORMTYPE, . . .)". Because the value is coming directly from the CE device and is not defined anywhere in an include file, you have to compare the returned string with the platform names you know. Table 4.5 lists all known platforms and their corresponding "SPI_GETPLATFORMTYPE" strings.

Table 4.5   Windows CE Platforms and Their "SPI_GETPLATFORMTYPE" Strings

Platform	SPI_GETPLATFROMTYPE	WCE Version	Remarks
Palm-size PC V1.0	Palm PC	2.01	
Palm-size PC V1.1	Palm PC	2.11	The "Wyvern" generation of palm-size PCs has the same platform type but the minor CE version number is different (2.11).
Palm-size PC V2.0 (Pocket PC V1.0)	Palm PC2	3.00	The Pocket PC generation of palm-size PCs has a new platform type. (Amazing the version chaos here.)
H/PC	HPC	1.0 and 2.0	"Pegasus" and "Mercury" handheld devices.
H/PC Professional (H/PC Version 3)	Jupiter	2.11	This might change because it is the code name of the professional edition. (Even more confusion.)

The following function, used often throughout the book, determines the Windows CE version and platform during runtime.

```
// *================================================================*
//
// GetCePlatform()
// Returns: HiWord: The Windows CE Version (three digits)
//          LoWord: The Windows CE platform (See table above)
//
// This function is optimized for use under Windows CE. You can easily
// add code to determine the desktop version to this function.
//
// *================================================================*
long GetCePlatform(void)
{
long result=CEP_DESKTOPPC;
int pltfrm=0;
TCHAR szPlatform[MAX_STRING_BUFFER];

    OSVERSIONINFO osVer;
    GetVersionEx(&osVer);
#ifdef UNDER_CE

        result=((osVer.dwMajorVersion*100+osVer.dwMinorVersion)<<16);
            switch (osVer.dwMajorVersion)
            {
                case 1:      // Check for all V1 Devices
                             if (SystemParametersInfo(
                                     SPI_GETPLATFORMTYPE,
                                     sizeof(szPlatform),
                                     szPlatform,0)!=0)
                             {
                                 if (lstrcmp(szPlatform,
                                         TEXT("HPC"))==0)
                                         result|=CEP_HPCV1;
                                 else
                                         result|=CEP_OEMV1X;
                             }
                             else
```

```
                          {     result|=CEP_OEMV1X;    }
            break;

      case 2: // Check for all V2 Devices
                if (SystemParametersInfo(
                SPI_GETPLATFORMTYPE,
                sizeof(szPlatform),szPlatform,0)!=0)
                {
                      if (lstrcmp(szPlatform,
                              TEXT("HPC"))==0)
                          result|=CEP_HPCV2;
                      else if (lstrcmp(szPlatform,
                              TEXT("Jupiter"))==0)
                          result|=CEP_HPCV3;
                      else if (lstrcmp(szPlatform,
                              TEXT("Palm PC2"))==0)
                          result|=CEP_PALMPCV3;
                      else if (lstrcmp(szPlatform,
                              TEXT("Palm PC"))==0)
                      {
                          switch (osVer.
                          dwMinorVersion)
                          {
                                case 1:
                                result|=CEP_PALMPCV1;
                                      break;
                                case 11:
                                result|=CEP_PALMPCV2;
                                      break;
                                default:
                                result|=CEP_PALMPC;
                                      break;
                          }
                      }
                      else
                      { result|=CEP_OEMV2X; }
                }
                else
                { // In doubt - running on Emulation?
                  HINSTANCE hDll =
                  LoadLibrary(TEXT("aygshell.dll"));
```

```
                         if (hDll)
                         {
                                switch (osVer.dwMinorVersion)
                                {
                                        case 1:
                                        result|=CEP_PALMPCV1;
                                                break;
                                        case 11:
                                        result|=CEP_PALMPCV2;
                                                break;
                                        default:
                                        result|=CEP_PALMPC;
                                                break;
                                }
                         }
                         else
                         { result|=CEP_OEMV2X; }
                }
           break;


      case 3:
                 if (SystemParametersInfo(
                 SPI_GETPLATFORMTYPE,
                 sizeof(szPlatform),szPlatform,0)!=0)
                 {
                        if (lstrcmp(szPlatform,
                                TEXT("Palm PC2"))==0)
                                result|=CEP_PALMPCV3;
                        else
                        { result|=CEP_OEMV3X; }
                 }
                 else
                 { // In doubt - running on Emulation?
                        HINSTANCE hDll =
                         LoadLibrary
                         (TEXT("aygshell.dll"));
                        if (hDll)
                        {
     typedef BOOL (*SHCREATEMENUBARPROC) (SHMENUBARINFO *pvParam);
     SHCREATEMENUBARPROC g_hSHCreateMenuBar=NULL;
#ifdef UNDER_CE
```

```
      g_hSHCreateMenuBar =(SHCREATEMENUBARPROC)
                          GetProcAddress(hDll, TEXT
                          ("SHCreateMenuBar"));
#else  // for emulation!
      g_hSHCreateMenuBar =(SHCREATEMENUBARPROC)
                          GetProcAddress(hDll, "SHCreateMenuBar");
#endif

                              if (g_hSHCreateMenuBar!
                              =NULL)
                                    result|=CEP_PALMPCV3;
                              else
                                    result|=CEP_OEMV3X;
                        }
                        else
                              result|=CEP_OEMV3X;
                  }
                  break;
            }
#else
            // Not a CE device.
#endif
      return result;
}
```

This function requires some defines that it returns together with the Windows CE version number. Here are the relevant defines. Add them to the top of your helper source.

```
#define MAX_STRING_BUFFER 255
// *====* Windows CE Platforms by categories
// 00-09 Non CE Devices
#define CEP_DESKTOPPC 0    // Not a Windows CE Device
// 10-19 H/PC Devices
#define CEP_HPC     10  // Any H/PC not one of the below
#define CEP_HPCV1   11  // H/PC V1 (first B/W devices)
#define CEP_HPCV2   12  // H/PC V2 (Color Devices)
#define CEP_HPCV3   13  // H/PC Professional
#define CEP_HPCEND  19
// 20-20 Palm-size PC devices
#define CEP_PALMPC    20 // Any Palm-size PC not on of the below
```

```
#define CEP_PALMPCV1  21 // Palm-size PC 1.0 B/W
#define CEP_PALMPCV2  22 // Palm-size PC 1.1 Color Devices
#define CEP_PALMPCV3  23 // Palm-size PC 2.0
#define CEP_PALMPCEND 29
// 30-49 Special Purpose Devices (expect some over time)
// 50-59 Non specified devices
#define CEP_OEMV1X  50 // based on CEV1.x
#define CEP_OEMV2X  51 // based on CEV2.x
#define CEP_OEMV3X  52 // based on CEV3.x
```

 The function "GetCePlatform()" can be found in the file "CeHelpers.cpp" in the "\Sources\helpers" directory of the companion CD.

4.6.4   Accessing Debug Messages in ActiveX Controls

At times, it is necessary to take a quick look at some values in an ActiveX control. The simplest way to get such instant feedback is to use the "OnDraw()" method to print debug information into the control's client area. Of course, to do so requires that the control be visible at runtime.

The ATL wizard creates a default "OnDraw()" method for you that prints "ATL 3.0 : <ClassName>" to the client area. To utilize this method for your debug strings, simply declare a private variable in the class declaration in the include file:

```
TCHAR m_szDebug[255]
```

Then delete the following line from the original "OnDraw()" method:

```
LPCTSTR pszText = _T("ATL 3.0 : Commander");
```

Replace "pszText" with "m_szDebug" in the line:

```
DrawText(di.hdcDraw, m_szDebug, -1, &rc, DT_CENTER | DT_VCENTER |
DT_SINGLELINE);
```

To avoid getting a strange string during insertion of the control in a container, set the "m_szDebug" variable to an empty string in the constructor of the class.

Now all you have to do is fill the variable "m_szDebug" with any value you like—for example, using the "wsprintf()" function—and then call the ATL method "FireViewChange()". This function internally calls the "OnDraw()" method and calculates the correct "ATL_DRAWINFO" structure. Never call "OnDraw()" directly.

4.6.5 Debugging ActiveX Controls

Debugging ActiveX controls is more complicated on Windows CE targets than it is on the desktop. The best way I have found is to use the runtime "pvbload.exe" of eMbedded Visual Basic in the emulation environment. Here is what you do to debug your control.

1. Create a small eVB test application and host your control in it.
2. Select "H/PC Pro 2.11", "Win32 (WCE x86em) Debug", and "Handheld PC Pro Emulation" in the WCE configuration toolbar.
3. Open the settings of your ActiveX project and select the "Debug" tab.
4. Select the "PVBLOAD.EXE" with its full path under "<VB InstallationPath>/eVB/sdk/hpcpro/Emulation/Runtime/ PVBLOAD.EXE" as "Executable for debug session".
5. Enter the name of your test application of Step 1 preceded by a forward slash "/" in the field "Program Arguments".
6.   Enter "/Windows/PVBLOAD.EXE" in the field "Remote Executable Path and File Name".

Now if you compile the ActiveX control project, it will download and register the control in the emulation environment. When you click the "Go (F5)" button, you will get two error messages that you can ignore. The debugger will now hit every breakpoint you set.

5
Chapter

The Thread-Example Pocket-CD-Manager

Throughout the rest of this book you will be working on a Windows CE application called a Pocket-CD-Manager (PCDM). In each subsequent chapter, you will develop different parts of this sample application. If you read the book chapter by chapter, the thread example will give you a systematic introduction to the features of Windows CE. Along with the extended thread example, each chapter will include a number of smaller, freestanding examples that will explain the specific features discussed in that chapter. Thus you need not follow the entire thread example in order to learn about a specific Windows CE feature; instead you can jump directly to the appropriate chapter and refer to the freestanding example. The thread example source can also be found, ordered by chapter, in the directory "Sources/ThreadExample". You will find all sources on the accompanying CD, ordered by chapter, in the "Sources" directory. The following list shows all the features your Pocket-CD-Manager will have when you are finished with the book.

5.1 The Pocket-CD-Manager Feature List

The Pocket-CD-Manager is a tool to manage your CDs on your Windows CE Device. The data from your CDs will be stored in an Access database on the desktop that your

Windows CE application will use to synchronize with a Pocket-Access database on your Windows CE device.

The Deluxe CD player comes with Windows 2000, and the Plus Pack for Windows 98 provides the database for the desktop. A helpful feature of this database is that the Deluxe CD player reads the information about the CD's tracks and other data from the Internet and stores the result in its own database. You can take advantage of this feature by using the Deluxe CD player as your front-end. Your database on Windows CE will contain a mirror of the "Titles" and "Tracks" tables of the database on the desktop. The "TitleID" will be linked to the CD table in such a way that you will be able to display all the track information of a given CD in one screen. The user will be able to send any CD's data via an infrared connection to another Windows CE device running the Pocket-CD-Manager.

The Pocket-CD-Manager will run on all devices running Windows CE 2.11 or higher, such as the palm-size PC Version 1.1/2.0 and the H/PC Professional with the full feature set. The application will have a help file that explains all the important user interface features. In addition, the installer for the Pocket-CD-Manager will be able to install the correct version of the application to the corresponding platform. Table 5.1 explains how you will implement these features.

Table 5.1 Technologies-to-Feature Mapping Table

PCDM Feature	Technology
Pocket-CD-Manager—main application	MFC application hosting several ActiveX controls
Data access to the Pocket-Access database, searching and retrieving of data	ADO for CE
Synchronization between the Windows CE database and the desktop database	ActiveSync, ADO synchronization, and RAPI
Displaying the track data in a CE dialog box	ListView ActiveX control for Windows CE
Displaying a bitmap inside the "About" box	GDI bitmap routines
Sending data to another Windows CE device	Winsock over IrDA
Help file	HTML Help for Windows CE, Word 2000, and FrontPage 2000 as authoring tools
Installer	Windows CE installer technology and Microsoft Installer (MSI) for desktop part
General configuration data and user profiles	CE-Registry access using an ActiveX control that you will write

Table 5.2 **PCDM Components**

PCDM Component	Framework	Used for	See Chapter
PCDM.EXE	MFC	The main executable	All chapters
PCDMUI.DLL	ATL supporting MFC	Wraps all UI technologies of the PCDM application	All chapters
PCDMDLL.DLL	ATL	Wraps all non-UI technologies	All chapters
PCDMSync.DLL	Pure C++	ActiveSync provider for the desktop that synchronizes the Deluxe CD database with the PCDM database on Windows CE	Section 9.3.2
DevPCDMSync.DLL	Pure C++	ActiveSync provider for Windows CE, the counterpart to PCDMSync.dll	Section 9.3.2
PCDM.INF	Installer	Installer script to install the PCDM application on Windows CE	Section 11.5.4
PCDM.MSI	MSI	Windows Installer database containing the desktop part of the PCDM installation	Section 11.5.5
AUTORUN.EXE	CE Installer	AutoRun package to run PCDM directly from a CF-Card	Section 11.5.6

As the framework for the Pocket-CD-Manager, I chose MFC because the application will be fairly large and it has some unique features that can be solved much more easily using MFC than Visual Basic. Table 5.2 shows the components of the PCDM application that you will write in the rest of the book.

5.2 Creating the Framework of Your Application

Before you create the framework for the PCDM application, it is important to review the architecture that you will be creating and using. Figure 5.1 shows the architecture diagram and how you will layer your software.

The PCDM MFC application never directly accesses any Windows CE feature. It either uses the PCDMUI component for UI tasks or the PCDMDLL component for

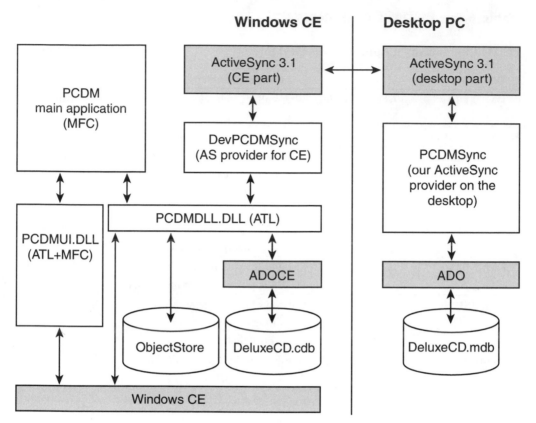

Figure 5.1   Pocket-CD-Manager architecture diagram

non-UI-related technologies. The ActiveSync provider on Windows CE also uses the PCDMDLL to access the underlying data store.

Here is the place to start in creating the first version of your application:

1. Start the eMbedded Visual C++ environment and select "New . . ." from the "File" menu.

2. In the upcoming dialog box, select "WCE MFC AppWizard (exe)", name the project "PCDM" for Pocket-CD-Manager, and press "OK".

3. In the first page of the upcoming MFC AppWizard, you can use the default setting "Single Document" and "Document/View architecture support" and click "Next".

4. In the second page, select all three "Windows Sockets", "Windows Help", and "ActiveX Controls".

5. In the setting frame for the control bar type, select "Basic CommandBar".

6. Do not set the "Printing (2.1 only)" and "Status Bar" flags.

7. In the next page, leave the default values intact and select "Next".

The final page will summarize these steps, and if everything is in order, you can select "Finish" to start the creation of your framework. Except for some minor differences in the pages of the wizard, you will no doubt be familiar with this wizard. Even the files the wizard created are nearly the same.

Next, as shown in Table 5.3, you want to create the same framework for the desktop and look at the differences between the two.

8. To create the framework for your desktop version of PCDM, start the "MFC AppWizard (exe)", choose a different location for the project, but give it the same name, "PCDM".

9. Then select the options shown in Table 5.3 in the MFC AppWizard.

Table 5.3   Creating the MFC for Desktop Equivalent

Setting	Select
AppWizard, page 1	
Type of application	Single document
Document/View architecture support	Check
AppWizard, page 2	
Database support	None
AppWizard, page 3	
Compound document support	Container
Compound file support	No, thank you
Other support	Only "ActiveX controls"

(continued)

Table 5.3 (continued)

Setting	Select
AppWizard, page 4	
Docking support	Check
Initial status bar	Check
Printing and print preview	Uncheck
Context-sensitive help	Check
3D controls	Check
MAPI support	Uncheck
Windows sockets	Check
Toolbar look	Normal
AppWizard, page 5	
Style of project	MFC standard
Source comments	Yes, please
MFC library	As a shared DLL
AppWizard, page 6	
Do not change anything	

5.3 Differences between the Desktop and Windows CE Versions

The first difference you will notice is that the desktop AppWizard generated some extra files that the CE AppWizard did not. If you take a closer look, you will find that the desktop version created a set of help files and the help file project. On Windows CE, you have to use HTML help, so the HPJ and all the RTF files would not help you. You will learn how to create Help files for Windows CE in Section 11.2.

The other file that the desktop wizard created is the file "cntrlitem.cpp". The desktop application is using this file to manipulate ActiveX controls. This is not supported under Windows CE, and it does not make sense for the CE AppWizard to create this file either. Here are the relevant files.

5.3.1 stdafx.h

Because you are using an MFC that requires features of Version 2.01, the stdafx.h for Windows CE makes sure that you are not compiling this application for any platform older than Version 2.01.

The next interesting thing you will notice is that the Windows CE version requires only the "afxdisp.h" to support OLE controls (ActiveX controls) in the application, whereas the desktop version requires a set of "afx<xxx>.h" include statements. The only include statement that is unique to the Windows CE version is "afxsock.h". So far there are no dramatic differences.

5.3.2 PCDM.CPP

You will notice a difference in the constructor of the "theApp" class. The MFC for Windows CE requires that the help file name be passed to the constructor of the application class. The files contain only two more differences.

First, the Windows CE application does not have to initialize OLE. Windows CE does not support any OLE functionality other than hosting ActiveX controls and in-process servers. The AfxOleInit() function on the desktop side initializes the application to be a "good citizen" in the OLE environment. The function prepares the application for in-place use in other applications. This is not necessary for Windows CE, since you just need to host ActiveX Controls running on the main-process thread, and in-place activation is not supported on Windows CE. If you want to have multi-threading in Windows CE, you will have to do everything yourself. A later chapter of this book will explain how to use multi-threading on Windows CE.

The second difference between the desktop and Windows CE versions is the activation of 3D controls on the desktop. These calls were legacy calls from the Windows NT 3.51 and Windows 3.11 versions but were not necessary in a pure NT4 (or higher) environment. Windows CE does not have different control types, so the call is not necessary. You will find out in reading this book that Microsoft has eliminated nearly all Win16 calls, as well as those that relate to Win32 prior to Version 4.0.

 The rule of thumb for old calls is: If there is a newer call (mostly ending with an "Ex" at the end—for example, "MoveToEx"), the old call does not exist in Windows CE.

5.3.3 Mainfrm.cpp

Nothing is really different here except that Windows CE toolbars are created differently from those on the desktop. Therefore the code is different, too. I will cover this issue in detail in Chapter 7.

5.3.4 PCDMDoc.cpp

The "PCDMDoc.cpp" file is the same in both systems except for the OLE "Cut" and "Paste" commands for the edit menu. The reason for this difference is simple: The Windows CE clipboard does not support OLE objects.

5.3.5 PCDMView.cpp

The file "PCDMView.cpp" is very different in the two operating systems. In the desktop version, the AppWizard created a lot of methods for adding ActiveX controls at runtime, manipulating ActiveX controls, and using in-place activation. Your Windows CE application will not add ActiveX controls at runtime, so the AppWizard for Windows CE avoids the work of creating all the calls relating to that feature.

5.3.6 Resources

The wizard creates the same resources for the desktop and Windows CE versions, with the exception of the ActiveX and in-place activation-supporting accelerators and menus. You will also note that Windows CE lacks the toolbar resource that can be found on the desktop side. This dissimilarity reflects differences in the creation of the command bar in Windows CE and the toolbar in the desktop version.

5.3.7 Differences in Project Settings

The last differences you need to consider are the "Project Settings". On the "General" tab, everything is the same. On the "Debug" tab, you will find an entry for a remote executable on the Windows CE side. This entry defines where the debugger will find the final application on the Windows CE device. You can add any valid Windows CE path here. Remember that Windows CE does not know anything about drive letters. A valid path could be "\Windows" or "\my folder\".

In the "C++" tab there are some preprocessor settings that should interest you:

```
UNDER_CE=$(CEVersion)
```

and

```
_WIN32_WCE=$(CEVersion)
```

These settings give you the opportunity to generate different code depending on which Windows CE version you are targeting. You can select the Windows CE version in the second combo box of the platform toolbar. In "stdafx.h", the AppWizard generated two lines of code using this pre-compiler setting:

```
UNICODE, _UNICODE
```

This setting is very important because Windows CE is only Unicode! If you remove this entry, your compilation will fail miserably.

```
$(CEConfigName)
```

This entry allows you to test for a configuration you have chosen. It reflects the third combo box in platform toolbar.

```
_WIN32_WCE_EMULATION
```

This entry tells you whether you are going to compile for emulation. It helps you exclude code paths that do not run under emulation or that you want to run differently.

```
$(CePlatform)
```

This entry allows you to exclude or include parts of your application code, depending on the platform you are compiling against. If you want to keep the same source code for all platforms but still use certain features of the Pocket PC, you can surround your code with the following lines:

```
#ifdef PSPC
// Special code for the Pocket-PC here
#endif
```

Once the compiler reads this code it will not compile the lines in between the "#if . . . #endif" statements if it is compiling for a handheld PC.

You will likewise find similar or even identical settings in the "Resource" tab. One more change can be found on the "Linker" tab. Microsoft eMbedded Visual Tools does not support incremental linking and profiling. Also the category "Output" does not exist. Windows CE requires the "wWinMainCRTStartup" to be set. It also requires a fixed stack size because, unlike the desktop version, Windows CE cannot shrink or expand its stack.

You can now compile the application. Select the "H/PC Pro 2.11; Win32 (WCE x86em Debug); Handheld Pro Emulation" environment first, and then press the "Compile" button. Visual C++ for CE will automatically download the application after it finishes the compiling process.

You can start the application with either "Execute CTRL-F5", to run it without debugging, or "Run F5", to debug it. Once the application starts, it should appear on the screen of your device as shown in Figure 5.2.

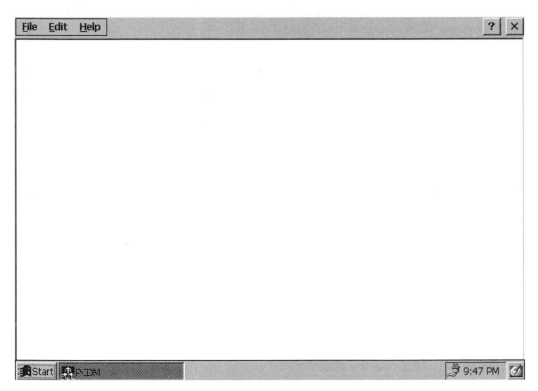

Figure 5.2 The "blank" Pocket-CD-Manager application

5.4 The User Interface of the Pocket-CD-Manager

I am a strong supporter of the idea that UI design has to come before the "life under the hood"—the core code. This is particularly true in the case of a UI-dominated application like the PCDM. Many companies go the other way and define the features of the runtime first and then build the UI in later. Sometimes they miscalculate and leave too little time for creating the user interface, which, because it is produced in a rush, is not optimized for ease of use.

 For any application, user satisfaction is the most important sales factor. If you spend a good portion of your time in designing the base frame of your UI, you will save yourself much trouble during the development of the core. Timely UI development also gives you the opportunity to get a prototype into the usability labs at an early stage to check for any design flaws.

The diagram in Figure 5.3 shows the basic user-interface interaction you will implement for the PCDM. The menu bar will contain the following two submenus.

5.4.1 "File"

Although the PCDM is not a file-based application, it has a "File" menu. Microsoft has not come up with a better name for the first menu of an application, even if it is not file-based. Your file menu will include these commands: "Send to", to send a CD description to an IrDA recipient; "Receive", to receive a CD description from an IrDA source; and "Exit". On the palm-size PC, this menu will also contain "Help" and "About", but not "Exit". The "Designed for Windows CE" logo for palm-size PCs requires that the user cannot terminate the application. This logo requirement is currently highly debated inside and outside of Microsoft. Indeed, it might have changed by the time this book is published. Section 11.6, "Rules to Make Your App Logo-Complaint", will summarize all logo requirements for the different devices and will explain what you have to do to take care of them.

5.4.2 "Help"

The "Help" menu contains three menu items: "Contents", "Search for Help On . . .", and "About". On a palm-size PC, the toolbar will not contain the "Edit", "Delete", or

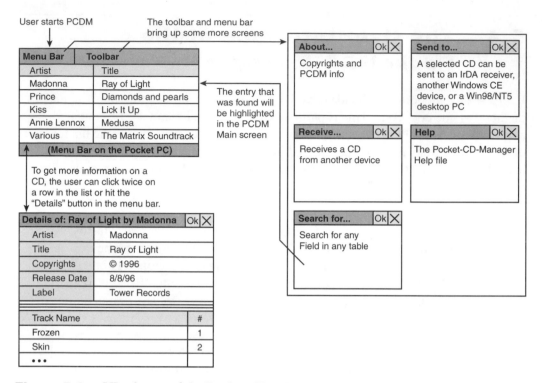

Figure 5.3 UI scheme of the Pocket-CD-Manager application

"Synchronize" buttons due to space limitations. Also, the "Help" menu will not be a separate menu, but instead will appear at the end of the "File" menu.

5.5   Creating a Prototype of PCDM

With the information in the previous section, it is now very easy to create a prototype that will pop up the dialog boxes with real content. I strongly recommend creating a prototype at this stage of the development process to get early feedback from real users.

If you do not want to reproduce the prototype in detail, you can find its source in the directory "\Sources\ThreadExample\PCDM VB Prototyp\Desktop" on the accompanying CD. The corresponding Windows CE version is located in the folder "\WCE" next to "\Desktop" folder. The next section explains how to convert a desktop Visual Basic project into a Windows CE project.

Visual Basic is the perfect tool to create this prototype because it creates user interfaces very quickly, and that is all you want to do with it. Unfortunately, Visual Basic has one big problem: you cannot compile an application for Windows CE and for the desktop PC with the same Visual Basic project. In Visual C++, you can at least use a common directory for your CE and NT applications, but this is not the case in Visual Basic.

5.5.1 Creating the Desktop Version of the Prototype

Here are the steps that you need to follow to create the desktop version of your prototype:

1. To create the prototype for the desktop, start Visual Basic 6.0 and launch the "Application Wizard" off the "New Project" dialog-box.
2. Fill out the wizard as described in Table 5.4.

Table 5.4 Settings for the eVB Application Wizard

Setting	Select
App Wizard, Page 1—No changes are needed.	
App Wizard, Page 2	
Type of application	Single Document Interface (SDI)
Name of the application	PCDM
App Wizard, Page 3	
Menus	Deselect "Edit", "View", and "Window", and select "Tools".
Submenu "File"	Deselect all but "Send . . ." and "Exit". Then use the "+" button to add "Receive" and "Show Details".
Submenu "Help"	Deselect "Search for Help on . . . ."
App Wizard, Page 4	
Remove all Button settings except "New"	Add "Find" and "Properties".
	For "Synchronize", choose "Button".

(continued)

Table 5.4 (continued)

Setting	Select
App Wizard, Page 5	
Save strings in resource file	For your prototype, you do not want to make this extra effort. If you are planning to write a real application with Visual Basic, you should choose "Yes" here.
App Wizard, Page 6	
Do you want to have Internet access?	Choose "No" here.
App Wizard, Page 7	
Splash screen	Uncheck
Logon dialog	Uncheck
Option dialog for custom settings	Uncheck
About box	Check
App Wizard, Page 8	
Start the "Create New Form" Wizard.	
Form Wizard, Page 1—No changes	
Form Wizard, Page 2	
Access setting	Remote (ODBC)
Form Wizard, Page 3	
ODBC connection data	Select the DSN "DeluxeCD" and leave everything else blank. The Deluxe CD player on first launch created this DSN entry. If you do not find its DSN entry, just start the Deluxe CD player and close it again.
Form Wizard, Page 4	
Name of the form	MainScreen
Form layout	Grid (Datasheet)
Binding type	ADO code

Setting	Select
Form Wizard, Page 5	
Record source	Titles
Selected fields	Choose only "Artist", "Title", and "TitleID".
Sort by	(None)
Form Wizard, Page 6	
Available controls	Check all
Form Wizard, Page 7—Just press "Finish".	

The wizard will ask you now if you want to have another data form created. Choose "Yes". The new wizard will only have four pages.

Setting	Select
Form Wizard, Page 1	
Form name	CDInfo
Form layout	Grid (Datasheet)
Binding type	ADO code
Form Wizard, Page 2	
Record source	Tracks
Selected fields	Only "TrackName"
Form Wizard, Page 3	
Clear all controls.	
Form Wizard, Page 4—Just press "Finish".	
Add another form.	
Form Wizard, Page 1	
Form name	CDEdit
Form layout	Single record
Binding type	ADO code

(continued)

Table 5.4 (continued)

Setting	Select
Form Wizard, Page 2	
Record source	Titles
Selected fields	Select all fields.
Form Wizard, Page 3	
Available controls	Check all.
Form Wizard, Page 1—Just press "Finish".	
This time do not add another form. The Form Wizard will end, and the Application Wizard will proceed.	
App Wizard, Final Page—Just press "Finish".	

Once the wizard is finished, your prototype is already half done. To finish the prototype, complete the following steps:

3. Open the two forms "frmMain" and "MainScreen".
4. Copy and paste the grid control from the "MainScreen" to the "frmMain" form.
5. Now copy the navigation bar from "MainScreen" to the "frmMain" form.

You have to select the picture box under the button to get the whole bar.

6. Now copy the following subroutines of "MainScreen" to the "frmMain" code:

```
Form_Resize()
From_KeyDown()
AdoPrimaryRS_MoveComplete ()
AdoPrimaryRS_WillChangeRecord()
CmdAdd_Click()
CmdDelete_Click()
CmdUpdate_Click()
CmdFirst_Click()
CmdLast_Click()
CmdNext_Click()
CmdPrevious_Click()
SetButtons()
```

7.   Then copy the code of "Form_Unload" and "Form_Load" from "Main-Screen" to the end of the corresponding subroutines in the "frmMain" code.

8.   Finally, copy the global variables from "MainScreen" to "frmMain".

If you press the Visual Basic "Run" button, you will see an application that already looks pretty close to your final goal.

9.   To clean up the prototype, you can now delete the form "MainScreen".

To do so, you also need to remove the subprocedure "mnuDataMainScreen_Click()" in the form "frmMain", or you will not be able to create an executable.

Now you need to set up the two toolbar buttons to show the CD-information and the track-information dialog boxes.

10.   Open the code window of the "CDEdit" form and add the following code lines:

```
Private m_ID As String
Public Sub SetID(ID As String)
    m_ID = ID
End Sub
```

11.   Now change the "Form_Load" function to the following code:

```
Private Sub Form_Load()
  Dim db As Connection
  Set db = New Connection
  db.CursorLocation = adUseClient
  db.Open "PROVIDER=MSDASQL;dsn=DeluxeCD;uid=;pwd=;"

  Set adoPrimaryRS = New Recordset
  adoPrimaryRS.Open "select TitleID,Artist,Title,Copyright,Label,"
          "ReleaseDate,NumTracks,NumMenus,PlayList,TitleQuery"
          "from Titles where TitleID=" & m_ID, _
              db, adOpenStatic, adLockOptimistic

  Dim oText As TextBox
  'Bind the text boxes to the data provider
  For Each oText In Me.txtFields
    Set oText.DataSource = adoPrimaryRS
  Next

  mbDataChanged = False
End Sub
```

12. The dialog box will only show one CD track, and you can get rid of the navigation bar and all the buttons except the "Close" button in the "CDEdit" Form.

Since this is a prototype you need not bother with deleting the code that corresponds to the deleted buttons. The only code you have to delete—or at least mark as a remark—is the content of the sub procedure "doPrimaryRS_MoveComplete". If you fail to do so, you will get an error during runtime.

13. To call the "CDEdit" form within "frmMain", add the following lines of code to the sub "tbToolBar_ButtonClick" in the case of "Properties":

```
Dim f As New CDEdit
f.SetID adoPrimaryRS("TitleID")
f.Show
```

14. Delete the MsgBox or put it in remarks.
15. You can also add the following code lines to launch the "CDEdit" form if the user double-clicks a row in your CD database:

```
Private Sub grdDataGrid_DblClick()
    Dim f As New CDEdit
    f.SetID adoPrimaryRS("TitleID")
    f.Show
End Sub
```

To display the track you have to edit the "CDInfo" form.

16. Open the "CDInfo" form and delete all the buttons except the "Close" button, as you did in the "CDEdit" form.

You can keep the navigation bar to navigate inside the track data table.

17. Then add the following code to the code view:

```
Private m_ID As String

Public Sub SetID(id As String)
    m_ID = id
End Sub
```

18. Now find the following line in the "Form_Load" procedure:

```
adoPrimaryRS.Open " select TrackName from Tracks ", db,_
            adOpenStatic, adLockOptimistic
```

19. Change it to:

```
adoPrimaryRS.Open " select TrackName from Tracks where TitleID=" &_
                m_ID, db, adOpenStatic, adLockOptimistic
```

These are the same changes that you made earlier to the "CDEdit" form.

20. To launch the "CDInfo" form, open the code view of the form "frmMain" and add the following code to the sub procedure "tbToolBar_ButtonClick" in the case of "Button":

```
Dim CDi As New CDInfo
CDi.SetID adoPrimaryRS("TitleID")
CDi.Show
```

This concludes the prototype of your Pocket-CD-Manager application. As you will remember, you simply want to test basic user-interface features. The final version will have several more features that are not important for an early prototype.

Start the prototype, and see if all your changes are working. At this point, it is not much of an application, but if you undertake too many fancy details too quickly, you will lose sight of the book's original purpose—introducing the basic technologies of Windows CE.

The final source code of this section can be found on the companion CD under "\Sources\ThreadExample\PCDM VB Prototype\Desktop".

5.5.2 Porting the Desktop Prototype to Windows CE

Many developers have existing Visual Basic projects that they want to port to Windows CE. Since this book is written for C++ developers, I will not go into each and every detail on the porting of eVB applications, but by porting the PCDM application I hope I can at least give you an initial jump start.

Here is the bad news: There is officially no way to convert a Visual Basic application to a Windows CE-compliant eVB project. But I will give you some hints on how to migrate such a project, taking advantage of the fact that eVB stores all its project information in text-readable files.

5.5.3 Preparing the DeluxeCD Database

Before commencing the porting process, you should change your desktop project into a Windows CE project and copy the prototype for the desktop into a different directory. You should also copy the Access database "DeluxeCD.mdb" to the "My Documents" folder of your Windows CE device. You can do this by dragging "DeluxeCD.mdb" onto the "My Documents" folder of your Windows CE device, using the Windows CE Services. As soon as you drop it into the folder, a dialog box will pop up asking you whether you want to keep the database synchronized with your desktop version. Keep all default options, as shown in Figure 5.4, and any change you make to either the desktop or Windows CE version of the file will be synchronized with the other database.

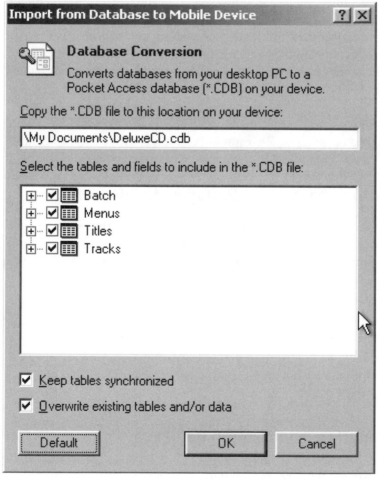

Figure 5.4   Synchronization options for the DeluxeCD database

5.5.4   Converting the Desktop eVB Project to an eVB Project

Since the introduction of Microsoft eMbedded Visual Tools and eMbedded Visual Basic, Microsoft changed the file extension used by Visual Basic projects for Windows CE.

1.   The first thing you need to do is change the file extension of the "PCDM.vbp" file to "PCDM.ebp".
2.   All forms likewise have to be renamed, from ".frm" to ".ebf".
3.   To tell eVB that your project is a Windows CE project, you have to open the "PCDM.EBP" file in a text editor like Notepad.

In this file you will find many parameters—surprisingly, most of them are the same for the desktop and Windows CE.

4.   The following changes have to be applied to the "PCD.VBP" file:

The parameter ExeName32="PCDM.exe" is not used in eMbedded Visual Basic projects.

5.   Now add the following parameter into the "PCDM.EBP" file:

```
PlatformGUID={74239C21-1DCA-11D2-9747-00A0240918F0}
DeviceGUID={00000000-0000-0000-0000-000000000000}
RemotePath=\Project1.vb
UpdateType=Ask
Form=Form1.ebf
```

The first three lines are important. They establish that the project is a Windows CE project and set the platform and device. The lines above define the project for an H/PC Professional device running Windows CE 2.11. Since you can create projects for other devices supporting Visual Basic, you have to change the platform and device identifier accordingly.

For a palm-size PC Version 1.1 (the Wyvern devices) you can set the same parameter because the palm-size Version 1.1 PCs use the same Windows CE platform as the H/PC Professionals. For H/PC Version 2.0, you have to set the following parameter:

```
PlatformGUID={0B7D1301-289F-11D2-974F-00A0240918F0}
```

For palm-size PC Version 2.0 (Rapier), you have to use the following parameter:

```
PlatformGUID={6D5C6210-E14B-11D2-B72A-0000F8026CEE}
```

The parameter "DeviceTarget" is different from device to device and can easily be evaluated by creating a dummy project with Visual Basic for Windows CE. Open the VBP file of this dummy project and copy the GUID from there into your VBP file.

6. Change also all ".frm" references to ".ebf".

You can now try to load the project in eMbedded Visual Basic again. You will get several warnings that some forms have errors and that they will be logged in the corresponding "<formname>.log" file. All ".log" files contain the error message:

```
"Line <x>: Class VB.PictureBox of control picButtons was not a loaded
control class."
```

Later in this section you will learn how to get rid of this error. If you try to run the project or make the PCDM.VB application, you will get numerous error messages because Visual Basic for Windows CE supports only a subset of the standard Visual Basic edition.

 Also remember that Visual Basic for Windows CE always takes "Sub Main", if it exists, as its start object no matter what you have selected in the project properties.

5.5.5 Migrating Forms and Code

eMbedded Visual Basic is closer to Visual Basic Script than it is to standard Visual Basic. Many of the errors that you will encounter while compiling your application result from this distinction. This section discusses how to clean up those errors. However, since this book is intended for C++ developers, I will not go into too much detail.

Before you do anything else, you need to fix some error-causing issues, using a text editor like Notepad, since it could be that eMbedded VB cannot load your form at all.

Indexed Controls Are Not Supported

The tab "lblLabels" and "txtFields" controls in the form "CDEdit" make use of indexed controls. But Visual Basic for Windows CE does not support this simple way of dealing with multiple controls of the same type. Since you can achieve the same functionality with conventional methods, Windows CE has saved the code for this feature. Unfortunately the Application Wizard uses this feature in several locations. The form "CDEdit" is nearly completely based on indexed forms. The fastest way to correct this is to load the "CDEdit.ebf" file into a text editor like Notepad and change each label and text box into a unique name and delete the "INDEX = x" entry. To compensate for the loss of the index, you have to give all controls unique names.

7.   Rename the labels and text boxes by adding the index number to the name of the control; in other words, rename the text field "txtFields" with the index 0 to "txtFields0".

Unsupported Properties

The next set of errors consists of methods and properties not supported by Windows CE, such as ".SetMaskColor" or ".Picture" and ".DataFld". The documentation of Visual Basic for Windows CE provides a list of supported properties per object.

8.   The fastest way to get rid of the ".SetMaskColor" property is to open all ".EBF" files in a text editor and manually delete the ".SetMaskColor" property.

For the ".Picture" and ".DataFld" properties, you have to do a little more.

The ".Picture" property allows you to assign a bitmap to a button on the desktop. This is not possible for standard buttons on the Windows CE side, but if you use a command bar instead of a toolbar, you can use an image list control to assign bitmaps to the buttons on the command bar. Since you are going to add a command bar in the section on "unsupported intrinsic controls," you should not get any more ".Picture" errors. If you still get errors, delete the ".Picture" property from the ".EBF" files using a text editor, as described above. You must also remove the ".DataFld" property from the ".EBF" files. The section on porting the desktop ADO to ADO for Windows CE will explain how to compensate for this lack of functionality in Windows CE.

You can also set the border style to "None" for the forms "frmMain" and "CDInfo" because the command bar on Windows CE takes over the functionality of the caption bar of a standard window.

Unsupported Intrinsic Controls

Next, the Visual Basic compiler will identify a series of intrinsic controls that you need to alter. For our small example, controls that the compiler complains about, such as the "line" and "picture Icon" controls in the form "frmAbout", can simply be deleted.

The error messages that are most difficult to remedy are those involving controls that are either in the toolbar or assigned to a Picture Box control, such as the one used as background for the ADO Navigation toolbar. Since Windows CE uses a command bar instead of a toolbar, you have to add the command bar control to your project.

9. To add a command bar to your project, you have to open the "Components" dialog box of Visual Basic and add "Windows CE Commandbar Control 6.0" and the "Windows CE ImageList Control 6.0" to the project toolbar.

10. Then add the command bar to the forms "frmMain" and "CDInfo". In the form "frmMain", make sure that the property "ShowOK" is set to "False".

This step will insure that your main application window will not be closed by an "OK" button.

Compared to the toolbar, the command bar does not support a rich set of visual propertics for defining its content; on the other hand, it supports more than just buttons as its content. Here is the code you have to insert into the forms to add the command bar functionality to the PCDM prototype.

11. Add the following code to the "Form_Load" sub of "frmMain":

```
InitCommandbar Me
```

12. Delete the menu from the form by entering the "Menu Editor" and deleting all menu items from the menu.

13. Then add the following subroutine and constants to "Module1.bas":

```
Const keySend = "Send"
Const keyReceive = "Receive"
Const keyExit = "Exit"

Const ID_NEW = 301
Const ID_DELETE = 302
Const ID_SEARCH = 303
Const ID_EDIT = 304
Const ID_TRACKS = 305
Const ID_ADONEXT = 306
Const ID_ADOPREV = 307
Const ID_ADOFIRST = 308
Const ID_ADOLAST = 309
Public Sub InitCommandbar(myForm)
  Dim mnuMain As CommandbarLib.CommandBarMenuBar
  Dim mnuFile As CommandbarLib.Item
  Dim cmdBtn As CommandBarButton

  ' Assigns the ImageList to the Command Bar
  myForm.ImageList1.Add App.Path & "\PCDMCE.bmp"
' You need to have PCDMCE.BMP Bitmap on you device to make this
happen
```

```
myForm.CommandBar1.ImageList = myForm.ImageList1.hImageList


' Adds the File Menu to the Command Bar
Set mnuMain = myForm.CommandBar1.Controls.Add(cbrMenuBar,
"MainMenu")
Set mnuFile = mnuMain.Items.Add(1, "File", "File")
mnuFile.SubItems.Add , keySend, "Send"
mnuFile.SubItems.Add , keyReceive, "Receive"
mnuFile.SubItems.Add , "", "", cbrMenuSeparator
mnuFile.SubItems.Add , keyExit, "Exit"


'Adds all our Buttons to the Command Bar
Set cmdBtn = myForm.CommandBar1.Controls.Add(cbrButton)
cmdBtn.Style = cbrSeparator
Set cmdBtn = myForm.CommandBar1.Controls.Add(cbrButton)
cmdBtn.Image = 0
cmdBtn.Caption = "N"
cmdBtn.Tag = ID_NEW
Set cmdBtn = myForm.CommandBar1.Controls.Add(cbrButton)
cmdBtn.Image = 1
cmdBtn.Caption = "D"
cmdBtn.Tag = ID_DELETE
Set cmdBtn = myForm.CommandBar1.Controls.Add(cbrButton)
cmdBtn.Style = cbrSeparator
Set cmdBtn = myForm.CommandBar1.Controls.Add(cbrButton)
cmdBtn.Image = 2
cmdBtn.Tag = ID_SEARCH
cmdBtn.Caption = "S"
Set cmdBtn = myForm.CommandBar1.Controls.Add(cbrButton)
cmdBtn.Image = 3
cmdBtn.Tag = ID_EDIT
cmdBtn.Caption = "E"
Set cmdBtn = myForm.CommandBar1.Controls.Add(cbrButton)
cmdBtn.Image = 4
cmdBtn.Caption = "T"
cmdBtn.Tag = ID_TRACKS
End Sub
```

For the prototype, you need not put code behind all the buttons. If you want to learn more about the command bar in eMbedded Visual Basic, you can look into the

CEPad that ships with the eMbedded Visual Basic toolset. Here is the event handler you have to put into the form "frmMain" to handle the buttons:

```
Private Sub CommandBar1_ButtonClick(ByVal Button As
CommandbarLib.CommandBarButton)
  Select Case CInt(Button.Tag)
  Case ID_NEW
  Case ID_DELETE
  Case ID_SEARCH
  Case ID_EDIT
  Case ID_TRACKS
  End Select
End Sub
```

You should also remove the menu entries from "frmMain" using an text editor. This book will cover the command bar for Visual C++ developers in detail in Section 7.1, "The Command Bar."

Unsupported ActiveX Controls

Your PCDM prototype for the desktop includes several ActiveX controls that are not supported under Windows CE. You have to remove them or exchange them with the Windows CE counterparts. Table 5.5 shows all the controls used in the PCDM prototype for the desktop, including those that have to be exchanged or removed.

"WithEvents" Not Supported

The first error that Visual Basic will identify involves the ADO Recordset being declared with events. Visual Basic supports only a limited set of COM features, and creating objects with events is not one of them.

1. Remove all appearances of the "WithEvents" statement that is used when your demo declares the ADO Recordset.

The forms using an ADO Recordset are "frmMain", "CDEdit", and "CDInfo". You can also delete "adoPrimaryRS_MoveComplete()" and "adoPrimaryRS_WillChangeRecord()", which are the corresponding methods. In your prototype, you will rewrite all the ADO code anyway (see Section 5.5.6 "Migrating ADO Desktop to ADO for Windows CE"), so do not spend too much time here.

Table 5.5   **ActiveX Controls Replacement Table**

Desktop	Windows CE	Our Control Name
Common Dialog In "Microsoft Common Dialog Control 6.0"	Microsoft CE Common Dialog Control 6.0	dlgCommonDialog (Can be removed for the prototype because you are not using it)
Image List In "Microsoft Common Dialog Control 6.0"	Microsoft CE Image List Control 6.0	ImlToolBarIcon (Can be removed for the prototype because you are not using it)
Data Grid Control In "Microsoft DataGrid Control 6.0 (OLEDB)"	Microsoft CE Grid Control 6.0	ListCDS (Set "View" property to "3—lvwReport")
Status Control In "Microsoft Common Dialog Control 6.0"	Remove	sbStatusBar
Toolbar Control In "Microsoft Common Dialog Control 6.0"	Microsoft CE command bar Control 6.0	tbToolBar

All Forms Are Created on Loading of the Application

The next set of errors will pop up for the "New" statement in conjunction with forms. Visual Basic creates all forms at an application's load time. Therefore

```
Dim tform as New CDEdit
```

would duplicate an existing form.

2.   In your prototype you can delete all lines that take the form

```
Dim <tempname> as new <FormName>
```

because you will call the methods of the forms directly using

```
<FormName>.<Method>.
```

Declares in Win32 API Do Not Work in Windows CE

In the code view of the form "frmMain" the Visual Basic Application Wizard inserted a declaration for the WinHelpA function. This function will not work for three reasons:

- The USER32 library that is referenced here does not exist in Windows CE.

- Windows CE does not use the old WinHelp APIs, but rather the new HTML-based help files.

- Windows CE only supports Unicode calls. Therefore Win32 API calls ending with ". . . A", which require ASCI parameters, are not supported.

3. Since you are not going to explore the help system for the prototype, you can remove this declaration and the corresponding call of the WinHelpA function.

Section 11.2 of this book discusses the Windows CE help system in great detail. You will also find the "Declare" statement in "frmAbout" for reading the path for the "MSINFO.EXE". This executable does not exist in Windows CE so you can delete the whole section containing the code to access the registry. A later chapter will come back to the issue of accessing the registry.

If you want to access Windows CE APIs, you can still use the declare statement. But of course you have to know what function is exposed in what DLL. Most functions that would be in User32 or Kernel32 of Win32 are in the "COREDLL.DLL". The API Viewer Tool from Visual Studio 6 can help you find and create the correct declare statement for Visual Basic for Windows CE. If you install the Toolkits for Windows CE, you will find a new text-based API file in the "WINAPI" folder, which contains all Windows CE APIs.

"On Error GoTo" Is Not Supported on Windows CE

The next set of errors you will get are syntax errors involving the "On Error" statement. Like Visual Basic Script, Visual Basic for Windows CE does not support "On Error GoTo". And as mentioned earlier in the book, Windows CE's designers chose to optimize it by placing less code in its system libraries and DLLs, and therefore removed a lot of redundant code. To a considerable extent, Visual Basic for Windows CE adopts the same principle. The "On Error" statement supports only the "Resume Next" declaration and the "Err" interpretation. In any case, using the "GoTo" command is not a very clean way of programming. The Visual Basic Wizard generated subs like:

```
Private Sub cmdDelete_Click()
  On Error Resume GoTo DeleteErr
```

```
  With adoPrimaryRS
    .Delete
    .MoveNext
    If .EOF Then .MoveLast
  End With
  Exit Sub
DeleteErr:
  MsgBox Err.Description
End Sub
```

This is very convenient for the developer, but uses the troublesome "GoTo" statement. Working with the "Resume Next" statement is a little more complex and time-consuming for developers, but in the end serves the same purpose as the "GoTo" statement.

4. With the following lines your code will not use the "GoTo" statement, but will still have the same functionality:

```
Private Sub cmdDelete_Click()
  On Error Resume Next
  With adoPrimaryRS
    .Delete
      If Err Then
      MsgBox Err.Description
      Else
      .MoveNext
            If Err Then
            MsgBox Err.Description
            Else
            If .EOF Then .MoveLast
                If Err Then
                    MsgBox Err.Description
                End if
            End if
    End If
  End With
End Sub
```

Of course, it involves a lot of work and a lot more code to cover all possible error conditions, but it is worth the effort. You will find appearances of the "On Error GoTo" statement in the forms "frmMain", "CDEdit", and "CDInfo". Do not change the appearances right now, just put the "On Error" statement into remarks because you will replace the complete ADO code later, and all "On Error" statements in the prototype are related to ADO code.

Declaration of Global Variables with Same Name Is Not Supported

Because all global "Dim" statements are public by default and eVB, unlike the desktop version, does not create an own stack for each form, Windows CE does not support the declaration of variables with the same name in different forms.

5. A good way to handle this limitation is to add the suffixes "CDE" and "CDI" to all the variables declared in the global section of a form.

6. For your prototype, you can just rename the "m_ID" to "m_IDCDE" and "m_IDCDI". Because you will not use any of the other variables, you can delete them.

"Sub Main" Must Be "Public Sub Main"

Windows CE cannot initialize the application if the sub "Main" is not declared as public. You also want to clean up the sub "Main" of code that is not necessary in Windows CE. You actually need only two lines of code inside this sub procedure:

```
Public Sub Main()
    frmMain.Show
End Sub
```

The "Unload Me" Method to End an Application Is "App.End"

Another curiosity from Microsoft is the way you end an eVB application in Windows CE. Instead of the (already strange) "Unload Me" method, Microsoft introduced a new method for the "App" object called "End". This method will not be visible in the new "Code-Tips" of Visual Basic 6.0 because it does not exist for the desktop, but, believe me, it is there. If you know what happens behind the curtain, it will be easier to understand why Microsoft was forced to include this new method.

A Visual Basic application for the desktop ends as soon as the last form has been unloaded. As mentioned earlier, forms on eVB are not explicitly loaded and unloaded, but are rather, to some extent, always there. Since there is no way to unload a form, an application would not end even if there were no forms loaded. And in fact, if you create a tiny application and include a "sub Main" but do not "Show" a form in it, the eVB runtime on the Windows CE device will show a message telling you that there are no forms loaded and it is about to end. If you put "App.End" into this "sub Main", you will not get the message.

If you want to remove a form from the screen, you have to use "Me.Hide" instead of "Unload Me" even if you never use the form again because—as I mentioned above—forms cannot be unloaded.

"Form_Load()" Is Always the First Method Called

Another confusing aspect of Windows CE is that "Form_Load()" will always be called before any other call to a forms method. If you are used to initializing data before you call the "Form.Show()" method, you will struggle with this one. In other words, using the desktop version of your prototype, you will call the method "SetID" of the form "CDEdit" and "CDInfo" before you show the form. Visual Basic for the desktop reacts as you would expect and calls the "SetID" method first and calls "Form_Load()" before the "Show()" is executed and the form is visible. You could discuss the merits of that procedure for a long time, but if you view "Form_Load()" as an initialization method simply for viewing a form, you just have to keep in mind the following tip.

 Only put code into the "Form_Load()" method that relates to the *visual* content of the form. Do not initialize data using this method.

To fix this problem in your prototype, you have to remove nearly all of the code from the "Form_Load" method and in its place create a "Refresh<FormName>" method that you will call after the "SetID" method. In the form "frmMain", you will call the refresh method from within the "From_Load" method—you do not call any method of this form before the show method, and your application will call this form only once during its lifetime. If "frmMain" gets closed, the application will end.

No Support for Any Double-Click Event

Double-clicking is one of the most difficult tasks for PC beginners. If you had ever seen my mother trying to start her Internet browser by double-clicking on an icon, you would know what I am talking about. Microsoft has recognized that fact for some time now and is trying to reduce the double-clicks wherever it can. On Windows CE, it is even worse since double-tapping requires precise taps at the same position. This can be challenging even for a professional. Only a very few parts of Windows CE require double-tapping, and the ListView control you will use for the CD list is not one of them. The resolution for your prototype is very simple:

 Try to avoid double-clicks whenever possible.

5.5.6 Migrating ADO Desktop to ADO for Windows CE

Migrating ADO Desktop to ADO for Windows CE is your next big task. The ".DataFld" property is used by Visual Basic to realize the Databinding of controls. Unfortunately, the Databinding function is not available on Windows CE, so you have to implement it manually. There are some differences between the desktop ADO and ADO for Windows CE implementations. Section 8.4, "ADO for Windows CE, " will explain those differences in detail. For your eVB prototype, you need only consider some differences that will affect your code.

ADO for Windows CE Knows Only Recordsets

The concepts of connections, Data Source Names (DSNs), and other OLEDB-related features are not supported on Windows CE because there is no OLEDB on Windows CE. Microsoft plans to include an OLEDB layer in a later version of Windows CE. The good news is that it makes ADO even easier to use on Windows CE than it is on the desktop. While you have to fight with connections, cursor locations, DSN, and connection string parameters on the desktop, ADO for Windows CE supports only pocket-access files (".CDB") or Windows CE's very own object store. Therefore the only object you have to define to use ADO on Windows CE is a Recordset. Windows CE uses a special version of the Recordset called "ADOCERedordSet". The Windows CE version of your prototype will not use a global variable for the Recordset, but rather two small global methods that return the Recordset in a two-dimensional array. You can see the code of those two methods in the third step of the ADO migration.

To define a Recordset for Windows CE use

```
Dim RS as ADOCERecordSet
```

ADO for Windows CE Supports Only ".CDB" and the Object Store

As mentioned above there is no OLEDB layer on Windows CE, ADO for Windows CE only supports pocket-access files (".CDB") and the native Windows CE object store. In case of accessing pocket-access files, the open method of the Recordset uses the full path to the ".CDB" file as the connection string parameter. If you want to access the object store, just use an empty string ("") as the parameter for the connection string.

For your prototype, you want to access "DeluxeCD.CDB" in the "My Documents" folder. The easiest way to do so is by defining a global constant with the path name.

```
Public Const DeluxeCDVolume = "\My Documents\DeluxeCD.cdb"
```

Of course, hard-coding a path to a file is not an elegant development style, but for the prototype it will suffice. Later in the book, you will put the path into the registry and have the chance to change it in the "Option" dialog box.

Databinding Replaced with Manual Initialization

Databinding is not available on Windows CE. This will require you to rewrite nearly all of your code that contains any ADO reference. You should start with the form "frmMain". In this form, you can delete all code that is related to ADO navigation, such as the methods "cmdNext_Click()" and "cmdFirst_Click()". Navigation in the Windows CE version of the prototype will be accomplished by means of the ListView control only.

First, you need to initialize the ListView control. Insert the following method immediately after the "Form_Load()" method:

```
Private Function InitlistCDS()
Dim GotRecord
Dim NewItem
Dim adoPrimaryRS as ADOCERecordSet
Dim CDRecord

    ' Initializes the Columns of the List View
    Set adoPrimaryRS = CreateObject("ADOCE.Recordset")
    listCDS.ColumnHeaders.Clear
    listCDS.ColumnHeaders.Add , , "Title", listCDS.Width / 2,
    lvwColumnLeft
    listCDS.ColumnHeaders.Add , , "Author", listCDS.Width / 3,
    lvwColumnLeft
    listCDS.ColumnHeaders.Add , , "ID", listCDS.Width / 6,
    lvwColumnLeft

    ' Fills the List View with the current data from our database
    listCDS.ListItems.Clear
    GotRecord = GetFirstCDRecord(adoPrimaryRS, "select
    Title,Artist,TitleID from Titles", CDRecord)
    Do While GotRecord
        Set NewItem = listCDS.ListItems.Add(, , CDRecord(0, 0))
        NewItem.SubItems(1) = CDRecord(1, 0)
        NewItem.SubItems(2) = CDRecord(2, 0)
        GotRecord = GetNextCDRecord(adoPrimaryRS, CDRecord)
    Loop
```

```
        currentID = istCDS.ListItems.Item(1).SubItems(2)
End Function
```

Add the following two methods to "Module1.bas" because you are using them in all the forms.

```
'********************************************************************
'*  GetFirstCDRecord() - Gets the first CD record, and place
'*                       it into the global
'*                       buffer.  Returns True if a record was found,
'*                       else returns False.
Public Function GetFirstCDRecord(tRS, sql, ByRef CDR) As Boolean

        tRS.Open sql, DeluxeCDVolume, adOpenKeyset, adLockReadOnly,
adCmdText
    If (tRS.EOF) Then
        ReDim CDR(tRS.Fields.Count, 0)
        tRS.Close
        GetFirstCDRecord = False
    Else
        CDR = tRS.GetRows(1)
        GetFirstCDRecord = True
    End If
End Function
'********************************************************************
'*  GetNextCDRecord()  - Gets the next record from the already open
'*                       recordset, and
'*                       place it into the global buffer.  Returns
'*                       True if a record was found, else returns
'*                       False.
'*                       Will close the recordset when no more
'*                       records are found.
Public Function GetNextCDRecord(tRS, ByRef CDR) As Boolean

    If (tRS.EOF) Then
        ReDim CDRecordCDE(tRS.Fields.Count, 0)
        tRS.Close
        GetNextCDRecord = False
    Else
```

```
        CDR = tRS.GetRows(1)
        GetNextCDRecord = True
    End If
End Function
```

The methods "GetFirstCDRecord" and "GetNextCDRecord" use the ADO syntax to retrieve fields from a record and are used in all forms. They return a record inside a two-dimensional array where the second dimension is always zero.

The method "InitlistCDS" fills the ListView control with data. To execute the code, you have to include the line "InitlistCDS" in the "form_Load()" method. Here is how the "form_Load()" method could look now:

```
Private Sub Form_Load()
  Left = (Screen.Width - Width) / 2
  Top = (Screen.Height - Height) / 2
  InitCommandbar Me
  InitlistCDS
End Sub
```

Now you want to show the "CDEdit" form whenever someone taps on a CD in the ListView control and hits the "Edit" button. First, add the following method to the form:

```
Private Sub listCDS_ItemClick(ByVal Index As Long)
    currentID = listCDS.ListItems.Item(Index).SubItems(2)
End Sub
```

Now add the two lines to the button handler of the command bar in the select section for "ID_EDIT":

```
    CDEdit.SetID currentID
    CDEdit.RefreshCDEdit
    CDEdit.Show
```

You can also add the following lines to the "ID_TRACKS" section:

```
    CDInfo.SetID currentID
    CDInfo.RefreshCDInfo
    CDInfo.Show
```

To bring the form "CDEdit" to life, you have to change the code inside that form as well. In this form you have to open an additional Recordset to display the CD details. Add the following method to the form:

```
Public Sub RefreshCDEdit()
Dim GotRecord
Dim CDRecordCDE
Dim adoPrimaryRSCDE As ADOCERecordset

    ' Fills the Text fields with the current data from our database
    Set adoPrimaryRSCDE = CreateObject("ADOCE.Recordset")
    GotRecord = GetFirstCDRecord(adoPrimaryRSCDE, "select * from
    Titles where TitleID=" & m_IDCDE, CDRecordCDE)
    Do While GotRecord
        txtFields0.Text = CDRecordCDE(0, 0)
        txtFields1.Text = CDRecordCDE(1, 0)
        txtFields2.Text = CDRecordCDE(2, 0)
        txtFields3.Text = CDRecordCDE(3, 0)
        txtFields4.Text = CDRecordCDE(4, 0)
        txtFields5.Text = CDRecordCDE(5, 0)
        txtFields6.Text = CDRecordCDE(6, 0)
        txtFields7.Text = CDRecordCDE(7, 0)
        txtFields8.Text = CDRecordCDE(8, 0)
        txtFields9.Text = CDRecordCDE(9, 0)
        GotRecord = GetNextCDRecord(adoPrimaryRSCDE, CDRecordCDE)
    Loop
    Set adoPrimaryRSCDE = Nothing
End Sub
```

Also add the event handler for the "Close" button:

```
Private Sub cmdClose_Click()
    Me.Hide
End Sub
```

For the form "CDInfo", you have to add one method as well:

```
Public Function RefreshCDInfo()
Dim GotRecord
Dim NewItem
```

```
Dim adoPrimaryRS as ADOCERecordSet
Dim CDRecord

    ' Initializes the Columns of the List View
    Set adoPrimaryRS = CreateObject("ADOCE.Recordset")
    listTracks.ColumnHeaders.Clear
    listTracks.ColumnHeaders.Add , , "TrackNo", listTracks.Width / 6,
lvwColumnLeft
    listTracks.ColumnHeaders.Add , , "Track Name", listTracks.Width -
listTracks.Width / 6, lvwColumnLeft

    ' Fills the List View with the current data from our database
    listTracks.ListItems.Clear
    GotRecord = GetFirstCDRecord(adoPrimaryRS, "select * from Tracks
where TitleID=" & m_ID, CDRecord)
    Do While GotRecord
        Set NewItem = listTracks.ListItems.Add(,, CDRecord(1, 0))
        NewItem.SubItems(1) = CDRecord(2, 0)
        GotRecord = GetNextCDRecord(adoPrimaryRS, CDRecord)
    Loop
End Function
```

Also add the event handler for the "Close" button;

```
Private Sub cmdClose_Click()
    Me.Hide
End Sub
```

You have to run the new CE version of your prototype on your Windows CE device since the desktop does not have the "DeluxeCD.cdb" database installed. Section 8.5.1 will explain how to get the DeluxeCD database into the emulation environment.

 The final source code of this section can be found on the companion CD under "\Sources\ThreadExample\PCDM VB Prototype\WCE".

5.6 Summary

If you compare the original prototype for the desktop and the final version for Windows CE you will find that you did not keep much of the code untouched. Since the

PCDM prototype is a very small application, you can imagine how difficult it would be to port a big Visual Basic application to your Windows CE device.

Table 5.6 summarizes the differences between Visual Basic for the desktop and Visual Basic for Windows CE and explains how to reconcile those differences.

Table 5.6   Differences between VB for the Desktop and eVB for Windows CE

Desktop	Windows CE
"WithEvents" in public variables.	Wrap the variable in an ActiveX control written in Visual C++ for Windows CE and insert this control in your form. Events of ActiveX controls are supported.
Allows declaration of public variables with the same names in different forms.	Rename all variables by giving them suffixes indicating the form name.
Strong type definition like "Dim bookmark as Boolean".	Remove strong definition because all variables are variants on Windows CE "Dim bookmark".
Instances of forms can be created with "Dim tForm as new <FormName>".	All forms are created at the start of the application; multiple instances are not allowed. Use "Dim tForm as <FormName>" to get the instance of the form.
Private Declares of Win32 API functions can be inserted into forms to access standard Windows API calls.	eVB supports that, too, but uses different DLLs and declaration syntax. You can find more on this topic in the Visual Basic for Windows CE documentation.
On Error GoTo	Use "On Error Resume Next" instead.
Intrinsic controls	Use the corresponding "Windows CE . . ." controls instead.
Other ActiveX controls	Only controls that are designated for Windows CE are supported. All other controls must be exchanged with their counterparts or must be removed.
Indexing of controls allows fast access to controls.	Each control must be addressed by its name. Indexing of controls is not supported.

Desktop	Windows CE
Properties	Some properties of controls are not supported. Please check the eVB documentation for details.
Toolbars	Convert to command bar.
Databinding	Use ADO Recordsets directly.
Sub Main	Public Sub Main
Unload Me	App.End
"Form_Load()" gets called when eVB app calls "Form.Show".	"Form_Load()" gets called before *any* call to a method of a form.
Double-click events	Only "single-click" events

These are the main differences between the two platforms. If you keep in mind that Visual Basic for Windows CE is based on VBScript, you will find your way through the migration path of eVB applications far more easily.

 Active Server Pages (ASP) and Internet Explorer client-side scripts also use VBScript, and porting those scripts to Windows CE is nearly a 1:1 port.

6
Chapter

COM for Windows CE

In this book, I emphasize the utility of the component object model (COM), which can be used for nearly every development task. Once you are familiar with the COM paradigm, I doubt that you will want to go back to the "old" API-based development style. Microsoft will continue to increase support for COM interfaces with each new version of Windows CE. This chapter discusses COM support for Windows CE and how to make use of it. It also explains how to design and host ActiveX controls and points out the differences between COM in Windows CE and in the desktop.

6.1   A Short Introduction to COM

As a professional in Windows desktop development, you may already be familiar with the COM paradigm. However, in case you are one of the many developers still writing applications the conventional way, this section will provide a brief introduction to COM.

 Basic definition: The whole purpose of COM is to help applications and components communicate with each other using a standardized object-oriented paradigm.

In the past—the "16-bit world"—communication between two applications was not very well organized. You could use shared-memory, files, Dynamic Data

Exchange (DDE), or any other method you invented to provide such communication. The operating system itself did not give you much help. The first "idea" of COM was implemented in the object linking and embedding (OLE) concept, which Microsoft introduced with Office 4.0. The first version of OLE made it possible to insert a document created by one application inside another document created by another application. The inserted document could then be activated directly by double-clicking on it. Looking back, this was not so much a real communication mechanism as a back-door approach to launching an application from within another application. During the 16-bit and Office evolution, Microsoft made this process more seamless, but it did not meet the main communication needs of the developers.

With application developers demanding usable object-oriented methods, Microsoft wanted to do things right in the 32-bit world from the very beginning. Thus came the invention of COM. Unfortunately, it carried over the name OLE (as in OLE controls or OCX), causing a lot of confusion in the developer community. Even today there are still initiatives and technologies on the market that have the word "OLE" in their name like "OLE for Health Care" or "OLE for Process Control". Both initiatives are actually based on COM and do not use any of the old OLE concept.

Current application architectures use COM as their standard communication "glue" between individual components. Over the years, Microsoft added more functionality to COM and now offers a wide variety of choices for communication within and between applications. If you are interested in learning more about the internals of COM, I recommend the book *Essential COM* by Don Box, published by Addison Wesley Longman.

6.1.1 How Does COM Work?

Since COM is the glue between two components, it always requires at least one server and one client. Of course, it also allows for one client communicating with multiple servers or one server communicating with multiple clients. Figure 6.1 shows the general way a client establishes a connection to a server, using the COM runtime. The COM runtime, although Microsoft never used this name in its documents, is simply a set of dynamic link libraries (DLLs)—for example, OLE32.DLL and OLEAUT32.DLL—that establishes communication between the client(s) and the server(s) and then lets them figure out the rest.

COM helps developers solve a variety of problems that they have had to struggle with since the invention of inter-process communication, including

- Versioning
- Early binding (which is no longer necessary)
- Communicating EXE to EXE
- Making remote communication as seamless as possible

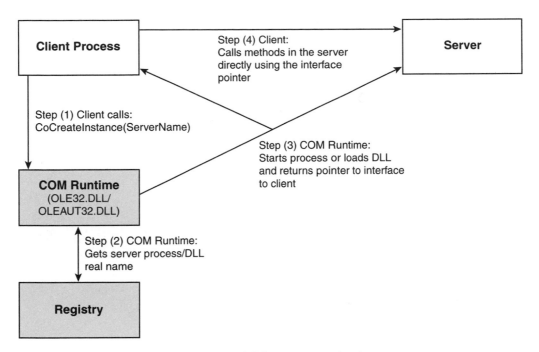

Figure 6.1   A simplified diagram of COM communication

6.1.2   Versioning

In the past, if you wanted to release a new version of a DLL, you also had to upgrade the application that used the DLL, or you had make sure that the order of exported functions (ordinal number) in the DLL stayed the same. With COM there is a separation between the interface (the name of a function) and the implementation of the function. If you want to upgrade a COM server, you can change the implementation in any way you want as long as the interface remains the same. If you export new functions in your new version, you simply add another interface with a different name to the interfaces of your existing server.

6.1.3   Early Binding No Longer Necessary

In the past, you could only link an application if all external functions had a proper library to which they were exported. The library was then bound to the application during the linking of the application. The only way to get around the early binding was to use LoadLibrary() and GetProcAddress(), which was rather clumsy and prone to error. Most errors happened while trying to load a library that was not there anymore because it had been moved or deleted. And if the parameter of the procedure had changed in a new version, GetProcAddress() would still return the correct function, but in most cases, your call would fail.

With COM, all you need is the interface description of the COM server. Since you are requesting the interface pointer from COM using CoCreateInstance() at runtime, you do not have to bind the server to your application during linking.

6.1.4   Communicating EXE to EXE

In the past, establishing communication between executables was a difficult problem. You either had to use shared memory, a Winsock loop back, or file-based communication. For a COM client, it does not really make a difference whether you are connecting to an EXE or hosting a DLL. The COM runtime will "figure out" how to connect the client to the server.

6.1.5   Making Remote Communication Seamless

Machine-to-machine communication was also a major challenge, especially making such communication seamless. Crossing machine boundaries introduced new concerns such as security, machine availability, and communication protocols; in addition, you had to do practically everything yourself. The only Windows support available was using NetDDE without any security.

DCOM, or Distributed COM, is the answer from the COM side. With DCOM, a COM client can communicate seamlessly with a remote server or a local server. The DCOM runtime takes care of everything.

6.2   COM Activation Methods

The COM runtime on the desktop supports several different methods for two applications to communicate. Unfortunately, on Windows CE not all of those methods are currently supported. Table 6.1 lists the types of communication supported for each version of Windows. As you can see, Microsoft already offers a wide variety of ways to use COM, and it promises to add more in the future.

Table 6.1   Communication Paths between Applications

OS and Version	In-Place Activation	ActiveX Controls	Inproc	EXE to EXE	MTS	DCOM	COM+ Services
Windows 3.x	Yes	No	No	No	No	No	No
Windows 95/98	Yes	Yes	Yes	Yes	Client only	Yes but limited	Only client-side
Windows NT 4.0	Yes	Yes	Yes	Yes	Yes (add on)	Yes	Yes (add on)
Windows 2000	Yes	Yes	Yes	Yes	Yes	Yes	Yes
Windows CE 1.0	No	No	No	No	No	No	No
Windows CE 2.x	No	Yes	Yes	No	No	Yes (using third-party deviceCOM)	No
Windows CE 3.0	No	Yes	Yes	Yes	Yes, but client only	Yes	Only MSQ client

6.2.1   In-Place Activation

In-place activation was also known as the old OLE during the 16-bit "dark ages." One application is able to include a data object of another application in its data file. When the user activates this blob, either by double-clicking on it or by selecting "Edit" from the context menu, the server application is launched and allowed to edit the object. You still find this legacy OLE mechanism inside the current Office suite of applications if you embed an Excel spreadsheet inside a Word document or place a bitmap in a PowerPoint slide.

6.2.2   ActiveX Controls

The ActiveX controls were the direct successors of the OLE in-place mechanisms, originally called OLE controls (OCX). When Microsoft realized that it took too much time to load a big application like Excel every time you just wanted to change the content of one cell, it turned to the Visual Basic team that had invented Visual Basic controls (VBX). The VBX concept was improved upon, extended, and generalized to support controls in languages besides Visual Basic. The result is ActiveX controls. Under Windows CE, many user interface controls in Visual Basic are implemented using ActiveX controls. It is also the most highly recommended way to build reusable code for all sorts of applications. As you will see, this book's PCDM application wraps nearly every important feature in ActiveX controls.

6.2.3 Inproc: In-Process Activation

In-process COM servers are basically ActiveX controls without a user interface or the corresponding interfaces needed to access the UI from the hosting client application. In-process activation of a COM server is very similar to using standard API calls that have been bound to the hosting application (client). Similar to API calls, the server (always a DLL) is loaded into the process space of the client, and the client calls the functions of the server using either the "Dispatch" interface or the vector-table. Since those calls do not have to go through process boundaries, the Inproc method is the fastest way to communicate between COM clients and servers. But it requires that the server be a DLL. The disadvantage of the Inproc activation is that it is possible for badly written servers to crash their hosts because they run in the same process space. This was the only way to use COM in Windows CE as late as CE Version 3.

6.2.4 EXE to EXE

With Windows 95 and Windows NT, the need to communicate between applications became more and more important. COM allows for application processes to communicate with each other even over process boundaries. EXE-to-EXE communication, also known as out-of-process communication, requires an Automation Interface. For this communication method, COM offers standard marshallers that, in effect, simulate a server-process DLL inside the client application, thereby allowing the client to call into the server. Marshallers were not available on Windows CE until Version 3.0.

Out-of-process calls are slower because they have to go through multiple layers of the operating system and carry security information that must be verified. Their big advantage is that a client does not crash if a server crashes.

6.2.5 MTS or DLLHOST.EXE

When the client calls COM's CoCreateInstance() function, it can specify that it always wants to run the server out-of-process in order to avoid getting clobbered by a failing server. To handle this scenario, Microsoft came up with the DLLHOST.EXE, a small surrogate that hosts the COM server DLL, simulating an external process. This gives crash-security to the COM DLL servers.

Further improvements came with the Microsoft Transaction Server (MTS). In addition to the function provided by DLLHOST.EXE, MTS provides transaction control and multi-threading for single-threaded servers. Currently, Windows CE does not support DLLHOST.EXE or MTS, but since Windows CE 3.0 will include DCOM, a Windows CE-based device can be a client to an MTS-hosted application on a desktop server.

6.2.6   DCOM

As the Internet age intensified, application developers were screaming for a solution to connect applications across machine boundaries. Microsoft's answer to this request was Distributed COM (DCOM), first available in Windows NT 4.0. With DCOM, a client uses the same mechanism to talk to a server whether it is running on the same machine or on another machine. With a tool called "DCOMConfig", the administrator is able to redirect the client call to any machine running the same server. Microsoft also extended the COM API with the CoCreateInstanceEx() function that had a new parameter to specify the target machine name directly via the application. While DCOM is not a high-speed protocol, is not very reliable, and is not designed to transfer huge amounts of data, it does provide seamless communication between two applications running on different machines. Windows CE Version 3.0 supports DCOM to connect to servers hosted on a desktop PC.

Intrinsyc, a Canadian company, has provided a DCOM-like solution for Windows CE 2.0-based devices, called "deviceCOM". You can find out more about deviceCOM at the end of this chapter.

6.2.7   COM+ Services

With Windows 2000, Microsoft will introduce the next step in COM development: COM+ services. The COM+ services feature new communication enhancements, including message queuing and events. Starting with Windows CE 3.0, only Microsoft Message Queuing (MSMQ) is available and only as a client.

6.3   Creating a Small COM Server

Now that you are familiar with COM support under Windows CE, the next step is putting that knowledge to use. As I have noted, this book will provide numerous examples of wrapping various sorts of functionality in COM components that can be reused and extended in your own applications.

As shown in Table 6.1, up to Version 3, Windows CE only provided support for COM servers activated and accessed in the same process as the client—in-process activation. Now you will create a simple COM server and load it into a hosting application.

6.3.1 Creating a COM Server for Windows CE

The most efficient way to create ActiveX controls is by using the ATL library that Microsoft ships with eMbedded Visual C++. The controls created with ATL are small, fast, and easy to maintain for the developer while still providing a lot of flexibility for enhancements.

1. Start eMbedded Visual C++ and select "New . . ." from the file menu.
2. In the "Open" dialog box select the "Projects" tab and choose the "WCE ATL COM AppWizard". Enter "MyCeServer" into the project name field and click "OK".

The "WCE ATL COM AppWizard" will appear and ask only one question: "Support MFC?" If you are familiar with the ATL wizard for the desktop, you will notice that the wizard for CE does not ask about the server type (DLL, EXE, or Service), MTS support, or proxy/stub merging. The reason is simple: those options are not supported in Windows CE.

3. For your test server you do not need support for MFC. To keep the server as small as possible, do not select it.
4. Click "Finish", and after confirming the summary page, your project workspace should look like the one shown in Figure 6.2.

The AppWizard will generate a COM server frame for you, providing all the necessary glue to compile a valid COM server. As you will see, it is the same global function as its desktop ATL counterpart. Next, you have to add the object type to the server.

5. Click on the "MyCeServer classes" root entry in the Class View with the right mouse button and select "New ATL object . . ." from the context menu.

In the "ATL Object" wizard you will see a subset of all the object types ATL supports for the desktop. Table 6.2 lists these object types and their respective purposes in life.

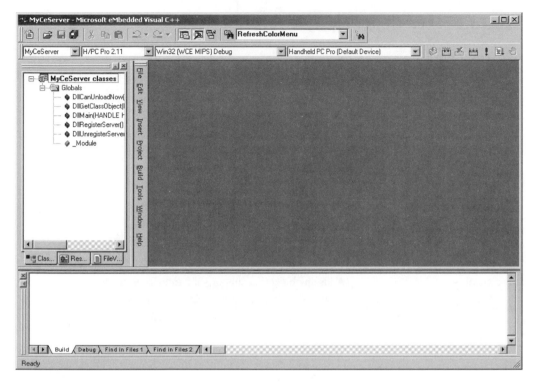

Figure 6.2   The eMbedded Visual C++ workspace

6.   For your small example, choose the "Simple Object" type in the category "Objects".

The wizard will ask you for information regarding the C++ class and the COM interface.

7.   Enter "TestMe" in the C++ "Short Name" field, and you will see that the wizard fills in the blanks.

If you switch to the "Attributes" tab of the wizard, you may note that the wizard for Windows CE disables several options that are available to you when you create an ATL server on the desktop.

8.   For this example, you will keep the default settings. Later in the book you will change some of those settings to get the desired response.

9.   As soon as you click on "OK", you will see the expected class and interface entries in the tree view of "MyCeServer Classes".

Now you need to add a method to your new control.

Table 6.2   ATL Object Types

Object Type	Used for
Category: Objects	
Simple object	No specialized use. Totally up to the developer.
Internet Explorer object	An object that can be used in Internet Explorer to be scriptable. It is available with Windows CE 2.12.
Component registration object	Implements the IcomponentRegistrar interface that lets you register individual objects in your control.
Category: Controls	
Full control	Adds an object that supports the interfaces for all containers.
Lite control	Adds an object that supports the interfaces needed by Internet Explorer, including support for a user interface.
Property page	Includes the interfaces required to display a property page from within a control.
Composite control	Adds a control that can host many other controls.
Lite composite control	Adds a composite control that can host other controls, but it supports only the interfaces needed by Internet Explorer.
Category: Miscellaneous	
Dialog	Adds an object that implements a dialog box.

10. Select the ItestMe interface in the "CTestMe" class and add the method ShowMe with the following "Parameters":

```
"[out,retval]short *nVal"
```

At this point, if you were to compare the respective Interface Definition Languages (IDLs) of the desktop control and the Windows CE control, you would find no difference. Microsoft did a very good job of keeping the IDL in sync.

11. Open the C++ implementation of the ShowMe method and enter the following line of code in the method body:

```
*nVal=4711;
```

12. Add a property to the object called AboutText. Define the property type as "BSTR" and keep all other default settings.

13. Add the following code to the implementation methods of get_AboutText and set_AboutText:

```
STDMETHODIMP CTestMe::get_AboutText(BSTR *pVal)
{
CComBSTR tbstr;
    tbstr=m_AboutTxt;
    *pVal=SysAllocString(tbstr);
    return S_OK;
}
STDMETHODIMP CTestMe::put_AboutText(BSTR newVal)
{
    m_AboutTxt= SysAllocString(newVal);
    return S_OK;
}
```

14. Declare the "m_AboutTxt" variable as follows in the "CTestMe" class:

```
BSTR m_AboutTxt;
```

15. Compile the control for "H/PC Pro 2.11", "Win32 (WCE x86em) Debug", and "Handheld PC Pro Emulation".

At the end of the compilation process, eMbedded Visual C++ for Windows CE will check whether all required system DLLs are on the device and will download them if they are not. The COM server requires the ATLCE211.DLL that eVC will download and register automatically.

eMbedded Visual C++ will also download and register your COM server. You can verify the successful registration by starting the Windows CE Remote Registry Editor and looking into the "HKEY_CLASSES_ROOT" folder of the emulation registry. Since the registry editor sorts the keys by name, scroll down to those starting with "M", and as shown in Figure 6.3, you should see

```
MyCeServer.TestMe
MyCeServer.TestMe.1
```

 You can find the source of this example COM server on the companion CD in the folder "\Sources\Chapter 6\6.1".

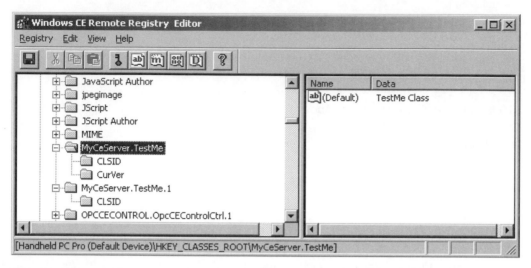

Figure 6.3 A Remote Registry Editor showing the two COM server keys

6.3.2 Generating the Desktop-Equivalent COM Server

In order to use the COM server in Visual Basic or in other programs that require the same COM server on the desktop as in Windows CE, you have to create the same "MyCeServer" project for the desktop. While Visual Studio 97 permitted adding a desktop configuration to the compiler bar, Microsoft decided to create eMbedded Visual Tools as separate tools from Visual Studio 98, making it a bit more complicated to generate a desktop equivalent. Here is the procedure you will use to generate a desktop project for your COM server.

1. Create a Win32 version of the control project with the same name as the original COM server "MyCeServer" using the ATL COM AppWizard, but store it in a different directory.

2. In the ATL wizard keep all defaults.

3. You will need to put the new ".dsp" and ".dsw" files in the same directory as the original COM server project.

4. Open the workspace "MyCeServer.dsw" in Visual C++ and add the file "TestMe.cpp" to the workspace.

If you have compiled your original COM server before you generated the desktop version, you will find some more files like "MyCeServerps.def", "MyCeServer_p.c", and "MyCeServer_i.c". Visual C++ generates those when you compile your project so those files do not need to be added to your project. Nor do you need to add the ".h" files to the workspace because Visual C++ includes them automatically after the first generation of the dependencies.

    5.   Compile the COM server as "Unicode Debug".

In the end, you will have two project workspaces that share the same source files. Unfortunately, the class wizard has a hard time keeping in sync between the two projects. If you are as addicted to the class wizard as I am, you will always have to do your changes in the eMbedded Visual C++ project. As long as you work under Windows NT and target a Windows NT desktop or server with your components, you can stick with the Unicode target. If you are targeting a Windows 9x desktop, you will need to use a non-Unicode target mode. In Appendix D you can find many tips that will help you to solve that challenge.

 NOTE: The class wizard of the desktop equivalent is not able to reproduce the complete class view as you see it in the project for Windows CE. If you want to use it to add methods, properties, or events, always load the Windows CE project and make your changes there.

 You can find the source of this example's COM server on the companion CD in the folder "\Sources\Chapter 6\6.2".

6.3.3   Calling the COM Server in C++

Next you will create a small client application that creates an instance of the COM server DLL and accesses the ShowMe() method that you developed in the last section. You will also use the "MyFirst" application from Chapter 4. It already contains all the framework code so you can concentrate on calling the COM server.

    1.   Copy the "MyFirst" project into a new directory and then load it into the Visual C++ environment.

    2.   To activate the support for COM in your application, you have to add the "afxdisp.h" include file to the "StdAfx.h". Add the following statement after the "afxext.h" include:

```
#include <afxdisp.h>        // MFC OLE automation classes
```

6.3.4   Using #import

You will use the new helper directive "#import" to include the COM server in your application. This is a very simple way of getting around the complex initialization of

COM interfaces in Visual C++. There are other easy methods of using COM components in client applications. In Section 6.7, you will learn to use a wrapper class that the class wizard will generate.

3. Add the following line to the "myFirstDlg.h" include file before the class definition "CMyFirstDlg":

```
#import "<myPathToTheDLLOfChapter6.3.2>\myceserver.dll"
rename_namespace("myce") raw_interfaces_only
```

You have to replace the <MyPathToTheDll> with the path to the location of your MyCeServer.DLL of Section 6.3.2. If you want to be path-neutral, you can use <myceserver.dll>, but then you have to set the path to the DLL in the Include Options of the eMbedded Visual C++ compiler environment. I do not recommend this method because you have to do this for all Windows CE target platforms and variations.

I recommend adding the parameter "raw_interfaces_only" to the "#import" directive. This parameter will prevent the compiler from generating a more complex wrapper code around the COM server methods.

Remember, in your COM server "MyCeServer", you had a method that returned a value "4711". Without the "raw_interfaces_only" directive, the compiler would generate a wrapper function that could be used as follows:

```
Int iRetValue=MyCeServer.ShowMe();
```

Compiling with the "raw_interfaces_only" directive results in a COM-defined function as

```
Int iRetValue;
MyCeServer.ShowMe(&iRetValue);
```

The second code is not only faster, but it also contains different error handling in the wrapper. If you look in the compiler-generated file "MyCeServer.tlh" in the target directory, you can see the wrapper for the COM server. It looks very straightforward and does not show anything unusual. If you compiled the "MyFirst" application now, you would not get any error messages because you are not yet calling the wrapper function. Now add the code to the OnButton1() method to call the COM server.

4. Change the content of the OnButton1() method to the following:

```
void CMyFirstDlg::OnButton1()
{
    ITestMePtr Conn1;
```

```
HRESULT hr=Conn1.CreateInstance( __uuidof( TestMe ) );
if (FAILED(hr))
{
MessageBox(TEXT("Creating the COM Server instance failed"));
return;
}
short a;
Conn1->ShowMe(&a);
CString ast;
ast.Format(TEXT("MyCeServer returned ShowMe=%d"),a);
MessageBox(ast);
}
```

5.   To tell the compiler that you are going to use the "MyCe" namespace in this code, you must add the following line after the include statements:

```
using namespace myce;
```

Now if you compile the application, you will get a linker error stating that the export function "com_issue_error" was not found. This error reflects a difference between COM in Windows CE and COM for the desktop. COM in Windows CE does not support exception handling, but the desktop ATL uses exception handling to handle the errors of any methods created with the "#import" directive.

Fortunately, Microsoft made it fairly simple to include your own error handler. You basically have to include a global function in your code called com_issue_error(HRESULT). For this small test, you need not put any code in that function, but you have to include it in order to get rid of the linker error.

6.   Add the following lines before the "use namespace . . ." statement:

```
void __stdcall _com_issue_error(HRESULT hr)
{
      // Error handling goes here!
}
```

7.   Compile the application and test it.

If everything is correct, the application should come up on your CE device, and as soon as you press "Button1", you should see the dialog box shown in Figure 6.4 with the content "MyCeServer returned ShowMe=4711".

 You can find the source of this COM server example on the companion CD in the folder "\Sources\Chapter 6\6.3".

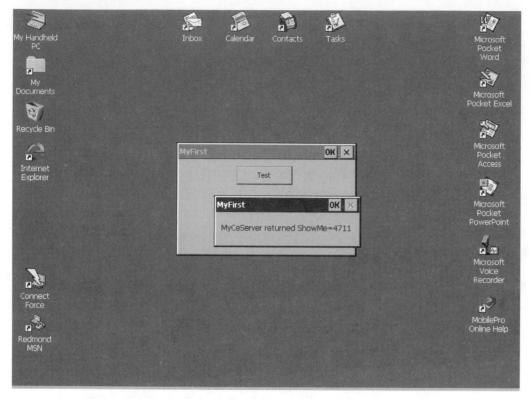

Figure 6.4 An MFC application MyFirst showing the ShowMe result

6.3.5 Calling the COM Server in Visual Basic

Calling a COM server in eMbedded Visual Basic is even simpler.

1. Create a new H/PC Pro project and add a button to the main form.

2. Double-click the button to get to the code view of the button and enter the following code to the "on_click" method of the button:

```
Private Sub Command1_Click()
Dim foo As Object
Dim a
    Set foo = CreateObject("MyCeServer.TestMe")
    foo.abouttext = "Hello World"
    a = foo.showme
    MsgBox a
```

```
    MsgBox foo.abouttext
End Sub
```

If you run this application, you will first see a message box containing the number "4711" followed by a message box containing "Hello world".

To use the code above, your control must use either plain C++ or ATL. Visual Basic for Windows CE does not currently support MFC COM servers.

 You can find the source of this COM server example on the companion CD in the folder "\Sources\Chapter 6\6.4".

6.4 Creating an ActiveX Control

ActiveX controls are perfect for encapsulating user interface controls and their intelligence. Visual Basic for Windows CE can only host ActiveX controls as user interface controls, including even those intrinsic controls that Visual Basic for the desktop has in its toolbar.

Throughout this book, you will encapsulate all user interface-related technologies as ActiveX controls. And for the Pocket-CD-Manager example, you will put all controls in one DLL named PCDMUI.DLL.

6.4.1 Creating an ActiveX Control for Windows CE

Creating an ActiveX control is as simple as creating a COM server.

1. Create a new "WCE ATL Wizard" project with eMbedded Visual C++ and name the project "MyFirstCtrl". The wizard will ask you if you want to support MFC, but for this minimal control you do not need MFC.

 The MFC enlarges your control by several KB. If you want to generate small, high-speed controls, try not to use it.

The wizard will then create the necessary framework to start adding the control-specific functions to the project.

2. Select the "MyFirstCtrl classes" root folder of the project and select "New ATL Object . . ."
3. In the dialog box select "Full Control".

4. The wizard will ask you for the name of the new control. Enter "HexConv", select the "Attributes" tab of the dialog box, and then select "Supports Connection Points".

The reason you want to support connection points is some ActiveX Containers want to be notified if a property has changed. Those containers can then trigger either small scripts or even transfer the property content automatically to other controls without polling the property.

You should be very familiar with the rest of the control dialog box. If you are wondering why the "apartment" setting for the control is not available, you have to remember that Windows CE does not support out-of-process COM and the apartment-threading model exists mainly for this purpose.

Adding Properties to the Control

As before, you can now add properties and methods to the control by selecting "Add Method . . ." or "Add Property . . ." in the object menu of the "IHexConv" interface.

5. Add two properties to the control named "InValue" and "OutValue" and select the type "long" for the two properties.

6. Select the "Attributes . . ." button and add the following attributes to the list:

   • Bindable

   • Requestedit

   • Displaybind

These attributes are necessary in order to notify the container of changes in the control and to prepare the control for data binding in the future. Unfortunately, eMbedded Visual Basic does not support this capability. Many vertical applications use this technology to reduce the number of scripts that have to be used to connect different ActiveX controls and exchange data between them.

Finally, you will add the implementation code for the properties and one small addition to the CHexConv class.

7. Open the "HexConv.H" include file and add the following lines to the end of the class:

```
private:
     long m_InValue,m_OutValue;
     CComBSTR m_DisplayStr;
```

The values "m_InValue" and "m_OutValue" will contain the content of the corresponding properties of your control. The method "SetDisplayString" will use the "m_DisplayStr" that you will add to the control.

In accordance with the strict concept of object-orientation—whereby all data are encapsulated inside objects and are only accessible through methods—you do not want to expose this value to the outside world. In the COM world, this means that data are only accessible through interfaces.

If you compared this code with that of a control created for the desktop, you would see no difference. Microsoft did a very good job of keeping the COM world in Windows CE as similar to the desktop as possible.

8. Open the "HexConv.cpp" file and insert the following code:

```
STDMETHODIMP CHexConv::get_InValue(long *pVal)
{
     *pVal=m_InValue;
     return S_OK;
}


STDMETHODIMP CHexConv::put_InValue(long newVal)
{
     m_InValue=newVal;
     put_OutValue(m_InValue);
     FireOnChanged(2);
     FireViewChange();
     return S_OK;
}


STDMETHODIMP CHexConv::get_OutValue(long *pVal)
{
     *pVal=m_OutValue;
     return S_OK;
}


STDMETHODIMP CHexConv::put_OutValue(long newVal)
{
     m_OutValue=newVal;
     FireViewChange();
     Fire_OnOutChange();
     return S_OK;
}
```

Other than the "put_ . . ." implementations, you do not see any unusual code. The "put_inValue" method copies the value of "m_InValue" into "m_OutValue" by calling the method "put_outValue". In the object-oriented world, it would read:

"copies the content of the property 'InValue' to the content of the property 'OutValue'". This method is much safer than just addressing the "m_OutValue" directly because the "put_OutValue" method may produce other side effects besides setting the member variable to "newVal", such as firing another event, doing some calculations, and validating data.

"OnFireChanged(2)" fires an event to the COM system to tell an interested host that the content of the property "OutValue" has changed. The host, which listens to that event, will then be able to read the new value by calling the method "get_outValue". Without the event or the connection points, the host would have to continuously poll the "OutValue" property in order to recognize a change. Of course, this is not very efficient. The parameter (2) of this function corresponds to the dispatch ID in the IDL of the control. If you open the file "MyFirstCtrl.IDL" and search for the "OutValue" property you will find the following lines:

```
[propget, id(2), helpstring("property OutValue"), bindable,
  displaybind, requestedit] HRESULT OutValue([out, retval] long *pVal);
[propput, id(2), helpstring("property OutValue"), bindable,
  displaybind, requestedit] HRESULT OutValue([in] long newVal);
```

The "id(2)" defines the dispatch ID number that you must use to call the "OnFireChanged()" method. It will tell the container that the property with the dispatch ID 2 has changed.

Design all properties of your controls to have connection points and event-triggered notification. This not only helps to enforce object-orientation in your code, but also is more efficient for processing changes by the container.

The helper method "FireViewChange();" of ATL calls the "OnDraw" method. As you can see, the "OnDraw" method requires an ATL_DRAWINFO structure parameter that is normally hidden from regular methods. The ATL code constructs that structure inside the "FireViewChange()" method and then calls "OnDraw".

Now you want to add a method to the control that sends a string to the control that will be shown in the display area of the control:

```
Fire_OnOutChange();
```

This method fires an event that you have to add to the control. eMbedded Visual Basic does not currently support data binding so you have to fire an event manually in order for Visual Basic to recognize changes in the property of the control.

Adding an Event to the Control

Next you will add an event to your control that will fire when the "OutValue" is changed.

9.   Locate the interface "_IHexConvEvents" and select "Add Method . . ." from its context menu.

10.   In the dialog box, select "void" as the return type, select "OnOutChange" as the method name, and specify no parameters.

The last change you need to make is to include the "IconnectionPoint" implementation in your project. The class wizard can help you with this, too.

11.   Select the class "ChexConv" with the right mouse button and select "Implement Connection Point . . ." from the context menu.

12.   In the dialog box you only have to set the checkbox for the interface "_IHexConvEvents". The class wizard will then create all the code in your project necessary to implement the event.

Unfortunately, the class wizard has a small bug: In the include file "HexConv.h", the wizard creates the new connection-point entry inside the connection-point map:

```
CONNECTION_POINT_ENTRY(IID__IHexConvEvents)
```

The correct entry should be

```
CONNECTION_POINT_ENTRY(DIID__IHexConvEvents)
```

By the time you read this, Microsoft may already have corrected this bug in a service pack that shipped prior to the book's release. If not, simply correct the error.

Adding a Method to the Control

Finally, you want to add a method to the control.

13.   Add the method "SetDisplayString" to the control and add the parameter "BSTR DisplayStr" to the method. The implementation code of this method is again very simple:

```
STDMETHODIMP CHexConv::SetDisplayString(BSTR DisplayStr)
{
    m_DisplayStr=SysAllocString(DisplayStr);
    FireViewChange();
    return S_OK;
}
```

You also need to change some code in the "HexConv.h" include file. First, you should initialize the new member variables in order to force a defined starting state.

14. Add the following lines to the "CHexConv" class constructor:

```
CHexConv()
{
    m_DisplayStr=TEXT(" ");
    m_InValue=0;
    m_OutValue=0;
}
```

The ATL wizard creates the implementation code for the constructor and for the "OnDraw" method inside the class definition in the include file.

```
m_DisplayStr=TEXT("");
```

The TEXT("") macro is necessary because Windows CE is fully Unicode-compliant; without the "TEXT" you would get an error during compilation. Another macro L"" would also work, but forces the string to be Unicode. This means that you cannot compile the same code for Windows 9x. Windows 9x still requires ANSI code, which would create a compiler error. See Appendix D for more details.

15. Select the "OnDraw" method of the control and change the code to:

```
HRESULT OnDraw(ATL_DRAWINFO& di)
{
    RECT& rc = *(RECT*)di.prcBounds;
    HBRUSH hBrush, hOldBrush;
    hBrush = (HBRUSH)GetStockObject(WHITE_BRUSH);
    hOldBrush = (HBRUSH)SelectObject(di.hdcDraw, hBrush);
    Rectangle(di.hdcDraw, rc.left, rc.top, rc.right, rc.bottom);
    SelectObject(di.hdcDraw, hOldBrush);

    TCHAR *pszText=(TCHAR *)LocalAlloc(LMEM_ZEROINIT,
                (UINT)(m_DisplayStr.Length()+20)*sizeof(TCHAR));
#ifdef UNICODE
        wsprintf(pszText,TEXT("%s %d=0x%x"),m_DisplayStr,
                        m_InValue,m_OutValue);
#else
        USES_CONVERSION;
        wsprintf(pszText,TEXT("%s %d=0x%x"),W2A(m_DisplayStr),
                        m_InValue,m_OutValue);
#endif
```

```
        DrawText(di.hdcDraw, pszText, -1, &rc,
                 DT_CENTER | DT_VCENTER | DT_SINGLELINE);
        LocalFree(pszText);
    return S_OK;
}
```

There is nothing very complicated about the "OnDraw" method. You simply create one big string that contains your display string and append the two values as decimal and hexadecimal values. You can also see that you have to do some special conversions for an ANSI target, but the nice helper macros of ATL come in handy for this job. More tips and tricks pertaining to the "Unicode versus ANSI" issue can be found in Appendix D.

Now you are ready to compile. Do not forget to set the compiler bar to the correct values corresponding to your Windows CE device.

You can find the source of this COM server example on the companion CD in the folder "\Sources\Chapter 6\6.5".

6.4.2 Generating the Desktop Equivalent

Generating the desktop equivalent for ActiveX controls works exactly as described in Section 6.3.2, except in this case, you need to add the file "HexConv.cpp" to the new project.

Now that both controls are ready to test, use the eVB Tools Control Manager to download and register the control on your device as well as the desktop Design Control for Visual Basic.

In my experience, you can install the device control faster if you first install it into the desktop Design Controls list.

6.4.3 Using the Control in eMbedded Visual C++

Using an ActiveX control in eMbedded Visual C++ is as straightforward as you would expect. If you are familiar with the desktop version of C++, you already know how to do this. The quickest way to get the ActiveX control into an application is to create a dialog-based MFC application.

1. Create a new "WCE MFC AppWizard" project and name it "CeOCXHost".

2. In the first page of the wizard select the "Dialog Based" application, and in the second page select support for ActiveX controls. Keep the default values for the other pages.

3. As soon as the wizard has done its work, open the "IDD_CEOCXHOST_DIALOG" dialog box in the Resource Editor.

4. Right-click the dialog box and select "Insert ActiveX control . . ." from the context menu.

5. Select the "HexConv Class" in the list of ActiveX controls that are installed on your PC, as illustrated in Figure 6.5.

6. Add three Edit controls and three buttons to the dialog box and name them as shown in Figure 6.6.

The next step is to generate a wrapper class for the control. The class wizard of Visual C++ can help with this task.

7. Right-click the "IDC_HEXCONV1" control and select the class wizard. In the class wizard select the "Member Variables" tab.

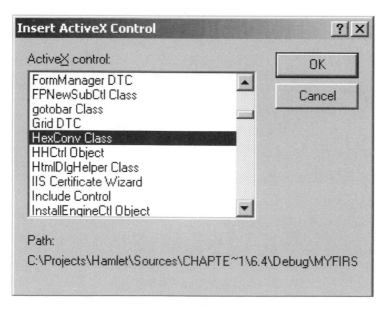

Figure 6.5   Selection dialog box for ActiveX controls in Visual C++

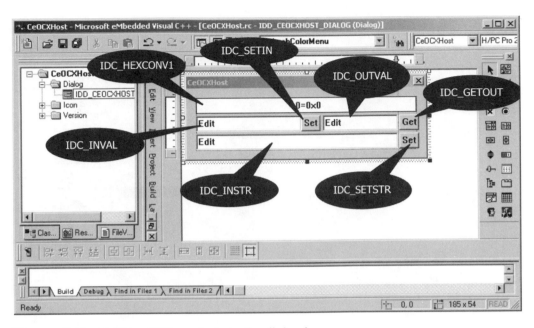

Figure 6.6   Adding Edit controls to the dialog box

8.   Double-click the "IDC_HEXCONV1" control. The wizard will ask you if you want to create a new class, assign it to the control, and add it to the project.

9.   Confirm the resulting message box and the wizard will ask you to name the new class, the include file, and the implementation file.

10.   Simply accept the defaults and select "OK".

The next dialog box will ask you for a variable name to use to address the control within your code.

11.   Name the control "m_ctrlHexConv" and close the dialog box by clicking "OK".

12.   Add member variables to the three Edit controls and name them as shown in Figure 6.7.

The last thing to do before actually writing code is to generate the event handler for the three buttons and the "IDC_HEXCONV1" control.

13.   To generate the event handler for the buttons, just double-click them in the dialog box. The class wizard will ask you for a method name. Just accept the suggestions of the wizard and press "OK".

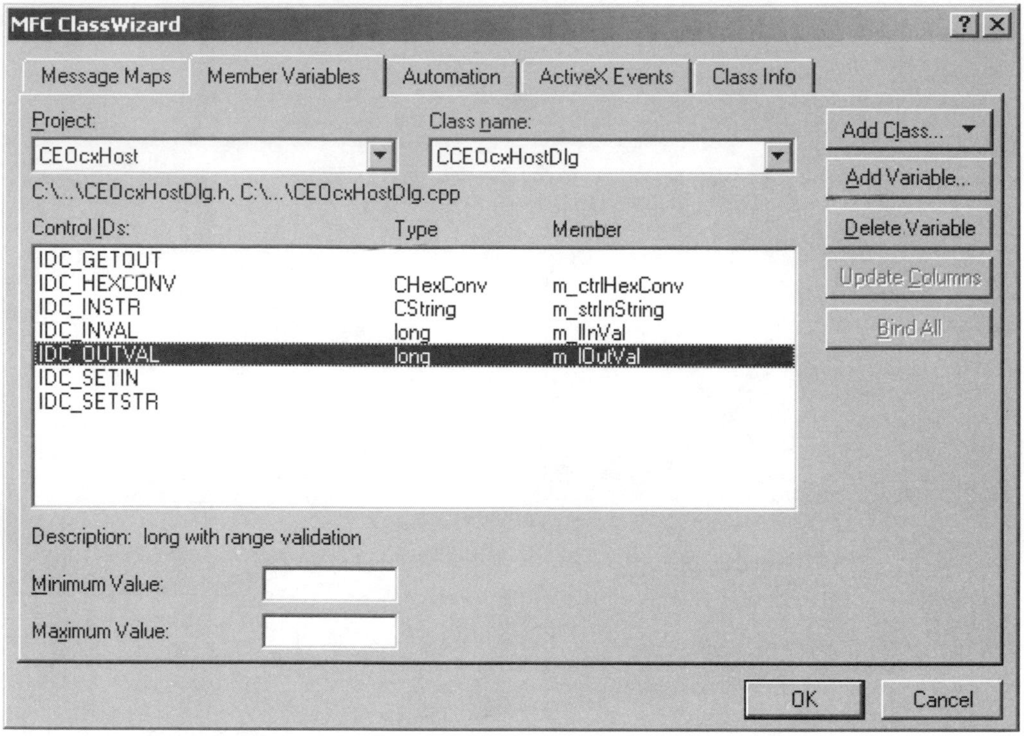

Figure 6.7 Member variables in the CEOcxHost dialog box

14. To generate the event handler for the "IDC_HEXCONV" control, you can also just double-click the control.

15. The wizard will suggest the name "OnOnOutChangeHexconv1", but change it to "OnOutChangeHexconv1".

16. Here again, the code you have to write is very simple. Add the following lines to the methods of the button event handlers and the "IDC_HEXCONV" event handler:

```
void CCEOcxHostDlg::OnSetin()
{
    UpdateData(TRUE);
    m_ctrlHexConv.SetInValue(m_lInVal);
}

void CCEOcxHostDlg::OnGetout()

{
```

```
        m_lOutVal=m_ctrlHexConv.GetOutValue();
        UpdateData(FALSE);
}

void CCEOcxHostDlg::OnSetstr()
{
        UpdateData(TRUE);
        m_ctrlHexConv.SetDisplayString(m_strInString);
}

void CCEOcxHostDlg::OnOutChangeHexconv()
{
        m_lOutVal=m_ctrlHexConv.GetOutValue();
        UpdateData(FALSE);
}
```

If you're wondering what the "UpdateData()" method does, it updates the member variables before you send them to the "m_ctrlHexConv" control. If the parameter is set to "TRUE", the MFC updates the controls with the content of their member variables. Setting the parameter to "FALSE" updates the member variables with the content of the controls.

This is standard MFC behavior; you will not find any difference here from a desktop application. Even the "EVENTSINK_MAP" is exactly as it would be on the desktop. Microsoft did a great job of keeping the behavior and code in sync between the Windows CE development and the desktop development.

    17.   Compile the application and test it on your device.

To test the application, enter "64" into the first edit field "IDC_INVAL". If it works correctly, the content of the second edit field "IDC_OUTVAL" should show the exact same value of "64". In the drawing area of your control you should see "64 = 0 × 40". And if you enter a string like "My Display String" into the third edit field "IDC_INSTR", the control should show "My Display String 64 = 0 × 40".

You can find the source of this example COM server on the companion CD in the folder "\Sources\Chapter 6\6.6".

6.4.4   Using the Control in eMbedded Visual Basic

You also want to test your control on eMbedded Visual Basic (eVB) and reproduce the same application you created in Visual C++.

1. Create a new Visual Basic project for H/PC Professionals.

2. Once Visual Basic has created the project framework, right-click the toolbar containing the eVB intrinsic controls and select "Components" from the context menu.

3. Select the "MyFirstCtrl V1.0 Type Library" and click on "OK".

If you do not see the type library in the selection box, make sure you have used the Control Manager to install the "MyFirstCtrl" on the desktop and on your Windows CE device.

You should instantly see a new control in the toolbar.

4. Add the new control, three Edit controls, and three buttons to the form "Form1". Arrange the controls on the form as shown in Figure 6.8.

5. Now add the following code to the event handler of the three command buttons and the "HexConv1" control:

```
Private Sub Command1_Click()
    HexConv1.InValue = Text1.Text
End Sub

Private Sub Command2_Click()
    HexConv1.SetDisplayString Text3.Text
End Sub
```

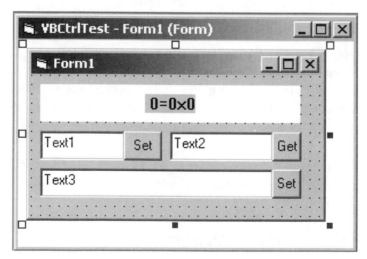

Figure 6.8   The main form of the VBCtrlTest application

```
Private Sub Command3_Click()
    Text2.Text = HexConv1.OutValue
End Sub

Private Sub HexConv1_OnOutChange()
    Text2.Text = HexConv1.OutValue
End Sub
```

6. Save the project, compile it, and run it. Your Windows CE screen should resemble Figure 6.9.

To test the application, you need to repeat what you did with the C++ application. Enter "64" into the "text1" field. If it works correctly, the content of the "Text2" field should also show "64". In the drawing area of your control you should see "64 =

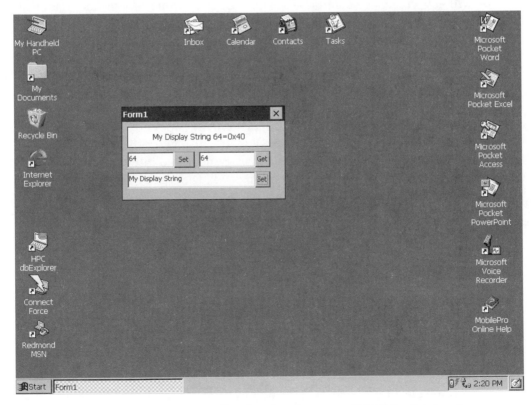

Figure 6.9   The VBCtrlTest application running on an H/PC Professional

0×40". And if you enter a string like "My Display String" into the field "Text3", the control should show "My Display String $64 = 0 \times 40$".

 You can find the source of this COM server example on the companion CD in the folder "\Sources\Chapter 6\6.7".

6.5 Creating the Wrapper Controls for the PCDM

As mentioned before, you want to wrap most of the Windows CE technologies in COM controls so as to be able to reuse them later and to be able to use them in Visual Basic.

You will now create two controls—one that wraps user-interface technologies and another that contains code without a user interface. The reason to split these two categories of features is simple: Windows CE can be run on devices without user interfaces. If you put all the features in a single control, it would carry a lot of unwanted functionality into those devices. You will call the two DLLs "PCDMUI.DLL" and "PCDMDLL.DLL".

The PCDMUI will contain multiple ActiveX controls that contain different Windows CE UI technologies. The other control, PCDMDLL, does not include any ActiveX controls and will be as small as possible. It will contain all non-UI technologies, such as registry management, database management, and infrared support. Both components will be created using the ATL framework, with the PCDMUI supporting the MFC and the PCDMDLL not supporting the MFC.

You will begin by creating the framework for the PCDMUI DLL.

1. Start Visual C++ and create a new project called "PCDMUI" using the "WCE ATL Wizard".

2. In the ATL wizard, set the "Support for MFC" flag and select "Finish".

3. Now, as explained in previous chapters, create the desktop equivalent to the Windows CE version by means of the following steps:

    • Create the same project with the "ATL COM Wizard" and select the support for MFC.

    • Copy the ".DSP" and ".DSW" files over into the original CE project.

Now do the same for the PCDM DLL, but do not select the MFC support this time.

You can find these two projects on the companion CD in the directories "\Sources\ThreadExample\PCDMUI\Step1" and "\Sources\ThreadExample\PCDMDLL\Step1".

6.6   DCOM: Distributed COM

As previously noted, DCOM is a technology to support remote COM calls via any network to another PC. Unfortunately, DCOM is not yet available for Windows CE because there is currently no RPC layer inside Windows CE.

To transmit parameters of method calls to another application, even on the same machine, DCOM requires a marshalling subsystem. On Windows NT, DCOM uses the Distributed Computing Environment-Remote Procedure Call (DCE-RPC) stack that is already many years old. This stack is currently not available on Windows CE, and thus neither is DCOM. Microsoft has DCOM on its roadmap for an upcoming version of Windows CE.

6.7   deviceCOM: The Industrial Version of DCOM

Intrinsyc, a Canadian company with headquarters in Vancouver, BC, is filling the communication gap for developers of Windows CE Version 2.*x* devices. The device-COM is a DCOM replica that provides the same look and feel to COM client/server applications as DCOM does. But under the hood, deviceCOM uses different communication techniques. While DCOM is based on DCE-RPC (built in the 1980s), device-COM is based on pure User Datagram Package (UDP), Transmission Control Protocol (TCP), or Inter-Process Connection (IPC) protocols.

Windows CE 2.*x* supports only in-process COM servers. Intrinsyc needed to come up with a solution to support access to out-of-process servers as well as to permit COM across machine boundaries. Figure 6.10 shows how Intrinsyc solved this challenge. A special deviceCOM interface proxy for the COM server is loaded together with the deviceCOM library into the COM client application. This proxy and the deviceCOM server provide the communication between the client and the server.

Because deviceCOM does not use DCE-RPC as its communication protocol, it is not possible to connect a deviceCOM client to a DCOM server directly or vice versa. To be able to communicate via deviceCOM, deviceCOM has to be installed on both sides—the Windows CE device and the desktop PC. The client and the server do not

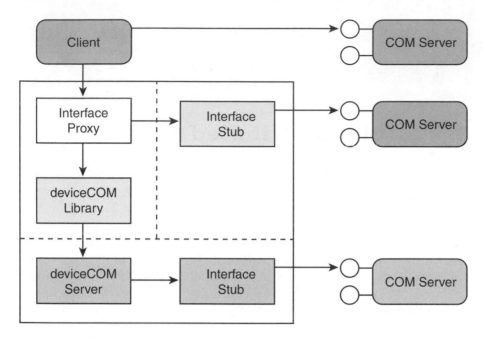

Figure 6.10 deviceCOM client/server interaction schematics

have to be changed to work with deviceCOM. Both DCOM and deviceCOM can coexist on the same PC.

6.7.1 Installation of deviceCOM

The deviceCOM ships as an Open Development Kit (ODK). The installation is extremely painless and easy to use. The samples in this book use Version 2.1, but it is possible that Intrinsyc has shipped a newer version since this book was printed.

To see how easy it is to set up a deviceCOM connection between a desktop PC and a Windows CE device, you are going to create a small desktop application that calls your PCDMDLL.DLL COM server remotely via deviceCOM.

1. First install the deviceCOM ODK V2.1. Use the default path for the installation directory.

 You can find a test and evaluation version of the ODK on the companion CD in the directory "\Tools\Intrinsyc\deviceCOM." In this evaluation version calls will fail after 15 minutes and any deviceCOM server has to be restarted.

The ODK installer will not install the deviceCOM runtime on your Windows CE device, even if it is connected. Intrinsyc chose to do it this way because it gives more flexibility to the developers. During application deployment and installation, you can decide how much of deviceCOM you want to ship with your product. It allows you to include the deviceCOM components in your standard setup.

2.   To install the deviceCOM runtime for Windows CE on your device, locate the binaries for the CPU in your device under the deviceCOM installation path. For development purposes, you will copy all files into the Windows directory on the Windows CE device.

Later in the installation chapter, you will only select those components that you really need in order to keep your setup as small as possible.

The core of deviceCOM (see Table 6.3) consists of only three DLLs and one additional transport DLL.

All DLLs of deviceCOM are COM in-process servers. Therefore, you have to register them. Intrinsyc was smart to include the complete registration in its helper surrogate "DCServer.EXE". If it is run without any parameter, it checks to see whether deviceCOM is registered, and if it is not, the surrogate simply registers

Table 6.3   The Components of deviceCOM

Component	Used for
EFC21.DLL	Intrinsyc's Embedded Foundation Classes. These classes are proprietary to Intrinsyc and not open for common developers . . . yet.
DcCore21.DLL	This DLL is the heart of deviceCOM. As the name suggests, it contains the core functions of deviceCOM. It has to be included or linked to if you are going to use special deviceCOM methods.
DcOlePs21.DLL	This DLL holds all OLE/COM-related functions of deviceCOM. In the real DCOM world you could compare this DLL with the OLEAUT32.DLL.
DCIPC21.DLL, DCUDP21.DLL, DCTCP21.DLL	The transport DLLs of deviceCOM. You need at least one of them to get deviceCOM talking.
DCServer.EXE	The DCServer.EXE is comparable to the DLLHOST.EXE on the desktop. It provides general surrogate functionality plus several special configuration services. A detailed description of this executable can be found in the deviceCOM help file.

all the components. Again, your installer will do that later automatically and you do not have to use the DCServer for it.

3. To register the deviceCOM components, start "DCServer.EXE" in your Windows directory.

4. To verify that the installation was correct, start the visual "Administration Utility" on the desktop PC.

You can find this tool in the "Intrinsyc deviceCOM Start" menu.

This utility shows all running deviceCOM servers on a given PC or device. You need to add either the IP address of your Windows CE device to the list of "Target Hosts" or select the "IP Broadcast" options in the modification dialog box. By the way, this is a great way of finding out the IP address of your serial link connection.

 An important note: A serial connection always has priority over an Ethernet connection if PC-Link or ActiveSync is established to a desktop PC. To force deviceCOM to route over the Ethernet link, disconnect the PC-Link or ActiveSync connection. It is not needed for deviceCOM anyway.

If the installation and registration were correct, you should see a "Listener" of your Windows CE device in the list of the server processes, as illustrated in Figure 6.11. I will come back to the Administration Utility after you have written the proxy DLL for your PCDMDLL COM server.

Running DCServer as listener allows you to do things like

• Remote registration of COM servers

• Starting and stopping any application from the desktop PC

• Configuring proxies and stubs for use with deviceCOM

• Adding servers to the list of deviceCOM servers

5. Try it out by selecting the "Listener" in the "Server Processes" list and clicking the "Remote Run . . ." button.

6. Then type "\Windows\Calc.exe" in the command field of the dialog box.

You should soon see the calculator pop up on the Windows CE device.

6.7.2 Starting DCServer as a COM Surrogate

Starting DCServer as a COM surrogate requires some parameters. You can do it very easily with the desktop Administration Utility of deviceCOM.

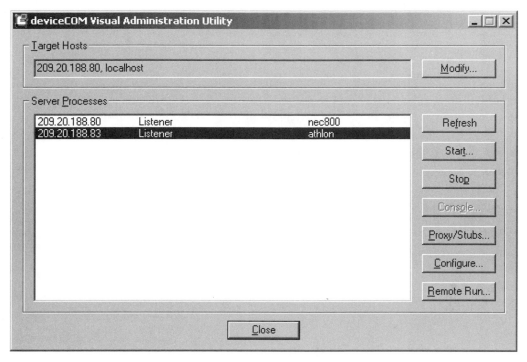

Figure 6.11   The deviceCOM Administration Utility

1. Start the deviceCOM Administration Utility and make sure that the "Listener" is running on your Windows CE device.
2. Select the "Listener" and press the "Start…" button.
3. In the dialog box you should see the IP address of your Windows CE device in the "Host Name" combo box.
4. To activate the surrogate you only have to select the protocol you want to use to connect to the device.

You can also select all protocols if you have them installed. The Console Output gives you a tracer-window for debugging messages. During the development process I recommend switching on the console.

The combo box labeled "Auto Load ProgID" allows you to specify a COM server that should get loaded automatically when the surrogate starts.

5. Click "OK" and in the list box of "Server Processes", you will see a new entry for your Windows CE device listing the ports that the surrogate will be listening to.

6.7.3 A Small deviceCOM Example

This simple example will help you to understand and configure deviceCOM. And for convenience you will use the "MyCeServer" example (Section 6.1) that you created at the beginning of this chapter. As the host application, you will also use an earlier example (Section 6.2), the "MyFirst" application. If fact, you will use the same example that you used to explore the in-process activation of the "MyCeServer" component.

Here is a short outline of what you are going to do: The "MyFirst" desktop application will call the "MyCeServer" component as in the earlier sample. But instead of loading the component directly into its process, you will host the "MyCeServer" component inside the "DCServer.EXE" of deviceCOM on the Windows CE device.

To accomplish this scenario you need to

- Create a proxy and a stub DLL for deviceCOM
- Register the proxy and server using the Administration Utility
- Modify the "MyFirst" application to use a wrapper class

At no time do you have to change the "MyCeServer.DLL" component.

Creating the deviceCOM Proxy/Stub

First, you need to activate the DevStudio plug-in of Intrinsyc.

1. Start Visual C++ and select the "Customize" item in the "Tools" menu.
2. Select the "Add-ins and Macro Files" tab and you will see the "DcAddin.DcAddin.1" plug-in.

If you do not see the plug-in, you probably installed deviceCOM before you installed your Visual Studio. You can then browse the deviceCOM directory and select the "DCAddIn60.dll". This will install the deviceCOM plug-in.

3. Check it if it is not checked and close the "Customize" dialog box.

A new toolbar icon will appear with the deviceCOM logo.

4. Click on the icon, and a dialog box called "deviceCOM-Developer Studio Addin-Proxy/Stub Project Generator" will appear.
5. Now click on the "Add . . ." button and select the "MyCeServer.IDL" file.

When you select the IDL file, the project is renamed "MyCeServerPs".

6. Now press "OK", and the plug-in will generate new Visual C++ projects called "MyCeServerPs_Vc6Ce.dsp" and "MyCeServerPs_Vc6Nt.dsp".
7. Finally, you need to load these projects and build them.

Easy, isn't it? Well, you should know that Intrinsyc is using its own IDL compiler that only supports a subset of the Microsoft IDL. Most of the unsupported tags are related to native DCOM and out-of-process servers and are not supported by Windows CE 2.x anyway. A full description of the supported IDL tags can be found in the device-COM ODK documentation.

 You can find these two projects on the companion CD in the directory "\Sources\Chapter 6\6.7".

Registering the deviceCOM Proxy/Stub

During the Visual C++ build process, the DLLs are automatically registered on the desktop and on your Windows CE device.

1.   To verify that the proxies are ready to be used, select the "Listener" process of your Windows CE device and click the "Proxy/Stub" button.

If the dialog box shows the "ItestMe" interface, the registration was successful. If it does not show up, use "RegSvr32.exe" on the desktop and "RegSvrCe.EXE" on your Windows CE device to register the DLLs.

This registration, however, does not provide all the information you will need to use deviceCOM. Unfortunately, since it would appear that you are already finished, the next steps may seem a bit confusing.

2.   First, you have to declare your "MyCeServer.DLL" to be exposed as a deviceCOM server. This is necessary for deviceCOM to activate its surrogate and determine how to load and handle the server.

3.   In the "Server Processes" list box of the Administrative Utility, select the "Listener" of your Windows CE device again, and this time select the "Configure" button.

You will see an empty list box for objects.

4.   Select the "Add Server . . ." button.

The dialog box asks for three values:

•   The Prog-ID or Class-ID of the server
•   The Type
•   The Category

Prog-ID or Class-ID defines the server. I normally recommend using the class ID. This will speed up the first communication that gets established between the client and the server. The Prog-ID always has to be resolved to a class ID internally and leads to registry round trips. For this sample, you will use the Prog-ID because it is easier to determine.

5.   Enter the Prog-ID "MyCeServer.TestMe.1".

The Type determines how the surrogate loads the server. There are three options:

• Shared—All clients share the same server instance.

• Multiple—Each client gets a new instance of the server.

• Single—Only one client can be connected to the server. All subsequent clients are rejected.

The Category allows the developer to specify a specific category to the server. The deviceCOM will create a new sub-key with the Category name underneath the server object's Prog-ID in the "HKEY_CLASSES_ROOT" branch of the registry.

Only the first value is mandatory; the two others can be left to their default values. Your next step is to register the proxy on your desktop PC.

6.   In the "Server Processes" list box select the "Listener" of the desktop PC and click on the "Configure . . ." button.

7.   In case the host name is still set to the IP address of the Windows CE device in the dialog box, change it to the IP Address of the desktop PC.

Click on "Add Proxy . . ." and you will get another dialog box. The dialog box asks for a multitude of entries, but fortunately Intrinsyc did a great job in helping to fill them out.

The first entry is the Prog-ID of the new proxy object. This Prog-ID will be used by your "MyFirst" application to address the COM server on the Windows CE device.

8.   You can enter any name here. For this example use "DcMyCeServer.TestMe.1".

The Administration Utility sets the Class-ID field automatically. It points the new Prog-ID to the deviceCOM communication layer.

The transport determines how you want to connect to the server. Currently, deviceCOM supports three means of communication:

• UDP—Very fast, asynchronous, but can be unreliable

• TCP—Standard TCP/IP communication; synchronous, slower, but more reliable

• IPC—Only for out-of-process communication, not for remote communication

The port depends on the transport selected above. If you do not have the default port in use by a different application, I recommend keeping the default port.

The remaining fields will be filled automatically if you use the deviceCOM server browser.

9. Click on the "Browse" button and select the IP address of your Windows CE device in the dialog box.

You should see the server object "MyCeServer.TestMe.1" that you added in Step 5.

10.   Select this object and press "OK".

11.   Once back in the "Configure Proxy Object" dialog box, click on "OK".

The new entry should now be visible in the list box of the configuration dialog box. You are now ready to use deviceCOM and the Windows CE server inside the host application.

Changing the Host Application

You have to change the host application because you were using the "#import" statement to include "myceserver.dll". This DLL is the *real* Windows CE component, not the proxy DLL. The correct name is now "MyCeServerPs.DLL". deviceCOM proxy DLLs are not type-library compatible, therefore the "#import" directive will not work. And, unfortunately, it is not possible to change the resulting ".TLH" and ".TLI" files because they are recreated every time the "#import" directive is interpreted by the compiler.

1. In creating the "MyFirst" application earlier in this chapter, you did not make a desktop version of "MyFirst", so do this now.

If you only follow the procedure described in Part 1 of this book, you will get an error during the compilation of the resources. The "MyFirst" application uses some special Windows CE resource tags that are not available for the desktop. Unfortunately, there is no easy way to fix this. You will either run into trouble with the desktop or with the Windows CE device.

2. For now just remove the following reference to "WCERES.RC" from the resource file using the text editor of Visual C++ and change the line

```
EXSTYLE WS_EX_APPWINDOW   | WS_EX_CAPTIONOKBTN
```

to

```
EXSTYLE WS_EX_APPWINDOW   // | WS_EX_CAPTIONOKBTN
```

3. The next change you need to make is deleting the "#import" statement in the "MyFirstDlg.h".

4. Delete both the definition of the com_issue_error() function and the declaration of the namespace in "MyFirstDlg.cpp".

Instead of using the "#import" statement, you will use the class wizard to create a new wrapper class for your COM server.

5. Open the class wizard and select "Add Class . . ./From a type library . . ." from the member variable tab.

6. Now browse to the original "MyCeServer.dll" COM server and click on "OK".

Do not select the proxy DLL that you created with the deviceCOM add-in. As mentioned before, the proxy DLL is not type-library compatible.

The class wizard will create a new class called "ItestMe" and add it to the project. Before you can use COM on the desktop, the COM subsystem has to be initialized.

7. You need to add the following structure to your application:

```
#ifndef UNDER_CE
struct InitOle {
     InitOle()  { ::CoInitialize(NULL); }
     ~InitOle() { ::CoUninitialize();   }
} _init_InitOle_;         // Global Instance to force load/unload of
                          OLE
#endif
```

You can place this code anywhere in the global area of your CPP files.

You also need to change the code that calls your method using the new wrapper class.

8. Open the code "OnButton1()" method of the "CmyFirstDlg" class and change it to the following:

```
void CMyFirstDlg::OnButton1()
{
     HRESULT hResult = S_OK;
     TCHAR tsProgID[]= TEXT("DcMyCeServer.TestMe.1");
     CLSID tClsid = GUID_NULL;

#ifdef UNICODE
     hResult = CLSIDFromProgID( tsProgID, &tClsid );
#else
     USES_CONVERSION;
     LPWSTR wszToken = A2W( tsProgID );
```

```
        hResult = CLSIDFromProgID( wszToken, &tClsid );
#endif
        if (FAILED( hResult )) return;

        LPVOID ipServer = NULL;
        hResult = CoCreateInstance(
                tClsid,
                NULL,
                CLSCTX_SERVER,
                IID_IUnknown,
                (void**)&ipServer);

        CString ast;
        if (hResult==S_OK)
        {
                ITestMe  Conn1((LPDISPATCH)ipServer);
                long a=Conn1.ShowMe();
                ast.Format(TEXT("MyCeServer returned ShowMe=%d"),a);
                Conn1.ReleaseDispatch();
        }
        else
        {
                ast=TEXT("CoCreateInstance Failed!");
        }
        MessageBox(ast);
}
```

I will concede that I take the easy way here. Relying on the "IID_IUnknown" interface in the "CoCreateInstance()" call is not the best way to use COM but, unfortunately, it works: you can actually ask the server for "IUnknown" and then call a method of a completely different interface. A better way would be to put the "ItestMe" interface here. Unfortunately, the class wizard wrapper does not include the UUID of the "ItestMe" interface.

9.   Now build the application and put a breakpoint on the "CoCreateInstance" call.

10.   On your Windows CE device, start DCServer from the "Start/Run" menu.

If you have selected "Broadcast" in the target host parameters, deviceCOM's Visual Administration Utility on the desktop will show the listener running on the Windows CE device.

11. Select your Windows CE device in the "Server Processes" list and hit the "Start" button. In the dialog box, select the protocol UDP, enter "DcMyCeServer.TestMe.1" into the field for "Auto Load ProgID", and enable the console for your desktop IP address.

12. Now start the MyFirst Application in the Visual C++ environment in debug mode and click on the button in the dialog box.

Once you step over "CoCreateInstance()" you will see a lot of traffic going to the Windows CE device. If everything is correct you will see "4711" in the message box that pops up at the end of the "OnButton1()" method.

If you had used the "Create Class from Type Library" method in your original application, you would only have needed to change the Prog-ID from "MyCeServer. TestMe.1" to "DcMyCeServer.TestMe.1".

 You can find these two projects on the companion CD in the directory "\Sources\Chapter 6\6.8".

6.7.4 Other Features of deviceCOM

deviceCOM offers advantages over DCOM that make it a very interesting technology for industrial applications.

Setting the deviceCOM Timeout

Unlike DCOM, you can change the timeout for deviceCOM either with a global registry setting or by special code in your proxy DLL per process. DCOM has a fixed timeout of 3×2 minutes. The default timeout for deviceCOM is 30 seconds. If you change/add the following entry to the registry you can set the timeout of deviceCOM in milliseconds:

```
HKEY_LOCAL_MACHINE\Software\Intrinsyc\DeviceCOM\DefaultTimeout=
<milliseconds>
```

Filters for the IDL

deviceCOM's IDL compiler allows you to filter out the interfaces that are not required or that you do not wish to include in the proxy DLL. A simple text file with the word "exclude:" in the first line lets you define which interfaces will be excluded.

6.8   Summary

To summarize the features of COM for Windows CE, here are some points you should keep in mind:

- Up to Windows CE 3.0, only in-process servers (COM servers and ActiveX controls) are supported.

- You cannot have a desktop and a Windows CE project in the same workspace of eMbedded Visual C++. See Section 6.3.2 on how to generate a desktop for a Windows CE project

- You cannot use eMbedded Visual Basic to create ActiveX controls for Windows CE.

- You can use the "#import" directive in Visual C++ to call COM servers, but you have to include and implement a function called "com_issue_error()".

- You must use ATL to create your COM servers because Visual Basic does not support MFC components.

You now know everything necessary about COM in order to use it intensively in the chapters to come. In your applications, I strongly recommend using the COM paradigm as often as possible in order to get the most out of reusable code.

II
Part

Windows CE
in Detail

7
Chapter

The Windows CE User Interface

Now that we have a reliably functioning workstation, we can enter the realm of hard-core Windows CE development. The second part of this book will go deep into all areas that make Windows CE a great operation system. Because COM is the most important interface technology that is available for Windows platforms, this book will use COM as often as possible. In the coming chapters I will discuss the following:

- **Basic technologies of Windows CE,** such as the command bar, common controls, Pocket PC enhancements, and other user-interface-related technologies

- **Storage concepts,** such as the registry, the file system, the object store, and most important—ADO for Windows CE

- **Remote connectivity**, including the implementation of acronyms like RAPI, RAS, IrDA, HTTP, DCOM, and ActiveSync

- **Advanced topics** like HTML help generation, building your own installer for Windows CE, creating a single binary that runs everywhere, writing a control panel applet, and satisfying the rules for the "Designed for Windows CE" logo

You will also read about some great third-party solutions, and, by time you have finished the final chapter, I hope that you will have solid ideas about using Windows CE in exciting development projects of your own.

Are you getting anxious to dive right into Windows CE? Well, before diving in, you need to explore the new and special functionalities of the CE user interface. Many Windows CE devices have user-interface and display configurations that are not found on desktop PCs. Microsoft developed alternatives for the smaller devices in order to increase the usable screen real estate and reduce the space taken up by such Windows controls as menus, toolbars, and status bars. The new CE designs are by no means the end of this evolution, but they offer an interim solution for porting applications from the desktop. One of the new user-interface controls invented for Windows CE is the command bar.

7.1 The Command Bar

System DLL:	COMMCTRL.DLL
Include file:	Commctrl.h
Library file:	Commctrl.lib
Help file:	CEGUIDE.CHM (MSDN 10/98 and later)
Available since:	Windows CE 1.0
API prefix/suffix:	CommandBar_<action>
InitCommonControlEx flag:	Not necessary
MFC class:	CceCommandBar

The command bar is a new control that combines a menu with a toolbar. Instead of using two "lines" of valuable screen space, the command bar uses only one. Introduced in Windows CE 1.0, the command bar can host menus, buttons, and combo boxes in one control. On a palm-size PC, however, it can be quite challenging to get all the buttons and menus that an application requires into this single line. With Internet Explorer 4.0, Microsoft introduced the "ReBar", also known as the "Cool-Bar", which offered new ways of saving space in the "command" area of an application. Windows CE 2.0 adopted this functionality and introduced the Command-Band, a nearly exact recreation of the desktop idea.

The order in which controls are added to the command bar is very sensitive. Microsoft did not do a very good job in designing those APIs. For example, if you use only the "Insert . . ." function of the command bar, you will get funny results, such as buttons appearing under the menu or combo boxes appearing over the menu. You will face this problem firsthand in the next section's example.

If you are planning to run your target application on all versions of Windows CE, including Version 1.0, you must use the command bar with its old style. If, on the other hand, you will be targeting devices for Windows CE 2.0 or higher, you can select the Command-Band. Section 7.2.2 shows you how to use the Command-Band.

7.1.1 Adding a Command Bar to an Application

Creating a command bar is fairly simple. Microsoft introduced a new set of functions to allow the creation of a command bar. All APIs start with the "CommandBar_" prefix. Unfortunately, there are several "gotchas" that you may run into and that can cost you a lot of time trying to figure out what is wrong if you don't know about them.

You can start learning about command-bar implementation with this small application. Actually, if you create a "Standard Hello-World" application, using the "WCE Application" wizard, the wizard will automatically create a command bar for you.

1. Create a "Standard Hello-World" application, using the "WCE Application" wizard and name it "CmdBarApp".

2. Open "CMDBarApp.cpp" and scroll to the WndProc function.

You will find API calls starting with CommandBar_ in the WM_CREATE and WM_DESTROY branches of the message switch.

The CommandBar_Create() function is the first call that has to be called to create a command bar in the window specified by the second parameter. The first parameter is the "HINSTANCE" of the current application. The last parameter is the identifier of the command bar. The return value is the new window handle of the command bar. If the return value is NULL, the creation failed.

The opposite call to CommandBar_Create is CommandBar_Destroy(hwndCB); and can be found in the WM_DESTROY branch of the message switch. To show and hide the toolbar you can use the function:

```
if (hwndCB)    CommandBar_Show(hwndCB, TRUE);
```

The second parameter of this function specifies whether the command bar is visible. The "Hello-World" application uses this function in the InitInstance() function. Since screen space is valuable on Windows CE devices, I recommend turning on the command bar only when the user needs it. A tap on the screen in an area where normally no tap is required could bring up the command bar and a button in the command bar can hide it again, or even auto-hide it when the user begins working with the application. You can add this functionality to your little test application.

3. Add the following lines before the WinMain function in the "CMDBarApp.cpp":

```
#define JCCMDBAR_OFF      0
#define JCCMDBAR_ON       1
#define JCCMDBAR_TOGGLE   2
int JCCMDBarUp;
```

```
void ToggleCMDBar(HWND hWnd,int how)
{
      switch (how)
      {
            case JCCMDBAR_OFF:
                        JCCMDBarUp=0;
                        CommandBar_Show(hWnd, TRUE);
                        break;
            case JCCMDBAR_ON:
                        JCCMDBarUp=1;
                        CommandBar_Show(hWnd, FALSE);
                        break;
            case JCCMDBAR_TOGGLE:
                        JCCMDBarUp=1-JCCMDBarUp;
                        ToggleCMDBar(hWnd, JCCMDBarUp);
                  break;
      }
}
```

4. To activate the new method if the user clicks in the window area of your application with the left mouse button add the following branch to the "WndProc":

```
case WM_LBUTTONDOWN:
      ToggleCMDBar(hwndCB,JCCMDBAR_TOGGLE);
      break;
```

The function CommandBar_IsVisible can be used to determine whether the command bar is visible CommandBar_Height helps you calculate the space remaining of your screen real estate for the application.

Returning to the WM_CREATE branch, the next command after the Command-Bar_Create call—CommandBar_InsertMenubar—adds a Menu to the command bar. The third parameter identifies the menu-resource that gets added to the command bar. The last parameter is unusual for Windows developers. You can set the position of the menú where you want to add it in the command bar. Theoretically, you could add buttons to the left of a menu in the command bar. Since this choice is neither recommended nor allowed under the "Designed for Windows CE" logo rules, you should only use the value zero here.

Windows CE already supports a CommandBar_InsertMenubarEx function. The only difference is that the new function requires a String instead of a Long as the menu identifier. Since Windows CE could drop support for all "non-ex" functions in the future, I recommend replacing the current call with its "ex"-equivalent:

```
CommandBar_InsertMenubarEx(hwndCB,hInst,MAKEINTRESOURCE(IDM_MENU),0);
```

The last API call in the WM_CREATE branch is the CommandBar_AddAdornments method. Adornments on Windows CE are the standard buttons:

- "?"—Help button (CMDBAR_HELP)
- "OK"—Button (CMDBAR_OK)
- "X"—Close button (will always be added if CommandBar_AddAdornment gets called)

With the function CommandBar_AddAdornment, you can add those buttons to the menu bar using the second parameter.

This function also contains a logo "gotcha". For palm-size PCs, an application should no longer have a Close button. But if you want to include a help button in your application and *no* Close button, you cannot use "CommandBar_AddAdornment" because it always creates the Close button when it is called. For more information on this particular logo requirement, see "The Missing 'X'-Close Button", in Section 11.6.3.

 Here is another interesting "gotcha": If the AddAdornment function is *not* the last one called, the adornment buttons will be "pushed" off the visible screen area with every menu, button, or combo box that you add to the command bar.

You will also need to include some buttons in your command bar.

5.   Add the following lines of code to the WM_CREATE branch:

```
case WM_CREATE:
     hwndCB = CommandBar_Create(hInst, hWnd, 1);
     CommandBar_InsertMenubar(hwndCB, hInst, IDM_MENU, 0);

     {
     int ii;
     CommandBar_AddBitmap(hwndCB, hInst, IDR_TOOLBAR,
                          2, 16, 16);
     CommandBar_AddButtons(hwndCB, sizeof(tbSTDButton)/
                     sizeof(TBBUTTON),tbSTDButton);
     CommandBar_InsertComboBox(hwndCB,hInst, 50,
                          NULL, 8, 1);
     szToolTips[0]=(LPTSTR)LocalAlloc(LMEM_ZEROINIT,
```

```
                                                sizeof(TCHAR));
        wsprintf(szToolTips[0],TEXT(""));
        for (ii=1;ii<MAX_CMDBAR_ITEMS;ii++)
        {
            LoadString(hInst,IDS_TOOLTIPSTART+ii,
                        szHello,MAX_LOADSTRING);
            szToolTips[ii]=(LPTSTR)LocalAlloc(
                        LMEM_ZEROINIT,
                        sizeof(TCHAR)*lstrlen(szHello));
            wsprintf(szToolTips[ii],szHello);
        }
        CommandBar_AddToolTips(hwndCB,
                        MAX_CMDBAR_ITEMS,szToolTips);
    }
    CommandBar_AddAdornments(hwndCB, CMDBAR_OK, 0);
    break;
```

The most important of these functions is CommandBar_AddButtons. Next to the menu and the adornments, it adds the third item class to the command bar. The first two parameters are once again straightforward, but the last is more interesting. It requires a pointer to the "TBBUTTON" structure. Since you are already familiar with the toolbar-button structure on the desktop, you will not find any surprises here. Just fill the structure as you would on the desktop, and it will work fine.

6. Here is the code you need to add to the global space of your "CmdBarApp.cpp":

```
#define MAX_CMDBAR_ITEMS        3
static TBBUTTON tbSTDButton[] = {
    {0,              0, TBSTATE_ENABLED, TBSTYLE_SEP,    0, 0},
    {STD_FILENEW,  33,TBSTATE_ENABLED, TBSTYLE_BUTTON, 0, 0},
    {STD_FILEOPEN, 34,TBSTATE_ENABLED, TBSTYLE_BUTTON, 0, 0},
};
LPTSTR szToolTips[MAX_CMDBAR_ITEMS];
```

If you want to insert the menu in a different location, such as to the left of all buttons, you have to call the CommandBar_AddButtons function first. If you want to use your own bitmaps for your buttons, you have to call the function CommandBar_AddBitmap first. Its parameter points to a bitmap containing the images of the buttons.

Here Microsoft created another tiny "gotcha": The toolbar resource of eMbedded Visual C++ is one pixel too low for a Windows CE command-bar button. It requires a height of 17 pixels instead of 16 as the desktop toolbar. It also does not make any difference if you use 17 as the pixel height in the CommandBar_AddBitmap() function. You have to paint the bitmaps with a height of 17 pixels.

By the way, if you do not want to use your own bitmaps, you can also use the two Windows CE internal stock objects of every application. The bitmap ID in the "TBBUTTON" structure then resolves to the images shown in Table 7.1. You can also use the stock bitmaps of the common control library that you have included in your application if you work with command bars or Command-Bands. The library contains two toolbar bitmaps:

- The standard buttons
- The view buttons

Table 7.1   Bitmap Stock Objects for a Toolbar Object

ID	Picture	Used for
0	✕	Close button
1	OK	OK button

They contain several more icons, as listed in Table 7.2, including small (16 × 16 pixels) and large (32 × 32 pixels) versions. These item IDs are defined in the "commctrl.h".

Table 7.2   Standard Bitmap Stock Objects Inside the commctrl.dll

ID	Item ID Name	Picture	Used for
Standard Buttons (IDB_STD_SMALL_COLOR and IDB_STD_LARGE_COLOR)			
0	STD_CUT	✂	Cut
1	STD_COPY	🗐	Copy
2	STD_PASTE	📋	Paste

(continued)

Table 7.2 (continued)

ID	Item ID Name	Picture	Used for
3	STD_UNDO		Undo
4	STD_REDO		Redo (funny spelling error in the commctrl.h)
5	STD_DELETE		Delete
6	STD_FILENEW		New in File menu
7	STD_FILEOPEN		Open in File menu
8	STD_FILESAVE		Save in File menu
9	STD_PRINTPRE		Print Preview
10	STD_PROPERTIES		Properties
11	STD_HELP		Help
12	STD_FIND		Find/Search
13	STD_REPLACE		Replace
14	STD_PRINT		Print

View Bitmaps (IDB_VIEW_SMALL_COLOR and IDB_VIEW_LARGE_COLOR)

ID	Item ID Name	Picture	Used for
0	VIEW_LARGEICONS		View list as large items
1	VIEW_SMALLICONS		View list as small items
2	VIEW_LIST		View list mode
3	VIEW_DETAILS		View list in details mode
4	VIEW_SORTNAME		Sort list by name
5	VIEW_SORTSIZE		Sort list by size
6	VIEW_SORTDATE		Sort list by date
7	VIEW_SORTTYPE		Sort list by type
8	VIEW_PARENTFOLDER		Select parent folder

ID	Item ID Name	Picture	Used for
9	VIEW_NETCONNECT		Connect to a drive. Because this function is not available in Windows CE, I suggest avoiding the use of this or the following icon.
10	VIEW_NETDISCONNECT		Disconnect a drive
11	VIEW_NEWFOLDER		Create a new folder

If you want to include these icons, use the instance handle of the common control library (HINST_COMMCTRL) instead of the one in your application. If you use the common control library's instance handle, the toolbar resource ID will be one of the four shown in Table 7.3. Unfortunately, you cannot mix them. Either you have to use the application's stock bitmaps, the common control stock bitmaps, or your own images for all buttons.

Another interesting function in your code is CommandBar_InsertComboBox. Windows CE allows adding combo boxes to the command bar. The parameters do not include any surprises, but remember that space in the command bar is limited; you should not create a monster combo box and forget to leave space for other more important buttons.

> Here is another funny Windows CE "gotcha": You cannot insert a combo box in a command bar that only contains a menu except to the left of it, which is—yes, you guessed it—against the logo rules. You have to add at least one button.

Table 7.3   Resource IDs for HINST_COMMCTRL Icons

ID	Used for
IDB_STD_SMALL_COLOR	Standard toolbar icons as shown in the previous table. The size of these icons is 16×17 pixels.
IDB_STD_LARGE_COLOR	Same icons but this time 32×32 pixels.
IDB_VIEW_SMALL_COLOR	Icons used in a "View" toolbar as shown in the previous table. The size of these icons is 16×17 pixels.
IDB_VIEW_LARGE_COLOR	Same icons as above, only 32×32 pixels.

In the code above, you will find another command-bar method called CommandBar_AddToolTips. Not only do the logo requirements ask for ToolTips, but ToolTips are also a great help for manual-reluctant users like me. If you force yourself to add them to your command bars from the beginning, you will not have the trouble of adding them later.

The CommandBar_AddToolTips function requires an array of strings containing the actual ToolTips. Please also remember to retrieve those strings from a resource file to keep your code as language-neutral as possible. Since you can add ToolTips only to buttons, you can NULL the entry for a menu or a combo box in the array. Let's say you follow the logo guidelines and add the menu to the left of all the buttons. Item zero in the array contains the menu's ToolTips, but since this entry cannot be retrieved with any user command, you can NULL it. The ToolTips require some resource strings.

7. Add the following strings to the string table of the "CmdBarApp" resource:

```
IDS_TOOLTIPSTART        "My Combo Box"
IDS_STRING5             "Separator"
IDS_STRING6             "Creates a new file"
IDS_STRING7             "Loads a file"
```

Only the first resource has to be labeled "IDS_TOOLTIPSTART". Since the other strings are following directly after this label, your small loader will find the correct strings.

How Do I Get Rid of a Command-Bar Item?

If you want to remove items from the command bar, you will be out of luck. Microsoft did not provide any such function, other than CommandBar_ Destroy(HWND). But this function kills the entire command bar, and you will have to recreate it from scratch.

8. You should also clean up the ToolTips by inserting the following code into the same WM_DESTROY branch:

```
{
    int     ii;
    for (ii=0;ii<MAX_CMDBAR_ITEMS;ii++)
        LocalFree(szToolTips[ii]);
}
```

Now compile the application and run it on your emulation environment or on your Windows CE device.

The source code in the directory "Sources\Chapter 7\7.1" on the companion CD contains an example how to use the command bar.

7.1.2   PCDMUI: Including the Command Bar

Your PCDM application will run on all Windows CE platforms, but not every technology that it will incorporate is available in the older versions of Windows CE. In such cases, you will either need to stub the unavailable technology out or replace it with one found in Version 1.x. For example, Version 1.x devices must use the command bar; Version 2.x devices can also take advantage of the new Command-Band control. In this section you will create an ActiveX control inside your "PCDMUI.DLL", which will use either the command bar, if it is on a Windows CE 1.x device, or the Command-Band, for Version 2.x devices. eMbedded Visual Basic already includes an ActiveX control for the command bar. But adding this new control will give the user a choice between the old command bar and the new Command-Band. It also offers simplified methods.

1.   Open the last version of the PCDMUI project with Visual C++.
2.   Add a new "Full control" to the PCDMUI classes using the "New ATL Object" wizard and name the control "PCDMCommander".
3.   In the "Attributes" tab of the wizard, select the "Support Connection Points" switch and keep the defaults.

Stock properties are quite convenient for controls because they are somewhat standardized and come with some nice built-in support. For example, a container can offer special property pages or connection options if a control exposes stock properties that the container knows about. The "Enabled" property, for example, can be used simply to enable or disable whole banks of controls if a container wants to change their states.

The "Mouse Pointer" property gives the container the option to change the mouse cursor to an application-specific cursor if desired. For your application, you are not going to use any of these properties, but feel free to experiment with them.

4.   After the wizard has created the new control, select the "OnDraw()" method and delete everything except "return S_OK".

I also recommend moving the implementations of "OnDraw", the constructor, and destructor out of the include file and into the CPP implementation file. This increases the readability of your code.

The first method you will implement is the "CreateBar" method. It will create a new command bar or menu bar on the Pocket PC. Later in the next chapter, you will add the Command-Band to this method.

5. Add the method "CreateBar" with the parameter "int ID" to the "IPCDMCommander" interface and add the following code to its implementation:

```
STDMETHODIMP CPCDMCommander::CreateBar(int ID)
{
      AFX_MANAGE_STATE(AfxGetStaticModuleState())
#ifdef UNDER_CE
      if (m_IDBAR==0)
      {
            m_hwndCB = CommandBar_Create(_Module.m_hInst, m_hWnd, ID);
            CommandBar_AddBitmap(m_hwndCB, _Module.m_hInst,
                                        IDR_TOOLBAR, 17, 16, 16);
            m_IDBAR=ID;
            m_bIsFresh=FALSE;
      }
#else       // Code for Desktop here
#endif
      return S_OK;
}
```

6. Add the private member variable to the the "CPCDMCommander" class:

```
private:
      HWND        m_hwndCB;
      int         m_IDBAR;
      BOOL        m_bIsFresh;
```

This step will create the command bar in the client area of the control. It is an interesting way to position the command bar anywhere on your client screen. Of course, to be logo compliant, you need to position the control on top of your client area. The "IDR_TOOLBAR" bitmap that gets inserted into the command bar contains the common icons for a toolbar (see Figure 7.1).

7. You have to add this bitmap to your PCDMUI project. Either paint a new toolbar or use the one provided on your companion CD ("TOOLBAR1.BMP").

Figure 7.1   IDR_TOOLBAR bitmap with common toolbar icons

8. The next method you need to add is called "InsertMenu", and, as shown in Table 7.4, it has two parameters.

9. Add the following code to the method's implementation:

```
STDMETHODIMP CPCDMCommander::InsertMenu(BSTR MenuName, int Index)
{
      AFX_MANAGE_STATE(AfxGetStaticModuleState())

      if (Index<MAXMENUS && m_MyPopup[Index]==NULL)
      {
            if (m_MyMenu==NULL)
            {
                  m_MyMenu=CreateMenu();
#ifdef UNDER_CE
                  if (m_hwndCB!=NULL)
                  {
                        CommandBar_InsertMenubarEx(m_hwndCB, NULL,
                                        (LPTSTR)m_MyMenu, Index);
                        SortToolTips(Index);
                  }
#else // Code for Desktop here
                  ::SetMenu(m_hWnd,m_MyMenu);
#endif
            }
            m_MyPopup[Index]=CreatePopupMenu();
            AppendMenu(m_MyMenu,MF_STRING|MF_POPUP,
                        (UINT)m_MyPopup[Index],MenuName);
      }
      return S_OK;
}
```

Table 7.4   InsertMenu() Parameters

Type	Variable Name	Used for
BSTR	MenuName	Name for the menu to be inserted.
Int	Index	Location in the command bar for the new menu. Should be zero.

This code is very straightforward. To keep it simple, the maximum number of menus is limited to 5 and the number of buttons is limited to 15.

10. Set the define statement in the "PCDMCommander.h" include file as follows:

```
#define MAXMENUS        5
```

The "Index" parameter is used to position the menu in the command bar, but once again note that the logo requirements require the menu to be the leftmost item in the command bar.

You might wonder what the "SortToolTips()" function is doing. Microsoft was trying to stay as close to the desktop toolbar as possible with the command-bar APIs. As mentioned previously, ToolTips are not added to individual buttons, as on the desktop, but rather to the entire command bar itself using an array of ToolTips. The indexes in the array are then assigned to the buttons. The "CPCDMCommander" class will add each button individually, passing the ToolTips as a parameter to the method call. But if you inserted a new item to the command bar at this point, the index of the buttons might shift, and the ToolTips would no longer fit. The function SortToolTips() corrects the array for the ToolTips. The code for this function is very simple:

```
void CPCDMCommander::SortToolTips(int index)
{
int i;
            for (i=MAXBUTTONS-1;i>index;i-)
                 m_szTTips[i]=m_szTTips[i-1];
            if (m_iMaxButtons<MAXBUTTONS) m_iMaxButtons++;
#ifdef UNDER_CE
            if (m_hwndCB!=NULL)
                 CommandBar_AddToolTips(m_hwndCB,
                            MAXBUTTONS,m_szTTips);
#else       // Code for Desktop here
#endif
}
```

11. Insert this function at the end of the "PCDMCommander.cpp" file.

12. Declare the function as a private method of the "CPCDMCommander" class.

You will find calls to this function in the "InsertComboBox()" and "InsertButton()" methods as well.

13. You also need to add three new private member variables to your "PCDMCommander" class:

```
HMENU      m_MyMenu;                    // Menu
HMENU      m_MyPopup[MAXMENUS];         // Popup Menus (max 5)
LPTSTR     m_szTTips[MAXBUTTONS         // ToolTip Text (max 15 per Band)
int        m_iMaxButtons;
```

14.   The next method adds menu items to the menu. Name it "InsertMenuItem" and give it the four parameters listed in Table 7.5.

15.   Add the following code to the implementation of the method:

```
STDMETHODIMP CPCDMCommander::InsertMenuItem(BSTR ItemName, int
MenuNo,
                                            int Index, int ID)
{
     AFX_MANAGE_STATE(AfxGetStaticModuleState())

     if (MenuNo<MAXMENUS)
     {
          if (ID==0)
               ::InsertMenu(m_MyPopup[MenuNo],Index,
                         MF_BYPOSITION|MF_SEPARATOR,NULL,NULL);
          else
               ::InsertMenu(m_MyPopup[MenuNo],Index,
                    MF_BYPOSITION|MF_STRING|MF_ENABLED,ID,
                    ItemName);
     }
     return S_OK;
}
```

No surprises here. The only remarkable fact is that this code runs on both Windows CE and the desktop without any changes.

Table 7.5   InsertMenuItem() Parameters

Type	Variable Name	Used for
BSTR	ItemName	Name for the menu item to be inserted.
Int	MenuNo	Number of the menu that will contain the new item.
Int	Index	Location of the new menu item inside the menu.
Int	ID	Command ID for the item. The CmdBarEvent handler will return command IDs.

The "InsertButton()" method you will add next contains the most interesting code. It allows you to set the ToolTip text with the same call that inserts the button.

16. Add this new method and define the five parameters listed in Table 7.6.

17. Add the following code to the implementation of the "InsertButton()" method:

```
STDMETHODIMP CPCDMCommander::InsertButton(int StockNo, int state,
                               int Index, int ID, BSTR ToolTipText)
{
     AFX_MANAGE_STATE(AfxGetStaticModuleState())

TBBUTTON lpButtons;
     lpButtons.idCommand=ID;
     lpButtons.fsState=state;
     if (ID==0) // If ID is 0 a Separation Space is created
     {
          lpButtons.iBitmap=0;
          lpButtons.fsStyle=TBSTYLE_SEP;
     }
     else
     {
          lpButtons.iBitmap=StockNo;
          lpButtons.fsStyle=TBSTYLE_BUTTON;
```

Table 7.6   InsertButton() Parameters

Type	Variable Name	Used for
Int	StockNo	Number of the stock icon in the IDR_TOOLBAR bitmap. A list of SBM_ defines can be found in the "CeHelpers.H" include file.
Int	State	Uses TBSTATE_ flags.
Int	Index	Location of the new menu item inside the menu.
Int	ID	Command ID for the item. The CmdBarEvent handler will return command IDs.
BSTR	ToolTipText	The text for the ToolTip of the new button.

```
      }
      lpButtons.iString=0;

#ifdef UNDER_CE
      if (m_hwndCB!=NULL)
      {
            CommandBar_InsertButton(m_hwndCB,Index,
                              (LPTBBUTTON)&lpButtons);
            if (Index<MAXBUTTONS)
            {
                  SortToolTips(Index);
                  if (ID!=0)
                  {
                     m_szTTips[Index]=(LPTSTR)LocalAlloc
                     (LMEM_ZEROINIT,
                              sizeof(TCHAR)*(lstrlen(ToolTipText)
                              +2));
                     wsprintf(m_szTTips[Index],ToolTipText);
                     if (Index>m_iMaxButtons) m_iMaxButtons=Index;
                  }
                  CommandBar_AddToolTips(m_hwndCB,
                                    m_iMaxButtons+1,m_szTTips);
            }
      }
#else       // Code for Desktop here
#endif
      return S_OK;
}
```

18. The "CPCDMCommander" class limits the number of buttons (and ToolTips) to 15; thus you will need to set in the "PCDMCommander.h" include file:

```
#define MAXBUTTONS     15
```

19. The next method, "InsertComboBox()", will add a combo box to the command bar. It takes three parameters, as shown in Table 7.7.

To deal with the combo box, you first have to define some structures and member variables that will be used to identify the combo box later.

Table 7.7   InsertComboBox() Parameters

Type	Variable Name	Used for
Int	Size	Size of the combo box in pixels.
Int	Index	Location of the new menu item inside the menu.
Int	ID	Command ID for the item. The "CmdBarEvent" handler will return command IDs.

20.   Add the following code to the "PCDMCommander" class definition file:

```
#define MAXCOMBOS        3
typedef struct tagCOMBOHANDLE
{
     HWND      hWnd;       // Combo Handle
     UINT      ID;              // Combo ID
     TCHAR     Text[255]; // Combo Text
} COMBOHANDLE;

typedef struct tagCOMBOSTUFF
{
     int                  curCnt;       // Combo Counter
     COMBOHANDLE       handle[MAXCOMBOS];
} COMBOSTUFF;
```

You will limit the number of possible combo boxes in the command bar to 3. Having more combo boxes in a Windows CE application would unnecessarily crowd the command bar.

21.   Do not forget to declare the member variable "m_ComboStuff" in the private section of the class definition:

```
COMBOSTUFF     m_ComboStuff;
```

22.   Returning to your "InsertComboBox", the implementation code is once again straightforward and looks like this:

```
STDMETHODIMP CPCDMCommander::InsertComboBox(int Size, int Index,
                                            int ID)
{
     AFX_MANAGE_STATE(AfxGetStaticModuleState())
```

```
#ifdef UNDER_CE
    if (m_hwndCB!=NULL)
    {
        m_ComboStuff.handle[m_ComboStuff.curCnt].ID=ID;
        m_ComboStuff.handle[m_ComboStuff.curCnt].hWnd=
            CommandBar_InsertComboBox(m_hwndCB,
                    _Module.m_hInst,Size,NULL,ID,Index);
        SortToolTips(Index);
        m_ComboStuff.curCnt++;
    }
#else       // Code for Desktop here
#endif
    return S_OK;
}
```

Now what good is a combo box if you can't add strings to it? Adding strings to the combo box will be your next step.

23.　To keep it simple, you will add another method to your class called "AddStringToComboBox" and give it two parameters, as shown in Table 7.8.

Adding strings to a combo box in the command bar works the same as it would with any other combo box.

24.　Add the following code to the "AddStringToComboBox" implementation:

```
STDMETHODIMP CPCDMCommander::AddStringToComboBox(int ID, BSTR text)
{
    AFX_MANAGE_STATE(AfxGetStaticModuleState())

    int tCombo=-1;
    for (int i=0;i<m_ComboStuff.curCnt;i++)
    {
        if (ID==(int)m_ComboStuff.handle[i].ID)
```

Table 7.8　AddStringToComboBox() Parameters

Type	Variable Name	Used for
Int	ID	ID of the combo box
BSTR	Text	String to be added to the box

```
            {
                    tCombo=i;
                    break;
            }
    }
    if (tCombo>=0)
    {
            if (lstrcmp(text,TEXT("<CLR>"))==0)
                    SendMessage(m_ComboStuff.handle[i].hWnd,
                            CB_RESETCONTENT,0,0);
            else
                    SendMessage(m_ComboStuff.handle[i].hWnd,
                            CB_ADDSTRING,0,(LPARAM)(LPCSTR)text);
    }
    return S_OK;
}
```

You can see that adding the string is as easy as promised. If the method is called with "<CLR>" as the text string, the combo box will be reset.

25. The next method you will need to add to the class is called "SetAdornments()", and it takes only one parameter (see Table 7.9).

26. And its implementation is also very simple:

```
STDMETHODIMP CPCDMCommander::SetAdornments(int Flags)
{
    AFX_MANAGE_STATE(AfxGetStaticModuleState())
#ifdef UNDER_CE
    if (m_hwndCB!=NULL)
    {
            CommandBar_AddAdornments(m_hwndCB, Flags,0);
    }
```

Table 7.9 SetAdornments() Parameter

Type	Variable Name	Used for
Int	Flags	The adornment flags

```
#else // Code for Desktop here
#endif
      return S_OK;
}
```

The last two things you need to do before you can test your application are (1) some initialization code in the "CPCDMCommander" constructor, and (2) add some declarations in the "CPCDMCommander" class declaration.

27.   Here is the constructor code:

```
CPCDMCommander()
{
int i;

      for (i=0;i<MAXMENUS;i++) m_MyPopup[i]=NULL;
      for (i=0;i<MAXBUTTONS;i++) m_szTTips[i]=NULL;
      m_iMaxButtons=0;
      m_MyMenu=NULL;
      m_hwndCB=NULL;
      m_ComboStuff.curCnt=0;
      m_bIsFresh=FALSE;
      m_IDBAR=0;
}
```

28.   To cross-check, here are the final declarations for the "CPCDMCommander" class:

```
private:
      void SortToolTips(int index);
      HWND       m_hwndCB;    // Command-Bar Window
      int        m_IDBAR;     // ID of the CommandBar
      BOOL       m_bIsFresh;  // Have the menus been redrawm already
      HMENU      m_MyMenu;    // Menu
      HMENU      m_MyPopup[MAXMENUS];         // Popup Menus (max 5)
      LPTSTR        m_szTTips[MAXBUTTONS];    // ToolTip Text (max
                                             15)
      int           m_iMaxButtons;           // Contains highest
                                             Button No
      COMBOSTUFF    m_ComboStuff;            // Text, Count and HWND
                                             and ID
                                             // of every Combo-Box
```

What good is a command bar if it doesn't fire any events? To keep it simple, you will only use one event, which will tell your host what was selected from the command bar.

29. Add the method "CmdBarAction()" to the "_IPCDMCommanderEvents" interface and give it two parameters, as shown in Table 7.10.

30. Select the "CPCDMCommander" class with the right mouse button and choose "Implement Connection Points" from the context menu.

31. In the dialog box, set the check mark for the "_IPCDMCommanderEvents".

As mentioned in Chapter 6, the Class wizard has a small bug and does not write the correct GUID to "CONNECTION_POINT_MAP". To correct the bug, change the map entry as follows:

```
BEGIN_CONNECTION_POINT_MAP(CPCDMCommander)
    CONNECTION_POINT_ENTRY(IID_IPropertyNotifySink)
    CONNECTION_POINT_ENTRY(DIID__IPCDMCommanderEvents)
END_CONNECTION_POINT_MAP()
```

The wizard will now create a "PCDMUICP.H" file that contains the implementation code for a method called "Fire_CmdBarAction()". You want to fire this event every time something happens to the command bar. For that purpose, you will need to add an event handler to the message map of your "CPCDMCommander" class.

In the ATL tutorial you will find the description of how to select the implementation class and choose "Add Windows Message Handler" from its context menu. On my own workstation, for some unknown reason, whenever I invoke this wizard the dialog box comes up empty. Well, here is what the wizard is supposed to do.

32. Add the following lines to "MSG_MAP(CPCDMCommander)":

```
BEGIN_MSG_MAP(CPCDMCommander)
    MESSAGE_HANDLER(WM_COMMAND, OnCommand)
    MESSAGE_HANDLER(WM_CLOSE, OnClose)
```

Table 7.10 CmdBarAction() Parameters

Type	Variable Name	Used for
Int	ID	The ID of the command-bar item that was selected
BSTR	Text	The combo box will also fire a string to the container.

```
    MESSAGE_HANDLER(WM_DESTROY, OnDestroy)
    NOTIFY_RANGE_HANDLER(0, 0xFFFF, NotifyHandler)
    CHAIN_MSG_MAP(CComControl<CPCDMCommander>)
    DEFAULT_REFLECTION_HANDLER()
END_MSG_MAP()
```

33.   Below "MSG_MAP" add the two prototypes:

```
LRESULT NotifyHandler(int idCtrl, LPNMHDR pnmh, BOOL& bHandled);
LRESULT OnCommand(UINT uMsg, WPARAM wParam, LPARAM lParam,
                  BOOL& bHandled);
LRESULT OnClose(UINT uMsg, WPARAM wParam, LPARAM lParam,
                BOOL& bHandled);
LRESULT OnDestroy(UINT uMsg, WPARAM wParam, LPARAM lParam,
                  BOOL& bHandled);
```

The implementation code is a bit more complex because you have to identify the correct combo box first and then check whether a new entry was made or an item was selected in the list box of the combo box. In case the user writes to the edit field of the combo box, you will fire the "CmdBarAction" event after every keystroke. This arrangement will give you the most flexibility—for example, for instant searching.

34.   Insert the following methods in the "PCDMCommander.cpp" source file:

```
LRESULT CPCDMCommander::OnCommand(UINT uMsg, WPARAM wParam,
                                  LPARAM lParam, BOOL& bHandled)
{
    if (HIWORD(wParam)!=0)          // Caught the Combo-Box
    {
        int tCombo=-1,u;
        for (int i=0;i<m_ComboStuff.curCnt;i++)
        {
            if ((HWND)lParam==m_ComboStuff.handle[i].hWnd)
            {
                tCombo=i;
                break;
            }
        }
        if (tCombo>=0)
        {
            switch (HIWORD(wParam))
            {
                case 5:
```

```
                                SendMessage((HWND)lParam,
                                        WM_GETTEXT,(WPARAM)255,
                                (LPARAM)m_ComboStuff.handle[tCombo].
                                Text);
                                Fire_CmdBarAction(LOWORD(wParam),
                        m_ComboStuff.handle[tCombo].Text);
                    break;
                        case 1:
                          u=SendMessage((HWND)
                          lParam,CB_GETCURSEL,0,0);
                          SendMessage((HWND)lParam,CB_GETLBTEXT,
                            (WPARAM)u,
                            (LPARAM)m_ComboStuff.handle
                            [tCombo].Text);
                            Fire_CmdBarAction(LOWORD(wParam),
                                    m_ComboStuff.handle[tCombo].Text);
                        break;
                      default:
                       break;
                }
            }
        }
    else
    {
        Fire_CmdBarAction(wParam,TEXT(""));
    }
    return S_OK;
}


LRESULT CPCDMCommander::OnClose(UINT uMsg, WPARAM wParam,
                        LPARAM lParam, BOOL& bHandled)
{
    Fire_CmdBarAction(IDCLOSE,TEXT(""));
    return S_OK;
}
LRESULT CPCDMCommander::OnDestroy(UINT uMsg, WPARAM wParam,
                        LPARAM lParam, BOOL& bHandled)
{
int i;

    for (i=0;i<MAXBUTTONS;i++)
```

```
                if (!m_szTTips[i])
                        LocalFree(m_szTTips[i]);
        return S_OK;
}
```

If you look into the description of "CommandBar_DrawMenuBar", you will find a very important hint—that you should call this function every time the menu is changed. This includes the creation of the menu. Unfortunately, you cannot call this function from within any member method of the ATL control. Instead, you need to use a notify handler that will call the "OnDraw" function the very first time it gets called. Since you cannot anticipate what ID your command bar will get, you will use the "NOTIFY_RANGE_HANDLER(0, 0xFFFF, NotifyHandler)" macro to ensure that your handler will be called.

Before you add the notify handler, you need to add some code to your control's "OnDraw" method.

35.   Add the following line to the method:

```
    HRESULT OnDraw(ATL_DRAWINFO& di)
    {
#ifdef UNDER_CE
        if (m_hwndCB!=NULL)
            CommandBar_DrawMenuBar(m_hwndCB,0);
#endif
        return S_OK;
    }
```

36.   The code for your notify handler looks like this:

```
LRESULT CPCDMCommander::NotifyHandler(int idCtrl, LPNMHDR pnmh,
                                        BOOL& bHandled)
{
    if (idCtrl==m_IDBAR && m_bIsFresh==FALSE)
    {
        FireViewChange();
        m_bIsFresh=TRUE;
    }
    return S_OK;
}
```

Now the control is done, and you can compile and download it. To test the control, you need to insert it into your PCDM application or into an eMbedded Visual Basic application.

You should also load the project "PCDMUI_Win32" now, add the file "PCDMCommander.cpp", and compile this project. You will need a registered desktop version of your control as well to insert into a host application.

 The final source code of this section can be found on the companion CD under "\Sources\ThreadExample\PCDMUI\Step2".

7.1.3   Testing the Control in eMbedded Visual Basic

To see whether your new control works, you will first test it in eMbedded Visual Basic. Before you can use the control in eVB, you have to use the Control Manager and install the control on the device as a design control.

1.   Start the "Windows CE Control Manager" and select the device you are using.

You will see at least three branches in the tree view:
- Emulation
- (Default Device)
- Desktop Design controls

If you have installed a new device using the Platform Manager, you will see this device here as well.

2.   Click on the entry "(Default Device)" or on your new device and you will get a list of all installed controls on the device.

Because eMbedded Visual C++ already has downloaded and registered your control, you will find the control "PCDMCommander Class" in the list but in the column "Design" it will read "No".

3.   Select the "Desktop Design Controls" area now and select the "PCDMCommander Class" with the right mouse button.

4.   From the context menu select "Install on Target" and select the desktop version of the control in the open dialog box.

After a short while the column "Design" reads "Yes". You are now ready to insert the control into eMbedded Visual Basic.

1.   Start the eVB environment and create a new project for Windows CE.

2.   Once "Form1" is visible in the eVB development environment, right-click the toolbar and select "Components" from the context menu.

3.   Scroll to "PCDMUI 1.0 Type Library" and select the check mark (see Figure 7.2).

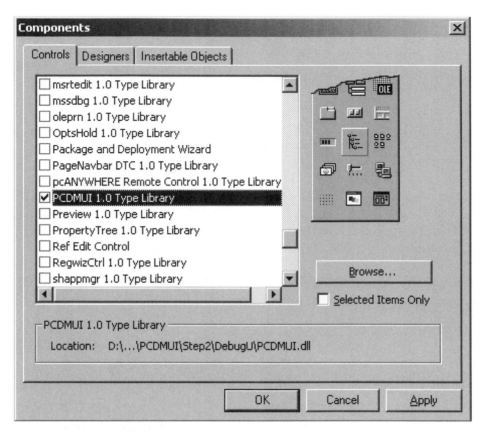

Figure 7.2   Selecting the PCDMUI control for use in eMbedded Visual Basic

You will now find a new icon in the toolbar for your control.

4.   Select the icon and insert the control on the form.

You will not see the control in your form because you deleted everything in the "OnDraw" method of that class. If you want to have at least a bounding rectangle, you simply need to bring back the code.

5.   Double-click the form and enter the following code into the "Form_Load()" function:

```
Private Sub Form_Load()
PCDMCommander1.CreateBar 100
PCDMCommander1.InsertButton SBM_SEP, TBSTATE_ENABLED, 0, 0, ""
PCDMCommander1.InsertButton SBM_NEW, TBSTATE_ENABLED, 1, 1001, "New
File"
```

```
PCDMCommander1.InsertButton SBM_SEP, TBSTATE_ENABLED, 2, 0, ""
PCDMCommander1.InsertButton SBM_OPEN, TBSTATE_ENABLED, 3, 1002,
"Opens a file"
PCDMCommander1.InsertButton SBM_SAVE, TBSTATE_ENABLED, 4, 1003,
"Saves a file"
PCDMCommander1.InsertComboBox 150, 4, 1008
PCDMCommander1.AddStringToComboBox 1008, "<CLR>"
PCDMCommander1.AddStringToComboBox 1008, "First Choice"
PCDMCommander1.AddStringToComboBox 1008, "Second Choice"
PCDMCommander1.InsertMenu "File", 0
PCDMCommander1.InsertMenuItem "New", 0, 0, 1001
PCDMCommander1.InsertMenuItem "", 0, 1, 0
PCDMCommander1.InsertMenuItem "Load", 0, 2, 1002
PCDMCommander1.InsertMenuItem "Save", 0, 3, 1003
PCDMCommander1.InsertMenu "Edit", 1
PCDMCommander1.InsertMenuItem "Undo", 1, 0, 1004
PCDMCommander1.InsertMenuItem "Copy", 1, 1, 1005
PCDMCommander1.InsertMenuItem "Paste", 1, 2, 1006
PCDMCommander1.SetAdornments 0
End Sub
```

To catch the events, you need to include an event handler for the "CmdBarAction" event.

6. Double-click the "PCDMCommander1" control in the form and eVB will automatically add an event handler for the "CmdBarAction" event because it is the only event exposed by your control.

7. Add the following code to the handler:

```
Private Sub PCDMCommander1_CmdBarAction(ByVal ID As Long, ByVal Text
As String)
    If ID = IDCLOSE Then
        App.End
    Else
        MsgBox "The ID " & ID & " fired the string <" & Text & ">"
End If
End Sub
```

8. The following lines have to be added after the "Option Explicit" declaration on top of the form code:

```
Const SBM_COPY = 0
Const SBM_CUT = 1
Const SBM_DELETE = 2
```

```
Const SBM_FIND = 3
Const SBM_HELP = 4
Const SBM_NEW = 5
Const SBM_OPEN = 6
Const SBM_PASTE = 7
Const SBM_PRINT = 8
Const SBM_PROP = 9
Const SBM_REDO = 10
Const SBM_SAVE = 11
Const SBM_SORTASC = 12
Const SBM_SORTDES = 13
Const SBM_UNDO = 14
Const SBM_SYNC = 15
Const SBM_SEND = 16
Const SBM_SEP = 99

Const TBSTATE_CHECKED = 1
Const TBSTATE_PRESSED = 2
Const TBSTATE_ENABLED = 4
Const TBSTATE_HIDDEN = 8
Const TBSTATE_INDETERMINATE = 16
Const TBSTATE_WRAP = 32

Const IDCLOSE = 8
```

Now run the project and you will see your command-bar control with two menus, four buttons, and a combo box. If you press any button, you will get a message box telling you the ID of the button you pressed and an empty string. If you type into the combo box or select an item from its list, you will see the ID of the combo box and the string that the combo box has in its edit field.

 The final source code of this section can be found on the companion CD under "\Sources\Chapter 7\7.2".

7.1.4   Calling the Control from the PCDM Application

In the PCDM framework that you created in Section 5.2, the MFC Application Wizard created a command bar. Since you want to use the new control, you need to change several things in the code.

1. Load the last PCDM project.

 If you do not have this project anymore, you can find it on the companion CD in the directory "\Sources\ThreadExample\PCDM CD\Step1".

2. Open the "CMainFrame" class and delete everything in the "OnCreate()" method so that it looks like this:

```
int CMainFrame::OnCreate(LPCREATESTRUCT lpCreateStruct)
{
        if (CFrameWnd::OnCreate(lpCreateStruct) == -1)
                return -1;
        return 0;
}
```

You want to base your "CPCDMView" on a "CFormView" instead of "Cview".

3. Replace all appearances of "CView" with "CFormView". You'll find them in "PCDMView.h" and "PCDMView.cpp".

4. Change the "CPCDMView" constructor to:

```
CPCDMView::CPCDMView()
        : CFormView(CPCDMView::IDD)
{
        // TODO: add construction code here

}
```

5. Add the following code to the definition of the "CPCDMView" class in the public "//Attributes" section:

```
//{{AFX_DATA(CPCDMView)
enum { IDD = IDD_MAINFORM };
//}}AFX_DATA
```

6. Add the following virtual method to "PCDMView.cpp":

```
void CPCDMView::DoDataExchange(CDataExchange* pDX)
{
        CFormView::DoDataExchange(pDX);
        //{{AFX_DATA_MAP(CPCDMView)
        //}}AFX_DATA_MAP
}
```

7. Make sure the declaration of this function was inserted into the "//{{AFX_VIRTUAL(CPCDMView)" section:

```
virtual void DoDataExchange(CDataExchange* pDX);
```

Without these AFX remarks the class wizard will not work correctly with the new form.

8. Add a dialog box to the resources of the PCDM application and set its ID to "IDD_MAINFORM". Choose the style "Child" with border "None" for the dialog box.

9. Add the "PCDMCommander Class" ActiveX control to this form and set its ID to "IDC_COMMANDER".

10. Click on the "IDD_MAINFORM" dialog box with the right mouse button and select the class wizard from the context menu.

The class wizard will tell you that no class has been attached to the form yet and ask you if you want to create or select one.

11. Choose "Select class" and select the "CPCDMView" class from the list of classes. The wizard will complain that the new class is not a dialog class, but since it is a "CFormView" class, you can ignore the warning.

12. Select the "Member Variable" tab of the wizard and double-click the "IDC_COMMANDER" control.

The wizard will ask you to create a new class for the control.

13. Accept all defaults and name the new variable "m_cmdBar".

14. Select the "Message Maps" tab again and add a function for the "CmdBarAction" event of the "IDC_COMMANDER" object.

Now you can call the methods of your control, using the "OnInitialUpdate()" function.

15. Select the "CPCDMView" in the "ClassView" and add a "Virtual Function" for "OnInitialUpdate".

16. Insert the following code in the implementation method of this handler:

```
void CPCDMView::OnInitialUpdate()
{
        CFormView::OnInitialUpdate();
        // Sizes the IDD_MAINFORM Dialog to the size of the Mainframe
        CRect myRect;
        GetParentFrame()->GetClientRect(&myRect);
        SetWindowPos(NULL, myRect.left,myRect.top,
```

```
                    myRect.right,myRect.bottom,SWP_NOZORDER);
    m_cmdBar.SetWindowPos(NULL,myRect.top,myRect.left,
                    myRect.right,30,SWP_NOZORDER);

    // Creates your Command Bar
    m_cmdBar.CreateBar(1);

    // Inserts Menus
    m_cmdBar.InsertMenu(TEXT("File"),0);
    m_cmdBar.InsertMenuItem(TEXT("Send to..")   ,0,0,30);
    m_cmdBar.InsertMenuItem(TEXT("Receive..")   ,0,1,36);
    m_cmdBar.InsertMenuItem(TEXT("Show Details"),0,2,31);
    m_cmdBar.InsertMenuItem(TEXT("")                 ,0,3,0);
    m_cmdBar.InsertMenuItem(TEXT("Help")             ,0,4,34);
    m_cmdBar.InsertMenuItem(TEXT("About")            ,0,5,35);
    m_cmdBar.InsertMenuItem(TEXT("")                 ,0,6,0);
    m_cmdBar.InsertMenuItem(TEXT("Exit")             ,0,7,IDCLOSE);

    // Inserts Toolbar Buttons
    m_cmdBar.InsertButton(SBM_SEP,TBSTATE_ENABLED,  1,0, TEXT(""));
    m_cmdBar.InsertButton(SBM_SEND,TBSTATE_ENABLED, 2,30,
                    TEXT("Send Entry to other Device"));
    m_cmdBar.InsertButton(SBM_OPEN,TBSTATE_ENABLED, 3,31,
                    TEXT("Show Details"));
    m_cmdBar.InsertButton(SBM_SEP,TBSTATE_ENABLED   4,0,
                    TEXT(""));
    m_cmdBar.InsertButton(SBM_FIND,TBSTATE_ENABLE   5,32,
                    TEXT("Search for CD"));
    m_cmdBar.InsertButton(SBM_SEP,TBSTATE_ENABLED,  5,0,
                    TEXT(""));
    m_cmdBar.InsertButton(SBM_HELP,TBSTATE_ENABLED,6,34,
                    TEXT("Help"));
    m_cmdBar.InsertButton(SBM_PROP,TBSTATE_ENABLED,7,35,
                    TEXT("About"));

    // Inserts the Search Combo Box
    m_cmdBar.InsertComboBox(100,3,1007);
    m_cmdBar.AddStringToComboBox(1007,TEXT("Madonna"));

    // Adds the Close Button
    m_cmdBar.SetAdornments(0);
}
```

17.   Add the include files "cehelpers.h" and "aygshell.h"to the "stdafx.h" of
your project:

```
#include <aygshell.h>
#include "<path2cehelpers.h>\cehelpers.h"
```

Before you can compile your new application you need to catch the
"CmdBarAction" event that the "PCDMCommander" class will fire if one of the
command-bar items is selected.

18.   Open the "IDD_MAINFORM" dialog box resource and right-click the
"PCDMCommander Class" control. In the context menu select "Events . . .".

19.   Select the "IDC_COMMANDER" object and the "CmdBarAction" event from
the list of "New Windows messages/events" and then press "Add and Edit".

20.   Name the new handler "OnCmdBarActionCommander".

21.   In the new member function "OnCmdBarActionCommander" that the wizard has created for you, add the following code:

```
void CPCDMView::OnCmdBarActionCommander(long ID, LPCTSTR text)
{
    if (ID==IDCLOSE)
        GetParentFrame()->DestroyWindow();
}
```

For now, you will only handle "IDCLOSE". You will add more fun to this method
later in the book.

Now compile and download the application. Since you have not done anything
with the event handler, there will not be much action at this point. For now, the application should exit if you select the "X" Close button. This will tell you that the event
handler and your container are working properly.

 The final source code of this section can be found on the companion CD
under "\Sources\ThreadExample\PCDM CE\Step2".

7.1.5   Summary

Here are some points to summarize the features and traps of the command bar:

- The command bar is the old style of creating menus and toolbars on Windows
  CE, but it is available on all platforms and versions of Windows CE.

- It was designed to closely resemble the desktop toolbar, but uses its own API
  calls starting with "CommandBar_".

- Inserting into the command bar can be tricky because it can cause strange overlapping redraw issues.
- Even though the function is called "AddBitmaps", it cannot be called more than once for a command bar.
- "DrawMenuBar" has to be called if you change, add, or remove a menu from the command bar.

7.2   The Command-Band

System DLL:	COMMCTRL.DLL
Include file:	Commctrl.h
Library file:	Commctrl.lib
Help file:	CEGUIDE.CHM (MSDN 10/98 and later)
Available since:	Windows CE 2.0
API prefix/suffix:	CommandBands_<action>
InitCommonControlEx flag:	ICC_COOL_CLASSES
MFC class:	Crebar

The Command-Band is the Windows CE equivalent of the ReBar or Cool Bar control that Internet Explorer 4.0 introduced to the desktop. The Command-Band is not all that different from the command bar. It is just a container of multiple command bars.

7.2.1   Adding the Command-Band to an Application

Unfortunately, the WCE Application Wizard does not create an application with the Command-Band, but you can reuse the project in which you created a command bar.

1. Load the "CmdBarApp" project, open the "CMDBarApp.CPP" source file, and select the "case WM_CREATE" branch of "WndProc".

Here are the commands that have to be added to this code branch: The function "CommandBand_Create" creates a new Command-Band. Compared with the "CommandBar_Create", it has two additional parameters—one for style flags and one for a list that holds images for items that get added to the Command-Band. The style flags of the Command-Band match the styles of the ReBar control that you may already be familiar with from your work on the desktop. Table 7.11 lists these flags and their uses.

Table 7.11   Command-Band Style Flags

Name	Use
RBS_AUTOSIZE	The band gets automatically reformatted if the size or position of the Command-Band is changed.
RBS_BANDBORDERS	Each band gets a one-pixel-wide border around it.
RBS_FIXORDER	The band can be moved, but it remains in its order between other bands.
RBS_SMARTLABELS	A very useful flag on Windows CE. If the band is minimized (by double-tapping), it will be shown with its icon. This flag exists only on Windows CE.
RBS_VARHEIGHT	Each row of bands in the Command-Band gets resized to the maximum size of a band in the row. If this flag is missing, all bands in the Command-Band get the same height regardless of their row.

The desktop flags "RBS_VERTICALGRIPPER" and "RBS_REGISTERDROP" are not supported under Windows CE. Most applications only use "RBS_SMARTLABELS" and "RBS_VARHEIGHT".

The other parameter of the "CommandBands_Create" function receives an image list. The creation of an image list on Windows CE is exactly the same as it is for the desktop. You are going to use the "IDR_TOOLBAR" bitmap you have already used for the command-bar example.

2. Here is the complete code to add at the beginning of the "WM_CREATE"-branch:

```
Case WM_CREATE:
{
int ii;
HBITMAP hBmp;
    hImLst=ImageList_Create(16,16,ILC_COLOR,2,0);
    hBmp=LoadBitmap(hInst,MAKEINTRESOURCE(IDR_TOOLBAR));
    ImageList_Add(hImLst,hBmp,NULL);
    DeleteObject(hBmp);
    hwndCB=CommandBands_Create(hInst,hWnd,1,
                            RBS_SMARTLABELS|RBS_VARHEIGHT,
                            hImLst);
```

3. Do not forget to declare "hImLst" at the beginning of your source file:

```
HIMAGELIST hImLst;
#define MAX_BANDS     3
```

The next command you need to add is "CommandBands_AddBands". Before you can call this function, you need to fill the "REBARBANDINFO" structure. You are probably familiar with this structure and will not find any surprises here: the structure members are the same as they are on the desktop. For this example, you are going to add three bands:

- A menu band
- A button-bar band
- A band with a combo box

4. Add the following code after the "CommandBands_Create()" call:

```
REBARBANDINFO trbi[MAX_BANDS];
int i;
HWND thwndCombo;
HWND thwndCBar;                   // The command bar handle

// Zero the RebarInfo Structure or you will get funny effects !
memset(trbi,0,sizeof(REBARINFO)*MAX_BANDS);
for (i = 0; i < MAX_BANDS; i++)
{
    trbi[i].cbSize = sizeof (REBARBANDINFO);
    trbi[i].fMask = RBBIM_ID | RBBIM_SIZE | RBBIM_STYLE;
    trbi[i].wID = IDR_TOOLBAR+i;
}

// First Band: The Menu - No Gripper here. You do not want to move it
trbi[0].fStyle = RBBS_FIXEDBMP | RBBS_NOGRIPPER;
// You have to guess the size because there is no measure
// method available
trbi[0].cx = 100;
trbi[0].iImage = 0;

// Second Band: The buttons
trbi[1].fMask |= RBBIM_TEXT;
trbi[1].iImage = 0;
trbi[1].lpText = TEXT ("Buttons");
// Guessing again. This time you can be more precise (2x16 + border)
trbi[1].cx = 40;
//trbi[1].fStyle = RBBS_FIXEDBMP;

// Third Band: A combo Box
```

```
thwndCombo = CreateWindow (TEXT ("COMBOBOX"), TEXT ("MyComboBox"),
                           WS_VISIBLE | WS_CHILD | WS_BORDER,
                           0, 0, 10, 5, hWnd, (HMENU)42, hInst,
                           NULL);

trbi[2].fMask |= RBBIM_TEXT | RBBIM_STYLE |
                 RBBIM_CHILDSIZE | RBBIM_CHILD;
trbi[2].hwndChild = thwndCombo;
trbi[2].cxMinChild = 0;
trbi[2].cyMinChild = 23;
trbi[2].cyChild = 55;
trbi[2].iImage = 0;
trbi[2].lpText = TEXT ("My ComboBox");
trbi[2].cx = 130;
trbi[2].fStyle = RBBS_BREAK|RBBS_CHILDEDGE;

// Add the bands.
CommandBands_AddBands (hwndCB, hInst, 3, trbi);
```

As I said, no surprises here. Next you have to bring the bands to life. And guess what: you will use the command-bar function to do so.

The button band requires a toolbar bitmap with two bitmaps.

5. Enter the resource editor and add two icons to a new toolbar resource labeled "IDR_TOOLBAR".

Instead of calling "CommandBar_Create()", you will call "CommandBands_ GetCommandBar". This call returns a HWND to the command bar inside the band and now allows all the command-bar calls that you utilized in Section 7.1. Except for the first line, the following code is identical to that used in the command-bar example.

6. Add the following code right after the "CommandBands_AddBands" call:

```
//hwndCB = CommandBar_Create(hInst, hWnd, 1);
// Instead of Creating a CommandBar you just get it
// from the first Band (Index 0)
    thwndCBar = CommandBands_GetCommandBar (hwndCB, 0);
    CommandBar_InsertMenubarEx(thwndCBar, hInst,
                               MAKEINTRESOURCE(IDM_MENU), 0);

// Now getting it from the second Band (Index 1)
    thwndCBar = CommandBands_GetCommandBar (hwndCB, 1);
```

```
CommandBar_AddBitmap(thwndCBar, hInst, IDR_TOOLBAR, 2, 16, 16);
CommandBar_AddButtons(thwndCBar,
                    sizeof(tbSTDButton)/sizeof(TBBUTTON),
                    tbSTDButton);

szToolTips[0]=(LPTSTR)LocalAlloc(LMEM_ZEROINIT, sizeof(TCHAR));
wsprintf(szToolTips[0],TEXT(""));
for (ii=1;ii<MAX_CMDBAR_ITEMS;ii++)
{
    LoadString(hInst,IDS_TOOLTIPSTART+ii,
            szHello,MAX_LOADSTRING);

    szToolTips[ii]=(LPTSTR)LocalAlloc(LMEM_ZEROINIT,
                                sizeof(TCHAR)*lstrlen
                                (szHello));
    wsprintf(szToolTips[ii],szHello);
}
CommandBar_AddToolTips(thwndCBar, MAX_CMDBAR_ITEMS,szToolTips);
// Not needed anymore. Band Three holds a combo box already
// You can still use this function but the method above is much
// more flexible
//CommandBar_InsertComboBox(hwndCB,hInst, 50, NULL, 8, 1);
```

To get the "OK" button and the "X" Close button in the Command-Band, you need to call the function "CommandBands_AddAdornments".

7. Add the following line at the end of the "WM_CREATE" branch:

```
CommandBands_AddAdornments(hwndCB, hInst, CMDBAR_OK, NULL);
}
```

This call allows you to change the settings and flags of the Command-Band.

The last command that the Command-Band has to offer is the function "CommandBands_GetRestoreInformation", which can be used to store the current details of the Command-Band's properties in the registry. After the call to this function, the "COMMANDBANDSRESTOREINFO" holds details on size, order, and style of each bar in the Command-Band. Call this function just before the Command-Band gets destroyed—best done in the "WM_DESTROY" branch of the "WinProc"—nd store the structure into the registry. When your application restarts, you can simply populate the "REBARINFO" structure with the saved values.

Before you can compile and run the code, you must initialize "ICC_COOL_CLASSES", using "InitCommonControlEx".

8. Add the following lines to the "InitInstance" function after "MyRegisterClass":

```
INITCOMMONCONTROLSEX icex;
icex.dwSize = sizeof (INITCOMMONCONTROLSEX);
icex.dwICC = ICC_COOL_CLASSES;
InitCommonControlsEx (&icex);
```

 The final source code of this section can be found on the companion CD under "\Sources\Chapter 7\7.3".

7.2.2 Updating the PCDMCommander Class

The "PCDMCommander" class in your PCDMUI control will support both the command-bar and the Command-Band interfaces. You will need to add some methods to your class to be able to use the features of the Command-Band. The idea behind the PCDMUI control is to be as simple for the application developer as possible. That's why you are going to do a lot of work for the application developer in the control class.

1. Load the "PCDMUI" project from the last chapter.

The first method you need to add sets the type of the command bar.

2. Add the method "SetCmdBarType" with an integer parameter named "type" to the "IPCDMCommander" interface.

3. Insert the following lines of code into the implementation of this method:

```
STDMETHODIMP CPCDMCommander::SetCmdBarType(int type)
{
        AFX_MANAGE_STATE(AfxGetStaticModuleState())

        if (type!=0)
                m_CmdBarType=CMDBAND;
        else
                m_CmdBarType=CMDBAR;

        return S_OK;
}
```

4. Define the two values "CMDBAR" and "CMDBAND" in the "PCDMCommander.h" include file as:

```
#define CMDBAR      0
#define CMDBAND     1
#define MAXBAN      5
```

5. Add the "int m_CmdBarType" variable to the private variable section of your "PCDMCommander" class.

To use the Command-Band control inside your command class, you must initialize the extended common control library. The new class will allow up to five different bars inside one band. To deal correctly with the ToolTips, you need to add a dimension to its definition. You must also initialize several member variables.

6. Here is the final constructor of your "PCDMCommander" class:

```
CPCDMCommander::CPCDMCommander()
{
int i,j;

        for (i=0;i<MAXMENUS;i++) m_MyPopup[i]=NULL;
        for (j=0;j<MAXBANDS;j++)
        {
                for (i=0;i<MAXBUTTONS;i++) m_szTTips[j][i]=NULL;
                m_iMaxButtons[j]=0;
        }
        m_MyMenu=NULL;
        m_hwndCB=NULL;
        m_bIsFresh=FALSE;
        m_IDBAR=0;
        // Command-Band addons
        m_BandCreated=FALSE;
        m_CmdBarType=CMDBAR;
        m_CurrentBar=0;

        INITCOMMONCONTROLSEX icex;
        icex.dwSize = sizeof (INITCOMMONCONTROLSEX);
        icex.dwICC = ICC_COOL_CLASSES;
        InitCommonControlsEx (&icex);
}
```

The declarations of the variables in the "PCDMCommander" class definition must be updated to reflect these changes.

7. Change the private declaration section of your control to:

```
private:
        void SortToolTips(int index);
        int      m_IDBAR;
```

```
BOOL      m_bIsFresh;
HWND      m_hwndCB;                    // Command-Bar Window
HMENU     m_MyMenu;                    // Menu
HMENU     m_MyPopup[MAXMENUS];         // Popup Menus (max 5)
LPTSTR m_szTTips[MAXBANDS][MAXBUTTONS];
                                       // ToolTip Text (max 15 per
                                       Band)
int    m_iMaxButtons[MAXBANDS]   // Contains highest Button No
TCHAR m_ComboTxt[255]            // Contains current Combo Box
                                       Text


// Command Band addons
int       m_CmdBarType;   // Bar Type: 0= Command Bar; 1=Command
                          Band
BOOL      m_BandCreated;           // TRUE if Band was created
                                   already
int       m_CurrentBar;            // Index of current Bar in
                                   Band
HIMAGELIST m_hImLst;               // ImageList of Band
HWND      m_hwndCBand;             // HWND of the Command Band
REBARBANDINFO m_trbi[MAXBANDS];        // Bar info
```

You changed the indexes of the "m_iMaxButtons" and "m_szToolTips" member variables. Therefore you will need to fix all appearances of those two variables in your code.

8. The first change is in "SortToolTips":

```
void CPCDMCommander::SortToolTips(int index)
{
int i;
      for (i=MAXBUTTONS-1;i>index;i-)
            m_szTTips[m_CurrentBar][i]=m_szTTips[m_CurrentBar][i-1];
      if (m_iMaxButtons[m_CurrentBar]<MAXBUTTONS)
            m_iMaxButtons[m_CurrentBar]++;
#ifdef UNDER_CE
            if (m_hwndCB!=NULL)
                  CommandBar_AddToolTips(m_hwndCB,
                              MAXBUTTONS,m_szTTips[m_CurrentBar]);
#else // Code for Desktop here
#endif
}
```

9. The second change is in "InsertButton":

```
STDMETHODIMP CPCDMCommander::InsertButton(int StockNo, int state,
                            int Index, int ID, BSTR ToolTipText)
{
    AFX_MANAGE_STATE(AfxGetStaticModuleState())

    TBBUTTON lpButtons;
    lpButtons.idCommand=ID;
    lpButtons.fsState=state;
    if (ID==0)        // If ID is 0 a Separation Space is created
    {
        lpButtons.iBitmap=0;
        lpButtons.fsStyle=TBSTYLE_SEP;
    }
    else
    {
        lpButtons.iBitmap=StockNo;
        lpButtons.fsStyle=TBSTYLE_BUTTON;
    }
    lpButtons.iString=0;

#ifdef UNDER_CE
    if (m_hwndCB!=NULL)
    {
        CommandBar_InsertButton(m_hwndCB,Index,
                        (LPTBBUTTON)&lpButtons);
        if (Index<MAXBUTTONS)
        {
            SortToolTips(Index);
            if (ID!=0)
            {
                m_szTTips[m_CurrentBar][Index]=
                        (LPTSTR)LocalAlloc(LMEM_ZEROINIT,
                    sizeof(TCHAR)*(lstrlen(ToolTipText)
                    +2));
                wsprintf(m_szTTips[m_CurrentBar][Index],
                        ToolTipText);
                if (Index>m_iMaxButtons[m_CurrentBar])
                        m_iMaxButtons[m_CurrentBar]=Index;
            }
```

```
                    CommandBar_AddToolTips(m_hwndCB,
                              m_iMaxButtons[m_CurrentBar]+1,
                              m_szTTips[m_CurrentBar]);
                }
        }
#else          // Code for Desktop here
#endif
        return S_OK;
}
```

As you saw in the previous section, you must create a band before you can fill the bars with controls. Making use of the methods from your "PCDMCommander" class, you can create the band inside the "CreateBar" method when it is called the first time. Every subsequent call to "CreateBar" will add another bar to the band. After every "CreateBar" call, you can create as many items as you want for this bar until the next "CreateBar". You will also need to add one parameter to this function in order to add styles to the bars.

To change the parameter of an ActiveX method, you have to change it at three locations:

- The class definition file ("PCDMCommander.h")
- The IDL file ("PCDMUI.IDL")
- The implementation file ("PCDMCommander.cpp")

10. At all three locations you have to add "int Styles" to the list of parameters for the "CreateBar" method.

 Do not change the files "PCDMUI.H" and "PCDMUI_p.c.". The eMbedded Visual C++ compiler updates them as soon as you recompile the project.

11. Locate the "CreateBar" implementation and change the code to:

```
STDMETHODIMP CPCDMCommander::CreateBar(int ID,int Styles)
{
        AFX_MANAGE_STATE(AfxGetStaticModuleState())

#ifdef UNDER_CE
        // New Command-Band Addons
        if (m_CmdBarType==CMDBAR)
        {
```

```
    // Original Code from Command-Bar version
    if (m_IDBAR==0)
    {
m_hwndCB = CommandBar_Create(_Module.m_hInst, m_hWnd,
ID);
    CommandBar_AddBitmap(m_hwndCB, _Module.m_hInst,
                        IDR_TOOLBAR, 17, 16, 16);
    m_IDBAR=ID;
    m_bIsFresh=FALSE;
    }
}
else
{
        if (m_BandCreated==FALSE)
        {
            HBITMAP hBmp;
            int i;

            // Create an Image List for the icons of
            // the Bars when they get minimized
            m_hImLst=ImageList_Create(16,16,ILC_COLOR,17,0);
            hBmp=LoadBitmap(_Module.m_hInst,
                        MAKEINTRESOURCE(IDR_TOOLBAR));
            ImageList_Add(m_hImLst,hBmp,NULL);
            DeleteObject(hBmp);
            m_hwndCBand=CommandBands_Create(_Module.m_hInst,
                    m_hWnd,4711,
                    RBS_SMARTLABELS|RBS_VARHEIGHT|RBS_AUTOSIZE,
                    m_hImLst);
            if (m_hwndCBand==NULL)
                    return S_FALSE;
            m_BandCreated=TRUE;

            // Initialize the REBARBANDINFO structure
            memset(m_trbi,0,sizeof(REBARINFO)*MAXBANDS);
        for (i = 0; i < MAXBANDS; i++)
        {
            m_trbi[i].cbSize = sizeof (REBARBANDINFO);
            m_trbi[i].fMask = RBBIM_SIZE;
              m_trbi[i].cx = 100;
        }
```

```
                }
                else
                {
                     m_CurrentBar++;
                }

                // Set the attributes of the new Bar
                m_trbi[m_CurrentBar].fMask |=
                                  RBBIM_ID | RBBIM_STYLE | RBBIM_ID;
                m_trbi[m_CurrentBar].wID = ID;
                if (Styles==0)    // Set NoGripper and Fixed
                                  // BMP as default values
                     Styles=RBBS_NOGRIPPER + RBBS_FIXEDBMP;
                m_trbi[m_CurrentBar].fStyle = Styles;
                CommandBands_AddBands (m_hwndCBand, _Module.m_hInst, 1,
                                  &m_trbi[m_CurrentBar]);
                UINT idx=SendMessage(m_hwndCBand,RB_IDTOINDEX,
                                  (WPARAM)(UINT)ID,0);
                m_hwndCB = CommandBands_GetCommandBar (m_hwndCBand, idx);
                 CommandBar_AddBitmap(m_hwndCB, _Module.m_hInst,
                                  IDR_TOOLBAR, 17, 16, 16);
        }

#else        // Code for Desktop here
#endif

        return S_OK;
}
```

The only other method you will need to change is "AddAddornments". As you know from the last section, the adornments can no longer be added to a bar, but must be assigned to the band itself.

12.   Locate the "AddAdornments" method and change the code to:

```
STDMETHODIMP CPCDMCommander::SetAdornments(int Flags)
{
        AFX_MANAGE_STATE(AfxGetStaticModuleState())

#ifdef UNDER_CE
        if (m_CmdBarType==CMDBAR)
        {
```

```
            if (m_hwndCB!=NULL)
                    CommandBar_AddAdornments(m_hwndCB, Flags,0);
    }
    else
    {
            if (m_hwndCBand!=NULL)
                    CommandBands_AddAdornments(m_hwndCBand,
                                            _Module.m_hInst,Flags,NULL);
    }
#else // Code for Desktop here
#endif
      return S_OK;
}
```

Compile the new control now and let it download and register on your device. Then load the "PCDMUI_win32" project and fully compile it. This finalizes the command class and its interface. Now you are ready to test the new class in Visual Basic.

Any change you want to make to the command-class interface definition should lead to a new interface like "IPCDMCommander2". But if you are only changing the implementation of the interface, you can stick with "IPCDMCommander".

The final source code of this section can be found on the companion CD under "\Sources\ThreadExample\PCDMUI\Step 3".

7.2.3 Testing the New PCDMCommander Class in eMbedded Visual Basic

Next, you will make use of "PCDMUI2", the eVB program that you wrote for the last section.

1. To run the project, simply load the project and add a "0" at the end of the parameters for the "PCDMCommander1.CreateBar" call.

The program should run with no visible change in the user interface.

2. Replace the line "PCDMCommander1.CreateBar" with the following two lines:

```
PCDMCommander1.SetCmdBarType 1
PCDMCommander1.CreateBar 100,0
```

This will set the command-bar type to use the Command-Band interface. Run the application again, and you should still see no difference.

The next step is to move the buttons and the combo box to a second bar.

3. Insert the following line before the first "InsertButton" call:

```
PCDMCommander1.CreateBar 101, RBBS_FIXEDBMP
```

4. You should also start the indexes of the bitmaps at zero, and you can remove the first separator from the button list.

5. The RBBS_ values are defined in the following code paragraph that you must insert into the global area of the Visual Basic code:

```
Const RBBS_BREAK = 1
Const RBBS_FIXEDSIZE = 2
Const RBBS_CHILDEDGE = 4
Const RBBS_HIDDEN = 8
Const RBBS_NOVERT = 16
Const RBBS_FIXEDBMP = 32
Const RBBS_VARIABLEHEIGHT = 64
Const RBBS_GRIPPERALWAYS = 128
Const RBBS_NOGRIPPER = 256
```

Run the application again and check your Windows CE device.

The last test that you need to make involves putting the combo box on a third bar.

6. Insert the following line before the "InsertComboBox" call and set the index of the combo box to zero:

```
PCDMCommander1.CreateBar 102, RBBS_FIXEDBMP + RBBS_BREAK
PCDMCommander1.InsertComboBox 150, 0, 1008
```

When you run the application, you should see the screen in Figure 7.3.

   The final source code of this section can be found on the companion CD under "\Sources\Chapter 7\7.4".

Figure 7.3 A Command-Band eVB test application

7.2.4 Using the PCDMCommander Class in the PCDM Application

Now you need to adjust your PCDM application to use the new "PCDMCommander" class. The tricky part here is not the calling of the methods, but rather the changing of the "PCDMCommander" class that the wizard created earlier. Since you only added one method and changed another, it is easier to change the class directly than to have the class wizard recreate the class.

1. Load the PCDM application project from the preceding section and open the "PCDMCommander.cpp" source file.

2. Add the following code at the end of the file:

```
void CPCDMCommander::SetCmdBarType(long Type)
{
```

```
        static BYTE parms[] = VTS_I4;
        InvokeHelper(0x8, DISPATCH_METHOD, VT_EMPTY, NULL,
                        parms, Type);
}
```

This is the wrapper function for the method "SetCmdBarType" that you created earlier.

 The dispatch ID of the "InvokeHelper" function could be different!
Check for the correct number in the IDL file of the "IPCDMCommander"
interface of your PCDMUI control.

3.   Locate the "CreateBar" wrapper function and add the new parameter "long
Styles" to it. The following text shown in bold highlights the parts you should
add:

```
void CPCDMCommander::CreateBar(long ID,long Styles)
{
        static BYTE parms[] = VTS_I4 VTS_I4;
        InvokeHelper(0x4, DISPATCH_METHOD, VT_EMPTY, NULL,
                        parms, ID, Styles);
}
```

Check the dispatch ID of this "InvokeHelper" function as well.

4.   Open the "PCDMCommander.h" include file and change the "CreateBar"
declaration to

```
void CreateBar(long ID, long Styles);
```

5.   Then add the following declaration for the "CreateBar" method:

```
void SetCmdBarType(long type);
```

Now you can change the "OnInitialUpdate" method in the "CPCDMView" class.

6.   Set the command-bar type to "1" and change the "CreateBar" method parameter:

```
m_cmdBar.SetCmdBarType(1);
m_cmdBar.CreateBar(1,0);
```

7.   Insert the following two lines before the buttons are inserted:

```
m_cmdBar.CreateBar(101,RBBS_FIXEDBMP);
m_cmdBar.InsertButton(SBM_SEP,TBSTATE_ENABLED,      0,0, TEXT(""));
```

8. Remove the first separator button, change the index of the buttons to start from zero, and do not forget to decrease the combo box's index by two.

Now you can compile, download, and start the new PCDM application.

Which do you prefer, a command bar or two command bars in a Command-Band? Well, especially for palm-size PCs the new bars are quite handy because if the menu bar is minimized, the toolbar can hold more buttons.

 The final source code of this section can be found on the companion CD under "\Sources\ThreadExample\PCDM CE\Step 3".

7.2.5 Summary

- The Command-Band is a container control that hosts command bars.
- Each of those command bars can be filled using the standard command-bar methods.
- The "AddAdornnent" method creates a bar that gets inserted into the Command-Band at the proper location.
- Separating the menu bar from the toolbar on two different command bars solves the redraw problem.
- The Command-Band requires Windows CE 2.0 or higher and the "Cool" classes initiated in the common control library.
- To keep user settings of the Command-Band, use the function "CommandBands_GetRestoreInformation" and save its values to the registry in the "HKLM_CURRENT_USER" section.

7.3 Special Palm-size PC Considerations

System DLL:	Aygshell.dll
Include file:	aygshell.h
Library file:	aygshell.lib
Help file:	CEGUIDE.CHM (MSDN 10/98 and later)
Available since:	Windows CE 2.01
API prefix/suffix:	SH . . .
InitCommonControlEx flag:	—
MFC class:	—

The latest generation of Pocket PCs has a new user interface unlike the interfaces of earlier devices. It moves the "Task" bar to the top of the screen and places all application menus at the bottom. Since the screen estate of the palm-size PC is quite limited, you should take care not to overload the toolbar or the menu bar.

To create this menu bar, Microsoft invented a new API call. "SHCreateMenuBar" takes a pointer to a SHMENUBAR structure that contains several flags and, most important, a resource identifier to a new type of resource. You can edit these new bars in the resource editor of eMbedded Visual C++.

If the call succeeds, the "hWND" member of the SHMENUBAR structure will contain a command-bar windows handle that can be used for all subsequent calls explained in the previous chapter, with the exception of "SetAdornment" and "InsertComboBox". The new menu bar does not support the "X" button or any other command-bar adornment; it also does not support a combo box inside.

7.3.1 Small Example Showing the Application Menu Bar

The following example shows everything you need to do to create an SDK-based application that runs on a palm-size PC 2.0 or any other older device.

1. Launch the eMbedded Visual C++ environment and create a new "WCE Application" named "MenuBarApp".

2. In the upcoming application wizard, select "Simple Hello World application".

Locate the "InitInstance" function in the "MenuBarApp.cpp" and add the following code to it:

```
BOOL InitInstance(HINSTANCE hInstance, int nCmdShow)
{
    HWND    hWnd;
    TCHAR   szTitle[MAX_LOADSTRING];
    TCHAR   szWindowClass[MAX_LOADSTRING];
    hInst = hInstance;
    LoadString(hInstance, IDC_MENUBARAPP, szWindowClass,
            MAX_LOADSTRING);
    MyRegisterClass(hInstance, szWindowClass);

    hAygDll = LoadLibrary(TEXT("aygshell.dll"));
    if (hAygDll)
    {
        g_hSHCreateMenuBar =(SHCREATEMENUBARPROC)
            GetProcAddress(hAygDll, TEXT("SHCreateMenuBar"));
        if (g_hSHCreateMenuBar) isRapier=TRUE;
```

```
    }

    LoadString(hInstance, IDS_APP_TITLE, szTitle, MAX_LOADSTRING);
    hWnd = CreateWindow(szWindowClass, szTitle, WS_VISIBLE,
                        0, 0, CW_USEDEFAULT, CW_USEDEFAULT, NULL,
                        NULL, hInstance, NULL);

    if (!hWnd)
    {
        return FALSE;
    }

    ShowWindow(hWnd, nCmdShow);
    UpdateWindow(hWnd);
    if (isRapier)
        if (hwndCB)
            CommandBar_Show(hwndCB, TRUE);
    return TRUE;
}
```

You will use "LoadLibrary" and "GetProcAddress" to get to the "SHCreateMenuBar" function. If you are running on an H/PC Professional or older palm-size PC, the "GetProcAddress" call will fail, so you cannot use it. The results will be stored in some global variables.

3.   Add the following lines before the "InitInstance" function:

```
#include <aygshell.h>
typedef      BOOL (*SHCREATEMENUBARPROC)(SHMENUBARINFO *pmbi);
SHCREATEMENUBARPROC          g_hSHCreateMenuBar = NULL;
HINSTANCE   hAygDll;
BOOL  isRapier=FALSE;
```

At this point, if you tried to compile the application for any device other than a palm-size PC, you would get an error message that "aygshell.h" could not be found. Since you are not using any function from "aygshell.lib", you can just copy "aygshell.h" from the palm-size PC 2.0 SDK to the other platform SDKs. You find the include file in the "include" directory.

 You have to put the new "aygshell.h" into the old palm-size PC SDKs as well because the definition of the SHMENUBARINFO structure is not found in the older versions.

The last modification in the code that you need to make is in the "WM_CREATE" branch of "WndProc". Change the code in the "WM_CREATE" branch to the following code:

```
case WM_CREATE:
    if (isRapier)
    {
        SHMENUBARINFO mbi;
        memset(&mbi, 0, sizeof(SHMENUBARINFO));
        mbi.cbSize      = sizeof(SHMENUBARINFO);
        mbi.hwndParent  = hWnd;
        mbi.nToolBarId  = IDR_MAIN_MENU;
        mbi.hInstRes    = hInst;
        mbi.nBmpId      = 0;
        mbi.cBmpImages  = 0;

        (*g_hSHCreateMenuBar)(&mbi);
        hwndCB = mbi.hwndMB;
    }
    else
    {
        hwndCB = CommandBar_Create(hInst, hWnd, 1);
        CommandBar_InsertMenubar(hwndCB, hInst, IDM_MENU, 0);
        CommandBar_AddAdornments(hwndCB, 0, 0);
    }
break;
```

All the magic for "SHCreateMenuBar" is going on in the SHMENUBARINFO structure. The most important entry is "mToolBarId", which points to a new resource in the eMbedded Visual C++ resource editor.

4. To create the new resource, open the resource editor and select "Insert . . ." on the main root.
5. In the upcoming dialog box, select "Menubar" and click "OK".

 This new resource type will be visible only if you have the "palm-size PC 3.00" platform selected. If you switch back to another platform, "MenuBar" will be changed to "Menu".

I recommend creating a second menu resource for the palm-size PC 2.0 in the PsPC2's resource editor.

6. Name the menu "File" and add one submenu item named "Exit" with the ID "IDM_FILE_EXIT"

Here comes a "gotcha": If you switch back to a different platform that does not support the new "MenuBar" resource, it will be changed to "Menu". As long as you do not touch the resource, it will remain intact. But as soon as you open it again, it will be reformatted as a regular menu.

If you try to compile it for H/PC Professional, you will get error messages informing you that several defines cannot be found.

7. To work around this, you can insert the following lines in the "Compile-time directives" field of the "Resource Includes" settings:

```
#include <commctrl.h>
#define I_IMAGENONE  (-2)
```

The "Resource Includes" can only be accessed in "Palm-size PC 2.0" mode. If you switch to H/PC before you add them, you cannot open the resources.

You will get some redefinition warnings, but you can ignore them.

Now compile and launch the program on your palm-size PC 2.0 device and on an H/PC Professional. You should see the two different menus on the corresponding devices.

 The final source code of this section can be found on the companion CD under "\Sources\Chapter 7\7.5".

7.3.2 Updating Your PCDMCommander Class

To update your "PCDMCommander" class, you will need to change the "CreateBar", "InsertMenu", and "InsertButton" methods of the class. Other changes that you will make affect functions that are not necessary or supported on the palm-size PC 2.0, such as adornments.

1. Load the latest version of the PCDMUI project and open the "CPCDMCommander.cpp" file.

2. Here is the new code for this method:

```
STDMETHODIMP CPCDMCommander::CreateBar(int ID)
{
      AFX_MANAGE_STATE(AfxGetStaticModuleState())

#ifdef UNDER_CE
      if (LOWORD(m_CePlatform)==CEP_PALMPCV3)
      {
            if (m_hwndCB!=NULL) return S_OK;
typedef BOOL (*SHCREATEMENUBARPROC)(SHMENUBARINFO *pvParam);
SHCREATEMENUBARPROC       g_hSHCreateMenuBar=NULL;
SHMENUBARINFO             mbi;
HINSTANCE                 hAygDll;

            hAygDll = LoadLibrary(TEXT("aygshell.dll"));
            if (hAygDll)
            {
                  g_hSHCreateMenuBar =(SHCREATEMENUBARPROC)
                  GetProcAddress(hAygDll, TEXT("SHCreateMenuBar"));
                  memset(&mbi, 0, sizeof(SHMENUBARINFO));
                  mbi.cbSize       = sizeof(SHMENUBARINFO);
                  mbi.hwndParent = m_hWnd;
                  mbi.dwFlags      = 0;
                  mbi.nToolBarId = IDR_MAIN_MENU;
                  mbi.hInstRes     = _Module.m_hInst;
                  mbi.nBmpId       = IDR_TOOLBAR;
                  mbi.cBmpImages = 17;

                  (*g_hSHCreateMenuBar)(&mbi);
                  m_hwndCB=mbi.hwndMB;
            }
            else
            {   return S_FALSE;   }

            return S_OK;
      }
///////// OLD code here.. ./////////
}
```

3. Insert the following two new includes in "stdafx.h":

```
#ifdef UNDER_CE
#include <aygshell.h>
#endif
#include "<path2Cehelpers.h>\cehelpers.h"
```

4. Add "CeHelpers.cpp" to your project files.

As you fill the SHMENUBARINFO structure, you will refer to an "IDR_MAIN_MENU" resource. This resource has to be created in the resource file. Unfortunately, it is not possible to create an empty menu bar and then dynamically add menus to it. This forces you to make a major decision: How many menus do you want in your menu bar?

For each menu, you have to create a resource in your ".RC" file. For your PCDMUI control, you will only need to support one menu.

5. Add the following lines to the "PCDM.RC" file:

```
IDR_MAIN_MENU MENU DISCARDABLE
BEGIN
    POPUP ""
    BEGIN
        MENUITEM "Exit",                          12345
    END
END

IDR_MAIN_MENU RCDATA DISCARDABLE
BEGIN
    IDR_MAIN_MENU, 1,
    I_IMAGENONE, ID_FILE, TBSTATE_ENABLED,
    TBSTYLE_DROPDOWN | TBSTYLE_AUTOSIZE, IDS_CAP_FILE, 0, 0,
END

STRINGTABLE DISCARDABLE
BEGIN
    IDS_CAP_FILE            "File"
END
```

The menu item with "Exit" is necessary because the resource editor does not support empty menus. You will delete that entry in your "InsertMenu" method. You could also delete it in the "CreateBar" method in case the "InsertMenu" method is never called. In that case, the "Exit" menu remains on your menu bar, which should not be a problem.

In the previous section of the book, you learned that the H/PC has difficulty in recognizing some defines in the resource.

6. Add the following lines to the "Compile-time directives" list of the "Resource Includes" dialog box:

```
#include <commctrl.h>
#define I_IMAGENONE  (-2)
```

 If you open the PCDMUI resources with eMbedded Visual C++ and enter "IDR_MENU_BAR" while you are in the H/PC mode, you will destroy the menu bar.

The next method you need to change is "InsertMenu".

7. Insert the following lines directly under the "AFX_MANAGE_STATE" macro:

```
STDMETHODIMP CPCDMCommander::InsertMenu(BSTR MenuName, int Index)
{
    AFX_MANAGE_STATE(AfxGetStaticModuleState())

    if (LOWORD(m_CePlatform)==CEP_PALMPCV3)
    {
        TBBUTTONINFO tbbi;
        tbbi.cbSize = sizeof(tbbi);
        tbbi.dwMask = TBIF_LPARAM;
        SendMessage(m_hwndCB,
                        TB_GETBUTTONINFO,
                        ID_FILE,
                        (LPARAM)&tbbi);

        m_MyPopup[Index]= (HMENU)tbbi.lParam;
        DeleteMenu(m_MyPopup[Index],12345,MF_BYCOMMAND);
        m_iMaxButtons[m_CurrentBar]=1;
        return S_OK;
    }
    // OLD CODE continues here
}
```

The next method that you need to change is "InsertButton". Here you will have to do quite a bit of work because Microsoft changed the behavior of the ToolTips on the menu bar. Both H/PCs and palm-size PCs introduced since Version 2.0 treat a separator as a button and theoretically could have a ToolTip. But on the palm-size PC 2.0, the separator is not considered a button. Hence, you will have to change the way in which you assign ToolTips to your buttons.

8.   Here is the new code for the "InsertButton" method:

```
STDMETHODIMP CPCDMCommander::InsertButton(int StockNo, int state,
                        int Index, int ID, BSTR ToolTipText)
{
      AFX_MANAGE_STATE(AfxGetStaticModuleState())

      TBBUTTON lpButtons;
      lpButtons.idCommand=ID;
      lpButtons.fsState=state;
      if (ID==0) // If ID is 0 a Separation Space is created
      {
            lpButtons.iBitmap=0;
            lpButtons.fsStyle=TBSTYLE_SEP;
      }
      else
      {
            lpButtons.iBitmap=StockNo;
            lpButtons.fsStyle=TBSTYLE_BUTTON;
      }
      lpButtons.iString=0;

#ifdef UNDER_CE
      if (m_hwndCB!=NULL)
      {
            CommandBar_InsertButton(m_hwndCB,Index,
                              (LPTBBUTTON)&lpButtons);
            if (Index<MAXBUTTONS)
            {
                  if (LOWORD(m_CePlatform)==CEP_PALMPCV3)
                  {
                        if (ID!=0)
                        {
                        m_szTTips[m_CurrentBar]
```

```
                              [m_iMaxButtons[m_CurrentBar]]=
                              (LPTSTR)LocalAlloc(LMEM_ZEROINIT,
                              sizeof(TCHAR)*(lstrlen(ToolTipText)+2));

                              wsprintf(m_szTTips[m_CurrentBar]
                                 [m_iMaxButtons[m_CurrentBar]],
                                 ToolTipText);
                              m_iMaxButtons[m_CurrentBar]++;
                        }
                  }
                  else
                  {
                        SortToolTips(Index);
                        if (ID!=0)
                        {
                           m_szTTips[m_CurrentBar][Index]=
                              (LPTSTR)LocalAlloc(LMEM_ZEROINIT,
                              sizeof(TCHAR)*(lstrlen(ToolTipText)+2));

                           wsprintf(m_szTTips[m_CurrentBar][Index]
                              ,ToolTipText);
                              if (Index>m_iMaxButtons[m_CurrentBar])
                                    m_iMaxButtons[m_CurrentBar]=Index;
                        }
                  }
                  CommandBar_AddToolTips(m_hwndCB,
                              m_iMaxButtons[m_CurrentBar]+1,
                              m_szTTips[m_CurrentBar]);
            }
      }
#else // Code for Desktop here
#endif

      return S_OK;
}
```

9. Add the following line to the "InsertComboBox", "AddStringToComboBox", and "SetAdornments" methods directly under the "AFX_MANAGE_STATE" macro:

```
if (LOWORD(m_CePlatform)==CEP_PALMPCV3) return S_OK;
```

This line ensures that those methods are not processed on the palm-size PC 2.0.

10. The "m_CePlatform" member variable has to be declared in your private section of the "PCDMCommander" class:

```
DWORD        m_CePlatform;
```

11. In the "PCDMCommander" constructor, add the following line to initialize the variable:

```
m_CePlatform=GetCePlatform();
```

Now compile and have the new control downloaded to your device. Do not forget to load the desktop version of your project, include "CeHelper.cpp" in the project files, and compile the application. You will need it in the following section to allow Visual Basic to find the correct control.

 The final source code of this section can be found on the companion CD under "\Sources\ThreadExample\PCDMUI\Step 4".

7.3.3 Testing the New Class in eMbedded Visual Basic for Palm-size PC 2.0

1. Start eMbedded Visual Basic and create a new PsPC 2.0 project. Before you can use your control, you will need to install it for design mode in the Control Manager.

2. Open the "Palm-size PC 3.00" branch (I wished Micrsoft would get its version chaos in order) and select the "Desktop Design Controls" branch.

3. In the right pane, select "Add new control . . ." from the object menu and choose the latest version of "PCDMUI.DLL".

After a short loading time, the new "PCDMCommander Class" should be visible in the list. You can close the Control Manager again. Back in eMbedded Visual Basic, the new "PCDMUI 1.0 Type Library" was added to the components in your toolbox.

4. Insert the new control into "Form1" and then double-click on "Form1" itself.

5.   Add the following code to its implementation:

```
Private Sub Form_Load()
PCDMCommander1.SetCmdBarType 1
PCDMCommander1.CreateBar 100, 0
PCDMCommander1.InsertMenu "File", 0
PCDMCommander1.InsertMenuItem "New", 0, 0, 1001
PCDMCommander1.InsertMenuItem "", 0, 1, 0
PCDMCommander1.InsertMenuItem "Load", 0, 2, 1002
PCDMCommander1.InsertMenuItem "Save", 0, 3, 1003
PCDMCommander1.InsertMenuItem "Exit", 0, 4, IDCLOSE
PCDMCommander1.InsertMenu "Edit", 1
PCDMCommander1.InsertMenuItem "Undo", 1, 0, 1004
PCDMCommander1.InsertMenuItem "Copy", 1, 1, 1005
PCDMCommander1.InsertMenuItem "Paste", 1, 2, 1006
PCDMCommander1.CreateBar 101, RBBS_FIXEDBMP
'PCDMCommander1.InsertButton SBM_SEP, TBSTATE_ENABLED, 0, 0, ""
PCDMCommander1.InsertButton SBM_NEW, TBSTATE_ENABLED, 1, 1001, "New
File"
PCDMCommander1.InsertButton SBM_SEP, TBSTATE_ENABLED, 2, 0, ""
PCDMCommander1.InsertButton SBM_OPEN, TBSTATE_ENABLED, 3, 1002,
"Opens a file"
PCDMCommander1.InsertButton SBM_SAVE, TBSTATE_ENABLED, 4, 1003,
"Saves a file"
PCDMCommander1.CreateBar 102, RBBS_FIXEDBMP + RBBS_BREAK
PCDMCommander1.InsertComboBox 150, 0, 1008
PCDMCommander1.AddStringToComboBox 1008, "<CLR>"
PCDMCommander1.AddStringToComboBox 1008, "First Choice"
PCDMCommander1.AddStringToComboBox 1008, "Second Choice"
PCDMCommander1.SetAdornments 0
End Sub
```

This code is almost exactly the same as that given in Section 7.2.3, with the exception of a few minor changes shown in bold. The palm-size PC 2.0 no longer supports cascading menus; therefore the second menu, "Edit", was attached to the top of the file menu.

6.   Double-click the "PCDMCommadbar1" control and add the same code to its event handler as you did in Section 7.2.3:

```
Private Sub PCDMCommander1_CmdBarAction(ByVal ID As Long, ByVal text
As String)
```

```
     If ID = IDCLOSE Then
         App.End
     Else
         MsgBox "The ID " & ID & " fired the string <" & text & ">"
     End If
End Sub
```

Before you can start the new program and see the menu bar in action, make sure that you copy the constants from Section 7.2.3 into this project.

7.3.4   Verifying Your PCDM Application

Verifying your PCDM application is simple. Just load the latest version of the PCDM CE project (from Section 7.2.4), compile it for palm-size PC 3.0, and run it. If everything works correctly, you should see the menu bar where it belongs. Only the menu itself will be in the wrong position.

To correct this problem, you will need to find out whether you are running on a palm-size PC 2.0. If so, do not call the "InsertButton" for the first separator.

1.   Add the "cehelpers.cpp" file to the PCDM project.

2.   Open "PCDM.cpp" and add the following code to the "CPCDMApp()" constructor method:

```
CPCDMApp::CPCDMApp(LPCTSTR lpszHelpName)
     : CWinApp(lpszHelpName)
{
     m_CePlatform=GetCePlatform();
}
```

3.   Declare the "m_cePlatform" variable in the public section of the "CPCDMApp" class.

```
class CPCDMApp : public CWinApp
{
public:
     CPCDMApp(LPCTSTR lpszHelpName);

// <BOOK_ADDON STEP4 Chapter 7.3.4>
     DWORD m_CePlatform;
// </BOOK_ADDON STEP4 Chapter 7.3.4>

// Overrides
     // ClassWizard generated virtual function overrides
```

```
//{{AFX_VIRTUAL(CPCDMApp)
public:
virtual BOOL InitInstance();
//}}AFX_VIRTUAL
```

```
// Implementation
```

```
    //{{AFX_MSG(CPCDMApp)
    afx_msg void OnAppAbout();
    //}}AFX_MSG
    DECLARE_MESSAGE_MAP()
};
```

4. Add the following line before the first "InsertButton" call in the "OnInitialUpdate" method of "PCDMView.cpp":

```
if (LOWORD((((CPCDMApp *)AfxGetApp())->m_CePlatform)!=CEP_PALMPCV3)
```

The insert button will only be executed if you are not running on a palm-size PC 2.0. Run the new version of the PCDM application and check whether the menu works correctly on all devices.

7.4   The List View Control

System DLL:	COMMCTRL.DLL
Include file:	Commctrl.h
Library file:	Commctrl.lib
Help file:	CEGUIDE.CHM (MSDN 10/98 and later)
Available since:	Windows CE 1.0 (Ex Version in 2.0)
API prefix/suffix:	CommandBar_<action>
InitCommonControlEx flag:	ICC_LISTVIEW_CLASSES
MFC class:	CListCtrl

The description of the list view control shows you that Windows CE common controls are very similar to those on the desktop. After going through the features of the list view, you will easily be able to use the other common controls supported by Windows CE. You will also need the list view for your PCDM application.

7.4.1 Including the List View Control in an Application

To illustrate the use of a list view control, you will include a list view in a typical "Hello World" application.

1. Start eMbedded Visual C++ and create a new project called "ListViewTest" using the "WCE Application Wizard".

2. Choose "A typical 'Hello-World' application" in the wizard option page.

You are going to create the "Ex" version of the list view control. Currently, this is not possible using MFC; that's why you will use the standard APIs with the list view control.

3. To activate the "Ex" version of the list view control, add the following code to the "WinMain" function:

```
int WINAPI WinMain(      HINSTANCE hInstance,
                         HINSTANCE hPrevInstance,
                         LPTSTR    lpCmdLine,
                         int       nCmdShow)
{
    MSG msg;
    HACCEL hAccelTable;

    INITCOMMONCONTROLSEX icex;
    icex.dwSize = sizeof (INITCOMMONCONTROLSEX);
    icex.dwICC = ICC_LISTVIEW_CLASSES;
    InitCommonControlsEx (&icex);

    // Perform application initialization:
    if (!InitInstance (hInstance, nCmdShow))
    {
        return FALSE;
    }

    hAccelTable = LoadAccelerators(hInstance,
                            (LPCTSTR)IDC_LISTVIEWTEST);

    // Main message loop:
    while (GetMessage(&msg, NULL, 0, 0))
    {
        if (!TranslateAccelerator(msg.hwnd, hAccelTable, &msg))
```

```
            {
                TranslateMessage(&msg);
                DispatchMessage(&msg);
            }
        }

        return msg.wParam;
}
```

The wizard generates standard "WM_CREATE" and "WM_PAINT" paths in the Windows procedure. You will keep the command bar the wizard created, but will need to get rid of the "WM_PAINT" code since you are using the client area of the application for your list view.

4.   Delete the code in the "WM_PAINT" branch of the Windows procedure.

5.   Add the following code to the "WM_CREATE" branch directly under the creation of the command bar and its function calls:

```
case WM_CREATE:
    HWND hwndLVC;
    LPCREATESTRUCT lpCreate=(LPCREATESTRUCT)lParam;
    int cmdBarHeight=CommandBar_Height(hwndCB);
    hwndLVC = CreateWindowEx (0, WC_LISTVIEW, TEXT ("MyList"),
                        LVS_REPORT|LVS_SINGLESEL|WS_VISIBLE |
                        WS_CHILD | WS_BORDER | WS_VSCROLL,
                        0,cmdBarHeight , lpCreate->cx,
                        lpCreate->cy-cmdBarHeight,
                        hWnd, (HMENU)42, hInst, NULL);
            if (hwndLVC)
            {
                // Add two Columns
                LVCOLUMN lvCol;
                lvCol.mask= LVCF_TEXT | LVCF_WIDTH |
                        LVCF_FMT | LVCF_SUBITEM;
                lvCol.pszText=TEXT("CD Name");
                lvCol.cx= lpCreate->cx/2-2;
                lvCol.fmt= LVCFMT_LEFT;
                lvCol.iSubItem=0;
                SendMessage(hwndLVC, LVM_INSERTCOLUMN,
                        0, (LPARAM)&lvCol);
                lvCol.mask= LVCF_TEXT | LVCF_WIDTH |
```

```
                             LVCF_FMT | LVCF_SUBITEM;
                 lvCol.pszText=TEXT("Author");
                 lvCol.cx= lpCreate->cx/2-2;
                 lvCol.fmt= LVCFMT_LEFT;
                 lvCol.iSubItem=1;
                 SendMessage(hwndLVC, LVM_INSERTCOLUMN,
                             1, (LPARAM)&lvCol);
            ListView_SetExtendedListViewStyle(hwndLVC,
   LVS_EX_FULLROWSELECT|LVS_EX_GRIDLINES | LVS_EX_FULLROWSELECT);
                 }
            }
       break;
```

Well, you get the point. I will stop here because everything else works just as it does on the desktop.

What Windows CE's List View Control Does Not Support

None of the flags, such as "LVS_EX_FLATSB", that Internet Explorer 4.0 added to the list view control are supported on Windows CE. In addition, you cannot set the "LVS_EX_ONECLICKACTIVATE" or "LVS_EX_TWOCLICKACTIVATE" flag. The default behavior is double-clicking to activate. This is interesting, if you consider a tapping device as being double-tap-unfriendly by nature.

 The final source code of this section can be found on the companion CD under "\Sources\Chapter 7\7.7".

7.4.2   Adding the List View Control to PCDMUI.DLL

The PCDM application requires a list view in two of its forms. Therefore, you will need to include the list view control in the PCDMUI ActiveX control. So as not to overload your control, you will include only a basic set of methods that correspond to the needs of your application.

Here is what you will implement:

- A control that will act like a grid control rather than like a list view.
- An "AddColumn" method to add new columns to the list view. You will not distinguish between sub-items and items. This will make it easier for the developer to use the control.
- An "AddItem" method that specifies content, row number, and column number.

- A "DeleteRow" method that allows deleting an item from the list.
- A "GetItem" method to retrieve the content of a specified row and column.
- A "Reset" method that removes all items from the list.
- A "SendCommand" method that will give you the ultimate freedom of being able to send any ListView message to your control in case you have special needs.
- A "RowSelected" event that gets fired when a user clicks on one of the items.

As always, you can find the source of the control on the companion CD. Please feel free to enhance "PCDMUI.DLL" as you like.

 Remember: You must create a new interface!

1. Load the most recent version of the PCDMUI project for Windows CE and add a new ATL "Full Control" named "PCDMList". Do not forget to check the "Supports Connection Points" checkbox in the "Attributes" tab.

2. In the constructor, add the following code:

```
CPCDMList::CPCDMList()
{
    INITCOMMONCONTROLSEX icex;
    icex.dwSize = sizeof (INITCOMMONCONTROLSEX);
    icex.dwICC = ICC_LISTVIEW_CLASSES;
    InitCommonControlsEx (&icex);

    m_hwndLVC=NULL;
    m_iLVCID=0;
    m_iColCnt=0;
}
```

You will need to initialize the "Common-Control-Ex" library again, this time for the extended flags of the list view control. Everything else is standard initialization code.

3. Declare the variables initialized in the constructor in a private section of the "PCDMList" class:

```
private:
    HWND       m_hwndLVC;
    int        m_iLVCID;
    int        m_iColCnt;
```

The list view will be created in the "OnCreate" message handler of the control.

4. Let the wizard create a new message handler for the "WM_CREATE" message and add the following code to the implementation of the "OnCreate" handler:

```
LRESULT CPCDMList::OnCreate(UINT uMsg, WPARAM wParam, LPARAM lParam,
BOOL& bHandled)
{
RECT rc;

        GetClientRect(&rc);
        TCHAR tStrWndName[100];
#ifdef UNDER_CE
        m_iLVCID=Random()%100;
#else
        m_iLVCID=rand()*100;
#endif
        wsprintf(tStrWndName,TEXT("PCDMList%d"),m_iLVCID);
        m_hwndLVC = CreateWindowEx(0, WC_LISTVIEW, tStrWndName,
                        LVS_REPORT|LVS_SINGLESEL|WS_VISIBLE |
                        WS_CHILD | WS_BORDER | WS_VSCROLL,
                        rc.left,rc.top, rc.right,
                        rc.bottom,        m_hWnd, (HMENU)
                                          m_iLVCID,
                        _Module.m_hInst, NULL);
        if (m_hwndLVC)
                ListView_SetExtendedListViewStyle(m_hwndLVC,
LVS_EX_FULLROWSELECT|LVS_EX_GRIDLINES | LVS_EX_FULLROWSELECT);
return S_OK;
}
```

You cannot take these steps in the constructor because the window of the ActiveX control will not yet exist. The window name is calculated with a random number generator so that you can have multiple list view controls in one dialog box and still be able to find the window. I know this approach is quick and dirty, but it's totally sufficient for your application. Please feel free to create a better way.

5. Delete the code from the "OnDraw" method and add the following code to it:

```
HRESULT CPCDMList::OnDraw(ATL_DRAWINFO& di)
{
     if (m_hwndLVC!=NULL)
     {
```

```
              RECT& rc = *(RECT*)di.prcBounds;
              ::MoveWindow(m_hwndLVC,rc.left,rc.top,
                          rc.right, rc.bottom, TRUE);
      }
      return S_OK;
}
```

The "OnDraw" method will fit your list view to the size of the parent ActiveX window.

6. Add the method "AddColumn" to the control using the parameters listed in Table 7.12.

7. Add the following code to its implementation:

```
STDMETHODIMP CPCDMList::AddColumn(long Size, BSTR Caption)
{
      AFX_MANAGE_STATE(AfxGetStaticModuleState())

      if (!m_hwndLVC)
            return S_OK;
      LVCOLUMN lvCol;
      lvCol.mask= LVCF_TEXT | LVCF_WIDTH | LVCF_FMT | LVCF_SUBITEM;
      lvCol.pszText=Caption;
      lvCol.cx=Size;
      lvCol.fmt= LVCFMT_LEFT;
      lvCol.iSubItem=m_iColCnt;
      SendMessage(m_hwndLVC, LVM_INSERTCOLUMN,
      m_iColCnt, (LPARAM)&lvCol);
      m_iColCnt++;

      return S_OK;
}
```

Table 7.12   AddColumn() Parameters

Type	Variable Name	Used for
Long	Size	Size of the new column in pixels
BSTR	Caption	Caption of the new column

There are no surprises here.

8. The next methods are "AddItem" and "GetItem". They have four parameters, as shown in Table 7.13.

The code of the AddItem method will handle the most of the LV_ITEM structure members internally.

9. Add the following code to the "AddItem" and "GetItem" implementations:

```
STDMETHODIMP CPCDMList::AddItem(long Row, long Column, long lParam,
                                BSTR Caption)
{
    AFX_MANAGE_STATE(AfxGetStaticModuleState())

    if (!m_hwndLVC)
        return S_OK;
    LVFINDINFO lvf;
    LVITEM pitem;
    memset((void *)&pitem,0,sizeof(LVITEM));
    int id;

    lvf.flags=LVFI_PARAM;
    lvf.lParam=lParam;
    lvf.vkDirection=VK_DOWN ;
    if ((id=ListView_FindItem(m_hwndLVC,-1,&lvf))<0)
    {
        pitem.mask=LVIF_TEXT | LVIF_PARAM;
        pitem.iItem=Row;
```

Table 7.13   AddItem() and GetItem() Parameters

Type	Variable Name	Used for
Long	Row	Row number (item) where the item will be inserted.
Long	Column	Column (sub-item) of the item to be inserted.
Long	Lparam	This item will be stored in the lParam field of a list item. It can hold a unique index of a row.
BSTR / ([out,retval] BSTR *for GetItem)	Caption	Text of the item.

```
                pitem.iSubItem=0;
                pitem.pszText=Caption;
                pitem.lParam=lParam;
                id=ListView_InsertItem(m_hwndLVC,&pitem);
        }
        else
        {
                pitem.mask=LVIF_TEXT;
                pitem.iItem=id;
                pitem.iSubItem=Column;
                pitem.pszText=Caption;
                id=ListView_SetItem(m_hwndLVC,&pitem);
        }
        return S_OK;
}


STDMETHODIMP CPCDMList::GetItem(long Row, long Column,
                                long lParam,BSTR *Caption)

{
TCHAR theContent[100]; // Be careful here!
                       // For simplicity its just hard coded

        AFX_MANAGE_STATE(AfxGetStaticModuleState())

        LVITEM        tLVI;
        memset((void *)&tLVI,0,sizeof(LVITEM));
        memset((void *)theContent,0,sizeof(TCHAR)*100);
        tLVI.iItem=Row;
        tLVI.iSubItem=Column;
        tLVI.mask=LVIF_TEXT;
        tLVI.pszText=theContent;
        tLVI.cchTextMax=100;
        ListView_GetItem(m_hwndLVC,&tLVI);
        *Caption=SysAllocString(theContent);

        return S_OK;
}
```

You will store the parameter "lParam" in the "LPARAM" of the "LV_ITEM" structure. This will allow you to keep track of an index that you do not want to see in the list view.

10. Add the other methods "Reset" and "DeleteRow". Here is the code for their implementation:

```
STDMETHODIMP CPCDMList::Reset()
{
        AFX_MANAGE_STATE(AfxGetStaticModuleState())

        if (!m_hwndLVC)
                return S_OK;
        ListView_DeleteAllItems(m_hwndLVC);

        return S_OK;
}


STDMETHODIMP CPCDMList::DeleteRow(long Row)
{
        AFX_MANAGE_STATE(AfxGetStaticModuleState())

        if (!m_hwndLVC)
                return S_OK;
        LVFINDINFO lvf;
        int id;

        lvf.flags=LVFI_PARAM;
        lvf.lParam=Row;
        lvf.vkDirection=VK_DOWN ;
        if ((id=ListView_FindItem(m_hwndLVC,-1,&lvf))>=0)
        {
                ListView_DeleteItem(m_hwndLVC,id);
                //SortRows: In case a row gets deleted
                // you have to resort the LPARAMs
        }

        return S_OK;
}
```

The parameter "Row" is not correctly named here since you are searching for the index in the "lParam" field of the "LVFINDINFO" structure.

The last feature that you will need to add is the event "RowSelected". Do you remember how to add an event to an interface? Well, in case you forgot, here it is again:

11. Locate the interface "_IPCDMLListEvents" in the class view and select "Add Method" from its context menu.

12. Add the method "RowSelected" and define the three parameters listed in Table 7.14.

13. Select the "CPCDMList" class and choose "Implement Connection Points" from its context menu.

14. In the dialog box, select the "_IPCDMListEvents" handler and click on "OK".

The wizard will now generate the "Fire_RowSelected" method in the connection point implementation file "PCDMUICP.H" that will be represented as "Cproxy_IPCDMListEvents<class T>" in the class view.

To call the event, you need to install a notification handler for the "NM_CLICK" message of the list view control. As I mentioned earlier, my eVC installation wizard did not help me by automatically creating the event handler, so I had to do it manually.

15. Open the "CPCDMList.h" include file and add the following line to the message map of the class:

```
NOTIFY_CODE_HANDLER(NM_CLICK, OnClickLVC)
```

16. Define the notification handler prototype with the following line below the message map:

```
LRESULT OnClickLVC(int idCtrl, LPNMHDR pnmh, BOOL& bHandled);
```

17. Add the following method to the "CPCDMList.CPP" source file:

```
LRESULT CPCDMList::OnClickLVC(int idCtrl, LPNMHDR pnmh, BOOL&
bHandled)
{
    if (idCtrl==m_iLVCID)
```

Table 7.14   AddItem() Parameters

Type	Variable Name	Used for
Long	Row	Row number of the item that was selected
Long	Column	Column of the item that was selected
Long	Lparam	Returns the lParam content of the selected row

```
        {
                NM_LISTVIEW* pLvdi = (NM_LISTVIEW*) pnmh;
                if (pLvdi->iItem>=0)
                {
                        LVITEM          tLVI;
                        tLVI.iItem=pLvdi->iItem;
                        tLVI.iSubItem=0;
                        tLVI.mask=LVIF_PARAM;
                        ListView_GetItem(m_hwndLVC,&tLVI);
                        Fire_RowSelected(pLvdi->iItem,
                                        pLvdi->iSubItem,tLVI.lParam);
                }
        }
        return S_OK;
}
```

Pretty simple, isn't it? Compared to the "NM_LISTVIEW" structure of the desktop, the Windows CE structure does not support "lParam" so you will need to retrieve this parameter with the "GetItem" message.

The last method, "SendCommand", sends the commands to your list view.

18. Add the method "SendCommand" and define its four parameters, shown in Table 7.15.

19. The code is very simple:

```
STDMETHODIMP CPCDMList::SendCommand(long Msg, long wParam, long
lParam,

                                                        long
                                                        *result)
```

Table 7.15 SendCommand() Parameters

Type	Variable Name	Used for
Long	Msg	The message that you want to send to the control
Long	Wparam	The Wparam of the SendMessage call
Long	Lparam	The Lparam of the SendMessage call
[out,retval] long *	result	Returns the result from the SendMessage function used in the method

```
{
        AFX_MANAGE_STATE(AfxGetStaticModuleState())

        *result::SendMessage(m_hwndLVC,Msg,wParam,lParam);
        return S_OK;
}
```

Now compile the control and let eVC download and register it. Before you go on to the next section, load the desktop version of the control, add "PCDMList.cpp" to the project, and compile it.

 The final source code of this section can be found on the companion CD under "\Sources\ThreadExample\PCDMUI\Step4".

7.4.3   Testing the New CPCDMList Class in Visual Basic

Here is how you can quickly test your new control in Visual Basic.

1. Just create a new H/PC Professional project and add the "PCDMUI.DLL" control to the toolbar.

You will see that two new controls are visible there. Because you have not changed the controls, they both look like the MFC/ATL icon.

2. Select the "PCDMList" control and insert it into the form.

You will not see anything in the area because "Create Window" will fail in the design mode of eMbedded Visual Basic. You cannot call your methods in the "OnLoad" method of the form because the control's "OnDraw" function has not been called yet; therefore your list view still has to be created.

3. Add a button to the form and insert the following code in its "OnClick" event:

```
Private Sub Command1_Click()
PCDMList1.AddColumn 200, "CD Name"
PCDMList1.AddColumn 300, "Author"
PCDMList1.AddItem 0, 0, 1, "Ray of Light"
PCDMList1.AddItem 0, 1, 1, "Madonna"
PCDMList1.AddItem 1, 0, 2, "Innuendo"
PCDMList1.AddItem 1, 1, 2, "Queen"
PCDMList1.AddItem 2, 0, 3, "Dark side of the moon"
```

```
PCDMList1.AddItem 2, 1, 3, "Pink Floyd"
End Sub
```

4. Double-click the invisible list control and add the following line to the "PCDMList1_RowSelected" event handler that will be visible:

```
Private Sub PCDMList1_RowSelected(ByVal row As Long, ByVal column As
Long, ByVal lParam As Long)
    MsgBox "Fired: " & row & "/" & column & " / " & lParam
    MsgBox PCDMList1.GetItem(row, column, lParam)
End Sub
```

If you did everything correctly, your screen should look similar to the one in Figure 7.4. If you click on one of the items in the list, you will get a message box telling you what row and what column you clicked and its "lParam" value. Then a message box containing the content of the field should pop up.

 The final source code of this section can be found on the companion CD under "\Sources\Chapter 7\7.8".

CD Name	Author	
Ray of Light	Madonna	
Innuendo	Queen	
Dark side of the moon	Pink Floyd	

Command1

Figure 7.4   A CPCDMList eVB test application

7.4.4   Using the New CPCDMList Class in the PCDM Application

Before inserting the control into your PCDM application, you should review the user-interface design schema. As you can see in Figure 7.5, you need to add the list view to two different screens of the PCDM application: the main screen and the "CD-Details" dialog box.

Updating the "Mainform"

In the previous step of the PCDM application, you transformed the main view into a form view.

1. Open the PCDM project and open the MAINFORM in the resources.
2. Right-click the form and add the ActiveX control "PCDMList Class" to the form, as illustrated in Figure 7.6.
3. Right-click on the control and name it "IDC_PCDMLIST".

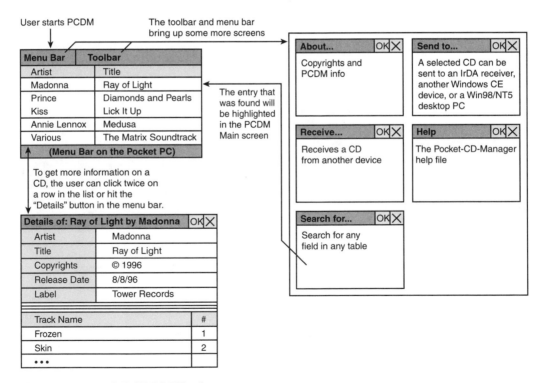

Figure 7.5   A PCDM UI schema

4. Start the class wizard and select the member variable tab.

If you try to add a member variable to the control, the wizard will ask you if it can create a wrapper class.

5. Just let the wizard do its work and name the member variable "m_LVC" when it is done.

6. Open the "CPCDMView" source file and locate the "OnInitialUpdate()" method.

This method should already contain the initialization code for the commander class.

7. Change the code of this method using the new bold statements:

```
void CPCDMView::OnInitialUpdate()
{
```

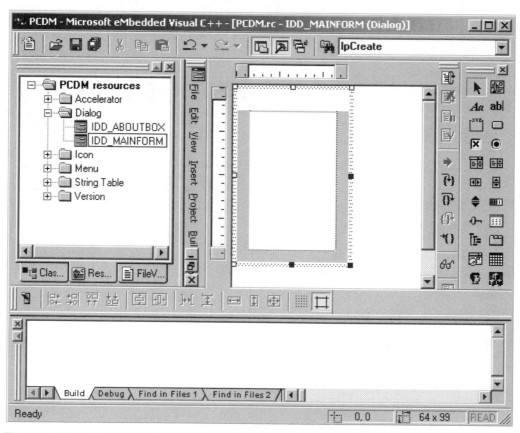

Figure 7.6 A source view of the PCDM MAINFORM

```
CFormView::OnInitialUpdate();

CRect myRect;
GetParentFrame()->GetClientRect(&myRect);
SetWindowPos(NULL,myRect.left,myRect.top,
         myRect.right,myRect.bottom,SWP_NOZORDER);
if (LOWORD(((CPCDMApp *)
    AfxGetApp())->m_CePlatform)==CEP_PALMPCV3)
    m_cmdBar.SetWindowPos(NULL,myRect.top,myRect.left,
                          myRect.right,1,SWP_NOZORDER);
else
    m_cmdBar.SetWindowPos(NULL,myRect.top,myRect.left,
                          myRect.right,25,SWP_NOZORDER);

// Creates your Command Bar
m_cmdBar.SetCmdBarType(1);
m_cmdBar.CreateBar(1,0);

// Inserts Menus
m_cmdBar.InsertMenu(TEXT("File"),0);
m_cmdBar.InsertMenuItem(TEXT("Send to..")    ,0,0,30);
m_cmdBar.InsertMenuItem(TEXT("Receive..")    ,0,1,36)
m_cmdBar.InsertMenuItem(TEXT("Show Details"),0,2,31);
m_cmdBar.InsertMenuItem(TEXT("")             ,0,3,0);
m_cmdBar.InsertMenuItem(TEXT("Help")         ,0,4,34);
m_cmdBar.InsertMenuItem(TEXT("About")        ,0,5,35);
m_cmdBar.InsertMenuItem(TEXT("")             ,0,6,0);
m_cmdBar.InsertMenuItem(TEXT("Exit")         ,0,7,IDCLOSE);

m_cmdBar.CreateBar(101,RBBS_FIXEDBMP);
if (LOWORD(((CPCDMApp *)
     AfxGetApp())->m_CePlatform)!=CEP_PALMPCV3)
     m_cmdBar.InsertButton(SBM_SEP,TBSTATE_ENABLED,
                          0,0, TEXT(""));
// Inserts Toolbar Buttons
m_cmdBar.InsertButton(SBM_SEND,TBSTATE_ENABLED,    1,30,
                     TEXT("Send Entry to other Device"));
m_cmdBar.InsertButton(SBM_OPEN,TBSTATE_ENABLED, 2,31,
                     TEXT("Show Details"));
m_cmdBar.InsertButton(SBM_SEP,TBSTATE_ENABLED,  3,0,
                     TEXT(""));
```

```
    m_cmdBar.InsertButton(SBM_FIND,TBSTATE_ENABLED, 4,32,
                          TEXT("Search for CD"));
    m_cmdBar.InsertButton(SBM_SEP,TBSTATE_ENABLED,  5,0,
                          TEXT(""));
    m_cmdBar.InsertButton(SBM_HELP,TBSTATE_ENABLED,6,34,
                          TEXT("Help"));
    m_cmdBar.InsertButton(SBM_PROP,TBSTATE_ENABLED,7,35,
                          TEXT("About"));

    // Inserts the Search Combo Box
    m_cmdBar.InsertComboBox(100,4,1007);
    m_cmdBar.AddStringToComboBox(1007,TEXT("Madonna"));

    // Adds the Close Button
    m_cmdBar.SetAdornments(0);
    if (LOWORD(((CPCDMApp *)
                AfxGetApp())->m_CePlatform)==CEP_PALMPCV3)
        m_LVC.SetWindowPos(NULL,5,0,myRect.right-10,
                           myRect.bottom-5,SWP_NOZORDER);
    else
        m_LVC.SetWindowPos(NULL,5,30,myRect.right-10,
                           myRect.bottom-35,SWP_NOZORDER);
    // Column for Author (Half the screen )
    m_LVC.AddColumn((myRect.right/2),TEXT("Artist/Author"));
    // Column for Title (Half the screen)
    m_LVC.AddColumn((myRect.right/2)-14,TEXT("Title"));
}
```

Now build the project, download it to your device, and run it. You will see that your application is starting to take shape.

Creating the New CD-Details Form

The "CD-Details" form will provide information about a selected CD. Therefore you will need to include a variety of information in this dialog box.

1. Create a new dialog box with the name "IDD_CDDETAILS" in the resource editor and assign the new class "CDetails" to it.

2. Add the controls and member variables shown in Table 7.16 to the dialog and position them on the form as shown in Figure 7.7.

Table 7.16   List of Controls for the CD-Details Form

Type	Identifier	Member Variable	Used for
Edit Field	IDC_ARTIST	Cstring M_strArtist	Name of the artist
Edit Field	IDC_TITLE	Cstring M_strTitle	Name of the CD
Edit Field	IDC_COPYRIGHT	Cstring M_strCopyright	Copyright date of the CD
Edit Field	IDC_RELEASE	Cstring M_strRelease	Release date of the CD
Edit Field	IDC_LABEL	Cstring M_strLabel	Record label of the CD
PCDMList Class	IDC_TRACKLIST	CPCDMList M_ctrlTrackLst	The list of tracks on the CD

Figure 7.8 shows another form with the name "IDD_CDDETAILSPALM" that represents the same dialog box for the palm-size PC.

3.   The easiest way to create this dialog box is to load the resource file into Visual C++ using the text mode, copy the original dialog box, rename it to "IDD_CDDETAILSPALM", and save the resource file again.

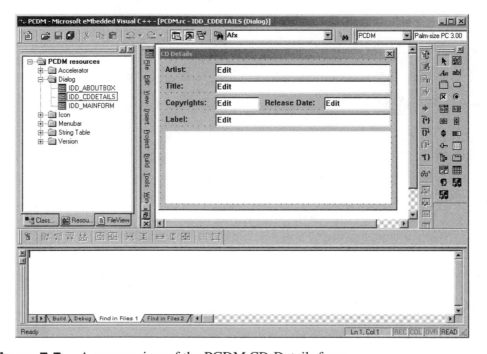

Figure 7.7   A source view of the PCDM CD-Details form

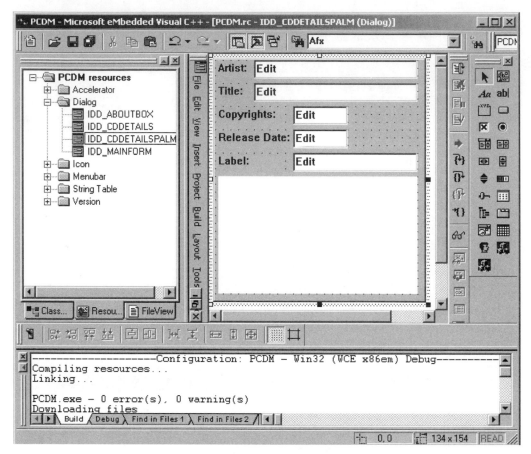

Figure 7.8 A source view of the PCDM CD-Details form for palm-size PCs

When you load the resource file with the eMbedded Visual C++ resource editor again, the name of the dialog box resource will be in quotes.

4. Correct the identifier in the property box of the dialog by removing the quotes. Then redesign the dialog box to fit on a palm-size PC.

 The maximum size of a dialog box on palm-size PCs is 134×154 dialog units if you retain the system font.

5.   To be able to use two dialog boxes with the same implementation class, you need to change the constructor of the "CDetails" class:

```
CDetails::CDetails(int IDD,long TitleID,CWnd* pParent /*=NULL*/)
   : CDialog(IDD, pParent)
```

6.   Add the following code to the constructor:

```
m_TitleID=TitleID;
```

7.   You will also need to change the definition of the constructor in the "Details.h" include file to

```
CDetails(int IDD,long TitleID, CWnd* pParent = NULL);
```

8.   Add the definition of the variable "Long m_TitleID;" to a private section of the class definition.

The variable "m_TitleID" will be used for data access in Chapter 8.
   Two more things and you will be done for now:

9.   Add a message handler for the "WM_INITDIALOG" message and include the following five lines of code:

```
BOOL CDetails::OnInitDialog()
{
    CDialog::OnInitDialog();
    SetWindowLong(this->m_hWnd,GWL_EXSTYLE,WS_EX_CAPTIONOKBTN);
    CRect myRect;
    m_ctrlTrackLst.GetClientRect(&myRect);
    m_ctrlTrackLst.AddColumn(myRect.right-34,TEXT("TrackName"));
    m_ctrlTrackLst.AddColumn(30,TEXT("#"));
    return TRUE;
}
```

The function "SetWindowLong" adds the "OK" button to the dialog box.

10.   Change the code of the method "OnCmdBarActionCommander" in the "CPCDMView" source to

```
void CPCDMView::OnCmdBarActionCommander(long ID, LPCTSTR Text)
{
    switch (ID)
    {
        case 31:
            if (m_LastRow!=-1)
            {
```

```
            CDetails *dlg;
            int plat;
            plat= LOWORD(((CPCDMApp *)
                        AfxGetApp())->m_CePlatform);
            if (plat>=CEP_PALMPC && plat<CEP_PALMPCEND)
                    dlg=new CDetails(IDD_CDDETAILSPALM,0);
            else
                    dlg=new CDetails(IDD_CDDETAILS,0);
            dlg->DoModal();
        }
    break;
case 32:
        {
        LONG Result=0,tRes=0;
        LV_FINDINFO FindIt;

        if (m_SearchString[0]==0)
        {
                CFindDlg *dlg;
                dlg=new CFindDlg();
                dlg->DoModal();
                wsprintf(m_SearchString,dlg->m_FindString);
                if (m_SearchString[0]==0)
                        break;
        }
        memset(&FindIt,0,sizeof(FindIt));
        FindIt.flags=LVFI_PARTIAL;
        FindIt.psz=m_SearchString;
        Result=m_LVC.SendCommand(LVM_FINDITEM,0,
                                (long)&FindIt);
        if (Result>=0)
        {
                tRes=m_LVC.SendCommand(LVM_ENSUREVISIBLE,
                                    Result,FALSE);
                LV_ITEM lvi;
                memset(&lvi,0,sizeof(lvi));
                lvi.stateMask=0x000F;
                lvi.state=LVIS_FOCUSED | LVIS_SELECTED;
                tRes=m_LVC.SendCommand(LVM_SETITEMSTATE ,
                                    Result,(long)&lvi);
                tRes=m_LVC.SendCommand(LVM_UPDATE ,Result,0);
                Result=tRes;
```

```
            }
          }
        break;
      case 1007:
            wsprintf(m_SearchString,text);
        break;
      case IDCLOSE:
            GetParentFrame()->DestroyWindow();
        break;
      default:
        break;
    }
}
```

11.   You need to include "Details.h" and "FindDlg.h" in "PCDMView.cpp" to be able to compile this program.

The "case 32:" branch will activate the "Find" button to scan through your list view for an author name and make this entry visible in the list view. In the case of the H/PC Professional and the palm-size PC Version 1.2, you will use the content of the combo box (ID=1007) to run the search. The Pocket PC will not show the combo box, so you need to create a tiny dialog box that asks for the string to look for. You will use the same dialog box on the H/PC Professional if the combo box is empty.

Here is the quick procedure to create this dialog box and its corresponding code:

12.   Create a new dialog resource named "IDD_FINDDLG", create a new class for it named "CFindDlg", add an edit box to the resource, and connect it to a member variable named "m_FindString".

Since you are using MFC, you do not have to make any changes to the class.

Returning to "PCDMView.cpp", the last method that you need to fill is the "OnRowSelected" event that the list view fires if the user taps on one of the items.

13.   Double-click "IDC_PCDMLIST" in the "IDD_MAINFORM" dialog box resource and add this code to the event handler that is created by the class wizard:

```
void CPCDMView::OnRowSelected(long row, long column, long lParam)
{
CDetails *dlg;
int plat;

    if (lParam==m_LastRow)
    {
    plat= LOWORD((((CPCDMApp *)AfxGetApp())->m_CePlatform);
```

```
        if (plat>=CEP_PALMPC && plat<CEP_PALMPCEND)
                    dlg=new CDetails(IDD_CDDETAILSPALM, lParam);
        else
                    dlg=new CDetails(IDD_CDDETAILS, lParam);
        dlg->DoModal();
}
m_LastRow=lParam;
}
```

The "lParam==m_LastRow" clause will allow you to launch the "CDetails" dialog only on the second click. You need to declare the "m_LastRow" variable in a private section of the "CPCDMView.cpp" class:

```
private:
        long m_LastRow;
        TCHAR       m_SearchString[255];
```

14.   Reset the variable in the "PCDMView" constructor to –1:

```
CPCDMView::CPCDMView() : CFormView(CPCDMView::IDD)
{
        m_LastRow=-1;
        m_SearchString[0]=0;
}
```

If the user selects the "Show Details . . ." menu item, clicks on the corresponding button in the toolbar, or taps on an item in the list view, the new dialog box "Details . . ." will come up. In Chapter 8, you will add life to this dialog box through the use of storage technologies.

 The final source code of this section can be found on the companion CD under "\Sources\ThreadExample\PCDM CE\Step5".

7.4.5 Summary

Here are the summary bullet points for the list view:

- The list view control of Windows CE is programmed in the same way as the desktop version.
- Most window messages to manipulate the list view control are wrapped in macros much as they are in the desktop version.

- Unsupported "Ex" flags are "LVS_EX_FLATSB", "LVS_EX_ONECLICKACTIVATE" and "LVS_EX_TWOCLICKACTIVATE".

7.5 Other Supported Common Controls

You are probably familiar with all the common controls on the desktop. Table 7.17 lists other controls that are supported in Windows CE and their respective limitations.

Table 7.17 **Supported Common Controls**

Name	API Starting with ... (Since)	MFC Class (Since)	Unsupported Features
DateTime Control	DateTime_ (2.0)	CDateTimeCtrl (2.10)	None
Header Control	Header_ (1.0)	CHeaderCtrl (1.0)	None
Month Calendar Control	MonthCal_ (2.0)	CMonthCal (2.10)	None
Tab Control (Property Page)	TabCtrl_ (1.0)	CTabCtrl (1.0)	No support for the obsolete function "SetItemExtra". All ToolTips-related methods, messages, and flags are also not supported.
Tree View	TreeView_ (1.0)	CTreeViewCtrl (1.0)	None
Property Page	—	CPropertyPage (1.0)	Windows CE does not support wizards yet. Therefore, all wizard-related messages and MFC methods are not supported
Propery Sheet	PropSheet_ (1.0)	CPropertySheet (1.0)	No wizard-related messages and MFC methods are supported. The PROPSHEETHEADER and PROPSHEETPAGE structures do not support all members. Property sheets on Windows CE are always modal.

(continued)

Table 7.17 (continued)

Name	API Starting with . . . (Since)	MFC Class (Since)	Unsupported Features
ListView	ListView_ (1.0 – EX since 2.0)	CListCtrl (1.0)	Method and messages relating to drag and drop are not supported.
Slider Bar (also known as Trackbar)	—	CSliderCtrl (1.0)	None
Spin Button Control	—	CSpinButtonCtrl (1.0)	On Windows CE, the buddy of a spin control must be an edit control.
Button Control	—	CButton (1.0)	Bitmap, icon, and cursor-related messages and MFC methods are not supported.
Combo Box	—	CComboBox (1.0)	Combo boxes on Windows CE cannot be owner-drawn. Therefore, all messages, flags, and methods related to owner-drawn combo boxes are not supported. The MFC method "Dir" is not supported.
Edit Control	—	CEdit (1.0)	GetHandle and SetHandle are not supported.
Static Control	—	CStatic (1.0)	Owner-drawn static controls are not supported. Also methods, messages, and flags related to cursors, icons, and meta files are not supported.
Status Bar Control	—	CStatusBarCtrl (1.0)	Methods, flags, and messages related to icons and ToolTips are not supported.
List Box Control	—	CListBox (1.0)	Owner-drawn controls are not supported. The MFC method "Dir" is not supported.

Name	API Starting with ... (Since)	MFC Class (Since)	Unsupported Features
Scroll Bar Control	—	CScrollBar (1.0)	None
ReBar Control	CommandBand_ (2.0)	CreBarCtrl (2.0)	Drag and drop is not supported.
Special Windows CE Controls			
Command Bar Control	CommandBar_ (1.0)	CCeCommandBar (1.0)	N/A

In general, you can say that none of the methods, messages, or flags related to the following technologies are supported on Windows CE:

- ToolTips
- Owner-draw
- Icons and bitmaps
- Cursor change if the mouse hovers over the control
- Legacy or obsolete methods that can be replaced by new or different methods
- Drag and drop

7.6   Common Controls That Are Not Supported

Not all controls are supported on Windows CE. Luckily, there are only a few that Microsoft had to exclude from the Windows CE API. Table 7.18 lists control classes that are not supported on Windows CE and explains why.

Table 7.18 Nonsupported Common Controls

Name	Desktop MFC Class	Use
Animate Control	CanimateCtrl	Up to Windows CE 3.0 there is no AVI playback in any form. The animate control only exists around AVIs and, therefore, its very basis is missing.
Hotkey Control	ChotkeyCtrl	Hotkeys only exist in the form of accelerators for menus. Microsoft is even considering moving away from the paradigm altogether because a key combination is even less user-friendly than a double-click.
Listbox with Check Marks	CcheckListBox	This control might appear in one of the next versions of the MFC.
Drag List Box	CDragListBox	This control requires a lot of screen real estate. That is why Microsoft decided not to support it. Also, there is currently no drag-and-drop support on Windows CE.
Rich Edit Control	CrichEditCtrl	This control is very big on the desktop and would explode a Windows CE device. The rich text format is dying on the desktop anyway in favor of HTML- or XML-based editors.
ToolTip Control	CtoolTipCtrl	ToolTips are realized differently on Windows CE. They can only be assigned to command bars and are integrated into the CommandBar API (see Section 7.3).

7.7 Printing in Windows CE

System DLL:	COMMDLG.DLL/core.dll
Include file:	Commdlg.h/wingdi.h
Library file:	Commdlg.lib/core.lib
Help file:	CEGUIDE.CHM (MSDN 10/98 and later)
Available since:	Windows CE 2.0
API prefix/suffix:	—
InitCommonControlEx flag:	—
MFC class:	—

Well, well, well . . . what do we have here? Printing on Windows CE? A tiny device with no parallel port or even a standard serial interface should print its screen or letters with no special formatting. Surely, it could use the infrared port and drain its valuable battery while printing a poorly formatted Excel spreadsheet. I don't think so!

Still, Microsoft included a printing subsystem in Windows CE. Even if I do not use this feature, I will at least describe how it works. The good news is that Microsoft kept the printing subsystem very simple. This means there is no special printing DC; instead, the display driver has to render the printer output. Likewise, there is no spool manager or print manager. All outputs go directly to a printer, if one is available. The entire printing process consists of seven steps:

1. Call PageSetupDlg() to get the printer information. The PrintDlg() call is obsolete and might not be supported in later versions of Windows CE.
2. Create a DC with information from the DEVNAMES structure.
3. Call StartDoc() to tell the printer the document has started.
4. Call StartPage() for any new page and render it to the DC.
5. Render something to the DC.
6. Call EndPage() to send a page of information to the printer.
7. Call EndDoc() to close the printing document.

Here is a tiny application that prints a nice test page to a connected printer.

1. Start Visual C++ and create a new "Hello World" project called "PrintIt" using the "WCE Application" settings.
2. In the "Resource View" add the menu item "Print" to the "File" menu and give it the identifier "ID_PRINT".
3. Open the source for "PrintIt.cpp" and add the following line to the include section of the file:

```
#include <commdlg.h>
```

4. Add the "commdlg.lib" to the linker import libraries to compile your small example.
5. Find "WndProc" and add the following variables to the top of the method:

```
PAGESETUPDLG pd;
HDC hDC;
LPDEVNAMES pDevNames;
DOCINFO pDoc;
RECT rect;
LPTSTR pDriver,pDevice,pOutput;
```

```
        PBYTE pOff;
        LOGFONT         MainFontRec;
        HFONT           hnewsfont,oldf;
```

6. Add the switch statement for the "ID_PRINT" menu item underneath the "IDM_FILE_EXIT" branch:

```
case ID_PRINT:
    // Initialize PAGESETUPDLG
    memset(&pd, 0,sizeof(PAGESETUPDLG));
    pd.lStructSize = sizeof(PAGESETUPDLG);
    pd.hwndOwner    = hWnd;
    pd.hDevMode     = NULL;
    pd.hDevNames    = NULL;
    pd.Flags        = PSD_INTHOUSANDTHSOFINCHES | PSD_MARGINS;

    if (PageSetupDlg(&pd)==TRUE)
    {
        pDevNames=(LPDEVNAMES)pd.hDevNames;
        pOff=(PBYTE)pDevNames;
        pDriver=(LPTSTR)(pOff+pDevNames->wDriverOffset);
        pDevice=(LPTSTR)(pOff+pDevNames->wDeviceOffset);
        pOutput=(LPTSTR)(pOff+pDevNames->wOutputOffset);
        hDC=CreateDC((LPCTSTR)pDriver,
                        (LPCTSTR)pDevice,
                        (LPCTSTR)pOutput,
                        NULL); //(LPDEVMODE)pd.hDevMode);
        // GDI calls to render output.
        if (hDC)
        {
            memset(&pDoc, 0,sizeof(DOCINFO));
            pDoc.cbSize= sizeof(DOCINFO);
            pDoc.lpszDocName=TEXT("My First Printed Document");
            StartDoc(hDC,&pDoc);
            StartPage(hDC);
                rect.bottom=500;
                rect.top=50;
                rect.left=50;
                rect.right=500;
            memset(&MainFontRec, 0,sizeof(LOGFONT));
            MainFontRec.lfHeight = -200;
            MainFontRec.lfWidth = 30;
```

```
                        MainFontRec.lfWeight = FW_NORMAL;
                        MainFontRec.lfCharSet = ANSI_CHARSET;
                        MainFontRec.lfOutPrecision = OUT_DEFAULT_
                        PRECIS;
                        MainFontRec.lfClipPrecision = CLIP_DEFAULT_
                        PRECIS;
                        MainFontRec.lfQuality = DEFAULT_QUALITY;
                        MainFontRec.lfPitchAndFamily =
                                    VARIABLE_PITCH | FF_ROMAN;
                        wsprintf(MainFontRec.lfFaceName,L"Tahoma");
                        hnewsfont =CreateFontIndirect(&MainFontRec);
                        oldf=(HFONT)SelectObject(hDC, hnewsfont);

                        DrawText(hDC,TEXT("A printer Test"),14,
                                    &rect,DT_CENTER);
                    SelectObject(hDC,oldf);
                    EndPage(hDC);
                    EndDoc(hDC);
                    DeleteDC(hDC);
            }
        if (pd.hDevMode)
                free (pd.hDevMode);
        if (pd.hDevNames)
                free (pd.hDevNames);

    }
    break;
```

I wish you good luck in finding a device to test the code on. The only way I found one was to hook my H/PC Professional to my local network, give it an IP address in my subnet, and let it print to a network printer. This does not work with the emulator. If you want to use the emulator, you have to have a printer connected to your local LPT port.

MFC does not reduce the code size of the example much since the API calls are already very simple. Basically, an MFC example would just use a CDC object instead of an HDC handle. For all you original equipment manufacturers (OEMs) and device designers out there, please include a very powerful battery, a parallel port, or write drivers for USB-based printers. Without one of those features, printing on Windows CE is just not worth the effort.

 The final source code of this section can be found on the companion CD under "\Sources\Chapter 7\7.9".

7.8 The Hardware Buttons on Palm-size PCs

The palm-size PC does not have a real keyboard for obvious reasons. Instead it comes with a Soft Input Panel (SIP) and some hardware buttons like an "Action" key, a "Cancel" or "Exit" key, and special application launch keys. All of those keys and the SIP require special programming, although some of them are just mapped to "KEYUP" messages.

7.8.1 The Action and Escape Keys

The two buttons every palm-size PC must have by design are the "Action" and "Escape/Exit" keys. The "Action" and "Escape/Exit" keys seem to fire a series of weird messages. The important KEYUP messages you should pay attention to are:

- VK_F23 or VK_RETURN for the "Action" key
- VK_F24 or VK_ESCAPE for the "Escape/Exit" key

7.8.2 The Application Launch Keys

System DLL:	Aygshell.dll
Include file:	aygshell.h
Library file:	Coredsip.lib
Help file:	Undocumented
Available since:	Windows CE 2.01
API prefix/suffix:	SHSip
InitCommonControlEx flag:	—
MFC class:	—

The application launch keys of the palm-size PC are reserved for the OS to launch applications. There is a way to use them, but since it requires the use of an undocumented function to access them, it is generally not recommended.

Having said that, here is what you have to do:

1. Unregister the current function of the key with the undocumented "UnregisterFunc1" call.

```
typedef            BOOL (*SHUNREGISTERFUNC1)(UINT one, UINT two);
HINSTANCE          h;
SHUNREGISTERFUNC1 g_hUnregisterFunc1=NULL;
    h = LoadLibrary(TEXT("coredll.dll"));
    g_hUnregisterFunc1=(SHUNREGISTERFUNC1)GetProcAddress(h,
                      TEXT("UnregisterFunc1"));
    (*g_hUnregisterFunc1)(MOD_WIN, VK_APP_LAUNCH<#>);
```

Replace "<#>" with the number of the key you want to unregister.

2. Use "RegisterHotKey" to get events to a window procedure.

```
RegisterHotKey(hwnd, VK_APP_LAUNCH<#>, MOD_WIN, VK_APP_LAUNCH<#>);
```

3. You have to handle "Activate" and "Deactivate" messages to get back to the original function:

```
case WM_ACTIVATE:
    fActive = LOWORD(wParam);           // activation flag
    if (WA_INACTIVE != fActive)
    {
      // Unregister the Hotkeys to use them in your app
    }
    else
    {
      // Release the Hotkeys back to their original function
    }
```

4. Release the hotkeys when you are done with them and restore the original state.

```
typedef    BYTE (*SHGETAPPKEYASSOCPROC)(LPCTSTR ptszApp);
TCHAR      szAppName[MAX_LOADSTRING];                    // window name
BYTE       byteButton;
HINSTANCE h;
SHGETAPPKEYASSOCPROC g_hSHGetAppKeyAssoc = NULL;

    UnregisterHotKey(hwnd, VK_APP_LAUNCH<#>);
    h = LoadLibrary(TEXT("aygshell.dll"));
    g_hSHGetAppKeyAssoc = (SHGETAPPKEYASSOCPROC)GetProcAddress(h,
                      TEXT("SHGetAppKeyAssoc"));
    FreeLibrary(h);
    if (byteButton = (*g_hSHGetAppKeyAssoc)(szAppName))
```

```
RegisterHotKey(hwnd, VK_APP_LAUNCH<#>, MOD_WIN,
byteButton);
```

5. Broadcast "WM_WININICHANGE: SPI_APPBUTTONCHANGE" to inform the OS of your actions at the end of your application:

```
SendMessage(HWND_BROADCAST, WM_WININICHANGE, SPI_APPBUTTONCHANGE, 0);
```

If anything "unnatural" happens to your application, there might be no way to give the keys back to the OS, forcing the user to push the reset button.

 My final tip, therefore, is this: Only use application launch keys if it is *absolutely* necessary.

7.9 The Soft Input Panel

System DLL:	Aygshell.dll
Include file:	aygshell.h
Library file:	Coredsip.lib
Help file:	CEGUIDE.CHM (MSDN 10/98 and later)
Available since:	Windows CE 2.01
API prefix/suffix:	Sip
InitCommonControlEx flag:	—
MFC class:	—

The SIP (Soft Input Panel) is the main input "device" for a palm-size PC. It is an input device like the keyboard or the mouse but uses the touch screen of the palm-size PC to send its "VK_KEY" messages to the application. Like the keyboard messages, all "VK_KEY" messages are sent to the window with the focus. Therefore using the SIP is very intuitive and simple. The SIP offers two input methods:

- The soft keyboard (Figure 7.9)
- The Jot Character Recognizer (see Figure 7.10)

7.9.1 A Simple Application Showing the SIP

Your choices for displaying the SIP are limited; all you can do is show it or hide it. The function that handles the SIP is called

```
SHSipInfo()
```

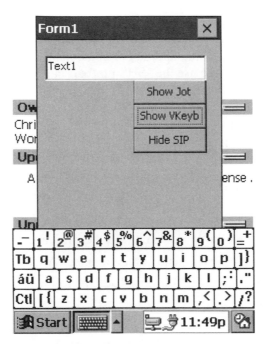

Figure 7.9   The soft keyboard SIP

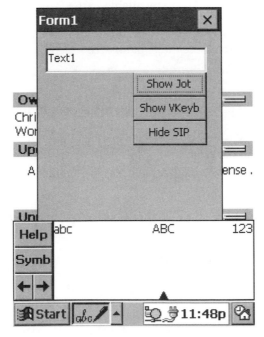

Figure 7.10   The Jot Character Recognizer SIP

Here is the trap of the SIP: It is available only on palm-size PCs and trying to call it from an application running on an H/PC Professional will fail with the infamous message "The application cannot find a library or component".

Therefore, the best way to use the "SHSipInfo()" call is first by using "LoadLibrary()" to load "aygshell.dll"; only when this function returns a valid library handle should you call the "SHSipInfo()" function.

Some people might even recommend using this method to detect at runtime whether your application is running on a palm-size PC. I do not recommend this procedure because it could happen that Microsoft or any OEM puts "aygshell.dll" on its "whatever" device and you would be fooled by its presence. In Section 4.6.4 you will find a much more reliable method to detect the platform your application is running on.

1. Create a new "Hello World" palm-size PC project called "SIPit".

2. To keep it simple, just add an edit field to the "About-Box" dialog.

3. In the "include" area of "SIPit.cpp" add the following code lines:

```
#include <aygshell.h>
typedef BOOL (*SHSIPINFOPROC)(UINT uiAction, UINT uiParam,
          PVOID pvParam, UINT fWinIni);
```

The include file "aygshell.h" is not available in the H/PC SDKs. You have three alternatives here:

- Copy "aygshell.h" from the latest palm-size PC SDK to the H/PC SDKs.
- Copy "aygshell.h" from the palm-size PC SDK to the eVC include directory.
- Address "aygshell.h" with the full path to the palm-size PC SDK.

I recommend the second choice. It is not a very clean method, but since this include file is not available on the desktop, it will not interfere with any desktop include file. And, as explained earlier, it will be available for the "Default" platform for devices that are yet to come.

4. Declare the following variables in the declaration section of "WndProc" of the "SIPit" application:

```
SHSIPINFOPROC  g_hSHSipInfo  = NULL;
HINSTANCE      hDll;
SIPINFO        si;
```

5. Add the following code in the "case IDM_HELP_ABOUT:" branch of the "message" switch in "WndProc" of the application:

```
case IDM_HELP_ABOUT:
hDll = LoadLibrary(TEXT("aygshell.dll"));
if (hDll)
{
     memset(&si, 0, sizeof(si));
     si.cbSize = sizeof(si);
     g_hSHSipInfo=(SHSIPINFOPROC)GetProcAddress(hDll,
                               TEXT("SHSipInfo"));

     (*g_hSHSipInfo)(SPI_GETSIPINFO, 0, &si, 0);
     // Switch the SIP ON
     si.fdwFlags = si.fdwFlags | SIPF_ON;
     // set new SIP state
     (*g_hSHSipInfo)(SPI_SETSIPINFO, 0, &si, 0);
     FreeLibrary(hDll);
}
DialogBox(hInst, (LPCTSTR)IDD_ABOUTBOX, hWnd, (DLGPROC)About);
break
```

To select a special input method (IM), you need to use the flag
"SPI_SETCURRENTIM" and enter the class ID of the IM. Here are
the class IDs for the virtual keyboard and the Jot recognizer:

- {42429667-AE04-11D0-A4F8-00AA00A749B9} = Virtual Keyboard
- {42429690-AE04-11D0-A4F8-00AA00A749B9} = Virtual Keyboard

If you try to run this application against the old palm-size PC 1.0 and 1.2 emulators, you will not see the SIP pop up. It appears that Microsoft has a bug in the emulator "aygshell.dll" that prevents the SIP from appearing. On a real palm-size PC or the emulator of a palm-size PC 2.0, you will see the SIP come up before the About Box is visible.

 The final source code of this section can be found on the companion CD under "\Sources\Chapter 7\7.10".

7.9.2 ShowSIP() for PCDMDLL.DLL

For any inputs into your Pocket-CD-Manager application, you will sometimes want to use the SIP to help the user. For this reason, you need to add an interface called "IPCDMInput" to the "PCDMDLL.DLL" control and install a method, "ShowSIP(int)", to open it. Although UI functionality is provided, there is no real

UI code involved in the "IPCDMInput" interface. Therefore you can put the functionality into the UI-less "PCDMDLL.DLL".

1. Load the last version of your PCDMDLL project and add a new "Simple ATL" object called "PCDMInput" to it.

2. Add the method "ShowSIP()" to the "IPCDMInput" interface and add one "int iShow" parameter to it.

The "iShow" parameter will determine how the SIP will be displayed:

- A "0" will hide the SIP.
- A "1" will show the virtual keyboard.
- Anything else will show the Jot Character Recognizer.

3. In the implementation of the method, add the following code:

```
STDMETHODIMP CPCDMInput::ShowSIP(int iShow)
{
#ifdef UNDER_CE
    SHSIPINFOPROC  g_hSHSipInfo=NULL;
    HINSTANCE      hDll;
    SIPINFO si;

    hDll = LoadLibrary(TEXT("aygshell.dll"));
    if (hDll)
    {
        memset(&si, 0, sizeof(si));
        si.cbSize = sizeof(si);
        g_hSHSipInfo =(SHSIPINFOPROC)GetProcAddress(hDll,
                                    TEXT("SHSipInfo"));
        switch (iShow)
        {
            case 0:
              (*g_hSHSipInfo)(SPI_GETSIPINFO, 0, &si, 0);
               // Switch the SIP OFF
              si.fdwFlags = si.fdwFlags & ~ SIPF_ON;
              (*g_hSHSipInfo)(SPI_SETSIPINFO, 0, &si, 0);
              break;
            case 1:
              (*g_hSHSipInfo)(SPI_SETCURRENTIM, 0,
                          (void *)&IID_IVKeyB, 0);
              (*g_hSHSipInfo)(SPI_GETSIPINFO, 0, &si, 0);
              si.fdwFlags = si.fdwFlags | SIPF_ON;
              (*g_hSHSipInfo)(SPI_SETSIPINFO, 0, &si, 0);
```

```
                        break;
                default:
                    (*g_hSHSipInfo)(SPI_SETCURRENTIM, 0,
                                    (void *)&IID_IJot, 0);
                    (*g_hSHSipInfo)(SPI_GETSIPINFO, 0, &si, 0);
                    si.fdwFlags = si.fdwFlags | SIPF_ON;
                    (*g_hSHSipInfo)(SPI_SETSIPINFO, 0, &si, 0);
                    break;
            }
            FreeLibrary(hDll);
        }
#endif
        return S_OK;
}
```

There is no big magic in these lines. The class IDs of the IMs are not defined in the Microsoft include files. This might be a sign that they could change in the future.

4. Next add these declarations to the top of your "PCDMInput.cpp":

```
#ifdef UNDER_CE
#include <aygshell.h>
typedef BOOL (*SHSIPINFOPROC)(UINT uiAction, UINT uiParam,
                              PVOID pvParam, UINT fWinIni);

#endif

#include <initguid.h>
DEFINE_GUID( IID_IVKeyB,0x42429667,
             0xAE04,0x11D0,0xA4,0xf8,0x00,0xAA,0x00,0xA7,0x49,0xB9 );
DEFINE_GUID( IID_IJot,0x42429690,
             0xAE04,0x11D0,0xA4,0xf8,0x00,0xAA,0x00,0xA7,0x49,0xB9 );
```

Compile the new class and register it on your Windows CE device or emulation. Then load the desktop version of the control, add the "PCDMInput.cpp" file to the project, and compile it, too.

 The final source code of this section can be found on the companion CD under "\Sources\ThreadExample\PCDMDLL\Step2".

7.9.3 Testing the New PCDMUI in Visual Basic

Now you can quickly test the new method in eMbedded Visual Basic.

1. Start eVB and create a new "Windows CE PsPC" project.

2. Add three buttons to "Form1":

- Button 1 (Command1) = "Show JOT"

- Button 2 (Command2) = "Show Vkeyb"

- Button 3 (Command3) = "Hide SIP"

3. Add the following code to the "OnClick" event of those buttons:

```
Private Sub Command1_Click()
    Dim II As PCDMInput
    Set II = CreateObject("PCDMDLL.PCDMInput.1")
    II.ShowSIP (2)
End Sub

Private Sub Command2_Click()
    Dim II As PCDMInput

    Set II = CreateObject("PCDMDLL.PCDMInput.1")
    II.ShowSIP (1)
End Sub

Private Sub Command3_Click()
    Dim II As PCDMInput

    Set II = CreateObject("PCDMDLL.PCDMInput.1")
    II.ShowSIP (0)
End Sub
```

Once you have started this application, you can hit the buttons on the screen and the corresponding SIP should show up.

 The final source code of this section can be found on the companion CD under "\Sources\Chapter 7\7.11".

7.10 Ink Control

System DLL:	ixresdll.dll, riresdll.dll, richink.dll, inkx.dll
Include file:	inkx.h
Library file:	inkx.lib

Help file:	Not documented
Available since:	Windows CE 2.11
API prefix/suffix:	—
InitCommonControlEx flag:	None, but InitInkX() must be called first
MFC class:	—

An Ink control is another way of putting data into a Windows CE device. For keyboard-less devices like the palm-size PCs, an Ink control offers an excellent alternative to storing the text you enter with the virtual keypad.

The control is also very easy to include in your application. Only three steps and you're done:

1. Add the InkX control to a dialog box resource.
2. Initialize Ink Control using "InitInkX()" in the "WinMain" function.
3. Use the standard "SendMessage()" call with either "IM_SETDATA" or "IM_GETDATA" to get/set the actual Ink from the screen.

7.10.1 Creating a Small Ink Control Application

As always, I want to provide a small application that hosts an Ink control and displays it in a dialog box.

1. Create a new "Hello World" project and call it "Inkit".

You will to use the About dialog box again to keep this example as small as possible.

2. Open the About dialog box resource and add a custom control to it.
3. In the properties of the control, enter "InkX" into the class field of the control and save the new dialog box.
4. Add the include file "inkx.h" to the includes of "InkIt.cpp".
5. Locate the "WinMain()" function of the "InkIt" application and add the following two lines before the "InitInstance()" call:

```
InitCommonControls();
InitInkX();
```

6. Locate the window procedure of the "About" box and add two variable definitions:

```
DWORD lBlobLen;
BYTE *inkBlob;
```

7. Add the following code in the "WM_COMMAND" branch of the "message"-switch:

```
if ((LOWORD(wParam) == IDOK) || (LOWORD(wParam) == IDCANCEL))
{
      if (LOWORD(wParam) == IDOK)
      {
            //Get the length of the ink data blob
            lBlobLen = SendDlgItemMessage(hDlg,
                              IDC_CUSTOM1, IM_GETDATALEN, 0, 0L);
            if (lBlobLen == 0)
            {
                  //Nothing in the control
                  EndDialog(hDlg, 0);
                  return TRUE;
            }

            //Allocate object pData
            inkBlob = (PBYTE) LocalAlloc(LMEM_FIXED, lBlobLen);
            if (!inkBlob)          return FALSE;

            //Retrieve ink data blob and store it in inkBlob.
            SendDlgItemMessage(hDlg, IDC_CUSTOM1,
                        IM_GETDATA, lBlobLen, (LPARAM)inkBlob);

            // ... Do Something with the inkBlob
      }
      EndDialog(hDlg, LOWORD(wParam));
      return TRUE;
}
break;
```

8. The last thing you need to do before you can compile this example is to add "inkx.lib" to the libraries for the linker.

If you compile your application now and start it on your device, you will see the Ink control in the "About" box. On older palm-size PCs (V1.0 and V1.2), you will also find a toolbar and even a menu bar inside the control. The new palm-size PC 2.0 switches them off by default.

9. If you want to get rid of those windows, add the following lines to the "WM_INITDIALOG" branch of the "message"-switch:

```
#define IDC_POSTSETUP WM_USER + 127
PostMessage(hDlg, WM_COMMAND, MAKELONG(IDC_POSTSETUP,
                  IDC_POSTSETUP), IDC_POSTSETUP);
```

This is necessary because the children windows of a dialog box are not yet ready when the dialog box runs through the "WM_INITDIALOG" message.

10. Of course, you must define "IDC_POSTSETUP" and add a case for "IDC_POSTSETUP" in the "WM_COMMAND" section of the "message" switch:

```
if (LOWORD(wParam) == IDC_POSTSETUP)
{
        HWND        hwndInk,hwndCB, hwndSB, hwndRI;
        RECT        rc;

        hwndInk=GetDlgItem(hDlg, IDC_CUSTOM1);
        // The commandbar of the InK Ctrl is Child 1
        hwndCB = GetWindow(hwndInk, GW_CHILD);
        // The scrollbar of the Ink Ctrl is Child 2
        hwndSB = GetWindow(hwndCB, GW_HWNDNEXT);
        // The main window (richink) is Child 3
        hwndRI = GetWindow(hwndSB, GW_HWNDNEXT);

        // simply hide what you dont like
        ShowWindow(hwndCB, SW_HIDE);
        ShowWindow(hwndSB, SW_HIDE);

        // resize RI window to be the same size as hwnd
        GetClientRect(hwndInk, &rc);
        InflateRect(&rc, -2, -2);
        SetWindowPos(hwndRI, hwndInk,rc.left, rc.top,
                        rc.right - rc.left + 1, rc.bottom - rc.top + 1,
                        SWP_NOZORDER);
        ShowWindow(hwndInk, SW_SHOW);
        break;
}
```

Start the application and check out the "About" box. You will see that the Ink control no longer shows the toolbar.

There is also a difference between palm-size PCs and H/PC Professionals. While the PsPCs show the writing pane by default, the H/PC Professionals show the typing pane.

11. To set a view mode, use the "IM_SETVIEW" message.

```
SendDlgItemMessage(hDlg, IDC_CUSTOM1, IM_SETVIEW, IX_TYPEVIEW,
                (LPARAM)NULL);
```

Unfortunately, those messages are not defined in the H/PC SDK but only in the palm-size SDK, and they only work with PsPCs.

7.10.2 Other Ink Control Functions

The Ink control also knows three other interesting functions. But since Microsoft has not yet fully documented this control, you cannot be sure that it will be there in a newer version of Windows CE.

InkToString()

As its name implies, this function tries to convert an Ink binary blob to a string.

Type	Variable Name	Used for
DWORD	Cb	Length of the Ink blob
BYTE *	Pb	Ink blob
LPWSTR *	Psz	Target string

You can play with this function in your sample application by adding the following two lines after the "SendDlgItemMessage(hDlg,IDC_CUSTOM1 . . .)" call:

```
LPWSTR testme;
InkToString(lBlobLen,(BYTE*)inkBlob,&testme);
```

But to be honest, I could never get any real string out of it . . .

ConvertInkFile()

With no documentation and only a few handles as parameters, it is hard even for a professional to guess what this function might do.

PrintInk()

This call would be very cool if the palm-size PCs had any significant printing capablity. And in the SDK for the H/PC Professionals, this call is missing. Otherwise it would be easy to use. It allows printing of an Ink blob to a given printer DC. All you need to do is to fill out the "P_PRINTINK structure" and give the size and pointer to the Ink blob to this function, and it does the rest.

 The final source code of this section can be found on the companion CD under "\Sources\Chapter 7\7.12".

8
Chapter

Storage

Just about every application that you will write will need to store some sort of state to a persistent media. Windows CE supports several persistent storage locations:

- The registry
- The file system
- The object store
- Databases, such as Pocket-Access or SQL for Windows CE

Some of these storage methods—the registry and object store, for example—are RAM-based and are therefore only kept alive by the internal battery. In the event of a cold reset, these data are lost. The file system can also use Flash-RAM cards to store data that survive a cold reset.

You are no doubt familiar with most of those storage concepts because they are quite similar to those used by the desktop. Therefore I will only touch on them, mainly to point out any differences between the desktop and Windows CE versions. The only Windows CE-specific storage is the object store, which I will address in detail. This is an important chapter for your PCDM application. It finally fills your screens with life.

8.1   The Windows CE Registry

System DLL:	COREDLL.DLL
Include file:	Coredll.h
Library file:	Coredll.lib
Help file:	CEGUIDE.CHM (MSDN 10/98 and later)
Available since:	Windows CE 1.0
API prefix/suffix:	Reg<action>
InitCommonControlEx flag:	Not necessary
ATL/MFC class:	CregKey (2.0 or later)
Store here:	Application settings, user settings, state of the application in case of a WM_CLOSE by the OS on a palm-size PC

The Windows CE registry is generally accessed in the same way as the registry on a desktop PC. Since Windows CE does not support the notion of different user profiles, the Windows CE registry has only three root keys:

- HKEY_LOCAL_MACHINE
- HKEY_CURRENT_USER
- HKEY_CLASSES_ROOT

Another difference to the desktop is the absence of any security-related parameters or calls.

To access the registry you have to write the standard registry code:

1. RegCreateKeyEx/RegOpenKeyEx
2. RegQueryValueEx/RegSetValueEx
3. RegCloseKey

Here is a very small code example that reads a key from the registry and writes it back into a backup key:

```
HKEY rhKey;
DWORD tlValType,BufferSize;
PBYTE bBuffer;
If (RegOpenKeyEx(HKEY_LOCAL_MACHINE,TEXT("Indent"),0,0,&rhKey)
    !=ERROR_SUCCESS)
{
    RegQueryValueEx(rhKey,TEXT("Name"),0,&tlValType,
```

```
                bBuffer,&BufferSize);
    RegSetValueEx(rhKey,TEXT("NameBak"),0,REG_SZ,bBuffer,0);
}
RegCloseKey(rhKey);
```

8.1.1   Adding **CPCDMAccessReg** to the **PCDMDLL.DLL**

For your thread-example application, you will need an easy access to the registry.
Therefore you need to add a simple control to the PCDMDLL.DLL that provides two
methods, "ReadRegistryKey" and "WriteRegistryKey".

1. Open the last version of the PCDMDLL.DLL and add a simple ATL object
   named "PCDMAccessReg".
2. Add two methods called "ReadRegistryKey" and "WriteRegistryKey".
3. Both methods will take two parameters, as shown in Table 8.1.
4. Now add the following code to the implementation of the methods:

```
STDMETHODIMP CPCDMAccessReg::ReadRegistryKey(BSTR Path, VARIANT
*Value)
{
HKEY hKey,rhKey;
DWORD      tlValType,BufferSize;
PBYTE      bBuffer;
int i;
DWORD ret;
BSTR tPath;

        VariantInit(Value);
        tPath=Path;
```

Table 8.1   The ReadRegistryKey() Parameters

Type	Variable Name	Used for
BSTR	Path	Points to the path of the registry key *Syntax:* **HK\<root>**\\\<KeyPath>\\\<ValueName>
VARIANT ([out, reval] *VARIANT for ReadRegistryKey)	Value	The value that gets stored/retrieved from the key

```
    if (CompareString(LOCALE_SYSTEM_DEFAULT,NORM_IGNORECASE,
                  TEXT("HKLM\\"),5,tPath,5)==CSTR_EQUAL)
        hKey=HKEY_LOCAL_MACHINE;
    else if (CompareString(LOCALE_SYSTEM_DEFAULT,NORM_IGNORECASE,
                       TEXT("HKCU\\"),5,tPath,5)==CSTR_EQUAL)
        hKey=HKEY_CURRENT_USER;
    else if (CompareString(LOCALE_SYSTEM_DEFAULT,NORM_IGNORECASE,
                       TEXT("HKCR\\"),5,tPath,5)==CSTR_EQUAL)
        hKey=HKEY_CLASSES_ROOT;
    else   // No valid Root Key specified
        return S_FALSE;

    i=lstrlen(tPath); while (tPath[i]!='\\' && i>0) i-;
    if (i==0) // Path contains no ValueName
        return S_FALSE;
    tPath[i]=0;

    if (RegOpenKeyEx(hKey,&tPath[5],0,0,&rhKey)!=ERROR_SUCCESS)
        return S_FALSE;

    BufferSize=4096;
    bBuffer=(PBYTE)LocalAlloc(LMEM_FIXED|LMEM_ZEROINIT,BufferSize);
    RegQueryValueEx(rhKey,&tPath[i+1],0,&tlValType,bBuffer,
                  &BufferSize);

    ret=S_OK;
    switch (tlValType)
    {
        case REG_SZ:
                    Value->vt=VT_BSTR;
                    Value->bstrVal=SysAllocString((TCHAR*)
                    bBuffer);
            break;
        case REG_DWORD:
                    Value->vt=VT_I4;
                    Value->lVal=(long)bBuffer;
            break;
        default:
                    ret=S_FALSE;
            break;
    }
```

```
        RegCloseKey(rhKey);
        return ret;
}
```

The "ReadRegistryKey" method reads the key and sets the appropriate variant type in the resulting value. Only "strings" and "double-words" are supported. All other values will return "S_FALSE".

```
STDMETHODIMP CPCDMAccessReg::WriteRegistryKey(BSTR Path, VARIANT
Value)
{
HKEY hKey,rhKey;
LPDWORD result=NULL;
Long tlVal;
Int tLen,i;
DWORD ret;
BSTR tPath,keyName;

        if (CompareString(LOCALE_SYSTEM_DEFAULT,NORM_IGNORECASE,
                        TEXT("HKLM\\"),5,Path,5)==CSTR_EQUAL)
            hKey=HKEY_LOCAL_MACHINE;
        else if (CompareString(LOCALE_SYSTEM_DEFAULT,NORM_IGNORECASE,
                        TEXT("HKCU\\"),5,Path,5)==CSTR_EQUAL)
            hKey=HKEY_CURRENT_USER;
        else if (CompareString(LOCALE_SYSTEM_DEFAULT,NORM_IGNORECASE,
                        TEXT("HKCR\\"),5,Path,5)==CSTR_EQUAL)
            hKey=HKEY_CLASSES_ROOT;
        else  // No valid Root Key specified
            return S_FALSE;

        i=lstrlen(Path); while (Path[i]!='\\' && i>0) i-;
        if (i==0) // Path contains no Value-Name
            return S_FALSE;

        tPath=&Path[5];
        keyName=&tPath[i-4];
        tPath[i-5]=0;

        if (RegOpenKeyEx(hKey,tPath,0,0,&rhKey)!=ERROR_SUCCESS)
        {
            RegCreateKeyEx(hKey,tPath,0,NULL,0,0,NULL,&rhKey,result);
```

```
        }
        if (rhKey==NULL) // Key could neither be created nor opened
                return S_FALSE;

        tLen=-1;
        ret=S_OK;
        switch (Value.vt)
        {
                case VT_I4:
                                tlVal=Value.lVal; tLen=4;
                        break;
                case VT_UI1:
                                tlVal=Value.bVal; tLen=4;
                         break;
                case VT_I2:
                                tlVal=Value.iVal; tLen=4;
                        break;
                case VT_EMPTY:
                                RegSetValueEx(rhKey,keyName,0,REG_SZ,
                                        (BYTE *)TEXT(""),0);
                        break;
                case VT_BSTR:
                                ret=RegSetValueEx(rhKey,keyName,0,REG_SZ,
                                  (BYTE *)Value.bstrVal,
                                  (lstrlen(Value.bstrVal)+1)*sizeof(TCHAR));
                        break;
                default:
                        ret=S_FALSE; // Unsupported Variant Type
        }
        if (tLen>0)
                RegSetValueEx(rhKey,keyName,0,REG_DWORD,(BYTE
                *)&tlVal,4);
        RegCloseKey(rhKey);
        return ret;
}
```

The "WriteRegistryKey" method parses the variant value to see what kind of key it has to write to the registry. Only strings and numbers are supported; everything else will be ignored.

The final source code of this section can be found on the companion CD under "\Sources\ThreadExample\PCDMDLL\Step3".

8.1.2 Testing the New CPCDMAccessReg in eMbedded Visual Basic

Here is a quick application that calls your new methods from within an eVB application:

1. Create a new eVB application and add a button and a text field to the main form.

2. Enter the following code to the "Command1_Click()" method:

```
Private Sub Command1_Click()
Dim foo As Object
Dim valler As Variant
    Set foo = CreateObject("PCDMDLL.PCDMAccessReg")
    foo.WriteRegistryKey "HKLM\Software\MyCompany\Name",
    "CompanyName"
    valler = foo.ReadRegistryKey("HKLM\Ident\Name")
    Text1.Text = valler
    Set foo = Nothing
End Sub
```

This application will create a new registry key called "Name" in the path "Software\ MyCompany" in the "HKEY_LOCAL_MACHINE" root. It then reads the current machine name of your Windows CE device from the registry and puts it in the text field.

 The final source code of this section can be found on the companion CD under "\Sources\Chapter 8\8.1".

8.2 The File System

System DLL:	COREDLL.DLL
Include file:	Coredll.h
Library file:	Coredll.lib
Help file:	CEGUIDE.CHM (MSDN 10/98 and later)
Available since:	Windows CE 1.0
API prefix/suffix:	—
InitCommonControlEx flag:	Not necessary
MFC class:	Cfile
Store here:	User documents

The file system is the only common storage location on all Windows CE platforms and versions. All Windows CE devices have a file system by definition, even those that only have battery-backed RAM. You access the file system in exactly the same way as you would on the desktop, using

- "CreateFile()"
- "WriteFile()"/"ReadFile()"
- "CloseHandle()"

You should already be familiar with the file system so I will not discuss it in detail. There are, however, several differences that I want to point out.

8.2.1 No Drive Letters

The file system on Windows CE has no notion of drive letters. All "drives," such as Flash-RAM cards or ATA disks, are mounted under the root directory. If a device has two slots for PC-Cards or CF-Cards (Compact-Flash) and you plug in a storage card in both slots, the one in the primary slot becomes "Storage Card" and the other becomes "Storage Card2". The number is assigned to the slot, not to the card. In other words, any storage card plugged into the secondary slot will always be named "Storage Card2". You have to find out which is your primary slot and which is your secondary slot. On the NEC MobilPro 800, the PC-Card slot is the primary slot.

8.2.2 The Name "Storage Card" Can Be Localized

If you are designing software that is supposed to run on foreign devices, you need to be aware of the localized name. Do not try to locate the storage card only by its English name. Microsoft created an API to find available storage cards that is very similar to the "FindFirstFile()/FindNextFile()" API. Unfortunately, this API is available only on palm-size PC devices. I hope that Microsoft will add the API to all devices, since it provides a solution for the localization problem.

System DLL:	Note_prj.dll
Include file:	Projects.h
Library file:	Note_prj.lib
Help file:	CEGUIDE.CHM (MSDN 10/98 and later)
Available since:	Windows CE 2.01
API prefix/suffix:	—
InitCommonControlEx flag:	—
ATL class:	—

Here is a small example that makes use of this API:

1.   Create a new "Hello World" application and name it "FindFlash".
2.   Add the file "Projects.h" to the list of includes in the "FindFlash.cpp" source file.
3.   Add the following method before the "WinMain" function:

```
void ShowFlashCard()
{
BOOL bContinue = TRUE;
HANDLE hFlashCard;
WIN32_FIND_DATA lpwfdFlashCard;

    hFlashCard = FindFirstFlashCard (&lpwfdFlashCard);
    if (hFlashCard == INVALID_HANDLE_VALUE)
        return;
    while (bContinue)
    {
        MessageBox(NULL,lpwfdFlashCard.cFileName,
                TEXT("FindFlash"),MB_OK);
        bContinue = FindNextFlashCard (hFlashCard,
                                    &lpwfdFlashCard);
    }
    FindClose (hFlashCard);  // Close the search handle.
}
```

4.   Locate the "WinMain" function and add the following line before the main message loop:

```
ShowFlashCard();
```

5.   Before you can compile and link the application, you need to add the library "note_prj.lib" to the list of libraries in the linker settings.

This library does not exist in the emulation environment.

As soon as you launch this application, you will get a message box with the real name of the storage card. For example, on a German palm-size PC you will get "Speicherkarte" instead of "Storage Card".

Remember, this API does not exist on H/PCs. To keep your code platform-neutral, you should use "LoadLibrary" and "GetProcAddress" again.

The final source code of this section can be found on the companion CD under "\Sources\Chapter 8\8.2".

8.2.3 "My Documents" on a Palm-size PC

In Chapter 7 you used the "OpenFileDialog()" method to get a file browser. On palm-size PC devices, "OpenFileDialog()" does not allow you to select any directory other than the "My Documents" folder. But it accesses all "My Documents" folders, even those created on storage cards. In order to store a document in a "My Documents" folder on a storage card using a palm-size PC application, you must use the API discussed in the previous section.

8.3   The Object Store

System DLL:	COREDLL.DLL
Include file:	Windbase.h
Library file:	Coredll.lib
Help file:	CEGUIDE.CHM (MSDN 10/98 and later)
Available since:	Windows CE 1.0
API prefix/suffix:	Ce . . .
InitCommonControlEx flag:	Not necessary
MFC class:	CCeDBDatabase, CCeDBEnum, CCeDBProp, CCeDBRecord
Store here:	Structured data

The object store is a technology that can only be found in Windows CE and is very similar to a database. It holds all Personal Information Manager (PIM) information, such as calendar data, contacts, mails, and tasks. If you open the Windows CE Explorer from ActiveSync, you will see a top-level icon called "Database", as shown in Figure 8.1. This icon represents the object store. The tables inside the database cannot be opened or accessed with Windows CE Explorer. You can only look at them and get information about their sizes. To help clarify the strange terminology of Microsoft's APIs and documentation, see the mapping in Table 8.2.

Another strange fact is that you do not have to specify the properties (fields) of a record at the time when you create the database (table). However, it is possible to specify the sort order during creation of the database. This could lead to missynchroniza-

Figure 8.1   The object store icon

tion between sort order and actual properties in the database. Moreover, not all records have to have the same number of properties. They can actually vary from record to record. And to make things even more interesting, a property (field) in one record can be of a different type in the next record, but can still use the same property ID (PID). To search through a database using the "CeSeekDatabase()" call, all records must share at least one common property.

Up to Version 2.x of Windows CE, the object store has a 16MB maximum limit. Likewise, each database (table) is limited to a maximum of 4MB. This limitation was eliminated with Windows CE 2.12. With Windows CE 2.10 and higher, it is possible to access database volumes similar to the object store from any file system location. To access a database inside such a volume, the volume has to be mounted first.

To access the database you need either Pocket-Access, which can only create and view new tables, or you have to use the object store APIs. In Section 8.5, I will discuss Pocket-Access; now I will concentrate on the object store APIs. Section 8.4 shows that you can also use ADO to access the object store. Since ADO is Microsoft's most important data access technology, I recommend using it. However, because ADO is not available on devices based on Windows CE 2.01 and older, I want to go through the object store APIs and MFC classes first.

Table 8.2   Terminology Mapping of Object Store versus Databases

Windows CE	General Database Language
Database volumes	Databases
Database	Table
Record	Record
Properties	Fields or columns
PID (property ID)	Name of a column in a record

8.3.1   A Simple API Application Accessing the Object Store

First, here is a brief example showing how to deal with the object store. Accessing the object store requires five steps:

- Mount a database volume. This is not necessary for the object store and is only supported with Windows CE 2.10 and higher.
- Enumerate the existing databases to see if a new one has to be created.
- Create or open the database.
- Read or write a record.
- Close the database.

The following example creates a new database, inserts two records, reads the two records again, and closes the database.

1.   Create a new "Hello World" application and name it "ObjectStoreIt".

2.   Add the following function before the "WinMain" function:

```
void AccessObjectStore (void)
{
// Variables for Step1 - Open/Create a database
HANDLE hDataBase;
CEOID      CeOid=0;
DWORD      dwErr;

// Variable for Step2 - Writing a record
CEPROPVAL    NewRecProps[4],*Fields;
SYSTEMTIME   SystemTime;
FILETIME     FileTime;
TCHAR        *lpStr;
LPVOID       lpBlob;

// Variables for Step3 - Reading a record
DWORD      dwIndex;
LPBYTE     pData=NULL;
CEPROPID PropId=1;
WORD       cPropID = 1;
DWORD      cbData = 0;

    // Step1 - Open/Create a database
    // *********************************************
```

```
hDataBase = CeOpenDatabase(&CeOid,TEXT("Book831"),0,
                                    0,NULL);
if (hDataBase == INVALID_HANDLE_VALUE)
{
      dwErr = GetLastError ();
      if (dwErr == ERROR_NOT_ENOUGH_MEMORY)
      {  }  // Handle not enough memory
      else
      { // Database does not exist - create it.
            CeOid = CeCreateDatabase(TEXT("Book831"),
            0,0,NULL);
            wprintf(TEXT(" : New Database Created\n\r"));
            if (CeOid != NULL)
                  hDataBase = CeOpenDatabase(&CeOid,
                              TEXT("Book831"),0, 0,NULL);
            else
                  return; // Handle Open Failure
      }
}
wprintf(TEXT("Step1 Complete: Database Opened\n\r"));

// Step2 - Writing a record
// ********************************************
NewRecProps[0].propid = MAKELONG( CEVT_I4, 0);
NewRecProps[0].wLenData = 0;
NewRecProps[0].wFlags = 0;
NewRecProps[0].val.lVal = 0xffffffff;

GetSystemTime(&SystemTime);
SystemTimeToFileTime(&SystemTime,&FileTime);
NewRecProps[1].propid = MAKELONG( CEVT_FILETIME, 1);
NewRecProps[1].wLenData = 0;
NewRecProps[1].wFlags = 0;
NewRecProps[1].val.filetime = FileTime;

lpStr = (TCHAR*)LocalAlloc(LMEM_FIXED, 50 * sizeof(TCHAR));
if ( lpStr )
    _tcscpy(lpStr, TEXT("This is a string property"));
NewRecProps[2].propid = MAKELONG( CEVT_LPWSTR, 2);
NewRecProps[2].wLenData = 0;
```

```
        NewRecProps[2].wFlags = 0;
        NewRecProps[2].val.lpwstr = lpStr;

        lpBlob = (LPVOID)LocalAlloc(LMEM_FIXED, 50 * sizeof(TCHAR));
        if ( lpBlob )
                _tcscpy((TCHAR*)lpBlob, TEXT("This is a blob property"));
        NewRecProps[3].propid = MAKELONG( CEVT_BLOB, 3);
        NewRecProps[3].wLenData = 0;
        NewRecProps[3].wFlags = 0;
        NewRecProps[3].val.blob.dwCount = 50 * sizeof(TCHAR);
        NewRecProps[3].val.blob.lpb = (LPBYTE)lpBlob;

        if(!CeWriteRecordProps(hDataBase, 0, 4, NewRecProps) )
        { return; } // Handle Write Failure
        wprintf(TEXT("Step2 Complete: New Record Written\n\r"));

        if( lpBlob ) LocalFree(lpBlob);
        if( lpStr ) LocalFree(lpStr);

        // Step3 - Reading a record
        // ***********************************************
        if (!CeSeekDatabase(hDataBase, CEDB_SEEK_BEGINNING,
                            0, &dwIndex) )
        { return; } // Handle Seek Failure

        if(!CeReadRecordPropsEx(hDataBase, CEDB_ALLOWREALLOC,
                                &cPropID,NULL, &pData,&cbData,NULL ))
        { return; } // Handle Read Failure

        Fields=(CEPROPVAL*)pData;
        wprintf(TEXT("Step3 Complete: Read %d records\n\r"),cPropID);
        for (int i=0;i<cPropID;i++)
                wprintf(TEXT(" : Prop/Field %d of Type %d\n\r"),
                        i+1,LOWORD(Fields[i].propid));

        // Step4 - Closing the Database
        CloseHandle(hDataBase);
}
```

3. Put the following line before "ShowWindow()" in the "InitInstance" function:

```
AccessObjectStore();
```

If you launch this application on your H/PC Professional you will see a console with your "wprintf" output strings. You can also verify that the new database "Book831" was created. Start Windows CE Explorer with Active Sync. The new database should show up in the "Databases" folder, as you can see in Figure 8.2.

 The final source code of this section can be found on the companion CD under "\Sources\Chapter 8\8.3".

8.3.2   A Simple MFC Application Accessing the Object Store

With MFC, accessing the object store is even easier. Three classes help with the databases in object store:

`CCeDBDatabase`

contains all necessary methods to access databases in the object store.

`CCeDBRecord`

deals with record-related issues, such as adding and deleting record properties, as well as with getting information on properties in the record.

`CCeDBProp`

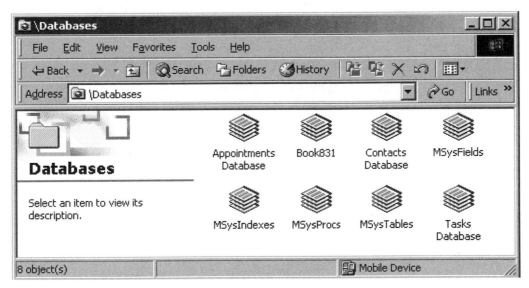

Figure 8.2   The "Book831" icon in the database folder

deals with the properties—in other words, the fields of a record. It also nicely abstracts the various supported property types. Table 8.3 shows a list of all supported properties and the CCeDBProp methods to access them. To store and retrieve Boolean or doubles properties, you have to use the API calls.

The following example will do exactly the same thing that your SDK sample did in the last section.

1. Create a new MFC dialog-based application using the Windows CE project wizard and name it "MFCObjectStore". Accept all defaults that the wizard offers.

2. Open the dialog resource "IDD_MFCOBJECTSTORE_DIALOG" and add a button to it. Keep the name and ID that eVC automatically assigns.

3. Double-click on the button and add the following code to the "OnButton1()" method:

```
void CMFCObjectStoreDlg::OnButton1()
{
CCeDBDatabase myDB;

        // Step1 - Open/Create a database
        // *********************************************
        if (!CCeDBDatabase::Exists(TEXT("Book831")))
              myDB.Create(TEXT("Book831"));
        myDB.Open(TEXT("Book831"));
        wprintf(TEXT("Step1 Complete: Database Opened\n\r"));
```

Table 8.3   The Property/Field Types of a Database in the Object Store

Property Type	SDK Define	CCeDBProp Method
Short	CEVT_I2	Set/GetShort()
Unsigned Short	CEVT_UI2	Set/GetUShort()
Long	CEVT_I4	Set/GetLong()
Unsigned Long	CEVT_UI4	Set/GetULong()
File-Time	CEVT_FILETIME	Set/GetFiletime()
String (always Unicode)	CEVT_LPWSTR	Set/GetString()
Binary Blob	CEVT_BLOB	Set/GetBlob()
Boolean	CEVT_BOOL	Not supported
Double	CEVT_R8	Not supported

```
// Step2 - Writing a record
// ********************************************
CCeDBRecord rec;
CCeDBProp props[4];
SYSTEMTIME  SystemTime;
FILETIME FileTime;
CEBLOB tBlob;

props[0] = CCeDBProp((long)0xffffffff, 0);
GetSystemTime(&SystemTime);
SystemTimeToFileTime(&SystemTime,&FileTime);
props[1] = CCeDBProp(FileTime,1);
props[2] = CCeDBProp(TEXT("This is a string property"),2);
tBlob.lpb=(LPBYTE)TEXT("This is a Blob property");
tBlob.dwCount=lstrlen((TCHAR *)tBlob.lpb)*sizeof(TCHAR);
props[3] = CCeDBProp(tBlob,  3);

rec.AddProps(props,4);
if(!myDB.AddRecord(&rec))
{ return; } // Handle Write Failure

// Step3 - Reading a record
// ********************************************
CCeDBProp *pProp;

if(!myDB.SeekFirst() || !myDB.ReadCurrRecord(&rec))
{ return; } // Handle Seek and Read Failure

for (int i=0;i<rec.GetNumProps();i++)
{
     pProp = rec.GetPropFromIdent(i);
     wprintf(TEXT(" : Prop/Field %d of Type %d\n\r"),
            i+1,pProp->GetType());
}
// Step4 - Closing the Database
// ********************************************
myDB.Close();
}
```

Another class, called "CCeDBEnum()", can be used to enumerate all existing databases in the object store. The MFC sample "WCDDbTst", which is included in the H/PC Professional SDK, demonstrates all MFC techniques for databases on Windows CE.

 The final source code of this section can be found on the companion CD under "\Sources\Chapter 8\8.4".

8.3.3 Adding Object Store Access to the PCDMDLL.DLL

You might ask why you would want to add this functionality to your PCDM application rather than simply step right into ADO implementation. The idea behind the class you are going to create is to have an abstraction for the application between ADO and the pure database API so that the application will run on older devices as well.

As I have mentioned, older Windows CE devices do not support ADO. This class will check the platform type it is running on and then decide whether it should use ADO to access a Pocket-Access file or the object store or whether it should use pure API calls to access the object store. This section will begin by having this class support the native calls to the object store.

Here is what you are going to do:

- Create a new simple object class called "PCDMAccessDB".
- Add several database access methods such as "Create/OpenTable", "Find/Read/WriteRecord", "MoveNext/Previous/First/Last", and "CloseTable".

In Section 8.4.2, you will add ADO code to all those methods. Since your new object "PCDMAccessDB" is UI-less, you will need to include the object in your "PCDMDLL.DLL".

Before you implement the class, it is important to review the call sequences that a client application will need to go through to create a database, read a record, and write a record. To create a database the client has to call

```
AddProperty(<PID>,<Type>,<Sorted>) // For every field
                          // that wants to have an index and then
CreateTable(<Location>,<Name>);
```

To write a record the client has to call

```
AddNewRecord(<DBHandle>); // Create a new record
SetValue(<PID>,<Value>); // per field in the record and then call
WriteRecord(<DBhandle>);
```

To read a record the client has to call first

```
ReadRecord(<handle>,<PropsRead>); // Reads record
GetValue(<PID>,<PtrValue>); // for each field in the record
CloseTable(<handle>); // Closes the Database
```

This sequence of calls nicely abstracts the underlying technology. In the next section, you will see that ADO has a very similar concept of accessing the data.
Note: You will need to put "#ifdef UNDER_CE" around the code in nearly all methods because the object store is neither available nor supported under Win32 for the desktop.

Now let's get down to work . . .

1. Load the latest version of "PCDMDLL.DLL" and add a new "Simple ATL Object" called "PCDMAccessDB" to it.

2. The first method to add is the "AddProperty()" method. It will take two parameters, as shown in Table 8.4.

3. Add the following code to the implementation of the method:

```
STDMETHODIMP CPCDMAccessDB::AddProperty(VARIANT PID, long Sorted)
{
#ifdef UNDER_CE
VARIANT tvPID;

    if (Sorted==TRUE)
    {
        VariantInit(&tvPID);
        VariantChangeType(&tvPID,&PID,0,VT_I4);
        m_DBSortOrder[m_SortCnt].propid=
                            MAKELONG(CEVT_LPWSTR,tvPID.lVal);
        m_DBSortOrder[m_SortCnt].dwFlags=CEDB_SORT_GENERICORDER;
        m_SortCnt++;
```

Table 8.4   PCDMAccessDB.AddProperty Parameters

Type	Variable Name	Used for
VARIANT	PID	The ID of the property. This ID will later be used to reference the property (field) within a record. ADO can have field names; that's why you use a VARIANT here.
LONG	Sorted	If this parameter is set to TRUE, it will be added to the sort order.

```
    }
#endif
    return S_OK;
}
```

As I noted earlier, the object store allows different types at the same position in two records.

4. The "m_DBSortOrder" variable must be declared in the "PCDMAccessDB" class. Add a "Private" section to the class definition and insert the following declarations to it:

```
private:
#ifdef UNDER_CE
    SORTORDERSPEC m_DBSortOrder[10];
#endif
    WORD          m_SortCnt;
```

A database in the object store supports a maximum of four indexes. Since you want to support up to ten properties (fields) in a database (table) in ADO later, you should use an array of ten instead.

5. The next method is the "CreateTable" method. It will take two parameters, as shown in Table 8.5.

6. The implementation of the "CreateTable" method looks like this:

```
STDMETHODIMP CPCDMAccessDB::CreateTable(BSTR FileLocation, BSTR Name)
{
#ifdef UNDER_CE
CEOID  CeOid=0;
HANDLE     tHandle;
```

Table 8.5   PCDMAccessDB.CreateTable Parameters

Type	Variable Name	Used for
BSTR	FileLocation	Using a Pocket-Access database (see Section 8.4) allows you to store the database at any location that you want. If the "FileLocation" parameter is empty, you can store the database in the object store.
BSTR	Name	The name of the new database.

```
       tHandle = CeOpenDatabase(&CeOid,Name,0,0,NULL);
       if (tHandle!= INVALID_HANDLE_VALUE)
       {
              CloseHandle(tHandle);
              CeDeleteDatabase(CeOid);
       }
       if ((CeOid = CeCreateDatabase(Name,PCDM_DB,
                                     m_SortCnt,m_DBSortOrder))==NULL)
              return S_FALSE;
#endif
       return S_OK;
}
```

"PCDM_DB" is a special identifier that can help you find your database if you want to enumerate all existing databases. All databases created with your "PCDMAccessDB" control class will have this identifier.

The "CreateDB" method will delete a database if it already exists.

7. Add the following define statement to the header of "PCDMAccessDB.CPP":

```
#define PCDM_DB 833
```

8. Add the "OpenTable" method to the "IPCDMAccessDB" interface and give it the four parameters shown in Table 8.6.

Table 8.6   PCDMAccessDB.OpenTable Parameters

Type	Variable Name	Used for
BSTR	FileLocation	Using a Pocket-Access database in Section 8.4 allows you to store the database at any location that you want. If the "FileLocation" parameter is empty, you can store the database into the object store.
BSTR	Name	The name of the new database.
VARIANT	PID	Property ID of the primary key, used while this database is open. It can be one of the IDs set with the SetProperty()/CreateTable() calls.
[out,retval] LONG *	Handle	The OpenTable method will return a handle to the open database.

9. Open the "PCDMAccessDB.cpp" source file and add the following code to the implementation of the "OpenTable" method:

```
STDMETHODIMP CPCDMAccessDB::OpenTable(BSTR FileLocation, BSTR Name,
VARIANT PID, long *Handle)
{
#ifdef UNDER_CE
CEOID CeOid=0;
HANDLE      hDataBase;
CEPROPID    tPID=0;
VARIANT tvPID;

        VariantInit(&tvPID);
        VariantChangeType(&tvPID,&PID,0,VT_I4);
        for (int i=0;i<m_SortCnt;i++)
        {
            if (HIWORD(m_DBSortOrder[i].propid)==tvPID.lVal)
            {
                tPID=MAKELONG(LOWORD(m_DBSortOrder[i].propid),
                        tvPID.lVal);
                break;
            }
        }
        hDataBase = CeOpenDatabase(&CeOid,Name,tPID,0,NULL);
        if (hDataBase == INVALID_HANDLE_VALUE)
        {
            *Handle=0;
            return S_FALSE;
        }
        *Handle=(long)hDataBase;
        VariantCopy(&m_ActPID,&PID);
#endif

        return S_OK;
}
```

You do not specify the "CEDB_AUTOINCREMENT" flag so as to make sure that you call "MoveNext" before you read the next record. This ensures compatibility with the later ADO implementation.

10. The variable "VARIANT m_ActPID;" must be declared in the private section mentioned in Step 4.

11. Add the "CloseClose" method and give it only one parameter, shown in Table 8.7.

12. Add the following code to its implementation:

```
STDMETHODIMP CPCDMAccessDB::CloseDB(LONG Handle)
{
#ifdef UNDER_CE
    m_SortCnt=0;
    m_rfldCnt=0;
    CloseHandle((HANDLE)Handle);
#endif
    return S_OK;
}
```

The "m_rfldCnt" and "m_wfldCnt" variables will count the number of fields written to or read from a record.

13. You must initialize this variable in the private section of the "PCDMAccessDB" class:

```
WORD m_rfldCnt,m_wfldCnt;
```

14. Add the navigation methods "MoveFirst", "MoveLast", "MoveNext", and "MovePrevious". They will have only one parameter, shown in Table 8.8.

15. The code for those navigation methods is simple:

```
STDMETHODIMP CPCDMAccessDB::MoveFirst(LONG Handle)
{
```

Table 8.7 PCDMAccessDB.CloseTable Parameter

Type	Variable Name	Used for
LONG	Handle	The handle of an open database.

Table 8.8 PCDMAccessDB.Move\<direction\> Parameter

Type	Variable Name	Used for
LONG	Handle	The handle of an open database.

```
#ifdef UNDER_CE
    if (!(m_curRec=CeSeekDatabase((HANDLE)Handle,
    CEDB_SEEK_BEGINNING,
                                     0, &m_dwIndex)))
            return S_FALSE;

#endif
    return S_OK;
}

STDMETHODIMP CPCDMAccessDB::MoveLast(LONG Handle)
{
#ifdef UNDER_CE
    if (!(m_curRec=CeSeekDatabase((HANDLE)Handle, CEDB_SEEK_END,
                                 0, &m_dwIndex)))
            return S_FALSE;
#endif
    return S_OK;
}

STDMETHODIMP CPCDMAccessDB::MoveNext(LONG Handle)
{
#ifdef UNDER_CE
    if (!(m_curRec=CeSeekDatabase((HANDLE)Handle, CEDB_SEEK_
    CURRENT,
                                     1, &m_dwIndex)))
            return S_FALSE;
#endif
    return S_OK;
}

STDMETHODIMP CPCDMAccessDB::MovePrevious(LONG Handle)
{
#ifdef UNDER_CE
    if (!(m_curRec=CeSeekDatabase((HANDLE)Handle,
    CEDB_SEEK_CURRENT,
                                     -1, &m_dwIndex)))
            return S_FALSE;

#endif
    return S_OK;
}
```

You do not need sophisticated error handling if the "CeSeekDatabase()" call does not succeed. This is up to the calling application.

16. The two private variables that you will need to declare for the "Move" methods are "DWORD m_dwIndex" and "CEOID m_curRec".

"m_dwIndex" holds the current record number, and "m_curRec" contains a CEOID to the current record. Since CEOIDs are not available on the desktop, put the "m_curRec" declaration in between the "#IFDEF UNDER_CE" clause.

17. The next method to be added is "FindRecord()". It will take three parameters, shown in Table 8.9.

The "FindRecord" method will start searching from the current position in the database. This allows for a "Search Next Record" using the same method.

18. Add the following code to its implementation:

```
STDMETHODIMP CPCDMAccessDB::FindRecord(LONG Handle, VARIANT PID,
                                       VARIANT Value)
{
#ifdef UNDER_CE
CEPROPVAL tPropVal;
DWORD     tdwIndex;
VARIANT tvPID,tvValue;

    VariantInit(&tvPID);
    VariantInit(&tvValue);
    VariantChangeType(&tvPID,&PID,0,VT_I4);
```

Table 8.9   PCDMAccessDB.FindRecord Parameters

Type	Variable Name	Used for
LONG	Handle	The handle of an open database.
VARIANT	PID	The property ID of a field. In ADO you can also use a field name, so you are using a VARIANT here.
VARIANT	Value	The value that you want to look for in the database. Again, to keep it simple in case of strings, you are comparing the value with the field content from the left. For example, a search for "Da" will find the first "Dagger" or "Dart."

```
  if (tvPID.lVal!=m_ActPID.lVal) return S_FALSE;
  tPropVal.wLenData = 0;
  tPropVal.wFlags = 0;
  VariantChangeType(&tvValue,&Value,0,VT_BSTR);
  tPropVal.propid=MAKELONG(CEVT_LPWSTR,m_ActPID.lVal);
  tPropVal.val.lpwstr=tvValue.bstrVal;

  tdwIndex=m_dwIndex;
  if (!(m_curRec=CeSeekDatabase((HANDLE)Handle,
                  CEDB_SEEK_VALUEFIRSTEQUAL,(DWORD)&tPropVal,
                  &tdwIndex)))
  {
      m_curRec=CeSeekDatabase((HANDLE)Handle,
                              CEDB_SEEK_BEGINNING, m_dwIndex,
                              &m_dwIndex);
      return S_FALSE;
  }
  m_dwIndex=tdwIndex;
#endif
return S_OK;
}
```

The first line of the method checks whether the supplied PID is identical to the sort order specified during the "OpenTable" call. If it is not the same, you return an error. To keep it simple, your PCDM table on Windows CE will only contain strings. The "FindRecord" method will search through the database, using the current primary key that was given with the "OpenTable" method.

Thus far you have only positioned the internal database pointer on a record that you want to manipulate. Now it is time to get to the two methods that will actually access the records. To keep it simple again, you will only deal with one open database (table), one record that you can read, and one record that you can write. The data of the record will be discarded as soon as the record is written to the database.

The first method that you have to create is the "AddNewRecord" method. It will reset the two variables "m_curRec" and "m_wfldCnt".

19. Add the "AddNewRecord" method with only one parameter, shown in Table 8.10.

20. Add the following code to its implementation:

```
STDMETHODIMP CPCDMAccessDB::AddNewRecord(LONG Handle)
{
#ifdef UNDER_CE
```

Table 8.10   PCDMAccessDB.AddNewRecord Parameter

Type	Variable Name	Used for
LONG	Handle	Handle of an open database

```
      m_curRec=0;
#endif
      m_wfldCnt=0;

      return S_OK;
}
```

This method exists solely to stay in sync with ADO (to be discussed later in this chapter). ADO requires an "AddNew" method before actual values can be written. The object store does not require this, so you are just using this method to initialize some values.

21.   Add the "SetValue()" method with the two parameters shown in Table 8.11.

22.   The code for the "SetValue" method is as follows:

```
STDMETHODIMP CPCDMAccessDB::SetValue(VARIANT PID, VARIANT Value)
{
#ifdef UNDER_CE
VARIANT tValue,tvPID;

      if (m_wfldCnt>9) return S_FALSE;
      VariantInit(&tValue);
      VariantChangeType(&tValue,&Value,0,VT_BSTR);
      VariantInit(&tvPID);
      VariantChangeType(&tvPID,&PID,0,VT_I4);
```

Table 8.11   PCDMAccessDB.SetValue Parameters

Type	Variable Name	Used for
VARIANT	PID	Property ID. If it matches with the PID of the OpenTable method it will be the primary key.
VARIANT	Value	The value to be written.

```
    m_wFields[m_wfldCnt].propid=MAKELONG(CEVT_LPWSTR, tvPID.lVal);
    m_BStr[m_wfldCnt]=SysAllocString(tValue.bstrVal);
    m_wFields[m_wfldCnt].val.lpwstr=m_BStr[m_wfldCnt];
    m_wFields[m_wfldCnt].wLenData = 0;
    m_wFields[m_wfldCnt].wFlags = 0;
    m_wfldCnt++;
#endif
    return S_OK;
}
```

You only support BSTR for your database (table) storage on Windows CE. Again the following variables have to be declared in your private section:

```
BSTR            m_BStr[10];
CEPROPVAL       m_wFields[10];
```

You support a maximum of ten properties per record. The "m_wFields" variable has to be located in between the "#IFDEF UNDER_CE" clause.

This was the hard part. The easy part is the "WriteRecord" method.

23.   Add the method "WriteRecord" to the "IPCDMAccessDB" interface and give it the parameter shown in Table 8.12.

24.   The implementation has only one line of code:

```
STDMETHODIMP CPCDMAccessDB::WriteRecord(LONG DBHandle)
{
#ifdef UNDER_CE
    if(!CeWriteRecordProps((HANDLE)DBHandle, m_curRec, m_wfldCnt,
                            m_wFields) )
            return S_FALSE;
    for (int i=0;i<m_wfldCnt;i++)
            SysFreeString(m_BStr[i]);
    m_fldCnt=0;
#endif
    return S_OK;
}
```

Table 8.12   PCDMAccessDB.WriteRecord Parameter

Type	Variable Name	Used for
LONG	DBHandle	The handle of a previously opened database

After you have written the record, you must invalidate the values in the "m_wFields" array by resetting "m_wfldCnt" to zero. You cannot write another record using the same methods as before.

The steps for the "ReadRecord" method are similar except that you will reverse the order of things. First, the application will call the "ReadRecord" method; then it will read out the values of the record using "GetValue".

25. Create the "ReadRecord" method and give it the two parameters shown in Table 8.13.

26. The code for "ReadRecord" looks like this:

```
STDMETHODIMP CPCDMAccessDB::ReadRecord(LONG DBHandle,LONG *Count)
{
#ifdef UNDER_CE
LPBYTE      pData=NULL;
DWORD       cbData=0;

    m_rfldCnt=0;
    if(!CeReadRecordPropsEx((HANDLE)DBHandle, CEDB_ALLOWREALLOC,
                        &m_rfldCnt,NULL,&pData,&cbData, NULL ))
    {
        DWORD err=GetLastError();
        m_rFields=NULL;
        return S_FALSE;
    }
    m_rFields=(CEPROPVAL*)pData;
    *Count=m_rfldCnt;
#endif
    return S_OK;
}
```

27. "ReadRecord" requires the declaration of the variable "CEPROPVAL *m_rFields;" in your private section of the "PCDMAccessDB" class.

Table 8.13 **PCDMAccessDB.ReadRecord Parameters**

Type	Variable Name	Used for
LONG	DBHandle	The handle of a previously opened database
[out, retval] LONG *	Count	Number of properties (fields) that were read

28. The last method that you will need to add to your class is the "GetValue" method. It will take the parameters shown in Table 8.14.

29. Here is the code for the "GetValue" method:

```
STDMETHODIMP CPCDMAccessDB::GetValue(VARIANT PID, VARIANT *Value)
{
#ifdef UNDER_CE
CEPROPVAL    *Flds=NULL;
VARIANT            tvPID;

     if (m_rFields==NULL || m_rfldCnt==0) return S_FALSE;
     VariantInit(Value);
     VariantInit(&tvPID);
     VariantChangeType(&tvPID,&PID,0,VT_I4);

     for (int i=0;i<m_rfldCnt;i++)
     {
          if (HIWORD(m_rFields[i].propid)==tvPID.lVal)
          {
               Flds=&m_rFields[i];
               break;
          }
     }
     if (Flds==NULL) return S_FALSE;

     Value->vt=VT_BSTR;
     Value->bstrVal=SysAllocString((TCHAR*)Flds->val.lpwstr);
#endif
     return S_OK;
}
```

You should check to make sure that your private section in the "PCDMAccessDB" class is correct:

```
private:
#ifdef UNDER_CE
     SORTORDERSPEC      m_DBSortOrder[10];
     CEOID              m_curRec;
     CEPROPVAL          m_wFields[10];
     CEPROPVAL          *m_rFields;
#endif
     BSTR         m_BStr[10];
     VARIANT      m_ActPID;
     WORD         m_SortCnt;
```

Table 8.14 **PCDMAccessDB.GetValue Parameters**

Type	Variable Name	Used for
LONG	PID	Property ID of the property you want to read.
[out, retval] VARIANT *	Value	This value will receive the value that was read. Again, you only support LONGs, BSTRings, and DATEs.

```
DWORD      m_dwIndex;
WORD       m_rfldCnt,m_wfldCnt;
```

Now add the following code to the constructor of the "PCDMAccessDB" class:

```
    CPCDMAccessDB()
    {
#ifdef UNDER_CE
        m_curRec=0;
        m_rFields=NULL;
#endif
        m_wfldCnt=0;
        m_rfldCnt=0;
        m_SortCnt=0;
        m_dwIndex=0;
        VariantInit(&m_ActPID);
    }
```

Before you test the class in eMbedded Visual Basic and integrate it into your PCDM application, remember to compile the Win32 desktop version as well.

 The final source code of this section can be found on the companion CD under "\Sources\ThreadExample\PCDMDLL\Step5".

8.3.4 Testing the New Class in eMbedded Visual Basic

Are you starting to get the drill? Once again you will be testing your new class in eVB first. To be consistent, you will do exactly the same as you have done previously with your small SDK and MFC applications.

1. Create a new eVB project.
2. Add a button and a list box to the main form.
3. Enter the following code to the button's "Command1_Click" event:

```
Private Sub Command1_Click()
Dim a As PCDMAccessDB
Dim DBhandle As Long
Dim vali As Variant
Dim i, tCnt As Long

List1.Clear
    Set a = CreateObject("PCDMDLL.PCDMAccessDB.1")
List1.AddItem "Class created"
    a.AddProperty 0, True
    a.AddProperty 1, False
    a.AddProperty 2, False
    a.CreateTable "", "Book835"
List1.AddItem "DB Created"
    DBhandle = a.OpenTable("", "Book835", 0)
List1.AddItem "DB Opened, handle=" & DBhandle
    a.AddNewRecord DBhandle
List1.AddItem "New Record Created"
    a.SetValue 0, 42234
    a.SetValue 1, Date
    a.SetValue 2, "This is a string"
List1.AddItem "Record prepared to be written..."
    a.WriteRecord DBhandle
List1.AddItem "...Record written"
    a.MoveFirst DBhandle
    tCnt = a.ReadRecord(DBhandle)
List1.AddItem "Properties read: " & tCnt
    For i = 0 To tCnt - 1
        vali = a.GetValue(i)
List1.AddItem "1st Value read: " & vali
    Next
    a.CloseTable DBhandle
    List1.AddItem "DB Closed, all done."
End Sub
```

4. The "CEVT_I2" value is defined in the following section that you can add to the top of your code view:

```
Option Explicit
Const CEVT_I2 = 2
Const CEVT_UI2 = 18
Const CEVT_I4 = 3
Const CEVT_UI4 = 19
Const CEVT_FILETIME = 64
Const CEVT_LPWSTR = 31
Const CEVT_BLOB = 65
Const CEVT_BOOL = 11
Const CEVT_R8 = 5
```

As soon as you start the application, you will get the results in the list box. If everything works well, your eMbedded Visual Basic application should show a screen similar to that in Figure 8.3.

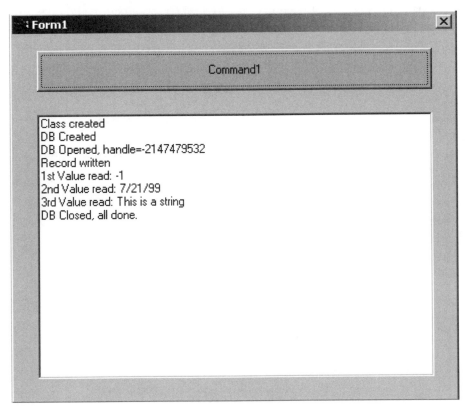

Figure 8.3 eMbedded Visual Basic test program showing the PCDMAccessDB calls

The final source code of this section can be found on the companion CD under "\Sources\Chapter 8\8.5".

8.3.5   Adding the PCDMAccessDB Class to the PCDM Application

So far, your PCDM application has a UI, but no actual data to play with. In this chapter, you will remedy that situation. The "PCDMAccessDB" class represents your access to data for the Pocket-CD-Manager application. Using this class, you will fill all list views of your application with data.

Because the database on your device is still empty, for now you will need to fill it with some sample data. In the next chapter, you will synchronize your desktop "Deluxe CD"-access database with a Pocket-Access database, using ADO to access it. This process will use the same class so that you will not need to change any of the code you are going to write now.

1. Load the most recent version of the PCDM CE application and open the "PCDMView.CPP" source file.

Before you can access any of the methods in the "PCDMDLL.DLL COM" server, you must install a reference to the DLL in your code. Do you remember how to do so?

2. Enter the following lines to the "stdafx.h" file:

```
#import "<Path to your DLL>\pcdmdll.dll" \
        rename_namespace("PCDMdll_space") raw_interfaces_only
    #define PCDM_PID_ID            0
    #define PCDM_PID_AUTHOR        1
    #define PCDM_PID_TITLE         2
    #define PCDM_PID_LABEL         3
    #define PCDM_PID_RELEASE       4
    #define PCDM_PID_COPYRIGHT     5
    #define PCDM_PID_CRC           6

    #define PCDM_PID_TRACKS_ID         0
    #define PCDM_PID_TRACKS_TITLE      1
    #define PCDM_PID_TRACKS_TRACKNO    2
```

CE uses the defines as property IDs (field names) for your tables.

3. Add the following lines to the "stdafx.cpp" file:

```
void __stdcall _com_issue_error(HRESULT hr)
{
```

```
      // Error handling goes here!
}
```

The "<path to your DLL>" points to the location of the desktop version of your "PCDMDLL.DLL"

4. Add the following lines to the top of the source file that contains the code that accesses the DLL— in this case, "PCDMView.CPP" and "Details.CPP":

```
using namespace PCDMdll_space;
```

As mentioned in Chapter 6, this will create a file called "PCDMdll.tlh" in the output directory that contains all the information on your "PCDMDLL" classes.

5. Locate the "OnInitialUpdate" method and add the following call to the end of it:

```
RefreshLVC();
```

This method of the "CPCDMView" class will be called on two occasions:

*   On initial update
*   After a CD was successfully received via IrDA

6. To add this new method, select the "CPCDMView" class in the class view and add a new private member function called "RefreshLVC". Do not give it any parameter, but set the "Function Type" to "BOOL".

7. Now add the following code to its implementation:

```
BOOL CPCDMView::RefreshLVC()
{
IPCDMAccessDBPtr   comDB;
long DBHandle;
VARIANT value,tvalue;
VariantInit(&value);
VariantInit(&tvalue);

      HRESULT hr=comDB.CreateInstance( __uuidof( PCDMAccessDB ) );
      if (FAILED(hr))
      {
      MessageBox(TEXT("Could not access the PCDMAccessDB Class"));
          return FALSE;
      }
```

```
hr=comDB->OpenTable(TEXT("\\My Documents\\PCDM.cdb"),
                    TEXT("PCDMCDs"),_variant_t((LONG)
                    PCDM_PID_ID),
                    &DBHandle);
if (hr!=S_OK) // If Database does not exist create sample data
{
        hr=comDB->AddProperty(_variant_t((LONG)PCDM_PID_ID),
        TRUE);
        hr=comDB->AddProperty(_variant_t(
                            (LONG)PCDM_PID_AUTHOR),FALSE);
        hr=comDB->AddProperty(_variant_t(
                            (LONG)PCDM_PID_TITLE),FALSE);
        hr=comDB->AddProperty(_variant_t(
                            (LONG)PCDM_PID_LABEL),FALSE);
        hr=comDB->AddProperty(_variant_t(
                            (LONG)PCDM_PID_RELEASE),FALSE);
        hr=comDB->AddProperty(_variant_t(
                            (LONG)PCDM_PID_COPYRIGHT),FALSE);
        hr=comDB->AddProperty(_variant_t(
                            (LONG)PCDM_PID_CRC),FALSE);

        hr=comDB->CreateTable(TEXT("\\My Documents\\PCDM.cdb"),
                            TEXT("PCDMCDs"));
        hr=comDB->OpenTable(TEXT("\\My Documents\\PCDM.cdb"),
                            TEXT("PCDMCDs"),_variant_t(
                                (LONG)PCDM_PID_ID),&DBHandle);

        hr=comDB->AddNewRecord(DBHandle);
        hr=comDB->SetValue(_variant_t((LONG)PCDM_PID_ID),
                            _variant_t(TEXT("1")));
        hr=comDB->SetValue(_variant_t((LONG)PCDM_PID_AUTHOR),
                            _variant_t(TEXT("Madonna")));
        hr=comDB->SetValue(_variant_t((LONG)PCDM_PID_TITLE),
                            _variant_t(TEXT("Ray of Light")));
        hr=comDB->SetValue(_variant_t((LONG)PCDM_PID_LABEL),
                            _variant_t(TEXT("Tower Records")));
        hr=comDB->SetValue(_variant_t((LONG)PCDM_PID_RELEASE),
                            _variant_t(TEXT("8/8/96")));
        hr=comDB->SetValue(_variant_t((LONG)PCDM_PID_COPYRIGHT),
                            _variant_t(TEXT("(c) 1996")));
        hr=comDB->SetValue(_variant_t((LONG)PCDM_PID_CRC),
```

```
                                          _variant_t(TEXT("0")));
              hr=comDB->WriteRecord(DBHandle);

              hr=comDB->AddNewRecord(DBHandle);
              hr=comDB->SetValue(_variant_t((LONG)PCDM_PID_ID),
                                 _variant_t(TEXT("2")));
              hr=comDB->SetValue(_variant_t((LONG)PCDM_PID_AUTHOR),
                                 _variant_t(TEXT("Queen")));
              hr=comDB->SetValue(_variant_t((LONG)PCDM_PID_TITLE),
                                 _variant_t(TEXT("Innuendo")));
              hr=comDB->SetValue(_variant_t((LONG)PCDM_PID_LABEL),
                                 _variant_t(TEXT("Queen Records")));
              hr=comDB->SetValue(_variant_t((LONG)PCDM_PID_RELEASE),
                                 _variant_t(TEXT("3/2/92")));
              hr=comDB->SetValue(_variant_t((LONG)PCDM_PID_COPYRIGHT),
                                 _variant_t(TEXT("(c) 1992")));
              hr=comDB->SetValue(_variant_t((LONG)PCDM_PID_CRC),
                                 _variant_t(TEXT("0")));
              hr=comDB->WriteRecord(DBHandle);
              hr=comDB->MoveFirst(DBHandle);
      } // Get rid of that code after testing your application...

      m_LVC.Reset();
      int cntRec=0;
      long CDID=0,FieldCnt;
      while (hr==S_OK)
  {
              hr=comDB->ReadRecord(DBHandle,&FieldCnt);
              if (hr==S_OK)
              {
                  for (int i=0;i<FieldCnt;i++)
                  {
                      VariantClear(&value);
                      hr=comDB->GetValue(_variant_t((LONG)
                                  (PCDM_PID_ID+i)),&value);
                      if (hr==S_OK)
                      {
                          switch (i)
                          {
                              case PCDM_PID_ID:
                                  VariantChangeType(&tvalue,
```

```
                                                    &value,0,VT_I4);
                                    CDID=tvalue.lVal;
                                    break;
                        case PCDM_PID_AUTHOR:
                                    m_LVC.AddItem(cntRec,
                                    0,CDID,
                                                value.bstrVal);
                                    break;
                        case PCDM_PID_TITLE:
                                    m_LVC.AddItem(cntRec,
                                        1,CDID,value.bstrVal);
                                    break;
                    }
                }
            }
            cntRec++;
        }
        hr=comDB->MoveNext(DBHandle);
    }
    comDB->CloseTable(DBHandle);
    return TRUE;
}
```

8. Open the "Details.cpp" file and add the following code to the end of "OnInitDialog":

```
IPCDMAccessDBPtr   comDB;
long DBHandle,FieldCnt;
VARIANT value,tvalue;


HRESULT hr=comDB.CreateInstance( __uuidof( PCDMAccessDB ) );
if (FAILED(hr))
{
    MessageBox(TEXT("Could not access the PCDMAccessDB Class"));
    return TRUE;
}
VariantInit(&value);
hr=comDB->OpenTable(TEXT("\\My Documents\\PCDM.cdb"),TEXT("Titles"),
                    _variant_t((LONG)PCDM_PID_ID),&DBHandle);
if (hr!=S_OK)
{
```

```
            MessageBox(TEXT("Could not open Titles Table"));
            return TRUE;
}
VariantInit(&value);
VariantInit(&tvalue);
value.vt=VT_I4;
value.lVal=m_TitleID;
hr=comDB->MoveFirst(DBHandle);
hr=comDB->FindRecord(DBHandle,_variant_t((LONG)PCDM_PID_ID),value);
if (hr!=S_OK)
{
            MessageBox(TEXT("CD Does not exits in database"));
            EndDialog(TRUE);
}
if (hr==S_OK)
{
            hr=comDB->ReadRecord(DBHandle,&FieldCnt);
            if (hr==S_OK)
            {
                    for (int i=0;i<FieldCnt;i++)
                    {
                            VariantClear(&value);
                            hr=comDB->GetValue(_variant_t((LONG)
                            (PCDM_PID_ID+i)),
                            &value);
                            if (hr==S_OK)
                            switch(i)
                            {
                                    case PCDM_PID_AUTHOR:
                                                m_strArtist=value.bstrVal;
                                         break;
                                    case PCDM_PID_TITLE:
                                                m_strTitle=value.bstrVal;
                                         break;
                                    case PCDM_PID_LABEL:
                                                m_strLabel=value.bstrVal;
                                         break;
                                    case PCDM_PID_RELEASE:
                                                m_strRelease=value.bstrVal;
                                         break;
                                    case PCDM_PID_COPYRIGHT:
```

```
                                        m_strCopyright=value.bstrVal;
                            break;
                    default:
                            break;
                }
            }
            UpdateData(FALSE);
        }
}
comDB->CloseTable(DBHandle);

// Fill Track list box
hr=comDB->OpenTable(TEXT("\\My Documents\\PCDM.cdb"),
                    TEXT("PCDMTracks"),_variant_t((LONG)PCDM_PID_ID),
                    &DBHandle);
if (hr!=S_OK) // If Database does not exist create sample data
{
        hr=comDB->AddProperty(_variant_t((LONG)PCDM_PID_TRACKS_ID)
        ,TRUE);
        hr=comDB->AddProperty(_variant_t((LONG)PCDM_PID_TRACKS_TITLE),
                        FALSE);
        hr=comDB->AddProperty(_variant_t((LONG)PCDM_PID_TRACKS_TRACKNO),
                        FALSE);
        hr=comDB->CreateTable(TEXT("\\My Documents\\PCDM.cdb"),
                        TEXT("PCDMTracks"));
        hr=comDB->OpenTable(TEXT("\\My Documents\\PCDM.cdb"),
                        TEXT("PCDMTracks"),
                        _variant_t((LONG)PCDM_PID_TRACKS_ID),
                        &DBHandle);
        hr=comDB->AddNewRecord(DBHandle);
        hr=comDB->SetValue(_variant_t((LONG)PCDM_PID_TRACKS_ID),
                        _variant_t(m_TitleID));
        hr=comDB->SetValue(_variant_t((LONG)PCDM_PID_TRACKS_TITLE),
                        _variant_t(TEXT("Skin")));
        hr=comDB->SetValue(_variant_t((LONG)PCDM_PID_TRACKS_TRACKNO),
                        _variant_t(1L));
        hr=comDB->WriteRecord(DBHandle);

        hr=comDB->AddNewRecord(DBHandle);
        hr=comDB->SetValue(_variant_t((LONG)PCDM_PID_TRACKS_ID),
                        _variant_t(m_TitleID));
```

```
        hr=comDB->SetValue(_variant_t((LONG)PCDM_PID_TRACKS_TITLE),
                          _variant_t(TEXT("Frozen")));
        hr=comDB->SetValue(_variant_t((LONG)PCDM_PID_TRACKS_TRACKNO),
                          _variant_t(2L));
        hr=comDB->WriteRecord(DBHandle);
        hr=comDB->MoveFirst(DBHandle);
} // Get rid of that code after testing your application...
int ListPos=0,cnt=0;
long CDID=0;
long tTitleID=-1;
while (hr==S_OK)
{
        hr=comDB->ReadRecord(DBHandle,&FieldCnt);
        if (hr==S_OK)
        {
                for (int i=0;i<FieldCnt;i++)
                {
                        hr=comDB->GetValue(_variant_t(
                                        (LONG)(PCDM_PID_ID+i)),&value);
                        switch (i)
                        {
                                case PCDM_PID_TRACKS_ID:
                                        VariantChangeType(&tvalue,
                                                        &value,NULL,VT_I4);
                                        tTitleID=tvalue.lVal;
                                        CDID=cnt;
                                        break;
                                case PCDM_PID_TRACKS_TITLE:
                                        m_ctrlTrackLst.AddItem(ListPos, i-1,
                                                        CDID,value.bstrVal);
                                        break;
                                case PCDM_PID_TRACKS_TRACKNO:
                                        m_ctrlTrackLst.AddItem(ListPos,i-1,
                                                        CDID,value.bstrVal);
                                        ListPos++;
                                        break;
                                default:
                                        break;
                        }
                        VariantClear(&value);
                        if (tTitleID!=m_TitleID)
```

```
                    break;
            }
            cnt++;
        }
        hr=comDB->MoveNext(DBHandle);
    }
    comDB->CloseTable(DBHandle);
```

Compile and run the application. If everything is correct, you should see two CD titles—a Queen CD and a Madonna CD—in the main form of your Pocket-CD-Manager. If you select the Madonna CD, you will see the details dialog box containing another list view and the two sample tracks you entered. If you click on the Queen CD, the list view in the details dialog box will be empty. You can get rid of the code that creates these two sample entries as soon as you address the access database in the next chapter.

 The final source code of this section can be found on the companion CD under "\Sources\ThreadExample\PCDM CD\Step6".

8.4 ADO for Windows CE

System DLL:	ADOCE.DLL, ADOCEDB.DLL, ADOCERES.DLL (V3: ADOCE30.dll, ADOCEDB30.DLL, ADOCEOLEDB30.DLL), ADOSYNC.DLL ActiveSync provider
Include file:	ADOCE30.H
Library file:	Not necessary, uses COM
Help file:	ADOCE30.CHM (MSDN 1/2000 and later)
Available since:	Add-on technology for Windows CE 2.11 (palm-size PC 1.2 and H/PC Professional) and Windows CE 3.0 (Pocket PC). See also Table 8.15.
API prefix/suffix:	ADOCE
InitCommonControlEx flag:	Not necessary
MFC class:	Not supported
Store here:	Structured data

One of my favorite Microsoft technologies is ADO. If you have past experience with Data Access Objects (DAO), Remote Data Objects (RDO), Open Database Connectivity (ODBC), Remote Data Services (RDS), or Transaction Sequential Query Language (TSQL), you will find that the Active Data Objects (ADO) provide a good mixture of those earlier technologies and are based on OLEDB (not an actual abbreviation).

To add some more abbreviations to the list above, ADO is part of Microsoft's Microsoft Data Access Components (MDAC) and part of Microsoft's Universal Data Access (UDA) strategy. Confused? Believe me, I'm quite sympathetic. Let me try to bring some order into this terminological confusion.

ADO is Microsoft's latest and strategically most important data access technology. It represents a nice COM abstraction layer of OLEDB, a low-level database "driver" (called a "provider") that was designed to access all kinds of data at high speed. To allow for a smooth migration from ODBC to OLEDB, Microsoft ships an OLEDB provider that uses ODBC data as its source and exposes that information as OLEDB data. ADO ships in the MDAC together with several OLEDB providers, RDS, and ODBC. Figure 8.4 illustrates the ADO object hierarchy.

On Windows CE, Microsoft did not have a very clear strategy for ADO until Windows CE Version 3.0. With Windows CE 3.0, ADOCE finally becomes a core part of the operating system and is based on OLEDB, just as it is on the desktop. Table 8.15 shows which version of ADOCE is available for the various versions of Windows CE and where to get it.

In the case of ADOCE 2.0, ADO is not layered on top of OLEDB because OLEDB did not exist at that time. If you are wondering why there was no Version 1.0

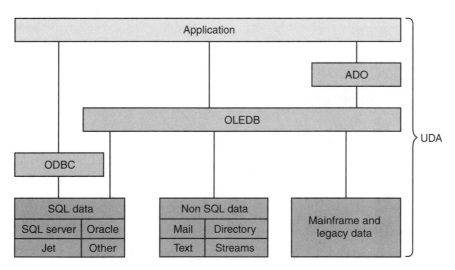

Figure 8.4 The object model of ADO for Windows CE

Table 8.15   The Availability of ADOCE for Windows CE

Windows CE Version	Platform	ADOCE Version	How/Where to Get . . .
1.0	H/PC 1.0	Not available	N/A
2.00	H/PC 2.0	ADOCE 2.0	http://support.microsoft.com/support/kb/articles/Q238/9/47.ASP or in the "Visual Basic for Windows CE 2.0" CD. To get it installed with ActiveSync 3.x, read http://support.microsoft.com/support/kb/articles/Q242/4/99.asp
2.01	PsPC 1.0	ADOCE 2.0	See above
2.11	PsPC 1.2, H/PC 3.0	ADOCE 2.0, ADOCE 3.0	http://www.microsoft.com/windowsce
2.12	Only embedded devices	ADOCE 2.0	Shipping with "Platform Builder 2.12"
3.00	PsPC 2.0 (Pocket PC)	ADOCE 3.0	Comes with the device

of ADOCE, here is the answer. There was an ADO control in the very first ActiveX control pack for Windows CE. This control pack had a very short lifespan and was quickly resolved into the controls now shipping with eVB. The ADO control disappeared into what's now known as ADOCE.

What Are the Benefits of ADO?

Easy-to-use COM interface: Compared to ODBC and OLEDB, ADO is an easy-to-learn and easy-to-use COM interface. Knowing its four essential commands, listed below in boldface print, you can already access fields in a table of a database:

- Create a connection object
- **Open a connection**
- Create a RecordSet object
- **Set the connection string of a RecordSet to connection object**
- **Execute or open the RecordSet using an SQL string**
- Read values from the RecordSet

Access to all kind of data: ODBC can only be used to access data from relational databases. ADO can access all kinds of structured data, including the file system, SQL-based databases, an exchange e-mail server, the ActiveDirectory, and so on.

Part of the OS, starting with Windows CE 2.12 and Windows 2000: Compared to ODBC, which was always an operating system add-on, ADO, beginning with Windows CE 2.12 and Windows 2000, has become a basic part of the OS. In addition, H/PC Professionals and some palm-size PC Version 1.2 devices already have ADOCE 2.0 preinstalled. ADOCE 2.0 can access two data sources:

- Object store
- Pocket-Access databases (.CDB)

ADOCE 3.0 has the potential to access even more data sources as soon as third parties create OLEDB providers for their data sources. Sybase Anywhere CE and Microsoft's SQL Server for Windows CE are already working on such implementations.

Differences between ADOCE and the Native Object Store

As shown in Table 8.16, there are some important differences between ADOCE and Windows CE's native object store technology, as shown in Table 8.15.

You might be wondering why Table 8.16 states, "Very similar technology is available on the desktop." Microsoft decided to give the "ADORecordset" on Windows CE a different name because it does not support all of the features of the desktop version. It is called "ADOCERecordset" instead. And, of course, the GUID is different, too. Unfortunately, this leads to source incompatibility between a desktop and a Windows CE application. With ADOCE 3.0, Microsoft again changed the GUID and added some methods to the ADOCE interfaces that bring ADOCE closer to the desktop version. Therefore a lot depends on how you create the ADOCE objects. If you look into the registry you will find two ProgIDs for ADOCE 3.0:

```
ADOCE.Recordset.3.0
ADOCE.Connection.3.0
```

Version 2.0 of ADOCE has two ProgIDs named:

```
ADOCE.Recordset
ADOCE.Recordset.1
```

Depending on how you create your object, you will get either a Version 2.0 or Version 3.0 ADO "RecordSet". There are at least two advantages to this state of affairs. You can have both versions on your device at the same time, and Microsoft

Table 8.16   Comparison between the Object Store Technology and ADO

Native Object Store	ADO
Object-oriented structure. Each property (field) in a record can be of a different type, even across different records.	Structured storage, but relational. Each field in a record is of the same type in subsequent records.
Records can consist of variable properties (fields).	Every record has the same number of fields.
API-based.	COM-based.
Direct access to (and only to) the object store.	ADOCE 2.0 allows direct access to the object store and to Pocket-Access files. ADOCE 3.0 layers on top of an OLEDB provider.
Supported since Windows CE 1.0.	Only supported on certain Windows CE devices and on CE versions subsequent to 1.x.
Rather complicated to use and still not very flexible.	Easy to use and very flexible.
No comparable technology available on the desktop.	Very similar technology is available on the desktop (see below).
No filtering and limited to four sort orders per database.	No limits and permits extensive filtering. With the object store, the same limitation of four sort orders.
MFC classes available.	Not yet supported by MFC for Windows CE.

can update either Version 2.0 or Version 3.0 without necessarily changing the other. Another way to find out which version of ADOCE you have installed is by trying to create a "Connection" object. If this fails, but the "RecordSet" object is created, you are in an ADOCE 2.0 environment. If both succeed you can be sure ADOCE 3.0 is installed.

There are also some other differences between ADO for the desktop and ADO for Windows CE. Table 8.17 contains a list of those differences. Luckily, these differences are minimal, and it should be fairly simple to write an abstraction call combining the two flavors. Since you already have abstracted the access to the object store with native calls and ADOCE, you are not going to add another abstraction to compensate for the desktop needs.

In Section 5.5, you had your first contact with ADO in eVB. You will now concentrate on eVC. The upcoming examples will show you how to write an application that runs on ADOCE 3.0 and ADOCE 2.0.

Table 8.17   Comparison between the ADO for CE and ADO for the Desktop

ADO for the Desktop	ADO for Windows CE
Connection Object:defines the provider for ADO	Not supported in 2.x—ADO for Windows CE has only fixed connection to the ADOCE database engine. With ADOCE 3.0 the Connection object is supported.
RecordSet Object	Same as on the desktop, ADOCE 2.0 does not support "Find", "Seek", "get/put_index", "get/put_filter", "get_Properties", or "get_State".
Field Object/Fields Collection	Same as on the desktop, ADOCE 2.0 does not support "get_numericscale" or "get_precision".
Command Object	All commands are sent using the Open method of the RecordSet object. ADOCE 3.0 supports the "Execute" method at the Connection object.
Error Object and Collection	Not supported in 2.0—use the "Err" object in eVB and "GetLastError()" in eVC. Supported in Version 3.0.
Property Object	Supported since Version 3.0.
ADOMD (OLAP and Cubes)	Not supported.
ADOX (Views, Procedures, User)	Not supported.

8.4.1   A Simple Application Using ADO

Here is an application to introduce you to the ADO technology. The example that follows it will do exactly the same thing as the previous examples of the native object store did.

1. Create a new "Hello World" application with eMbedded Visual C++ and name it "ADOSample".

2. To add the ADOCE 3.0 interfaces and VARIANT declarations, add the following two includes to your project:

```
#include <COMDEF.H>
#include <ADOCE30.h>
void __stdcall _com_issue_error(HRESULT hr)
```

```
{
    // Error handling goes here!
}
```

The code above does not work correctly if you do not have the "ADOCE30.h" include file in your include path. You can copy the "ADOCE30.h" file into the include directory of your platform SDK if it is not already available there. In case ADOCE 3.0 is not installed on the target device, the "CoCreateInstance" call will fail, and you will have to deal with this condition at runtime.

3. Locate the "WinMain" procedure and insert the following code before the "InitInstance" call:

```
_Connection              *Conn1;                // new in ADOCE3.0
VARIANT                   varConn1;
BOOL                      bADOCE3=FALSE;
_Recordset               *Rs1;
Fields                   *Fields;
Field                    *Field;
// <BOOK Necessary due to Compatibility Wrapper in ADOCE30.h>
Field20                  *Field20;
// </BOOK Necessary due to Compatibility Wrapper in ADOCE30.h>

VARIANT_BOOL             tBOF,tEOF;
long                     FldCnt;
VARIANT                  value;
VARIANT                  vaEmpty;
SYSTEMTIME               MyTime;

const IID IID__Recordset = {0x113033F6,0xF682,0x11D2,
                            {0xBB,0x62,0x00,0xC0,0x4F,0x68,0x0A,0xCC}};
const IID IID__Connection = {0x113033DE,0xF682,0x11D2,
                            {0xBB,0x62,0x00,0xC0,0x4F,0x68,0x0A,0xCC}};
// <BOOK Necessary due to Compatibility Wrapper in ADOCE30.h>
const IID IID__Recordset20 =    {0x4BEB93D5,0x28D8,0x11D1,
                            {0x83,0x21,0x00,0xA0,0x24,0xA8,0x81,0x10}};
// </BOOK Necessary due to Compatibility Wrapper in ADOCE30.h>
TCHAR tsADOCE30ConnProgID[]= TEXT("ADOCE.Connection.3.0");
TCHAR tsADOCE30RSProgID[]= TEXT("ADOCE.Recordset.3.0");
TCHAR tsADOCE20RSProgID[]= TEXT("ADOCE.Recordset.1");
CLSID tClsid;
VariantInit(&varConn1);
```

```
VariantInit(&vaEmpty);
HRESULT hr;

if (FAILED(CoInitializeEx(NULL, COINIT_MULTITHREADED)))
            return FALSE;
// Step1 - Open/Create a database
// **********************************************
hr = CLSIDFromProgID( tsADOCE30ConnProgID, &tClsid );
if (!FAILED(hr))
{       // ADOCE3.0 found !!
      hr=CoCreateInstance(tClsid,NULL,CLSCTX_INPROC_SERVER,
                          IID__Connection, (LPVOID *)&Conn1);
      hr=Conn1->put_Provider(TEXT("cedb"));
      hr=Conn1->Open(TEXT(""),TEXT(""),TEXT(""),adOpenUnspecified);

      hr=CLSIDFromProgID( tsADOCE30RSProgID, &tClsid );
      hr=CoCreateInstance(tClsid,NULL,CLSCTX_INPROC_SERVER,
                          IID__Recordset,(LPVOID *)&Rs1);
      varConn1.pdispVal=Conn1;
      varConn1.vt=VT_DISPATCH;
      hr=Rs1->put_ActiveConnection(varConn1);
      bADOCE3=TRUE;
}
else
{       // Is at ADOCE2.0 there ?
      if (FAILED(CoInitializeEx(NULL, COINIT_MULTITHREADED)))
            return FALSE;
      hr=CLSIDFromProgID( tsADOCE20RSProgID, &tClsid );
      hr=CoCreateInstance(tClsid,NULL,CLSCTX_INPROC_SERVER,
                          IID__Recordset20 ,(LPVOID *)&Rs1);
}
if (FAILED(hr)) return FALSE; // No ADOCE there... leave

hr=Rs1->Open(_variant_t(TEXT("DROP TABLE Book841")),vaEmpty,
            adOpenForwardOnly , adLockReadOnly ,adCmdUnknown);

hr=Rs1->Open(_variant_t(TEXT("CREATE TABLE Book841 (MyInt integer,
MyDate datetime, MyString varchar(200), MyBlob long varbinary)")),
            _variant_t(TEXT("")),adOpenForwardOnly , adLockReadOnly ,
            adCmdUnknown);
if (FAILED(hr)) return FALSE;       // Error handling
```

```
wprintf(TEXT("Step1 Complete: Database Created\n\r"));

// Step2 - Writing a record
// ***********************************************
hr=Rs1->Open(_variant_t(TEXT("select * from Book841")),
             _variant_t(TEXT("")), adOpenKeyset , adLockOptimistic ,
             adCmdUnknown);
if (FAILED(hr)) return FALSE;        // Error handling

hr=Rs1->AddNew(vaEmpty,vaEmpty);

hr=Rs1->get_Fields(&Fields);
hr=Fields->get_Count(&FldCnt);
for (int i=0;i<FldCnt;i++)
{
     if (bADOCE3)
           hr=Fields->get_Item(_variant_t((long)i),&Field);
     else
           hr=Fields->get_Item(_variant_t((long)i),
                             (struct Field **)&Field20);
     VariantInit(&value);
     switch (i)
     {
          case 0:
                     if (bADOCE3)
                            hr=Field->put_Value(_variant_t(-1L));
                     else
                            hr=Field20->put_Value(_variant_t(-1L));
               break;
          case 1:
                     value.vt=VT_DATE;
                     GetSystemTime(&MyTime);
                     SystemTimeToVariantTime(&MyTime,&value.date);
                     if (bADOCE3)
                            hr=Field->put_Value(value);
                     else
                            hr=Field20->put_Value(value);
               break;
          case 2:
                     if (bADOCE3)
                            hr=Field->put_Value(
```

```
                                        variant_t(TEXT("This is a string")));
                        else
                                hr=Field20->put_Value(
                                _variant_t(TEXT("This is a string")));
                    break;
            case 3:
                        if (bADOCE3)
                                hr=Field->put_Value(
                                _variant_t(TEXT("This is a
                                blob-string")));
                        else
                                hr=Field20->put_Value(
                                _variant_t(TEXT("This is a
                                blob-string")));
                    break;
            default: break;
        }
}
hr=Rs1->Update(vaEmpty,vaEmpty);
if (FAILED(hr)) return FALSE;        // Error handling
// or
//hr=Rs1->Open(_variant_t(TEXT("INSERT INTO Book841 "
//                       "(MyInt,MyDate,MyString) VALUES "
//                       "(1,'1/1/1999 12:12','This is a string')")),
//                       _variant_t(TEXT("")),
//                       adOpenForwardOnly , adLockReadOnly , 1);
wprintf(TEXT("Step2 Complete: New Record Written\n\r"));

// Step3 - Reading a record
// *********************************************
Rs1->MoveFirst();

int RecCnt=0;
Rs1->get_BOF(&tBOF);
Rs1->get_EOF(&tEOF);
if(!(tBOF==VARIANT_TRUE && tEOF==VARIANT_TRUE))
{
    while (tEOF!=VARIANT_TRUE)
    {
        Rs1->get_Fields(&Fields);
        Fields->get_Count(&FldCnt);
```

```
            for (int i=0;i<FldCnt;i++)
            {
                    VariantInit(&value);
                    if (bADOCE3)
                    {
                            hr=Fields->get_Item(_variant_t((long)i),
                                                &Field);
                            hr=Field->get_Value(&value);
                    }
                    else
                    {
                            hr=Fields->get_Item(_variant_t((long)i),
                                        (struct Field **)&Field20);
                            hr=Field20->get_Value(&value);
                    }
            VariantChangeType(&vaEmpty,&value,0,VT_BSTR);
            if (vaEmpty.vt==VT_BSTR)
        wprintf(TEXT("Property #%d = <%s>\n\r"),i, vaEmpty.bstrVal);
            }
            Rs1->MoveNext();
            Rs1->get_EOF(&tEOF);
            RecCnt++;
    }
}
wprintf(TEXT("Step3: Read %d Records\n\r"),RecCnt);

// Step4 - Closing the Database
// *********************************************
Rs1->Close();
Rs1->Release();
if (bADOCE3)
      Conn1->Release();
CoUninitialize();
wprintf(TEXT("Step4 Complete: All closed\n\r"),RecCnt);
```

The boldface code shows where ADOCE 2.0 and ADOCE 3.0 differ. In ADOCE 3.0, the "Field" interface got two new members that were added before the "get_value" and "put_value" methods in the COM V-Table. If you did not use the new interface with ADOCE 2.0, COM would try to jump behind the actual V-Table inside ADOCE and would crash. To avoid this crash, you must define a new

"Field20" variable, using the interface from the old ADOCE 2.0 include file ("ADOCE.H"):

```
Field20      *Field20;
```

Since you cannot include "ADOCE.H" because some enumerations conflict with existing enumerations in "ADOCE30.H", you must include "ADOCE.H"'s entire "IADOCE_Fields" interface in the header of your "ADOSample.CPP".

4. Load the "ADOCE.H" from the ADOCE2.0 SDK and search for the lines:

```
#ifndef __IADOCEField_INTERFACE_DEFINED__
#define __IADOCEField_INTERFACE_DEFINED__
// A lot of interface definition code here
#endif       /* __IADOCEField_INTERFACE_DEFINED__ */
```

5. Copy everything that is between those lines beneath the void "__stdcall _com_issue_error(HRESULT hr)" function that you added earlier.

6. Locate the following line:

```
interface DECLSPEC_UUID("4BEB93D7-28D8-11D1-8321-00A024A88110")
IADOCEField : public IDispatch
```

7. Change it to

```
interface DECLSPEC_UUID("4BEB93D7-28D8-11D1-8321-00A024A88110")
Field20 : public IDispatch
```

One of the new RecordSet interface methods is "PutRef_ActiveConnection". It is inserted before the "get_ActiveConnection" method in the V-Table, rendering "get/put_ActiveConnection" and "get_ErrorDescription" invalid using the ADOCE 3.0 "_Recordset" pointer with ADOCE 2.0. To write clean code, you should insert a similar "_Recordset20" interface as that shown for the "Field20" interface. As mentioned before, the RecordSet objects ADOCE 2.0 and ADOCE 3.0 have different GUIDs. Therefore you need to define "IID__Recordset20" inside your code.

```
const IID IID__Recordset20 = {0x4BEB93D5,0x28D8,0x11D1,
                    {0x83,0x21,0x00,0xA0,0x24,0xA8,0x81,0x10}};
```

These changes are necessary because Microsoft included "Compatibility Wrappers" in "ADOCE 30.H" that map all the old interfaces to new ones. The benefit of this is that you can recompile your ADOCE 2.0 code without changing it, and it should run under ADOCE 3.0. Unfortunately, if you want to support both versions, these wrappers create more work.

8. No matter whether you use ADOCE 2.0 or ADOCE 3.0, before you can compile the code, you must add "OLE32.LIB" and "OLEAUT32.LIB" to the linker import libraries.

The code looks more complicated than it is. Let's have a closer look. The "_Recordset", "Fields", and "Field" pointers are defined in the "ADOCE30.H" file and are the main objects of ADO for Windows CE.

While you need to create a "_Connection" object first when using ADOCE 3.0 or the desktop version, ADOCE 2.0 for Windows CE starts with the Recordset and its "Open" method. Like the desktop version, the "Open" method takes five parameters. The most interesting parameter is the second one. This is where ADO normally takes the active Connection object as a parameter. Under Windows CE it is basically the same. Using ADOCE 2.0, this parameter allows only two Connection strings:

- No string (blank)—points to the object store
- A full path to a Pocket-Access (.CDB) file

If you are using ADOCE 3.0, you should use the connection object and put the connection to the RecordSet before you open it. The connection parameter of such a RecordSet should be empty.

All other parameters are more or less the same as on the desktop, except that Windows CE does not allow all cursor and locking combinations. Table 8.18 lists the valid cursors, and Table 8.19 lists the valid locks.

The last parameter of the "Open" method tells ADO how it should interpret the first parameter. Table 8.20 shows the possible settings.

 IMPORTANT: If you try to access a database (called a "table" in the ADO language) in the object store created with the native object store APIs, you will get an error because custom-made databases (tables) are not added to the "MsysTables" of the object store.

ADO for Windows CE was originally developed for Visual Basic. This has resulted in a rather unfriendly library for VC programmers. All "get_" methods normally point to properties of the corresponding object. Instead of writing

```
if (!(Rs1->BOF && Rs1->EOF))
```

Table 8.18   ADO Cursors for Windows CE

Constant (Value)	Description
AdOpenForwardOnly (0)	Forward-only cursor (default setting).
AdOpenKeyset (1)	Keyset cursor, which allows all kinds of movements through a table.

No other cursors are supported. If you specify another cursor to keep parity with the desktop, ADOCE will assume "adOpenKeyset".

Table 8.19   ADO Lock Types for Windows CE

Constant (Value)	Description
AdLockReadOnly (1)	Read only. No changes in table allowed (default setting).
AdLockOptimistic (3)	Allows changing, deleting, and adding records as well as all kinds of movements through a table.

"Pessimistic" and "batch locking" are not supported on ADOCE.

Table 8.20   Command-Interpreting Enumerations for ADO for Windows CE

Constant (Value)	Description
AdCmdText (1)	The first parameter will be interpreted as an SQL statement.
AdCmdTable (2)	The first parameter will be interpreted as a table name from "MSysTables".
AdCmdStoredProc (4)	The first parameter will be interpreted as a stored procedure in "MsysProcs".
AdCmdUnkown (8)	The type of the first parameter is unknown (default setting).
AdCmdTableDirect(512)	Evaluates the "CommandText" parameter of the "Open" method as a table name whose columns are all returned.

you have to write this more complicated-looking code:

```
Rs1->get_BOF(&tBOF);
Rs1->get_EOF(&tEOF);
if(!(tBOF==VARIANT_TRUE && tEOF==VARIANT_TRUE))
```

To get a value of a field in a record, you always have to go through the following order of commands:

- RecordSet->get_Fields()—Returns the "Fields" collection
- Fields->get_Field()—Returns a "Field" object
- Field->get/put_Value()—Retrieves or stores a value into a field

Instead of using the "SELECT" statement with a "Keyset" cursor and an "optimistic" lock, you could use the "INSERT INTO" SQL statement. But you cannot put anything in the "long varbinary" field using this statement. Table 8.21 contains a list of all SQL statements supported by ADO for Windows CE.

 The final source code of this section can be found on the companion CD under "\Sources\Chapter 8\8.6".

Table 8.21   Supported SQL Statements of ADO for Windows CE

Statement	Description
ALTER TABLE	Changes a table definition; you can ADD, DROP, RENAME, or MOVE a table.
CREATE DATABASE	Creates a new database of the type "CDB". This SQL statement was undocumented in ADOCE 2.0, but worked.
CREATE INDEX	Creates a new index. Remember, the object store only supports four indexes.
CREATE TABLE	Creates a new table.
DROP DATABASE	Deletes a database.
DROP TABLE	Deletes a table.
DROP INDEX	Deletes an index.
DELETE	Deletes a record from a table.
INSERT	Adds a new record to a table.
SELECT	Retrieves a set of records (RecordSet). You can specify filters using the "WHERE" and "ORDER BY" clauses. You can also specify one "INNER JOIN".

8.4.2 Adding ADO to the PCDMAccessDB Class

Before you update the "PCDMAccessDB" class with ADO, look at Table 8.22, which shows the mapping of native object store calls to the ADO methods that you will be using. Now let's add an ADO capacity to all your "AccessDB classes".

Your "AccessDB" class will use ADO by default and will only revert back to the object store if ADO is not available on the device. If the "CLSIDFromProgID" call to the ProgID of ADOCE 3.0 fails, you should try ADOCE 2.0, and if this fails as well, assume that ADO is not available on the device. If so, you should set the "m_useADO" variable to FALSE and use the native object store code instead. For your PCDMAccessDB class you will not use the connection object in order to keep the code as simple as possible.

1. Load the latest version of your PCDMDLL project and open the "PCDMAccessDB.H" file.

2. To get access to the ADO methods you need to include the "ADOCE30.H" directive in "PCDMAccessDB.H":

```
#include <comdef.h>
#ifdef UNDER_CE
#include <adoce30.h>
#endif
```

3. Do not forget to add the error handler to the top of "PCDMAccessDB.cpp":

```
void __stdcall _com_issue_error(HRESULT hr)
{
```

Table 8.22 Map of Native Object Store Calls to ADO for Windows CE

Native Object Store	ADO	Description
CeCreateDatabase	Recordset.Open("create table . . .")	ADO uses an SQL statement to create a table.
CeOpenDatabase	Recordset.Open("Tablename . . .")	ADO can either use a table name or an SQL statement.
CeSeekDatabase	Recordset.Move<direction>	
CeReadRecordPropsEx	Recordset.Fields.Field.get_Value()	In ADO there is no real concept of reading a record.
CeWriteRecordProps	Recordset.Update	Very similar concepts.
CloseHandle	Recordset.Close	

```
        // Error handling goes here!
}
```

You also require the interface definition for the "Field20" class of the ADO example in the previous section.

4. Follow the procedure from the previous section to get the interface description to the top of your "PCDMAccessDB.H" file.

5. Add the following definitions to the "PCDMAccessDB.H" file:

```
#define     PCDMADO_NONE     0
#define     PCDMADO_V2       2
#define     PCDMADO_V3       3
```

6. Add the following code to the constructor of the "PCDMAccessDB" class:

```
#ifdef UNDER_CE
CLSID tClsid;
HRESULT hr;
m_RS=NULL;
const IID IID__Recordset = {0x113033F6,0xF682,0x11D2,
                            {0xBB,0x62,0x00,0xC0,0x4F,0x68,0x0A,0xCC}};
const IID IID__Recordset20 = {0x4BEB93D5,0x28D8,0x11D1,
                            {0x83,0x21,0x00,0xA0,0x24,0xA8,0x81,0x10}};
TCHAR tsADOCE30RSProgID[]= TEXT("ADOCE.Recordset.3.0");
TCHAR tsADOCE20RSProgID[]= TEXT("ADOCE.Recordset.1");
    hr = CLSIDFromProgID( tsADOCE30RSProgID, &tClsid );
    if (!FAILED(hr))
    {      // ADOCE3.0 found !!
        hr=CoCreateInstance(tClsid,NULL,CLSCTX_INPROC_SERVER,
                            IID__Recordset,(LPVOID *)&m_RS);
        m_useADO=PCDMADO_V3;
    }
    else
    {      // Is at ADOCE2.0 there ?
        hr=CLSIDFromProgID( tsADOCE20RSProgID, &tClsid );
        if (!FAILED(hr))
        {
        hr=CoCreateInstance(tClsid,NULL,CLSCTX_INPROC_SERVER,
                    IID__Recordset20 ,(LPVOID *)&m_RS);
        m_useADO=PCDMADO_V2;
}
    }
```

```
if (FAILED(hr)) m_useADO=PCDMADO_NONE;
#endif
```

7. Define the following two variables in your "private" section:

```
WORD                    m_useADO;
#ifdef UNDER_CE
_Recordset              *m_RS;
#endif
```

8. To be sure that your RecordSet will be closed—even if the
    "PCDMAccessDB" object gets destroyed before somebody calls
    "CloseTable"—add the following destructor to the class:

```
~CPCDMAccessDB()
{
CloseTable(0L);
#ifdef UNDER_CE
        if (m_RS!=NULL)
                m_RS->Release();
#endif
    }
```

The first method you will update is "AddProperty". Since ADO requires strong
field types and names, this method must be called for each field that you want to add
to a database.

9. Change the code of the "AddProperty" implementation as follows:

```
STDMETHODIMP CPCDMAccessDB::AddProperty(VARIANT PID, LONG Sorted)
{
#ifdef UNDER_CE
    if (m_useADO != PCDMADO_NONE)
    {
        if (m_SortCnt<10)
        {
            VariantInit(&tvPID);
            VariantChangeType(&tvPID,&PID,0,VT_I4);
            m_DBSortOrder[m_SortCnt].propid=
                        MAKELONG(CEVT_LPWSTR,tvPID.lVal);
            if (Sorted==TRUE)
                m_DBSortOrder[m_SortCnt].dwFlags=
                                CEDB_SORT_GENERICORDER;
            else
```

```
                                   m_DBSortOrder[m_SortCnt].dwFlags=0;
                        m_SortCnt++;
                }
                return S_OK;
        }
//… old code continues…
```

You can see that the only diffcrence between the native object store and the ADO part is that you are going to store all properties in the "m_DBSortOrder" structure rather than only the sorted properties.

The next method that you need to edit is the "CreateTable" method.

10.   Change the code of this method to:

```
STDMETHODIMP CPCDMAccessDB::CreateTable(BSTR FileLocation, BSTR Name)
{
#ifdef UNDER_CE
        if (m_useADO!=PCDMADO_NONE)
        {
                wsprintf(strSQL,TEXT("CREATE DATABASE '%s'"),
                FileLocation);
                HRESULT hr=m_RS->Open(_variant_t(strSQL),
                                      _variant_t(TEXT("")),
                                      adOpenForwardOnly,
                                      adLockReadOnly , 1);
                wsprintf(strSQL,TEXT("DROP TABLE %s"),Name);
                hr=m_RS->Open(_variant_t(strSQL),
                             _variant_t(FileLocation),
                             adOpenForwardOnly , adLockReadOnly , 1);
                wsprintf(strSQL,TEXT("CREATE TABLE %s ("),Name);
                for (int i=0; i<m_SortCnt; i++)
                {
                        wsprintf(tStr,TEXT("Fld%d varchar(200)"),
                                       HIWORD(m_DBSortOrder[i].propid));
                        wcscat(strSQL,tStr);
                        if (i<m_SortCnt-1)
                                wcscat(strSQL,TEXT(","));
                        else
                                wcscat(strSQL,TEXT(")"));
                }
                hr=m_RS->Open(_variant_t(strSQL),
```

```
                        _variant_t(FileLocation),
                         adOpenForwardOnly ,
                         adLockReadOnly , 1);
           m_SortCnt=0;
           return hr;
       }
//... old code continues ...
```

Before you create the new table, you should try to drop it first. The "for . . . next" loop constructs the SQL statement to create the new table. Since ADO requires real field names in the SQL statement, you are constructing a string-based field name consisting of the prefix "Fld" and the PID. For your application, you will only support "varchar" fields.

11.   The new "OpenTable" method uses a similar "for . . . next" loop to construct the "Order by" clause of the "SELECT" statement:

```
STDMETHODIMP CPCDMAccessDB::OpenTable(BSTR FileLocation, BSTR Name,
                                      VARIANT PID, LONG *Handle)
{
#ifdef UNDER_CE
CEOID      CeOid=0;
HANDLE     hDataBase;
CEPROPID    tPID=0;
VARIANT tvPID;

    VariantInit(&tvPID);
    VariantChangeType(&tvPID,&PID,0,VT_I4);
    if (m_useADO !=PCDMADO_NONE)
    {
        TCHAR strSQL[1024],tStr[200];
        HRESULT hr;
          wsprintf(strSQL,TEXT("SELECT * FROM %s "),Name);
          wsprintf(tStr,TEXT("Order By Fld%d "),tvPID.lVal);
          wcscat(strSQL,tStr);
          hr=m_RS->Open(_variant_t(strSQL),
                        _variant_t(FileLocation),
                        adOpenKeyset , adLockOptimistic , 1);
          *Handle=(long)m_RS;
          return hr;
    }
//... old code continues...
```

Again ADOCE requires the field name for the "Order by" clause of the "SELECT" statement. Therefore you need to get the field name from the PID and construct the "Order By" clause with the "Fld" suffix.

The "OpenDB" ADO implementation will open a RecordSet and store the result in the member variable "m_RS". The handle you will return is not really important since you will not use it in any other call. The "FileLocation" property will now determine whether you will use a Pocket-Access file or the object store as the container for your new table. If the "FileLocation" is left empty, the object store will be your container. Otherwise, the "FileLocation" must point to an existing Pocket-Access file.

12. To close the RecordSet and free its reference update, use the "CloseDB" method, as follows:

```
STDMETHODIMP CPCDMAccessDB::CloseTable(LONG Handle)
{
#ifdef UNDER_CE
    m_SortCnt=0;
    m_rfldCnt=0;
    if (m_useADO !=PCDMADO_NONE)
    {
        HRESULT hr=m_RS->Close();
        return hr;
    }
    CloseHandle((HANDLE)Handle);
#endif
    return S_OK;
}
```

The "Move . . ." methods of this class are modeled after the ADO move methods. Therefore the implementation of those methods is fairly simple.

13. Change the code of the methods "MoveFirst", "MoveLast", "MoveNext", and "MovePrevious" to the following code:

```
STDMETHODIMP CPCDMAccessDB::MoveFirst(LONG Handle)
{
#ifdef UNDER_CE
    if (m_useADO !=PCDMADO_NONE)
    {
        HRESULT hr=m_RS->MoveFirst();
        return hr;
    }
    if (!(m_curRec=CeSeekDatabase((HANDLE)Handle,
```

```
                                     CEDB_SEEK_BEGINNING, 0, &m_dwIndex)))
            return S_FALSE;

#endif
      return S_OK;
}


STDMETHODIMP CPCDMAccessDB::MoveLast(LONG Handle)
{
#ifdef UNDER_CE
      if (m_useADO !=PCDMADO_NONE)
      {
            HRESULT hr=m_RS->MoveLast();
            return hr;
      }
      if (!(m_curRec=CeSeekDatabase((HANDLE)Handle, CEDB_SEEK_END,
                                    0, &m_dwIndex)))
            return S_FALSE;
#endif
      return S_OK;
}


STDMETHODIMP CPCDMAccessDB::MoveNext(LONG Handle)
{
#ifdef UNDER_CE
      if (m_useADO !=PCDMADO_NONE)
      {
            HRESULT hr=m_RS->MoveNext();
            return hr;
      }
      if (!(m_curRec=CeSeekDatabase((HANDLE)Handle,
      CEDB_SEEK_CURRENT,
                                    1, &m_dwIndex)))
            return S_FALSE;
#endif
      return S_OK;
}


STDMETHODIMP CPCDMAccessDB::MovePrevious(LONG Handle)
{
#ifdef UNDER_CE
```

```
    if (m_useADO !=PCDMADO_NONE)
    {
        HRESULT hr=m_RS->MovePrevious();
        return hr;
    }
    if (!(m_curRec=CeSeekDatabase((HANDLE)Handle,
CEDB_SEEK_CURRENT,
                                     -1, &m_dwIndex)))
        return S_FALSE;

#endif
    return S_OK;
}
```

Your next step is to add the "FindRecord" method. This step also clearly reveals some of the problem areas in ADOCE. For example, ADOCE 2.0 for Windows CE does not support "Find" or "Filter" on RecordSets. ADOCE 3.0 requires an OLEDB provider that supports "Find" and "Filter," but since the object store and Pocket-Access files do not use an OLEDB provider, you will need to use the conventional method even for those databases. Thus you will need to implement your "FindRecord" method with conventional ADOCE calls in ADOCE 2.0, but you will be able to use the "Find" method of ADOCE 3.0.

14.   Here is the new code of the "FindRecord" method:

```
STDMETHODIMP CPCDMAccessDB::FindRecord(long Handle, VARIANT PID,
                                        VARIANT Value)
{
#ifdef UNDER_CE
VARIANT tvPID,tvValue;

VariantInit(&tvPID);
VariantInit(&tvValue);
VariantChangeType(&tvPID,&PID,0,VT_I4);
VariantChangeType(&tvValue,&Value,0,VT_BSTR);
    switch (m_useADO)
    {
        case PCDMADO_V2:
        case PCDMADO_V3:
            {
                Fields          *pFields;
                Field20          *pField20;
```

```
                        HRESULT hr;
                        TCHAR tFldName[10];
                        VARIANT_BOOL        tBOF,tEOF;
                        VARIANT value,tBookMark;

                        VariantInit(&tBookMark);
                        m_RS->get_Bookmark(&tBookMark);
                        m_RS->get_BOF(&tBOF);
                        m_RS->get_EOF(&tEOF);
                        if(!(tBOF==VARIANT_TRUE &&
                        tEOF==VARIANT_TRUE))
                        {
                                while (tEOF!=VARIANT_TRUE)
                                {
                                        m_RS->get_Fields(&pFields);
                        wsprintf(tFldName,TEXT("Fld%d"),tvPID.lVal);
        if (m_useADO==PCDMADO_V3)
        {
#ifdef UNDER_CE
                hr=pFields->get_Item(_variant_t(tFldName),
                                (struct Field **)&pField);
#else
                hr=pFields->get_Item(_variant_t(tFldName),
                                (struct ADOField **)&pField);
#endif
                pField->get_Value(&value);
        }
        else
        {
#ifdef UNDER_CE
                hr=pFields->get_Item(_variant_t(tFldName),
                                (struct Field **)&pField20);
#else
                hr=pFields->get_Item(_variant_t(tFldName),
                                (struct ADOField **)&pField20);
#endif
                pField20->get_Value(&value);
        }
                                VariantChangeType(&value,
                                &value,0,VT_BSTR);
                                        if (value.vt==VT_BSTR &&
```

```
                                tvValue.vt==VT_BSTR)
                        {
                                if (!(CompareString(
                                        LOCALE_USER_DEFAULT,
                                        NORM_IGNORECASE,
                                        value.bstrVal,-1,
                                        tvValue.bstrVal,
                                        -1)-2))
                                {
                                        hr=S_OK;
                                        break;
                                }
                        }
                        hr=m_RS->MoveNext();
                        hr=m_RS->get_EOF(&tEOF);
                }
        }
        if (FAILED(hr) || tEOF==VARIANT_TRUE)
        {
                m_RS->put_Bookmark(tBookMark);
                if (tEOF==VARIANT_TRUE)
                        hr=ERROR_NO_MORE_FILES;
        }
        return hr;
    }
    break;
case PCDMADO_OLEDB:
    {
        VARIANT tBookMark;
        TCHAR tFldName[10];
        VariantInit(&tBookMark);

        HRESULT hr=m_RS->get_Bookmark(&tBookMark);
        wsprintf(tFldName,TEXT("Fld%d='%s'"),
                        tvPID.lVal,tvValue.
                        bstrVal);
        hr=m_RS->Find(tFldName,0,
                    adSearchForward,tBookMark);
        if (FAILED(hr))
                m_RS->put_Bookmark(tBookMark);
        return hr;
```

```
                      }
                      break;
              default:
//</BOOK_ADDON STEP5 Chapter 8.4.2> *********************************
                      CEPROPVAL tPropVal;
                      DWORD      tdwIndex;

                      if (tvPID.lVal!=m_ActPID.lVal) return S_FALSE;
                      tPropVal.wLenData = 0;
                      tPropVal.wFlags = 0;
                      tPropVal.propid=MAKELONG
                      (CEVT_LPWSTR,m_ActPID.lVal);
                      tPropVal.val.lpwstr=tvValue.bstrVal;

                      tdwIndex=m_dwIndex;
                      if (!(m_curRec=CeSeekDatabase(
                              (HANDLE)Handle,CEDB_SEEK_
                              VALUEFIRSTEQUAL,
                              (DWORD)&tPropVal, &tdwIndex)))
                      {
                              m_curRec=CeSeekDatabase((HANDLE)Handle,
                                      CEDB_SEEK_BEGINNING, m_dwIndex,
                                      &m_dwIndex);
                              return S_FALSE;
                      }
                      m_dwIndex=tdwIndex;
                      break;
      }
#endif

      return S_OK;
}
```

You use the "Bookmark" property to remain in the same record in case you don't find a matching result in the RecordSet. The code is already prepared for the use of an OLEDB provider. Microsoft SQL for Windows CE will include such a provider and is able to run the much simpler code.

Next are the data manipulation methods. To write a record you will need to modify the "AddNewRecord" and "SetValue" methods first. Your "AddNewRecord" method is again modeled after ADO, and, therefore, its ADO implementation is very simple.

15. Add the following code to the implementation of "AddNewRecord":

```
STDMETHODIMP CPCDMAccessDB::AddNewRecord(LONG Handle)
{
#ifdef UNDER_CE
      if (m_useADO==TRUE)
      {
_variant_t  vaEmpty;
            HRESULT hr=m_RS->AddNew(vaEmpty,vaEmpty);
            return hr;
      }
// … Old Code continues…
```

The "SetValue" method is also easy to implement. Here you will see the strength of ADO. Since ADO is using VARIANT all over the place, you really only have to write some tiny lines of code to use ADO. Unfortunately, you have to differentiate between ADOCE 2.0 and 3.0 again.

16. Here is what the final "SetValue" method should look like:

```
STDMETHODIMP CPCDMAccessDB::SetValue(VARIANT PID, VARIANT Value)
{
#ifdef UNDER_CE
VARIANT tValue,tvPID;

      if (m_wfldCnt>9) return S_FALSE;
      VariantInit(&tValue);
      VariantChangeType(&tValue,&Value,0,VT_BSTR);
      VariantInit(&tvPID);
      VariantChangeType(&tvPID,&PID,0,VT_I4);
      if (m_useADO!=PCDMADO_NONE)
      {
            Fields      *pFields;
            Field       *pField;
            Field20      *pField20;
            TCHAR tFldName[10];

            HRESULT hr=m_RS->get_Fields(&pFields);
            wsprintf(tFldName,TEXT("Fld%d"),tvPID.lVal);

            if (m_useADO==PCDMADO_V3)
            {
                  hr=pFields->get_Item(_variant_t(tFldName),&pField);
```

```
                                hr=pField->put_Value(tValue);
                }
                else
                {
                        hr=pFields->get_Item(_variant_t(tFldName),
                                          (struct Field **)&pField20);
                        hr=pField20->put_Value(tValue);
                }

                return hr;
        }
        m_wFields[m_wfldCnt].propid=MAKELONG(CEVT_LPWSTR,tvPID.lVal);
        m_BStr[m_wfldCnt]=SysAllocString(tValue.bstrVal);
        m_wFields[m_wfldCnt].val.lpwstr=m_BStr[m_wfldCnt];
        m_wFields[m_wfldCnt].wLenData = 0;
        m_wFields[m_wfldCnt].wFlags = 0;
        m_wfldCnt++;
#endif
        return S_OK;
}
```

17.   The "WriteRecord" method contains basically only one line of code:

```
STDMETHODIMP CPCDMAccessDB::WriteRecord(LONG DBHandle)
{
#ifdef UNDER_CE
        if (m_useADO!=PCDMADO_NONE)
        {
                _variant_t       vaEmpty;
                HRESULT hr=m_RS->Update(vaEmpty,vaEmpty);
                return hr;
        }
//… old code continues …
```

The "ReadRecord" method is very simple, too.

18.   You just need to get the number of fields in a record back to the caller:

```
STDMETHODIMP CPCDMAccessDB::ReadRecord(LONG DBHandle,LONG *Count)
{
#ifdef UNDER_CE
        if (m_useADO!=PCDMADO_NONE)
        {
```

```
        Fields                    *pFields;
        long tCnt;

        HRESULT hr=m_RS->get_Fields(&pFields);
        hr=pFields->get_Count(&tCnt);
        *Count=tCnt;
        return hr;
    }
// … old code continues…
```

Nor are there any surprises in the "GetValue" function. Its implementation is actually identical to the "SetValue" implementation, except for one line.

19.   Change the code of "GetValue" as follows:

```
STDMETHODIMP CPCDMAccessDB::GetValue(VARIANT PID, VARIANT *Value)
{
#ifdef UNDER_CE
    if (m_useADO!=PCDMADO_NONE)
    {
        Fields                  *pFields;
        Field                   *pField;
        Field20                 *pField20;
        long tCnt;
        HRESULT hr;
        TCHAR tFldName[10];

        VariantInit(Value);
        m_RS->get_Fields(&pFields);
        hr=pFields->get_Count(&tCnt);
        wsprintf(tFldName,TEXT("Fld%d"),PID);
        if (m_useADO==PCDMADO_V3)
        {
            hr=pFields->get_Item(_variant_t(tFldName),&pField);
            hr=pField->get_Value(Value);
        }
        else
        {
            hr=pFields->get_Item(_variant_t(tFldName),
                            (struct Field **)&pField20);
            hr=pField20->get_Value(Value);
        }
```

```
        return hr;
    }
// … Old code continues…
```

Finally, you will add a new method to your class that you will want to use in a later chapter.

20. Add a new method to the "PCDMAccessDB" class and name it "Execute". Give it the two parameters shown in Table 8.23.

21. Now add the following code to the implementation of the method:

```
STDMETHODIMP CPCDMAccessDB::Execute(BSTR FileLocation, BSTR Command)
{
#ifdef UNDER_CE
    if (m_useADO !=PCDMADO_NONE)
    {
        HRESULT hr=m_RS->Open(_variant_t(Command),
                              _variant_t(FileLocation),
                              adOpenForwardOnly ,
                              adLockReadOnly , 1);
        return hr;
    }
#endif
    return S_OK;
}
```

You are now finished with your updates and can test the new class in eVB.

 The final source code of this section can be found on the companion CD under "\Sources\ThreadExample\PCDMDLL\Step5".

Table 8.23   PCDMAccessDB.Execute Parameters

Type	Variable Name	Used for
BSTR	FileLocation	Database name
BSTR	Command	A command string that contains an executable SQL statement

8.4.3 Retesting ADO Changes in eMbedded Visual Basic

Load the eVB application from Section 8.3.5 and change the database name to "Book843". This is necessary since ADO cannot access databases created with the object store native's APIs. If you run the application, the result will be exactly the same as in Section 8.3.5. You can also run the last version of the PCDM application. It should now use ADO instead of the object store API and still produce the same result.

 The final source code of this section can be found on the companion CD under "\Sources\Chapter 8\8.7".

8.5 Pocket-Access Files

So far, you have only worked with play data. Now it is time to get some real data to work with. Since Version 2.11 and the H/PC Professionals became available, Windows CE includes Pocket-Access. Pocket-Access on Windows CE is actually just a nice, friendly front-end for ADO for Windows CE. This means that everything it offers can be written by third parties as well, and you can also look at the data that you added in the previous chapter.

Just start Pocket-Access on your H/PC Pro or palm-size PC Professional and cancel the "Open . . ." dialog. You will find a table called "Book841" in the object store. Double-tap it and you will see a screen similar to that shown in Figure 8.5. For your Pocket-CD-Manager Application, you want to use a database that the Deluxe CD player of Windows 2000 uses as well. In case you never started the Deluxe CD player before, it is located in the "Start" menu at "Programs\Accessories\Entertainment\CD Player". The first time that you start the Deluxe CD player it creates the "Deluxe CD.MDB" database in the directory "Documents and Settings\<username>\Application Data\Microsoft\CD Player" on Windows 2000. It also creates an ODBC entry for this database. The ".MDB" file is an Access 2000 database containing four tables: "Batch", "Menus", "Titles", and "Tracks". For your PCDM application you will only use the two tables "Titles" and "Tracks". The Deluxe CD player not only adds a new entry for each new Audio CD that you put into your CD-ROM, but also tries to retrieve the title and track names from the Internet.

8.5.1 Copying an Access 2000 Database to the Emulation

If you think you can simply copy an ".MDB" file into emulation as you can do with a real Windows CE device, you will soon find out that there is actually no documented

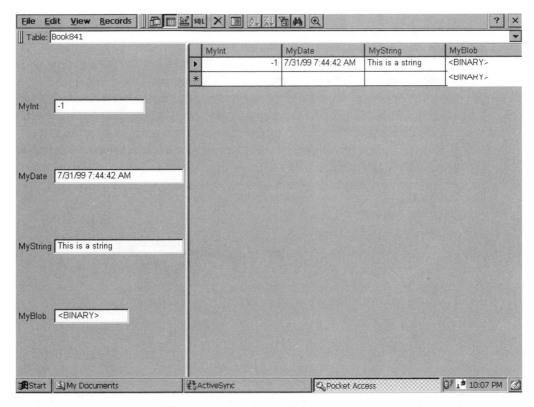

Figure 8.5 The "Book841" table in Pocket-Access

way to do it. Microsoft has not made it easy to learn how. In fact, the documentation and release notes do not explain anything about how to do this. And to make matters worse, you basically have to write code to get it done.

After a lot of digging—and with help from some friendly guys on Microsoft's documentation team—I can share the following complicated procedure for accomplishing what would seem so "simple" a task. On the "Visual Basic for Windows CE 6.0" CD you will find a directory called "ADOCE". This directory contains a setup for the ADOCE SDK. In fact, it is just a collection of samples and the binaries of ADOCE 2.0 for Windows CE 2.0. To make things even more difficult, installation of this SDK requires an old version of the Windows CE Services. But do not be afraid. Luckily, you can use a backdoor to install it, or at least those parts that you need to use.

1. If you double-click "MSADOCE2.EXE", it will tell you that it only supports H/PC 2.0 devices, not the palm-size PC. Ignore this message and click "OK"

Next it will ask you where to copy the temporary files.

2. Select a directory where you'll be able to go back and find the temporary files again, and start the extraction.

As soon as the setup is finished copying the files to that directory, the main ADOCE 2.0 setup will start. However, other than the nice greeting message, you won't get much further if you have ActiveSync 3.0 or higher installed. The setup will tell you that it requires Version 2.0 of the Windows CE Services, and then it will quit.

If you have Windows CE Services 2.x installed, the setup will continue and store the ADOCE SDK in a directory of your choice. You can then skip the next two steps. If you have ActiveSync 3.x installed, it would normally end here, but luckily the files in the temporary directory from Step 2 are all that you need.

3. Open File Explorer and navigate to the temporary directory.

The file called "ADOCE1.CAB" contains everything you need. You will need to use an unzip utility such as WinZIP 7.0 to open this file.

4. Open the "ADOCE1.CAB" file and extract the content to any directory. I recommend using "\Windows CE Tools\ADOCE".

In the target directory, you will now find a series of samples and the H/PC installation CAB files for MIPS ("adoMIPS.CAB") and for SH3 ("adoSH3.CAB"). To install those on an H/PC Version 2 device, just copy the CAB files into the device's temporary directory and double-tap them. Windows CE will install them correctly. You can also follow the knowledge-base article on the Microsoft Web site to install ADOCE 2.0 on your desktop PC: http://support.microsoft.com/support/kb/articles/Q242/4/99.asp.

The sample application that you will need to use in copying your Access 2000 database to the emulation environment is called "EmulDemo". The directory contains two eVB projects:

- "vbEmulDB.vbp"—converts the ".MDB" to ".TDB" and copies the ".TBD" to the emulation
- "EmulDB.vbp"—converts the ".TDB" into tables of the object store

Don't worry, you will fix the second project so that it stores the tables in a ".CDB" file rather than in the ObjectStore.

But don't think you can simply load the eVB project, run it, and be done. . . . Remember, you are dealing with Access 2000! The demo was written for Access 97, and therefore you have to do some extra work in order to use it. If you are still using Access 97, you can skip the next two steps. Another interesting side note: the demo was written using DAO on the desktop and not using ADO. What an irony!

To be able to use EmulDemo you will need to change an object reference of the "vbEmulDB" project from "Microsoft DAO 3.51 Object Library" to "Microsoft DAO 3.6 Object Library".

5. Open the "vbEmulDB" project into eVB and select "References" from the "Project" menu.

6. In the upcoming "Reference" dialog box, uncheck the "Microsoft DAO 3.51 Object Library" and check the "Microsoft DAO 3.6 Object Library".

7. To be able to use the "vbEmulDB" project, you first have to copy the application "EMPFILE.EXE" to either the Windows directory or the directory containing the eVB project.

"EMPFILE.EXE" is located in the following directory:

```
\Windows CE Tools\WCE<version>\<Platform>\emulation\<platform>\Windows
```

To be able to use "vbEmulDB", you must make some modifications. You must keep those modifications to a minimum so as not to be distracted from your major goal—copying "DeluxeCD.MDB" into the emulation environment.

8. Navigate to the subroutine "cmdCopyEmul_Click()" and find the line:

```
xfer = "empfile -c " & Chr(34) & LogFilePath & Chr(34) & " " &
Chr$(34) & "WCE:" & filename & Chr$(34)
```

9. Change that line to

```
xfer = "empfile -c " & Chr(34) & LogFilePath & Chr(34) & " " &
Chr$(34) & "WCE:\windows" & Chr$(34)
```

The old line would lead to an error message of "EMPFILE.EXE", indicating that the target directory was not found because EMPFILE adds the name of the source file to the target file. If you did not change the line, the target directory would be "WCE:\ DeluxeCD.TDB\DeluxeCD.TDB"—not quite what you want.

I also found that with "DeluxeCD.MDB", the "vbEmulDB" application creates strange, long strings with zeros inside that would totally confuse the "Windows CE File Control" used by EmulDB later.

10. To fix this issue, change the "StripChar" subroutine to the following code:

```
Function StripChar(ByVal FieldVal As Variant) As String
    Dim ReplaceChar As Variant
    Dim TxtFieldVal As String
    Dim ChrPos As Integer
    TxtFieldVal = FieldVal
    For Each ReplaceChar In Array(Chr$(13), Chr$(10), Chr(34))
        Do
            ChrPos = InStr(1, TxtFieldVal, ReplaceChar)
```

```
                If (ChrPos > 0) Then
                     Mid(TxtFieldVal, ChrPos, Len(ReplaceChar)) = " "
                End If
           Loop While (ChrPos > 0)
       Next ReplaceChar
       ChrPos = 1
       While Mid(TxtFieldVal, ChrPos, 1)  Chr$(0) And _
             ChrPos < Len(TxtFieldVal)
           ChrPos = ChrPos + 1
       Wend
       TxtFieldVal = Left(TxtFieldVal, ChrPos - 1)
       StripChar = Chr(34) & TxtFieldVal & Chr(34)
End Function
```

11. Now launch it, select your "DeluxeCD.MDB", convert it, and copy it to the emulation using the buttons on the form.

On Windows 2000, "DeluxeCD.MDB" is located in the directory:

```
"<SystemDrive>:\Documents and Settings\<YourUserName>\Application
Data\Microsoft\CD Player"
```

If you look into the "My Documents" folder on the emulation, you will see the new file "DeluxeCD.TDB". You can also open the "DeluxeCD.TDB" file on your desktop, and you will find it to be a series of SQL statements recreating the entire database.

You can probably guess what the EmulDB project does . . . it simply loads the file and executes all the statements in it. On H/PC Version 2 devices there was no Pocket-Access. Hence the "EmulDB" project creates those tables in the object store. For example, you should have a "DeluxeCD.CDB" in the "My Documents" folder in order to debug your PCDM application. Luckily, there is an SQL statement that was not documented in ADOCE 2.0

```
CREATE DATABASE '<DatabaseName.CDB>'
```

Thus you will need to change the code of the EmulDB project slightly to get the tables created in the "DeluxeCD.CDB". But first you must install the "Windows CE File Control 6.0" to the emulation because EmulDB uses that control.

12. Start "Windows CE Control Manager" from the "Windows CE" menu in eMbedded Visual Basic and install "Windows CE File System Control 6.0" in your emulation environment.

13.   Load the EmulDB project in eVB and locate the subroutine "CreateTable(Path)".

14.   Add the following code to the top of the subroutine:

```
Dim rs
Set rs = CreateObject("ADOCE.Recordset")
rs.Open "CREATE DATABASE '\My Documents\DeluxeCD.cdb'"
```

15.   In the subroutine "Rs_Open(SQLStr)", locate the line:

```
rs.Open SQLStr, , 2, 3
```

and change that line to

```
rs.Open SQLStr, "\My Documents\DeluxeCD.CDB", 2, 3
```

Now download the EmulDB application and run it. Once it succeeds, you can see the new tables in Pocket-Access when you open "DeluxeCD.CDB" in the "My Documents" folder. If the "EmulDB" reports any error, you can manually fix the "Deluxe CD.TDB" file on the desktop and copy it down to the emulation using the command:

```
empfile -c "<path>\DeluxeCD.tdb" "WCE:\windows"
```

If you run "EmulDB" twice, it will tell you that the tables already exist. In that case, open Pocket-Access and delete the tables manually.

The emulation environment is really not a good environment in which to test an ADO application. I hope the emulation that Microsoft has announced for its next-generation tools will solve these issues.

 The final source code of this section can be found on the companion CD under "\Sources\Chapter 8\EmulDB".

8.5.2   Synchronizing Pocket-Access with Access 2000 Databases

This sounds more complicated than it is. But since ActiveSync can only synchronize tables that have a primary key, you will need to open "DeluxeCD.MDB" in Access 2000 and add a primary key, at least to the two tables you will use in your PCDM application.

Beware: If you do so, the Deluxe CD player will no longer be able to store new albums in the database. For some reason, the Deluxe CD player was written to be very sensitive to changes to the database schema. In Section 9.3, you will write an ActiveSync provider that will not change the DeluxeCD database.

1. Locate the "DeluxeCD.MDB" in your "Documents and Settings" folder and double click it to load it into Access 2000.

2. Select the "Titles" table and click on the "Design" button.

3. Select the "TitleID" row and click on the "Key" button in the toolbar, as shown in Figure 8.6.

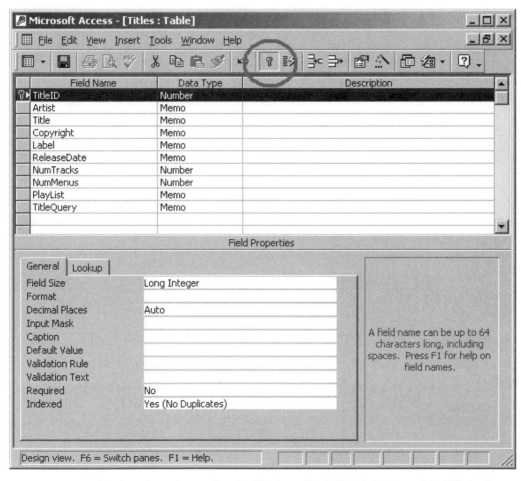

Figure 8.6 Setting the primary key in "DeluxeCD.MDB" for the table "Titles"

Unfortunately, the author of the Deluxe CD player did not do a good job in designing the database. Some of the fields in the "Titles" tables do not contain any data and remain blank although the property "Allow Zero Length" is set to "No".

4. To ensure proper synchronization you must set the "Allow Zero Length" property of the fields "Copyright", "Label", "ReleaseDate", "PlayList", and "TitleQuery" to "Yes".

5. Save the design and open the "Tracks" table in design mode.

6. The "Tracks" table does not contain any field that can be used as a primary key yet. Therefore you need to create a new field that can be used as primary key, as shown in Figure 8.7.

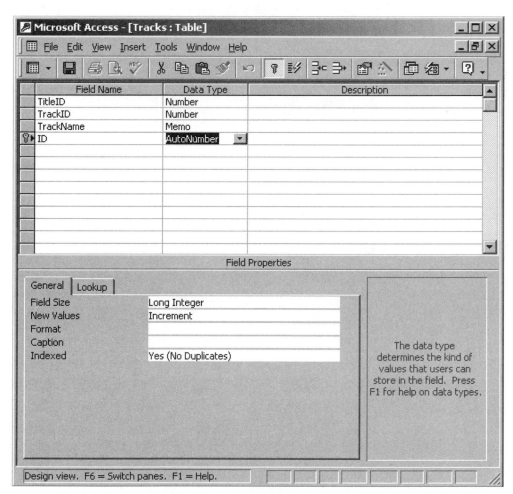

Figure 8.7 Creating a new field in the "Tracks" table

7. Add the field name "ID" to the list of fields and give it the data type "Autonumber". Then create the primary key by selecting the "Key" button in the toolbar again.

As soon as you save the new design of the "Tracks" table, Access creates a unique number for all records in the table.

Next you just need to use ActiveSync to drag and drop the "DeluxeCD.MDB" file into your connected device, and ActiveSync will take care of the synchronization.

8. Click on "Explore" in the ActiveSync toolbar. Once the content of your mobile device shows up, drag and drop the "DeluxeCD.MDB" file into the explorer.

It actually does not matter where you drop the file because ActiveSync will automatically put the target file into the "My Documents" folder.

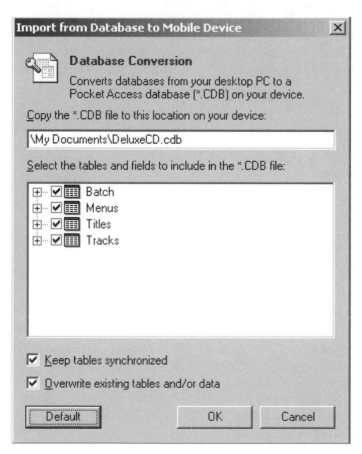

Figure 8.8   The "DeluxeCD.MDB" synchronization settings

As soon as ActiveSync recognizes that you are copying an Access database, it will ask you about the synchronization settings, as shown in Figure 8.8. ActiveSync allows you to select exactly what you want to synchronize with your mobile device. You can even select the specific fields that you want to synchronize for each table in the database.

9. For your Pocket-CD-Manager application, you only need the "Titles" and "Tracks" tables, but you may also keep the defaults if you wish.

As soon as you hit "OK", ActiveSync will convert "DeluxeCD.MDB" into "DeluxeCD.CDB" and put it into the "My Documents" folder. At the end of the conversion, ActiveSync shows a log explaining what it did and what went wrong.

As you can see in Figure 8.9, if you have selected "Batch" and "Menus" as well, ActiveSync tells you that those two tables cannot be synchronized because they do not have a primary key. The "Titles" and "Tracks" tables, on the other hand, have primary keys and can be synchronized.

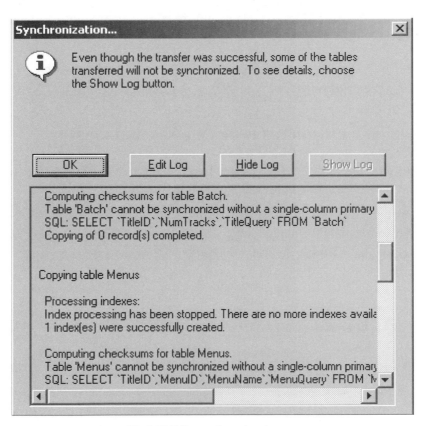

Figure 8.9 The "DeluxeCD.MDB" synchronization errors

Since you only care about "Titles" and "Tracks", you can ignore these error messages.

10.   To test whether the database was converted correctly, open Pocket-Access on the mobile device and select "DeluxeCD.CDB".

You should see the four tables. If you double tap the "Titles" table, you should get a list of all the CDs that you had in the Deluxe CD player.

11.   Change one of the titles in the "Titles" database. Reconnect the device or press the "Sync" button in ActiveSync and you will see that ActiveSync synchronizes this change with the desktop version of the database.

12.   Load the desktop version of "DeluxeCD.MDB" into Access and verify the change you made.

During the first synchronization, ActiveSync creates several tables that contain errors that might occur during synchronization, as shown in Table 8.24.

For example, if you had changed the "Allow Zero Length" property of the "Copyright" field, the "MsysCeCTitles" table would contain an error pointing to the changed record with the "Reason":

```
"[Microsoft][ODBC Microsoft Access Driver] Field 'Titles.Copyright'
cannot be a zero-length string."
```

8.5.3   Updating the PCDM to Use the New Database

The only thing left to do is to change three lines of code in your PCDM application in order to use the tables in the new "DeluxeCD.CDB" database.

1.   Open the last version of the PCDM application and locate the "OnInitialUpdate" method in the "PCDMView.CPP" file.

2.   Locate the "OpenTable" call to your "PCDMAccessDB" class and change it to:

Table 8.24   **ActiveSync Synchronization Tables**

Table Name	Used for
MsysCeConflicts	Contains a list of all tables that show conflicts during synchronization
MsysCeC<TableName> (For each table)	Contains the errors that happened during the synchronization

```
hr=comDB->OpenDB(TEXT("\\My Documents\\DeluxeCD.cdb"),
                TEXT("Titles"),PCDM_PID_ID,&DBHandle);
```

3. Open "Details.cpp" and make similar changes to the two "OpenTable" calls in its "OnInitialUpdate" method:

```
...
hr=comDB->OpenDB(TEXT("\\My Documents\\DeluxeCD.cdb"),
                TEXT("Title"),PCDM_PID_ID,&DBHandle);

...
hr=comDB->OpenDB(TEXT("\\My Documents\\DeluxeCD.cdb"),
                TEXT("Tracks"),PCDM_PID_TRACKS_ID,&DBHandle);

...
```

4. You can also delete the code that creates the sample data.

Now run the Pocket-CD-Manager application. If everything works correctly, you will see all of your CD titles in the list view of the PCDM application. If you tap on one of the entries, the "Details of . . . " dialog box will appear, giving the names of all tracks on the selected CD. In coming chapters, you will continue working with the "PCDM.CDB" database and the "PCDMCDs" and "PCDMTracks" tables, and will synchronize them with the ActiveSync provider, to which I will turn in the next chapter.

9
Chapter

Remote and Connectivity

This is another important chapter if you plan on writing killer applications. Even at this early stage in the growth of the Internet, it is clear that no application will be successful if it remains an island, cut off from the broader distributed world of connectivity. But if you don't think that we're still in the dark ages of connected computing, just show me a way to program my VCR over the Internet. . . .

Windows CE devices are "mostly disconnected" devices, meaning that most of the time they are not connected to a network or another entity. It will still take some time before the first "constantly connected" mobile devices reach the market. The main reason is the short battery life of all mobile devices.

From a software point of view, this means that you will have to live with a "mostly disconnected" state for quite a while. Your application cannot count on a connected state and must be able to run in disconnected environments. Once reconnected to its partner entity, it has to synchronize all changes made to the data in your application or to the relevant data on the partner entity.

Most solutions available today make the Windows CE application basically passive, once it is docked in its docking station. All necessary actions are initiated and controlled by the partner entity, which in the case of ActiveSync is the desktop PC. In an enterprise environment, though, it may be necessary to initiate calls and actions from the Windows CE device to a back-end server.

This chapter explains several methods of accessing data remotely from a desktop PC and also shows ways to initiate and communicate with a back-end server. Table 9.1 shows all the technologies and features that this chapter will cover. Microsoft has also announced support for Message Queuing in Windows CE 3.0. Unfortunately, I was unable to secure any information on MSMQ before the book went to print.

Table 9.1   Connectivity Technologies on Windows CE

Name	Initiated by	Queued	Base Protocol	Features	Used for
RAPI	PC	No	ActiveSync	Remote access to file system, registry, and object store.	Administration and configuration.
ActiveSync	PC	Yes	2.x TCP/IP 3.0 ActiveSync over serial and TCP/IP over Ethernet	Detection of changed application data and automatic synchronization.	Synchronization of user data in applications on the desktop PC.
DCOM/ deviceCOM	Both	No	TCP/IP	Calling of COM methods via a TCP/IP connection.	General connectivity between a client and a server application. Client or server can be on Windows CE. DCOM support is in Windows CE 3.0. Older devices (2.x) can use deviceCOM by Intrinsyc (see Section 6.7, "deviceCOM: The Industrial Version of DCOM").
Winsock	Both	No	TCP/IP	Low-level, TCP/IP-based transport. Offers a maximum of flexibility but requires that developer creates his or her own "protocol".	Used for fast communication that does not require a secure, predefined, or standard protocol.
IrDA	Both	No	TCP/IP IrDA	Very close to Winsock with two exceptions: 1) Only one partner.	Quick exchange of small amounts of data without having to set up a cable.

Name	Initiated by	Queued	Base Protocol	Features	Used for
				2) No wire necessary.	
HTTP	Both	No (but can be cached)	TCP/IP	Very common standard spoken by nearly all devices now.	User interface data, help files, exchange of information using forms. Very UI driven.

9.1   Using RAS as TCP/IP Provider

As you can see in Table 9.1, most connectivity technologies are based on TCP/IP. Until Version 3.0 of ActiveSync, the Windows CE Services were also using TCP/IP to communicate with Windows CE devices. To get a TCP/IP connection, using either a modem or a serial cable between your Windows CE device and your desktop PC or server, you must use the Remote Access Services (RAS). If you have an Ethernet card in your Windows CE device, you will have TCP/IP and can run ActiveSync via this protocol. This section will explain how you get ActiveSync 3.0 to use RAS even with a local serial cable.

9.1.1   Install the Communication Cable between Two PCs

The first component you must install is the communication cable between the two computers. Then manually set the COM ports to their maximum speed.

1. To install the communication cable, start the control panel applet "Phone and Modem Options" (Figure 9.1) and select the "Modems" tab.
2. Select the "Add . . ." button. The wizard to install a new modem will appear.
3. On the first page, select "Don't detect my modem; I will select it from a list" and click "Next".
4. On the second page, choose the "Standard Modem Types" and "Communications cable between two computers" (Figure 9.2).

The next page asks for the port. You can put the cable on both ports if you like. If you are using one port for any other use—for example, a digital camera—do not

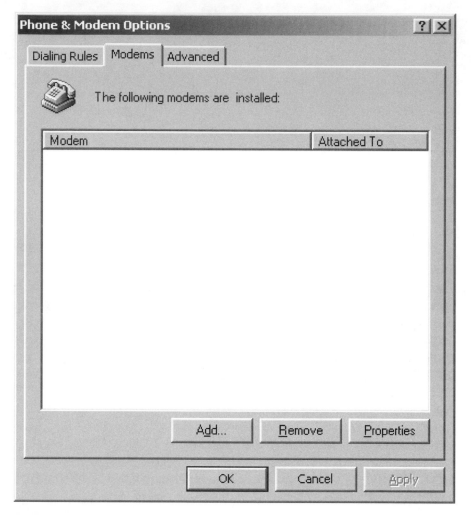

Figure 9.1   The control panel's "Phone and Modem Options" applet

assign the cable to that port because it will prevent your digital camera from working. If you have installed ActiveSync before you do this procedure, it will already use one port. To get the port back for RAS, you will need to go into the ActiveSync communication settings and disable the COM port access. You cannot switch it back on once RAS is set up. All further connection will have to go through the RAS subsystem.

Once Windows 2000 has installed the cable, you will see a new modem listed in the "Modems" tab, as shown in Figure 9.3. But do not close the "Modems" tab yet: you still need to set the cable speed.

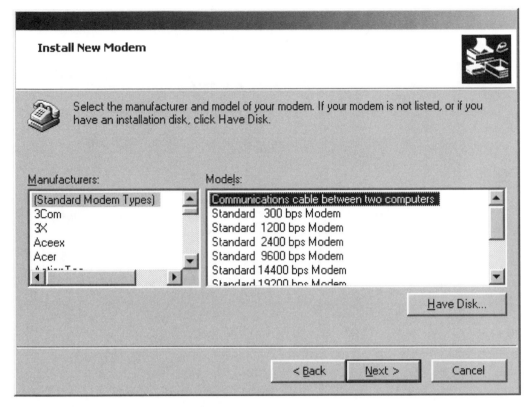

Figure 9.2 Select "Communications cable between two computers"

9.1.2 Setting the Baud Rate of the Communication Cable to 115K

The default communication speed for Windows CE 2.0 devices is 19,200 baud. This is terribly slow. Microsoft has learned that a developer needs to download his or her application hundreds of times during the development process, and at that slow speed, downloads seem to take forever. On some devices using Windows CE Version 2.01 (palm-size PC) and 2.11 (H/PC Professional), Microsoft increased the default speed to 57,600. I think that is still too slow, so I recommend using the highest speed possible: 115,200 baud. Some older PCs may not be able to connect at this speed, but I would give it a try first and only slow down if necessary.

To make the speed of the communication cable 115K baud, do the following:

1. Select the "Properties" button of the cable and set the "Maximum Port Speed" in the "General" tab to "115200".

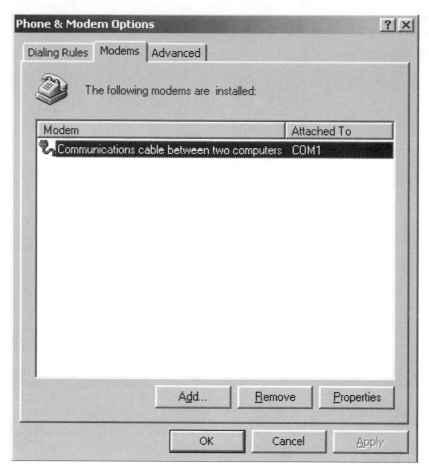

Figure 9.3 The cable is now installed

2. Select the "Advanced" tab and press the "Change Default Preferences" button. Verify that the port speed in the "General" tab shows "115200" (Figure 9.4).

3. Click on "OK" to close the default preferences and click again on "OK" to close the cable properties.

With those settings, your PC is ready to synchronize with your Windows CE device, using the maximum speed that the device is able to support.

9.1.3 Set Up Windows 2000 Incoming Connections

Now you need to set your Windows 2000 installation to accept calls on the newly installed cable.

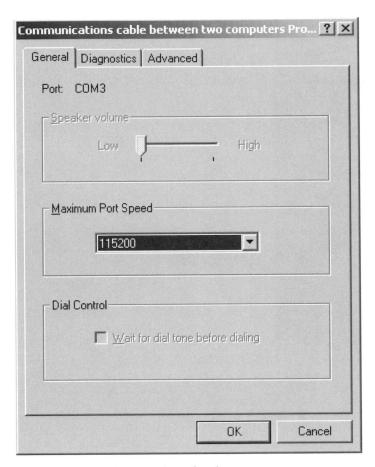

Figure 9.4 Change the default settings for the port

1. To set up this feature, locate the "My Network Places" icon on the desktop and right-click it. Select "Properties" from the object menu that will show up after you clicked it.

This is the new Windows 2000 area for dial-up and incoming connections. You will find a wizard template icon labeled "Make New Connection" here.

2. Double-click that icon and the "Network Connection Wizard" will pop up. See Figure 9.5.

3. Skip the introductory page and select "Accept Incoming Connection" on the second page of the wizard.

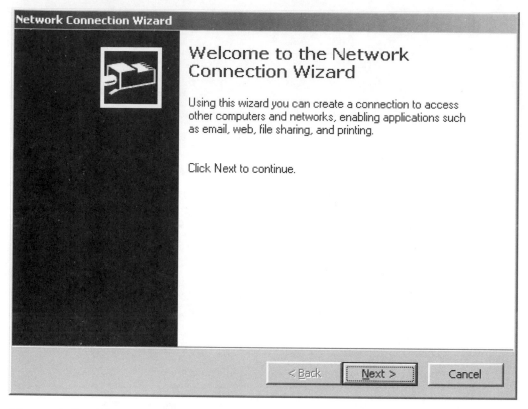

Figure 9.5 The Windows 2000 "Network Connection Wizard"

If your server belongs to a domain controller, the wizard will tell you that you have to use the Routing and Remote Access system console to continue. You can find instructions on how to use this console in Section 9.1.1, "Install the Communication Cable between Two PCs".

4. On the wizard's third page, you can select the well-known "Communications cable between two computers".

On the next page, you will be asked if you want to allow virtual connections. This setting would activate the Point-to-Point Tunneling Protocol (PPTP) that allows the setup of virtual private networks (VPNs) on your workstation.

5. This does not really matter for a Windows CE device, so select "Do not allow virtual connections".

The next page is important. Here you select the account that will have permissions to log in to your workstation. The administrator account is selected by default;

the guest account is not. I recommend leaving the defaults as is and using the administrator account to connect with your Windows CE device. If for any reason you are not allowed to use the administrator account, then create a new account rather than using the guest account. The reason is simple: If you want to use the guest account, you have to enable it in the User Manager. But with an enabled guest account, you basically open up holes in your security, since any user can log in to your machine without credentials using the guest account. With the guest account disabled, an intruder at least needs to know some user credentials on the workstation in order to get access. The better way is to create a new account for your Windows CE device log on.

6.   Click the "Add . . ." button to create a new user (Figure 9.6).

In the upcoming dialog box, enter a user name and password that you like and will remember; you will need them later for the Windows CE device logon.

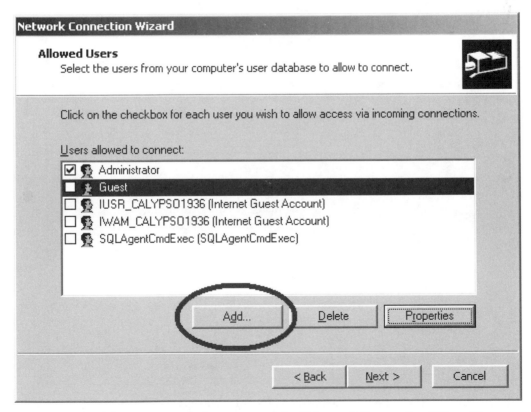

Figure 9.6   The user permissions page of the "Network Connection Wizard"

7. For the examples in the book, choose "CEPC" as the user name and a small "a" as the password. As soon as you click "OK", you will see the new user added to the list of allowed users.

8. Select "Next" to get to the wizard's last page.

Normally, everything that you need is already selected here. Check that "Internet Protocol (TCP/IP)" is selected. Click on "Properties" after you select the Internet Protocol. The upcoming dialog box defines how your Windows CE device will get its IP address (Figure 9.7).

The first setting is very interesting. It will determine whether your Windows CE device will be able to access the entire local network. If you select "Allow callers to access my local area network", your Windows 2000 workstation will work as a router

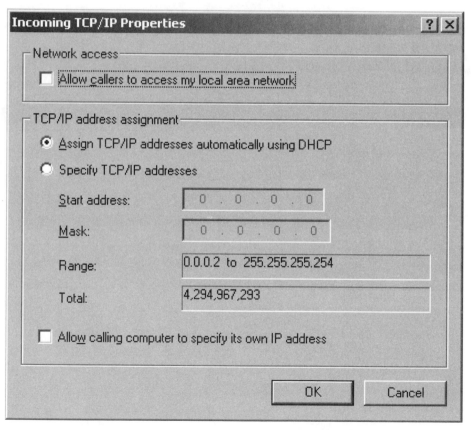

Figure 9.7 This dialog box determines what IP address your Windows CE device will get

and your Windows CE device will be able to access any PC on your local area network. I always check this setting in case I want to access some files from my server or even access the Internet with my device.

The TCP/IP address assignment allows you to choose between automatically assigned IP addresses using Dynamic Host Configuration Protocol (DHCP) or manual specification of TCP/IP address range.

9.   If you have a DHCP server running in your local area network, I recommend using it. If not, you have to set the IP range to the settings shown in Table 9.2.

I also recommend setting the "Allow calling computer to specify its own IP address". This setting allows you to set a fixed IP address on the Windows CE device side. Sometimes this can be important if you want to use software to access the Windows CE device that needs to know exactly what IP address it is using.

10.   Close this page and continue to the final page.

The final page names the new settings "Incoming Connections" and creates a new entry in the "Network and Dial-Up Connection" folder. You can change any of those settings by selecting "Incoming Connections" with the right mouse button and choosing "Properties" in the object menu. Please also note an interesting setting in the "Users" tab of those properties: "Always allow directly connected devices such as palmtop computers to connect without providing a password". I found that this setting actually does not do anything yet. I assume it is an option for a later version of the Windows CE Services that might make use of this setting.

9.1.4   Windows 2000 Server in a Domain Environment

If you are installing Windows 2000 Server and have upgraded it to a domain server instead of Windows 2000 Professional, you will have to install and configure the RAS server before you can connect to any Windows CE device. If you are using Windows 2000 Professional, you can skip this section and proceed with the installation of the tools. Here is what you need to do.

The steps to install the Communication cable are the same as those described above for the Windows 2000 Professional installation.

Table 9.2   IP Settings

Start address	192.168.55.98
Mask	255.255.255.0

1. Under "Start/Programs/Administrative Tools" select the "Routing and
    Remote Access". See Figure 9.8.

"Routing and Remote Access Management" is a plug-in for the Microsoft Management Console (MMC). Many options of Windows 2000 will be set using MMC plug-
ins. First, you need to install the Remote Access Services.

2. To do so, click with the right mouse button on the node in the Tree View that
    has the name of your computer.

You will get an object menu with several options to choose from.

3. Select the one that reads "Configure and Enable Routing and Remote
    Access".

You will be presented with a wizard that allows you to set several options for the
Routing and Remote Access Services, shown in Table 9.3.

The address range 192.168.$x.x$ is reserved for private intranets by the RFC1918
standard and can be used for your "private Windows CE intranet". Once you have
configured and started the service as described above, the RAS Management Console
should show a state similar to that in Figure 9.9.

4. Select the "Ports" folder and verify that the communication cable is displayed
    on the right side and reads "Inactive".

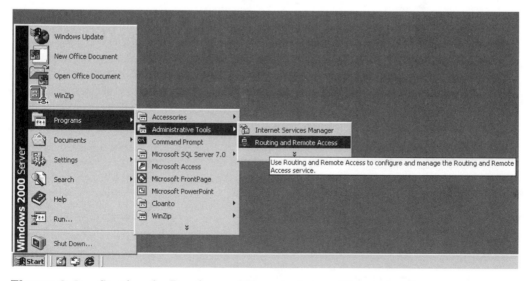

Figure 9.8   Starting the Routing and Remote Access Management

Table 9.3   Routing and Remote Access Service Settings

Name of the Setting	Your Configuration
Wizard, Page 1: Introductory page	
Wizard, Page 2: Common configurations	
Remote Access Services (RAS)	Select this option
Wizard, Page 3: Remote client protocols	
TCP/IP should be in the list of protocols	Do not change anything here
Wizard, Page 4: IP address assignment	
Depending on whether you have a DHCP server in your network, you can go with the "Automatic" option or will have to select the "From a specific range of addresses" option. For now select the second option.	
Wizard, Page 5: if you selected "specific IP range" **Select "New . . ." and add:**	
Start IP address	192.168.55.0
End IP address	192.168.55.255
Wizard, Page 6: (page 5 if you selected the automatic option in page 4)	
"No, I don't want to set up this server to use RADIUS now"	Select this option
You are done! Press "Finish" on the last page, and after a short loading time, Windows 2000 will ask you if you want to start the service. Select "Yes", and Windows 2000 will start the service.	

5. Now you need to launch "Active Directory Management for Users and Computers" from the "Administrative Tools" menu under "Start Menu/Programs/Administrative Tools".

You will get a tree view containing your domain name as a folder.

6. Open this folder and you will see several new folders, including one labeled "Users". Right-click on "Users", and you get a large object menu. Select the menu item "New/User", and a dialog box will pop up.

A domain controller requires a lot more information than a regular server does.

7. Type in the data shown in Table 9.4.

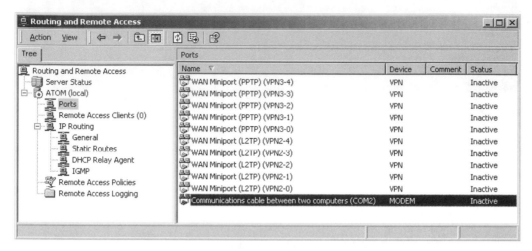

Figure 9.9   The Routing and Remote Access Management Console

Once you are finished with the wizard, you will see a new entry in the list of users called "CE PC". The last setting you will need to create is the permission to dial in.

8.   Right-click the new user "CE PC" and select "Properties" in the object menu.

A property dialog box will pop up and present you with a lot of tabs.

9.   Select the "Dial-In" tab, switch the "Remote Access Permission" setting to "Allow access", and then close the properties.

Table 9.4   Create New Object (User)-Wizard

Setting	Value
Wizard, Page 1	
First name	CE
Last name	PC
Name is filled out automatically	
User logon name	CEPC
Wizard, Page 2	
Password	Small "a"
Confirm password	Small "a"
Password never expires	Select
All other options	Leave unselected
On the final page, just press "Finish"	

Table 9.5 **Differences between RAS and Native ActiveSync 3.0 Connectivity**

Feature	ActiveSync Native	ActiveSync via RAS
Auto baud detection	Yes	No (fixed through modem settings)
Fast connection	Very fast	Slower, due to protocol and security negotiations
Underlying protocol	Proprietary	TCP/IP
Synchronization between Pocket-Outlook and Outlook	Yes	Yes
Web browsing via desktop PC	No	Yes (if DHCP gives IP address in the company's subnet)
RAPI	Yes	Yes
DCOM/deviceCOM	No	Yes
Easy to set up (PC)	Yes	Not really
Easy to set up (CE)	No difference	No Difference
Security	No	Yes

 An important note: ActiveSync 3.x cannot share a port with RAS.

Once you add a cable connection to the RAS service it will be blocked by RAS and can no longer be used by ActiveSync. Nearly all PCs these days have two COMports. You can keep one port for ActiveSync natively and assign the second port for RAS. Table 9.5 shows the differences between connection to a PC using RAS or ActiveSync 3.0

9.2　Remote API

System DLL:	RAPI.dll, RAPILIB.dll, CEUTIL.DLL (on the desktop)
Include file:	Rapi.h
Library:	rapi.lib
Help file:	wcesdkr.chm
Available since:	Windows CE 1.0

(continued)

API prefix/suffix:	Ce . . .
InitCommonControlEx flag:	—
MFC class:	—

The first technology I will discuss is Remote API (RAPI). RAPI has been available since Windows CE 1.0 and serves as a way to remotely configure applications and data on a Windows CE device. Although it has some calls that could be used to exchange data with a Windows CE device, it is not really a good choice for this purpose.

As mentioned before, RAPI offers calls to access remotely the following areas on the Windows CE device:

- The file system
- The registry
- Databases in the object store

Most RAPI functions are exactly modeled after or are even duplicates of their local subsidiaries and therefore do not require any special documentation. As Table 9.6 shows, there are also some RAPI calls that do not exist in the local Windows CE API.

 Important note: All string parameters on any RAPI call must be Unicode. Windows CE devices only know Unicode, so any ANSI string would produce strange effects.

9.2.1 A Small RAPI Example

Here is a small example that creates a file on the Windows CE device, writes to it, and reads it again.

1. Create a new "Hello World" application and name it "RAPITest".

 This is a desktop application. Do not use eMbedded Visual C++ to create this example, but rather the regular Visual C++ 6.0.

2. Add the following two includes to the header section of "RAPITest.CPP" and the three functions below it:

```
#include <Objidl.h>
#include <rapi.h>
```

Table 9.6   RAPI Calls That Do Not Exist in the Windows CE API

API Name	Used for
CeRapiInit<Ex>	Initializes the underlying communication layer, while CeRapiInit waits until it is successful. If your device is not connected, this could lead to a deadlock. The "Ex" function uses an event instead and therefore is nonblocking.
CeRapiInvoke	Can be used to remotely call any function in any DLL on the Windows CE device.
CeRapiUninit	Closes all connections to the Windows CE device and unloads the communication layer.
CeGetPassword	Compares the given parameter string to the current password on the CE device and returns "True" if they match.
CeGetDesktopDeviceCaps	Retrieves the desktop capabilities of the Windows CE device (its CE counterpart is GetDeviceCaps).
CeRapiFreeBuffer	Frees memory that was allocated, using CeFindAllDatabases or CeReadRecordProps.

```
void WriteFile2CE()
{
HANDLE hFile;
DWORD nByteWritten;
TCHAR szText[]=TEXT("This is a test");
// Use L"" Macro to define an Unicode string

        hFile = CeCreateFile(L"\\TEMP\\RAPITEST.TMP",
                        GENERIC_WRITE,(DWORD)0,NULL,
                        CREATE_ALWAYS,(DWORD)NULL, NULL);
        if (hFile!= INVALID_HANDLE_VALUE)
        {
                CeWriteFile(hFile,szText,strlen(szText)*sizeof(TCHAR),
                        &nByteWritten,NULL);
}
        CeCloseHandle(hFile);
}
```

```
void ReadFileFromCE()
{
HANDLE hFile;
DWORD nByteWritten;
TCHAR szText[300];

        hFile = CeCreateFile(L"\\TEMP\\RAPITEST.TMP",
                             GENERIC_READ,(DWORD)0,NULL,
                             OPEN_EXISTING ,(DWORD)NULL, NULL);
        if (hFile!= INVALID_HANDLE_VALUE)
        {
                CeReadFile(hFile,szText,300,&nByteWritten,NULL);
        }
        CeCloseHandle(hFile);
}


void DoStuff()
{
HRESULT hRapiResult;

        hRapiResult = CeRapiInit ();

        if (FAILED(hRapiResult))
                return;      // Error handler

        WriteFile2CE();
        ReadFileFromCE();

        CeRapiUninit ();
}
```

"Objidl.h" defines the "IStream" interface that RAPI will use to communicate.

    3.   Add the following line before the "MessageLoop" in the "WinMain" function:

```
DoStuff();
```

    4.   Add "RAPI.LIB" to the library list of the linker settings.

You will find the "RAPI.H" and "RAPI.LIB" in the directory:

```
/Windows CE Tools/WCE<CEVersion>/<Platform>/Desktop/inc
/Windows CE Tools/WCE<CEVersion>/<Platform>/Desktop/lib
```

I always recommend using the latest version of "RAPI.H" and its matching "RAPI.LIB". If Microsoft added features to RAPI, they are defined in that latest version. Microsoft promises that new features will be compatible with earlier versions.

Before you can run the example, your PC has to be connected to your Windows CE device. If your device is not connected, the application will stop at the "CeRapiInit()" call. Now run the example in debug mode and step through the "DoStuff()" function. If everything succeeds, you will see the "szText" string variable containing the "This is a test" message in the "ReadFileFromCE" call. You can also see the new file "RAPITEST.TMP" in the "TEMP" folder of your Windows CE device. Load it with Pocket-Word. It should contain the same test string.

 The final source code of this section can be found on the companion CD under "\Sources\Chapter 9\9.1".

9.2.2 Converting ObjectStoreIt to a Desktop Application

To show that the RAPI calls are really identical to the local Windows CE APIs, you will to use the "ObjectStoreIt" example from Section 8.3.1 and convert it to a desktop project, making only some minor modifications.

1. Create a desktop project, as described in Chapter 6, using the example in Section 8.3.1.
2. Open the resource file with the text editor and delete the following line from the "IDD_ABOUTBOX" dialog resource.

```
EXSTYLE WS_EX_CAPTIONOKBTN
```

3. Now add the two include files to the "ObjectStoreIt.cpp" header as before:

```
#include <objidl.h>
#include <rapi.h>
```

If you were to compile the project now, you would get four kinds of errors:

- All strings passed to any "Ce<Name>" call are not Unicode yet.
- The command bar used by the "Hello World" project on Windows CE is, of course, not supported on Win32.
- The "wprintf" function does not work on the desktop.
- The "CeReadRecordPropertyEx" method is not supported in RAPI.

4. Locate the "CommandBar" calls and put a "#ifdef UNDER_CE" around them. They are located in "WndProc" and at the end of the "InitInstance" function of the "ObjectStoreIt.cpp" source file.

5. Put all "wprintf" calls in remarks.

To deal with the Unicode issue, you need to make several changes.

6. Change all TEXT(" ") macros to the "L" macro.

As an example, the new "CeOpenDatabase" line would look like this:

```
hDataBase = CeOpenDatabase(&CeOid,L"Book922",0, 0,NULL);
```

7. Change all "TCHAR" definitions and type-casts to "WCHAR".

8. Change all "_tcscpy" instances to "wcscpy" and all "_tsclen" instances to "lstrlen".

If your application targets only Windows NT or Windows 2000, you can just set the "UNICODE" define in the C++ preprocessor settings, and you will have a lot less work to do.

9. The last error, regarding "CeReadRecordPropsEx", is easy to eliminate, since you are not using the "Ex" functionality—the heap—anyway. Just change the call to "CeReadRecordProps" and remove the last NULL pointer.

10. Add "CeRapiInit()" before the "CeOpenDatabase" call and "CeRapiUninit()" at the end of the "AccessObjectStore" function.

11. Also change the "CloseHandle" call to "CeCloseHandle" to close the remote handle rather than a local one.

12. The last addition you need to make to your example is to add "RAPI.LIB" to the libraries for your linker.

Now compile the example and debug it. You will see that all calls work as expected.

The final source code of this section can be found on the companion CD under "\Sources\Chapter 9\9.2".

9.2.3 Updating Your PCDM Application with RAPI

RAPI is a desktop-only technology. Therefore it does not make sense to put RAPI in your PCDM application on the Windows CE side. There is one part of the application where RAPI can be helpful, at least for some potential future enhancements. The "PCDMDLL.DLL" currently has a lot of "#IFDEF UNDER_CE" inside excluding code that cannot be compiled on the desktop. Using RAPI, you can get rid of most of those "#IFDEF" statements and even use your "PCDMDLL.DLL" control to access the object store on the Windows CE device. Here is what you need to do.

1. Load the last version of the PCDMDLL project for the desktop and open the "PCDMAccessDB.h" include file.

2. Change the header of the include file to:

```
// PCDMAccessDB.h : Declaration of the CPCDMAccessDB

#ifndef __PCDMACCESSDB_H_
#define __PCDMACCESSDB_H_

#include "resource.h"        // main symbols

#include <comdef.h>
#ifndef UNDER_CE
#include <rapi.h>
#include <adoint.h>
typedef Field          Field20;
#else
#include <adoce30.h>
//… old code continues here with Field20 description
```

"RAPI.H" is located in the "Desktop\Inc" directory of your platform SDK. As stated in the previous section, you can add this path to the "include" settings of the Visual C++ directory options.

3. With those changes, you can remove almost all the "#IFDEF UNDER_CE" statements from the include file.

The only "#IFDEF UNDER_CE" statement left is the one around the "Field20" interface description. This "#IFDEF" has to remain because ADO for the desktop is in no way compatible with this old version of ADOCE 2.0. The "typedef" under the "<ADOINT.H>" include will avoid compiler errors except for those caused by the "(struct Field **)" cast.

4. To get rid of these errors you need to put "#IFDEF UNDER_CE" around these calls. To have clean code without holes, you can add the following code:

```
#ifdef UNDER_CE
    hr=pFields->get_Item(_variant_t(tFldName),
                         (struct Field **)&pField20);
#else
    hr=pFields->get_Item(_variant_t(tFldName),
                         (struct ADOField **)&pField20);
#endif
```

Including "<ADOINT.H>" will allow you to compile the ADO code, and since you hard-coded the IIDs for ADOCE, you can even run the component without problems on the desktop. The "CLSIDFromProgID" call will fail, and "m_useADO" will be set to "PCDMADO_NONE", activating the RAPI calls.

5. Add the initialization of RAPI to the constructor of the "PCDMAccessDB" class.

```
//.. .. old construction code here
#ifndef UNDER_CE
    CeRapiInit ();
#endif
}
```

This is not a very efficient or good way to do it, but it keeps the example simple. For now, you are not going into asynchronous event mode.

6. Remove the "#IFDEF UNDER_CE" statements from the "PCDMAccessDB.cpp" source file, too.

You will also need to address some issues pertaining to the database handle.

7. Locate all "CloseHandle" calls and replace them with the following code:

```
#ifdef UNDER_CE
        CloseHandle(Handle);
#else
        CeCloseHandle((HANDLE)Handle);
#endif
```

There are two occurrences of "CloseHandle": one in the "CloseTable" method and one in the "CreateTable" method. Before you can compile the changed class, add "RAPI.LIB" to the libraries of your project. The next section will test your new RAPI control.

The final source code of this section can be found on the companion CD under "\Sources\ThreadExample\PCDMDLL\Step6".

9.2.4 Testing the Class in Visual Basic for the Desktop

To test your changes, you can simply use the code from Section 8.3.4, "Testing the New Class in eMbedded Visual Basic."

1. Create a new Visual Basic version for the desktop project and copy the code of the "OnLoad()" method of the CE project into the "OnLoad" method of your desktop project.

2. Change the table name from "Book843" to "Book924".

3. To get the right object reference for the "Dim a as PCDMAccessDB" definition you must either include a reference to the "PCDMAccessDB" class in the Visual Basic settings or change the dimension line to:

```
Dim a as Object
```

If your device was connected and you stepped through the code, you would find that it works exactly like the project for Windows CE. If you did not have your device connected, the application would wait in the "CreateObject" call until it was connected. Unfortunately, your Visual Basic application will appear to be "hanging" during that time.

 The final source code of this section can be found on the companion CD under "\Sources\Chapter 9\9.3".

9.3 ActiveSync: Keep in Sync with Your Data

System DLL:	None
Include file:	CESYNC.H
Library file:	None
Help file:	Wcesdkr.chm
Available since:	Windows CE 1.0
API prefix/suffix:	Irepl . . .
InitCommonControlEx flag:	—
MFC class:	—

ActiveSync is the synchronization technology that ships with every Windows CE device in the form of the ActiveSync 3.1 tool. During the past three years, it has been through quite a series of name changes. During the time of Windows CE 1.x devices, it was called "Windows CE Explorer". With the first Windows CE 2.0 devices, Microsoft renamed it "Windows CE Services" and for the first time introduced the AppInstaller and the plug-in concept that you will be learning about next.

With the latest generation of palm-size PC 2.0 devices, Microsoft arrived at the name "ActiveSync". Well, at least Microsoft has kept the versioning of these tools consistent over the years; the latest ActiveSync version is 3.1. I predict that they are still not done and that an upcoming release might even be on the market before this book hits the shelves. But for now, let's concentrate on the existing plug-in technology that Microsoft includes in the ActiveSync product.

9.3.1 The Concept of ActiveSync

ActiveSync has two components:

- One running on the desktop PC (WCESMgr.exe)
- One running on the Windows CE device (CEMGRC.EXE)

Both components can be extended with a plug-in to synchronize any data you desire. If you look at the ActiveSync application window, shown in Figure 9.10, you can see

Figure 9.10   Standard ActiveSync services for an H/PC Professional

a list of services that are synchronized by ActiveSync out of the box. You can add a new service to this list for your own data.

ActiveSync consists of two so-called ActiveSync providers. One runs on the desktop, the other on the Windows CE device. Both parts only check their local store for changes and then send the changes to the other side.

9.3.2 Creating an ActiveSync Service Provider for the PCDM

The ActiveSync provider wizard is designed to synchronize three different sorts of containers:

- A store containing one or more . . .
- Folders containing one or more . . .
- Items . . .

Table 9.7 translates those three synchronization objects into their real-life implementations. The folder level determines whether the two stores, one on the desktop and one on the Windows CE device, are out of sync. If they are, the items will be synchronized.

ActiveSync is a very complex technology, and to cover each and every detail would require a book of its own. The following example will concentrate on the essentials that you will need in order to get ActiveSync up and running. To familiarize yourself with ActiveSync, you will write an ActiveSync service provider for your PCDM application. As you learned in Chapter 8, the Deluxe CD player will not work once you change anything using Access 2000. Thus your ActiveSync service provider will use the unchanged Deluxe CD database and will synchronize it with your Windows CE database using your PCDMDLL.DLL COM component.

Before you can start writing code, you need to install the "ActiveSync Service Provider Wizard". However, at the time that I wrote this chapter, this wizard was not part of eMbedded Visual Tools 3.0, and Microsoft had not disclosed how the wizard would be distributed.

Table 9.7 Mapping of the ActiveSync Containers to Example Objects

ActiveSync Name	File System Example	PCDM Application
Store	Directory	DeluxeCD database
Folder	File	CD table
Item	Content of file	Tracks table

1. The wizard is contained in a file called "syncwiz.awx" and has to be copied into the directory:

`"\Program Files\Microsoft Visual Studio\Common\MSDev98\Template"`

2. Now launch Visual Studio 98 and select the "ActiveSync Service Provider Wizard" in the list of new project templates. Name the project "PCDMSync".

3. In the first page of the wizard select "a simple file sync provider" and then select "Next".

You will use the file sync provider because it already contains a lot of code that you can reuse.

4. Fill the second page of the wizard with the entries shown in Figure 9.11.

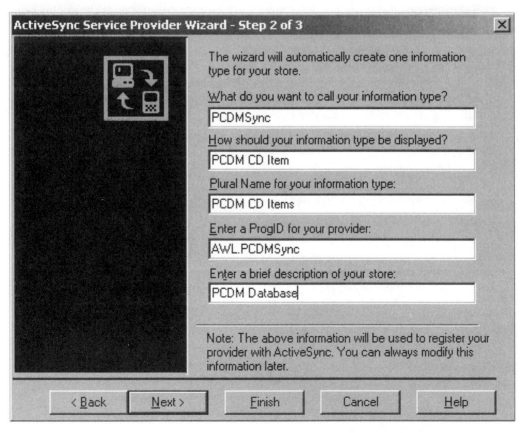

Figure 9.11 The "ActiveSync Service Provider Wizard" description page

5.   In the wizard's last page, select the middle option, "Poll my provider when the ActiveSync window is activated".

You only want to synchronize your database permanently if ActiveSync is running on the desktop. The other two options are for those real-time synchronization requirements.

As soon as you hit "Finish", the wizard will create two projects:

- The desktop part of the ActiveSync provider
- The device part of the ActiveSync provider in a subdirectory named "device"

The Desktop Side of ActiveSync

Now take a look at the desktop part created by the wizard. If you open the class view of the project, you will find nine classes and a series of methods in those classes. Seeing that, you will no doubt conclude that writing an ActiveSync service provider without the wizard would not be one of the easiest tasks in the Windows CE design process. Figure 9.12 shows a simplified flowchart of the ActiveSync calls going back and forth between ActiveSync and your provider. To stick to the essentials, I am not

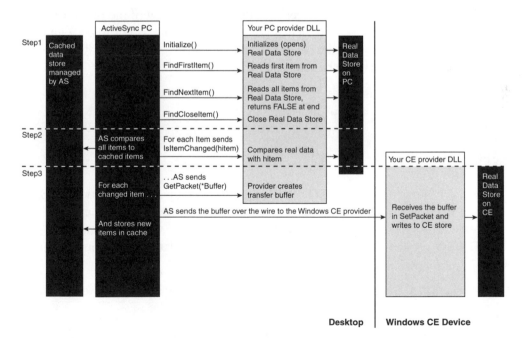

Figure 9.12   A simplified ActiveSync flowchart driven from the desktop side

going to explain all the functions in the provider, but rather tell you where and what you have to add to get your provider up and running. If you want to learn more about the possibilities and features of the provider, you can look through the code that the wizard generates. It contains detailed remarks on where you have to do what, although it gives very little information about the order in which the various methods are called.

Nearly all of the changes you will make to the code will take place in the "CPCDMSyncFolder" and "CPCDMSyncObjHandler" classes. The only other change you will make is in the "CPCDMSyncStore" class. The wizard always generates the same number for a new ActiveSync store. You have to change that number to a unique one in order to ensure the uniqueness of your store.

1. Open the "PCDMSyncStore.cpp" file and locate the "GetStoreInfo" method.

One line above the very last line in this method you will find

```
*puId=12345;
```

2. Change this line to

```
*puId=14499;
```

The new number 14499 will now identify your PCDM database synchronization store. The same number has to be entered in the device version of the provider. Another change you need to make in this file and in "replobjs.h" has to do with the example's focus on file synchronization. The define "*MAX*_PATH" of 240 is too small for your provider and needs to be replaced by MAXDATASIZE.

3. Change all occurrences of "*MAX*_PATH" with "MAXDATASIZE" in the files "PCDMSyncStore.cpp" and "replobjs.h".

4. Add the following define to the top of the "replobjs.h" file:

```
#define MAXDATASIZE     8000
```

To synchronize the Deluxe CD database on the desktop and on Windows CE, you are going to use ADO on the desktop and your PCDMDLL component on Windows CE. As mentioned before most of the ActiveSync work happens in the "CPCDMSyncFolder" and "CPCDMSyncObjHandler" classes. Therefore you have to add support for ADO to those classes.

5. Open "PCDMSyncFolder.h" and add the following lines to the top of the file:

```
#undef EOF
#import <\Program Files\Common Files\System\ado\msado15.dll> \
        rename_namespace("ado15")
```

```
using namespace ado15;
```

6.   Add the following private class to the "CPCDMSyncFolder" class:

```
private:
      _ConnectionPtr  m_Conn1;
      _RecordsetPtr   m_Rs1;
      HRESULT BuildItemStrNCrc(_RecordsetPtr RS,_bstr_t *str,
                               FILETIME *ft);
      HRESULT BuildItem(HREPLITEM *phItem, BOOL *pfExist);
```

Before you add the code to the "CPCDMSyncFolder" class methods, have a look back at the flowchart in Figure 9.12. As you can see, the most important stage of the synchronization is the loop through "FindFirstItem"/"FindNextItem" and "FindItemClose". There are some other methods that are called during the synchronization that you will need to fill with code. But ActiveSync calls those methods only when they are required. In order to get your provider up and running, you will only need to change the methods that are shown in boldface in Table 9.8.

You will find a lot of "OutputDebugStrings" inside the code. As you will see in Section 9.3.3, "Some Debugging Tips," debugging is not easy. Therefore it is useful to put some verbose outputs in your code. Start with the initialization.

7.   Change the code of the initialization method to the following:

```
HRESULT CPCDMSyncFolder::Initialize(IUnknown **ppObjHandler)
{
OutputDebugString(TEXT("In Initialize...\n\r"));
      _variant_t        vaEmpty;
      _bstr_t                 bsEmpty = L"";

      HRESULT hr=m_Conn1.CreateInstance( __uuidof( Connection ) );
      if (FAILED(hr)) return hr;
      m_Conn1->ConnectionString =
L"Provider=MSDASQL.1;Persist Security Info=False;Data Source=
DeluxeCD";
      hr=m_Conn1->Open( bsEmpty, bsEmpty, bsEmpty, -1 );
      if (FAILED(hr)) return hr;
      hr=m_Rs1.CreateInstance( __uuidof( Recordset ) );
      if (FAILED(hr))      return hr;
OutputDebugString(TEXT("I:Out..\n\r"));

      *ppObjHandler = NULL;
```

Table 9.8 **CPCDMSyncFolder Methods Called by ActiveSync During Synchronization**

Method	Purpose	Will Be Called . . .
Initialization	Initializes the desktop store for synchronization	At the beginning of the synchronization
FindFirstItem	Starts the item iteration loop like the "FindFirstFile" API call	Once per synchronization iteration (ActiveSync runs through the list of items about four times.)
FindNextItem	Constructs the item that will be compared with the CE store	For each item in the folder
FindItemClose	Closes the iteration loop	Once per synchronization iteration
IsValidObject	Determines if an object in a folder was deleted	If ActiveSync cannot verify if the item is still valid
IsFolderChanged	Allows the provider to skip the synchronization of the folder at the current time	If ActiveSync starts the synchronization process
IsItemChanged	Determines if an existing item has changed	If ActiveSync cannot verify if the item has changed
IsItemReplicated	Allows the provider to skip an item during synchronization	For each item during synchronization
RemoveDuplicates	Allows the provider to remove duplicate items	Only if duplicate items are found
UpdateItem	Updates an OID in the ActiveSync store	If a change was applied to the corresponding item in the CE store
GetObjTypeUIData	Retrieves all the UI elements from the provider to be shown in the ActiveSync dialog box	During startup of the synchronization
ActivateDialog	Allows the user to select options for the provider	If the user double-clicks the provider in the ActiveSync dialog box
GetConfictInfo	Resolves conflicts between the desktop and the CE store	If an item was changed on the desktop and the CE store
DeleteItem	Allows deletion of an item that was deleted from the CE store	If ActiveSync found a deleted item in the CE store

```
        CPCDMSyncObjHandler *pObj = new CPCDMSyncObjHandler(this);
        if(pObj == NULL)
                return E_OUTOFMEMORY;

        hr = pObj->QueryInterface(IID_IUnknown,
                                    reinterpret_cast<void**>
                                    (ppObjHandler));
        pObj->Release();
        return hr;
}
```

You will only use the initialization method to create an ADO connection to the Deluxe CD database. The next method to be patched is the "FindFirstItem" method.

8.   Change the code to the following lines:

```
HRESULT CPCDMSyncFolder::FindFirstItem(HREPLITEM *phItem,
                                        BOOL *pfExist)
{
    *phItem  = NULL;
    *pfExist = FALSE;

OutputDebugString(TEXT("In FindFirstItem...\n\r"));
        _bstr_t             bsSel(L"SELECT * FROM Titles");
        m_Rs1->PutRefActiveConnection( m_Conn1 );
        m_Rs1->Open(bsSel,vtMissing,adOpenKeyset,
                    adLockBatchOptimistic,-1);
        BuildItem(phItem,pfExist);
OutputDebugString(TEXT("FFI:Out..\n\r"));
        return S_OK;
}
```

Next you will need to open the "Titles" table of the Deluxe CD database and create the first synchronization item, using a private helper method named "BuildItem".

9.   "BuildItem" and its helper method "BuildItemStrNCrc" need to be added next:

```
int PCDMCDsIDs[]= { 0,1,2,4,5,3,-1,-1,-1,-1,-1,-1 };

HRESULT CPCDMSyncFolder::BuildItemStrNCrc(_RecordsetPtr RS,
                                        _bstr_t *str, FILETIME *ft)
{
```

```
int         i,max;
VARIANT     value;
VariantInit(&value);
LPCSTR      tP;
_bstr_t     bsSel(L"");
WCHAR       tStr[1000];

OutputDebugString(TEXT("In BuildItemStrNCRC...\n\r   "));
     max=RS->Fields->GetCount();
     for (i=0;i<max;i++)
     {
          if (PCDMCDsIDs[i]>=0)
          {
               bsSel+=L"&";
               VariantClear(&value);
               VariantCopy(&value,
                    &RS->Fields->Item[(long)
                    PCDMCDsIDs[i]]->Value);
               if (PCDMCDsIDs[i]==0)
                    ft->dwHighDateTime=value.lVal;
               VariantChangeType(&value,&value,0,VT_BSTR);
               if (lstrlenW(value.bstrVal)!=0)
                    wsprintfW(tStr,L"Fld%d=%s",i,value.bstrVal);
               else
                    wsprintfW(tStr,L"Fld%d=n.a.",i);
               bsSel+=tStr;
          }
     }
     ft->dwLowDateTime=0;
     tP=(LPCSTR)bsSel;
     for (i=0;i<lstrlen(bsSel);i++)
          ft->dwLowDateTime+=(int)*tP++;
     wsprintfW(tStr,L"&Fld6=%d",ft->dwLowDateTime);
     bsSel+=tStr;
     bsSel+=L";";
     max=lstrlen(bsSel);

     if (str!=NULL)
          str->Assign(bsSel);
OutputDebugString(bsSel);
OutputDebugString(TEXT("\n\rBISNC:Out\n\r"));
```

```
        return S_OK;
}

HRESULT CPCDMSyncFolder::BuildItem(HREPLITEM *phItem, BOOL *pfExist)
{
        if  (!m_Rs1->EOF)
        {
                FILETIME crc={0,0};
                _bstr_t              bsSel;

                BuildItemStrNCrc(m_Rs1,&bsSel,&crc);

                CReplItem *pItem = new CReplItem(bsSel);
                if(pItem == NULL)
                        return E_OUTOFMEMORY;

                pItem->SetModified(crc);
                *phItem = reinterpret_cast<HREPLITEM>(pItem);
                *pfExist = TRUE;

        }

        return S_OK;
}
```

A synchronization item consists of two properties: a TypeID as a string and a modification date as a FILETIME. For your provider, you need to put all fields of a record from the "Titles" table into the TypeID string using the URL syntax from your "PCDMUtils" class (See Appendix B, "The PCDMUtils Class"). The "PCDMCDsIDs" array is used to correctly arrange the fields of the desktop table to your table on Windows CE.

The FILETIME structure consists of two DWORDs normally used for "high-time" and "low-time" longs. In your provider, you will use them for a different purpose:

- The "dwHighDateTime" member of the structure will contain the "TitleID" of a CD title.
- The "dwLowDateTime" will contain a checksum of the TypeID string.

With these two values, it will be possible to detect changes inside a record of the "Titles" table and your "PCDMCDs" table in the Windows CE store.

10.   The "FindNextItem" method contains only four lines of code:

```
HRESULT CPCDMSyncFolder::FindNextItem(HREPLITEM *phItem, BOOL
*pfExist)
{
        *pfExist = FALSE;
OutputDebugString(TEXT("In FindNextItem...\n\r"));
        m_Rs1->MoveNext();
        BuildItem(phItem,pfExist);
OutputDebugString(TEXT("FNI:Out..\n\r"));
        return S_OK;
}
```

11.   "FindItemClose" is even smaller:

```
HRESULT CPCDMSyncFolder::FindItemClose()
{
OutputDebugString(TEXT("In FindItemClose...\n\r"));
        m_Rs1->Close();
OutputDebugString(TEXT("FIC:Out..\n\r"));
        return S_OK;
}
```

As noted above, you will only add code to some of the remaining methods. The first such method is "IsValidObject".

12.   Add the following code to its implementation:

```
    HRESULT CPCDMSyncFolder::IsValidObject(HREPLITEM hObject,
                                             UINT uFlags)
{
    CReplItem *pReplItem = reinterpret_cast<CReplItem *>(hObject);
    if(pReplItem == NULL)
        return RERR_CORRUPT;

OutputDebugString(TEXT("In IsValidObject...\n\r"));
        _bstr_t             bsSel(L"SELECT * FROM Titles where
                                TitleID=");
        _RecordsetPtr       tRs;
        HRESULT             hr;
        TCHAR               id[20];

        hr=tRs.CreateInstance( __uuidof( Recordset ) );
        if (FAILED(hr))        return hr;
        FILETIME& ftOld=pReplItem->GetModified();
```

```
        wsprintf(id,TEXT("%d"),ftOld.dwHighDateTime);
        bsSel+=id;
        tRs->PutRefActiveConnection( m_Conn1 );
        tRs->Open(bsSel,vtMissing,adOpenKeyset,adLockBatchOptimistic,
        -1);
        if (tRs->EOF)
                hr=RERR_OBJECT_DELETED;
        else
                hr=S_OK;
        tRs->Close();
OutputDebugString(TEXT("IVO:Out..\n\r"));
        return hr;
}
```

This method will look in the "Titles" table for a special "TitleID" stored in the "Item Modify" flag. If it is not found, the method returns "RERR_OBJECT_DELETED", and ActiveSync asks the Windows CE store to delete the corresponding item. The "IsItemChanged" method has a similar function. It helps ActiveSync in determining whether an item has changed. For that purpose, the method recreates the checksum in the "Modify" flag of the item and compares it to the one coming from the CE store.

13.   Here is the code for this method:

```
BOOL CPCDMSyncFolder::IsItemChanged(HREPLITEM hItem)
{
        CReplItem *pReplItem = reinterpret_cast<CReplItem *>(hItem);
        FILETIME& ftOld = pReplItem->GetModified();

OutputDebugString(TEXT("In IsItemChanged...\n\r"));
        _bstr_t              bsSel(L"SELECT * FROM Titles where
                             TitleID=");
        _RecordsetPtr        tRs;
        HRESULT              hr;
        FILETIME             ftNew={0,0};
        TCHAR                id[20];
TCHAR              tStr[200];
        wsprintf(id,TEXT("%d"),ftOld.dwHighDateTime);
        bsSel+=id;
        hr=tRs.CreateInstance( __uuidof( Recordset ) );
        if (FAILED(hr))        return hr;
        tRs->PutRefActiveConnection( m_Conn1 );
        tRs->Open(bsSel,vtMissing,adOpenKeyset,adLockBatchOptimistic,-1);
```

```
        if (tRs->EOF)
              hr=FALSE;
        else
        {
              BuildItemStrNCrc(tRs,NULL,&ftNew);
wsprintf(tStr,TEXT("Old:<%d>,<%d> New:<%d>,<%d>\n\r"),
                  ftOld.dwHighDateTime,ftOld.dwLowDateTime,
                  ftNew.dwHighDateTime,ftNew.dwLowDateTime);
OutputDebugString(tStr);
              hr=::CompareFileTime(&ftOld, &ftNew);
        }
        tRs->Close();

OutputDebugString(TEXT("IIC:Out..\n\r"));
        return hr;
}
```

The important line of this method is the one containing "::CompareFileTime". If both
DWORDs in the two FILETIMEs are equal, the item has not changed. In your case, it
refers to the "TitleID" of a CD and the calculated checksum.

The next method, "UpdateItem", will be called if "ActiveStore" has successfully
updated a record in the store on Windows CE. It requests you to correct the checksum
(FILETIME) in the ActiveSync cache. ActiveSync has to bring the internal cache
back in sync—otherwise the record would be selected as dirty during the next synchronization and sent back to the CE device.

14.   Here is the implementation of this method:

```
HRESULT CPCDMSyncFolder::UpdateItem(HREPLITEM hItem)
{
    CReplItem *pReplItem = reinterpret_cast<CReplItem *>(hItem);

OutputDebugString(TEXT("In UpdateItem...\n\r"));
        FILETIME& ftOld = pReplItem->GetModified();
        _bstr_t            bsSel(L"SELECT * FROM Titles where
                           TitleID=");
        _RecordsetPtr      tRs;
        HRESULT            hr;
        FILETIME           ftNew;
        TCHAR              id[20];
        wsprintf(id,TEXT("%d"),ftOld.dwHighDateTime);
        bsSel+=id;
```

```
        hr=tRs.CreateInstance( __uuidof( Recordset ) );
        if (FAILED(hr))         return hr;
        tRs->PutRefActiveConnection( m_Conn1 );
        tRs->Open(bsSel,vtMissing,adOpenKeyset,adLockBatchOptimistic,-
        1);
        if (tRs->EOF)
                hr=FALSE;
        else
        {
                BuildItemStrNCrc(tRs,NULL,&ftNew);
                pReplItem->SetModified(ftNew);
        }
        tRs->Close();
OutputDebugString(TEXT("UI:Out..\n\r"));
        return S_OK;
}
```

The important line here contains "pReplItem->SetModified(ftNew);". It corrects the checksum in the ActiveSync cached item.

The last method you will change is the "DeleteItem" method. It will be called if a record was deleted in the CE store. It needs to be deleted on the desktop store as well.

15.   The code looks like this:

```
HRESULT CPCDMSyncFolder::DeleteItem(HREPLITEM hItem)
{
    CReplItem *pReplItem = reinterpret_cast<CReplItem *>(hItem);
OutputDebugString(TEXT("In DeleteItem...\n\r"));
        _bstr_t          bsSel(L"delete from Titles where TitleID=");
        _variant_t       vaEmpty;
        TCHAR            id[20];
        FILETIME&        ftOld=pReplItem->GetModified();
        wsprintf(id,TEXT("%d"),ftOld.dwHighDateTime); bsSel+=id;
OutputDebugString(bsSel);
OutputDebugString(TEXT("\n\r"));
        HRESULT hr=m_Conn1->Execute(bsSel,&vaEmpty,0);
        bsSel=L"delete from Tracks where TitleID=";
        bsSel+=id;
OutputDebugString(bsSel);
OutputDebugString(TEXT("\n\r"));
        hr=m_Conn1->Execute(bsSel,&vaEmpty,0);
OutputDebugString(TEXT("DI:Out..\n\r"));
```

```
        return S_OK;
}
```

You need to delete the CD in the "Titles" table and the corresponding tracks in the "Tracks" table.

There is one more minor change that you need to apply to this class. The ActiveSync wizard created a method called "GetSyncFileName". This method contains the name of the file that the example wants to synchronize. In your provider that name does not make any sense. And since the class uses the same method to get the text for the "szSyncText" member of the "POBJUIDATA" structure of the "GetObjTypeUIData" method, you need to change it.

```
const LPTSTR CPCDMSyncFolder::GetSyncFileName()
{
        return _T("Synchronizing the PCDM-DB...");
}
```

This concludes the changes made to the "CPCDMSyncFolder" class. Next you need to make some changes to the "CPCDMSyncObjHandler" class. This class does the marshalling of desktop items to the CE store and vice versa. The order in which the methods will be called is very simple, as Table 9.9 shows.

In case a record is out of sync with the CE store, you will transfer the CD data and its corresponding track data to the CE store using the URL syntax of your "PCDMUtils" class. The Windows CE side will send TSQL strings up to the desktop, which you can then execute in the "SetPacket" method.

Table 9.9   CPCDMSyncObjHandler Methods Called during Synchronization

Method	Purpose	Will Be Called . . .
Setup	Initializes the transfer buffer for the synchronization data	Before GetPacket or SetPacket will be called
GetPacket	Reads the data from the desktop store and streams it into the transfer buffer	Once per out-of-sync object if the item in the CE store has to be updated
SetPacket	The provider has to interpret the transfer buffer and write the item into the desktop store	Once per out-of-sync object if the item in the desktop store has to be updated
Reset	Destroys the transfer buffer	After GetPacket or SetPacket is called

16.   This leads to the following implementation of the "GetPacket" and
      "SetPacket" methods:

```
int PCDMTracksIDs[]= { 0,2,1 };
STDMETHODIMP CPCDMSyncObjHandler::GetPacket(LPBYTE *lppbPacket,
                                DWORD *pcbPacket, DWORD cbRecommend)
{
      if((lppbPacket == NULL)||(pcbPacket == NULL))
            return E_INVALIDARG;

      *lppbPacket = NULL;
      *pcbPacket  = NULL;
      CReplItem *pItem =
            reinterpret_cast<CReplItem*>(m_pReadSetup->hItem);
      if(pItem == NULL)
            return RERR_BAD_OBJECT;

OutputDebugString(TEXT("In GetPacket...\n\r"));
      _RecordsetPtr        tRs;
      _ConnectionPtr       tConn;
      _variant_t           vaEmpty;
      _bstr_t              bsEmpty = L"";
      HRESULT              hr;
      TCHAR                id[20];
      int                  i,max;
      WCHAR                tStr[255];
      VARIANT              value,tValue;
      VariantInit(&value); VariantInit(&tValue);
      _bstr_t
strBuffer(L"PCDMSync://PCDM/PCDMAccessDB?Command=1&Table=PCDMCDs");

      hr=tConn.CreateInstance( __uuidof( Connection ) );
      if (FAILED(hr)) return RERR_BAD_OBJECT;
      tConn->ConnectionString =
L"Provider=MSDASQL.1;Persist Security Info=False;Data
Source=DeluxeCD";
      hr=tConn->Open( bsEmpty, bsEmpty, bsEmpty, -1 );
      if (FAILED(hr)) return RERR_BAD_OBJECT;

      hr=tRs.CreateInstance( __uuidof( Recordset ) );
      if (FAILED(hr))        return RERR_BAD_OBJECT;
```

```
        _bstr_t  bsSel(L"SELECT * FROM Tracks where TitleID=");

        FILETIME& ftOld=pItem->GetModified();
        wsprintf(id,TEXT("%d"),ftOld.dwHighDateTime);
        bsSel+=id;
        tRs->PutRefActiveConnection( tConn );

        strBuffer+=pItem->GetId();
        tRs->Open(bsSel,vtMissing,adOpenKeyset,adLockBatchOptimistic,-
        1);
        while (!tRs->EOF)
        {
                strBuffer+=
L"PCDMSync://PCDM/PCDMAccessDB?Command=1&Table=PCDMTracks&";
                max=tRs->Fields->GetCount();
                for (i=0;i<max;i++)
                {
                        VariantClear(&value); VariantClear(&tValue);
                        VariantCopy(&value,
                                        &tRs->Fields->Item[(long)i]->Value);
                        VariantChangeType(&tValue,&value,0,VT_BSTR);
                        if (lstrlenW(tValue.bstrVal)!=0)
                                wsprintfW(tStr,L"Fld%d=%s",PCDMTracksIDs[i],
                                        tValue.bstrVal);
                        else
                            wsprintfW(tStr,L"Fld%d=n.a.",PCDMTracksIDs[i]);
                        strBuffer+=tStr;
                        if (i<2)
                                strBuffer+=L"&";
                        else
                                strBuffer+=L";";
                }
                tRs->MoveNext();
        }
        hr=RWRN_LAST_PACKET;

OutputDebugString(strBuffer);
OutputDebugString(TEXT("\n\r"));
        memset(m_pReadPacket,0,MAXDATASIZE);
        memcpy(m_pReadPacket,(WCHAR *)strBuffer,
                        (strBuffer.length()+1)*sizeof(WCHAR));
```

```
      *lppbPacket = m_pReadPacket;
      *pcbPacket  = (strBuffer.length()+1)*sizeof(WCHAR);
      tRs->Close();
OutputDebugString(TEXT("GP:Out..\n\r"));
    return hr;
}

STDMETHODIMP CPCDMSyncObjHandler::SetPacket(LPBYTE lpbPacket, DWORD
cbPacket)
{
      if(lpbPacket == NULL)
            return E_INVALIDARG;

      CReplItem *pItem = NULL;
      if(!(m_pWriteSetup->dwFlags & RSF_NEW_OBJECT))
      {
          pItem = reinterpret_cast<CReplItem*>(m_pWriteSetup->hItem);
      }
        else
      {
          pItem = new CReplItem(m_pFolder->GetSyncFileName());
          m_pWriteSetup->hItem = reinterpret_cast<HREPLITEM>
          (pItem);
      }
OutputDebugString(TEXT("In SetPacket...\n\r"));
      _ConnectionPtr     tConn;
      _variant_t         vaEmpty;
      _bstr_t            bsEmpty = L"";
      PSYNCBUFFERUP      pSync=(PSYNCBUFFERUP)lpbPacket;
      _bstr_t            bsSel((WCHAR *)pSync->str);

      HRESULT hr=tConn.CreateInstance( __uuidof( Connection ) );
      if (FAILED(hr)) return S_OK;
      tConn->ConnectionString =
L"Provider=MSDASQL.1;Persist Security Info=False;Data
Source=DeluxeCD";
      hr=tConn->Open( bsEmpty, bsEmpty, bsEmpty, -1 );
      if (FAILED(hr)) return S_OK;
OutputDebugString(bsSel);
OutputDebugString(TEXT("\n\r"));
```

```
        IPCDMUtilsPtr              comUtils;
        hr=comUtils.CreateInstance(__uuidof( PCDMUtils ) );
        if (FAILED(hr))
        {
OutputDebugString(TEXT("SP: No access to PCDMUtils Class\n\r"));
            return S_OK;
        }
        int idx=0;
        BSTR strURL;
        while (comUtils->GetURL(idx,bsSel,&strURL)==S_OK)
        {
            hr=tConn->Execute(strURL,&vaEmpty,0);
            idx++;
        }

        FILETIME oldft;
        oldft.dwHighDateTime=pSync->ID;
        pItem->SetModified(oldft);
            return S_OK;
}
```

The "SetPacket" method uses the "PCDMUtils" class of Appendix B. The "PCDMTracksIDs" array is used to map the fields of the "Tracks" table to the fields in your "PCDMTracks" table on Windows CE.

17.   To enable the class you need to put the following code at the top of the "PCDMSyncObjHand.cpp" file:

```
#include "syncbuffer.h"
#import "<Path2DesktopVersionofPCDMDLL.DLL>\pcdmdll.dll"
        rename_namespace("PCDMdll_space") raw_interfaces_only

using namespace PCDMdll_space;
```

The "SyncBuffer.h" include file contains the structure definition used for the transfer between the CE provider and the desktop provider.

18.   Review the content of "SyncBuffer.h":

```
#define MAXDATASIZE        8000

typedef struct tagSYNCBUFFERUP
{
```

```
        DWORD       ID;                         // TitleID
        WCHAR       str[MAXDATASIZE];           // ExecuteString/URL
} SYNCBUFFERUP, *PSYNCBUFFERUP;
```

You are now ready to compile the desktop side of your provider. Since Visual C++ registers the provider automatically, you can immediately activate the provider in ActiveSync. To do so, select the "Options" button in the toolbar of the ActiveSync dialog box, and you will see your new provider "PCDMSync – PCDM Database", as shown in Figure 9.13.

19. Select the new provider and close the "Options" dialog box.

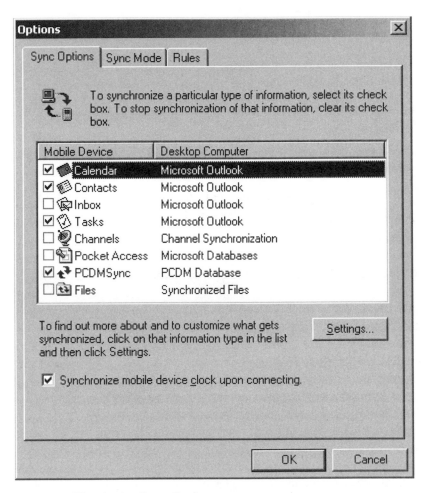

Figure 9.13 The ActiveSync Options page

Before you can actually use the new provider you at least have to compile and install the device part of the provider. You can find the eMbedded Visual Tools project in the "device" directory under your provider folder. To debug the desktop part of the provider, enter the following file as the "Executable for debug session:" entry in the "Debug" settings of your project:

```
\Program Files\Microsoft ActiveSync\WCESMgr.exe
```

For more tips on debugging your ActiveSync provider, refer to Section 9.3.3.

 The final source code of this section can be found on the companion CD under "\Sources\ThreadExample\PCDMSync".

The Windows CE Side of ActiveSync

Before you make any changes to the CE side of the ActiveSync provider, quickly compile the "DevPCDMSync" project and install it on the CE device.

1. Load the "DevPCDMSync" project from the "device" folder under the "PCDMSync" directory and compile it.

The eMbedded Visual C++ compiler will download the final DLL, but does not enter the correct values into the as registry as required for an ActiveSync provider.

2. To get this done, you have to edit "register.bat" in the "device" folder and enter the path of "Cabwiz.exe" where the batch asks you.

"Cabwiz.exe" normally resides in the following directory:

```
\Windows CE Tools\WCE<version>\<platform>\support\appinst\bin
```

Once you have updated the batch file, run it and you will see that the CE device will quickly install the necessary registry values.

You are now ready for a dry run of your ActiveSync provider. Of course, not all entries in the desktop store are able to synchronize, and since the CE part of the provider still does not work, you will never get the PCDM database synchronized. But at least you can debug through the desktop part of the provider. Figure 9.14 shows a simplified flowchart of ActiveSync on the Windows CE side.

In Figure 9.14, you can see that you need to do some different work in your code for the Windows CE side of ActiveSync. Nearly all of your work will take place in the "ObjectNotify" method. It will complete the necessary checking of your database and will fill the "pNotify" structure in case you have new or changed records. Table 9.10 shows the methods that you need to implement.

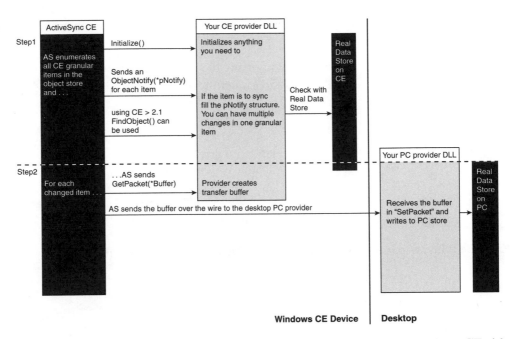

Figure 9.14   A simplified ActiveSync flowchart driven from the Windows CE side

The ActiveSync wizard generated a lot of helper functions, such as "UpdateFileTime" and "IsFileDirty", that you will not use. All these methods are called from within the "ObjectNotify" method.

As you learned in Chapter 8, you create the "PCDMAccessDB" class in your "PCDMDLL.DLL" component so as to keep the application from directly modifying

Table 9.10   CPCDMSyncFolders Methods Called during Synchronization

Method	Purpose	Will Be Called …
Initialize	Initializes your SyncObjHandler class	At the startup of ActiveSync on CE
ObjectNotify	Allows you to check for differences in the store to be synchronized	ActiveSync calls this method once per item in the object store
GetObjTypeIndo	Tells the user interface of ActiveSync about the things to come	At startup of ActiveSync on Windows CE
UnInitialize	Closes whatever you opened during Initialize	At the end of the synchronization process

the database. In your ActiveSync provider for Windows CE, you will again use this class to keep the provider away from your database.

3. As in all Windows CE applications using the "#import" statement you have to put the "COM_ISSUE_ERROR" function into your code:

```
void __stdcall _com_issue_error(HRESULT hr)
{
    // Error handling goes here!
}
```

You will use the "Initialize" method to create the "PCDMAccessDB" class.

4. Add the following lines to the "Initialize" method:

```
BOOL CPCDMSyncFolder::Initialize(IReplObjHandler **ppObjHandler,
                                 UINT uPartnerBit)
{
    if(ppObjHandler == NULL)
        return FALSE;

    *ppObjHandler = new CPCDMSyncObjHandler(this);
    if(*ppObjHandler == NULL)
        return FALSE;

    if(uPartnerBit & 0x01)
        m_uPartner = 0;
    else if(uPartnerBit & 0x02)
        m_uPartner = 1;

    ::CoInitializeEx(NULL,COINIT_MULTITHREADED);
    HRESULT hr=comDB.CreateInstance( __uuidof( PCDMAccessDB ) );
    if (FAILED(hr))
    {
        printf("ERR: No access to PCDMAccessDB HR=<%d>\n\r",hr);
        return TRUE; // Returing False would cancel ActiveSync...
    }
printf("PCDMAccessDB Initialized!\n\r",hr);
    m_bScanned=FALSE;
    m_cntPCDMCDs=ScanDatabase(NULL,SD_JUSTSCAN);
    m_plstCOID=(UINT *)LocalAlloc(LMEM_ZEROINIT,
                                  m_cntPCDMCDs*sizeof(UINT));
```

```
m_plstCOID2=(UINT *)LocalAlloc(LMEM_ZEROINIT,
                               m_cntPCDMCDs*sizeof(UINT));


    return TRUE;
}
```

You will find some "printf" and "wprintf" calls inside the code. These are for debugging purposes and can be removed as soon as you are happy with the provider.

Before you change the "ObjectNotify" method, you must do some work in the "GetObjTypeInfo" method. The Windows CE ActiveSync user interface uses this method to show the user what is going on.

5. Change the code of the "GetObjTypeInfo" method as follows:

```
BOOL CPCDMSyncFolder::GetObjTypeInfo(POBJTYPEINFO pInfo)
{
    ::wcscpy(pInfo->szName, TEXT("Record goes here"));
printf("In GetObjTypeInfo...\n\r");

    m_cntPCDMCDs=ScanDatabase(NULL,SD_GETALLRECORDS);
    pInfo->cObjects = m_cntPCDMCDs;
    pInfo->cbAllObj = m_cntPCDMCDs*256;     // You are guessing here
printf("GetObjTypeInfo set to <%d>,<%d>\n\r",pInfo->cObjects,
       pInfo->cbAllObj);
    pInfo->ftLastModified.dwLowDateTime=4321;  // not important
    pInfo->ftLastModified.dwHighDateTime=1234; // ditto

    return TRUE;
}
```

"ObjTypeInfo" and several other methods use a helper function called "ScanDatabase". This function will do most of the work for you.

6. Here is the code for this function:

```
long CPCDMSyncFolder::ScanDatabase(void *pNotify,int iScanMode)
{
int       cntRec=0;
UINT      OID;
long      CRC=0,FieldCnt=0;
long      DBHandle=0;
POBJNOTIFY            tNO=(POBJNOTIFY)pNotify;
```

```
PFINDOBJINFO          tFO=(PFINDOBJINFO)pNotify;
VARIANT value,tvalue;

     VariantInit(&value);
     VariantInit(&tvalue);

     switch (iScanMode)
     {
          case SD_NOTIFYOBJ:
               tNO->cOidChg=0;
               tNO->cOidDel=0;
               break;
          case SD_FINDOBJECTS:
               tFO->cChg=0;
               tFO->cUnChg=0;
               break;
          default:
               break;
     }

printf("in ScanDatabase...\n\r");
     HRESULT hr=comDB->OpenTable(TEXT("\\My Documents\\PCDM.cdb"),
                    TEXT("PCDMCDs"),_variant_t((LONG)PCDM_PID_ID),
                    &DBHandle);
     if (hr!=S_OK)
     if (hr!=S_OK)
     {      // Create the database if it was not there
          hr=comDB->AddProperty(_variant_t((LONG)PCDM_PID_ID),
          TRUE);
          hr=comDB->AddProperty(_variant_t((LONG)PCDM_PID_AUTHOR),
                         FALSE);
          hr=comDB->AddProperty(_variant_t((LONG)PCDM_PID_TITLE),
                         FALSE);
          hr=comDB->AddProperty(_variant_t((LONG)PCDM_PID_LABEL),
                         FALSE);
          hr=comDB->AddProperty(_variant_t((LONG)PCDM_PID_RELEASE),
                         FALSE);
          hr=comDB->AddProperty(_variant_t((LONG)PCDM_PID_COPY-
          RIGHT),
                         FALSE);
          hr=comDB->AddProperty(_variant_t((LONG)PCDM_PID_CRC),
```

```
                                          FALSE);
               hr=comDB->CreateTable(TEXT("\\My Documents\\PCDM.cdb"),
                                      TEXT("PCDMCDs"));
               hr=comDB->AddProperty(_variant_t((LONG)PCDM_PID_TRACKS_
               ID),
                                      TRUE);
               hr=comDB->AddProperty(_variant_t((LONG)
                                      PCDM_PID_TRACKS_TITLE),FALSE);
               hr=comDB->AddProperty(_variant_t((LONG)
                                      PCDM_PID_TRACKS_TRACKNO),FALSE);
               hr=comDB->CreateTable(TEXT("\\My Documents\\PCDM.cdb"),
                                      TEXT("PCDMTracks"));
               hr=comDB->OpenTable(TEXT("\\My Documents\\PCDM.cdb"),
        TEXT("PCDMCDs"),_variant_t((LONG)PCDM_PID_ID),&DBHandle);
        }
        while (hr==S_OK)
        {
               hr=comDB->ReadRecord(DBHandle,&FieldCnt);
               if (hr==S_OK && iScanMode!=SD_GETALLRECORDS)
               {
                      VariantClear(&value); VariantClear(&tvalue);
                      hr=comDB->GetValue(_variant_t((LONG)(PCDM_PID_ID)),
                                                   &value);
                      if (hr==S_OK)
                      {
                             hr=VariantChangeType(&tvalue,&value,0,VT_I4);
                             OID=tvalue.lVal;
                             VariantClear(&value); VariantClear(&tvalue);
                             hr=comDB->GetValue(_variant_t((LONG)
                                          (PCDM_PID_CRC)),&value);
                             if (hr==S_OK)
                             {
                                    hr=VariantChangeType(&tvalue,
                                                 &value,0,VT_I4);
                                    if (hr!=S_OK)
                                          CRC=0;
                                    else
                                          CRC=tvalue.lVal;
printf("SD: CRC=<%d>, OID=<%d>; Record#:<%d>\n\r",CRC,OID,cntRec);
                                    switch (iScanMode)
                                    {
```

```
                                case SD_NOTIFYOBJ:
                                    switch (CRC)
                                    {
                                        case 0:
                                m_plstCOID[tNO->cOidChg]=OID;
                                            tNO->cOidChg++;
                                            cntRec++;
                                        break;
                                        case -1:
                                m_plstCOID2[tNO->cOidDel]=OID;
                                            tNO->cOidDel++;
                                            cntRec++;
                                        break;
                                        default:
                                            break;
                                    }
                                break;
                                case SD_FINDOBJECTS:
                                    if (CRC==0)
                                    {
                                m_plstCOID2[tFO->cChg]=OID;
                                        tFO->cChg++;
                                        cntRec++;
                                    }
                                    else
                                        tFO->cUnChg++;
                                break;
                                default:
                                    if (CRC==0)
                                        cntRec++;
                                break;
                            }
                        }
                    }
                }
            if (iScanMode==SD_GETALLRECORDS)
                cntRec++;
            hr=comDB->MoveNext(DBHandle);
    }
    comDB->CloseTable(DBHandle);
    printf("SD: Record <%d> read.\n\r",cntRec);
```

```
        switch (iScanMode)
        {
                case SD_FINDOBJECTS:
                        memcpy(&m_plstCOID[tFO->cUnChg],m_plstCOID2,
                                tFO->cChg*sizeof(UINT));
                        tFO->poid=m_plstCOID;
                        break;
                case SD_NOTIFYOBJ:
                        memcpy(&m_plstCOID[tNO->cOidChg],m_plstCOID2,
                                tNO->cOidDel*sizeof(UINT));
                        tNO->poid=m_plstCOID;
                        break;
                default:
                        break;
        }


        return cntRec;
}
```

If the "ScanDatabase" method is called with "iScanMode" equal to "SD_
GETALLRECORDS", you just return the amount of records in your CE store. In case
of "SD_NOTIFYOBJ", you will treat the "pNotify" pointer as a pointer to an
"OBJNOTIFY" structure and fill its members correspondingly. The "iScanmode" of
"SD_FINDOBJECTS" is not yet used by your code.

7.   Add the prototype of this method to the "CPCDMSyncFolder" class:

```
BOOL ScanDatabase(void *pNotify,int iScanMode);
```

8.   Change the "ObjectNotify" method to the following code:

```
BOOL CPCDMSyncFolder::ObjectNotify(POBJNOTIFY pNotify)
{
        if(pNotify->cbStruct < sizeof(OBJNOTIFY))
            return FALSE;
        if(::lstrcmpi(GetName(), pNotify->szObjType))
            return FALSE;
        if(pNotify->uFlags & ONF_CLEAR_CHANGE)
            return !UpdateFileTime();

if (m_bScanned==TRUE)
        return FALSE;
printf("In ObjectNotify...\n\r");
```

```
        m_bScanned=TRUE;
        ScanDatabase(pNotify,SD_NOTIFYOBJ);
printf("ON: ChangedObjs=<%d> Delete=<%d>\n\r",
        pNotify->cOidChg,pNotify->cOidDel);
        if (pNotify->cOidChg>0)
            return TRUE;
        return FALSE;
}
```

In Windows CE 2.1, Microsoft introduced a new method for the Windows CE part of ActiveSync called "FindObject". If ActiveSync finds this method, it does not enumerate all objects in the object store, but calls "FindObjects" just once. Unfortunately, the "FindObject" method cannot be used in your example because it requires a more complex management of what is changed in the CE store. Therefore you will not use this method.

If you decide to implement it, you need to make some additional changes to the code. To make sure that ActiveSync calls the function, you have to declare it in your "DevPCDMSync.def" export table.

9. Load the "DevPCDMSync.def" file and add the following line:

```
; DevPCDMSync.def - Declares the module parameters for the DLL.

LIBRARY DEVPCDMSYNC.DLL

EXPORTS
        InitObjType
        ObjectNotify
        GetObjTypeInfo
        ReportStatus
        FindObjects
```

The "FindObjects" method has to be included as an "EXTERN_C" function in order to work in ActiveSync.

10. Add the following function to the end of the "DevPCDMSync.cpp" file:

```
EXTERN_C BOOL FindObjects(PFINDOBJINFO pFindObjInfo)
{
        return _Store.FindObjects(pFindObjInfo);
}
```

As you can see, you are following exactly the way the ActiveSync wizard modeled your code. The next addition you have to make to your code is to add the "FindObjects" method to the "CPCDMSyncStore" class.

11.   Add the "FindObjects" method to the "CPCDMSyncStore" class while using the same parameter as for the "EXTERN_C" definition:

```
BOOL FindObjects(PFINDOBJINFO pFindObjInfo);
```

12.   The code for its implementation looks similar to the code found in the "CPCDMNotifyObject" method:

```
BOOL CPCDMSyncStore::FindObjects(PFINDOBJINFO pFindObjInfo)
{
    if(pFindObjInfo == NULL)
        return FALSE;
    CBaseFolder *pFolder = GetFolderByName(pFindObjInfo->
    szObjType);
    if(pFolder)
        return pFolder->FindObjects(pFindObjInfo);
    else
        return FALSE;
}
```

13.   Hold on—just two more changes!

14.   Following the model of the wizard, you have to add the "FindObjects" definition to the list of virtual methods in the "CbaseFolder" class:

```
virtual BOOL FindObjects(PFINDOBJINFO pFindObjInfo) = 0;
```

Now for the final change and the actual code that does all the work in "FindObjects".

15.   Add the method "FindObjects" to the "CPCDMSyncFolder" class, using again the "PFINDOBJINFO" parameter:

```
BOOL CPCDMSyncFolder::FindObjects(PFINDOBJINFO pFindObjInfo)
```

 But remember: Once you put the "FindObjects" line in the ".DEF" file, your code in the "ObjectNotify" method will no longer be called on Windows CE devices running ActiveSync 2.1 or later.

Before you can test your new provider, you need to implement the "GetPacket" and "SetPacket" methods of the "CPCDMSyncObjHandler" class. Their implementation is very similar to the comparable implementation on the desktop. In Figures 9.12 and 9.14, you can see that the desktop "GetPacket" method is mapped to the CE "SetPacket" method and vice versa. You just have to "unpack" the transport buffer and write the records into your CE store using "SetPacket". In the "GetPacket" method, you read from your CE store using the "CPCDMAccessDB" class and create ADO strings that your desktop part will execute.

16. Here is the code for the "SetPacket" and "GetPacket" methods:

```
STDMETHODIMP CPCDMSyncObjHandler::GetPacket(LPBYTE *lppbPacket,
                              DWORD *pcbPacket, DWORD cbRecommend)
{
     if((lppbPacket == NULL)||(pcbPacket == NULL))
          return E_INVALIDARG;

     *lppbPacket = NULL;
     *pcbPacket  = NULL;

     CEOIDINFO oidInfo;
          ::memset(&oidInfo, NULL, sizeof(oidInfo));

printf("GetPacket: OID=<%d>\n\r",m_pReadSetup->oid);
     TCHAR tStr[1024];
     VARIANT value,tvalue;
     int cntRec=0,i;
     long CRC=0,FieldCnt=0,lCnt=0;
     long DBHandle=0;
     PSYNCBUFFERUP pSync=(PSYNCBUFFERUP)m_pReadPacket;

          ::memset(m_pReadPacket,0,MAXDATASIZE);
          ::memset(tStr,0,1024*sizeof(TCHAR));
          VariantInit(&value); VariantInit(&tvalue);
          pSync->ID=m_pReadSetup->oid;

          wsprintf(tStr,L"DELETE FROM Titles WHERE TitleID=%d;",
                         m_pReadSetup->oid);
          wcscat(pSync->str,tStr);
          wsprintf(tStr,L"INSERT INTO Titles (TitleID, Artist,
          Title, Label, ReleaseDate, Copyright) VALUES
          (%d,",m_pReadSetup->oid);
```

```
wcscat(pSync->str,tStr);
HRESULT hr=m_pFolder->comDB->OpenTable(
      TEXT("\\My Documents\\PCDM.cdb"),TEXT("PCDMCDs"),
      _variant_t((LONG)PCDM_PID_ID),&DBHandle);
if (hr!=S_OK)
      return RERR_BAD_OBJECT;
hr=m_pFolder->comDB->MoveFirst(DBHandle);
hr=m_pFolder->comDB->FindRecord(DBHandle,
                  _variant_t((LONG)PCDM_PID_ID),
                  _variant_t((long)
                  (m_pReadSetup->oid)));
if (hr!=S_OK)
{
      m_pFolder->comDB->CloseTable(DBHandle);
      *lppbPacket = (LPBYTE)pSync;
      *pcbPacket  = 0;
      return RERR_USER_SKIP; //RERR_BAD_OBJECT;
}
hr=m_pFolder->comDB->ReadRecord(DBHandle,&FieldCnt);
if (hr==S_OK)
{
      for (i=PCDM_PID_AUTHOR;i<PCDM_PID_CRC;i++)
      {
            VariantClear(&value);
            hr=m_pFolder->comDB->GetValue(
                  _variant_t((LONG)(i)),&value);
            if (hr==S_OK)
            {
                  if (i!=PCDM_PID_COPYRIGHT)
                  wsprintf(tStr,L"'%s',",value.bstrVal);
                  else
                  wsprintf(tStr,L"'%s');",value.bstrVal);
                  wcscat(pSync->str+lCnt,tStr);
            }
      }
}
hr=m_pFolder->comDB->SetValue(
            _variant_t((LONG)(PCDM_PID_CRC)),
            _variant_t(TEXT("1")));
hr=m_pFolder->comDB->WriteRecord(DBHandle);
m_pFolder->comDB->CloseTable(DBHandle);
```

```
            wsprintf(tStr,L"DELETE FROM Tracks WHERE TitleID=%d; ",
                        m_pReadSetup->oid);
            wcscat(pSync->str,tStr);
wprintf(TEXT("GP1: Value=<%s>; \n\r"),pSync->str);

            hr=m_pFolder->comDB->OpenTable(
            TEXT("\\My Documents\\PCDM.cdb"),TEXT("PCDMTracks"),
            _variant_t((LONG)PCDM_PID_TRACKS_ID),&DBHandle);
            while (hr==S_OK)
            {
                hr=m_pFolder->comDB->ReadRecord(DBHandle,
                &FieldCnt);
                if (hr==S_OK)
                {
                    for (i=0;i<FieldCnt;i++)
                    {
                        VariantClear(&value);
                        VariantClear(&tvalue);
                        hr=m_pFolder->comDB->GetValue(
                            _variant_t((LONG)(i)),&value);
                        if (i==PCDM_PID_TRACKS_ID &&
                                VariantChangeType(&tvalue,
                                &value,0,VT_I4)==S_OK)
                        {
                            if (tvalue.lVal!=m_pReadSetup->oid)
                                break;
                            wcscat(pSync->str,
L"INSERT INTO PCDMTracks (TitleID, TrackName,TrackID) VALUES (");
                        }
                        VariantChangeType(&value,
                                        &value,0,VT_BSTR);
                        if (i!=PCDM_PID_TRACKS_TRACKNO)
                            wsprintf(tStr,L"'%s',",
                                            value.bstrVal);
                        else
                            wsprintf(tStr,L"'%s');",
                                            value.bstrVal);
                        wcscat(pSync->str+lCnt,tStr);
                    }
                }
                hr=m_pFolder->comDB->MoveNext(DBHandle);
```

```
                    }
                    m_pFolder->comDB->CloseTable(DBHandle);
                    hr=RWRN_LAST_PACKET;
wprintf(TEXT("GP2: Value=<%s>; \n\r"),pSync->str);
                    *lppbPacket = (LPBYTE)pSync;
                    *pcbPacket  = ((lstrlen(pSync->str)+1)*
                              sizeof(WCHAR))+sizeof(DWORD);
        return RWRN_LAST_PACKET;
}


STDMETHODIMP CPCDMSyncObjHandler::SetPacket(LPBYTE lpbPacket,
                                              DWORD cbPacket)
{
        if(lpbPacket == NULL)
                return E_INVALIDARG;


IPCDMUtilsPtr          comUtils;
wprintf(L"SetPacket:<%d>:<%s>\n\r",cbPacket,(WCHAR *)lpbPacket);

        HRESULT hr=comUtils.CreateInstance(__uuidof( PCDMUtils ) );
        if (FAILED(hr))
                return hr;
        hr=comUtils->AnalyzeURL((WCHAR *)lpbPacket);
wprintf(L"SetPacketOut\n\r");
        return S_OK;
}
```

   17.   You also need to include the "SyncBuffer.h" file that you created for the
         desktop at the top of "DevPCDMSyncobjhand.cpp":

```
#include "..\syncbuffer.h"
```

Now compile the new provider and have it copied to the device. Disconnect and
reconnect your device, and you should find that the provider works. If your Windows
CE database was empty, the ActiveSync provider will have copied the database from
the PC to the Windows CE device.

A Final Word about the Provider

The provider does not handle each and every scenario possible with ActiveSync. You
are very likely to get the two stores out of sync if you try to change either of them manually. Also the provider is not very fast since you did nothing to optimize it for speed.

All the round trips to your PCDMAccessDB, ADOCE/ADO, and the "PCDMUtils" class cost a lot of time that could be optimized. I do not recommend synchronizing a DeluxeDB database that has more than 30 CDs inside. The provider on CE does not yet deal with deleted items. Since your application does not delete anything that the desktop DeluxeCD player does not delete as well, you are in good shape.

One more thing: You have to delete the code inside the PCDM application that generates the sample entries. Otherwise you will have new records on the desktop and new records on the CE Device. This would normally call for the item resolver in ActiveSync that you did not implement. In case your CE store already has the entries inside, you can delete "PCDM.CDB" on your Windows CE device. This will trigger synchronization during the next start of ActiveSync.

9.3.3 Some Debugging Tips

Debugging the ActiveSync provider is extremely difficult because you can only debug the desktop side. As mentioned before, to debug the desktop side you need to put the "WCESMgr.exe" into your project's "Executable for debug session" setting. Then you must make sure that this task is not running before you launch it. If it was running before—for example, if your device is connected—the debugger will start, but will not hit any breakpoints.

Once the ActiveSync window is open, deselect all other providers except for the one you want to debug. Otherwise, you will have to go through their synchronization steps every time. If you want to download a new version of your ActiveSync provider for CE, you must first deselect it in the "Options" dialog box of the desktop side. This will unload your CE DLL, and you can download a new version. To test the new version, just select it in the "Options" dialog box again, and your DLL will immediately be loaded. With this procedure you can stay connected to your device most of the time.

The only time that you need to disconnect is when you change desktop providers. For that purpose, follow these steps in the order listed:

- Deselect your provider in the "Options" dialog box of ActiveSync.
- Disconnect your device.
- Compile your new desktop provider.
- Run it in debug mode.
- Reconnect your device.

The procedure to download and "debug" a new CE provider is as follows:

- On the desktop, deselect your provider in the "Options" dialog box of ActiveSync.
- Compile and download your CE provider while staying connected.
- Select your provider again in the "Options" dialog box.

As mentioned before, you cannot debug the CE side of your provider. The best way of testing and getting some output is to put "printf" and "wprintf" functions inside your code in order to secure at least some explanatory information.

 The final source code of this section can be found on the companion CD under "\Sources\ThreadExample\PCDMSync\Device".

9.3.4 Summary

- Writing an ActiveSync provider is not an easy task.
- Before you start, think about how to enumerate the items in your CE store.
- You also need a way of storing the "last-synchronized" data on the CE device. Luckily the desktop version of ActiveSync does this for you.
- Debugging, though not easy, is doable.
- If you want to read more about ActiveSync development, you can find the documentation in

```
Microsoft eMbedded Visual C++ Version 3.0
Platform Builder 2.12 Exported SDK
          Connection Services
               Synchronizing Data
                    Creating an ActiveSync provider
```

This information is located in the MSDN or eMbedded Visual Tools 3.0 documentation.

9.4 Distributed COM

DCOM and its third-party pendant deviceCOM have already been discussed in Sections 6.6 and 6.7, respectively. Here you will take an abstract look at the differences between DCOM and deviceCOM in order to help you determine which technology to use for what kind of project. Table 9.11 shows the basic differences between DCOM for Windows CE by Microsoft and deviceCOM for Windows CE by Intrinsyc.

One of the biggest issues with DCOM for CE is its footprint. Its large size has probably convinced a number of independent hardware vendors (IHVs) to choose deviceCOM instead, in order to save valuable ROM space. This being the case, your application should support deviceCOM and provide deviceCOM proxy and stub DLLs. Many industrial Windows CE devices will have deviceCOM as their

Table 9.11   Comparison of DCOM and deviceCOM

Feature	DCOM	deviceCOM
Footprint	Ca. 1MB	Ca. 350KB
Transport layer	DCE RPC via TCP/IP	TCP, UDP, IPC; More in the works at Intrinsyc.
Connects natively to DCOM on desktops (no special runtime marshaller required)	Yes	No, requires deviceCOM for NT/Win9x to be installed on the target desktop.
Timeouts (COM will not show any error until the timeout is over. To the user, the application will appear to be "hanging.")	Fixed, six minutes (three pings every three minutes)	Can be set with a registry entry. With APIs can even be set per process.
Supports notification for "dead" servers in the "one client—multiple servers" scenario	No, client has to "guess" what server is gone.	Yes, client can get a notification from deviceCOM via an API as to which server is dead.
Supports notification for "dead" clients in the "multiple clients—one server" scenario	No, server has no way of cleaning up "dead" clients. An application-specific callback ping mechanism has to be realized by the server and client application.	Yes, server can request a notification from deviceCOM with the client handle if the client is dead.
Support for Windows CE 2.x	No	Yes
Support for Windows CE 3.0	Yes	Yes
Add-on for existing devices	No, has to be modeled into the device ROM image	Yes
Support for UPnP (Universal Plug-and-Play)	No	Yes, deviceCOM supports the "discovery mechanism" to locate servers automatically on the network and then to CoCreateInstanceFromURI() to those servers.
Security	Windows NT: NT-based; Windows CE: NT/98 hybrid-only verification against domain possible	DeviceCOM 2.x: No security; DeviceCOM 3.0: certificate-based

Feature	DCOM	deviceCOM
Automation support (IDISPATCH, BSTR marshaller)	No	Yes
Deployment tools	No	DeviceRMS can deploy, install, and configure deviceCOM-enabled COM components.
Remote configuration	No (DCOMCNFG runs on Windows CE device.)	Yes
Cross-platform development framework	ATL requires GDI, so headless devices cannot use DCOM and ATL components.	DeviceCOM ships with its own framework that is not ATL-compatible but offers similar functionality. This framework does not depend on GDI and therefore can run on headless devices.
Included in Windows CE Platform Builder	CE2.x: no; CE3.x: yes (free)	No, has to be licensed from Intrinsyc either by the ISV (independent software vendor) or IHV (independent hardware vendor).
MIDL interface compiler	Standard Microsoft	Intrinsyc version of MIDL

preinstalled primary COM transport mechanism, to offer the greatest stability for enterprise connectivity. DCOM for CE, on the other hand, requires no special knowledge of proprietary IDL compilers, nor does it require any special knowledge about its installation.

An IHV will go through the following questions, and if it answers most of them "yes," it will probably decide to have deviceCOM on its device rather than DCOM:

- Is my application running on a headless device with only the Windows CE kernel installed?
- Is the size of the footprint an issue for me; is my ROM size limited?
- Do I need fast and reliable connections?
- Do I still need to use Windows CE 2.x for some reason?
- Is native connectivity to desktop DCOM not an issue for me?
- Do I require deployment and remote management tools?

To summarize, I would in any case recommend that you build the deviceCOM proxy and stubs for your application. In this way, you will make sure that you will be able to run using either distributed COM solution.

9.5 Winsock

System DLL:	WINSOCK.dll
Include file:	winsock.h
Library:	winsock.lib
Help file:	wcesdkr.chm
Available since:	Windows CE 1.0
API prefix/suffix:	WSA . . .
InitCommonControlEx flag:	—
MFC class:	CSocket, CAsyncSocket, CCeSocket

Windows Sockets, or Winsock, is the most common way of accessing remote data. It requires a TCP/IP connection, so it will not work with only a native ActiveSync 3.x connection. Since Winsock is one of the basic layers of TCP/IP, there is no standard for packets flying back and forth between devices. On the other hand, it offers considerable flexibility, and many higher-level standards use Winsock as their transport layer. Winsock has been supported ever since Windows CE 1.0 and therefore offers a way to communicate even to very old devices.

Because Winsock development for Windows CE is nearly identical to that on the desktop, I want to point out the differences and give some hints on how to compensate for any shortcomings.

WSAAsyncSelect Is Missing

If you have used Winsock on the desktop before, you probably used the "WSAAsyncSelect" function to notify your Windows Message Handler of any changes in the socket. Unfortunately, this function is missing in the Windows CE version of Winsock.

To work around the lack of this function, you need to create a thread that waits on the socket using "recvfrom". When a valid package arrives at the socket, you send an appropriate message to your Windows Message Handler. MFC includes a class called "CCeSocket" that can deal with asynchronous sockets natively.

9.5.1 A Tiny Winsock Example

The example below is an application that runs on the desktop and on the Windows CE device, using the same code. It simply sends a packet to its counterpart application and pops up a message box. You will also implement a series of helper functions that might be useful to you later.

InitServer(HWND)

This function initializes Winsock, creates a socket for your communication, and creates the receiving thread for incoming packets. It will call two helpers called "CreateSocket" and "ResetSocket" that will do the socket plumbing for you.

The HWND that gets passed to "InitServer" will be passed to a thread that parses any incoming Winsock packets. In case of a valid packet, the thread sends the packet data to your main window message loop.

SceThread(LPVOID)

This function is your receiving thread. As mentioned before, Windows CE does not support "WSAAsyncSelect". This thread recreates the behavior of that missing function.

SendWSockPacket(SOCKET,<length>,BYTE*,<PacketCode>,IP-Address)

This function will send a buffer to the IP address given as the last parameter. You can create your own telegram structure for the packet. The "PacketCode" parameter will tell the receiver what type of telegram it will get. For your example, you just pass the Windows Message you want to send to the Windows Message Loop at the receiver.

SendPacket(,String>,<code>,<IPAddress>)

This function abstracts the "SendWSockPacket" function to a string. You will put IrDA support in this call in Section 9.6.

CloseServer()

This function cleans up Winsock and ends the thread.
Now let's get started:

1. Create a new "Hello World" application for Windows CE and name it "SendIt".

2. Open the resource editor for the new application and create a new menu entry in "IDM_MENU" named "Send Packet . . .".

3. Give it the ID "ID_SENDPACKET".

Next, you need a couple of defines, typedefs, and other global variables.

4. Add the following definitions to the head of "SendIt.CPP":

```
#include <winsock.h>
#define DESIRED_WINSOCK_VERSION    0x0101  // you like winsock ver
                                           1.1...
#define MINIMUM_WINSOCK_VERSION    0x0001  // ...but you'll take ver
                                           1.0
#define MAX_BUF_LEN                1000    // max telegram size
#define PACKET_TYPE_FILE           0x46494c45L    // "FILE"
#define PACKET_TYPE_NACK           0x4e41434bL    // "NACK"
#define MPPort                     4321    // Using Port 4321
#define WM_SOCKET_SELECT           (WM_USER + 100)      // WSOCK
Packet
                                                        // received
typedef INT            SOCKERR;            // A socket error code.
typedef struct _PACKET_FILE     // Your Telegram Structure
{
    DWORD       type;                      // Must be PACKET_TYPE_FILE.
    DWORD       cbFile;                    // Use data size
    DWORD       PakSize;                   // Packet size
    DWORD       Code;                      // Windows Message for
                                           receiver
    CHAR        szFile[MAX_BUF_LEN];       // The use data
} PACKET_FILE, FAR * LPPACKET_FILE;

SOCKET           sCommand = INVALID_SOCKET; // Command socket.
CRITICAL_SECTION m_csec;                     // Critical Section handle
BOOL             MPServerRunning=FALSE      // is TRUE if thread runs
```

5. Add two helper functions to your "InitServer" function:

```
SOCKERR ResetSocket( SOCKET sock )
{
    LINGER linger;
    if( sock == INVALID_SOCKET )
        return 0;
    linger.l_onoff  = TRUE;
```

```
        linger.l_linger = 0;
        setsockopt( sock,
                    SOL_SOCKET,
                    SO_LINGER,
                    (CHAR FAR *)&linger,
                    sizeof(linger) );
        return closesocket( sock );
    }   // ResetSocket

SOCKERR CreateSocket( SOCKET FAR * psock,
                      INT           type,
                      ULONG         address,
                      WORD          port )
{
    SOCKET  sNew;
    SOCKERR serr;
    sNew = socket( PF_INET, type, 0 );
    serr = ( sNew == INVALID_SOCKET ) ? WSAGetLastError() : 0;
    if( serr == 0 )
    {
        SOCKADDR_IN sockAddr;
        sockAddr.sin_family    = AF_INET;
        sockAddr.sin_addr.s_addr = address;
        sockAddr.sin_port      = port;
        if( bind( sNew, (SOCKADDR FAR *)&sockAddr,
                  sizeof(sockAddr) ) != 0 )
        {
            serr = WSAGetLastError();
        }
    }
    if( serr != 0 )
    {
        ResetSocket( sNew );
        sNew = INVALID_SOCKET;
    }
    *psock = sNew;
    return serr;
}   // CreateSocket
```

   "ResetSocket" will close a socket and empty its buffer if it is not already empty. It will also terminate your thread because a "recvfrom" on a close port will fail and set "endless" to FALSE. "CreateSocket" creates the socket and prepares Winsock to receive something at the given port.

6. Add the code for the thread:

```
DWORD WINAPI    SCeThread( LPVOID pParam )
{
INT             cbRead;               // Bytes read
PACKET_FILE     filePacket;           // buffer for a datagramm
SOCKADDR_IN     addrClient;           // The address of the sender
INT             cbAddrClient;         // Size of the addrClient buffer
BYTE            *tBuffer=NULL;        // a temporary buffer for the use
// data
int             endless;              // a loop flag

    cbAddrClient = sizeof(addrClient);
    endless=TRUE;
    while (endless==TRUE)
    {
        cbRead = recvfrom(sCommand,
                (CHAR FAR *)&filePacket,sizeof(filePacket),
                0,(SOCKADDR FAR *)&addrClient,&cbAddrClient );
        // This command blocks until something comes into the
        // WinSock Buffer
        if (cbRead<1)       // Socket was reset cvRead is zero
        {                           // you use this to end the thread
            endless=FALSE;
            if (cbRead==SOCKET_ERROR)
            {
                cbRead=WSAGetLastError();
                if (cbRead==WSAEWOULDBLOCK)
                {
                    endless=TRUE;
                    continue;
                }
            }
        }
        EnterCriticalSection(&m_csec);
        // You do not want other thread interrupting you while
        // reading the WINSOCK buffer
        switch (filePacket.type)
        {
```

```
              case PACKET_TYPE_FILE:  // A well know telegram
              arrived
                if (filePacket.cbFile>0)
                {
                      tBuffer = (BYTE *)LocalAlloc(LMEM_ZEROINIT,
                                             filePacket.cbFile);
                      memcpy(tBuffer,filePacket.szFile,
                                     filePacket.cbFile);
                }
                PostMessage((HWND)pParam, filePacket.Code,
                           (WPARAM)tBuffer,
                           (LPARAM)addrClient.sin_addr.s_addr);
              break;
            case PACKET_TYPE_NACK:
              endless=FALSE;
              break;
            default:
              // Ignore Packet
              break;
        }
        LeaveCriticalSection(&m_csec);
    }
    return TRUE;
}
```

7. Add the InitServer function:

```
BOOL InitServer(HWND hwnd)
{
WSADATA          wsadata;
SOCKERR          serr;
DWORD ThreadId = 0L;
HANDLE           m_pCeThread;                    // thread handle

    if (MPServerRunning)       return TRUE;

    serr = WSAStartup( DESIRED_WINSOCK_VERSION, &wsadata );
    if( serr != 0 )   return FALSE;       // More error handling
                                          here
    if( wsadata.wVersion < MINIMUM_WINSOCK_VERSION ) return FALSE;
    serr = CreateSocket( &sCommand, SOCK_DGRAM,
                  htonl( INADDR_ANY ), htons(MPPort));
```

```
            if( serr != 0 )  return FALSE;           // More error handling
                                                      here

            m_pCeThread = CreateThread( NULL, 0, SCeThread,
                                        hwnd,0L,&ThreadId);
                                        //Pass hWnd to Thread
        CloseHandle(m_pCeThread);
        InitializeCriticalSection(&m_csec);
        MPServerRunning=TRUE;

            return TRUE;
}
```

8. The cleanup code for the thread and Winsock looks like this:

```
BOOL CloseServer(void)
{
        if (MPServerRunning)
        {
                ResetSocket(sCommand);
                WSACleanup();
                MPServerRunning=FALSE;
        }
        return TRUE;
}
```

9. Add the "SendWSockPacket" and "SendPacket" functions:

```
SOCKERR SendWSockPacket( SOCKET sock, int  len, BYTE *Buffer,
                         DWORD code, TCHAR *tIP)
{
PACKET_FILE filePacket;
INT         cbWritten;
SOCKADDR_IN saUdpServ;
char        mpip[20]; // yep, the IP Address has to be ANSI !!
in  i;

        if (tIP==NULL) return 0;
        for (i=0;i<(int)lstrlen(tIP);i++) mpip[i]=(char)tIP[i];
        mpip[i]=0;       // Converting the tIP Parameter to ANSI
        saUdpServ.sin_family = AF_INET;      // This is Important !!
                    // It tells you are using the WINSOCK TCP/IP Layer
saUdpServ.sin_addr.s_addr = inet_addr(mpip);
```

```
        saUdpServ.sin_port = htons(MPPort);        // supplying the
        Port Number

        // Preparing your telegram structure
        memset(filePacket.szFile,0,sizeof(filePacket.szFile));
        filePacket.type   = PACKET_TYPE_FILE;        // Packet Type
        filePacket.cbFile = len;
        filePacket.PakSize= len+(4*sizeof(DWORD));
        filePacket.Code       = code;
        memcpy( filePacket.szFile, Buffer, len);

        cbWritten = sendto( sock,
                        (CHAR FAR *)&filePacket,
                        filePacket.PakSize,  0,
                        (SOCKADDR *) &saUdpServ,
                        sizeof ( SOCKADDR_IN ));
        return ( cbWritten == SOCKET_ERROR )
                ? WSAGetLastError() : 0;
}    // SendWSockPacket

BOOL SendPacket(WCHAR *Buffer, DWORD code,TCHAR *tIP)
{
BOOL ret;
long len;

        len=(wcslen(Buffer)+1)*sizeof(WCHAR);
            // Buffer = String incl. Terminating zero
        ret=SendWSockPacket( sCommand, len, (BYTE *)Buffer,code, tIP);
        if( ret != 0 ) return FALSE;   // more error handling goes here
        return TRUE;
}
```

This concludes your helper functions. Now you need to call them in the code of the "Hello World" application.

10. Put "CloseServer()" at the end of the "WinMain" function of your "SendIt.cpp" right before the "return msg.mParam;" line.

11. Add "InitServer(hWnd)" to the end of the "InitInstance()" function.

12. In "WndProc" Windows Message Procedure, locate the "WM_COMMAND" switch and add the following code right after the branch for the "IDM_FILE_EXIT" handler:

```
case ID_SENDPACKET:
#ifdef UNDER_CE
      SendPacket(L"This was sent from Windows CE",
                WM_SOCKET_SELECT,TEXT("<IP Address of PC>"));
#else
      SendPacket(L"This was sent from Windows NT/98",
                WM_SOCKET_SELECT,TEXT("<IP Address of CE
                device>"));
#endif
   break;
```

You can find out the IP address of your machines, depending on your platform, by following the steps shown in Table 9.12.

The last modification to "WndProc" will be your "WM_SOCKET_SELECT" message.

13. Add the following code before the "WM_PAINT" handler in "WndProc":

```
case WM_SOCKET_SELECT:
         TCHAR wsu[100];
         if (sizeof(TCHAR)==sizeof(WCHAR))
              wsprintf(wsu,TEXT("%s"),(TCHAR *)wParam);
         else
         {
              WCHAR *tTxt=(WCHAR *)wParam;
              for (int i=0;i<(int)wcslen(tTxt);i++)
                   wsu[i]=(TCHAR)tTxt[i];
              wsu[i]=0;
         }     // Some Unicode to ANSI conversion...
         MessageBox(hWnd,wsu,TEXT("SendIt"),MB_OK);
      break;
```

14. You can also change the code of the "WM_DESTROY" branch to close the partner application on the other side:

```
#ifdef UNDER_CE
      CommandBar_Destroy(hwndCB);
      SendPacket(L"",WM_CLOSE,TEXT("<IP Address of PC>"));
#else
      SendPacket(L"",WM_CLOSE,TEXT("<IP Address of CE device>"));
#endif
```

Table 9.12   How to Find the IP Address of a Platform

Platform	What to Do . . .
Windows 9x	Start the application "WINTCPCFG.EXE" and select your LAN card in the combo box. You will then see your TCP/IP address in the corresponding field.
Windows NT/Windows 2000	Launch the DOS prompt and type in "IPCONFIG". The program will reveal the IP address, subnet mask, and default gateway.
Windows CE (H/PC Professional)	Download the Power Toys from http://www.microsoft.com/windowsce/products/download/powtoy30.asp. They contain a tool named "Handheld PC's IP Address" that tells you the IP address of your CE device.
Pocket PC (palm-size PCs)	Double-click the small network icon in the start bar and read the device's IP address.
Windows CE (general)	If you have any device besides an H/PC Professional, you must look into your RAS server and select the current connection. 1. On Windows 2000, right-click the "My Computer" icon on the desktop and select "Manage". 2. In the upcoming MMC (Microsoft Management Console) window, open the "Services and Application/Routing and Remote Access/Ports" branch. 3. Double-click the current connected port, and you will see the IP address of the Windows CE device in the bottom part of the dialog box.

15. Add "winsock.lib" to your project settings.

16. Convert project to a desktop application project, which you do the same way as was described in Chapter 6:

   • Put some #ifdefs around the "CommandBar" functions.
   • Remove "WS_EX_CAPTIONOKBTN" from the "About" dialog box resource.
   • Add the following two lines to the "Compile-time directives" in the "Resource Includes" dialog box. Remember, you have to do this while your CE project is loaded in "Palm-size PC 3.0" mode.

```
#include <commctrl.h>
#define I_IMAGENONE  (-2)
```

- Change the "_tsclen(): into a "lstrlen()".
- Add the menu to the CreateWindow function.
- Do not forget to add "WSOCK32.LIB" to the linker settings of your project before compiling it.

Now run the application on both sides and check the result. If you select "Send Packet . . ." on the desktop, you should see "This was sent from Windows NT/98". If you select the same menu on the Windows CE device, you should see the corresponding "This was sent from Windows CE" message on your desktop.

 The final source code of this section can be found on the companion CD under "\Sources\Chapter 9\9.4".

9.5.2 The PCDM Application

Sending information to another device using Winsock requires, at the very least, knowing the partner device's IP address. Accomplishing this in the most user-friendly manner is very complex, since broadcast mechanisms, locator servers, or other negotiating protocols must be used. In the future, I foresee extensive use of the new UPnP (Universal Plug and Play) standard to accomplish this initial discovery and communication. Infrared is a much more user-friendly, although it is limited in functionality.

This section is one of the few in which you do not apply the chapter's technology topic directly by updating the thread example. Section 9.6, however, will update the PCDM example again, so just read on. . . .

9.6   IrDA or Infrared: The Wireless Wire

System DLL:	WINSOCK.dll
Include file:	af_irda.h (includes in the DDK for the desktop starting with Windows 2000)
Library file:	winsock.lib
Help file:	wcesdkr.chm
Available since:	Windows CE 1.0
API prefix/suffix:	WSA . . .
InitCommonControlEx flag:	—
MFC class:	CSocket, CasyncSocket, CCeSocket

The Infrared Data Association (IrDA) is an association of companies from around the globe providing infrared standards to ensure interoperability of the infrared technology. More information on the IrDA standard can be found at http://www.IrDA.org.

Here is the good news: The infrared port is just a special case of Winsock and is programmed in nearly the same way. It basically uses the same functions as the regular Winsock, but employs special parameters and structures. Since the partner can be gone at any time, it also requires the use of "getsockopt" to check whether the connection is still active.

On the other hand, IrDA is not supported on the early Win32 operating systems like Win95 and Windows NT 4. If you want to run your examples, you will need either Windows 98 or Windows 2000.

9.6.1   Adding IrDA Support to Your Winsock Example

In the following example, you are going to add IrDA capacity to the "SendIt" application from Section 9.5.1. As mentioned before, IrDA is a special case of Winsock and using it is very similar to using Winsock. You need to write a new thread to handle the incoming packets and a new "SendIrDAPacket" function to send telegrams over to the client, but you do not have to change any other code.

1. Open the "SendIt" example from the last section and add the "#include <af_irda.h>" file to the header section of the "SendIt.cpp" source file.

You'll find this include file in the DDK of Windows 98 or Windows 2000. I do not know why Microsoft chooses not to put it into the regular SDK or even to ship it with the eMbedded Visual Tools.

2. Now add the following code for your new thread right before your Winsock thread:

```
DWORD WINAPI IrDAThread( LPVOID pParam )
{
SOCKET          ClientSock; // Socket for the Client
                // The IrDA address for the server
SOCKADDR_IRDA   address = {AF_IRDA, 0, 0, 0, 0, "SendItReceiver"};
BYTE            *tBuffer=NULL;
int             endless;
PACKET_FILE     filePacket;
BYTE            *recBuf;
INT             cbRead;
SOCKERR         serr;
```

```
sCommand = socket(AF_IRDA, SOCK_STREAM, 0);
bind(sCommand, (struct sockaddr *)&address, sizeof(address));
listen(sCommand, 1);

endless=TRUE;
while (endless==TRUE)
{
      // Wait for a client to contact you.  Blocking call.
      ClientSock = accept(sCommand, 0, 0);
      if (ClientSock==SOCKET_ERROR)
      {
            endless=FALSE;
            serr=WSAGetLastError();
      }
      // Receive a string from the client
      recBuf=(BYTE *)&filePacket;
      cbRead=recv(ClientSock, (char *)recBuf,
                  sizeof(filePacket), 0);
      if (ClientSock==INVALID_SOCKET)
            endless=FALSE;

      // Now comes the same code as in the WINSOCK Thread
      EnterCriticalSection(&m_csec);
      switch (filePacket.type)
      {
        case PACKET_TYPE_FILE:
         if (filePacket.cbFile>0)
         {
            tBuffer = (BYTE *)LocalAlloc(LMEM_ZEROINIT,
                                        filePacket.cbFile);
            memcpy(tBuffer,filePacket.szFile,
            filePacket.cbFile);
         }
         PostMessage((HWND)pParam,filePacket.Code,
         (WPARAM)tBuffer,(LPARAM)filePacket.cbFile);
         break;
        case PACKET_TYPE_NACK:
            endless=FALSE;
         break;
        default:
            // Ignore Packet
```

```
            break;
        }
        LeaveCriticalSection(&m_csec);
        closesocket(ClientSock); // Close Client Socket
    }
    return(TRUE);
}
```

Check out the "SOCKADDR_IDRA" structure. It is related to the "SOCKADDR_IN" structure you used for the Winsock thread, but contains all the information needed for an infrared connection. You have to enumerate your IrDA devices using the "getsockopt" function call and put the result in the structure's "irdaDeviceID" array. The last parameter holds a string containing an identifier to your application.

To use your new thread, update the "InitServer" function. To keep this example simple, just use an exclusive "if . . . else" branch around the two communication options.

3.   Update the "InitServer" function with this new code:

```
BOOL InitServer(HWND hwnd)
{
WSADATA              wsadata;
SOCKERR              serr;
DWORD ThreadId = 0L;
HANDLE               m_pCeThread;                    // thread handle

    if (MPServerRunning)       return TRUE;

    serr = WSAStartup( DESIRED_WINSOCK_VERSION, &wsadata );
    if( serr != 0 )    return FALSE;     // More error handling here
    if( wsadata.wVersion < MINIMUM_WINSOCK_VERSION ) return FALSE;
    if (0==0)
    {
        m_pCeThread = CreateThread( NULL, 0, IrDAThread,
                                    hwnd, 0L, &ThreadId);
    }
    else
    {
    serr = CreateSocket( &sCommand, SOCK_DGRAM,
                         htonl( INADDR_ANY ), htons(MPPort));
    if( serr != 0 ) return FALSE; // More error handling here
    m_pCeThread = CreateThread( NULL, 0, SCeThread,
                                hwnd,0L,&ThreadId);
```

```
                        //Pass hWnd to Thread
        }
        CloseHandle(m_pCeThread);
        InitializeCriticalSection(&m_csec);
        MPServerRunning=TRUE;

        return TRUE;
}
```

4. Add the "SendIrDAPacket" function to the example.

```
BOOL SndIrDA(int len, BYTE *Buffer, DWORD code)
{
#define NumRetries      5       // You try five time to send then fail
SOCKET              sock;
SOCKADDR_IRDA       address = {AF_IRDA, 0,0,0,0, "SendItReceiver"};
DEVICELIST          devList;
SOCKERR             serr   = 0;
int                 devListLen = sizeof(devList),
                    cnt = 0,idx=0;
PACKET_FILE         filePacket;
INT                 cbWritten;
BOOL                ret=TRUE;

    sock = socket(AF_IRDA, SOCK_STREAM, 0);
    devList.numDevice = 0; // initialize number of devices to zero
    // Make NumRetries (5) attempts to find server device
    while ((devList.numDevice == 0) && (cnt <= NumRetries))
    {
        // see if device exists & retrieve its device identifier
        getsockopt(sock, SOL_IRLMP, IRLMP_ENUMDEVICES,
                (char *)&devList, &devListLen);
        if (devList.numDevice!=0) break;
        cnt++;
        Sleep(500); // Wait half a second before retrying
    }
    if  (cnt > NumRetries)
        return FALSE;
    else // You found a server
    {       // Get socket address of server
        for (idx = 0; idx <= 3; idx++)
```

```
            address.irdaDeviceID[idx] =
        devList.Device[0].irdaDeviceID[idx];
        connect(sock, (struct sockaddr *)&address,
                sizeof(SOCKADDR_IRDA));
        memset(filePacket.szFile,0,sizeof(filePacket.szFile));
        filePacket.type   = PACKET_TYPE_FILE;
        filePacket.cbFile = len;
        filePacket.PakSize= len+(4*sizeof(DWORD));
        filePacket.Code        = code;
        memcpy( filePacket.szFile, Buffer, len);
        cbWritten = send( sock,(CHAR FAR *)&filePacket,
                        len+(4*sizeof(DWORD)), 0 );
        serr = ( cbWritten == SOCKET_ERROR ) ? WSAGetLastError() : 0;
        if( serr != 0 ) ret=FALSE;
        closesocket(sock);
    }
    return ret;
}
```

The last addition you are going to make will fix the "SendPacket" function.

5.   Update the "SendPacket" function with the following code:

```
BOOL SendPacket(WCHAR *Buffer, DWORD code,TCHAR *tIP)
{
BOOL ret;
long len;

    len=(wcslen(Buffer)+1)*sizeof(WCHAR);
            // String incl. Terminating zero

    if (0==0)
        ret=SndIrDA(len,(BYTE *)Buffer,code);
    else
        ret=SendWSockPacket( sCommand, len, (BYTE *)Buffer,code,
        tIP);

    if( ret != 0 ) return FALSE;      // more error handling goes
    here
    return TRUE;
}
```

Before you can compile the Win32 version of your project, you must add a pre-processor definition to the compiler settings named "_WIN32_WINDOWS". The "AF_IRDA.H" include file will show you an error if you do not do so. Also include the "WINSOCK.LIB" in the linker settings of your project. Now compile the example for Windows CE and for the desktop, and run it on both sides. Of course, you must have an IrDA port on your desktop PC to run this example via infrared. Most notebooks have such a port these days.

Select the "SendPacket . . ." menu from either the Windows CE or the desktop side. You should see a message box pop up, showing the example string "This was sent to you from <platform>". If you still encounter difficulties running the example, here are some hints about why the IrDA connection might not work:

- If you are connected with ActiveSync, IrDA does not work. Disconnect your ActiveSync connection.

- If your devices are not correctly aligned, IrDA will not work. The H/PCs and the palm-size PCs have only a limited range. A notebook can go further. It might be that the notebook detects your Windows CE device but not vice versa.

- If you have another IrDA device in range, it might be interfering with your testing device. Make sure that there is no printer or scanner within range of the test devices. On a notebook, you can check the IrDA icon in the taskbar to see whether it detects your device or another one.

- On Windows 2000, you need administrator privileges to use the RAW socket support.

- If your notebook supports FastIrDA, you will not be able to connect to the CE device. Both ends have to use plain IrDA to communicate.

 The final source code of this section can be found on the companion CD under "\Sources\Chapter 9\9.5".

9.6.2 Adding IrDA Support to the PCDMDLL

Now that you are familiar with Winsock and IrDA technology, it is time to apply your knowledge to the PCDM thread example. As you have probably seen from other applications, such as the Contact Manager, you can send contacts back and forth between two Windows CE devices using infrared. This is exactly the feature you will add to your PCDM application.

You will add a class called "PCDMTransfer" to your "PCDMDLL.DLL" component, which implements two methods called "SendString" and "ReceiveString". "SendString" will send a CD description, including its "Tracks" to another device that receives the string with the "ReceiveString" method. A third method called "CancelReceive" will end the "ReceiveString" thread, which is created to wait for incoming IrDA packets.

The packet you are going to send contains a string that assembles a map to the API calls of your "PCDMAccessDB" class that you will recognize from the ActiveSync provider implementation. Table 9.13 shows that there are two ways of implementing an IrDA communication in an application.

For your "PCDMDLL.DLL", you are going to use the second implementation because you do not want to block the IrDA port to other applications whenever the PCDM application is running. Also, you do not want to have new entries popping up in your database without the user receiving confirmation.

Start with the new "PCDMTransfer" class.

1. Open the last version of the "PCDMDLL" project and add a new ATL "Simple Object" named "PCDMTransfer" to it.

2. Add the method "SendString" to the class using the following parameter:

Type	Variable Name	Used for
BSTR	Text	The string that gets sent via IrDA to the receiver

Table 9.13   Two Ways to Implement IrDA Receiving

Benefit	Disadvantage	Used for
1) Having the "IrDAThread" running from the start of the application.		
No user interaction required to receive a telegram.	The infrared port is blocked for all other applications as long as your application is running.	Games or applications that need to exchange telegrams permanently.
2) Having a "Receive . . ." menu item that launches the "IrDAThread" and waits for a certain amount of time in a modal state until a telegram arrives.		
The infrared port is only blocked for other applications as long as your application is in the modal state.	The user explicitly has to tell the application to receive an IrDA package.	Applications that only need to exchange data at a certain defined moment or where user interaction is even requested.

3. Now add the following code to its implementation:

```
STDMETHODIMP CPCDMTransfer::SendString(BSTR Text)
{
#define NumRetries      500

SOCKET              sock;
SOCKADDR_IRDA       address = {AF_IRDA, 0,0,0,0, "PCDMIrDA"};
DEVICELIST          devList;
SOCKERR             serr    = 0;
int                 devListLen = sizeof(devList),
                    cnt = 0,idx=0,len;
PACKET_FILE         filePacket;
INT                 cbWritten;
HRESULT             ret=S_OK;
BYTE                *Buffer;

    if (wsainit!=0)
        return S_FALSE;        // Could not init WINSOCK
    len=(lstrlen(Text)+1)*sizeof(BSTR);
    Buffer=(BYTE *)Text;


    if ((sock = socket(AF_IRDA, SOCK_STREAM, 0))==INVALID_SOCKET)
        return S_FALSE;        // Could not init WINSOCK
devList.numDevice = 0; // initialize number of devices to zero

while ((devList.numDevice == 0) && (cnt <= NumRetries))
  {
        getsockopt(sock, SOL_IRLMP, IRLMP_ENUMDEVICES,
                (char *)&devList, &devListLen);
        cnt++;      // This time no wait !
  }
  if  (cnt > NumRetries)
        return S_FALSE;
  else // You found a server
  {        // Get socket address of server
        for (idx = 0; idx <= 3; idx++)
            address.irdaDeviceID[idx] =
                    devList.Device[0].irdaDeviceID[idx];
        serr=connect(sock, (struct sockaddr *)&address,
                sizeof(SOCKADDR_IRDA));
```

```
        serr=( serr == SOCKET_ERROR ) ? WSAGetLastError() : 0;

        if( serr != 0 )        ret=S_FALSE;

        memset(filePacket.szFile,0,sizeof(filePacket.szFile));
        filePacket.type   = PACKET_TYPE_FILE;
        filePacket.cbFile = len;
        filePacket.PakSize= len+(4*sizeof(DWORD));
        filePacket.Code       = WM_SOCKET_SELECT;
        memcpy( filePacket.szFile, Buffer, len);
        cbWritten = send( sock,(CHAR FAR *)&filePacket,
                          len+(4*sizeof(DWORD)), 0 );
        serr=( cbWritten == SOCKET_ERROR ) ? WSAGetLastError() : 0;

        if( serr != 0 )        ret=S_FALSE;

        closesocket(sock);
    }
    return ret;
}
```

The "ReceiveString" method is a bit trickier. While the "SendString" method just retries five times and then returns, "ReceiveString" contains a blocking call. Since you do not want to be blocked forever in the "ReceiveString" method, you can choose one of two methods:

- Create a thread inside the "PCDMTransfer" class and wait with a timeout on to receive something, and, if nothing is received, cancel the thread.
- Create a thread inside the calling application and block inside the "ReceiveString" until it is canceled by the calling application.

The first of these methods would require putting up a dialog box showing the user that it is waiting for incoming packets. This dialog box would have to be written in the "PCDMTransfer" class. Since your "PCDMDLL.DLL" is a headless control and can even be running on a remote machine, you really do not want a dialog box popping up. Therefore you should use the second method.

4. Add the method "ReceiveString" to the class and give it the following parameter:

Type	Variable Name	Used for
[out,retval] BSTR *	Text	Returns the string that was received via IrDA

5.   Add the following code to its implementation:

```
STDMETHODIMP CPCDMTransfer::ReceiveString(BSTR *Text)
{
SOCKET                  ClientSock;
SOCKADDR_IRDA           address = {AF_IRDA, 0, 0, 0, 0, "PCDMIrDA"};
BYTE                    *tBuffer=NULL;
int                     endless;
PACKET_FILE             filePacket;
BYTE                    *recBuf;
INT                     cbRead;
SOCKERR                 serr;
HRESULT                 ret=S_FALSE;
TCHAR                   tStr[200];

    if (wsainit!=0)
    {
    wsprintf(tStr,TEXT("ERR: WsaInit Failed code=<%d>,<%d>,<%d>"),
            WSAGetLastError(),wsainit, wsadata.wVersion);
        *Text=SysAllocString(tStr);
        return S_FALSE;
    }

  if ((sCommand = socket(AF_IRDA, SOCK_STREAM, 0))==SOCKET_ERROR)
    {
        wsprintf(tStr,TEXT("ERR: Socket code=<%d>"),
                WSAGetLastError());
        *Text=SysAllocString(tStr);
        return S_FALSE;
    }
    if (bind(sCommand, (struct sockaddr *)&address,
        sizeof(address))==SOCKET_ERROR)
    {
        wsprintf(tStr,TEXT("ERR: Bind Failed code=<%d>"),
                WSAGetLastError());
        *Text=SysAllocString(tStr);
        return S_FALSE;
    }
    listen(sCommand, 1);

    endless=TRUE;
```

```
while (endless==TRUE)
{
      ClientSock = accept(sCommand, 0, 0);
      if (ClientSock==SOCKET_ERROR)
      {
            endless=FALSE;
            serr=WSAGetLastError();
      }
      recBuf=(BYTE *)&filePacket;
      cbRead=recv(ClientSock,(char *)recBuf,
                  sizeof(filePacket), 0);
      if (ClientSock==INVALID_SOCKET)
            endless=FALSE;
      EnterCriticalSection(&m_csec);
      switch (filePacket.type)
      {
            case PACKET_TYPE_FILE:
                  if (filePacket.cbFile>0)
                  {
                        *Text=SysAllocString(
                              (TCHAR*)filePacket.szFile);
                        endless=FALSE;
                        ret=S_OK;
                  }
                  break;
            default:
                  // Ignore all other Packets
                  break;
      }
      LeaveCriticalSection(&m_csec);
    closesocket(ClientSock); // Close Client Socket
}
return ret;
}
```

As you can see, the method will now block at the "accept" call. You cannot even stop the method if foreign packets other than those with your designation "PACKET_TYPE_FILE" come in. To unblock the call, you must write a "CancelReceive" method that resets the socket of the "accept" call and forces it to continue with a "SOCKET_ERROR", which you will use to terminate the thread.

6. Now add the "CancelReceive" method without parameters and add this code to its implementation:

```
STDMETHODIMP CPCDMTransfer::CancelReceive()
{
LINGER linger;

    if (wsainit!=0) return S_FALSE;        // Could not init WINSOCK
    if( sCommand != INVALID_SOCKET )
    {
        linger.l_onoff  = TRUE;
        linger.l_linger = 0;
        setsockopt(sCommand,SOL_SOCKET, SO_LINGER,
                    (CHAR FAR *)&linger,sizeof(linger) );
        closesocket( sCommand );
    }

    return S_OK;
}
```

You might recognize this code from the example in Section 9.5.2. It is the same code you already wrote for the "ResetSocket" function.

7. To be able to compile this class you also have to add the following "#includes", "#defines", and "typedefs" to the header of your "PCDMTransfer" class:

```
#include <winsock.h>
#ifdef UNDER_CE
#undef _WIN32_WINNT
#endif
#include "af_irda.h"
#define DESIRED_WINSOCK_VERSION    0x0101
#define MINIMUM_WINSOCK_VERSION    0x0001
#define MAX_BUF_LEN                1000
#define PACKET_TYPE_FILE           0x46494c45L    // "FILE"
#define PACKET_TYPE_NACK           0x4e41434bL    // "NACK"
#define MPPort                     4322      // New Port !
#define WM_SOCKET_SELECT           (WM_USER + 100)
typedef INT                        SOCKERR;
typedef struct _PACKET_FILE
{
```

```
        DWORD         type;
        DWORD         cbFile;
DWORD             PakSize;
DWORD             Code;
        CHAR          szFile[MAX_BUF_LEN];
} PACKET_FILE, FAR * LPPACKET_FILE;
```

The "#undef" around the "_WIN32 WINNT" define is necessary because ATL for CE devices defines it, which would lead to an invalid initialization of the IrDA defines on Windows CE.

8. You also have to add some initialization and cleanup code to the constructor and destructor of your class:

```
CPCDMTransfer()
{
        InitializeCriticalSection(&m_csec);
        wsainit = WSAStartup( DESIRED_WINSOCK_VERSION, &wsadata );
        if(wsainit==0 && wsadata.wVersion<MINIMUM_WINSOCK_VERSION )
                wsainit=-1;
}
~CPCDMTransfer()
{
        CancelReceive();
        WSACleanup();
}
```

9. Define the three private variables: "m_csec", containing the handle for the "Critical Section"; "sCommand", for the receiver socket; and "wsainit", containing the state of the Winsock system.

```
private:
        CRITICAL_SECTION        m_csec;
        SOCKET                  sCommand;
        SOCKERR                 wsainit;
        WSADATA                 wsadata;
```

Do not forget to include "WINSOCK.LIB" into the linker settings of your project. Now compile the PCDMDLL for Windows CE and the desktop, and you are ready to test it in eMbedded Visual Basic.

 The final source code of this section can be found on the companion CD under "\Sources\ThreadExample\PCDMDLL\Step7".

9.6.3 Test the New PCDMDLL in eMbedded Visual Basic

To test the DLL, you will write an eVB application that waits for a string using the "ReceiveString" method and a PC application that sends a string using "SendString".

1. Create a new desktop VB application EXE and add a two buttons to the main form. Name them "Send" and "Receive".

2. Add the following code to the "Click" methods of the buttons:

```
Private Sub Command1_Click()
Dim irda As Object
    Set irda = CreateObject("PCDMDLL.PCDMTransfer")
    irda.SendString "Send from Windows 2000"
End Sub

Private Sub Command2_Click()
Dim foo
Dim test
    Set foo = CreateObject("PCDMDLL.PCDMTransfer.1")
    test = foo.ReceiveString
    MsgBox "Received:" & test
End Sub
```

3. Create a new eVB application and add the same buttons.

4. Add the following code to its button "Click" method:

```
Private Sub Command1_Click()
Dim irda
    Set irda = CreateObject("PCDMDLL.PCDMTransfer")
    irda.SendString "Send from Windows CE"
End Sub

Private Sub Command2_Click()
Dim foo
Dim test
    Set foo = CreateObject("PCDMDLL.PCDMTransfer.1")
    test = foo.ReceiveString
    MsgBox "Received:" & test
End Sub
```

Run the two examples and select the "Receive" button on one device first. Then click the "Send" button on the other device. You should get a message box on the Windows

CE device stating "Received: Sent from <device>". Then repeat the same steps in reverse order.

You have to send a string to the receiving application because it will remain blocked until it receives a valid packet. If you have to end the application, you will need to kill it using the task manager. In eMbedded Visual C++ you can put the "Receive" method in a separate thread and end it by calling the "CancelReceive" method.

 The final source code of this section can be found on the companion CD under "\Sources\Chapter 9\9.6".

9.6.4 Implementing "Send to . . ."/"Receive . . ." in the PCDM Application

At last, you will fill the code in the PCDM application's "Send to . . ." and "Receive . . ." handlers. In Chapter 7, you added those two menu items to the "File" menu. In this chapter, you will add the code to the "OnCmdBarActionCommander" method of the "CPCDMView" class.

1. Load the last version of the PCDM CE application and add two dialog box resources to the project, one using the ID "IDD_SENDWAIT" and one using the ID "IDD_RECVWAIT".

2. Both dialog boxes should just contain a static text telling the user to wait either for the send to happen or that your application is waiting for a packet to arrive.

3. Besides the static text, keep the "Cancel" button, but remove the "OK" button.

4. Double-click one of the two dialog boxes and create a new MFC dialog box class called "CWaitDlg".

You are going to reuse this class for both dialog boxes to keep the code simple. The "CwaitDlg" will also contain all the IrDA communication.

5. Now open the "waitdlg.h" header file and add the following line to the top of the file:

```
using namespace PCDMdll_space;
```

As you might recall, this code makes the interface references for your PCD-MDLL component accessible by the "CwaitDlg" class.

6. Change the code of the "CwaitDlg" class definition to the following:

```
class CWaitDlg : public CDialog
{
```

```
// Construction
public:
      CWaitDlg(int IDD,BSTR bStr,CWnd* pParent = NULL);
      IPCDMTransferPtr  mcomTRANS;
      BSTR m_SendString,m_RecvString;
      int m_IDD;
      ~CWaitDlg()
      {
            if (mcomTRANS!=NULL)
                  mcomTRANS->Release();
      }

// Dialog Data
      //{{AFX_DATA(CWaitDlg)
      enum { IDD = IDD_SENDWAIT };
//... old code...
```

7. In the implementation file of "CwaitDlg.cpp", change the constructor to

```
CWaitDlg::CWaitDlg(int IDD,BSTR bStr,CWnd* pParent /*=NULL*/)
      : CDialog(IDD, pParent)
{
      m_SendString=m_SendString=SysAllocString(bStr);
      m_IDD=IDD;
      //{{AFX_DATA_INIT(CWaitDlg)
      // NOTE: the ClassWizard will add member initialization here
      //}}AFX_DATA_INIT
}
```

Instead of using the enumeration IDD to reference the dialog box resource, you need to set the ID during the creation of the class.

8. You need three Windows message handlers for "OnCancel", "OnInitDialog", and "OnTimer". You can create all of them using the class wizard.

9. Add the following code to their implementation:

```
void CWaitDlg::OnCancel()
{
      if (m_IDD==IDD_RECVWAIT)
            mcomTRANS->CancelReceive()        // Cancels the Receive
                                              Thread

      CDialog::OnCancel();
}
```

If you are in the "Receive" dialog box, you must cancel the receive thread using the "CancelReceive" call to the PCDMDLL component.

```
BOOL CWaitDlg::OnInitDialog()
{
     CDialog::OnInitDialog();
     HRESULT hr=mcomTRANS.CreateInstance( __uuidof( PCDMTransfer ) );
     if (FAILED(hr)) mcomTRANS=NULL;

     if (m_IDD==IDD_SENDWAIT && mcomTRANS!=NULL)
          this->SetTimer(111,1000,NULL);
     else
     {
          DWORD dwThreadId, dwThrdParam = 1;
          HANDLE hThread;
          hThread = CreateThread(NULL,0,
                                   ThreadFunc,this,
                                   0,&dwThreadId);
             if (hThread != NULL)
                 CloseHandle( hThread );
     }
     return TRUE;

}
```

For the "Send" dialog box, you will try to send the string every second until it succeeds. Otherwise, you create a receiving thread that waits for the packet.

```
void CWaitDlg::OnTimer(UINT nIDEvent)
{
     if (nIDEvent==111)
     {
          HRESULT hr=mcomTRANS->SendString(m_SendString);
          if (hr==S_OK)
               EndDialog(0);
     }
     CDialog::OnTimer(nIDEvent);
}
```

   10.   Add the code for the thread:

```
DWORD WINAPI ThreadFunc( LPVOID lpParam )
```

```
{
CWaitDlg *pwdlg;
    pwdlg=(CWaitDlg *)lpParam;
    pwdlg->mcomTRANS->ReceiveString(&pwdlg->m_RecvString);
    pwdlg->EndDialog(0);
    return 0;
}
```

The thread's parameter is a pointer to your "CWaitDlg" class. This approach works because your PCDM application is running in the apartment-threading model.

11. Locate the "OnCmdBarActionCommander" method in "PCDMView.cpp" and change the code of the method by adding the following lines, displayed in bold:

```
void CPCDMView::OnCmdBarActionCommander(long ID, LPCTSTR Text)
{
CDetails *dlg;
int plat;
#define RETRIES       5
CWaitDlg           *tDlg;
BSTR               tBstr;
IPCDMAccessDBPtr   comDB;
IPCDMUtilsPtr      comUtils;
long               DBHandle,FieldCnt;
HRESULT            hr;
TCHAR              tStr[255];
VARIANT            value,tvalue;

    switch (ID)
    {
        case 31:
                plat=LOWORD(GetCePlatform());
                if (plat>=CEP_PALMPC && plat<CEP_PALMPCEND)
                    dlg=new CDetails(IDD_CDDETAILSPALM,0);
                else
                    dlg=new CDetails(IDD_CDDETAILS,0);
                dlg->DoModal();
            break;
        case 36:
                tDlg=new CWaitDlg(IDD_RECVWAIT,TEXT(""));
                tDlg->DoModal();
```

```
                tBstr=SysAllocString(tDlg->m_RecvString);
                delete tDlg;
//MessageBox(tBstr,TEXT("Received")); // <BOOK Include to check
Buffer
                hr=comUtils.CreateInstance(__uuidof( PCDMUtils ) );
                if (FAILED(hr))
                {
        MessageBox(TEXT("Could not access the PCDMUtils Class"));
                    break;
                }
                hr=comUtils->AnalyzeURL(tBstr);
                if (hr==ERROR_DUP_NAME)
        MessageBox(TEXT("Sorry but this CD is already in the
        Database"));
                else
                    RefreshLVC();
            break;
        case 30:
        {
                if (m_LastRow==0) break;
                _bstr_t
bsSel(L"PCDMIrDA://PCDM/PCDMAccessDB?Command=1&Table=PCDMCDs&IDX=0&");
                hr=comDB.CreateInstance(__uuidof( PCDMAccessDB ) );
                if (FAILED(hr))
                {
                MessageBox(TEXT("Could not access the
                PCDMDll.DLL"));
                    break;
                }
                hr=comDB->OpenTable(TEXT("\\My
                Documents\\PCDM.cdb"),
                                TEXT("PCDMCDs"),
                                _variant_t((long)PCDM_PID_ID),
                                &DBHandle);
                if (FAILED(hr))
                {
                    hr=comDB->OpenTable(TEXT(""),TEXT("PCDMCDs"),
                        _variant_t((long)PCDM_PID_ID),
                        &DBHandle);
                    if (FAILED(hr))
                    {
```

```
            MessageBox(TEXT("Database could not be opened"));
                    break;
        }
}
VariantInit(&value);
value.vt=VT_I4;
value.lVal=m_LastRow;
hr=comDB->MoveFirst(DBHandle);
hr=comDB->FindRecord(DBHandle,
                    _variant_t((long)PCDM_PID_ID),
                    value);
if (hr==S_OK)
{
        hr=comDB->ReadRecord(DBHandle,&FieldCnt);
        if (hr==S_OK)
        {
                for (int i=0;i<FieldCnt;i++)
                {
                        VariantClear(&value);
                        hr=comDB->GetValue(_variant_t(
                        (long)(PCDM_PID_ID+i)),&value);
                        if (!FAILED(hr))
                        {
                                wsprintf(tStr,
                                        TEXT("Fld%d=%s"),i,
                                    value.bstrVal);
                                bsSel+=tStr;
                                if (i<FieldCnt-1)
                                        bsSel+=TEXT("&");
                        }
                }
        }
        comDB->CloseTable(DBHandle);
        hr=comDB->OpenTable(
                TEXT("\\My Documents\\PCDM.cdb"),
                TEXT("PCDMTracks"),
                _variant_t((LONG)PCDM_PID_
                TRACKS_ID),
                &DBHandle);
        if (hr==S_OK)
        {
```

```
                                VariantInit(&tvalue);
                                while (hr==S_OK)
                                {
                                        hr=comDB->ReadRecord(
                                                DBHandle,&FieldCnt);
                                        if (hr==S_OK)
                                        {
                                                for (int
                                                i=0;i<FieldCnt;i++)
                                                {
                                                VariantClear(&value);
                                                hr=comDB->GetValue(
                                                _variant_t((LONG)
                                                (PCDM_PID_TRACKS_ID+i)),
                                                &value);
                                                if (i==PCDM_PID_TRACKS_ID)
                                                {
                                                        VariantChangeType(
                                                        &tvalue,&value,
                                                        NULL,VT_I4);
                                                        if (tvalue.lVal!=m_LastRow)
                                                            break;
                                                        else
bsSel+=L";PCDMIrDA://PCDM/PCDMAccessDB?Command=1&Table=PCDMTracks&";
                                                }
                                                if (!FAILED(hr))
                                                {
                                                wsprintf(tStr,
                                                        TEXT("Fld%d=%s"),i,
                                                        value.bstrVal);
                                                        bsSel+=tStr;
                                                        if (i<FieldCnt-1)
                                                            bsSel+=TEXT("&");
                                                }
                                                }
                                        }
                                        hr=comDB->MoveNext(DBHandle);
                                }
                                comDB->CloseTable(DBHandle);
                        }
                        bsSel+=TEXT(";");
```

```
//MessageBox(bsSel);        // <BOOK Include to check Buffer
                tDlg=new CWaitDlg(IDD_SENDWAIT,bsSel);
                tDlg->DoModal();
                delete tDlg;
        }
        else

                comDB->CloseTable(DBHandle);

}
  break;
case IDCLOSE:
        GetParentFrame()->DestroyWindow();
  break;
default:
  break;
}
}
```

Now compile the application and run it on two Windows CE devices. Try the new "Send . . ." and "Receive . . ." features from the "File" menu. As you can see, you are transmitting a string formatted in a URL-like style. To analyze the URL, you are using the "PCDMUtils" class. The "PCDMUtils" class provides a neat way of doing this—and nicely demonstrates the use of IrDA. The source for this class can be found in Appendix B, "The PCDMUtils Class".

Extended Markup Language (XML) provides another way of implementing data exchange between two applications. XML provides a way of describing complex data structures in clear text. All kinds of industries have shown a growing interest in XML, and it is just a matter of time before the first XML parsers are available for Windows CE.

 The final source code of this section can be found on the companion CD under "\Sources\ThreadExample\PCDM CE\Step7".

9.7   HTTP: Integration of the Internet

A very important aspect of application development these days is Internet integration. This section discusses the integration of HTTP and other Internet-related client technologies within Windows CE applications.

9.7.1 Wininet: The Client Internet API

System DLL:	WININET.DLL
Include file:	Wininet.h
Library file:	Wininet.lib
Help file:	wcesdkr.chm
Available since:	Windows CE 2.0
API prefix/suffix:	Internet . . .
InitCommonControlEx flag:	—
MFC class:	CHttp . . ./Cinternet . . .

Just as on desktop Windows, you can use Wininet to access the two most common protocols on the Internet: HTTP and FTP. Windows CE does not support all Wininet features found on the desktop Windows version. Here are some of the exceptions:

- "InternetErrorDlg" and "InternetSetOption" are not supported.
- "InternetSetCookie" and "InternetGetCookie" are not supported.
- "InternetWriteFile" is not supported.
- Text coming back from "InternetOpenUrl" and "InternetReadFile" is in ASCII, although the APIs are in Unicode.
- H/PC 2.0 does not have the FTP functions of Wininet, and therefore you cannot use FTP on H/PC2 with Wininet.

Unfortunately, there is no ActiveX control that parses HTML or even takes a URL as a property on Windows CE. Writing your own parser is beyond the scope of this book and will not be covered.

9.7.2 A Small Wininet Example

To give you at least a head start with your Internet integration, the following example will show you how to retrieve a file or Web page using the Wininet API.

1. Create a new dialog box-based "WCE MFC Application", using all MFC wizard defaults and name it "WebIt".

You are going to use the MFC framework to concentrate on the Wininet essentials. The code you are going to add is pure SDK code and runs even in non-MFC applications.

2. Open the "IDD_WEBIT_DIALOG" resource and add three controls to it. Then use the class wizard to assign the variables in Table 9.13 to the controls.

3. Set the "Multiline" and "Vertical Scroll" flags for the "IDC_PAGE" and "IDC_HEADER" edit box.

4. Double-click the "Go" button and add the following code to the implementation of the button's "OnGo" method:

```
void CWebItDlg::OnGo()
{
HINTERNET hOpen = NULL,
         hConnect  = NULL,
         hRequest = NULL;
DWORD        dwSize = 0,
         dwFlags = INTERNET_FLAG_RELOAD |
INTERNET_FLAG_NO_CACHE_WRITE;
char        *lpBufferA,*lpHeadersA;
TCHAR        *lpBufferW, *lpHeadersW;
// You accept only "Text" pages.
LPTSTR        AcceptTypes[2] = {TEXT("text/*"), NULL};

  // Initializes the use of the Windows CE Internet functions.
     hOpen = InternetOpen (TEXT("CeHttp"),
                          INTERNET_OPEN_TYPE_PRECONFIG,
```

Table 9.14   The Controls for the WebIt Dialog Box

Type	ID	Member Variable	Used for
EDIT Box	IDC_URL	Cstring m_URL	Allows the user to enter a URL
BUTTON	IDC_GO		Starts the browser to retrieve the URL
EDIT BOX	IDC_HEADER	Cedit m_Header	Shows the header of the retrieved page (set flags "Vertical Scroll" and "Multiline")
EDIT Box	IDC_PAGE	Cedit m_Page	Shows the body of the page retrieved (set flags "Vertical Scroll" and "Multiline")

```
                    NULL, 0, 0);        // In case you need a
                                           proxy
                                        // server you can enter it here
if (!hOpen)       return;        // Error handling
UpdateData(TRUE); // get the URL from the Dialog Box
// Opens an HTTP session for a given site by lpszServer.
if (!(hConnect = InternetConnect (hOpen, m_URL,
                                INTERNET_INVALID_PORT_NUMBER,
                                NULL, NULL,
                                INTERNET_SERVICE_HTTP,
                                0, 0)))
        goto exit; // Error handling

// Opens an HTTP request handle.
if (!(hRequest = HttpOpenRequest (hConnect,TEXT("GET"),
                                NULL, HTTP_VERSION,
                                NULL, (LPCTSTR*)AcceptTypes,
                                dwFlags, 0)))
        goto exit;        // Error handling

// Sends a request to the HTTP server.
if (!HttpSendRequest (hRequest, NULL, 0, NULL, 0))
        goto exit;

// Call HttpQueryInfo to find out the size of the headers.
HttpQueryInfo (hRequest, HTTP_QUERY_RAW_HEADERS_CRLF,
                NULL, &dwSize, NULL);

// Allocates a block of memory for lpHeadersA.
lpHeadersA = new CHAR [dwSize];

// Call HttpQueryInfo again to get the headers.
if (!HttpQueryInfo (hRequest, HTTP_QUERY_RAW_HEADERS_CRLF,
                    (LPVOID) lpHeadersA, &dwSize, NULL))
        goto exit;

// Terminate headers with NULL.
lpHeadersA [dwSize] = '\0';

// Get the required size of the buffer receives the UNICODE string.
```

```
dwSize= MultiByteToWideChar (CP_ACP, 0, lpHeadersA, -1, NULL,
0);
 // Allocates a block of memory for lpHeadersW.
lpHeadersW = new TCHAR [dwSize];
// Convert headers from ASCII to UNICODE
MultiByteToWideChar (CP_ACP, 0, lpHeadersA, -1,
                    lpHeadersW, dwSize);

// Put the headers in the edit control.
m_Header.SetWindowText(lpHeadersW);

// Free the blocks of memory.
delete[] lpHeadersA;
delete[] lpHeadersW;

// Now do the same thing for the body of the Page
lpBufferA = new CHAR [32000];
do
{
    if (!InternetReadFile (hRequest, (LPVOID)lpBufferA,
                        32000, &dwSize))
        goto exit;
    if (dwSize != 0)
    {
        lpBufferA [dwSize] = '\0';
        dwSize = MultiByteToWideChar (CP_ACP, 0, lpBufferA,
                                    -1, NULL, 0);
        lpBufferW = new TCHAR [dwSize];
        MultiByteToWideChar (CP_ACP, 0, lpBufferA, -1,
                            lpBufferW, dwSize);
        m_Page.SetWindowText(lpBufferW);
        delete[] lpBufferW;
    }
} while (dwSize);

delete[] lpBufferA;
exit:
    // Closes the internet handles.
    if (hOpen) InternetCloseHandle (hOpen);
    if (hConnect) InternetCloseHandle (hConnect);
    if (hRequest) InternetCloseHandle (hRequest);
```

```
        return;
}
```

Now compile and run the example. Once the dialog box comes up, enter a Web address you know without the "HTTP://" prefix. You already coded the "InternetConnect" to use HTTP and do not have to parse the namespace part of the URL. After a short time, you should see the header of that page in the "IDC_HEADER" edit box and the body in the "IDC_PAGE" box. Of course, you have to be connected to the Internet to get to an Internet address. If you are connected with ActiveSync to your desktop PC, you won't be able to reach the Web server on your desktop PC. As described in Section 9.1, you need to install RAS to get to that Web server.

Without an HTTP parser, you will only be able to see the pure HTML page. However, you can use Wininet to look for updates. The function "HttpOpenRequest" allows you to specify certain media types. You could specify "application/<YourSubType>" here. Your Web server needs to understand that subtype and stream down the updated file to your client.

The most common data transport type in the future will be "*/XML". Since XML requires an XML parser to interpret the Internet file, to write an XML parser for Windows CE could be a lucrative opportunity.

 The final source code of this section can be found on the companion CD under "\Sources\Chapter 9\9.7".

9.7.3   The Web Server Issue

Another way of integrating the Internet into your application is to use a Web server and its extension model. Unfortunately, Windows CE up to Version 3.0 does not include an HTTP server, and no information was available on the HTTP server in Version 3.0 at the time this book went to press. There is, however, a third-party technology available that offers an HTTP server. deviceWEB by Intrinsyc even has an extension model similar to a CGI interface. If you want more information on deviceWEB go to the Intrinsyc Web site at http://www.intrinsyc.com.

10
Chapter

Graphics and Sounds

Graphics and sounds are very important features of applications these days. This chapter will introduce you to the basics of graphics and sounds on Windows CE. But before you dive into the technology, here is some background on Microsoft's design decisions.

Back in 1996, in the early days of Windows CE when the first Pegasus devices—like the Cassiopeia A10—appeared on the market, Windows CE only supported black-and-white screens with a resolution of 480×240 in four gray-scale shades. This left the developer with a hard task, since virtually no tool on the desktop supported this display mode. Converting a bitmap for use in a Windows CE application would require one of the two following tricks:

- Using the eMbedded Visual C++ internal bitmap converter by compiling a bitmap in a resource file.
- Copying a color bitmap to the device, using the Windows CE Explorer to convert it to four gray-scale shades. This involved renaming the file extension of the target bitmap to an unknown extension to prevent the Windows CE Explorer from converting it back on the way up, then copying it back to the desktop.

Since there are plenty of black-and-white devices out there, especially the first generation of palm-size PCs, you can use these two methods should you need to produce the appropriate bitmaps.

Generally, I recommend putting bitmaps into the resource files of an application or at least into a resource DLL. The reason is very simple, too.

Unlike the desktop, Windows CE does not copy a bitmap from the resource file into RAM. If you call the "LoadBitmap" API, the "HBITMAP" handle will point to the memory location of the bitmap inside the resource DLL.

This is very memory-friendly because bitmaps can be fairly large and would cost too much memory if copied all the time. There is a tradeoff in this.

 Bitmaps loaded from resource files cannot be manipulated directly. To do this, you must first copy them into a memory-DC; then you can apply changes to that DC.

If you changed the bitmap, you would change the actual bits of your application or DLL. Windows CE runs an application in place: the application's location remains the same on the storage media and all resources also stay on the media. CE does not load any DLL into RAM like the desktop. It just sets the program pointer to the start of the DLL function. A very effective way to use memory!

10.1 Loading Bitmaps

There are several ways to load bitmaps in Windows CE:

- Use "LoadBitmap()" to load a bitmap from a resource
- Use "SHLoadDiBitmap()" to load a bitmap from a file
- Use custom code, including "LoadDibSection()"

Using the DirectX API, you can load formats other than BMP, but then you need to use DirectX for the drawing, too. Since Windows CE devices that support DirectX have not yet been released, I will not discuss this option in this book. Moreover, with the continuing importance of the Internet, BMP will become less and less significant in comparison with compressed file formats such as the Joint Photographic Experts Group Format (JPG) and the Graphic Interchange Format (GIF).

10.1.1   Using LoadBitmap( )

System DLL:	CORE.DLL
Include file:	Core.h
Help file:	CEGUIDE.CHM (MSDN 10/98 and later)
Available since:	Windows CE 1.0
API prefix/suffix:	—
InitCommonControlEx flag:	—
MFC class:	Cbitmap

As mentioned before, "LoadBitmap()" lets you load a bitmap from a resource file. You probably know this function very well because it is no different from the desktop version. Just remember these important points:

- Bitmaps from resources cannot be manipulated because Windows CE does not "load" them, but simply provides pointers to the bitmaps' memory locations inside the resources.

- Bitmaps will be converted to the color specification of your target device during the linking of your application. This will happen by default for all Windows CE 2.0 devices. You can switch the conversion off by setting this linker option: /noconvert. Or you can force the conversion by using this linker option: /convert.

You should be familiar with "LoadBitmap" already from your desktop development experience; therefore I will skip any example for now.

10.1.2   Using SHLoadDiBitmap( )

System DLL:	CESHELL.DLL
Include file:	Shlobj.h
Help file:	CEGUIDE.CHM (MSDN 10/98 and later)
Available since:	Windows CE 1.0
API prefix/suffix:	SH
InitCommonControlEx flag:	—
MFC class:	—

This call is as easy to use as "LoadBitmap()". The difference is that you specify a file name rather than a bitmap resource. As with the "LoadBitmap()" call, you will get an HBITMAP in return. Unlike "LoadBitmap()", "SHLoadDiBitmap()" loads the bitmap into a memory-DC and allows you to change it directly.

A small source code example for "SHLoadDiBitmap" looks like this:

```
HBITMAP hBmp=SHLoadDiBitmap(L"C:\\My Documents\mypicture.bmp");
```

This function is not available on desktop Windows. You should work with "LoadLibrary" and "GetProcAddress". You can use the "L" macro here because there is no ANSI version of this call.

10.1.3 Using Custom Code

System DLL:	CORE.DLL
Include file:	Core.h
Help file:	CEGUIDE.CHM (MSDN 10/98 and later)
Available since:	Windows CE 1.0
API prefix/suffix:	—
InitCommonControlEx flag:	—
MFC class:	—

For those of you who like to have the most control over your bitmap, here is a piece of custom code that loads a bitmap into memory and "blits" it on a target HDC. "Blit" is a word that derives from the "blitter," a part of the graphics engine whose sole purpose is to copy a memory area into the graphics buffer. These days, this graphics engine is integrated into most graphics cards and is hardware accelerated.

Here is an approach that I find especially useful when I want to load a bitmap from a file containing multiple bitmaps. I simply use an offset pointer to load a bitmap from the middle of a file. Another advantage of this code is that it only requires the "CORE.DLL" of Windows CE. The tradeoffs are that you have to write a lot more code than the one-liners of previous sections and that the bitmap is stored uncompressed.

The following procedure creates a tiny "Hello-World" application that blits a bitmap into the client area of its windows.

1. Create a new Windows CE project and name it "BlitIt", using the "Simple Hello World Application" template of the "WCE Application" wizard.

2. Locate the WndProc message handler function and change the "WM_PAINT" branch as follows:

```
case WM_PAINT:
    RECT rt;
    hdc = BeginPaint(hWnd, &ps);
    GetClientRect(hWnd, &rt);
    DrawBitmapFromFile(hdc,TEXT("\\Windows\\Startup.bmp"),0,
                       rt.left,rt.top,rt.right,rt.bottom,
                       TRUE);
    LoadString(hInst, IDS_HELLO, szHello,MAX_LOADSTRING);
    DrawText(hdc, szHello, _tcslen(szHello), &rt,
             DT_SINGLELINE | DT_VCENTER | DT_CENTER);
    EndPaint(hWnd, &ps);
break;
```

The next functions are described in the order they are called by the application. You must declare each of these functions in the header of "BlitIt.h" along with its prototype. The first function you need to add is "DrawBitmapFromFile". It will allocate some memory, read the bitmap from file into a DIB memory, and blit it into the HDC given as a parameter.

3.   Add the following code to the end of "BlitIt.cpp":

```
void DrawBitmapFromFile(HDC hdc,LPCTSTR FileName,DWORD Offset,int x,
                        int y, int dx, int dy,BOOL stretch)
{
LPBYTE lpDIB= NULL;

    if( (lpDIB=ReadBMPFile(FileName,Offset)) == NULL )
        return;        // Error - do nothing
    BlitDIB(hdc, (LPBITMAPINFO)lpDIB, x,y,dx,dy, stretch );
    free( lpDIB );
}
```

4.   Add a function to read the file from the disk and convert it to a DIB buffer.

```
LPBYTE ReadBMPFile( LPCTSTR szFileName, DWORD Offset )
{
HANDLE            hFile;
BITMAPFILEHEADER  bfh;
DWORD             dwBytes;
LPBYTE            lpDIB = NULL, lpTemp = NULL;
WORD              wPaletteSize = 0;
DWORD             dwBitsSize = 0;
```

```
    // Open the file
    if( (hFile=CreateFile( szFileName, GENERIC_READ, 0, NULL,
                           OPEN_EXISTING, FILE_ATTRIBUTE_NORMAL,
                           NULL))
          == INVALID_HANDLE_VALUE )
        return NULL;
    if( SetFilePointer( hFile, Offset, NULL, FILE_BEGIN ) ==
          0xffffffff )
    {
        CloseHandle( hFile );
        return NULL;
    }
    // Read the header
    if((! ReadFile(hFile,&bfh,sizeof(BITMAPFILEHEADER),&dwBytes,
    NULL))
        || ( dwBytes != sizeof( BITMAPFILEHEADER ) ) )
    {
        CloseHandle( hFile );
        return NULL;
    }
    // Does it look like a BMP file?
    if((bfh.bfType != 0x4d42) || (bfh.bfReserved1!=0) ||
       (bfh.bfReserved2!=0) )
    {
        CloseHandle( hFile );
        return NULL;
    }
    // Allocate memory for DIB
    if( (lpDIB = (LPBYTE) malloc( sizeof( BITMAPINFO ))) == NULL )
    {
        CloseHandle( hFile );
        return NULL;
    }
    // Read in the BITMAPINFOHEADER
    if( (!ReadFile(hFile,lpDIB,sizeof(BITMAPINFOHEADER),
    &dwBytes,NULL))
        || (dwBytes!=sizeof(BITMAPINFOHEADER)) )
    {
        CloseHandle( hFile );
        free( lpDIB );
        return NULL;
```

```
    }
    if( ((LPBITMAPINFOHEADER)lpDIB)->biSize !=
        sizeof( BITMAPINFOHEADER ) )
    {
        CloseHandle( hFile );
        free( lpDIB );
        return NULL;
    }
    wPaletteSize = PaletteSize((LPSTR)lpDIB);
    dwBitsSize = ((LPBITMAPINFOHEADER)lpDIB)->biHeight *
                BytesPerLine((LPBITMAPINFOHEADER)lpDIB);
    // realloc to account for the total size of the DIB
    if( (lpTemp = (LPBYTE)realloc(lpDIB, sizeof( BITMAPINFOHEADER ) +
                                wPaletteSize + dwBitsSize )) ==
                                NULL)
    {
        CloseHandle( hFile );
        free( lpDIB );
        return NULL;
    }
    lpDIB = lpTemp;
    // If there is a color table, read it
    if( wPaletteSize != 0 )
    {
        if( (!ReadFile( hFile, ((LPBITMAPINFO)lpDIB)->bmiColors,
            wPaletteSize, &dwBytes, NULL ))
            || (dwBytes!=wPaletteSize) )
        {
            CloseHandle( hFile );
            free( lpDIB );
            return NULL;
        }
    }
    if( bfh.bfOffBits != 0 )
    {
        if( SetFilePointer( hFile, bfh.bfOffBits+Offset, NULL,
                        FILE_BEGIN ) == 0xffffffff )
        {
            CloseHandle( hFile );
            free( lpDIB );
            return NULL;
```

```
        }
    }
    // Read the image bits
    if( (!ReadFile( hFile, FindDIBBits((LPSTR)lpDIB), dwBitsSize,
                &dwBytes, NULL )) || (dwBytes!=dwBitsSize) )
    {
        CloseHandle( hFile );
        free( lpDIB );
        return NULL;
    }
    // clean up
    CloseHandle( hFile );
    return lpDIB;
}
```

Now you have the bitmap as a DIB in memory. Next you will blit it into the target HDC.

5. Add the following "BlitDIB" function to the end of "BlitIt.CPP":

```
BOOL BlitDIB( HDC JChdc,LPBITMAPINFO lpSrcDIB, int x,int y,int dx,
            int dy,BOOL bStretch )
{
LPBITMAPINFO        lpbmi = NULL;
LPBYTE              lpSourceBits;
HDC                 hDC = NULL, hSourceDC;
HBITMAP             hSourceBitmap, hOldSourceBitmap;
DWORD               dwSourceBitsSize;

    hDC = GetDC( NULL );
    hSourceBitmap = CreateDIBSection( hDC, lpSrcDIB, DIB_RGB_COLORS,
                                    (void **)&lpSourceBits, NULL, 0 );
    hSourceDC = CreateCompatibleDC( hDC );

    dwSourceBitsSize = lpSrcDIB->bmiHeader.biHeight *
                    BytesPerLine(&(lpSrcDIB->bmiHeader));
    memcpy( lpSourceBits, FindDIBBits((LPSTR)lpSrcDIB),
            dwSourceBitsSize );

    hOldSourceBitmap = (HBITMAP)SelectObject
    (hSourceDC,hSourceBitmap);
```

```
    if( bStretch )
        StretchBlt( JChdc, x, y, x+dx, y+dy, hSourceDC, 0, 0,
                    lpSrcDIB->bmiHeader.biWidth,
                    lpSrcDIB->bmiHeader.biHeight, SRCCOPY );
    else
        BitBlt( JChdc, x, y, x+dx, y+dy, hSourceDC, 0, 0, SRCCOPY );

    // Clean up and delete the DCs
    SelectObject( hSourceDC, hOldSourceBitmap );
    DeleteDC( hSourceDC );
    ReleaseDC( NULL, hDC );
    DeleteObject( hSourceBitmap );
    free( lpbmi );

    return TRUE;
}
```

The following four helper functions need to be added as well. "FindDIBBits" locates the image bits in a "CF_DIB"-formatted DIB and returns the pointer to the "CF_DIB" memory block:

```
LPSTR FindDIBBits( LPSTR lpbi )
{
    return ( lpbi + *(LPDWORD)lpbi + PaletteSize( lpbi ) );
}
```

"DIBNumColors" returns the number of entries in the color table:

```
WORD DIBNumColors( LPSTR lpbi )
{
    WORD wBitCount;
    DWORD dwClrUsed;

    dwClrUsed = ((LPBITMAPINFOHEADER) lpbi)->biClrUsed;

    if (dwClrUsed)
        return (WORD) dwClrUsed;

    wBitCount = ((LPBITMAPINFOHEADER) lpbi)->biBitCount;

    switch (wBitCount)
```

```
    {
        case 1: return 2;
        case 2: return 4;
            case 4: return 16;
        case 8:        return 256;
        default:return 0;
    }
    return 0;
}
```

"PaletteSize" returns the actual size in bytes of the color table:

```
WORD PaletteSize( LPSTR lpbi )
{
    return ( DIBNumColors( lpbi ) * sizeof( RGBQUAD ) );
}
```

"BytesPerLine" returns the number of bytes in one scan line. The result is DWORD aligned:

```
DWORD BytesPerLine( LPBITMAPINFOHEADER lpBMIH )
{
    return WIDTHBYTES(lpBMIH->biWidth * lpBMIH->biPlanes
                    * lpBMIH->biBitCount);
}
```

Do not forget to add function prototypes to either "BlitIt.h" or the top of "BlitIt.cpp". You also require a macro and a structure that are used in the code:

```
void DrawBitmapFromFile(HDC hdc,LPCTSTR FileName,DWORD Offset,
                        int x,int y, int dx, int dy,BOOL stretch);
LPBYTE ReadBMPFile( LPCTSTR szFileName, DWORD Offset );
BOOL BlitDIB( HDC JChdc,LPBITMAPINFO lpSrcDIB, int x,int y,int dx,
            int dy,BOOL bStretch );
LPSTR FindDIBBits( LPSTR lpbi );
WORD DIBNumColors( LPSTR lpbi );
WORD PaletteSize( LPSTR lpbi );
DWORD BytesPerLine( LPBITMAPINFOHEADER lpBMIH );
#define WIDTHBYTES(bits)      (((((bits) + 31)>>5)<<2)
```

Now compile the application and run it. You should see a "Hello World" application with the Windows CE startup bitmap in the top left corner.

The final source code of this section can be found on the companion CD under "\Sources\Chapter 10\10.1".

10.1.4 Adding a Picture Class to the PCDMUI.DLL

"PCDMUI.DLL" will include a new class for loading and displaying bitmaps in a window. You will include three ways of loading a bitmap, as was discussed in Sections 10.1.1, 10.1.2, and 10.1.3. This section will add the "loading" part of the class. In the next section you add the displaying part.

1. Load the latest version of "PCDMUI.DLL" and add a new "Full Control" ATL object named "PCDMPicture" to it. You do not need to change any of the attributes.

2. Add a method called "Load" to it and give it two parameters, as shown in Table 10.1.

3. Add the following code to the implementation of the method:

```
STDMETHODIMP CPCDMPicture::Load(BSTR Path, LONG ResourceID)
{
    AFX_MANAGE_STATE(AfxGetStaticModuleState())

    if (!m_hBitmap)    DeleteObject(m_hBitmap);
    if (!m_lpSrcDIB) free(m_lpSrcDIB);
    if (lstrlen(Path)==0)
        m_hBitmap=LoadBitmap(_Module.m_hInst,
                          MAKEINTRESOURCE(ResourceID));
    else
```

Table 10.1 **The Parameters for Method "Load"**

Type	Variable Name	Used for
BSTR	Path	This parameter will point to a file location or a resource name (if ResourceID is −1) of a bitmap. If it is empty (" "), the ResourceID will point to a bitmap by its resource ID in the current module.
LONG	ResourceID	This value is either the resource ID (if Path is set to " ") or an offset into the file given with Path.

```
        {
            switch (ResourceID)
            {
                case 0:
#ifdef UNDER_CE
                    m_hBitmap=SHLoadDIBitmap(Path);
#else
                    m_lpSrcDIB=ReadBMPFile(Path,0);
#endif
                    break;
                case -1:
                    m_hBitmap=LoadBitmap(_Module.m_hInst,Path);
                    break;
                default:
                    m_lpSrcDIB=ReadBMPFile(Path,ResourceID);
                    break;
            }
        }
    return S_OK;
}
```

4. For bitmap management, you will need two private class member variables:

```
private:
    HBITMAP                 m_hBitmap;
    LPBYTE                  m_lpSrcDIB;
```

5. Reset them to NULL in the class constructor:

```
    CPCDMPicture()
    {
        m_hBitmap=NULL;
        m_lpSrcDIB=NULL;
    }
```

6. Free the object on class destruction:

```
    ~CPCDMPicture()
    {
        if (!m_hBitmap)
            DeleteObject(m_hBitmap);
        if (!m_lpSrcDIB)
            free(m_lpSrcDIB);
    }
```

7. Add private member functions to the "CPCDMPicture" class named "ReadBMPFile", "FindDIBBits", "DIBNumColors", "PaletteSize", and "BytesPerLine"—using the same calling syntax as that of the example in Section 10.1.3 and adding the code from that example to their implementation.

8. Do not forget to add the "WIDTHBYTES" macro definition to the top of the implementation file.

Now compile the project and update the corresponding "PCDMUI_Win32" project. Since you are just loading the bitmap without actually doing something, you are not going to update the PCDM application just yet. Section 10.2 will add the blit function to your class. You can debug through the code to test it if you like.

 The final source code of this section can be found on the companion CD under "\Sources\ThreadExample\PCDMUI\Step6".

10.2 Displaying Bitmaps Using GDI

System DLL:	CORE.DLL
Include file:	Core.h
Help file:	CEGUIDE.CHM (MSDN 10/98 and later)
Available since:	Windows CE 1.0
API prefix/suffix:	Blt
InitCommonControlEx flag:	—
MFC class:	—

Bitmaps get "blitted" into a device context in the same way as they are on blitted on desktop windows. "BitBlt" and "StretchBlt" are supported on all Windows CE platforms and versions. Exceptions, of course, are platforms without the GDI subsystems, such as the AutoPC and headless devices. On Windows CE 1.x, only four raster operations are supported:

- SRCAND
- SRCCOPY
- SRCINVERT
- SRCPAINT

If you are targeting Windows CE 1.x, you might have to call "BitBlt" multiple times in order to get the same result as a later raster operation. In Section 10.1, you "blitted" a bitmap into a window using the "BitBlit" and "StretchBlt" functions; therefore I will skip the usual code snippet for now and will jump right to the "PCDMUI.DLL" update.

10.2.1 Updating the OnDraw Method of the PCDMPicture Class

To get the bitmap out on the device context of your control is actually pretty simple. All you have to do is update the "OnDraw" method of the class and force the control to call the "OnDraw" method. As you know, you should not just call the "OnDraw" method, but rather use the ATL method "FireViewChange".

1. Add the following two lines of code to the end of the "Load" method before "return S_OK;":

```
if (m_hBitmap!=NULL || m_lpSrcDIB!=NULL)
    FireViewChange();
```

The only other change you need to make is to update the "OnDraw" method.

2. Change the "OnDraw" method with the following code:

```
HRESULT CPCDMPicture::OnDraw(ATL_DRAWINFO& di)
{
RECT& rc = *(RECT*)di.prcBounds;
RECT            bRC;
HDC             hSourceDC;
HBITMAP         hSourceBitmap, hOldSourceBitmap;

    if (m_hBitmap==NULL && m_lpSrcDIB==NULL)        return S_OK;

    hSourceDC = CreateCompatibleDC( di.hdcDraw );
    bRC.left=0; bRC.top=0;
    if (m_lpSrcDIB!=NULL)
    {
        LPBITMAPINFO lpbmi = (LPBITMAPINFO)m_lpSrcDIB;
        LPBYTE       lpSourceBits;
        DWORD        dwSourceBitsSize;

        hSourceBitmap = CreateDIBSection( di.hdcDraw, lpbmi,
                    DIB_RGB_COLORS, (void **)&lpSourceBits,
```

```
                              NULL, 0 );
            dwSourceBitsSize = lpbmi->bmiHeader.biHeight *
                              BytesPerLine(&(lpbmi->bmiHeader));
            memcpy( lpSourceBits, FindDIBBits((LPSTR)lpbmi),
                    dwSourceBitsSize );
            bRC.right=lpbmi->bmiHeader.biWidth;
            bRC.bottom=lpbmi->bmiHeader.biHeight;
    }
    else
    {

            BITMAP bm;

            hSourceBitmap=m_hBitmap;
        GetObject (m_hBitmap, sizeof(BITMAP), &bm);
            bRC.right=bm.bmWidth;
            bRC.bottom=bm.bmHeight;
    }


    hOldSourceBitmap = (HBITMAP)SelectObject( hSourceDC,
hSourceBitmap );
    if( rc.right-rc.left!= bRC.right ||
  rc.bottom-rc.top!=bRC.bottom)
        StretchBlt( di.hdcDraw, rc.left,  rc.top, rc.right,
  rc.bottom, hSourceDC, 0, 0, bRC.right,
  bRC.bottom, SRCCOPY );
    else
        BitBlt( di.hdcDraw, rc.left,  rc.top, rc.right,
rc.bottom, hSourceDC, 0, 0, SRCCOPY );

    // Clean up and delete the DCs
    SelectObject( hSourceDC, hOldSourceBitmap );
    DeleteDC( hSourceDC );
    return S_OK;
}
```

That was quick. Now test it in eMbedded Visual Basic, but first load and compile the PCDMUI-component desktop project.

 The final source code of this section can be found on the companion CD under "\Sources\ThreadExample\PCDMUI\Step7".

10.2.2 Testing the PCDMPicture Class in eMbedded Visual Basic

As usual, begin with a quick test in eVB.

1. Create a new H/PC Professional project.
2. Add the "PCDMUI Library" to the list of custom controls and add the "PCDMPicture" control and a button to the form.
3. Add the following line of code to the button's "OnClick" method:

```
PCDMPicture1.Load "\Windows\Startup.bmp",0
```

Now launch the application and click on the button. The startup bitmap should be visible as soon as you hit the button.

 The final source code of this section can be found on the companion CD under "\Sources\Chapter 10\10.2"

10.2.3 Updating the PCDM Application

Let's add some fun to your PCDM application. So far, you have a pretty boring "About" box. Let's liven it up with a nice bitmap.

1. Load the last version of the PCDM application project and open the "IDD_ABOUTBOX" dialog box resource.
2. Add the "PCDMPicture" control to dialog box and let the class wizard generate the "CPCDMPicture" class for it. Name the member variable "m_Picture".
3. Now open the "PCDM.cpp" file and locate the "CaboutDlg" class. Copy everything that belongs to the class and move it into the "PCDMView.CPP" file.

An even better option is to create a separate implementation and header file for the class.

4. Now locate the "OnInitDialog" method of the "CAboutDlg" class and add the following line before the "CenterWindow()" call:

```
m_Picture.Load(TEXT("\\windows\\startup.bmp"),0);
```

The last addition to your code is the following new "case" branch for the "OnCmdBarActionCommander" method of the "PCDMView" class:

```
case 35:
{
      CAboutDlg aboutDlg;
      aboutDlg.DoModal();
}
```

If you start the PCDM application again, you will see the familiar "startup.bmp" in the "About" box. Please feel free to add whatever bitmap you'd like to see there. If you try to give a resource ID to the "PCDMPicture" class that resides inside the PCDM application, you will not see it. The "Load" method of this class looks for the resource inside "PCDMUI.DLL". You can add it to the resources of that DLL if you like.

 The final source code of this section can be found on the companion CD under "\Sources\ThreadExample\PCDM CE\Step8".

10.3   Playing Sounds Using the Windows CE API

System DLL:	CORE.DLL
Include file:	Core.h
Help file:	CEGUIDE.CHM (MSDN 10/98 and later)
Available since:	Windows CE 1.0
API prefix/suffix:	—
InitCommonControlEx flag:	—
MFC class:	—

This section will be the shortest of all. Up to Version 2.11, Windows CE only supports one high-level sound function: "SndPlaySound." It is used in the same way that you would use it on the desktop. Therefore I will not discuss it in any detail.

I do want to mention an error in the Windows CE SDK documentation and platform SDK. The "SndPlaySound" function is supported in Windows CE 1.0 and does not require the "mmsystem.h" include file. The standard "core.h" contains the function prototype, and unlike on the desktop, "SndPlaySound" is exposed through "CORE.DLL" instead of through the multimedia DLL. If you are interested in programming the low-level audio waveform drivers, please refer to the documentation of the Windows CE DDK.

10.3.1 Adding a Sound to the PCDM Application

This will be just a tiny add-on to your application.

1. Change the code of the "CaboutDlg::OnInitDialog()" method to

```
BOOL CAboutDlg::OnInitDialog()
{
    CDialog::OnInitDialog();

    m_Picture.Load(TEXT("\\windows\\startup.bmp"),0);
    sndPlaySound(TEXT("\\windows\\exclam.wav"),SND_ASYNC);
    CenterWindow();

    return TRUE;
}
```

As soon as you hit the "About" button, you will hear a tiny sound.

 The final source code of this section can be found on the companion CD under "\Sources\ThreadExample\PCDM CE\Step8".

10.4 DirectX on Windows CE

If your application requires high-speed graphics and video playback, DirectX is your only alternative. Microsoft has shipped a DirectX pack to its OEMs in addition to the Windows CE 2.12 Platform Builder. At the time this book went to press, no DirectX device was available.

11 Chapter

Miscellaneous Topics

This chapter describes a lot of interesting technologies that you might encounter during your own development for Windows CE.

11.1 Enhancements for Pocket PC Devices

System DLL:	Aygshell.dll
Include file:	aygshell.h
Library file:	Coredsip.lib
Help file:	CEGUIDE.CHM (MSDN 10/98 and later)
Available since:	Windows CE 3.00
API prefix/suffix:	SH . . .
InitCommonControlEx flag:	—
MFC class:	—

The latest addition to the family of companion devices adds another round of funny versioning issues to the Windows CE world. The new palm-size PC (Version 2.0), officially named the "Pocket PC" and code-named "Rapier," runs Windows CE Version 3.0. With it, Microsoft introduced a completely new user interface for the first time. The new user interface shows several improvements:

- The taskbar was relocated to the top of the screen.
- The Special Input Panel (SIP) is now on the application menu bar located on the bottom of the screen and appears automatically if it is needed.
- All controls are flattened with no cascading menus in order to improve readability.
- Child windows and dialog boxes are full pages.

As you learned in Section 7.3, to support this new UI the developer has to do some extra work. In this section of the book you will learn about some additional features and issues to watch for. Some of them are already requirements for the "Designed for Pocket PC" logo requirement.

11.1.1 Window Size Must Be Calculated Differently

Figure 11.1 shows the new design of the Pocket PC user interface. As you can see, the client area that can be used by an application is now smaller than it was on the older devices.

The application menu bar on the bottom of the screen and the caption bar on the top of the screen have to be calculated in your application before you create your main window. The following code shows you how to get the correct size, even taking into consideration whether the SIP is open.

```
int iDelta, x = CW_USEDEFAULT, y = CW_USEDEFAULT,
            cx= CW_USEDEFAULT, cy= CW_USEDEFAULT;
SIPINFO si = {0};
HWND hwnd = NULL;
si.cbSize = sizeof(si);
SHSipInfo(SPI_GETSIPINFO, 0, &si, 0);
iDelta = (si.fdwFlags & SIPF_ON) ? 0 : MENU_HEIGHT;
// MENU_HEIGHT is 26
cx = si.rcVisibleDesktop.right - si.rcVisibleDesktop.left;
cy = si.rcVisibleDesktop.bottom - si.rcVisibleDesktop.top - iDelta;
hwnd = CreateWindow(lpClassName, lpWindowName, dwStyle,
                    x, y, cx, cy, NULL, NULL, hInstance, lpParam);
```

Most of your legacy code—and even the code that the eVC application wizard generates—continues to use "CW_USEDEFAULT" only for the "cx" and "cy" coordinates of the window and "0, 0" for the x and y coordinates. As a result, the window will be 26 pixels too large and the top 26 pixels will be beneath the taskbar. If you use

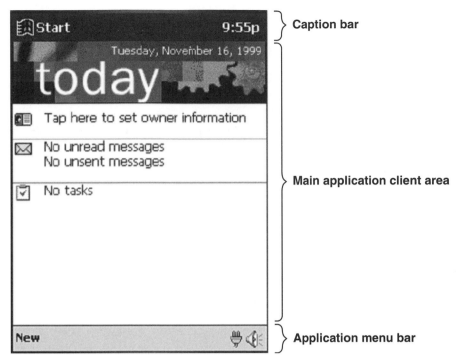

Figure 11.1   A Pocket PC emulation window

"CW_USEDEFAULTS" for the x and y coordinates as well, you get at the right position of the window under the caption bar. Check out the next section for a small code sample using this technique.

11.1.2   Only Full-Screen Dialog Boxes

Here comes one of the logo requirements: All dialog boxes on the Pocket PC must be full-screen. Microsoft completed a lot of usability studies with the older versions of the palm-size PC and found that most non-Windows users of the palm-size PC had difficulty in understanding the concept of dialog boxes. To remedy this, Microsoft now requires that all dialog boxes be full-screen windows.

For that purpose Microsoft has introduced a new API call that initializes a dialog box for Pocket PC full-screen mode called "SHInitDialog". As you know, all APIs starting with "SH . . ." are related to the "Shell" and are contained in the "aygshell.dll". This new method is no exception. Since that DLL is not present on other devices, a developer has to be sure that he or she is running on a Pocket PC device before calling this function. In general, I recommend the procedure shown in Section 7.9.1, "A Simple Application Showing the SIP," to deal with the "aygshell.dll". The MFC uses the right dialog box method automatically, so the developer does not have to worry about it.

11.1.3   A Tiny Example

Here is a tiny application for the Pocket PC that deals with the issues of full-screen dialog boxes and shows how to correctly calculate window size.

1. Launch eVC and create a new project called "SizeIt", using the "WCE Application" template.

2. In the "WCE Application Wizard", select "A typical "Hello World" application".

In the "InitInstance" method you will find that the "CreateWindow" call is still using "0,0,CW_USEDEFAULTS,CW_USEDEFAULTS".

3. Rewrite the "InitInstance" method to

```
BOOL InitInstance(HINSTANCE hInstance, int nCmdShow)
{
        HWND        hWnd;
        TCHAR       szTitle[MAX_LOADSTRING];        // The title bar text
        TCHAR       szWindowClass[MAX_LOADSTRING];// The window class
name

        hInst = hInstance; / Store instance handle in your global
        variable
        // Initialize global strings
        LoadString(hInstance, IDC_SIZEIT, szWindowClass,
        MAX_LOADSTRING);
        MyRegisterClass(hInstance, szWindowClass);

        LoadString(hInstance, IDS_APP_TITLE, szTitle, MAX_LOADSTRING);

        int iDelta, x = CW_USEDEFAULT, y = CW_USEDEFAULT,
                    cx= CW_USEDEFAULT, cy= CW_USEDEFAULT;

        hAygDll = LoadLibrary(TEXT("aygshell.dll"));
        if (hAygDll)
        {
                g_hSHInitDialog =(SHINIDIALOGPROC)GetProcAddress(hAygDll,
```

```
                                                TEXT
                                                ("SHInitDialog"));
          if (g_hSHInitDialog) isRapier=TRUE;

          SIPINFO si = {0};
          si.cbSize = sizeof(si);
          g_hSHSipInfo =(SHSIPINFOPROC)GetProcAddress(hAygDll,
                                            TEXT("SHSipInfo"));
          (*g_hSHSipInfo)(SPI_GETSIPINFO, 0, &si, 0);
          MENU_HEIGHT = (isRapier) ? 26 : 0;
          iDelta = (si.fdwFlags & SIPF_ON) ? 0 : MENU_HEIGHT;

          cx = si.rcVisibleDesktop.right -
          si.rcVisibleDesktop.left;
          cy = si.rcVisibleDesktop.bottom - si.rcVisibleDesktop.top -
              iDelta;
     }
     hWnd = CreateWindow(szWindowClass, szTitle, WS_VISIBLE,
          x, y, cx, cy, NULL, NULL, hInstance, NULL);

     if (!hWnd)
     {
          return FALSE;
     }

     ShowWindow(hWnd, nCmdShow);
     UpdateWindow(hWnd);
     if (!isRapier)
          if (hwndCB)
              CommandBar_Show(hwndCB, TRUE);

     return TRUE;
}
```

As you can see, you are probing to see whether "aygshell.dll" is present. Only if the "SHInitDialog" function returns a valid program address can you be sure that you are running on a Pocket PC device. You could also use your "GetCePlatform" helper from Section 4.6.3 to determine this.

4. The following section declaring some global variables has to be inserted before the "InitInstance" method:

```
#include <aygshell.h>
typedef BOOL (*SHCREATEMENUBARPROC)(SHMENUBARINFO *pmbi);
typedef BOOL (*SHINIDIALOGPROC)(PSHINITDLGINFO pshidi);
typedef BOOL (*SHSIPINFOPROC)(UINT uiAction, UINT uiParam, PVOID
pvParam, UINT fWinIni);
        SHSIPINFOPROC        g_hSHSipInfo        = NULL;
        SHINIDIALOGPROC      g_hSHInitDialog     = NULL;
        SHCREATEMENUBARPROC  g_hSHCreateMenuBar  = NULL;
        HINSTANCE       hAygDll;
        BOOL        isRapier=FALSE;
        int         MENU_HEIGHT;
```

You learned in Section 7.3 that the Pocket PC has a new "application menu bar" that comes with new resources. To show an application's "About" box, you must make three changes.

5. Open the "sizeIt.RC" file in text mode and add the following lines. Start by changing "IDM_MENU" menu resource:

```
IDM_MENU MENU DISCARDABLE
BEGIN
    POPUP "&File"
    BEGIN
        MENUITEM "&About",     IDM_HELP_ABOUT
        MENUITEM "E&xit",      IDM_FILE_EXIT
    END
END

IDR_MAIN_MENU RCDATA DISCARDABLE
BEGIN
  //Popup menu name
  IDM_MENU,
  //Count of items to put on the menu
  1,
  I_IMAGENONE, IDM_MAIN_MENUITEM2, TBSTATE_ENABLED,
  TBSTYLE_DROPDOWN | TBSTYLE_AUTOSIZE,
  IDS_MAIN_MENUITEM2, 0, 0,
END

STRINGTABLE DISCARDABLE
BEGIN
```

```
        IDS_MAIN_MENUITEM2        "File"
END
```

6.   Add the definition of "IDR_MAIN_MENU" to "resource.h":

```
#define IDR_MAIN_MENU                      100
#define IDS_MAIN_MENUITEM2                 203
#define IDM_MAIN_MENUITEM2                 303
```

You can also use the resource editor to make these changes. To get to the Pocket PC's resource editor, you have to switch to the palm-size PC 3.0 mode first. Otherwise you will see the standard menu editor. Also, to be able to compile the same application for an H/PC Professional or other Windows CE device, you must insert the following two lines into the "Resource Includes" dialog box:

```
#include <commctrl.h>
#define I_IMAGENONE   (-2)
```

Next, change the "WM_CREATE" branch of the main window message handler "WndProc":

```
        case WM_CREATE:
    if (isRapier)
    {
        SHMENUBARINFO mbi;
        memset(&mbi, 0, sizeof(SHMENUBARINFO));
        mbi.cbSize      = sizeof(SHMENUBARINFO);
        mbi.hwndParent = hWnd;
        mbi.nToolBarId = IDR_MAIN_MENU;
        mbi.hInstRes    = hInst;
        mbi.nBmpId      = 0;
        mbi.cBmpImages = 0;

        g_hSHCreateMenuBar =(SHCREATEMENUBARPROC)
        GetProcAddress(hAygDll, TEXT("SHCreateMenuBar"));
        (*g_hSHCreateMenuBar)(&mbi);
        hwndCB = mbi.hwndMB;
    }
    else
    {
        hwndCB = CommandBar_Create(hInst, hWnd, 1);
```

```
        CommandBar_InsertMenubar(hwndCB, hInst, IDM_MENU, 0);
        CommandBar_AddAdornments(hwndCB, 0, 0);
    }
    break;
```

The last change that you need to make is in the "About" box's message handler. Here you will add a section to the "WM_INITDIALOG" branch to activate the full-screen attributes of this dialog box.

7. Change the "WM_INITDIALOG" branch of the "About" box message handler to the following code:

```
case WM_INITDIALOG:
    if (isRapier)
    {
        SHINITDLGINFO shidi;
        shidi.dwMask = SHIDIM_FLAGS;
        shidi.dwFlags = SHIDIF_DONEBUTTON |
                        SHIDIF_SIPDOWN |
                        SHIDIF_SIZEDLGFULLSCREEN;
            shidi.hDlg = hDlg;
            (*g_hSHInitDialog)(&shidi);
        }
        else
        {
            if (GetWindowRect(hDlg, &rt1)) {
            GetClientRect(GetParent(hDlg), &rt);
            DlgWidth     = rt1.right - rt1.left;
            DlgHeight    = rt1.bottom - rt1.top ;
            NewPosX= (rt.right - rt.left - DlgWidth)/2;
            NewPosY= (rt.bottom - rt.top - DlgHeight)/2;
// if the About box is larger than the physical screen
            if (NewPosX < 0) NewPosX = 0;
            if (NewPosY < 0) NewPosY = 0;
            SetWindowPos(hDlg, 0, NewPosX, NewPosY,
                    0, 0, SWP_NOZORDER | SWP_NOSIZE);
            }
        }
        return TRUE;
```

You can now run your application. You should see "Hello World" in the middle of the screen. If you select "About" in the application menu on the bottom, you will see the full-screen "About" box. For your PCDM application you will not need to do anything because the MFC will take care of the new features for the Pocket PC.

 The final source code of this section can be found on the companion CD under "\Sources\Chapter 11\11.1".

11.1.4   Summary

Let me recap the various improvements made in the new Pocket PC and their implementation. The Pocket PC

- Has a new user interface that requires some new API calls. Those APIs can be found in "aygshell.dll", but might not be available on other platforms. The best way to remain source-code compatible is to work with "LoadLibrary" and "GetProcAddress".

- Has a new application menu bar, located on the bottom of the screen, and uses "SHCreateMenuBar" to create it (see Sections 7.3 and 11.1.3 for sample code).

- Requires full-screen dialog boxes you have to initialize in the "WM_INIT-DIALOG" message handler (see Section 11.1.2 for details).

- Automatically deals with the SIP and has a screen 26 pixels smaller than older palm-size PCs. Therefore you have to create any application window "CW_USEDEFAULT" for all coordinates and length parameters of "CreateWindow" (see Section 11.1.3 for sample code).

- Has flattened controls with no cascading menus in its UI. You actually do not have to do anything for this. Just be aware that you cannot create pop-up menus anymore.

- Allows instant installation and runs from Compact Flash RAM cards (CF-Card). You can copy your application's CAB file to a CF-Card and create a special "autorun.exe" to run install the application from the CF-Card when it is inserted. Using the new CEF (Common Executable Format), you can even give your application processor independence (see Section 11.5.3).

11.2   Creating Help Files for Your Application

This section explains the Windows CE help system. Although the need for tons of help files on a small device is debatable—especially if you can keep them on the desktop—this section will describe how to design, create, and use Windows CE help files.

The Windows CE help system is based wholly on HTML. Back in Windows CE Version 2.0, Microsoft used the file extension ".HTP". With Version 2.01, Microsoft changed the extension to ".HTM" to keep it in sync with the desktop. But other than the file extension, the files are identical.

Help files for Windows CE are created the same way as they are for the desktop:

- First, create your help files.
- Then create an index.
- And then link it to your application.

"PegHelp.exe" is responsible for displaying the help file during runtime and for reacting when the user presses ALT-H or the "Help" button in applications.

Before you add the help page for your PCDM application, here are some tips and some differences between HTML on the desktop and in Windows CE:

- The Windows CE Help/HTML engine does not support JPG and GIF yet. If you want to include images, you must use the ".2BP", two-color bitmap format.
- To create multiple help topics in a single ".HTM file", you can use the following tag:

```
<!-- PegHelp --!>
```

- With the following tag, you can create page breaks inside topics. This will improve the help file's readability, especially on palm-size PCs:

```
<!- **Topic Break** -!>
```

- To create an index, just create a list of "<A HREF . . . >" tags.
- If you want to jump to a bookmark within the same file, you still have to use the file name in the HREF address. In other words, if you want to jump to the bookmark "Test" in the file "PCDM.HTM", you must use the following HREF:

```
<A HREF="PCDM.HTM#Test">
```

11.2.1　Creating a Help File for the PCDM Application

To keep it simple, your PCDM application will have a help file that explains the working menu commands and includes two short "How to . . ." sections. You can use FrontPage to create the help file. If you prefer the world-famous HTML editor NotePad, you can use it instead.

First, you need to create the topics for the help file. Then you will create the index.

1. Start your HTML editor, create a new HTM file named "PCDM.HTM", and add the following topics to it:

```
<A NAME="Send_To"></A><B>Send to...</B>
<blockquote>
  <p>Sends a CD description to another Windows CE device,
running the Pocket-CD-Manager.</p>
  <p>To receive a CD description, select this item on the
target device first, then select &quot;Send To...&quot; on the
source device.</p>
</blockquote>

<B>See Also</B><BR>
<A HREF="PCDM.htm#Receive">Receive...</A><BR>
<A HREF="PCDM.htm#Send_a_file">How to send a CD description</A><BR>
<BR CLEAR=ALL >
<!- PegHelp ->
<HR>
<!- **********Topic Break********** ->
<A NAME="Receive"></A><B>Receive...</B>
<blockquote>
  <p>Receives a CD description from another Windows CE device,
running the Pocket-CD-Manager.</p>
  <p>To receive a CD description, select this item on the target
device first, then select &quot;Send To...&quot; on the
source device.</p>
</blockquote>

<B>See Also</B><BR>
<A HREF="PCDM.htm#Send_to">Send to...</A><BR>
<A HREF="PCDM.htm#Send_a_file">How to send a CD description</A><BR>
<BR CLEAR=ALL >
<!- PegHelp ->
<HR>
<!- **********Topic Break********** ->
<A NAME="Details"></A><B>Show Details</B>
<blockquote>
  <p>Sends a CD description to another Windows CE device,
running the Pocket-CD-Manager.</p>
</blockquote>
<!- PegHelp ->
```

```
<HR>
<!- **********Topic Break********** ->
<A NAME="About"></A><B>About</B>
<blockquote>
  <p>Shows the actual information of the Pocket-CD-Manager.</p>
</blockquote>
<!- PegHelp ->
<HR>
<!- **********Topic Break********** ->
<A NAME="Exit"></A><B>Exit</B>
<blockquote>
  <p>Quits the Pocket-CD-Manager.</p>
</blockquote>
<!- PegHelp ->
<HR>
<!- **********Topic Break********** ->
<A NAME="send_a_file"></A><B>How to send a CD description</B>
<blockquote>
  <ol>
    <li>Select &quot;Receive...&quot; on the target device</li>
    <li>Select the record you want to send on the source device</li>
    <li>Select &quot;Send to...&quot; on the source device</li>
    <li>In case you are using the IrDA port, line up the two
devices</li>
  </ol>
  <p>If the transfer was successful, you will see the new description
 on the target device.</p>
</blockquote>
<!- PegHelp ->
<HR>
<!- **********Topic Break********** ->
<A NAME="synchronize"></A><B>How to synchronize with the desktop</B>
<blockquote>
  <p>Synchronization of the Pocket-CD-Manager database is
automatically done if you connect to the desktop. Just make sure
that the Access file synchronization is installed in the ActiveSync
on the desktop.</p>
</blockquote>
<!- PegHelp ->
<HR>
<!- **********Topic Break********** ->
```

In the topics "Send to . . ." and "Receive . . ." you will find a "See Also" section that is simply done with "<A HREF>" tags.

2. Add the following index to the top of the file:

```
<!DOCTYPE HTML PUBLIC "-//W3C//DTD HTML 3.2 Final//EN">
<HTML>
<HEAD>
<META HTTP-EQUIV="Htm-Help" CONTENT="pcdm.htm#Main_Contents">
<TITLE>Pocket-CD-Manager Help</TITLE>
</HEAD>
<BODY BGCOLOR="#FFFFFF" TEXT="#000000">
<!- PegHelp ->
<P><A NAME="Main_Contents"></A><B>Pocket-CD-Manager Help</B></P>
<p>Welcome to the Pocket-CD-Manager<p>
<p>Learn how to...</P>
<blockquote>
<A HREF="PCDM.htm#Send_To">Send to...</A><BR>
<A HREF="PCDM.htm#Receive">Receive...</A><BR>
<A HREF="PCDM.htm#Details">Show Details</A><BR>
<A HREF="PCDM.htm#About">About</A><BR>
<A HREF="PCDM.htm#Exit">Exit</A><BR>
<A HREF="PCDM.htm#Send_a_file">How to send a CD Description</A><BR>
<A HREF="PCDM.htm#synchronize">How to synchronize</a><br>
</blockquote>
<BR CLEAR=ALL>
<!- PegHelp -><HR>
<!- **************************TOPIC BREAK************************** ->
```

The "<META>" tag in the header of the help file tells "PegHelp.exe" where to find the content of the file and that this ".HTM" file is a Windows CE help file. Now you can copy the new "PCDM.htm" file into your device's "Windows" directory and launch it from the "Start, Run" menu with the following command:

```
Peghelp.exe \PCDM.HTM
```

The first time you launch "PegHelp.exe" you will see the help file with all topics. But as soon as you click on one of the links in the index, you will see only the topic you selected. Clicking on the "Contents" button in the help system menu bar will also show the content without all the other topics.

If you click on "Help" in the start menu, you get a list of all available help files on your Windows CE device. You can get this list by selecting "All Topics" in the help system menu bar, too.

3. To integrate the "Pocket-CD-Manager" help file you have to create a tiny file named "Pocket-CD-Manager.lnk" and copy it to the directory "\Windows\ help". The content of the file looks like this:

```
18#\windows\PCDM.htm
```

The Windows CE documentation tells you that the "18" describes the number of characters in the "PCDM.HTM" file. I tried using different numbers and found that all of them worked.

As soon as you copy this file into the "\Windows\help" directory, you can select the "Help" menu from the "Start" menu and you will see "Pocket-CD-Manager" in the list of all "Help Contents".

 The final source code of this section can be found on the companion CD under "\Sources\ThreadExample\PCDMHelp".

11.2.2   Calling the Help File from within the PCDM Application

Calling your new help file from the PCDM application is very simple. The only thing you have to do is to call the "PegHelp" application from your command-bar message handler.

1. Load the latest version of the PCDM application and open "CPCDMView.cpp".
2. Locate "OnCmdBarActionCommander" and add the following new branch to the "ID" switch:

```
case 34:
    {
        CreateProcess(TEXT("peghelp.exe"),
                    TEXT("file:PCDM.htm#Main_Contents"),
                    NULL, NULL, FALSE, 0, NULL,
                    NULL, NULL, NULL);
    }
  break;
```

Copy and download the new version and test it on your device.

 The final source code of this section can be found on the companion CD under "\Sources\ThreadExample\PCDM CE\Step9".

11.3   Creating a Control Panel Application

The way you create an applet for Windows CE is exactly the same as creating one for the desktop. There is a very nice article in MSDN on how to do this using MFC. You'll find this article in the MSDN documentation under:

```
Technical Articles
    Visual Tools
        Visual C++
            Visual C++ 2.0
              478Creating Win32 Control Panel Applets with
              Visual C++
```

Creating a control panel applet is as simple as creating a regular DLL. The only difference is that you have to support one specific entry point "CplApplet" to make your DLL become a control panel applet. You also have to install the DLL into the "\Windows" directory and give it the file extension ".CPL". You can export multiple virtual control panel applet applications from one ".CPL" file. The "CplApplet" function will be called for each of those applications.

 One major difference between desktop Windows and Windows CE is that you have to process the "CPL_NEWINQUIRE" message instead of the "CPL_INQUIRE" message.

Let's create a very tiny control panel application that just shows a message box.

1. Create a new "Simple WCE Link Library" with eMbedded Visual C++ named "ClpIt" and open "ClpIt.cpp" in the source editor.

2. Add the following function "CplApplet" to the file:

```
#include "cpl.h"
#include "resource.h"
HANDLE  hinst = NULL;

LONG CALLBACK CPlApplet(HWND hwndCPL, UINT uMsg, LPARAM lParam1,
LPARAM lParam2)
{
int i;
```

```
LPCPLINFO lpCPlInfo;
LPNEWCPLINFO lpNewCPlInfo;

    i = (int) lParam1;

    switch (uMsg) {
        case CPL_INIT:        // first message
                              // save hInstance in case you need it
            hinst = GetModuleHandle(TEXT("CplIt.cpl"));
            return TRUE;

        case CPL_GETCOUNT:  // second message
            return 1; // Number of virtual Applet "Applications"
            break;

        case CPL_INQUIRE: // third message, sent once per application
                          // Will not be called under Windows CE
            lpCPlInfo = (LPCPLINFO) lParam2;
            lpCPlInfo->lData = 0; // Semd as lParam2 to CPL_DBLCLK
            lpCPlInfo->idIcon = IDI_ICON1;
            lpCPlInfo->idName = IDS_NAME;
            lpCPlInfo->idInfo = IDS_DESC;
            break;
        case CPL_NEWINQUIRE: // third message,sent once per
        application
            lpNewCPlInfo = (LPNEWCPLINFO) lParam2;
            lpNewCPlInfo->dwSize = sizeof(NEWCPLINFO); // Important
            lpNewCPlInfo->dwFlags = 0;
            lpNewCPlInfo->dwHelpContext = 0;
            lpNewCPlInfo->lData = 0;
            lpNewCPlInfo->hIcon = LoadIcon((HINSTANCE)hinst,
                                           MAKEINTRESOURCE
                                           (IDI_ICON1));
            wcscpy(lpNewCPlInfo->szName, TEXT("My First Applet"));
            wcscpy(lpNewCPlInfo->szInfo,
                   TEXT("My First Control Panel Applet"));
            wcscpy(lpNewCPlInfo->szHelpFile, TEXT(""));
            break;

        case CPL_DBLCLK:     // application icon double-clicked
            MessageBox(NULL,TEXT("My first Control-Panel Applet"),
```

```
                        TEXT("CplIt.CPL"),MB_OK);
            break;

        case CPL_STOP:    // sent once per application before CPL_EXIT
            break;

        case CPL_EXIT:    // sent once before FreeLibrary is called
            break;

        default:
            break;
    }
    return 0;
}
```

As mentioned before, the "CplApplet" function is the main function called by the control panel. Without it your applet will not work.

3. Now you only have to add the two resource strings "IDS_NAME" and "IDS_DESC", add the "IDI_ICON1", and define the "CplApplet" function in a "Clpit.def" file that looks like this:

```
; CplIt.def : Declares the module parameters for the DLL.

LIBRARY        "CPLIT"
;DESCRIPTION   'CPLIT Windows CE Dynamic Link Library'

EXPORTS
    ; Explicit exports can go here
CPlApplet
```

4. Name the strings as you like and paint an icon, or use one you already have.

You can now compile the applet, but eMbedded Visual Tools will copy the applet into the root of your Windows CE device.

5. Rename it to "CplIt.cpl" and copy it to the "\Windows" directory.

If you now launch the control panel you will see your new applet. On the Pocket PC the applet is showing up in the System category of the control panel.

 The final source code of this section can be found on the companion CD under "\Sources\Chapter 11\11.2".

11.4   Adding an Icon to the Taskbar

Another advanced topic some applications will have to deal with is to putting an icon in the notification area of the taskbar. On palm-size PCs this has become an interesting method to bring an application that is running in the background to the foreground.

The work a developer has to do is very simple. All you need is to add one API call to your application to add, delete, or modify the icons in the taskbar:

```
BOOL Shell_NotifyIcon(DWORD dwMessage, PNOTIFYICONDATE pnid);
```

The "PNOTIFYICONDATE" structure requires a handle to your application window that will deal with mouse messages like "WM_MOUSEMOVE" or "WM_LBUTTONDOWN". The only difference between desktop Windows and Windows CE is the missing support of tool tips on Windows CE.

11.4.1   Adding a Taskbar Icon to Your PCDM Application

Adding an "Alive" icon to the taskbar is a task for the PCDM application itself rather than for any of your components.

1. Load the last version of the PCDM application project and open the "Mainframe.cpp" file.

The definitions for the shell functions are in the include file "ShellAPI.h".

2. Add "#include <ShellAPI.H>" to the top of the "mainframe.cpp" file.

3. Now locate the "Cmainframe::OnCreate" method and change it to the following code:

```
int CMainFrame::OnCreate(LPCREATESTRUCT lpCreateStruct)
{
    if (CFrameWnd::OnCreate(lpCreateStruct) == -1)
        return -1;


NOTIFYICONDATA nid;

    nid.cbSize=sizeof(NOTIFYICONDATA);
    nid.hWnd=this->GetSafeHwnd();
    nid.uID=222;
    nid.uFlags=NIF_ICON|NIF_MESSAGE;
    nid.uCallbackMessage=WM_PCDM_TASKBARNOTIFY;
```

```
nid.hIcon=(HICON)::LoadImage(::AfxGetInstanceHandle(),
           MAKEINTRESOURCE(IDR_MAINFRAME),IMAGE_ICON,16,16,0);
nid.szTip[0]='\0';
Shell_NotifyIcon(NIM_ADD,&nid);
return 0;
}
```

4. The "WM_PCDM_TASKBARNOTIFY" message has to be defined in "Mainframe.h":

```
#define WM_PCDM_TASKBARNOTIFY      (WM_USER + 222)
```

The "nid.uID" identifier for your icon ensures that you can delete it as soon as "CMainFrame" gets destroyed. This code will now add an icon to the taskbar as soon as "CMainFrame" is created. To be a good citizen, you are going to remove the icon before your application exits. Many applications do not do this step and leave a "dead" icon behind.

5. Create a new message handler for the "WM_DESTROY" message and add the following code to its implementation:

```
void CMainFrame::OnDestroy()
{
     CFrameWnd::OnDestroy();
NOTIFYICONDATA nid;

     memset(&nid,0,sizeof(nid));
     nid.cbSize=sizeof(NOTIFYICONDATA);
     nid.hWnd=this->GetSafeHwnd();
     nid.uID=222;
     Shell_NotifyIcon(NIM_DELETE,&nid);
}
```

Now you have the icon in the toolbar, but you also want it to do something if the user single-taps on it: You simply want to bring your application window to the front. To implement this, you have to add your message handler for the "WM_PCDM_TASKBARNOTIFY" message to the chain of MFC messages. Therefore you have to make three additions to the "CMainFrame" class.

6. First add the following line immediately before the "DECLARE_MESSAGE_MAP()" macro in the "CMainFrame" class definition in "mainframe.h":

```
afx_msg void OnPCDMTaskbarNotify(WPARAM wParam,LPARAM lParam);
```

7. Then add the bold line to the message map in "Mainframe.cpp":

```
BEGIN_MESSAGE_MAP(CMainFrame, CFrameWnd)
    //{{AFX_MSG_MAP(CMainFrame)
    ON_WM_CREATE()
    ON_WM_HELPINFO()
    ON_WM_DESTROY()
    //}}AFX_MSG_MAP
    // Global help commands
    ON_MESSAGE(WM_PCDM_TASKBARNOTIFY,OnPCDMTaskbarNotify)
    ON_COMMAND(ID_HELP, CFrameWnd::OnHelp)
END_MESSAGE_MAP()
```

8. Add the following method to "Mainframe.cpp":

```
void CMainFrame::OnPCDMTaskbarNotify(WPARAM wParam,LPARAM lParam)
{
    switch(lParam)
    {
        case WM_LBUTTONDOWN:
        case WM_RBUTTONDOWN:
                    this->SetForegroundWindow();
            break;
        case WM_MOUSEMOVE:
        case WM_LBUTTONDBLCLK:
        default:
            break;
    }
}
```

If you now compile and run your application, you will find a new icon in the taskbar. Hide the PCDM application by starting Windows CE Explorer. Now click on the icon in the taskbar. The PCDM application should come to the front.

 The final source code of this section can be found on the companion CD under "\Sources\ThreadExample\PCDM CE\Step10".

11.5 Installation for Windows CE

Installation has become a big part of development for any Windows-based application. Windows CE is no different. It even requires a two-step installation procedure. First, the bits have to be installed on your desktop PC and then they must be installed on the actual device. This section will show you how to create a setup for Windows CE and the corresponding desktop part using the new MSI (**M**icrosoft **I**nstaller for Windows) technology.

11.5.1   Installation Targeting Windows CE

To avoid the same installation chaos that was common on the desktop for a long time, Microsoft created a common installer technology for Windows CE from the ground up. Whereas for Windows CE 1.0 you had to call a certain API function in a provided DLL, for Windows CE 2.0 the CE Application Manager (CeAppMgr.exe) in the ActiveSync directory takes over the desktop part of managing the installation.

An installation for Windows CE consists of three major parts:

- An ".INF" file that describes everything that has to be done during the installation.
- A cabinet file (".CAB") for each platform and CPU that contains the compressed files that have to be installed. The ".CAB" is the result of a compiled ".INF" file.
- A ".INI" file containing the names of all ".CAB" files.

11.5.2   The Installer Information File (.INF)

The ".INF" file is structured like an early ".INI" file and consists of sections and parameters and their values except that the INF file can also contain parameter lists without values. If you compare this ".INF" file with a standard installer file on Windows for drivers you will find similarities as well as with the installation description files of the SMS Server (System Management Server). In essence, all three follow the same concept, but due to the nature of Windows CE, there are some special sections in the ".INF" file that do not exist in the other installer files. Once you are done creating the .INF file it will be compiled together with your binaries to a cabinet file (".CAB") file.

Table 11.1 shows you a list of all sections that are important for Windows CE and explains how they have to be used.

As I mentioned earlier, there is a set of predefined strings available for you to use in the INF file. Table 11.2 shows these strings.

Finally, Table 11.3 contains a current list of all CPUs and their platform type IDs.

11.5.3   Creating the Installer File for Your PCDM Application

Now you are ready to move from dry theory to practical use—creating a CE installer for your Pocket-CD-Manager application. Your deliverables consist of three DLLs, an

Table 11.1   .INF Sections for Windows CE Installations

Name	Used for	Contains
[Version]	Identification of the .INF file	Signature = "$Chicago$" The old Windows 95 name that is still being used inside all .INF files on all Win32-based operating systems. CESignature = "$Windows CE$" A new signature showing Windows CE as the target provider = "<Your Company>"
[CEStrings]	Strings that are used on CE	InstallDir = %CE2% Defines the default installation directory. Table 11.2 explains the meaning of %CE2%. AppName = "<Application Name>".
[CEDevice.<CPUID>]	This section is required for each different CPU and platform type. Most commonly the CPUID is just the name of the CPU, but it is basically a value that you can choose.	ProcessorType = <Processor ID Number> This number is defined in the "WINNT.H" file of Windows CE. You can also find a list in Table 11.3. UnsupportedPlatforms = "Palm PC", "HPC", "Jupiter" This parameter tells which platforms this CEDevice type does not support. In other words, if you have different binaries for a palm-size PC and a H/PC, but both are based on the same CPU type, you have to create two "CEDevice" sections, one named "[CEDevice.PSH3]" and the other called "[CEDevice.HSH3]". Both sections would contain the same ProcessorType value, but the PSH3 contains UnsupportedPlatforms = "HPC", and the HSH3 section contains the setting UnsupportedPlatforms = "Palm PC". You can also add parameters for

Name	Used for	Contains
		"VersionMin", "VersionMax", "BuildMin", and "BuildMax".
[SourceDisksNames.<CPUID>]	Contains a list of all disks included in the setup.	Since most installations for Windows CE are rather small, the most common entry here is <Disk Number> = ,"<CPU> Files", <DirectoryName> The directory must exist during compile time of the .INF file.
[SourceDisksFiles]	Contains a list of all files and their source disk numbers.	<Filename> = <Disk Number>
[DestinationDirs]	Contains a list of directories and their default paths.	Most common entries are Files.Cpu.Windows = ,%InstallDir% For files that should go to the Windows directory: Files.Cpu.InstDir = ,%InstallDir% or DefaultDestDir = ,%InstallDir% for the main installation directory.
[DefaultInstall]	This section contains the main execution sequence for the installation.	A valid list could look like this: CopyFiles = Files.Cpu.Windows, Files.Cpu.InstDir AddReg = <Registry_Section_ Name> CEShortcuts = <Shortcut_Section_Name> This will first copy the files from the sections "Files.Cpu.Windows" and then the files from "Files.CPU.InstDir". Once they are copied, the installer will create the registry entries defined in the "Reg.Version.1" section and, at the end, will create the shortcuts defined in "CEShortcuts".
[Files.Cpu.<Target>]	Contains a list of all files for a certain target location.	You can have as many of these sections as you want as long as you add all of them to the "CopyFiles" list

(continued)

Table 11.1 **(continued)**

Name	Used for	Contains
		in the "DefaultInstall" section. All files also have to have a location in the "SourceDiskFiles" section.
[<Registry_Section_ Name>]	Contains a list of all registry entries your application needs.	An entry looks like this: <ROOTKey>,<keyname>,<Value>, <Type>,<Data>
[<Shortcut_Section_ Name>]	Contains a list of all shortcuts required for your application.	The syntax of a shortcut is <Shortcut_Name>,<shortcut_type>, <source_file_name>, <Source_Directory>
[Strings]	Contains a list of user-defined strings.	Instead of using hard-coded strings for the values, you can use either predefined strings, as shown in Table 11.2, or define your own strings. The syntax is: <String_Name> = "<Value>" To define such a string, use the %<Stringname>% macro. The difference between the "Strings" section and the "CEStrings" section is that the "Strings" section is only valid during the compile time of the .INF file.

executable, and a help file. You will also create a shortcut in the "Start" menu and add some registry values. To create the "PCDM.INF" file, use either the eMbedded Visual Tools environment or Notepad, the best-known source-code editor.

1. Add the [Version] section and add the following settings:

```
[Version]
Signature      = "$Windows NT$"
CESignature    = "$Windows CE$"
Provider       = "<YourCompanyName>"
```

2. Add the [CEStrings] section and add two parameters:

```
[CEStrings]
InstallDir  = %CE1%\<YourCompany>\Pocket-CD-Manager V1.0
AppName     = "Pocket-CD-Manager V1.0"
```

Table 11.2   Predefined Strings for Use in .INF Sections

Name	Description
%CE1%	Path to "\Program Files"
%CE2%	\Windows
%CE3%	\Windows\Desktop
%CE4%	\Windows\Startup
%CE5%	\My Documents
%CE6%	\Program Files\Accessories
%CE7%	\Program Files\Communication
%CE8%	\Program Files\Games
%CE9%	\Program Files\Pocket Outlook
%CE10%	\Program Files\Office
%CE11%	\Windows\Programs
%CE12%	\Windows\Programs\Accessories
%CE13%	\Windows\Programs\Communications
%CE14%	\Windows\Programs\Games
%CE15%	\Windows\Fonts
%CE16%	\Windows\Recent
%CE17%	\Windows\Favorites
%InstallDir%	Contains the path to the target directory selected by the user during installation. It is declared in the "CEStrings" sections.
%AppName%	Contains the application name, defined in the "CEStrings" section.

3. Add the [Strings] section with at least the following strings:

```
[Strings]
sh3_cpu     = 10003     ; SH3 processor
sh4_cpu     = 10005     ; SH3 processor
mips_cpu    = 4000      ; MIPS processor
arm_cpu     = 2577      ; StrongARM processor
shortcut_name       = "Pocket-CD-Manager V1.0"
key_install     = "Software\Apps"
val_version     = "Version"
data_version= "1.0"
exec_file = "PCDM.exe"
```

Table 11.3   Currently Supported CPUs and Their Platform IDs

CPU Type	Platform ID
INTEL_386	386
INTEL_486	486
INTEL_PENTIUM	586
INTEL_860	860 (Not yet supported by Windows CE)
MIPS_R2000	2000
MIPS_R3000	3000
MIPS_R4000	4000
HITACHI_SH3	10003
HITACHI_SH4	10005
PPC_403	403
PPC_601	601
PPC_603	603
PPC_620	620
PPC_821	821
STRONGARM	2577
ARM_720	1824
ARM_820	2080
ARM_920	2336
CEF	$0 \times 494F$ (Virtual processor for CEF installations) 0 for auto-run

The first two sections are mandatory for each installation. You should always start with them. The third one is optional, but it enhances the readability and reusability of your ".INF" file.

Next you need to add a [CEDevice.<name>] section for each processor that you are going to support. Depending on how you compiled the DLLs and the executable, you may need to add several [CEDevice] sections for special platforms. You will probably want to compile for H/PC Version 2.00. This is currently the only way to get your code running on *all* current Windows CE devices with Windows CE Version 2.0 and higher installed, including all palm-size and H/PC PCs. Of course, the H/PC does not support all technologies added in later versions of Windows CE. Your PCDM application will only run on devices with Windows CE 2.11 or higher. Therefore you need not include H/PC and the first palm-size PC generation in your installer.

If you have code that runs on all devices, your [CEDevice.<name>] section would look pretty simple:

```
[CEDevice.SH3_ALL]
ProcessorType   = %sh3_cpu%
[CEDevice.MIPS_ALL]
ProcessorType   = %mips_cpu%
```

The "%..%" macros will be replaced by the values defined in the strings section.

For the palm-size PC V1.0 running Windows CE 2.01, you would add the following sections:

```
[CEDevice.SH3_PSPC1]
ProcessorType          = %sh3_cpu%
UnsupportedPlatforms   = "Jupiter","HPC"
VersionMax             = 2.01
 [CEDevice.MIPS_PSPC1]
ProcessorType          = %mips_cpu%
UnsupportedPlatforms   = "Jupiter","HPC"
VersionMax             = 2.01
```

To support the H/PC Professional platform, you would add sections for the MIPS, ARM, SH3, and SH4 processors. Since ARM and SH4 were not supported with Windows CE 2.0, you must have the binaries of those, compiled with the H/PC Professional setting.

4.   Add these two sections to the ".INF" file:

```
[CEDevice.SH3_HPRO]
ProcessorType       = %sh3_cpu%
UnsupportedPlatforms = "Palm PC","HPC"

[CEDevice.MIPS_HPRO]
ProcessorType       = %mips_cpu%
UnsupportedPlatforms = "Palm PC","HPC"
[CEDevice.SH4_HPRO]
ProcessorType          = %sh4_cpu%
UnsupportedPlatforms = "Palm PC","HPC"
[CEDevice.ARM_HPRO]
ProcessorType       = %arm_cpu%
UnsupportedPlatforms = "Palm PC","HPC"
```

Since there are three different versions of palm-size PCs out on the market using different versions of Windows CE (2.01, 2.11, and 3.0), you will need to add even more sections:

5. Add the following two sections for the palm-size PCs running Windows CE 2.11 (Wyvern):

```
[CEDevice.SH3_PSPC2]
ProcessorType         = %sh3_cpu%
UnsupportedPlatforms  = "Jupiter","HPC"
VersionMax            = 2.11
 [CEDevice.MIPS_PSPC2]
ProcessorType         = %mips_cpu%
UnsupportedPlatforms  = "Jupiter","HPC"
VersionMax            = 2.11
```

6. Add the two following sections for the new Pocket PCs running Windows CE 3.0:

```
[CEDevice.SH3_PSPC3]
ProcessorType         = %sh3_cpu%
UnsupportedPlatforms  = "Jupiter","HPC"
VersionMin            =3.0
VersionMax            =3.01
 [CEDevice.MIPS_PSPC3]
ProcessorType         = %mips_cpu%
UnsupportedPlatforms  = "Jupiter","HPC"
VersionMin            =3.0
VersionMax            =3.01
```

Since the Pocket PC uses the same platform type as the palm-size PC ("Palm PC"), the only way to distinguish between the two types is by their Windows CE version numbers. The Windows CE version of the Pocket PC is 3.00. Therefore we can use the "VersionMin" entry to uniquely define the Pocket PC. The "VersionMax" entry is currently optional because currently there is no Windows CE version greater than 3.0.

Here again is the complete list of sections that you will need to add if you plan to compile a special binary for each platform and version:

```
; H/PC Professional (CE 2.11)
[CEDevice.SH3_HPRO]
ProcessorType         = %sh3_cpu%
UnsupportedPlatforms  = "Palm PC","HPC"
[CEDevice.MIPS_HPRO]
```

```
ProcessorType         = %mips_cpu%
UnsupportedPlatforms = "Palm PC","HPC"
[CEDevice.SH4_HPRO]
ProcessorType            = %sh4_cpu%
UnsupportedPlatforms = "Palm PC","HPC"
[CEDevice.ARM_HPRO]
ProcessorType         = %arm_cpu%
UnsupportedPlatforms = "Palm PC","HPC"
; Palm-size PC 1.2 (Wyvern CE 2.11)
[CEDevice.SH3_PSPC2]
ProcessorType         = %sh3_cpu%
UnsupportedPlatforms = "Jupiter","HPC"
VersionMax            = 2.11
 [CEDevice.MIPS_PSPC2]
ProcessorType         = %mips_cpu%
UnsupportedPlatforms = "Jupiter","HPC"
VersionMax            = 2.11
; Pocket PC (Palm-size PC 2.0) (Rapier CE 3.0)
[CEDevice.SH3_PSPC3]
ProcessorType         = %sh3_cpu%
UnsupportedPlatforms = "Jupiter","HPC"
VersionMax            =3.0
 [CEDevice.MIPS_PSPC3]
ProcessorType         = %mips_cpu%
UnsupportedPlatforms = "Jupiter","HPC"
VersionMax            =3.0
```

The next section you need to add is the [SourceDiskFiles] section. It contains a list of all files that need to be installed on the device.

7. For your PCDM setup create the following section:

```
[SourceDisksFiles]
PCDMDLL.DLL               = 1      ; The Uiless component
PCDMUI.DLL                = 1      ; The User Interface Component
DevPCDMSync.DLL           = 1      ; The ActiveSync provider
PCDM.EXE                  = 1      ; the Main application
PCDM.HTM                  = 2      ; The Help File
Pocket CD Manager.LNK     = 2      ; The Help File Shortcut
```

The number behind the file name refers to the source disk or directory that contains the file.

The next series of sections is mandatory. These sections will tell the CAB compiler where to find the binaries for the [CEDevice] sections.

8. For each [CEDevice.<NAME>] you have to define a [SourceDisksNames.<NAME>] section:

```
[SourceDisksNames]
2 = ,"Help Files",,PCDMHelp

[SourceDisksNames.SH3_HPRO]
1 = ,"HPC Pro/SH3 Files",,HPCPRO\SH3
[SourceDisksNames.MIPS_HPRO]
1 = ,"HPC Pro/Mips Files",,HPCPRO\MIPS
[SourceDisksNames.SH4_HPRO]
1 = ,"HPC Pro/SH4 Files",,HPCPRO\SH4
[SourceDisksNames.ARM_HPRO]
1 = ,"HPC Pro/ARM Files",,HPCPRO\ARM

 [SourceDisksNames.SH3_PSPC2]
1 = ,"Wyvern/SH3 Files",, PSPC2\SH3
[SourceDisksNames.MIPS_PSPC2]
1 = ,"Wyvern/Mips Files",, PSPC2\MIPS
[SourceDisksNames.SH3_PSPC3]
1 = ,"Rapier/SH3 Files",, PSPC3\SH3
[SourceDisksNames.MIPS_PSPC3]
1 = ,"Rapier/Mips Files",, PSPC3\MIPS
```

The first section refers to the help files. You will have a single help file that works under all devices. To save the work of copying this file into all directories, you will work with the default section [SourceDisksNames]. To make this work you have to create a directory structure under the directory that contains the ".INF" file as shown in Figure 11.2.

To fill all those directories you currently have to follow a quite painful procedure:

• Compile one target platform.
• Copy the files into the target directory.
• Compile the next target platform and copy its binaries to the designated target directory.
• Continue in this manner until you have all binaries in the correct place.

I hope that in the near future Microsoft will find a better way to target multiple platforms by means of a single source code. A nice "Super-Batch-Mode" would also be a great new feature.

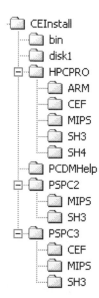

Figure 11.2   The directory structure for the PCDM installation

But you are not yet done with your ".INF" file. The next section you will add tells the installer how to copy the files from the CAB file to the target directory. You will put "PCDM.EXE" into the installation directory and the three DLLs into the "\Windows" directory.

9.   You need two [CopyFiles] sections:

```
[Files.Cpu.Windows]
PCDMUI.DLL,,,0xC0000002
PCDMDLL.DLL,,,0xC00000002
DevPCDMSync.DLL,,,0x400000002
PCDM.HTM,,,0x40000002

[Files.Cpu.HelpDir]
Pocket CD Manager.LNK,,,0x40000002

[Files.Cpu.InstDir]
PCDM.EXE,,,0x40000002
```

Set the "Shared DLL" flag to ensure that the DLLs do not get uninstalled should someone else happen to use them at the same time.

10.   In the next section [DestinationDirs], you will declare the desired target directory.

```
[DestinationDirs]
Files.Cpu.Windows    = ,%CE2%
Files.Cpu.InstDir    = ,%InstallDir%
Files.Cpu.HelpDir    = ,%CE2%\Help
Shortcuts            = 0, %CE11%
```

Three more sections and you will be done . . .

11. To add a shortcut into the "Start" menu of your Windows CE device, you will add the following section and entry:

```
[Shortcuts]
%shortcut_name%,0, %exec_file%, %CE11%
```

Using strings here helps keep this section independent, so that changes have to be made in the [Strings] section.

The last information section is the [AddReg] section that adds values and entries to the Windows CE registry during the installation.

12. Since your PCDM application does not require any special registry values, you need only add the "Good Citizen" entry for the Windows CE Application Manager.

```
[Reg.Version1]
HKLM,Software\Apps\%AppName%,%val_version%,0,%data_version%
HKLM,Windows CE
Services\Synchronization\Objects\PCDMSync,Store,0,\windows\
DevPCDMSync.dll
```

Once again you are using strings from the [Strings] and [CEStrings] sections to keep the install script universal for changes. The second entry will install the ActiveSync provider discussed in Section 9.3.

The final section that you need to add is the [DefaultInstall] section. This section determines the actual installation sequence.

13. Add the following [DefaultInstall] section to your ".INF" file:

```
[DefaultInstall]
CopyFiles = Files.Cpu.Windows, Files.Cpu.HelpDir, Files.Cpu.InstDir
AddReg = Reg.Version1
CEShortcuts = Shortcuts
CESelfRegister = PCDMDLL.DLL, PCDMUI.DLL
```

You can see that "CopyFiles" is referring to your [CopyFiles] sections, "AddReg" references your [AddReg] section, and "CEShortcuts" points to your [Shortcuts] section.

During installation, the installer will first copy the DLLs to the "Windows" directory, then place "PCDM.EXE" in the target directory, then add one entry to the registry, and finally add the shortcut to the "Start" menu in the "Programs" menu. At the very end, your two COM components will be self-registered.

Now that you are done with the ".INF" file, you can compile it. To compile a Windows CE ".INF" file, you need to use the "CABWIZ.EXE" found in the directory "<Drive>\Windows CE Tools\<CEVersion>\<Platform>\support\appinst\ BIN".

14. Copy the content of this directory into a directory called "BIN" under the directory containing the "PCDM.INF" file.

I recommend always using the latest version of "CABWIZ.EXE" in case Microsoft introduces new platforms that require new platform IDs, CPU types, or anything else. Since you have quite a few platforms listed in your ".INF" file, the command line for the compiler will be quite long.

15. To avoid typing in this long string every time you want to compile, create a tiny batch file named "COMPILE.BAT" and add the following string to it:

```
"bin\cabwiz.exe PCDM.inf /err PCDM.err /cpu SH3_HPRO SH4_HPRO
MIPS_HPRO ARM_HPRO SH3_PSPC2 MIPS_PSPC2 SH3_PSPC3 MIPS_PSPC3"
```

Once you start this batch, the CABWIZ will spin off several different windows containing the actual compilation process. At the end you should see a ".CAB" and a ".DAT" file for each "<CPU><PLATFORM>/CPU" entry.

You will also find a "PCDM.ERR" file containing three warnings for each CPU entry:

```
Warning: Section [DestinationDirs] key "Files.Cpu.Windows" is not
using the string "%InstallDir%"
Warning: Section [DestinationDirs] key "Files.Cpu.HelpDir" is not
using the string "%InstallDir%"
Warning: Section [DestinationDirs] key "Shortcuts" is not using the
string "%InstallDir%"
```

These three warnings can be ignored. They just tell you that your shortcuts and target directories point to a different directory that the user did not choose during the installation.

Once the CAB files have been copied to the Windows CE device, you can double-tap them to install the application. At this time, in fact, you can already do so. Since you have to find the correct CAB file for your device, you should know that there is an easier way to do this:

16. Create another file using Notepad called "PCDM.INI".

This file will tell the "CeAppMgr.exe" on your desktop PC which CAB files belong to the installation, and it will select the correct CAB file for you, download it to the device, and have the device's "WCELOAD.EXE" install it.

17. For your PCDM installation, "PCDM.INI" looks like this:

```
[CEAppManager]
Version = 1.0                 ; DO NOT CHANGE !!!!
Component = PCDM

[PCDM]
Description = AWL Pocket-CD-Manager V1.0
CabFiles =
PCDM.SH3_HPRO.CAB,PCDM.SH3_PSPC2.CAB,PCDM.SH3_PSPC3.CAB,PCDM.SH4_HPRO
.CAB,PCDM.MIPS_HPRO.CAB,PCDM.MIPS_PSPC2.CAB,PCDM.MIPS_PSPC3.CAB,PCDM.
ARM_HPRO.CAB
DeviceFile = PCDM.exe
DeviceIcon = PCDM.exe
IconFile=PCDM.EXE
```

The easiest way to test whether your ".INI" file and everything else works is to create a shortcut on the desktop pointing to "CeAppMgr.EXE" in the "Microsoft ActiveSync" directory. Then drag and drop the "PCDM.INI" file onto the shortcut, and the installation should start.

 The final source code of this section can be found on the companion CD under "\Sources\Thread Sample\PCDMSetup\CEInstall".

11.5.4 Creating a CEF Installation for PCDM

CEF is the new "Common Executable Format" first introduced for the H/PC Professional. It is a CPU-independent binary format for executables and DLLs that get compiled to the native CPU binary format either on install or on first runtime. CEF has great advantages for application writers who want to support all devices of a platform with a single executable. It also helps handle the possibility that Microsoft might support a different CPU later in the design process of a platform that was not in the initial release of the platform SDKs. This has happened with the StrongARM support for the H/PC Professionals. Customers of the HP Journada had to wait quite a while until the software vendors were able to support this platform. With CEF, a new CPU would be supported immediately on its release.

1. To create a CEF setup for your PCDM application you need to compile all controls and the "PCDM.EXE", using the CEF compiler. The ActiveSync provider does not as yet support CEF.

2. Once you have these binaries, create a new directory named "CEF" under "HPCPRO" and "PSPC3" and copy the CEF binaries from the release directories to the corresponding directories as you learned in the last section.

CEF does not care about the CPU so you can dramatically cut down the "PCDM.INF" file for the CEF setup.

Here is how the final "CEFPCDM.INF" looks:

```
[Version]
Signature      = "$Windows NT$"
CESignature    = "$Windows CE$"
Provider       = "Addison Wesley"

[CEStrings]
InstallDir  = %CE1%\Addison Wesley\Pocket-CD-Manager V1.0
AppName     = "Pocket-CD-Manager V1.0"

[Strings]
shortcut_name      = "Pocket-CD-Manager V1.0"
key_install       = "Software\Apps"
val_version       = "Version"
data_version= "1.0"
exec_file = "PCDM.exe"

[SourceDisksFiles]
PCDMDLL.DLL       = 1
PCDMUI.DLL        = 1
PCDM.EXE       = 1
PCDM.HTM       = 2
Pocket CD Manager.LNK = 2
cesetup.dll       = 1

[SourceDisksNames]
1 = ,"Pocket-PC/CEF Files",,PSPC3\CEF
2 = ,"Help Files",,PCDMHelp

[Files.Cpu.Windows]
PCDMUI.DLL,,,0xc0000002
```

```
PCDMDLL.DLL,,,0xc00000002
PCDM.HTM,,,0x40000002

[Files.Cpu.HelpDir]
Pocket CD Manager.LNK,,,0x40000002

[Files.Cpu.InstDir]
PCDM.EXE,,,0x40000002

[DestinationDirs]
Files.Cpu.Windows     = ,%CE2%
Files.Cpu.InstDir     = ,%InstallDir%
Files.Cpu.HelpDir     = ,%CE2%\Help
Shortcuts = 0, %CE11%

[Shortcuts]
%shortcut_name%,0, %exec_file%, %InstallDir%

[Reg.Version1]
HKLM,Software\Apps\%AppName%,%val_version%,0,%data_version%

[DefaultInstall]
CopyFiles = Files.Cpu.Windows, Files.Cpu.HelpDir, Files.Cpu.InstDir
CESetupDLL  = cesetup.dll
AddReg = Reg.Version1
CEShortcuts = Shortcuts
CESelfRegister = PCDMDLL.DLL, PCDMUI.DLL
```

There are two new lines in the script highlighted in bold. These two lines refer to a small DLL that will be called on Install initialization and Uninstall initialization for any custom action that you want to perform. The next section of this book involves implementing this DLL to launch the PCDM application as soon as the installation is finished. It will also close the PCDM application if it was running when the uninstallation began.

 The final source code of this section can be found on the companion CD under "\Sources\Thread Sample\PCDMSetup\CEInstall".

11.5.5 Writing a Custom SetupDLL

To allow the software developer to run some very specific custom actions on installation start and end, and on uninstallation start and end, Microsoft created the option of writing a "hook" DLL that gets called into specific functions during these events.

Since the built-in uninstallation cannot detect anything that you do in this DLL, I strongly recommend that you not use this DLL for any persistent installation procedures.

Launching PCDM at the End of the Installation

For your PCDM application's CEF setup, you will use hooks to launch the application as soon as the installation has been successfully completed. You will also close the application if it was running when the uninstallation was activated.

1.   To create this DLL, start eMbedded Visual C++ and create "An empty Windows CE DLL project" named "CeSetup".

2.   Create a new file named "CESETUP.CPP" and insert the code:

```
#include <windows.h>
#include <tchar.h>
#include <ce_setup.h>    // in the SDK dir

const TCHAR c_szFILE_APP[]      = _T("PCDM.exe");
const TCHAR c_szWNDCLASS_APP[]  = _T("PCDM");

BOOL WINAPI DllMain(HANDLE hMod, DWORD dwReason, LPVOID lpvReserved)
{
    return TRUE;
}

codeINSTALL_EXIT Install_Exit(
    HWND      hwndParent,
    LPCTSTR   pszInstallDir,
    WORD      cFailedDirs,
    WORD      cFailedFiles,
    WORD      cFailedRegKeys,
    WORD      cFailedRegVals,
    WORD      cFailedShortcuts
    )
    {
    WORD      cFailed = cFailedDirs + cFailedFiles;
    TCHAR     szFile[MAX_PATH];
    SHELLEXECUTEINFO    si;

    if (!cFailed)
    {
        wsprintf(szFile, _T("%s\\%s"), pszInstallDir, c_szFILE_APP);
```

```
        ZeroMemory(&si, sizeof(si));
        si.cbSize = sizeof(si);
        si.lpFile = szFile;
        ShellExecuteEx(&si);
    }
    return codeINSTALL_EXIT_DONE;
}

codeUNINSTALL_INIT Uninstall_Init(
    HWND    hwndParent,
    LPCTSTR pszInstallDir
)
{
    HWND    hwnd = NULL;
    USHORT  ix;

    // close app if it is running
    hwnd = FindWindow(c_szWNDCLASS_APP, NULL);
    if (hwnd)
    {
        SendMessage(hwnd, WM_CLOSE, 0, 0L);

        // wait a bit for the app to close
        for (ix = 0; ix < 10; ix++)
        {
            hwnd = FindWindow(c_szWNDCLASS_APP, NULL);
            if (hwnd)
                Sleep(1000);    // wait one second
            else
                break;
        }
    }
      if (hwnd)
          return codeUNINSTALL_INIT_CANCEL;
      else
        return codeUNINSTALL_INIT_CONTINUE;
}
```

With the "Uninstall_Init" function, you are trying to close the application. If it fails after ten tries, cancel the uninstallation. Otherwise the code does not contain any surprises. Unfortunately, you are not told the name of the installed application and have to hard-code it here to launch the application. If you want to write more sophisticated code, you can read the name of the application from a registry key that you wrote during the installation.

To compile the "CEFPCDM.INF" file, create a new batch named "compileCEF.BAT" and add the following line:

```
bin\cabwiz.exe CEFPCDM.inf /err CEFPCDM.err
```

 The final source code of this section can be found on the companion CD under "\Sources\Thread Sample\PCDMSetup\CESetup".

11.5.6   CF-Card Instant-Installer for the Pocket PC

What would you say if you could ship your application on a small Compact-Flash RAM card and have it only run as long as the card was in the CF slot of your palm-size PC? A great feature, I think.

With the new Pocket PC you can create just such behavior. All you need to do is create a special executable file that is named "AUTORUN.EXE", store it in a CPU-specific directory off the CF-Card's root directory, and store your application's CAB file in the card's root. The CPU-specific sub-folders are named after the platform IDs found in Table 11.3.

"AUTORUN.EXE" is executed as soon as the CF-Card is inserted into the CF slot of your Pocket PC. When the CF-Card is inserted, "AUTORUN.EXE" will be called with the command line parameter "install". Upon ejection of the card, no parameter will be supplied. With this in mind you can create a tiny auto-run application that installs your application on "insert" and uninstalls it again on "eject."

Creating a PCDM Auto-Installer for the Pocket PC

The steps to create a simple auto-installer for your PCDM application are not too complicated.

1. Create a new "Simple Windows CE Application" project, using eMbedded Visual C++, named "AUTORUN".

2. Add the following include statement and variables to the top of the "AUTORUN.CPP" file:

```
#include <tchar.h>

const WCHAR tstrINSTALL[]  = L"install";
const WCHAR tstrROOT[]     = L"\\*";
```

```
const WCHAR tstrCAB[]       = L"CEFPCDM.CAB";
const WCHAR tstrUNINST[]       = L"\\Windows\\unload.exe";
const WCHAR tstrUNINST_APP[]=L"Addison Wesley Pocket-CD-Manager
V1.0";

// a top-level dir with these attributes is a flash card
const DWORD dwATTRIB_CF     = FILE_ATTRIBUTE_DIRECTORY |
FILE_ATTRIBUTE_TEMPORARY;
```

Next you need to add two functions that handle the "on insert" and "on eject" events of the CF-Card:

```
void OnCardInsert()
{
    HANDLE  hFind   = NULL;
    BOOL    fLoop   = FALSE;
    WCHAR   szwFile[MAX_PATH];

    WIN32_FIND_DATA     fd;
    SHELLEXECUTEINFO    si;

    // search all top-level dirs
    ZeroMemory(&fd, sizeof(fd));
    hFind = FindFirstFile(tstrROOT, &fd);
    if (INVALID_HANDLE_VALUE == hFind)
        return;

    szwFile[0] = 0;
    do
    {
        // check the dir attributes
        if (dwATTRIB_CF == (dwATTRIB_CF & fd.dwFileAttributes))
        {
            // you have found the first CF Card
            lstrcpy(szwFile, fd.cFileName);
            break;
        }
        fLoop = FindNextFile(hFind, &fd);
    } while (fLoop);
    FindClose(hFind);
```

```
    // exit if you did not find a CF Card
    if (!szwFile[0]) return;

    // create the full filename of the CAB file
    lstrcat(szwFile, L"\\");
    lstrcat(szwFile, tstrCAB);

    // run the CAB
    ZeroMemory(&si, sizeof(si));
    si.cbSize = sizeof(si);
    si.lpFile = szwFile;
    ShellExecuteEx(&si);

    return;
}

void OnCardEject()
{
    SHELLEXECUTEINFO    si;

    // run the uninstall program to uninstall your app
    ZeroMemory(&si, sizeof(si));
    si.cbSize = sizeof(si);
    si.lpFile = tstrUNINST;
    si.lpParameters = tstrUNINST_APP;
    ShellExecuteEx(&si);
}
```

The code is extremely simple. First, find the name of the CF-Card in the slot. You can also use the "FindFirstFlashCard" API for the enumeration of the Flash cards. Since the "FindFirstFlashCard" API is only available on palm-size PCs, it might be better to use the "FindFirstFil" API here because Microsoft plans to add the auto-run capacity to a future generation of H/PCs.

After you determine the correct file name, simply execute the ".CAB" file using the "ShellExecuteEx" function that will detect the ".CAB" extension and launch it with the corresponding executable associated with the extension. The "eject" method will call the "Unload.exe" with the installation name used in the "PCDM.CAB/.INF" file. One change to the "WinMain" function, and your little auto-start application will be ready.

3. Add the following line to the body of the "WinMain" function:

```
int WINAPI WinMain(       HINSTANCE hInstance,
                          HINSTANCE hPrevInstance,
                          LPTSTR    lpCmdLine,
                          int       nCmdShow)
{
    if (0 == lstrcmpi(lpCmdLine, tstrINSTALL))
        OnCardInsert();
    else
        OnCardEject();
      return 0;
}
```

Now compile "AUTORUN.EXE" with the CEF compiler, but do not download it to your device. You are using CEF here to be completely CPU neutral. As mentioned before, CEF is the new Common Executable Format that is compiled at runtime.

4. Create the following tree structure on a CF-Card:

```
CF-Root
    \0
    \10003
    \2577
    \4000
```

You will recognize the numbers from Table 11.3 as platform IDs for various CPUs. If you now copy "CEF AUTORUN.EXE" into all of these directories and "CEFPCDM.CAB" into the root of your CF-Card, the PCDM application will be installed and launched as soon as you insert the CF-Card into your device. When you eject the card, the PCDM application will be terminated and automatically uninstalled. This is an optimal way of conserving the tight space of the palm-size PC.

You have to set the READ-ONLY flag for the ".CAB" file to prevent "WCELOAD.EXE" from deleting the CAB file as soon as it is installed.

The final source code of this section can be found on the companion CD under "\Sources\Thread Sample\PCDMSetup\Autorun".

Reading the Serial Number of the CF-Card

With serial number imprints of CF-Cards, you can even implement a simple copy protection by probing for the serial number of the CF-Card before you install the application.

The only place where the check makes sense is in the "CESetup.dll" file that you have in your CAB file. Otherwise, someone could just copy the CAB file from the Flash-Card, and it would run fine on any other card or Windows CE device. Here is how to add a serial-number protection to the "CESetup.DLL" that you created in Section 11.5.5.

1. Load the CESetup project and open the "CESetup.cpp" source file.

2. Add the following definition and the new function to the source:

```
const WCHAR tstrROOT[]      = L"\\*";
const DWORD dwATTRIB_CF      = FILE_ATTRIBUTE_DIRECTORY |
FILE_ATTRIBUTE_TEMPORARY;
typedef struct _STORAGE_IDENTIFICATION {
      DWORD      dwSize;
      DWORD      dwFlags;
      DWORD      dwManufactureIDOffset;
      DWORD      dwSerialNumOffset;
} STORAGE_IDENTIFICATION, *PSTORAGE_IDENTIFICATION;


// From DISKIO.H of the Windows CE 3.0 Platform Builder *************
#define FILE_DEVICE_DISK              0x00000007
#define IOCTL_DISK_BASE FILE_DEVICE_DISK
#define CTL_CODE( DeviceType, Function, Method, Access ) (          \
((DeviceType) << 16) | ((Access) << 14) |((Function)<< 2)|(Method) \
)
#define METHOD_BUFFERED               0
#define FILE_ANY_ACCESS               0
#define IOCTL_DISK_GET_STORAGEID   \
    CTL_CODE(IOCTL_DISK_BASE, 0x709, METHOD_BUFFERED,
FILE_ANY_ACCESS)
// From DISKIO.H of the Windows CE 3.0 Platform Builder *************

codeINSTALL_INIT Install_Init(
    HWND         hwndParent,
    BOOL         fFirstCall,
    BOOL         fPreviouslyInstalled,
```

```
    LPCTSTR      pszInstallDir
)
{
HANDLE  hFind    = NULL;
BOOL    fLoop    = FALSE;
WCHAR   szwFile[MAX_PATH];
PSTORAGE_IDENTIFICATION pStoreInfo;
HANDLE  hVolume;
DWORD   BytesRet;
codeINSTALL_INIT ret;
BYTE   *SerialNo;
WIN32_FIND_DATA      fd;
TCHAR tStr[200];

    // search all top-level dirs
    memset(&fd, 0,sizeof(fd));
    hFind = FindFirstFile(tstrROOT, &fd);
    if (INVALID_HANDLE_VALUE == hFind)
        return codeINSTALL_INIT_CONTINUE;       // Root is corrupt

    szwFile[0] = 0;
    do
    {
        // check the dir attributes
        if (dwATTRIB_CF == (dwATTRIB_CF & fd.dwFileAttributes))
        {
            // you have found the first CF Card
            lstrcpy(szwFile, fd.cFileName);
            break;
        }
        fLoop = FindNextFile(hFind, &fd);
    } while (fLoop);
    FindClose(hFind);

    // exit if you did not find a CF Card: No CF Install!
    // to enforce a CF-CARD inside, return codeINSTALL_INIT_CANCEL
    if (!szwFile[0]) return codeINSTALL_INIT_CONTINUE;

    wsprintf(tStr,L"\\%s\\Vol:",szwFile);
    ret=codeINSTALL_INIT_CONTINUE;
    hVolume=CreateFile(tStr,GENERIC_READ|GENERIC_WRITE,0,NULL,
```

```
                        OPEN_EXISTING,0,NULL);
    if (hVolume)
    {
            pStoreInfo=(STORAGE_IDENTIFICATION *)
                          GlobalAlloc(GMEM_ZEROINIT,3000);
            if (DeviceIoControl(hVolume,IOCTL_DISK_GET_STORAGEID,
                            NULL,0,(LPVOID)pStoreInfo,3000,
                            &BytesRet,NULL)!=FALSE)
            {
                        SerialNo=(((BYTE *)pStoreInfo)+
                        pStoreInfo->dwSerialNumOffset);
                    int i=0;
                    while (SerialNo[i]!=0 && i<(int)(BytesRet-
            pStoreInfo->dwSerialNumOffset) && i<200)
                        {
                                tStr[i]=(TCHAR)SerialNo[i];
                                i++;
                        }
                        tStr[i]=0;
//wsprintf(szwFile,TEXT("Serial =<%s>"),tStr);
//MessageBox(NULL,szwFile,TEXT("PCDM Install"),MB_OK);
                    if (!CompareString(LOCALE_USER_DEFAULT,
                    NORM_IGNORECASE,tStr,-1,TEXT("<SERIAL HERE>"), -1)-2)
                    {
                            ret=codeINSTALL_INIT_CONTINUE;
                    }
                    else
                    {
                            MessageBox(NULL,TEXT("Sorry, but this
Installation does not match your CF-Card. Installation will be
canceled"),TEXT("PCDM Install"),MB_OK);
                            ret=codeINSTALL_INIT_CANCEL;
                    }
            }
            else
            {
                    wsprintf(tStr,TEXT("Error %d"),GetLastError());
                    MessageBox(NULL,tStr,tStr,MB_OK);
            }

            GlobalFree(pStoreInfo);
```

```
        CloseHandle(hVolume);
    }
    // To enforce a CF-CARD inside, return codeINSTALL_INIT_CANCEL
    return ret;
}
```

This code will be called before Windows CE starts the installation. You are reading the CF-Card serial number and comparing it to the one you require. You can make the restriction even stronger if you change all "codeINSTALL_INIT_CONTINUE" insances to "codeINSTALL_INIT_CANCEL" in case of any error.

 But be careful if you do so. Your CAB file can be installed from a PC only if the corresponding CF-Card is in the slot.

3. To allow WCELoad to find the function you have to add the following line to the CESetup.DEF:

```
EXPORTS

Install_Exit
Uninstall_Init
Install_Init
```

Now compile the new DLL and run "CompileCEF.BAT" again. Test the new CAB file with a CF-Card. Since you probably do not know the serial number of the card, remove the remark markers around the message box. Then fix the code, compile everything, and run it again.

 The final source code of this section can be found on the companion CD under "\Sources\Thread Sample\PCDMSetup\CESetup".

11.5.7 Creating an Installation for the Desktop

All right, you may be saying, "Isn't all this getting a bit off the main topic"? As I promised at the beginning of the book, you will have a chance to create an application from start to ready-for-shipping finish. This includes the installer for the desktop.

Early in 1999, Microsoft released a new technology called MSI, (Microsoft Installer), which has since been renamed the "Windows Installer". The idea behind this technology was to end the chaos of installation once and for all. MSI includes features like

- Auto-repair
- Auto-deployment
- Just-in-time installation
- Easy-to-use interfaces

The concept behind MSI is very simple: An MSI file is a database containing a series of tables that are interpreted by a Windows NT service or, on Windows 9x, an executable. Depending on the entries of the tables the installation will perform its tasks. You can compare the tables to the sections from the ".INF" file. And if you take a closer look, you will find nearly all of those sections again in the MSI file. However, to build a complete MSI setup from scratch would take far too much space to include in this book.

Creating a New Basic MSI Project

I prepared a small procedure to create a basic MSI database that contains the most important entries that every setup must have using "InstallShield for Windows Installer". You can find an evaluation version of this product in the "Evals" directory on the companion CD.

1. Launch the "InstallShield for Windows Installer" IDE and create a new project using the "Project Wizard" with the name "CEDefaultMSI".

2. In the second page of the wizard, enter the application name "Pocket-CD-Manager" and your company data in the corresponding fields.

3. Skip the third page and remove the "DefaultHelpFiles" and "DefaultTemplates" features from the fourth page.

These features are only important if you want to ship help files that stay on the desktop. Do the same thing on the fifth page.

4. Delete all the components except the "Global_Default_Executable". Do not change any other parameter.

5. Skip the sixth page and add all ".CAB" files from the previous section of this book to the list of files as well as the "PCDM.INI" file.

As soon as you select the files and press "OK", a dialog box will pop up, asking for a path variable. This is the way ISW (InstallShield for Windows Installer) creates relative paths.

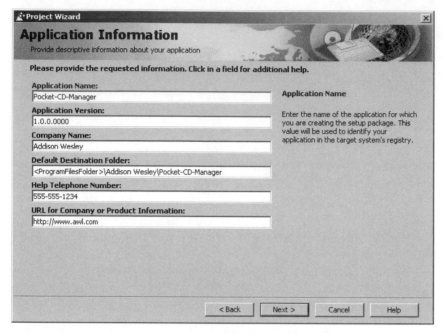

Figure 11.3 InstallShield for Windows Installer Application Information page

6. Enter the name "CEINSTALL" in the "Path Variable Name" field of the box, as shown in Figure 11.4.

Normally, MSI would require a separate component for each DLL or executable. But since auto-repair and install-on-demand will not work with the Windows CE "CeAppMgr.EXE", you can simply put all the files that belong to your Windows CE installation into one component. The ActiveSync provider for the desktop "PCDMSync.DLL" will be stored later in its own component. You still should assign a key file, which is essential to the installation. In your case it is the "PCDM.INI" file.

7. Select "PCDM.INI" and click on the "Set Key File" button.

8. You do not require any shortcut or registry data, so you can just skip the wizard's next two steps.

The wizard's "Dialogs" step lets you choose the user interface for your installation.

9. To keep the setup as simple as possible, you will only use the "Welcome" dialog. All other dialog boxes are optional and can be deselected.

10. On the last page, keep the defaults and press "Finish".

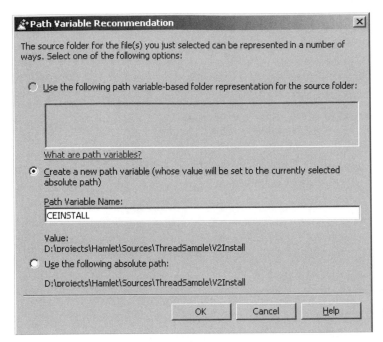

Figure 11.4 Setting the path variable to the directory containing the CAB files

If everything went well, the compiler at the end will show you a result similar to that shown in Figure 11.6.

By default, ISW creates a network image of the source files, a "Setup.exe" file, and a "Pocket-CD-Manager.MSI" file. You can find those files at

```
"<Drive>:\MySetups\CEDefaultMSI\Build Label 1\My Release-1\
DiskImages\Disk1"
```

The final source code of this section can be found on the companion CD under "\Sources\Thread Sample\PCDMSetup\MSI".

Adding a New Component for the ActiveSync Provider

As mentioned earlier, you need to add a component to the MSI project for your ActiveSync provider. "PCDMSync.DLL" will remain on the desktop and has to be registered for the use with ActiveSync.

MSI distinguishes between "Features" and "Components". An installation can have multiple features that themselves have multiple components. A component, on

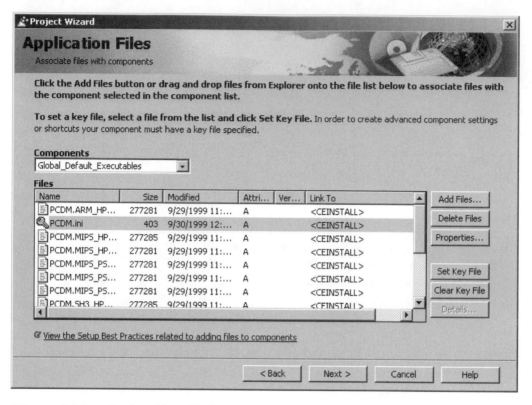

Figure 11.5 Setting a key file for the "Global_Default_Executables" component

the other hand, cannot have sub-components. A component is the most granular, atomic part of an installation. It holds all data belonging to it.

In your case, you only have a self-register file. In the case of an application, the component would hold the application's registry entries, shortcuts, and file types. Users would only see features, never components, in any "custom" view for selecting among the product's features. The "ActiveSyncProvider" component, for example, will belong to the "DefaultProgram" feature. Since this application has no custom screen, you can just install the "DefaultProgram" feature without asking the user whether he or she wants something different. The installation choice is simple: all or nothing.

Here is what you need to do:

1. In the ISW user interface, select the "Setup Design" button in the sidebar.

You will see the "DefaultProgram" feature and underneath it, the "Global_Default_ Executables" component that you created in the project wizard.

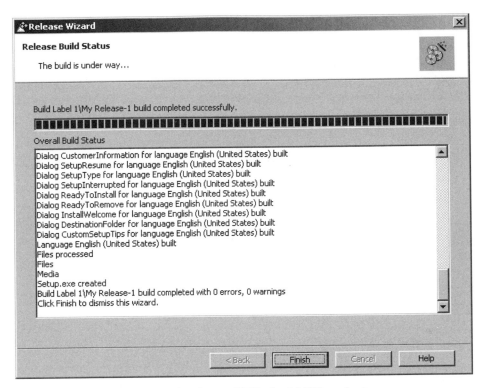

Figure 11.6   Compiler result of your CEDefaultMSI project

2.   To add a new component, select "New Component" in the object menu of the "DefaultProgram" feature.

3.   Label the new component "ActiveSyncProvider."

4.   In the right pane you see several options for the component. Your "PCDMSync.DLL" uses the self-register feature so you can select this option. All other settings remain at their default values.

   It is no longer recommended that you use self-register because an installation cannot be completely undone if the control's "UnRegister" function fails to work properly. A better way would be to create a ".REG" file with all the information required in the registry and import it into the IDE.

5.   Select the "Files" folder and click into the right pane to get the object menu.

6. Select "Add . . ." and browse for your ActiveSync provider DLL "PCDMSync.DLL".

If your provider is in a different directory from your CAB files, ISW will ask you for a "Path variable".

7. Enter "PCDMSYNCDIR" as the "Path Variable Name", hit "OK", and set the file as the key file using the object menu on the file.

You are done! Since the "ActiveSyncProvider" component belongs to the "DefaultProgram" feature, it will be installed as soon as the user hits "Next" on the welcome screen.

8. Repeat the same procedure for the desktop version of "PCDMDLL.DLL" since the ActiveSync provider for the desktop requires this DLL (see "The Desktop Side of ActiveSync", in Section 9.3.2.).

 The final source code of this section can be found on the companion CD under "\Sources\Thread Sample\PCDMSetup\MSI".

Adding the Windows CE-Specific Custom Actions

This section will explain how the MSI file has to be modified to install your PCDM CAB files on the desktop PC in a logo-compliant way. The logo requirements for Windows CE state that "Every Windows CE application has to be installed on the desktop PC in a directory under the 'Microsoft Active Sync' directory. The location of this directory can be located in the registry in the path 'SOFTWARE\Microsoft\Windows\CurrentVersion\App Paths\CEAPPMGR.EXE'."

Since MSI is based on interpretation of data in tables and rows of a database, you cannot script anything like what you might be used to with InstallShield Professional. The entries you are going to undertake in this section of the book are useful for all kinds of Windows CE installations. You will only need to make changes in one entry in order for it to work with your application.

Some Background on MSI

MSI has a wide range of predefined actions that can be called at certain times during the installation sequence. You can see the order in which these actions are called by clicking on the "Sequences" button in the ISW workspace toolbar.

There are three kinds of sequences:

- Installation—The sequence for a regular installation launched by the user.
- Advertisement—The sequence executed if the administrator has assigned this MSI file on your domain in the Active Directory. This is a "Windows 2000-only" feature.

- Administration—A sequence visible only to administrators of Active Directory domains.

The "Installation" sequence is sub-structured into "User Interface" and "Execution":

- User Interface—Describes all the actions that will be executed if the user does not launch the setup in batch mode.
- Execute—Batch-mode, UI-less installation of the setup.

If you open the "Execute" or "User Interface" branch, you will see a list of actions. Some have an icon showing a dialog box, others have a clapboard icon. The MSI database has several cross-references from one table to others and so on, which makes MSI very flexible but rather confusing for a first-time developer.

You must add a few MSI database entries in order to set your installation's target directory to the path whose parent directory is located in the registry and, later, to start "CeAppMgr.EXE" with the full path of the "PCDM.INI" file. You will need to

- Add properties called "CEAPPMGREXENAME" and "INIKEY" to the "Property" table.
- Add a path variable called "CEAPPMGR" to the "Directory" table.
- Add two records to the "RegLocator" table, reading their values into signatures.
- Add two records to the "AppSearch" table, copying the signature values to the property and path variables.
- Create three custom actions to call the "CeAppMgr.exe" with the full path to the "PCDM.INI" and to show the "CeAppMgr.exe" during the uninstallation.
- Add the custom actions to "User Interface" sequences.

And since ISW does not have a special user interface for this, you will need to use either the "Power Editor" in the "Tools" menu of ISW or "ORCA", a tool that ships with the MSI-SDK. You can find "MSI.SDK" in the "Evals" directory on the companion CD.

If you want to continue working with ISW to enhance your setup, you will need to use the ISW "Power Editor", since ORCA works directly with the MSI file. All changes that you make to the MSI file will be lost if you later decide to work with ISW. Here is how to make the necessary enhancements . . .

The "Property" Table

A property is comparable to a variable. It can hold a string value that is used later as a parameter to other actions. Your installation requires two custom properties, shown in Table 11.4.

Table 11.4   Property Table Entries

Property	Value
INIKEY	PCDM.INI
CEAPPMGREXENAME	—

The "Property" table is exposed in the regular user interface of the ISW IDE.

1. Select the "Project" icon in the workspace toolbar and select the "Project" branch in the "Property Manager" folder.

2. Scroll to the end of the "Property" table and add the two properties and their values as you can see in Figure 11.7.

The "INIKEY" property holds the name of the ".INI" file that you give to the "CeAppMgr.EXE" at the end of the installation. The "CEAPPMGREXENAME" property contains the full path to "CeAppMgr.EXE", which you are going to call at the end of the installation.

 The "INIKEY" entry is the only entry that you will need to change if you want to reuse the setup for your own application.

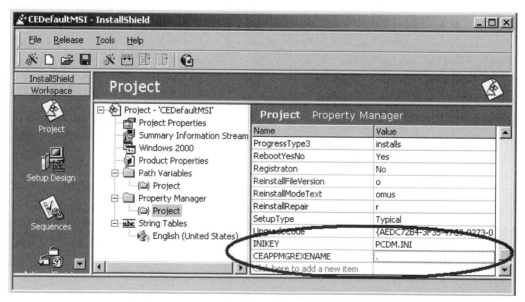

Figure 11.7   The ISW Property table

The "Directory" Table

The "Directory" table is similar to the "Property" table. Instead of holding any string, the "Directory" table holds only paths. It also contains an entry for the parent directory of a directory. This permits rather flexible path names. The target directory for your installation will have the following syntax:

```
<Active Sync Directory>\<Company Name>\<Application Name>
```

To establish this hierarchy, you need to create three entries in the "Directory" table, as shown in Table 11.5.

3. To add these entries you have to use the "Power Editor".

If you chain those three entries together by putting the "Directory_Parent" in front of the "DefaultDir" name, you will get the "FINALTARGETDIR":

```
<PathToProgramFiles>\AWL\Pocket-CD-Manager
```

The "." in the "Default" directory column just fulfills the "Not Nullable" option of that column. The "." is interpreted as "the same directory as the 'Directory_Parent'".

In one of the latter actions, the "CEAPPMGR" directory variable will be filled with the path to the "ActiveSync" directory. If the user has not installed "ActiveSync" yet, the "DefaultDir" will be empty and "ProgramFilesFolder" will be used instead. This is exactly the behavior you want to have, and it fulfills the logo requirements. ISW still puts its own "INSTALLDIR" entry into this table if you do not make the following change:

4. Select the "Project Properties" folder of the project view and clear the entry for the "Destination" folder.

Early ISW editions still create an "INSTALLDIR" even if none is specified in the IDE. To compensate for this, you need to open the final MSI file with the SDK tool

Table 11.5 **Directory Table Entries**

Directory	Directory_Parent	DefaultDir
INSTALLDIR	COMPANYDIR	Pocket-CD-Manager
COMPANYDIR	CEAPPMGR	AWL
CEAPPMGR	ProgramFilesFolder	

"ORCA" and correct two entries in the "Component" table. You do this at the end of your procedure.

The "AppSearch" Table

If you look back into the sequences, you will find an action called "AppSearch". This action corresponds to the "AppSearch" table in the "Power Editor" and interprets its content. The purpose of this table is to set properties and path variables with content that is evaluated in other tables, referenced with the "Signature" entry.

For your installation you need two entries in this table, as shown in Table 11.6.

5. To enter these two entries, you must open the "Power Editor" from the "Tools" menu.

If the installation sequence now executes the "AppSearch" action, this action will try to locate any action "signed" with the signature in the "AppSearch" table, execute it and return the result in the "Property/Directory" defined here. In this case, both signatures point to the "RegLocator" table.

The "RegLocator" Table

The "RegLocator" table has five columns that exactly reflect the structure of a registry key. For your installation you need the two entries shown in Table 11.7.

Table 11.6   AppSearch Table Entries

Property	Signature
CEAPPMGR	CEAPPMGRREGLOC
CEAPPMGREXENAME	CEAPPMGREXEREGLOC

Table 11.7   RegLocator Table Entries

Signature	Root	Key	Type
CEAPPMGRREGLOC	2	SOFTWARE\Microsoft\Windows\CurrentVersion\App Paths\CEAPPMGR.EXE	1
CEAPPMGREXEREGLOC	2	SOFTWARE\Microsoft\Windows\CurrentVersion\App Paths\CEAPPMGR.EXE	2

Table 11.8   Valid Root Settings

Value	Root Key
0	HKEY_CLASSES_ROOT
1	HKEY_CURRENT_USER
2	HKEY_LOCAL_MACHINE
3	HKEY_USERS

Table 11.9   Valid Type Settings

Value	Description
0	Key path is a directory. The directory name will be returned.
1	Key path is a file name. The directory name will still be returned. The file name gets stripped off the value.
2	Key is a raw string. The raw string will be returned without interpretation.

No surprises here. The root can be one of the entries in Table 11.8, and its type can correspond to any of the settings specified in Table 11.9.

For your setup you need the path to the "CeAppMgr.exe" in the CEAPPMGR directory and the full path plus the executable name in the property "CEAPPMGREXENAME" to execute it later.

The "Custom Action" Table

The next table you have to edit is the "Custom Action" table. Since ISW has an IDE for this table you can use the ISW's "Custom Action Wizard".

6. Select the "Actions/Script" button in the "Workspace" toolbar and right-click the "Custom Actions" branch in the "Actions/Scripts" tree to start the "Custom Action Wizard".

7. Name the custom action "Install2Ce" and select "Next".

8. Keep the type as "Launch an executable" in the wizard's following page, but change the location setting to "Stored in the Property Table".

By "Stored", ISW is referring to the path and name of the executable.

9. In the next page of the wizard, select the source "CEAPPMGREXENAME" and write "[INSTALLDIR][INIKEY]" in the "Target" field.

You need to include the quotes; otherwise it will not work if the path to INSTALLDIR has a space inside.

The MSI engine will launch an executable that is referenced as:

```
<CEAPPMGREXENAME> "<INSTALLDIR><INIKEY>"
```

Resolved, this string might look like:

```
"D:\Program Files\Microsoft Active Sync\CeAppMgr.EXE" "D:\Program
Files\Microsoft Active Sync\AWL\Pocket-CD-Manager\PCDM.INI"
```

The wizard's last page will ask you about some special options for the processing.

10. It is very important that you select "Ignore Custom Action return code" here!

"CeAppMgr.EXE" returns "1" rather than "0," even if everything is successful. MSI, on the other hand, interprets everything other than zero as an error. Thus the installation will cancel—even with a successful CE installation—unless you select the "ignore" option.

11. You can leave all other options in their default settings.

You should also create a custom action for uninstalling the PCDM. During uninstallation, you should only launch "CeAppMgr.EXE" without the INI file as parameter. This will allow the user to uninstall the PCDM manually, since it cannot be done automatically.

12. Repeat Step 5 through Step 10 and change only two entries:

- Step 7: Instead of naming the custom action "Install2Ce", name it "UnInstallFromCe".
- Step 9: Leave the "Target" field blank.

The "InstallUISequence" Table

The last table you need to edit is the "InstallUISequence" table. InstallShield has created a tree view editor for this table, which allows you to define the entries in their UI.

13. Select the "Sequences" button in the "Workspace" toolbar and open the "Installation\User Interface" branch.

14. On the very last entry, "ExecuteAction", click the right mouse button and select "Insert" from the context menu.

15. In the next dialog box, select "Custom Actions" from the list box at the top of the dialog box and then select the "Install2Ce" action.

16. Note: Only launch this action under certain conditions:

```
(Not Installed Or _IsMaintenance="Reinstall" or
_IsMaintenance="Change") And Not CEAPPMGREXENAME="."
```

You should only launch "Install2Ce" under one of the following conditions:

1. The installation was completed successfully.
2. The setup is in "Reinstall Mode".
3. The setup is in "Change Mode".

In any case, you should only launch it if ActiveSync is installed. If ActiveSync is not installed, the "RegLocater" will fail, filling the property "CEAPPMGREXENAME" with a valid value, and it will remain with its default value.

17. Repeat Step 12 through Step 15 for the "UnInstallFromCe" action and enter the following condition for the action:

```
_IsMaintenance = "Remove" And Not CEAPPMGREXENAME="."
```

You should only call this action if the MSI engine is in the "Remove" mode and ActiveSync is installed.

InstallShield also puts a funny blocker to the "AppSearch" action in the "User Interface" and "Execute" sequences. The "AppSearch" action will only execute if a property called "APP_TEST" is defined as "True".

18. Just remove this blocker and the "RegLocator" and all your other changes will work.

The last thing you might want to do is to package the final MSI file better. InstallShield offers you a variety of choices. Start the "Release Wizard" and play with the wizard's settings.

Also, for an optimized download from your Web site, you should choose "Compress all Files" in Step 5 of the wizard and deselect the option "Create Installation Launcher (Setup.Exe)" in Step 7. This step requires that end users have the MSI engine already installed on their computers. Windows 2000 integrates the MSI engine by default, but Win9x and NT4 users will need to download it, either from Microsoft or from your Web site.

Before you are finished with this setup, you will need to change the "Component" table in the final MSI file, as mentioned earlier.

19. Right-click the final "Pocket-CD-Manager.MSI" file and select "Edit with ORCA" in the upcoming object menu.

If this menu item is not available, you probably do not have ORCA installed. You can find the installation description in the next section.

20. In the left pane, select the "Component" entry and you will see two entries of this table in the right pane.

The column "Directory_" reads "dir22", but it should read "INSTALLDIR".

21. Double-click the entry and correct it with the "INSTALLDIR". Now save the MSI file and quit ORCA.

Attention: If you are running the ISW build wizard again, this entry will be reset and you will have to redo it.

More details on ORCA can be found in the next section. Congratulations! You just created a fully logo-compliant setup for Windows CE.

You can find the ISW project in the directory "\Sources\Thread Sample\ PCDMSetup\MSI" on the companion CD.

Creating the MSI File with MSI-SDK Tools

For those who do not like to work with the InstallShield tool, here are some tips on how you can work with ORCA to create your setup. ORCA is a tool that ships with the MSI SDK. You can find it in the "Tools" folder of the SDK. Once installed, ORCA will let you open any MSI file, either by using the right mouse button on the file or by starting ORCA and using its file menu.

If you want to have a compressed, all-in-one MSI file at the end, you need to complete some manual steps before and after using ORCA. However, if you use InstallShield, the tool itself will do all these steps automatically. Here is what you need to do:

- Create the CAB file for the MSI file using the "MakeCab.EXE" tool.
- Edit the tables "files" and "Media" in the MSI file, using "ORCA.EXE".
- Store the CAB file into a second-named stream of the MSI file using the "MSIDB.EXE" tool.
- Sign the MSI file with some properties to be recognized by the MSI engine using the "MSIINFO.EXE" tool.

MakeCab

The first step requires a CAB description file. This is similar to the one used for Windows CE, but since it is aimed at the desktop it has a lot more functionality. A complete description of this DDF file can be found in the MSDN library.

1.   For your PCDM application, the "PCDM.DDF" file would look like this:

```
;*** PCDM CAB Files Directive
;
.Set DiskLabel1=Setup
.Set CabinetNameTemplate=DATA*.CAB
.Set MaxDiskSize=1.44M

;** stored, compressed, in cabinet files
.Set Cabinet=on
.Set Compress=on
PCDM.ini
PCDM.ARM_HPRO.CAB
PCDM.MIPS_HPRO.CAB
PCDM.MIPS_PSPC2.CAB
PCDM.MIPS_PSPC3.CAB
PCDM.SH3_HPRO.CAB
PCDM.SH3_PSPC2.CAB
PCDM.SH3_PSPC3.CAB
PCDM.SH4_HPRO.CAB
```

 Note: The DDF file and the "Files" table in the MSI file are case-sensitive. Do not mix cases here. It takes forever to track down that sort of a bug! Also, the order of the files inside the DDF file is very important and must be the same order used in the "Files" table of your MSI file.

Once you are done with your "PCDM.DDF", you can compile it with:

```
makecab/f PCDM.DDF
```

The resulting "DATA1.CAB" can be found in a directory named "Disk1" under the current directory.

"Files" and "Media" Tables in ORCA

Now you have to verify that the "Files" and "Media" table entries are correct. The "Media" table, in particular, would have to be changed if you decided to store the CAB file in a second stream of the MSI file. If you open ORCA, you will see a split window. The left pane shows all the tables, and the right pane shows the content of the table.

2.   Select the "Media" table and verify the "Cabinet" entry.

For a network location, this field is empty, but for a CAB file stored in a stream, you must enter the CAB file name with a "#" as the first letter.

3.   In this case, enter "#DATA1.CAB".

Once again, watch out for the case sensitivity of this entry.

Storing the CAB File in an MSI Stream and Signing the Final MSI File

Next, you need to use the tool "MSIDB.EXE" to store the CAB file in a stream of the MSI file. Finally, you need to sign the final MSI file with a unique GUID so that the MSI engine will recognize it.

I created two batch files that will do this job for you. One batch file is generic and does not have to be changed for any other application. The other batch calls the first batch file with the application-specific data. Both batches are located in the "Disk1" directory.

The generic batch "FinalizeMSI.BAT" looks like this:

```
del %1.msi
copy CEApp.MSI %1.MSI
..\..\msidb -d %1.MSI -a DATA1.CAB
..\..\MsiInfo.exe %1.msi /V %3 /o %2 /a Chrism@C-Labs.com
del t.log
msival2 %1.msi darice.cub -f -l t.log
pause
```

I recommend that you not store the CAB file in the MSI file that you are working with. Therefore the first two lines of the batch delete the final MSI file and copy the working MSI file "CEApp.MSI" to make it the final MSI file. Then the "MSIDB" tool stores the "DATA1.CAB" file in a stream of the final MSI file.

The next command uses "MSIINFO" to sign the final MSI file with a GUID, a remark, and an e-mail address of the author. The last two lines are very interesting. "MSIVAL2" is a validation tool that checks the MSI files for common errors. It will help you hunt down errors that might appear later during the use of the MSI file.

The "Darice.cub" file contains a series of cross-reference checks of the MSI database. If one of the cross-references is invalid, it will produce an error. It can also check for "must-have" parameters and entries.

The "Go.bat" has only one command line:

```
FinalizeMSI PCDM "For All CE Devices" {53E7eeee-D637-40E8-A505-
1277326F0E0C}
```

Please remember to generate your own GUID for each of your applications. This GUID will be stored in the MSI system to find your installation. If you choose the same one over and over you will always start the same installation. Again, this GUID is case-sensitive; all letters in the GUID must be capital letters.

If the MSIVAL.2 logfile "T.LOG" does not show any errors or warnings, you have a perfect installation file. Now the only people who may complain will be the end users . . .

 The final source code of this section can be found on the companion CD under "\Sources\Thread Sample\PCDMSetup\CEInstall\Disk1".

Summary

MSI is the new Windows Installer technology that will help developers and support people simplify the mess that proprietary installations sometimes produced in the past. MSI is available on Windows 9x, NT4, and 2000.

I strongly encourage you to take a closer look at the MSI technology. For more details, SDKs, and white papers, visit the Microsoft Web site:

http://www.microsoft.com/Windows/professional/technical/whitepapers/Installer.asp

MSI is already a requirement for the new Windows 2000 logo programs.

11.6   Rules to Make Your App Logo-Compliant

In this book, you have learned a lot about logo requirements for Windows CE. There are some additional requirements, which this section will explain to you. If you want to examine the logo requirements in detail, download the latest logo handbooks from the following links:

H/PC Handheld Edition: ftp://ftp.veritest.com/mslogo/hpcedition.exe

Palm-size/Pocket PC Edition:
ftp://ftp.veritest.com/mslogo/pce_handbook.exe

AutoPC Edition: ftp://ftp.veritest.com/mslogo/AutoPC_handbook.exe

11.6.1   Logo Requirements of All Target Platforms

Each Windows CE logo requirements handbook has a set of common rules.

32-Bit Requirement

This logo requirement is the same for all versions of Windows. Compared to the desktop, where it is still possible to write 16-bit code, on Windows CE one has to use 32-bit code exclusively. Therefore all Windows CE programs fulfill this logo requirement.

Use Windows CE Application Installation Mechanisms

In Section 11.5, you learned how to install an application on your Windows CE device. Using ActiveSync for the installation is also a common logo requirement for all Windows CE devices. If you want to install to an embedded device, you will find this difficult because the ActiveSync part for Windows CE is not yet part of the Platform Builder.

To meet the logo requirements, you must also register all processor versions with ActiveSync. This requirement has a "gotcha". If Microsoft supports a new processor after the release of a platform, a "logo-ed" application must ship a new version as soon as the processor becomes available. This has already happened with the ARM processor and the H/PC Professional line. Moreover, if you want your application to get the logo, you must ship supporting binaries for all processor flavors. You can fulfill this requirement if you compile your code using the new CEF compiler. Since CEF is compiled during install time, it remains processor-neutral during compilation. The trade-off is that CEF applications are up to 20% slower and up to 20% larger than binary compiled applications.

Another very important installation requirement is that your application be able to run from a storage card. If you install your application to a storage card, remove the card, and reset the device, all the icons in your "Start" menu will be reset to the standard Windows icon. To restore the correct icons, you must insert the card and reset it again.

There are three more recommendations for the installation that might become requirements in the future. Two of them relate to the location of the installation files on the desktop. If you return to Section 11.5, you will see that you are already following those recommendations. In order to be logo-certified, applications must include a copy of the ".CAB" files and ".INI" files on the desktop in a folder under the "ActiveSync" directory. This will allow the reinstallation of the application at any time, should new Windows CE devices be connected to the desktop.

The last recommendation asks for a single executable. Most Windows CE applications these days consist of a single executable and multiple DLLs. Your PCDM application follows the same principle.

Regarding user data, the logo standards recommend either removing the data or informing the user that the uninstallation did not, in fact, remove user data and that the user should copy the data to a secure location in order to access them later. I strongly advise against automatically removing any user data during uninstallation. If a user accidentally uninstalls an application, he certainly will not want his data removed. Imagine if Microsoft Word removed all ".DOC" files every time that you uninstalled Word to clean your machine!

The Registry

This is very easy: All registry entries created by your application, either during installation or during runtime, must be removed. This includes user data. The registry contains an application's configuration data, which are a form of user data, but unlike user files in the file system, which contain data that the user might use again, the registry entries are very much tied to the application.

UI/Shell Requirements

Most of the UI and shell requirements are exactly the same as for the desktop. There are some additional ones, such as "You shall not duplicate the Address book or MessageStore APIs." For Pocket PCs, you must deal with your application's SIP virtual keyboard and your application must resize according to the taskbar settings.

An interesting logo recommendation is that applications should launch and close immediately. This design will give the user an impression of rapid task-change, especially on palm-size PC devices.

HTML help (see Section 11.2) and a default lack of caption bars for applications (see Chapter 7) are currently recommended, but I assume they will become requirements in the near future.

General Functionality

This section refers to communication (RAPI, Winsock, and IrDA, discussed in Chapter 9) and other general features related to the functionality of your application. There are only a few differences between the desktop and Windows CE applications. For example, there is a very strict sentence in the logo handbook:

 "Applications are not allowed to use proprietary methods of accessing the palm-size PC from the desktop."

If you rigorously followed this rule, you would not be able to use any form of remote COM (either DCOM or deviceCOM), or HTTP, or anything else except RAPI to connect your desktop to your device. Since older devices did not have any choice but RAPI, this requirement at least prevented ISVs from writing their own proprietary protocols. But with the emergence of widely available alternatives, such as HTTP and DCOM, this restriction must be lifted.

The section on long file name support is the same for Windows CE and the desktop.

Hibernation

Hibernation is a message (WM_HIBERNATE) the Windows CE operating system sends to all applications if memory gets short. An application is then required to free all unused resources and so reduce its memory usage by at least 25%. In the past (H/PC Version 2), an application was required to free 25% of its memory usage, which produced considerable discontent among software vendors. With H/PC Version 3, the logo requirement was relaxed to a "recommended 25%". In any case, Windows CE applications are normally designed to use minimal resources and cannot easily "just free 25%." But if you have sound effects, additional graphics, or cache allocations, you can free those in order to get the necessary 25%. But your PCDM application, for example, will not be able to release 25% of memory usage during runtime because it is so highly memory efficient as written.

11.6.2 Special H/PC Logo Requirements

Here are some special H/PC logo requirements that are neither valid nor even possible on palm-size PCs.

Mouse Cursor Support

Some H/PC Professional devices, such as the HP Journada and the NEC MobilPro, support mouse cursors. Your application thus needs to support the mouse cursor as well. There is really no reason to challenge this requirement. Since the logo does not require certain right-button features, you can choose the level of mouse support to incorporate into your application. The PCDM application, for example, does not use an object menu or anything else from the right mouse button, but it can be operated entirely by mouse.

11.6.3 Special Palm-size PC Requirements

The palm-size PC has even more special requirements than does the H/PC because of its unique keyboard-less design.

The Missing "X"-Close Button

This requirement has caused some heavy discussion between Microsoft and the software vendor community. The logo states:

 "Required: No user-exposed method for closing the application."

Many palm-size PC users do not understand that they cannot close any running application and have complained to software vendors. Most of those users were accustomed to closing applications on the desktop, but on palm-size PCs, the Windows CE shell closes an application when a new application is started and needs more memory or resources than are available. This requirement—along with that regarding state recovery—works very well on palm-size PCs. However, many software vendors have decided to include an "Exit" or "X" button anyway. In Chapter 7, you checked for the runtime platform first and then decided whether to include the exit and "X" button in the UI.

State Recovery

Without compliance with this logo requirement, the automatic closure of a running application would be fatal. State recovery is necessary to return an application closed by the shell to exactly the state that it had before it was closed. The simplest way to comply with this requirement is to save all necessary state information in the WM_CLOSE branch of your message loop. The shell will send a WM_CLOSE to your application before it tries to kill the process with a more "nasty" method if you ignore the WM_CLOSE branch.

Graceful Shutdown

Behind this logo requirement is the idea of getting rid of the "Are you sure?" before an application is terminated. Basically, if the shell tries to close an application and asks the user "Are you sure?," it neither knows what the user should be sure about, nor where this box is coming from. In order to comply with this rule, do not use any dialog box in the WM_CLOSE branch.

Hide the File System

 "Thou shalt not expose the file system."—Microsoft logo requirement, loosely translated.

The idea behind this logo requirement is to keep the user away from changes in the file system. Sooner or later, the desktop logo requirements will probably follow suit. To be honest, what does a user want from the file system anyway? Everything that the user needs or wants is accessible through applications. So if you are planning to create a file-explorer application for palm-size PCs, you can rest assured that it will not win you the palm-size PC logo.

Single Instance of Application

This requirement is related to the fact that the shell might close your application at any time. If the device were running multiple instances of your application, the shell might close them all at the same time, including the one then running in the front. Since your PCDM application is based on the MFC framework, it automatically contains code to ensure that your application only runs once. For an SDK application, you can use the following code to ensure a single instance:

```
if (hWnd=FindWindow(TEXT(<MainWindowClass>),
                     (LPTSTR)TEXT(<MainWindowName>)))
{
     BringWindowToTop(hWnd);
     ShowWindow(hWnd,SW_SHOWNORMAL);
     return(FALSE);
}
```

12 Chapter

Conclusions and Visions

12.1 A Word about Your PCDM Application

Agreed, your Pocket-CD-Manager is a very basic application that would require a lot of improvement in order to be marketable. Desirable features might include some of the following:

- The ability to delete a record off the table
- The ability to edit a record
- Performance enhancements in the synchronization/"PCDMUtils" class
- Better sorting and filtering capabilities

Another nice feature would be the playback of tracks that have been ripped from a CD and downloaded to the Windows CE device. But as I said in the beginning, the only purpose in life for the PCDM application is to serve as a real-world example that we have created from scratch to final production stage.

12.2 What's Next?

Thus far, you have learned a lot about the features and possibilities of Windows CE. But what can you do with it besides write cool tools or games for the mobile companions? This chapter should give you some ideas about the possibilities at hand.

You might wonder why this book includes a vision statement at all. Well, as you know, people like Bill Gates have often surprised the industry with new and exciting visions that have changed the world. In the area of Windows CE and the "tiny devices," I believe these visions are currently not expressed very loudly so as to avoid shocking the public or hurting partners in the PC OEM community.

But believe me, there are new visions. And Microsoft and other companies, including Siemens, Compaq, NEC, GE, and many Japanese firms—Sony, Mitsubishi, and Sega, among them—are already working to make these visions a reality.

Just sit back, look around, and think about the devices in your vicinity that in the future could be intelligent and networked. As I write this paragraph, I am sitting in the business class of a United Airlines jet fitted with those newly designed multi-function chairs. If I used a laptop, I could plug it right into a power outlet on the chair. But since I am using my fully charged Windows CE based H/PC Professional, I don't need to worry about power for the next eight hours. This fancy chair has a telephone that would let me connect my H/PC directly to my server at home and start a terminal session surfing the Web using my full T1 line. Only the fact that the telephone company still charges an arm and a leg for every minute prevents me from doing so.

Although this fancy chair is certainly well tricked out, it would have so much more potential if it became "intelligent." So far, the integrated video system allows me to select one of eight different video programs. The color screen embedded into the seat has a resolution of 640 × 480 and could be used perfectly well for Web browsing. Instead of renting only headphones to the customers, the airlines could also rent out keyboards like many hotels have begun doing.

And why stop there? I am a big fan of personal customization features. I already have a travel profile with United and could find my personal settings for the chair, position of the footrest, headrest, the setting of the new massage in the chair, volumes and language of the radio and so on, already set when I sit down. The chair could also connect to my home automation system via the Internet and check whether I have mail and whether my house alarm system is working properly. With the Web browser inside the video entertainment system, I could then connect to my home server and read my e-mail, which, of course, through unified messaging also shows my voice mails. In case I have to return earlier than expected from my trip, which happens to me all the time, I could change the temperature of my air conditioning at home so that I would feel comfortable as soon as I arrived. On my way home from the airport, I could pick up groceries, using a list that my refrigerator had automatically prepared at home and that my Pocket PC had downloaded while I sat in my comfortable seat on the airplane.

This fridge knows its contents exactly, it knows my favorite foods, and it keeps tabs on what I have had for dinners and lunches over the past couple of months (his brother, the oven, and his sister, the microwave, tell him). Whenever I add or remove an item, the refrigerator notes the "inventory" change by scanning a wireless tag that contains such information as the item's expiration date, category, and even appropriate recipes. It's not a reality yet, but it soon could be.

Of course, in the future you will no longer use the unfriendliest tool—the keyboard—to communicate with your computer, but rather natural language. To hear those commands all over your house there will be microphones in tiny devices that preprocess speech and transmit it either directly to the target device or to the central home computer. There will, of course, always be other input methods in addition to voice recognition for environments that do not permit voice input like libraries, loud factories, or that chair in the airplane. There will also be input methods that take into account the needs of those who either cannot speak or cannot speak clearly, for example, due to stroke. Still, I anticipate that the keyboard will undertake a huge evolution toward intelligent touch displays that transform themselves with every touch and therefore use much less space.

Since you would not want to discover that you could not switch on your lights whenever the central computer went down, the ideal technology here would be distributed intelligence. A light switch will talk directly to the lightbulb and, of course, can be routed to another lightbulb very easily. Have you ever tried to rewire a light switch? Well, you will love that feature. The same applies to your stereo and video equipment. Firewire (IEEE 1394) outlets in every room allow plugging in a DVD player, video camera, or television set anywhere and streaming the media to all the other rooms.

Speaking of the television, we finally get to your main input device. Guess what is the most ergonomic, easy to use, and widespread electronic device in the consumer market? The TV. And almost everybody can handle the remote, control for your TV set.

If you have monitored recent mergers between telecommunications and cable companies, you can no doubt forecast what the next conversion will bring. Web TV, game consoles, home automation controlled via your TV remote, and digital MP3 audio are just the beginning.

Coming back to distributed intelligence, a customer will never accept the necessity of turning on his TV in order to open his garage, adjust the temperature of his air conditioning, or cook a meal. Therefore all appliances will need to act and react independently of the central managing device and yet still be able to talk to one another.

12.2.1 How Small Will It Become?

Processors and RAM will not only become smaller and cheaper, but will also reduce their power consumption to the point that a single solar cell no larger than the eye of a needle could power one for days. The sensitivity of measurement sensors devices will increase in such a way that regular power lines can be used even for high-speed data transfer. Universal Plug-and-Play (UPnP) will allow the upgrade, exchange, or expansion of any setup without the hassle of configuration, programming, or other human intervention. To answer the question: smaller than a dime.

12.2.2 The Dark Side of the New World

Of course, all that has its dark side. If you have seen movies like *Enemy of the State, The Net,* or *Fair Game,* you have seen the potential negative side of those technologies. Not only would this be the old fear that "Big Brother is watching," but there would also be the new fear—that anybody could be watching. Nothing is 100% safe from hackers or crackers, and as soon as you have the means to access your home security system over the Web, it is potentially vulnerable to hackers. What can we do to protect ourselves?

It is my strong belief that total protection will not be possible. But there is also no sure protection against a sudden death by a falling rock, a drunken driver, or an insane shooter. The trick will be to make life as secure as possible without reducing the features of this new freedom.

As you have learned in this book, Windows CE only provides a basic set of security mechanisms. Instead, it places the responsibility on the application to include its own security. Microsoft will have some work here to improve that state without creating such a complicated security system that the only way of figuring it out is to switch it off.

Security must be distributed as well, even down to the smallest light switch and motion sensor. If a device enters a new domain space—for example, if you buy a new lamp—the device must be registered in its new domain. Again, this registration must not be complicated, or the average user will not do it. Data transfer from and to any device has to be encrypted, and any device must be able to function without a central server. Given the fact that you probably do not want to buy all your devices from one vendor, the encryption, security, and data transition protocols have to be unified and standardized—and in the competitive world of information electronics, such standardization is far from easy.

Another big threat is software viruses. With open and remote interfaces through the Internet, a new breed of viruses could spread through your home automation network and cook you spaghetti every day of the week, buy you foods that you hate, or just turn on all your lights in the middle of the night.

12.2.3   What Can You Do to Take Part?

If you have to design a device, know the industry standards, network protocols, and security standards that are relevant for the area in which you want to deploy the device. Integrate as much as you can, even if it might not make sense at the point when you want to deploy.

Do not skimp on RAM or ROM space. Check out the market; sometimes a chip with higher capacity is even cheaper than a smaller one. Design a good remote update strategy, especially in home automation. Customers do not want to update their toasters with complicated Web downloads, but if the toaster could complete an update by the press of a button, the user would be far more likely to do so. Finally, make sure that you do not forget security, because in a world of interconnectivity, having a software virus in the toaster might threaten many other devices—and could ruin countless perfectly good breakfasts as well.

Protect your code with certificates or some other protection mechanisms in order to prevent or at least decrease the opportunities for viruses.

12.3   Where Is the Technology Now?

Guess what . . . nearly all of the devices and ideas that I just mentioned are already possible with today's technologies. The only barriers to mass deployment and widespread availability are price and size. Once those two features come down, you will see an explosion of these devices on the market.

I am pretty sure that Bill Gates has already revised his vision for "a computer on every desk in every home" to "a computer *in* every desk in every home . . . and in every light switch and lightbulb and TV and stereo and garage door and fire alarm and . . . and . . . and . . ."

III

Part

Appendices

A
Appendix

Frequently Asked Questions

Why Did Microsoft Choose ADO over ODBC for Database Connectivity on Windows CE?

ODBC (Open Database Connectivity) was developed to access only relational data. It lacks any way of accessing other structured data like e-mail, object-oriented databases, or even the hierarchic file system. ADO includes all of those options and is therefore Microsoft's preferred technology. In the future, ODBC will not be enhanced or updated, but ADO will be. Since ADO is a COM abstraction layer for lower-level OLEDB interfaces, it is currently slower than ODBC. On Windows CE, ADOCE accesses the database natively on Windows CE 2.x, which is already as fast as possible. Starting with Windows CE 3.0, ADOCE will sit on top of the new OLEDB. More details on ADOCE can be found in Section 8.4.

Why Do You Recommend Windows 2000 over Windows NT4 at this "Early" Stage of Windows 2000?

Once you work with Windows 2000 or on Windows 2000, you will discover that Microsoft included many enhancements in Windows 2000 that can make your life easier and more productive. Since time is money these days, everything that speeds up your productivity is worth a lot.

But enough marketing babble. Here are some specifics that explain why I chose Windows 2000 over NT4:

- Multi-monitor support—Gives more screen estate for sources and the emulator.
- Infrared support—You will need this to exchange data with Windows CE.
- Plug and Play—No more manual-interrupt configuration.
- Better scalability—Try running Windows 2000 on a dual Pentium, and you will see what I mean.
- System files protection—It is not as easy to mess up a PC as it used to be.
- Notebook support—ACPI support, Instant-On, suspend, and Plug-and-Play make it a much better notebook OS than NT 4.

Why Do You Not Support Windows 9x?

Microsoft does not support the Windows 9x platform for Windows CE development due to Windows 9x's instability and its lack of Unicode support. Since Windows CE emulators do not work on Windows 9x, I do not recommend using Windows 9x as a development platform. A more detailed explanation can be found in Chapter 3.

When Do I Need to Install the RAS Services Manually?

Section 9.1 explains the circumstance under which you need to install RAS manually.

Why Do You Set the Baud Rate of the Modem to 115,200?

Downloading and debugging with the default rate of 19,200 is no fun. Most devices on the market support this high a baud rate without difficulty.

Do I Have to Install Office 2000?

To get the ActiveSync feature setup, you need Outlook 2000. You do not need to have Office 2000 installed for the examples or anything else in this book.

Why Is There So Little about AutoPC or SEGA Dreamcast in this Book?

The AutoPC and the SEGA Dreamcast game console are very different platforms from the H/PC or the palm-size PC. They have different UI concepts and support only a tiny subset of Windows CE. Given the differences, it would take an extra book to write about those two platforms. In the case of the Dreamcast console, there is not even a publicly available SDK because SEGA requires ISVs to sign up for the development program and checks out vendors before they are permitted any access to the SDK. This procedure is their way of ensuring the quality of games for the Dreamcast console.

Why Do You Recommend Creating the UI Before Adding the Core Code to an Application?

This is part of an ongoing dispute between UI people and core people. Who is more important to the application? Well the answer is: *They are both equally important.* With the exception of drivers and other UI-less components, the UI is, as its name announces, the interface to the user. If the user cannot handle or does not like the interface, she will not buy the product—even if the core is much better than its competition. A good example of this is UNIX versus Windows. The core of UNIX (or Linux) may be far better than the core of Windows 3.x and Win9x, but Linux/UNIX lost a lot of accounts due to Windows' much friendlier UI.

The earlier you have a UI prototype, the earlier you can do usability studies. You simply cannot do this with pure core code. You have to hope the user will accept it when it is done. Since I mentioned the driver, here is a small rule of thumb that shows which application type should start with which feature area:

- Servers, drivers, compilers, and business logic components should start off with the core technologies.

- Utilities, IDEs, Games, productivity applications (Word, Excel), and all other applications that involve a lot of user interaction should start with the UI design.

B

Appendix

The PCDMUtils Class

The PCDMUtils class does not actually use any special Windows CE technology. Since some of sections of the book (for example, Section 9.3, on ActiveSync, and Section 9.6, on IrDA) use this class, it is included here for your reference.

The purpose of the class is to analyze a BSTRing that contains one or more URLs. These URLs have the following syntax:

```
PCDMIrDA://PCDM/<PCDMClass>?<CommandString>;
```

- **"PCDMIrDA://"** is the protocol moniker.
- **"PCDM"** refers to the address of the target machine/device to receive the URL. In this case, you have a defined target machine and use the address for the application name.
- **"<PCDMClass>"** is the name of the class that will run the command string. In your parser only "PCDMAccessDB" is implemented.
- **"<CommandString>"** contains the command that has to be executed against the "PCDMAccessDB" class. It has the following syntax:

```
Command=<CommandID>[&<ParameterString>…]
```

Your parser only knows one CommandID ("1"). This is used to insert a new record into the database. CommandID "1" requires at least the following parameters in the <ParameterString>:

```
Table=<TableName>[&IDX=<indexFieldNumber>]&Fld<FieldNumber>=<Value>[&…]
```

- **"<TableName>"** refers to the table the new fields will be inserted in.
- **"<IndexFieldNumber>"** refers to the "Fld" parameter that contains the index of the new record. If the value of that field exists in the database, the new record will not be inserted. This parameter is optional. If it does not exist in the parameter string, the parser will not check the existence of the record index and will not write the new record into the database. This PCDMTracks table does not contain an index. Multiple records can have the same TitleID, and therefore you should not use the "IDX" parameter here.
- **"Fld<FieldNumber>"** addresses the name of the field.
- **"<value>"** holds the value that will be put into the corresponding field. There can be multiple Fld#=Value entries in the parameter string.

The parser follows the rules of URL construction, although its implementation is very basic and does not allow for any tolerance errors.

The PCDMUtils class requires a series of methods that you will also expose via COM in case you want to use them from your hosting application. Here is what you have to do to get the class added to the PCDMDLL project:

1. Open the PCDMDLL project to which you want to add the PCDMUtils class and select "New ATL Object . . ." on the root of the class view tree.

2. Select the "Simple object" and name it "PCDMUtils".

The first method you will add is the "AnalyzeURL" method. It is the main loop extracting URLs from the incoming BSTRing; it parses the class and sends it to the "Execute" method.

3. "AnalyzeURL" takes the parameter shown in Table B.1.

The implementation of this method looks like this:

```
STDMETHODIMP CPCDMUtils::AnalyseURL(BSTR bstrURL)
{
int i=0,idx=0;
long CmdClass=0;
BSTR strURL,strCMD;
HRESULT hr;
```

Table B.1 Parameter of the AnalyzeURL() Method

Type	Variable Name	Used for
BSTR	BstrURL	The caller inserts one or more URLs to be analyzed by this method.

```
    while (GetURL(idx,bstrURL,&strURL)==S_OK)
    {
            hr=GetClass(strURL,&CmdClass);
            if (hr==S_OK && CmdClass==PCDMCLASS_ACCESSDB)
            {
                    if (GetCommand(strURL,&strCMD)==S_OK)
                    {
                            hr=ExecuteADBCmd(strCMD);
                            if (hr==ERROR_DUP_NAME)
                                    return hr;
                    }
            }
            idx++;
    }
    return S_OK;
}
```

The line in bold shows that you are only supporting the PCDMAccessDB class. If you want to support the other classes of the PCDMDLL control, you need to add a new "Execute<Class>Cmd" method for each of those classes.

4. The next method you will add is "GetURL". It has the parameters listed in Table B.2.

5. Its implementation is as follows:

```
STDMETHODIMP CPCDMUtils::GetURL(LONG Index, BSTR InURL, BSTR *OutURL)
{
int pos,oldPos,j;

    pos=0;
    for (j=0;j<Index+1;j++)
```

Table B.2   **Parameters of the GetURL() Method**

Type	Variable Name	Used for
LONG	Index	Index of the URL inside the "InURL" Bstring.
BSTR	InURL	The caller inserts one or more URLs to be analyzed by this method.
[out,retval] BSTR *	OutURL	This BSTR will contain the extracted URL.

```
        {
                oldPos=pos;
                pos=InstrPos(InURL,pos,TEXT(";"));
                if (pos<0)        break;
        }
        if (pos>0)
                MidStr(InURL,oldPos,pos-1,OutURL);
        else
                return S_FALSE;
        return S_OK;
}
```

No big surprises here. You are just looking for the termination ";" character and read out the string.

The next method, "GetClass", is referenced in the "AnalyzeURL" method. It returns the "ClassID" of your PCDMDLL classes. This method already supports all your classes.

6.   The parameters of this method are shown in Table B.3.

7.   Here is the implementation of this class:

```
STDMETHODIMP CPCDMUtils::GetClass(BSTR InURL, LONG *ClassID)
{
BSTR ClassStr;
long pos=-1,startpos=-1,endpos=-1;

        pos=InstrPos(InURL,0,TEXT("://"));
        if (pos>=0)
                startpos=InstrPos(InURL,pos,TEXT("/"));
```

Table B.3   Parameters of the GetClass() Method

Type	Variable Name	Used for
BSTR	InURL	The BSTR containing the URL to be parsed.
[out,retval] LONG *	ClassID	The resulting ClassID. If it was not found the class ID is zero and the method returns S_FALSE.

```
    if (startpos>=0)
        endpos=InstrPos(InURL,startpos,TEXT("?"));
    if (endpos-1>0)
    {
        *ClassID=0L;
        MidStr(InURL,startpos,endpos-1,&ClassStr);
        if (!CompareString(LOCALE_USER_DEFAULT,
        NORM_IGNORECASE,ClassStr,-1,TEXT("PCDMAccessDB"), -1)-2)
            *ClassID=PCDMCLASS_ACCESSDB;
        else if (!CompareString(LOCALE_USER_DEFAULT,
        NORM_IGNORECASE,ClassStr,-1,TEXT("PCDMAccessReg"), -1)-2)
            *ClassID=PCDMCLASS_ACCESSREG;
        else if (!CompareString(LOCALE_USER_DEFAULT,
        NORM_IGNORECASE,ClassStr,-1,TEXT("PCDMUtils"), -1)-2)
            *ClassID=PCDMCLASS_UTILS;
        else if (!CompareString(LOCALE_USER_DEFAULT,
        NORM_IGNORECASE,ClassStr,-1,TEXT("PCDMInput"), -1)-2)
            *ClassID=PCDMCLASS_INPUT;
        else if (!CompareString(LOCALE_USER_DEFAULT,
        NORM_IGNORECASE,ClassStr,-1,TEXT("PCDMTransfer"), -1)-2)
            *ClassID=PCDMCLASS_TRANSFER;
    }
    else
        return S_FALSE;
    return S_OK;
}
```

8. The "PCDMCLASS_<name>" constants are defined in the PCDMUtils.h include file:

```
#define PCDMCLASS_ACCESSREG    1
#define PCDMCLASS_INPUT        2
#define PCDMCLASS_ACCESSDB     3
#define PCDMCLASS_UTILS        4
#define PCDMCLASS_TRANSFER     5

#define     ADBCMD_INSERT      1
```

9. The "GetCommand" method will extract the command string from the URL. It takes two parameters, shown in Table B.4.

10. Its implementation is pretty short:

Table B.4   Parameters of the GetCommand() Method

Type	Variable Name	Used for
BSTR	InURL	The BSTR containing the URL to be parsed
[out,retval] BSTR *	Command	The command string

```
STDMETHODIMP CPCDMUtils::GetCommand(BSTR InURL, BSTR *Command)
{
int pos=-1;
     pos=InstrPos(InURL,0,TEXT("?"));
     if (pos>=0)
          MidStr(InURL,pos,lstrlen(InURL),Command);
     else
          return S_FALSE;
     return S_OK;
}
```

11. The "GetTagValue" method returns a tag value to a given tag name from a command string. It takes three parameters, as shown in Table B.5.

12. Here is the code for this method:

```
STDMETHODIMP CPCDMUtils::GetTagValue(BSTR InCMD, BSTR TagName,
                                     BSTR *TagValue)
{
int pos=0,endpos=-1;
TCHAR tTagName[255];

     wsprintf(tTagName,TEXT("%s="),TagName);
     pos=InstrPos(InCMD,0,tTagName);
     if (pos>=0)
```

Table B.5   Parameters of the GetTagValue() Method

Type	Variable Name	Used for
BSTR	InURL	The BSTR containing the URL to be parsed
BSTR	TagName	The name of the tag you are looking for
[out,retval] BSTR *	TagValue	On success, contains the corresponding tag value

```
        endpos=InstrPos(InCMD,pos,TEXT("&"));
if (endpos-1>0 || (pos<lstrlen(InCMD) && pos>=0))
{
        if (endpos<pos) endpos=lstrlen(InCMD)+1;
        MidStr(InCMD,pos,endpos-1,TagValue);
}
else
        return S_FALSE;
return S_OK;
}
```

All the above methods use two functions named "InstrPos" and "MidStr".

13. These private functions of the "CPCDMUtils" class and are defined as follows (see Tables B.6 and B.7).

Table B.6   Parameters of the InstrPos() Method

Type	Variable Name	Used for
TCHAR *	InSTR	The string to be parsed
Long	Start	The position in the string to start parsing
TCHAR *	Tchar	The string you are looking for in the InSTR

Table B.7   Parameters of the MidStr() Method

Type	Variable Name	Used for
TCHAR *	InSTR	The string containing the partial string that you want
Long	StartPos	The position in the string where your new string starts
Long	EndPos	The position in the string where your new string ends
BSTR *	OutSTR	The resulting string

```
long CPCDMUtils::InstrPos(TCHAR *InSTR, LONG Start, TCHAR *tChar)
{
unsigned int i;

        if (Start>(long)lstrlen(InSTR)) return -1;
        i=Start;
        while (i<=(lstrlen(InSTR)-lstrlen(tChar)) &&
                CompareString(LOCALE_USER_DEFAULT,
                NORM_IGNORECASE,&InSTR[i],lstrlen(tChar),tChar,
                lstrlen(tChar))-2)
                i++;
        i+=lstrlen(tChar);
        if (i>lstrlen(InSTR)) i=-1;
        return (long)i;
}

BOOL CPCDMUtils::MidStr(TCHAR *InSTR, long StartPos, long EndPos,
                        BSTR *OutSTR)
{
TCHAR tmpStr[500];
long j=0,i;

        for (i=StartPos;i<EndPos;i++)
        {
                tmpStr[j]=InSTR[i];
                j++;
        }
        tmpStr[j]=0;
        *OutSTR=SysAllocString(tmpStr);
        return TRUE;
}
```

Finally, you have your command string and know that it belongs to the PCDMAccessDB class.

The next method, "ExecuteADBCmd", will take the command string, parse it, and execute it against the PCDMAccessDB class. As mentioned before, you need to create similar "Execute" methods for the other classes.

14.   The method has only one parameter, shown in Table B.8.

Table B.8   Parameter of the ExecuteADBCmd() Method

Type	Variable Name	Used for
TCHAR *	InSTR	The string containing the command

15.   Here is the implementation of the method:

```
STDMETHODIMP CPCDMUtils::ExecuteADBCmd(BSTR Command)
{
BSTR Cmd,Table,Value,IDX;
VARIANT      tValue,t1Value;
TCHAR tStr[20];
HRESULT hre,hret=S_OK;

    VariantInit(&tValue);
    VariantInit(&t1Value);
    HRESULT hr=GetTagValue(Command,TEXT("Command"),&Cmd);
    if (hr==S_OK)
    {
        tValue.vt=VT_BSTR;
        tValue.bstrVal=SysAllocString(Cmd);
        VariantChangeType(&t1Value,&tValue,0,VT_I4);
        switch (t1Value.lVal)
        {
            case ADBCMD_INSERT:
            {
            int i=0;
            long DBHandle;
            hr=GetTagValue(Command,TEXT("Table"),&Table);
            if (hr==S_OK)
            {
                CComObject<CPCDMAccessDB>* comDB = new
                        CComObject<CPCDMAccessDB>();
                HRESULT hr = comDB->FinalConstruct();
                hr=GetTagValue(Command,TEXT("IDX"),&IDX);
                if (hr!=S_OK)
                    IDX=SysAllocString(TEXT("0"));
```

```
hre=comDB->OpenTable(
            TEXT("\\My Documents\\PCDM.cdb")
            ,Table,_variant_t(IDX),&DBHandle);
if (FAILED(hre)) break;
if (hr==S_OK)
{
    wsprintf(tStr,TEXT("Fld%s"),IDX);
    hr=GetTagValue(Command,tStr,&Value);
    if (hr!=S_OK)
    {
        comDB->CloseTable(DBHandle);
        hret=ERROR_INVALID_PARAMETER;
        break;
    }
    hr=comDB->FindRecord
            (DBHandle,_variant_t(IDX),
            _variant_t(Value));
    if (hr==S_OK)
    {
        comDB->CloseTable(DBHandle);
        hret=ERROR_DUP_NAME;
        break;
    }
}
hr=comDB->AddNewRecord(DBHandle);
if (FAILED(hr)) break;
do
{
    wsprintf(tStr,TEXT("Fld%d"),i);
    hr=GetTagValue(Command,tStr,&Value);
    if (hr==S_OK)
      hr=comDB->SetValue(_variant_t
      ((LONG)i),
                            _variant_t
                            (Value));
    i++;
} while (hr==S_OK);
hr=comDB->WriteRecord(DBHandle);
comDB->CloseTable(DBHandle);
}
}
```

```
            break;
            default:        // Add more commands here...
            break;
        }
    }
    return hret;
}
```

You can see that the code only supports one command named "ADBCMD_INSERT". If you want support more commands, just add the corresponding "case" branches.

As mentioned above, the book uses the "AnalyzeURL" method in Sections 9.3 and 9.6, which discuss ActiveSync and IrDA, respectively. If you want to experiment with this class, you could add the command parsers of the other classes. By sending URLs to a PCDM application, you could do interesting things in a remote device like writing strings into the registry, changing values in a database, or just popping up the SIP on the remote device.

The final source code of this section can be found on the companion CD under "\Sources\ThreadExample\PCDMDLL\Step6".

C

Appendix

Glossary and Abbreviations

Active Data Objects (ADO)

Microsoft has designated ADO as its most strategic data access technology. It thus replaces the old technologies RDO (Remote Data Objects), DAO (Data Access Objects), ODBC (Open Database Connectivity), and RDS (Remote Data Services). It is a developer-friendly interface for OLEDB (no real abbreviation). OLEDB is the fastest way to get to data, except with data held in relational databases, where ODBC still holds a slight edge. But Microsoft is working to give OLEDB superior performance in every respect. OLEDB was designed to access not only relational databases, but also all kinds of structured data like Mail Application Programmable Interface (MAPI), Active Directory Service Interface (ADSI), and even the file system. To access a data source using OLEDB, the data source must provide an "OLEDB provider," which, in fact, provides nothing but a more "interesting" name for a driver to access the data source with OLEDB. There is also an OLEDB provider that can be plugged on top of ODBC because there are a lot of databases out there that only have ODBC interfaces. Section 8.4 covers this technology in detail.

Application Programmable Interface (API)

Before Microsoft introduced COM and the Windows world widely adopted this new concept, every application had to interface with another application via API calls. An API call is an exported function mostly from a DLL (dynamic link library). In newer application architectures, COM interfaces are used more often than exported functions (API). Many operation system functions, especially old and legacy calls, are still based on APIs and require a LIB (library) to be bound to your application. In the COM world this is not longer necessary.

Active Template Library (ATL)

The ATL is an application framework technology that helps developers to build small and lightweight components. The focus of ATL is on ActiveX controls and COM servers, but you can also use ATL to create standard DLLs. You will find that ATL is used throughout this book.

Common Object Model (COM)

A brief explanation of COM would be that it is the successor to API. Instead of loading the exported function using a static or dynamic library, the client application asks the COM runtime (OLE32.DLL or OLEAUT32.DLL) to connect it to the server application. It is not necessary to bind a library to the client application during the development of an application. See Chapter 6 to learn how you can use COM on Windows CE.

Distributed COM (DCOM)

DCOM is a remote protocol, based on DCE-RPC, that invokes COM components and calls their methods on distant Windows computers. Starting with Windows CE 3.0, DCOM also became available on selected Windows CE devices. Windows CE 2.x devices can use a third-party technology called deviceCOM to achieve the same goal. Chapter 6 and Section 9.4 explain the use of these technologies in more detail.

Dynamic Host Configuration Protocol (DHCP)

For a TCP/IP network to function correctly, a lot of configuration parameters need to be defined and set. A DHCP server can issue these parameters automatically to clients with Ethernet cards. This is very convenient and easy to administer.

Dynamic Link Library (DLL)

Before COM moved to the fore, the only way to create component-based applications was by means of DLLs. Those dynamic link libraries were loaded to the application either statically, during link time, or dynamically, using the command "LoadLibrary". Most COM controls are still packaged on DLLs, but they no longer have to be loaded with "LoadLibrary" or statically. The COM API call "CoCreateInstance" now does this for you.

Hypertext Transfer Protocol (HTTP)

HTTP is thus far one of the IT industry's most important inventions. The Hypertext Transfer Protocol is the main foundation of the Internet and permits the transmission of data between an HTTP (Web) server and an HTTP (browser) client. Section 9.7 shows you how you can make use of this protocol in Windows CE.

Integrated Development Environment (IDE)

An IDE represents the shell a developer is working in. Visual Studio currently has three IDEs: the Visual Basic IDE, the Visual Interdev IDE, and the Visual C++ IDE. Microsoft plans to combine all three in the future to reduce the training times for new developers and to encourage cross-language development.

Interface Definition Language (IDL)

IDL fulfills a similar task as the class description of a C++ class. The only difference is that an interface of a COM component can span and include methods of multiple classes. An interface represents the public description of a COM component. Without it, a COM component cannot be accessed by any other application. In Visual Basic the interface of a class module is generated automatically for each method with the "public" keyword in front. Visual C++ developers have to create the interface, using the IDL. C++ frameworks like ATL and MFC generate the IDL for you.

Interprocess Communication (IPC)

This protocol is used to communicate between two applications running on the same machine.

Infrared Data Association (IrDA)

IrDA is an organization devoted to creating a unified international standard for the exchange of data via infrared technology. All Windows CE devices support this standard. Section 9.6 explains more about IrDA. You can also visit the Web site of the IrDA: http://www.irda.org.

Information Technology (IT)

You should be familiar with this abbreviation. If you are reading this book, you are most likely tilling the fields of IT.

Marshaller: A Code/Object Converter/Transformer

In working with COM, you will often hear the term "marshaller". Marshalling data simply means converting it from one format into another. In the case of COM, a marshaller converts the data of one class to general RPC data and then back into the format in which the target application wants it. No marshalling is necessary in using C++ and in-process components, but as soon as the data leave process boundaries, or even machine boundaries, a marshaller has to step in.

Object Menu/Context Menu

Context or object menus are tiny menus (they should have a maximum of 11 entries) that pop up directly above an object on the screen as soon as you click on that object with the right mouse button.

Open Database Connectivity (ODBC)

With ODBC Microsoft tried for the first time to give the developer community a standard API for accessing data in databases. Since its introduction, various companies have written ODBC drivers for all kinds of databases, such as Sybase, Oracle, and, of course, the Microsoft databases, Access and SQL server. These days ADO and OLEDB are much richer in functionality and will eventually replace ODBC completely.

Object Linking and Embedding (OLE)

OLE was the first incarnation of Microsoft's object-oriented strategy. Unfortunately, Microsoft changed its name repeatedly and thus created a lot of confusion over the years. OLE, ActiveX, and COM all describe the same concept. There are just years between them—and some slight redefinitions. OLE's original purpose was to permit one object to link or point into another object, as, for example, in having an Excel spreadsheet inside a Word document. OLEDB and OLE Automation are technologies closer to the new COM concept that define a common communication architecture between two objects. The word OLE inside OLEDB and OLE Automation is rather confusing and has nothing to do with the original "Object Linking and Embedding."

Pocket-CD-Manager (PCDM)

This book's central thread example is named the Pocket-CD-Manager.

Remote API (RAPI)

Windows CE devices needed a way to become remotely configurable. Microsoft decided to create a new API called RAPI, (Remote API). Basically, it lets a desktop application call any function on a Windows CE device after a short initialization. Since it is a one-way protocol (a desktop application can call into Windows CE but not vice versa), it should not be used for application-to-application communication, but only for configuration. Better technologies to deal with the app-2-app challenge are DCOM or HTTP World Wide Web-based solutions. Section 9.2 explains the technology in more detail.

Remote Access Services (RAS)

Starting with ActiveSync 3.0, RAS is no longer required to connect your Windows CE device to your desktop. Microsoft was using RAS during the days of "Windows CE Services" because it wanted to use a standard Windows technology to realize the connection. Unfortunately, RAS is complicated to set up, and, faced with increasing complaints from Windows CE customers, Microsoft has abandoned its original plan. If you want to connect to your desktop PC using a modem, you still need to install and configure RAS. Section 9.1 explains how you can do this.

Transmission Control Protocol (TCP)

Defined in RFC 793, the TCP is a more complex synchronous protocol that ensures that packages get delivered to the receiver. However, TCP does not determine how long the transmission may take or the order in which packages are delivered.

User Datagram Protocol (UDP)

UDP, defined in RFC 768, is an asynchronous protocol used for high-speed data transfer over the Internet. Since it is asynchronous you cannot be sure whether your packages are actually reaching the recipients. The TCP protocol is used to ensure delivery.

User Interface (UI)

The UI encompasses the dialog boxes, button controls, and windows that a user uses to interact with an application. You will also find the related term "graphical user interface" (GUI) used in some of the literature.

Universal Plug-and-Play (UPnP)

UPnP is a new initiative to make it easier for users to discover and configure devices on a network. Based on XML and HTTP, UPnP provides an easy-to-exercise protocol to find out what is on your network. If you want to read more about this initiative visit: http://www.upnp.com.

Extended Markup Language (XML)

XML is the mother of all the markup languages (MLs), which include Hypertext Markup Language (HTML), which is used throughout the Internet, and Structured Graphics Markup Language (SGML), which is used for many documentations. The difference between HTML and XML is that HTML is used to describe the representation of data and XML describes the data itself. In HTML and SGML, only certain specific tags are known and can be rendered by a browser. With XML all kinds of tags are allowed. The trick is to agree upon a single schema, at which point a sender/server can exchange data with a client/browser. XML is currently the most widely accepted data communication format across a large variety of industries. Since it is essentially text-based, it is very easy to write servers and browsers. I would not be surprised if there will be new marshallers for COM in the future that marshall in XML instead of in a binary format. Sure, it would create bigger telegrams and more traffic overhead, but you could also send the telegrams over e-mail or the Web.

D

Appendix

Tips and Tricks for Unicode versus ANSI

Windows CE only supports Unicode applications and controls. If you only plan to target Windows CE and Windows NT/2000, this restriction will not bother you much. But as soon as you try to target Windows 9.x, you will run into trouble. This appendix offers some tips on how to use much the same code on all platforms.

Use TEXT(" ") instead of L""

You might be familiar with the L"" and TEXT(" ") macros that convert a regular string to a UNICODE string. The difference between L and TEXT is that L always creates a UNICODE string and, if passed to an ANSI call under Win9x, will create a conversion error. TEXT, on the other hand, is target-depending. If you compile for Unicode or Windows CE, it will create a Unicode string; if you compile for an ANSI target, it will create an ANSI string.

Use "TCHAR" for All String Definitions

There is a similar issue with regard to the definition of strings and string arrays. Do not use WCHAR or CHAR to declare your strings but rather the target-dependent TCHAR. You should use CHAR only in very rare circumstances—for example, in the

IP address for the socket description—or WCHAR—for example, in calls that require Unicode strings even under Win9x.

Use "wsprintf" for String Formatting

If you are used to the "sprintf" function in C to format a string, you will have to get used to the "wsprintf" function instead. It works with TEXT and TCHAR declared strings.

Use "lstrlen" instead of "strlen"

Another no-brainer is the use of "lstrlen" instead of "strlen".

Use the ATL- or MFC-Provided Conversion Macros

If you use the ATL or MFC for your application, you can use the macros that those frameworks provide. To activate those macros you have to add the following line to the top of the function or method in which you wish to use the conversion macros:

```
USES_CONVERSION;
```

Now you can use the following macros to convert ANSI to Unicode strings and vice versa. Table D.1 lists the macros and how they are used.

Table D.1   ATL Conversion Macros

Name	Converts	to	Usage	Remarks

A2(C)W	CHAR	LP(C)STR	WCHAR *twStr;
			`twStr=A2W`
			`("ANSI String")`
				The "C" in front of the "W" defines the return value as being a LPCSTR. Many API calls require the "constant" version of the LPSTR.

W2(C)A	LPSTR	LP(C)STR	CHAR *taStr;
			`taStr=W2A`
			`(L"Uni-String");`
				Remember that LPSTR is ANSI on Win9x and Unicode on Windows CE.

T2(C)OLECHAR
T2(C)OLE
	LPSTR	OLECHAR	OLECHAR *tstr;
			`Tstr=T2OLECHAR`
			`(TEXT("string"));`
				OLECHAR is still used by many old desktop API calls and remains in ATL for compatibility purposes.

OLECHAR2(C)T
OLE2(C)T
	OLECHAR	LPSTR	TCHAR *tstr;
			`Tstr=OLECHAR2T`
			`(L"String");`	

Index

A

AboutText object, 121

Access 2000 database
copying to emulation, 334–339
Pocket-Access synchronized with, 339–344

Access import wizard
setting field break lines in, *39*

Active Data Object, 31, 57, 58, 59, 61, 273, 280, 305, 557
cursors for Windows CE, *317*
lock types for Windows CE, *317*
over ODBC for database connectivity on Windows CE, 541
for Windows CE, 157

Active Directory Service Interface, 557

Active Server Pages, 109

ActiveStore, 382

ActiveSync, 26, 30, 31, 34, 35, 272, 277, 347, 369–405, 555
concept of, 370–371
connection dialog, *33*
CPCDMSyncFolder methods called by, during synchronization, *376*

creating service provider for PCDM, 371–373
debugging tips for, 404–405
DeluxeCD.MDB synchronization by, 342, 343, 344
desktop side of, 373–390
development documentation, 405
features, 15
mapping of containers to example objects, *371*
options, *32*
options page, *389*
processor versions registered with, 528
and provider, 371, 403–404
and RAS, 349, 350
and remote connectivity, 157
simplified flowchart driven from desktop side, *373*
simplified flowchart driven from Windows CE side, *391*
synchronization tables, *344*
Windows CE side of, 390–403
ActiveSync button (Start bar), 34

Note: *Italicized page numbers denote locations of figures/tables*

ActiveSync 3.0 connectivity
  differences between RAS and, *361*
ActiveSync 3.1, 27
ActiveSync provider
  for desktop PCDMSync.DLL, 512
  dry run of, 390
  installing, 496
  new component added to, 513–516
  PCDMDLL used by, 74
  Wizard, 371, 384
ActiveSync Service Provider Wizard
  description page, *372*
Active Template Library, 153, 558
  controls created with, 118
  conversion macros in, 566, *567*
  object types in, *120*
  wizard, 69
ActiveX containers, 128
ActiveX controls, 77, 116, 153, 558
  creating, 118, 127–140
  creating inside PCDMUI.DLL, 167
  debugging, 70
  desktop equivalent generated for, 133
  difference between desktop and Windows
    CE versions, 77
  events added to, 131
  generating desktop equivalent for, 133
  methods added to, 131–133
  and PCDMView.cpp, 78
  properties added to, 128–130
  removing, 43
  replacement table, *97*
  selection dialog box for, in Visual C++,
    134
  unsupported, 96
  using in eMbedded Visual Basic,
    137–140
  using in eMbedded Visual C++, 133–137
  for Windows CE, 44
ActiveX method
  changing parameters of, 199
AddAdornments method, 201, 206
AddColumn() parameters, *225*
AddItem() parameters, *226, 229*

AddNewRecord method, 288, 329, 330
AddProperty method, 321
AddStringToComboBox() parameters, *175*
Administrator account
  selecting, 354–355
ADO. *See* Active Data Objects
ADOCE, 541
  differences between native object store
    and, 307–308
  problem areas in, 326
ADOCE for Windows CE
  availability table for, *306*
ADOCE.H, 315
ADOCERecordSet, 102, 307, 308
ADOCE SDK, 335, 336
ADOCE 2.0, 305, 314, 315, 316, 319, 326,
    330, 336
ADOCE 3.0, 309, 314, 315, 316, 319, 326,
    330
ADOCE30.h include file, 310
ADO Desktop
  migrating, to ADO for Windows CE,
    102–107
ADO for desktop
  ADO for Windows CE compared to, *309*
ADO for Windows CE, 304–334
  ADO for desktop compared to, *309*
  benefits of, 306–307
  command interpreting enumerations for,
    317
  map of native object store calls to, *319*
  object model for, *305*
  recordsets known by, 102
  simple application using, 309–334
  supported SQL statements of, *318*
  supports only .CDB and Object-Store,
    102–103
ADO Recordset, 96
Adornments, 161, 201
ADSI. *See* Active Directory Service
    Interface
Advanced Graphics Port, 13
AfxOleInit() function, 77
AGP. *See* Advanced Graphics Port

AnalyzeURL() method, 548, 555
    parameters of, *546*
ANSI
    code, 132, 133
    tips and tricks for Unicode *versus*,
        565–567
API. *See* Application Programmable
    Interface
API Viewer Tool, 98
App.End, 100
AppInstaller, 369
Applets control panel, 479–481
Appliance management, 535
Application Programmable Interface,
    558
Applications
    API, accessing object store, 274–277
    command-band added to, 190–195
    command bar added to, 159–167
    ink control, 259–262
    list view controls included in, 220–222
AppSearch table, 520–521
    entries, *520*
AppWizard
    desktop *versus* Windows CE, 76
    MFC, 75–76
ARM, 59, 491, 528
ASPs. *See* Active Server Pages
ATA disks, 270
ATL. *See* Active Template Library
ATL_DRAWINFO structure, 69
Auto-complete, 53
Automation Interface, 116
AutoPC, 16, 58, 459, 543
    form technology developed for, 59
AUTORUN.EXE, 503, 506
aygshell.dll, 473

B
Backup keys, 264
Baud rate
    setting, 543
    setting of communication cable, 351–352

Binding, early
    lack of necessity for, 113–114
BitBlit, 459, 460
Bitmap display with GDI, 459–463
    PCDM application updated, 462–463
    PCDMPicture Class tested in eMbedded
        Visual Basic, 462
    updating OnDraw of PCDMPicture
        Class, 460–461
Bitmap loading, 448–459
    custom code use, 450–457
    picture class added to PCDMUI.DLL,
        457–459
    using LoadBitmap(), 449
    using SHLoadDiBitmap(), 449–450
Bitmap management
    private class member variables for, 458
Bitmaps, 447–448
Bitmap stock objects
    for toolbar object, *163*
BlitDIB function, 454
Blitter, 450
Blitting, 450, 459, 460
BMP, 448
Book831 icon
    in database folder, *277*
Bookmark property, 329
Box, Don, 112
BSTRing, 545
BuildItem method, 377
Buttons, 170
    adornment, 161
    in command bar, 158
    ToolTips assigned to, 166, 214
BytesPerLine, 456

C
C++
    COM server called in, 123
CAB files, 485
    copying to CF-Card, 473
    copying to Windows CE device, 497
    files copied from, to target directory, 495

CAB files (*cont.*)
  and logo requirements, 528
  setting path variable to directory
    containing, *513*
  testing with CF-Card, 510
Cable speed
  setting, 350, 351–352
CABWIZ.EXE, 497
Calendar data, 272
CancelReceive method, 425, 429,
    430, 433
Cassiopeia A10, 447
CCeDBDatabase class, 277
CCeDBEnum() class, 279
CCeDBProp class, 277
CCeDBRecord class, 277
CCeSocket, 408
.CDB file
  ADO for Windows CE support for,
    102–103
CD-Details form
  creating, 236–242
  list of controls for, *237*
  source view of, for palm-size PCs, *238*
  source view of PCDM, *237*
CDEdit form, 92
CD-ROM
  DVD-ROM over, 15
CEDevice sections
  binaries for, 494
CEF. *See* Common Executable Format
CEF compiler, 528
CeOCXHost dialog box
  member variables in, *136*
CEOID m_curRec, 287
CEPC, *17*
$(CEPlatform)
  translations of definition at compile
    time, *63*
$(CEPlatform) compiler
  preprocessor definition, 63
CeRapiInit() call, 365
Certificates, 537
CeSeekDatabase() call, 273, 287

CF-Card Instant-Installer
  for Pocket PC, 503–510
CF-Cards (Compact-Flash), 270, 473
  reading serial number of, 507–510
CHAR, 565
ChaseFolder class, 399
Class wizard, 187
  bug correction for, 178
Client applications
  using COM components in, 124
Client-sided scripting, 58
Close button
  adding, 188
CloseDB method, 324
CloseHandle(), 270, 368
CloseServer() function, 409
CloseTable method, 321, 368
CMainFrame, 483
CmdBarAction event
  catching, 189
CmdBarAction() method, 178
CmdBarAction() parameters, *178*
CoCreateInstance(), 114, 116, 151, 152, 310
CoCreateInstanceEx() function, 117
Cold resets, 263
Color, 61
Color bitmaps, 447
COM. *See also* Common Object Model
COM activation methods, 114–117
  ActiveX controls, 115–116
  COM+ services, 117
  DCOM, 117
  EXE to EXE, 116
  in-place activation, 115
  inproc: in-process activation, 116
  MTS or DLLHOST.EXE, 116–117
Combo boxes, 79, 145, 158, 179, 241
  adding to command bar, 165, 173, 174
  IDs of, 185
  strings added to, 175
  in toolbars in eVC environment, 53–54
Command-Band, 61, 158, 167, 190–206
  adding to application, 190–195
  eVB Test application, *204*

PCDMCommander Class used in PCDM application, 204–206
style-flags, 190, *191*
testing new PCDMCommander Class in eMbedded Visual Basic, 202–204
CommandBand_Create, 190
CommandBands_AddAdornments, 194
CommandBands_AddBands, 192
CommandBands_Create function, 191
CommandBands_GetCommandBar, 193
CommandBands_GetRestoreInformation, 194, 206
Command bar, 93, 157, 158–190
  adding to application, 159–167
  buttons added to, 95
  combo boxes added to, 165, 173, 174
  control called from PCDM application, 185–189
  creating, 188
  file menu added to, 95
  ImageList assigned to, 94–95
  items removed from, 166–167
  PCDMUI: command bar included, 167–182
  summary on features/traps of, 189–190
  testing control in eMbedded Visual Basic, 182–185
CommandBar_AddAdornments methods, 161
CommandBar_AddBitmap() function, 162, 163
CommandBar_AddButtons, 162
CommandBar_AddToolTips, 166
CommandBar_Create, 190
CommandBar_Create() function, 159
CommandBar_Destroy(HWND), 166
CommandBar_Destroy(hwndCB), 159
CommandBar_DrawMenuBar, 181
CommandBar_Height, 160
CommandBar_InsertComboBox, 165
CommandBar_InsertMenubar, 160
CommandBar_InsertMenubarEx function, 160
CommandBar_IsVisible function, 160

commctrl.dll
  bitmap stock objects inside, *163–165*
Common Executable Format, 54, 473, 506
  compiling files, 54
  for PCDM, 498–500
Common Object Model, 558
  basic definition of, 111
  calling in C++, 123
  communication paths between applications, *115*
  and early binding, 112, 113–114
  feature summary for Windows CE, 153
  how it works, 112
  introduction to, 111–112
  seamless remote communication with, 112, 114
  simplified diagram of communication, *113*
  versioning, 112, 113
  See also deviceCOM; Distributed COM
Communication cable
  installing, 349–350
  setting baud rate of, 351–352
Compaq, 534
Compatibility wrappers
  in ADOCE 30.H, 315–316
Compiler errors
  removing, 367–368
Compile-time platform detecting, 62–63
Compile-time version checking, 61–62
Components, 513, 514
COM port access, 350
COM server
  calling in C++, 123
  calling in Visual Basic, 126–127
  creating small, 117–118
  generating desktop equivalent, 122–123
  registering, 121
  using #import directive, 123–125
  for Windows CE, 118–121
COM+ services, 117
COM subsystem
  initializing, 150
COM V-TABLE, 314

CONNECTION_POINT_MAP, 178
Connectivity, 347
  baud rate of communication cable,
    351–352
  modem installation, *351*
  with Windows CE, *348–349*
Console Output
  deviceCOM, 145
Constantly connected mobile devices, 347
Contacts, 272
Containers, 189
  and ActiveSync provider wizard, 371
  See also Command-Band
Control Manager, 43–44, *44*
Control panel application
  creating, 479–481
Controls
  databinding of, 102
Conversion macros
  in ATL or MFC, 566, *567*
ConvertInkFile() function, 262
Cool Bar, 158, 190
CopyFiles sections, 495
CORE.DLL, 450
COREDLL.DLL, 98
  tips for, 5
CPCDMAccess Reg
  adding to PCDMDLL.DLL, 265–268
  testing in eMbedded Visual Basic, 269
CPCDMCommander class, 170
  constructor code for, 177
  declarations for, 177
CPCDMList
  eVB test application, *232*
  testing in Visual Basic, 231–232
  using new, in PCDM application,
    233–242
CPCDMNotifyObject method, 399
CPCDMSyncFolder class, 374, 375,
    380–384, 399
CPCDMSyncFolders method
  called during synchronization, *391*
CPCDMSyncObjHandler class, 374,
    384–389, 400

CPCDMSyncObjHandler methods
  called during synchronization, *384*
CPCDMSyncStore class, 374
CPCDMView class, 433
Crackers, 536
CreateBar method, 167, 199, 211, 213
CreateFile(), 270
Create New Object (User)-Wizard, *360*
CreateObject call, 369
CreateSocket, 412
CreateTable method, 322, 368
CreateWindow(), 4
CreateWindowEx(), 4
Custom Action table, 521–522
Custom code
  using, 450–457
Custom SetupDLL
  writing, 500–503
CWaitDlg class, 433, 434, 435, 436

D
Data Access Objects, 304, 557
Database management, 140
Databases
  creating, 280
  terminology mapping of object store
    versus, *273*
Databinding
  of controls, 102
  manual initialization replacing,
    103–107
.DataFld property, 93, 102
Data loss, 263
Data Source Names, 102
DCE-RPC. *See* Distributed Computing
    Environment-Remote Procedure Call
DCOM. *See* Distributed COM
DCOMConfig tool, 117
DCOM/deviceCOM, 24
DCServer
  running as listener, 144
  starting as COM surrogate, 144–145
DDE. *See* Dynamic Data Exchange

Debugger, 46
  eMbedded Visual Basic, *49*
Debugging, 375, 393
  ActiveSync provider, 390, 404–405
  ActiveX controls, 70
Declaration of global variables
  unsupported, with same name, 100
DefaultProgram feature, 514, 515
Defines, 61
  adding to top of helper source, 68–69
DeleteItem method, 383
DeluxeCD.CDB, 344
  DeluxeCD.MDB converted to, 343
Deluxe CD database, 374
  ADO connection to, 377
  preparing, 89–90
  synchronization options for, *90*
DeluxeCD.MDB, 338
  primary key set in, for table Titles, 340
  synchronization errors, *343*
  synchronization settings, *342*
Deluxe CD Player, 72, 334
Design Control for Visual Basic, 133
Designed for Pocket PC logo requirement,
  466
Designed for Windows CE logo rules, 157,
  160
Desktop
  HTML on, 474
  installation created for, 510–527
Desktop equivalent COM server
  generating, 122–123
Desktop eVB project
  converting to eVB project, 91–92
Desktop machine, locating, 34
Desktop Windows Platform SDK
  Spy++ in, 41
Development task
  choosing right framework for, 57–61
Development tools
  installing, 24–27
deviceCOM, 117, 141–152, 405, 530
  Administration Utility of, 144, *145*
  client/server interaction schematics, *142*

communication means supported by, 148
components of, *143*
DCOM compared to, *406*
DCServer started as COM surrogate,
  144–145
installation of, 142–144
other features of, 152
registering, 143–144
small example, 146–152
See also Distributed COM
deviceCOM proxy/stub
  changing host application, 149–152
  creating, 146–147
  registering, 147–149
deviceCOM timeout
  filters for the IDL, 152
  setting, 152
Device connections
  tray icon show status of, *27*
DevStudio plug-in
  activating, 146
DHCP. *See* Dynamic Host Configuration
  Protocol
DHTML, 58
Dialog boxes
  creating hard copies of, 55
  full-screen, for pocket PCs, 467–468
DIB buffer, 451
Digital MP3 audio, 535
Digital Versatile Disk, 7
Direct dial-up connection
  with 115K baud, 28–29
Directory table, 519–520
  entries, *519*
DirectX, 448
  on Windows CE, 464
Dispatch interface, 116
Display Properties, 13
Distributed COM, 57, 141, 157, 405–408,
  530, 558
  advantages of deviceCOM over, 152
  deviceCOM compared to, *406*
  and seamless remote communications, 114
  See also deviceCOM

Distributed Computing Environment-Remote Procedure Call, 141
Distributed intelligence, 535
DLL. *See* Dynamic Link Library
DLLHOST.EXE, 117
Domain controller, 31, 359
Domain environment
  Windows 2000 server in, 357–361
Domain name entries
  by operating system, *30*
DoStuff() function, 365
DrawBitmapFromFile, 451
Drive letters, 270
DSNs. *See* Data Source Names
Dual monitor
  scenario, *15*
  support, 12–13
DVD. *See* Digital Versatile Disk
DVD-ROM
  over CD-ROM, 15
DWORDm_dwIndex, 287
Dynamic Data Exchange, 111–112
Dynamic Host Configuration Protocol, 357, 559
Dynamic Host Control Protocol, 31
Dynamic Link Library, 4, 5, 40, 112, 116, 558, 559

E
EIDE. *See* Enhanced Integrated Drive Electronics
E-mail, 541
eMbedded Visual Basic, 153
  ADO changes retested in, 334
  command bar in, 95–96
  COM server called in, 126–127
  CPCDMAccess Reg tested in, 269
  debugger, *49*
  eMbedded Visual C++ *versus*, 44–46
  New Project dialog box, *47*
  PCDMCommander Class tested in, 202–204
  PCDMDLL tested in, 432–433

PCDMPicture Class tested in, 462
selecting PCDMUI Control for use in, *183*
testing control in, 182–185
testing new class in, 293–296
testing new class in, for Palm-size PC 2.0, 216–218
testing program showing PCDMAccessDB calls in, *295*
using ActiveX control in, 137–140
eMbedded Visual Basic environment, 46–49
  creating, downloading, and debugging small eVB application, 47–49
eMbedded Visual C++, 44, 121
  ActiveX control used in, 133–137
  debugger, 39
  development environment, *52*
  eMbedded Visual Basic *versus*, 44–46
  internal bitmap converter, 447
  new project dialog box, *51*
  resource editor, 210, 238
  workspace, *119*
eMbedded Visual C++ environment, 49–56
  creating, downloading, and debugging small C++ application, 50–56
  Windows CE Platform Manager, 54–56
eMbedded Visual Tools, 21, 22, 35, 91, 122
eMbedded Visual Tools 3.0
  installation, 26
Embedded Windows NT
  positioning with Windows CE, *9*
  Windows CE *versus*, 7, *8*
Emulation, 339
  Access 2000 database copied to, 334–339
Emulator
  and printing, 249
EmulDemo, 336
Enabled property, 167
Encryption
  standardizing, 536
Enemy of the State, 536
Enhanced Integrated Drive Electronics, 13
Err interpretation, 98

Errors
  ActiveX controls unsupported, 96
  all forms created at application load time,
    97
  declaration of global variables with same
    name not supported, 100
  declares on Win32 not working on
    Windows CE, 98
  double clicking unsupported, 101
  Form_Load() as first method called, 101
  indexed controls not supported,
    92–93
  intrinsic controls unsupported,
    93–96
  linker, 125
  on Error GoTo unsupported on Windows
    CE, 98–100
  properties unsupported, 93
  sub Main must be declared public, 100
  Unload Me to end application is
    App.End, 100–101
  WithEvents unsupported, 96
Essential COM (Box), 112
Ethernet, 7
  adapter, 14
  cable, 35
  card, 30, 349
  connections, 34, 144
Ethernet PC-card
  NE2000 compatible, 31
eVB application wizard
  settings for, *83–86*
eVB for Windows CE
  differences between VB for Desktop and,
    109–109
eVB project
  converting desktop eVB project to,
    91–92
eVB Tools Control Manager, 133
Event handlers, 189, 229
  for CmdBarAction events, 184
Events, 117
  adding to interfaces, 228–229
EVENTSINK_MAP, 137

Examples
  application menu bar for palm-size PC,
    207–210
  deviceCOM, 146–152
  Pocket PC enhancements, 468–473
  remote API, 362–365
  Wininet, 441–445
  Winsock, 408–418
Exception handling
  unsupported, 125
Executables
  communicating between with COM, 114
ExecuteADBCmd() method
  parameters of, *552*
EXE-to-EXE communication, 116
Extended Markup Language, 440, 445, 563

F
Fair Game, 536
FastIrDA, 424
FAT32, 24
File Menu
  added to Command Bar, 95
  PCDM, 81
Files table
  in ORCA, 525
File system, 263, 269–272
  localizing storage card, 270–272
  My Documents on palm-size PC, 272
  no drive letters, 270
FILETIME structure, 379
Filters
  for deviceCOM's IDL, 152
FindDIBBits, 455
FindFirstFil API, 505
FindFirstFlashCard API, 505
FindFirstItem method, 377
FindNextItem method, 379
FindObjects method, 398, 399
FindRecord method, 288, 287, 326
Fire_CmdBarAction() method, 178
Fire_RowSelected method, 229
FireViewChange, 69, 130, 460

Firewire outlets, 535
Flash-RAM cards, 263, 270
Footprint
  for DCOM for CE, 405, 407
Form_Load function, 87
Form.Show() method, 101
Frameworks
  available, by device, *58*
  choosing for development task,
    57–61
  decision table, *59–60*
frmMain form, 103
FrontPage, 474
FTP
  Wininet for accessing, 441
Full-screen dialog boxes
  on Pocket PC, 467–468

G
Game consoles, 535
Gates, Bill, 534, 537
GDI
  bitmap display using, 459–463
gdi32.dll, 5
GE, 534
GetCePlatform() function, 69
GetCePlatform helper, 469
GetClass() method
  parameters of, *548*
GetCommand() method
  parameters of, *550*
GetFirstCDRecord method, 105
GetItem message, 230
GetItem() parameters, *226*
GetNextCDRecord method, 105
GetObjTypeInfo method, 393
Get_outValue method, 130
GetPacket method, 385, 400
GetProcAddress(), 114
GetStoreInfo method, 374
GetSyncFileName method, 384
GetTagValue() method
  parameters of, *550*

GetURL() method
  parameters of, *547*
GetValue function, 332
GetValue method, 292
GIF. *See* Graphic Interchange Format
Global_Default_Executables component
  setting key file for, *514*
Global Positioning System devices, 7
Graphical User Interface, 563
Graphic cards, 13
Graphic Interchange Format, 448
Graphics, 447
  displaying bitmaps using GDI, 459–463
  loading bitmaps, 448–459
Graphics buffer, 450
Graphics cards, 450
Guest accounts, 355
GUI. *See* Graphical User Interface

H
Hackers, 536
Handheld (H/PC) emulation, 13
Handheld PC, *16–17*, 79
Hard disks, 13–14
HBITMAP, 448, 450
Headless devices, 5
Hello-World application, 159, 456
  and bitmap, 450–451
  list view in, 220
  in Winsock example, 415
Help files, 473–478
  for PCDM application, 474–478
  for Windows Ce, 76
Help generation, 157
Help menu, PCDM, 81–82
Hibernation, 530
HINST_COMMCTRL icons
  resource IDs for, *165*
HKEY_CLASSES_ROOT, 264
HKEY_CURRENT_USER, 264
HKEY_LOCAL_MACHINE, 264, 269
Home automation systems, 534–536, 537
Hotkeys, 251

H/PC Professional, 18, 210, 241, 491, 528, 534, 543
  and ink control, 261
  logo requirements, 530
  standard ActiveSync services for, *370*
  StrongARM support for, 498
  VBCtrlTest application running on, *139*
  See also Palm-size PCs
H/PC Version 2.0, 18
HP Journada, 498
  mouse cursor support for, 530
HTML. *See* Hyper Text Markup Language
HTTP. *See* Hyper Text Transfer Protocol
Hyper Text Markup Language, 57, 58, 157
  Extended Markup Language *versus*, 563
  Windows CE help system based on, 474
Hyper Text Transfer Protocol, 157, 530, 559
  and integration of the Internet, 440–445
  Wininet for accessing, 441

I
Icons
  adding to taskbar, 482–484
  and storage cards, 528
IDC_HEXCONV1 control, 135, 136
IDC_INVAL, 137
IDC_OUTVAL, 137
IDE. *See* Integrated Development Environment
IDL. *See* Interface Definition Language
IDL compiler (deviceCOM)
  filters for, 152
IDR_TOOLBAR bitmap, 191
  with common toolbar icons, *168*
IDs
  of combo boxes, 185
#IFDEF UNDER_CE statements, 366, 367, 368
IHVs. *See* Independent Hardware Vendors
IM. *See* Input method
ImageList, 191
  assigns to Command Bar, 94

#import directive, 149, 150, 153
  using, 123–125
Independent Hardware Vendors, 405, 407
Indexed controls, 92–93
Index parameter, 170
INF file. *See* Installer Information File
Information Technology, 560
Infrared
  devices, 7
  ports, 247, 419
  support, 140
  Windows CE support, 542
Infrared: wireless wire, 418–440
  IrDA support added to PCDMDLL, 424–431
  IrDA support added to Winsock example, 419–424
  PCDMDLL tested in eMbedded Visual Basic, 432–433
  Send to.../Receive... implemented in PCDM application, 433–440
Infrared Data Association, 157, 419, 529, 555, 560
INIKEY property, 518
Initialize method, 392
InitInstance function, 159, 195, 207, 208
InitServer function, 413
  updating, 421
InitServer(HWND), 409
Ink Blob, 262
Ink control, 258–262
  functions, 262
  small application, 259–262
InkToString() function, 262
Inproc: In-process activation, 116
Input methods, 255, 257
InsertButton method, 170, 172, 211, 214
InsertButton() parameters, *172*
InsertComboBox() method, 170, 173
InsertComboBox() parameters, *174*
INSERT INTO SQL statement, 318
InsertMenuItem() parameters, *171*
InsertMenu method, 169, 211, 213
InsertMenu() parameters, *169*

Installation
    of development tools, 24–27
    of operating system, 23–24
    PC, 21–23
Installation for desktop, 510–527
    adding new component for ActiveSync
        provider, 513–516
    AppSearch table, 520
    CAB stored in MSI stream/signing final
        MSI file, 526–527
    Custom Action table, 521–522
    Directory table, 519–520
    Files and Media tables in ORCA,
        525–526
    InstallUISequence table, 522–524
    MakeCab, 524–525
    MSI background, 516–517
    MSI Database creation, 511–513
    MSI file created with MSI-SDK tools,
        524
    Property table, 517–518
    RegLocator table, 520–521
    Windows CE-specific custom actions
        added, 516
Installation for Windows CE, 484–527
    CEF installation created for PCDM,
        498–500
    CF-Card Instant-Installer for Pocket PC,
        503–510
    for desktop, 510–527
    Installer File created for PCDM
        application, 485, 488–498
    Installer Information File, 485
    targeting Windows CE, 485
    writing Custom SetupDLL, 500–503
Installer Information File, 485, 495, 496
    and logo requirements, 528
    predefined strings for use in sections of,
        489
    sections for Windows CE installations,
        486–488
InstallShield, 523, 524
InstallShield for Windows Installer, 511
    Application Information page, *512*

InstallShield Professional, 516
Install-Time-Compiler, 54
InstallUISequence table, 522–524
InstrPos() method
    parameters of, *551*
Integrated Development Environment, 559
Interface Definition Language, 120, 147,
    560
Interfaces
    events added to, 228–229
Internet, 536
    integration of, 440–445
Internet Explorer 4.0, 158
Internet Explorer client-sided scripts, 109
Internet Information Server 5.0, 12
Internet Protocol
    selecting, 356
Interprocess Communication, 148, 560
Inter-Process Connection, 141
Intrinsic controls
    unsupported, 93–96
Intrinsyc, 117, 141, 143, 147, 405, 445
InvokeHelper function
    dispatch ID of, 205
IP addresses
    entering manually, 32
    of platform, *417*
IPC. *See* Interprocess Communication
IPCDMCommander, 202
IPCONFIG results, *32*
IP settings, *357*
IrDA. *See* Infrared Data Association
IrDA receiving
    ways to implement, *425*
iScanMode, 397
iShow parameter, 256
IsItemChanged method, 381
Istrlen, 566
IsValidObject method, 380
ISW Property Table, *518*
IT. *See* Information Technology
Item Ids
    in commctrl.h, 163
ItestMe class, 150, 151

J

Joint Photographic Experts Group Format, 448

Jot character recognizer SIP, *253*

Jot recognizer
  class IDs for, 255

JPG. *See* Joint Photographic Experts Group Format

K

kernel32.dll, 5

Keyboards, 535

L

LAN card
  using to connect to PC, 31–34

Linker errors, 125

Linker import libraries, 316

Linux, 543, 544

List view control, 101, 219–243
  adding to PCDMUI.DLL, 222–231
  CPCDMList Class used in PCDM application, 233–243
  including in application, 220–222
  initializing, 103
  initializing columns of, 107
  summary points for, 242–243
  testing new CPCDMList Class in Visual Basic, 231–232
  unsupported items in, 222

L macro, 565

LoadBitMap(), 448, 449

LoadDibSection(), 448

LoadLibrary(), 114

Load method parameters, *457*

Localized names, 270

.log files
  error messages in, 92

Logo compliance, 527–532

Logo handbooks, 527

Logo requirements, 81

Designed for Pocket PC, 466
  dialog boxes on Pocket PC, 467
  for Windows CE, 516

LVFINDINFO structure, 228

LV_ITEM structure, 227

M

Macros, 61
  conversion of, 566, *567*

Mail Application Programmable Interface, 557

Mails, 272

MAINFORM
  source view of PCDM, *234*
  updating, 233–236

Mainfrm.cpp, 78

MakeCab, 524–525

Make New Connection wizard, *28*

Manual initialization
  databinding replaced with, 103–107

MAPI. *See* Mail Application Programmable Interface

Marshaller
  code/object converter/transformer, 560–561

Matrox G200 PCI, 13

m_ctrlHexConv control, 137

MDAC. *See* Microsoft Data Access Components

Media table
  in ORCA, 525

Memory, 7
  leak detection in, 36, 37–39
  with Windows CE devices, 51

Menus
  changes in, 181
  in command bar, 158
  inserting, 188
  positioning of, in command bar, 170

Message Queuing, 117
  in Windows CE 3.0, 347

MFC
   AppWizard, 75–76
   control enlargement, 127
   conversion macros in, 566
   creating, for desktop equivalent, *75–76*
MFC application
   accessing object store, 277–280
Microsoft, 534
   Windows CE development by, 4
Microsoft Data Access Components, 305
Microsoft Development Network, 26
   Library CDs on DVD, 15
Microsoft Installer, 510, 527
   background on, 516–517
   files, 511
Microsoft Management Console, 358
Microsoft Message Queuing, 117
Microsoft Office 4.0, 112
Microsoft Tools, 21
Microsoft Transaction Server, 117
MidStr() method
   and InstrPos() method, *551*
Migrating forms and code, 92–101
MIPS, 59
Mitsubishi, 534
MMC. *See* Microsoft Management
   Console
Mobile devices
   short battery life of, 347
Modem
   installing new, *351*
Mouse cursor support, 530
Mouse Pointer property, 167
MoveFirst method, 324
MoveLast method, 324
MoveNext method, 324
MovePrevious method, 324
MSDN. *See* Microsoft Development
   Network
MSI. *See* Microsoft Installer
MSI Database
   creating basic, 511–513
MSI file
   signing final, 526

MSI-SDK tools
   MSI file created with, 524
MSI stream
   CAB stored in, 526
MSIVAL2, 526
MSMQ. *See* Microsoft Message
   Queuing
m_szDebug variable, 69
mToolBarId, 210
MTS. *See* Microsoft Transaction Server
Multi-monitor support, 12–13
Multithreading
   for single-threaded servers, 117
   on Windows CE, 77
MyCeServer component, 124, 146
MyCeServer project
   creating for desktop, 122–123
My Documents
   on palm-size PC, 272
MyFirst application, 149
   with ShowMe result, *126*

N
NEC, 534
NEC MobilPro
   mouse cursor support, 530
NEC MobilPro 800, 270
NE2000 compatible Ethernet PC-Card, 31
Net, The, 536
NetBEUI, 34
NetDDE, 114
Network Connection Wizard, 353, *354*
   user permission page of, *355*
Network Interface Card, 14–15
New Project dialog box
   eMbedded Visual Basic, *47*
NIC. *See* Network Interface Card
NM_LISTSERV structure, 230
Non-Unicode target, 123
Notebooks
   infrared ports for, 424
Notepad, 92, 93, 474, 488
Notification handlers, 229

Notify handler
    code for, 181
NTFS. *See* Windows NT File System

O
Object Linking and Embedding, 112, 561
Object menu/context menu, 561
ObjectNotify method, 390, 391, 393
Object-oriented databases, 541
Object store, 157, 263, 272–304
    adding access to PCDMDLL.DLL,
        280–293
    ADO compared to, *308*
    APIs, 316
    icon, *273*
    PCDMAccessDB Class added to PCDM
        application, 296–304
    property/field types of database in, *278*
    simple API application accessing,
        274–277
    simple MFC application accessing,
        277–280
    terminology mapping of, *versus*
        databases, *273*
    testing new class in eMbedded Visual
        Basic, 293–296
ObjectStoreIt
    converting to desktop application,
        365–366
OCX. *See* OLE controls
ODBC. *See* Open Database Connectivity
ODK. *See* Open Development Kit
Old calls
    rule of thumb for, 77
OLE. *See* Object Linking and Embedding
OLEAUT32.LIB, 316
OLE controls, 112, 115
    difference between desktop and Windows
        CE versions, 77
OLEDB, 305
OLEDB layer
    lack of, on Windows CE, 102
OLE32.LIB, 316

OnButton() method, 152
OnButton1() method, 124
OnCancel, 434
OnCmdBarActionCommander method,
    433, 436
OnDraw method, 69, 130, 132, 133, 167,
    181, 224, 225, 460–461
On Error GoTo
    unsupported, 98–100
OnInitDialog, 434
OnInitialUpdate() function, 187
OnTimer, 434
Open Database Connectivity, 304–305, 557,
    561
    ADO over, for database connectivity on
        Windows CE, 541
Open Development Kit, 142
Open method, 316
OpenTable method, 288, 323
Operating system, 7
    decision table for, *22–23*
    domain name entries by, *30*
    installing, 23–24
    segmentation pyramid, *6*
Oracle, 561
ORCA, 523, 524
    Files and Media tables in, 525–526
OS. *See* Operating system
Outlook 2000, 26, 543
Out-of-process communication, 116

P
PageSetupDlg(), 247
PaletteSize, 456
Palm-size PCs, *16*, 18, 158, 161, 206, 447,
    492, 543
    Action and Escape keys, 250
    and ActiveSync, 370
    application launch keys on, 250–252
    application menu bar example,
        207–210
    emulation, 13
    file menu, 81

Palm-size PCs (*cont.*)
  hardware buttons on, 250–252
  help menu, 81–82
  ink control for, 259, 261
  and localized names, 270
  logo requirements for, 530–532
  maximum size of dialog box on, 238
  My Documents on, 272
  parameter setting for, 91
  PCDMCommander Class updates,
    211–216
  Soft Input Panel for, 252–258
  source view of PCDM CD-Details form
    for, *238*
  special considerations with, 206–219
  testing New Class in eMbedded Visual
    Basic for Palm-size 2.0, 216–218
  verifying PCDM application, 218–219
  See also H/PC Professional
Palm-size PC 1.0, 491
Palm-size PC 1.2, 241
Palm-size PC 2.0, 214, 216–218
Parsers, 545, 546, 555
PC-Cards, 270
PCDM. *See* Pocket-CD-Manager
PCDMAccessCE Class
  ADO added to, 319–334
PCDMAccessDB.AddNewRecord
    parameters, *289*
PCDMAccessDB.AddProperty parameters,
    281
PCDMAccessDB Class, 296–304, 392, 547,
    552
PCDMAccessDB.CloseTable parameters,
    285
PCDMAccessDB.CreateTable parameters,
    282
PCDMAccessDB.Execute parameters, *333*
PCDMAccessDB.FindRecord parameters,
    287
PCDMAccessDB.GetValue parameters,
    292
PCDMAccessDB.Movedirection
    parameters, *285*

PCDMAccessDB.OpenTable parameters,
    283
PCDMAccessDB.ReadRecord parameters,
    291
PCDMAccessDB.SetValue parameters,
    289
PCDMAccessDB.WriteRecord parameters,
    290
PCDM Auto-Installer
  for Pocket PC, 503–506
PCDMCommander Class
  testing in eMbedded Visual Basic,
    202–204
  updating, 195–202, 211–216
  using in PCDM application, 204–206
PCDM.CPP
  difference between desktop and Windows
    CE versions, 77
PCDMDLL
  IrDA support added to, 424–431
  for non-UI technologies, 73–74
PCDMDLL.DLL, 140, 371
  CPCDMAccessReg to, 265–268
  object store access added to, 280–293
  ShowSIP() for, 255–257
PCDMDoc.cpp, 78
PCDM MFC application, 73
PCDMUI
  including command bar, 167–182
  testing in Visual Basic, 257–258
  for UI tasks, 73
PCDMUI Control
  selecting for use in eMbedded Visual
    Basic, *183*
PCDMUI.DLL, 127, 140
  list view control added to, 222–231
  Picture Class added to, 457–459
  picture class added to, 457–459
PCDM UI-schema, *233*
PCDMUI2, 202
PCDMUtils Class, 440, 545–555
PCDMView.cpp
  difference between desktop and Windows
    CE versions, 78

PC-Link
  setting default connection for, 29–30
Pegasus devices, 447
PegHelp.exe, 477
Personal computer
  choosing, 11–15
  installing, 21–23
  preparing for Windows CE, 11–19
  testing connection to, 30–31
Personal Information Manager, 272
Personal Web Server, 12
Phone and Modem Options applet, *350*
PhotoDraw 2000, 26
Picture class
  adding to PCDMUI.DLL, 457–459
.Picture property, 93
PID. *See* Property ID
PIM. *See* Personal Information Manager
Platform Builder, 528
Platform Manager
  transport configuration, *55*
  using, 54–56
Platforms
  Windows CE versions of, *27*
Plug-and-PLay
  of Windows 2000, 24
PNOTIFYICONDATE structure, 482
Pocket-Access, 263, 273
  Book841 table in, *335*
  synchronizing with Access 2000
    databases, 339–344
  on Windows CE device, 72
Pocket-access files, 102, 334–345
  copying an Access 2000 database to
    emulation, 334–339
  synchronizing with Access 2000
    databases, 339–344
  updating PCDM to use new database,
    344–345
Pocket-CD-Manager 127, 561
  architecture diagram, *74*
  blank application, *80*
  compiling application, 80
  components, *73*

creating framework of application, 73–76
desirable features for, 533
differences between desktop and
    Windows CE versions, 76–80
feature list, 71–73
help file, 478
technologies to feature mapping
    table, *72*
updating to use new database, 344–345
user interface of, 81–82
wrapper controls created for, 140–141
Pocket-CD-Manager application, 263
  calling control from, 185–189
  calling help file from within, 478
  CEF installation created for, 498–500
  CPCDMList Class used in, 233–242
  directory structure for installation, *495*
  help files for, 474–478
  installer file created for, 485, 488–498
  launching at end of CEF installation,
    501–503
  and logo requirements, 528
  PCDMAccessDB Class added to,
    296–304
  PCDMCommander Class used in,
    204–206
  Send to.../Receive... implemented in,
    433–440
  sound added to, 464
  taskbar icon added to, 482–484
  updating, 462–463
  updating with RAPI, 366–368
  verifying, 218–219
Pocket-CD-Manager prototype
  converting desktop eVB project to eVB
    project, 91–92
  creating, 82–107
  creating desktop version of, 83–89
  migrating ADO desktop to ADO for
    Windows CE, 102–107
  migrating forms and code, 92–101
  porting desktop prototype to Windows
    CE, 89
  preparing DeluxeCD database, 89–90

Pocket PC, 79, 465, 492
  CF-Card Instant-Installer for, 503–510
  emulation window, *467*
  improvements summary, 473
  resource editor, 471
  window size calculation for, 466–467
  See also H/PC Professional; Palm-size
    PC
Pocket PC devices enhancements, 465–473
  example, 468–473
  full-screen dialog boxes, 467–468
  window size calculation, 466–467
Pocket-Word, 365
Point-to-Point Tunneling Protocol, 354
Port assignment, 361
Ports, infrared, 419
Power consumption, 7
P_PRINTINK structure, 262
PPTP. *See* Point-to-Point Tunneling
  Protocol
Primary keys, 343
  setting in DeluxeCD.MDB, 339, *340*
PrintDlg(), 247
Printing
  support for, 61
  on Windows CE, 246–249
PrintInk() function, 262
Processes, killing, 40
Prog-ID, 147, 148
Project settings
  difference between desktop and Windows
    CE versions, 78–80
Property ID, 273
Property table, 517–518
Provider
  with ActiveSync, 403–404
Proxim Wireless LAN Card
  RangeLAN2, 31
Public sub mains, 100
Publisher 2000, 26
Put_inValue method, 129
Put_outValue method, 129, 130
PutRef_ActiveConnection, 315
PWS. *See* Personal Web Server

R
RAM, 12, 536
RangeLAN2, 31
RAPI. *See* Remote API
Rapier, 62. *See also* Pocket PC
RAPI.H, 365, 367
RAPI.LIB, 365, 366
RAS. *See* Remote Access Service
raw_interfaces_only directive, 124
RDO. *See* Remote Data Objects
RDS. *See* Remote Data Services
ReadFileFromCE call, 365
ReadRecord method, 291, 331
ReadRegistryKey method, 265, 267
ReadRegistryKey() parameters, *265*
ReBar, 158, 190
REBARBANDINFO structure, 192
ReceiveString method, 424, 425, 427, 432,
  433
Redundant code
  elimination of, 6
RefreshCDEdit(), 106
RefreshCDInfo(), 106
RefreshFormName method, 101
RegisterHotKey, 251
Registration, 257
Registry, 157, 263, 264–269
  access, 98
  CPCDMAccessReg added to
    PCDMDLL.DLL, 265–268
  and logo requirements, 529
  management, 140
  root keys, 264
  testing new CPCDMAccessReg in
    eMbedded Visual Basic, 269
Registry code, standard, 264
RegLocator table
  entries, *520*
Remote Access Service, 14, 24, 157, 358,
  562
  differences between ActiveSync 3.0
    connectivity and, *361*
  and manual installation, 542
  and Web, 445

Remote Access Services as TCP/IP
    provider, 349–361
    baud rate setting of communication cable,
        351–352
    communication cable install between two
        PCs, 349–350
    Windows 2000 incoming connections set
        up, 352–357
    Windows 2000 server in domain
        environment, 357–361
Remote API, 157, 361–369, 530, 562
    calls not existing in Windows CE API,
        363
    example, 362–365
    and logo requirements, 529
    ObjectStoreIt converted to desktop
        application, 365–366
    testing class in Visual Basic for desktop,
        368–369
    updating PCDM application with,
        366–368
Remote communication
    seamless, with COM, 114
Remote connectivity, 157
Remote data
    access, 347
    and Winsock, 408–418
Remote Data Objects, 304, 557
Remote Data Services, 305, 557
Remote File Viewer, 35–36, *36*
Remote Heap Walker, 36–39
Remote Process Viewer, 40, *40*
Remote Registry Editor, *41*, 121
    COM server keys shown in, *122*
Remote Spy++, 41–42
    in action, *42*
Remote tools, 31
Remote update strategies, 537
Remote Zoomin, 42
Removable hard drives, 24
RERR_OBJECT_DELETED, 381
ResetSocket, 411
Resource IDs
    for HINST_COMMCTRL icons, *165*

Resources, 78
Resource strings, 166
Resume Next declaration, 98, 99
Routing and Remote Access
    service settings, *359*
    starting, *358*
    system console, 354
Routing and Remote Access Management
    Console, *360*
RowSelected event, 228
Runtime version checking, 63–69

S
Sales
    and user satisfaction, 81
ScanDatabase method, 393, 397
SceThread(LPVOID), 409
Scriptlets, 58
SDKs
    Windows CE platform, 26–27
Search combo box
    inserting, 188
Security, 7, 536, 537
    and guest accounts, 355
    and remote communications, 114
Sega, 534
SEGA Dreamcast game console, 543
Self-register
    proviso about, 515
SendCommand() parameters, *230*
SendIrDAPacket function, 419, 422
SendPacket function, 409, 414
    updating, 423
SendString method, 424, 427, 432
SendWSockPacket function, 409, 414
Sequence types, 516–517
Serial cable, 35
    configuring, *29*
Serial connections, 144
Serial-number protection
    adding to CeSetup.DLL, 507
Server-sided scripting, 58
Service Pack of Visual Studio, 26

SetAdornments() parameter, *176*
SetCmdBarType method, 205
SetID method, 101
.SetMaskColor property
  removing, 93
SetPacket method, 384, 385, 388, 400
SetValue method, 329, 330
SetWindowsLong function, 239
SGML. *See* Structured Graphics Markup
  Language
Shared DLL, 50
SHCreateMenuBar function, 208, 473
ShellExecuteEx function, 505
Shell logo requirements, 529
SH4, 491
SHInitDialog function, 467, 469
SHLoadDiBitmap(), 448
  using, 449–450
SHMENUBARINFO structure, 209, 210,
  212
SHMENUBAR structure, 207
ShowFlashCard(), 271
ShowMe() method, 120, 123
ShowMe result
  MyFirst application showing, *126*
ShowSIP()
  for the PCDMDLL.DLL, 255–257
SHSipInfo() function, 252, 254
SH3, 59
Siemens, 534
SIP. *See* Soft Input Panel
16-bit related calls
  elimination of, with Windows CE, 6
Smaller code, 6
SndPlaySound, 463
SOCKADDR_IDRA structure, 421
SOCKADDR_IN structure, 421
SOCKET_ERROR, 429
Soft Input Panel, 250, 252–258, 468
  Jot character recognizer, *253*
  simple application showing, 252–255
  soft keyboard, *253*
Software viruses, 536, 537
Sony, 534

SortToolTips() function, 170, 197
Sounds, 447
  with Windows CE API, 463–464
SourceDiskFiles, 493
SourceDisksNames, 494
Space saving
  with command bar, 158
Special Input Panel, 466
Speed, 5, 51
SPI_GETPLATFORMTYPE strings
  Windows CE platforms and, *64*
Spy++ program
  in Desktop Windows Platform SDK, 41
SQL for Windows CE, 263
SRCAND, 459
SRCCOPY, 459
SRCINVERT, 459
SRCPAINT, 459
State recovery
  logo requirement for palm-size PCs, 531
stdafx.h
  difference between desktop and Windows
    CE versions, 77
Stock objects
  inside commctrl.dll, *163–165*
Storage, 263–345
  ADO for Windows CE, 304–334
  of CAB into MSI stream, 526
  cards, 270, 528
  file system, 269–272
  object store, 272–304
  pocket-access files, 334–345
  Windows CE registry, 264–269
StretchBlt, 459, 460
String arrays, 565
Strings, 565
  adding to combo box, 175
Strlen, 566
Structured Graphics Markup Language, 563
Style-flags
  of Command-Band, 190, *191*
Surrogates
  options for loading server, 148
Sybase, 561

Synchronization
  CPCDMSyncFolders methods called
    during, *391*
  CPCDMSyncObjHandler methods called
    during, *384*
System Management Server, 485

T
Taskbar
  icon added to, 482–484
TBButton-structure, 162
TCHAR
  for string definitions, 565–566
TCP. *See* Transmission Control Protocol
TCP/IP, 24
  address assignment, 357
  Winsock connection, 408
TCP/IP link
  setting up direct link to Windows CE
    device, 54–56
TCP/IP properties
  incoming, *356*
TCP/IP provider
  RAS used as, 349–361
TEXT macro, 132, 565
32-bit logo requirement, 528
Thread example, 3, 18
  Pocket-CD-Manager, 71–89
  source directory, 71
  See also Pocket-CD-Manager
3D controls, 77
3DFX Banshee AGP, 13
Timeouts
  deviceCOM, 152
Toolbar buttons
  inserting, 188
Toolbar objects
  bitmap stock objects for, *163*
Tools
  installation order of, *24–25*
ToolTips, 53, 56, 166, 170, 196, 214
Tracks table, 342
  new field created in, *341*

Transaction Sequential Query Language,
  305
Transmission Control Protocol, 141, 148,
  562
Transmission Control Protocol/Internet
  Protocol. *See* TCP/IP
TSQL. *See* Transaction Sequential Query
  Language
Type-Complete, 53
TypeID string, 379

U
UDA. *See* Universal Data Access
UDP. *See* User Datagram Protocol
UI. *See* User Interface
Unicode, 132, 133, 362, 366
  target, 123
  tips and tricks for, *versus* ANSI, 565–567
  Windows CE support for calls, 98
Uninstall_Init function, 502
Universal Data Access, 305
Universal Plug and Play, 418, 536, 563
Universal Serial Bus, 7
UNIX, 543, 544
Unload Me method, 100
UpdataData() method, 137
UpdateItem method, 382
UpnP. *See* Universal Plug and Play
URLs
  BSTRing containing, 545
USB. *See* Universal Serial Bus
User Datagram Package, 141
User Datagram Protocol, 148, 562
user32.dll, 5
User documentation
  remote Zoomin for, 42
User Interface, 543, 563
  controls, 127
  logo requirements, 529
  of Pocket-CD-Manager, 81–82
  See also Windows CE user interface
User Manager, 355
User satisfaction, 81

V
VARIANTS, 330
  declarations, 309
VBCtrlTest application
  on H/PC Pro, *139*
  main form of, *138*
VbEmulDB, 336, 337
VBScript, 109
VBX. *See* Visual Basic controls
Vector-table, 116
Virtual connections, 354
Virtual keyboard
  class IDs for, 255
Virtual Private Networks, 354
Viruses, 536, 537
Visual Basic, 91
  all forms created at application load time,
    97
  COM server called in, 126–127
  controls, 116
  testing new CPCDMList Class in,
    231–232
  testing new PCDMUI in, 257–258
Visual Basic for Desktop
  differences between eVB for Windows
    CE and, *108–109*
Visual Basic for Windows CE 6.0 CD, 335
Visual Basic IDE, 559
Visual Basic project
  converting into Windows CE project,
    83–107
Visual Basic Wizard
  subs generated by, 98
Visual C++, 53, 83, 389
  selection dialog box for ActiveX controls
    in, *134*
Visual C++ IDE, 559
Visual C++ 6.0, 53
Visual C++ Version 1.0, 61
Visual Interdev IDE, 559
Visual Studio
  IDEs in, 559
Visual Studio 6
  API Viewer Tool from, 98

Visual Studio 97, 61
Visual Studio 98, 122
  installation, 26
Voice recognition, 535
VPNs. *See* Virtual Private Networks

W
WCDDbTst
  MFC sample, 279–280
WCE Application wizard
  command bar creation by, 159
WCE ATL COM AppWizard, 118
WCE MFC AppWizard (EXE), 50
WCHAR, 566
WebIt dialog
  controls for, *442*
Web pages
  retrieving with Wininet API, 441–445
Web servers
  and Internet integration, 445
Web TV, 58, 535
WinDiff, 37
Window Message Handler, 408
Windows CE
  and ActiveSync, 390–403
  ActiveX control created for, 127–128
  ADO cursors for, *317*
  ADO for, 304–334
  ADO lock types for, *317*
  ADO over ODBC for database
    connectivity on, 541
  application installation mechanisms,
    528–529
  bitmap loading in, 448–459
  COM feature summary for, 153
  COM server created for, 118–121
  connectivity technologies, *348–349*
  CORE.DLL of, 450
  described, 4
  DirectX on, 464
  disadvantages with, 54
  embedded Windows NT *versus*, 7, *8*
  flexibility with, 7

graphics and sounds on, 447–464
help system, 98, 473–478
HTML in, 474
HTTP integration within, 440–445
installation for, 484–527
lack of 16-bit APIs for, 4
logo requirements for, 528–532
market for, 6
migrating ADO desktop to ADO for, 102
modular to fit into small devices, 4–5
optimal development workstation for, *19*
platform versions, *27*
porting desktop prototype to, 89
positioning with embedded Windows NT, *9*
properties not supported by, 93
registry, 264–269
Remote Registry Editor, 121
setting up, to connect to workstation, 28–34
supported common controls in, *243–245*
unsupported common controls with, 245, *246*
Winsock development for, 408
writing successful applications for, 3
XML parser for, 445
Windows CE API
  playing sounds using, 463–464
Windows CE development tips, 61–70
  compile-time platform detecting, 62–63
  compile-time version checking, 61–62
  debugging ActiveX controls, 70
  debug messages accessed in ActiveX controls, 69
  runtime version checking, 63–69
Windows CE Development Tools, 31
Windows CE development workstation
  setup components for, *22*
  software components for, *21*
Windows CE device
  choosing, 15, *16–17*, 18
Windows CE Explorer, 447
Windows CE File Control 6.0, 338

Windows CE installation
  CPUs supported and their platform IDs, *490*
  valid root and type settings, *521*
Windows CE 1.x, 459
Windows CE Platform Manager, 54–56
Windows CE 3.0
  message queuing in, 347
Windows CE tools, 35–44
  Control Manager, 43–44
  remote File Viewer, 35–36
  remote Heap Walker, 36–39
  remote Process Viewer, 40
  remote Registry Editor, 41
  remote Spy++, 41–42
  remote Zoomin, 42
Windows CE 2.*1*, 141
Windows CE user interface, 157–262
  command bar, 158–190
  Command-Band, 190–206
  hardware buttons on palm-size PCs, 250–252
  ink control, 258–262
  list view control, 219–243
  printing on Windows CE, 246–249
  Soft Input Panel, 252–258
  special palm-size PC considerations, 206–219
  supported common controls, 243–245
  unsupported common controls, 245–246
Windows CE version and platform
  determining during runtime, 65–68
Windows File Explorer, 36
Windows Installer, 510
Windows 95, 11, 116
Windows 98, 11
Windows 9x, 24, 123, 542, 565
Windows NT, 4, 6, 23, 116. *See also* Embedded Windows NT
Windows NT4, 542
Windows NT5, 12
Windows NT/2000, 565
Windows Office 2000
  installation, 26

Windows 2000
  display properties of, *14*
  dual-monitor environment configuration,
    13
  installing, 24
  over Windows NT4, 542
  server in domain environment, 357–361
  setting up incoming connections,
    352–357
Windows 2000 Professional, 12, 22
Windows 2000 Server
  advantages with, 12
WinHelpA function, 98
Wininet, 445
  Client Internet API, 441–445
  example, 441–445
WinMain function, 220, 505, 506
WinMain procedure, 310
Win16 calls, 77
Winsock, 14, 24, 408
  example, 409–418
  IrDA support added to example, 419–424
  and logo requirements, 529
  PCDM application, 418
  thread, 419–421
WINSOCK.LIB, 424
WINS Server, 34
Win32, 77
  API calls, 98
WithEvents statements
  unsupported, 96

WM_CLOSE, 531
WM_CREATE, 221
WM_DESTROY, 416
WM_INITDIALOG branch, 472
WM_INITDIALOG message handler, 473
WM_PAINT, 221, 416
WM_SOCKET_SELECT message, 416
Workstation
  Windows CE set up, to connect to,
    28–34
Wrapper classes, 150
Wrapper controls
  for PCDM, 140–141
WriteFile()/ReadFile(), 270
WriteRecord method, 290, 331
WriteRegistryKey method, 265, 268
WSAAsyncSelect
  missing in Windows CE version of, 408
wsprintf function, 69
  for string formatting, 566
wWinMainCRTStartup, 80
Wyvern devices, 91
Wyvern directory, 62

X
X-close button
  logo requirement for palm-size
    PCs, 531
XIP (eXecute In Place), 51
XML. *See* Extended Markup Language

Addison-Wesley Professional

How to Register Your Book

Register this Book

Visit: **http://www.aw.com/cseng/register**

Enter the ISBN*

Then you will receive:

- Notices and reminders about upcoming author appearances, tradeshows, and online chats with special guests
- Advanced notice of forthcoming editions of your book
- Book recommendations
- Notification about special contests and promotions throughout the year

*The ISBN can be found on the copyright page of the book

Visit our Web site

http://www.aw.com/cseng

When you think you've read enough, there's always more content for you at Addison-Wesley's web site. Our web site contains a directory of complete product information including:

- Chapters
- Exclusive author interviews
- Links to authors' pages
- Tables of contents
- Source code

You can also discover what tradeshows and conferences Addison-Wesley will be attending, read what others are saying about our titles, and find out where and when you can meet our authors and have them sign your book.

We encourage you to patronize the many fine retailers who stock Addison-Wesley titles. Visit our online directory to find stores near you.

Contact Us via Email

cepubprof@awl.com

Ask general questions about our books.
Sign up for our electronic mailing lists.
Submit corrections for our web site.

cepubeditors@awl.com

Submit a book proposal.
Send errata for a book.

cepubpublicity@awl.com

Request a review copy for a member of the media interested in reviewing new titles.

registration@awl.com

Request information about book registration.

Addison-Wesley Professional
One Jacob Way, Reading, Massachusetts 01867 USA
TEL 781-944-3700 • FAX 781-942-3076

CD-ROM Warranty

Addison-Wesley warrants the enclosed disc to be free of defects in materials and faulty workmanship under normal use for a period of ninety days after purchase. If a defect is discovered in the disc during this warranty period, a replacement disc can be obtained at no charge by sending the defective disc, postage prepaid, with proof of purchase to:

> Editorial Department
> Addison-Wesley Professional
> 75 Arlington Street, Suite 300
> Boston, MA 02216

After the ninety-day period, a replacement disc will be sent upon receipt of the defective disc and a check or money order for $10.00, payable to Addison-Wesley.

Addison-Wesley makes no warranty or representation, either expressed or implied, with respect to this software, its quality, performance, merchantability, or fitness for a particular purpose. In no event will Addison-Wesley, its distributors, or dealers be liable for direct, indirect, special, incidental, or consequential damages arising out of the use or inability to use the software. The exclusion of implied warranties is not permitted in some states. Therefore, the above exclusion may not apply to you. This warranty provides you with specific legal rights. There may be other rights that you may have that vary from state to state. The contents of this CD-ROM are intended for personal use only.

More information and updates are available at:
http://www.awl.com/cseng/titles/0-201-61642-4